The Athenæum Press

GINN AND COMPANY · PRO-
PRIETORS · BOSTON · U.S.A.

LEMNIAN ATHENA

TO THE MUSES

Whether on Ida's shady brow,
  Or in the chambers of the East,
The chambers of the sun, that now
  From ancient melody have ceas'd;

Whether in Heav'n ye wander fair,
  Or the green corners of the earth,
Or the blue regions of the air,
  Where the melodious winds have birth;

Whether on crystal rocks ye rove,
  Beneath the bosom of the sea,
Wandering in many a coral grove,
  Fair Nine, forsaking Poetry:

How have you left the ancient love
  That bards of old enjoyed in you!
The languid strings do scarcely move,
  The sound is forc'd, the notes are few!

WILLIAM BLAKE

O antique fables! beautiful and bright
 And joyous with the joyous youth of yore;
O antique fables! for a little light
 Of that which shineth in you evermore,
To cleanse the dimness from our weary eyes,
And bathe our old world with a new surprise
 Of golden dawn entrancing sea and shore.

JAMES THOMSON

PREFACE

In this new edition of "The Classic Myths in English Literature" the former order of materials has been altered in accordance with the advice of the teachers who have had longest experience with the use of the book; the old material has been thoroughly revised; and much new material has been added. Since most people prefer to begin a story at its beginning, and not with the career of its author and his genealogy, I have reserved the history of the myths for the conclusion of the text. Some of the myths have been restated in more careful form. Some short narratives, before omitted, have been included. The sketches of the Iliad and the Odyssey have been considerably expanded; and an outline — which, I hope, will be deemed adequate — of Wagner's version of the Ring of the Nibelung has been appended to the account of Norse and German mythology. That version is, of course, not English literature; but it has come to be received as the classic modern version of the story; and the story is needed, at some time or other, by every lover of music. Fresh examples of the employment of myth in English verse have, where practicable, been incorporated in the text; and some new references will be found in the Commentary.

I have thoroughly revised the list of illustrative cuts, have interpreted the more difficult of the ancient figures, and indicated the sources. The pictures themselves are a decided improvement upon those in the former edition. In the determination of sources for reproduction, I have had the valuable assistance of Dr. E. von Mach, the author of more than one well-known work on ancient art; and to him I am indebted, in addition, for the section on The Classic Myths in Art, which is included in my Introduction. With this new equipment the book should prove more useful to those who here make their first acquaintance with art, especially the art of the ancients, as well as to those who have been in the habit of using it as a guide to paintings and sculptures of mythological subjects in foreign galleries.

Much of our best English poetry lies beyond the imaginative reach of many readers because of their unfamiliarity with the commonplaces of literary allusion, reference, and tradition. Of such commonplaces few are more frequently recurrent than those furnished by the literature of myth.

In view of this consideration, the Academic Council of the University of California, some twenty years ago, introduced into its requirements for entrance in English the subject of Classical Mythology in its relation to English Literature, and recommended, as a textbook for preparation, Bulfinch's " Age of Fable." The experience of English and classical teachers in the schools of the state attested the wisdom of the requirement; but the demand for some textbook adapted to the needs of the classroom made necessary the preparation of this volume. For while " The Age of Fable " offered a tempting collection of Greek, Norse, and Oriental narratives, it was designed neither as a schoolbook nor as a systematized presentation and interpretation of the myths that have most influenced English literature.

At the request of my publishers I undertook at that time such a revision and rearrangement of the materials of "The Age of Fable" as might adapt it to the purposes of teacher and pupil, and to the taste of readers somewhat more advanced in years than those addressed by the original work or by the edition which bore the name of the Reverend Edward Everett Hale. But after a year's work I found that half my material for copy was new, and that the remainder differed in many important respects from the book upon which it was based. Consequently, while the obligation to " The Age of Fable " was acknowledged in full, a different title was selected for the resulting volume. For neither my publishers nor I desired that the scholarship or the taste of Mr. Bulfinch should be held accountable for liberties that were taken with his work.

In " The Classic Myths in English Literature and in Art," Chapters XXIII–XXVII, containing sketches of the Fall of Troy, the Odyssey, the Æneid, and of certain Norse lays, are a revision of corresponding chapters in " The Age of Fable." Chapters VII–XX, and XXII, comprising Myths of the Greater Divinities of Heaven, Earth, the Underworld, and the Waters, Myths of the Lesser Divinities of the same regions, Myths of the Older Heroes and Myths of the Younger Heroes, and the outline of the Trojan War, represent a total rearrangement and recomposition of the original material, section by section, and frequently paragraph by paragraph, — such portions of " The Age of Fable " as have been retained being abridged or rewritten, and, in places too frequent to enumerate, supplemented by new and necessary sentences, paragraphs, and sections. The Introduction, the first six chapters (on the Greek Myths of the Creation, and the attributes of Greek and Roman divinities), Chapters XXI and XXVIII–XXXII (on the Houses concerned in the Trojan War, the Saga of the Volsungs, the Lay of the Nibelungs, Wagner's Ring of the Nibelung, and on the origin, elements, distribution, and preservation of myth), the choice of poetic and artistic illustration, the footnotes referring to sources, and the Commentary are wholly, or essentially, my own. In fact, there is little but the scaffolding of " The Age of Fable " now remaining in the book.

Although in the Index of Mythological Subjects and their Sources the more common myths of some other nations are briefly stated, no myths save those known to the Greeks, Romans, Norsemen, or Germans have been included in the body of the text. The scope of selection has been thus confined for three reasons: first, the regard for necessary limits ; second, the desirability of emphasizing only such myths as have actually acclimated themselves in English-speaking lands and have influenced the spirit, form, and habit of English imaginative thought ; third, the necessity of excluding all but the unquestionably classic. The term *classic*, however, is, of course, not restricted to the products of Greece and Rome ; nor is it employed as synonymous with Classical or as antithetical to Romantic. From the extreme Classical to the extreme Romantic is a far cry; but as human life knows no divorce of necessity from freedom, so genuine art knows neither an unrelieved Classical nor an unrestrained Romantic. Classical and Romantic are relative terms. The Classical and the Romantic of one generation may merit equally to be the classics of the next. Therefore certain Hellenic myths of romantic spirit or construction have been included in this work, and certain Norse and German myths have not been excluded. Whatever is admitted, is admitted as first-class : first-class, because simple, spontaneous, and beautiful; because fulfilling the requirements of perennial freshness, of æsthetic potency, and of ideal worth.

In the matter of illustrative English and American poems the principle of selection has been that the . verses shall translate a myth from the classic original, or exemplify the poetic idealization and embellishment of the subject, or suggest the spirit and mien of ancient art. But in each case regard has been had to the æsthetic value of the poem or the citation. In the search for suitable examples I have derived valuable assistance from Mr. E. C. Guild's "Bibliography of Greek Mythology in English Poetry of the Nineteenth Century" (Bowdoin College, *Library Bulletin No. 1*). The student is also referred to A. E. Sawtelle's "Sources of Spenser's Mythology," C. G. Osgood's "Classical Mythology of Milton," and R. K. Root's "Classical Mythology in Shakespeare" (Holt, 1896, 1900, and 1903, respectively).

In the Commentary four things have been attempted : first, an explanation, under each section, of ordinary textual difficulties; second, an unpretentious exposition of the myth or a brief statement of the more evident interpretations advanced by philologists or ethnologists; third, an indication of certain additional poems or verses that illustrate the myth ; fourth, special mention of such masterpieces of ancient and modern sculpture and painting as may serve to introduce the student or the general reader to a field of æsthetic profit neglected by the great mass of our people. For the poetic conception of most of the myths contained in Chapters I–XXIV, we are indebted to the Greek imagination ; but since this book is intended for students of English poetry, and since in English poetry Latin names of mythological characters are much more frequently employed than Greek, the Latin designations or Latinized forms of Greek names have been, so far as possible, retained ; and such variations as Jupiter, Jove — Proserpina, Proserpine, freely used. In the chapters, however, on the attributes of the Greek gods, names exclusively Greek have been placed in parentheses after the usual Roman equivalents, Latin appellations, or designations common to both Greek and Roman usage. In the transliteration of Greek names I have followed, also, the prevalent practice of our poets, which is, generally speaking, the practice of the Romans. The diphthong ει, for instance, is transliterated according to the accepted English pronunciation, which in individual words perpetuates the preference of the Latins for the *e* sound or the *i* sound respectively. So Ἀτρείδης becomes Atrīdes ; Ἰφιμέδεια, Iphimedīa. But, on the other hand, Κυθέρεια becomes Cytherēa ; Πηνειός, Penēus ; and Μήδεια, Medēa ; while owing to purely popular English custom, such a name as Φειδίας has become, not Pheidias nor even Phīdias, but — *Phĭdias*. A few names of islands, towns, persons, etc., that even in Latin retain their Greek forms, — such as Delos, Naxos, Argos, Aglauros, Pandrosos, — have been transferred without modification. So also has Poseidon, because that is the common English spelling. In short, the practice aimed at has been not that of scientific uniformity, but of acknowledged poetic usage. In the titles of the illustrative cuts, Greek names have been used for works of Greek origin, Latin for the Roman.

For the benefit of readers who do not know the fundamental rules for the pronunciation of Greek and Latin proper names in English, a brief statement of rules is prefixed to the Index ; and in the Index of Mythological Subjects and their Sources names are not only accented, but, when necessary, diacritically marked.

In the preparation of the Text and Commentary more or less use has been made of : Roscher's Ausführliches Lexikon der griechischen und römischen Mythologie (Lieferungen 1–21, Teubner, Leipzig); Preller's Griechische Mythologie (2 Bde., Berlin, 1861); Max Müller's Chips from a German Workshop, Science of Religion (London, 1873), Science of Language (7th ed., 2 vols., London, 1873), Oxford Essays (1856); Sir G. W. Cox's Mythology of the Aryan Nations (2 vols., London, 1878); Frazer's Golden Bough; W. Warde Fowler's Roman Festivals (London, 1899); Welcker's Griechische Götterlehre; Baumeister's Denkmäler des klassischen Alterthums; Murray's Manual of Mythology (New York, 1880); Smith's Dictionary of Greek and Roman Biography and Mythology; Duruy's Histories of Rome and Greece; Keightley's Greek and Roman Mythology; Kelsey's Outline of Greek and Roman Mythology (Boston, 1889); Horn's Geschichte der Literatur des skandinavischen Nordens (Leipzig, 1880); Cleasby and Vigfusson's Icelandic Dictionary; Lüning's Die Edda (Zürich, 1859); Vigfusson and Powell's Corpus Poeticum Boreale (2 vols., Oxford, 1883); Paul's Grundriss der germanischen Philologie, 1 Bd., 5 Lfg. (article *Mythologie*, by E. Mogk); Grimm's Teutonic Mythology (translated by Stallybrass, 3 vols.); Werner Hahn's Das Nibelungenlied; Lang's Myth, Ritual, and Religion (2 vols., London, 1887), and *Mythology* (Encyc. Brit., Vol. 9); Tylor's Anthropology (New York, 1881) and Primitive Culture (2 vols.); J. W. Powell's Annual Reports of the Bureau of Ethnology (7 vols., beginning 1879–1880, Washington, D.C.); Keary's Outlines of Primitive Belief; Fiske's Myths and Myth-makers (Boston); Whitney's Oriental and Linguistic Studies; W. P. Johnston's The Origin of Myth; and of other works to which due reference is made in the footnotes and Commentary. The student is also referred to F. B. Jevons' edition of Plutarch's Romane Questions, translated by Philemon Holland (London, 1892) (introduction on Roman Mythology); and to C. G. Leland's Etruscan-Roman Remains in Popular Tradition (London, 1892). The Maps,

furnished by Messrs. Ginn and Company from other of their pub-
lications, have, with the kind consent of the authors of those works,
in some instances been adapted by me to suit the present purpose.

The principal authorities used in the selection of the illustrations of this new edition are: Baumeister, Denkmäler des
klassischen Alterthums (3 vols., Munich, 1888); Furtwängler,
Masterpieces of Greek Sculpture (London, 1905); Ernest Gardner, Ancient Athens (New York and London, 1902); Percy
Gardner, A Grammar of Greek Art (New York and London,
1905); and Sculptured Tombs of Hellas (London, 1896); Percy
Gardner and Jevons, A Manual of Greek Antiquities (London,
1895); Gerhard, Auserlesene griechische Vasenbilder (1840–1858);
Gusman, Pompei (London, 1900); Harrison and Maccoll, Greek
Vase Paintings (London, 1894); E. von Mach, Handbook of
Greek and Roman Sculpture (Boston, 1905); and Greek Sculp-
ture, Its Spirit and Principles (Boston, 1903); A. S. Murray,
Handbook of Greek Archæology (London, 1892); History of
Greek Sculpture (2 vols., London, 1883); and Sculptures of the
Parthenon (London, 1903); A. S. Murray and C. A. Hutton,
Greek Bronzes and Terra Cotta Statuettes (London, 1898); C. O.
Müller, Denkmäler der alten Kunst (Göttingen, 1832); Overbeck,
Griechische Kunstmythologie (1871——); Emil Presuhn, Pompeji,
1874–1881 (Leipzig, 1882); Salomon Reinach, Peintures de
vases antiques (including the collections of Millin, 1808, and
Millingen, 1813 (Paris, 1891)), and Apollo (Paris, 1907); H.
Roux Aîné, Herculaneum and Pompei; Roscher, Ausführliches
Lexikon der griechischen und römischen Mythologie (1884——)
(Lieferungen 1–17 in Vol. I, 18 on in Vol. II); Anton Springer,
Handbuch der Kunstgeschichte (I _Alterthum_, Leipzig, 1904);
Charles Waldstein, The Argive Heræum (2 vols.); and the archæ-
ological periodicals as cited in the List of Illustrations.

The acknowledgment of assistance made in the former edition
is here renewed.

CHARLES MILLS GAYLEY

CONTENTS

PART II

THE HISTORY OF MYTH

LIST OF ILLUSTRATIONS

FULL-PAGE ILLUSTRATIONS AND MAPS

INTRODUCTION

THE STUDY OF MYTHOLOGY IN CONNECTION WITH ENGLISH POETRY AND WITH ART

Our American educational methods too frequently seek to produce the effect of polish upon a kind of sandstone information that will not stand polishing. With such fatuity many of our teachers in the secondary schools exercise their pupils in the study of English masterpieces and in the critical estimate of æsthetic qualities before acquainting them with the commonplace facts and fables that, transmitted through generations, are the material of much of our poetry because the material of daily converse, imagination, and thought. These commonplaces of tradition are to be found largely in the literature of mythology. Of course the evil would be neither so widespread nor so dangerous if more of the guardians and instructors of our youth were at home even among the Greek and Latin classics. But for various reasons, — some valid, as, for instance, the importance of increased attention to the modern languages and the natural sciences ; others worthless, as the so-called utilitarian protest against the cultivation of " dead " languages, — for various reasons the study of the classics is at present considerably impaired. It is, therefore, incumbent upon our universities and schools, recognizing this fact and deploring it, to abate so far as possible the unfortunate consequences that proceed therefrom, until, by a readjustment of subjects of instruction and of the periods allotted them, the Greek and Latin classics shall be reinstated in their proper place as a means of discipline, a humanizing influence, the historic background against which our present appears. For, cut off from the intellectual and imaginative sources of Greece and Rome, the state and statesmanship, legislation and law, society and manners, philosophy, religion, literature, art, and even artistic appreciation, run readily shallow and soon dry.

Now, one evident means of tempering the consequence of this neglect of the classics is the study of them through translations and summaries. Such secondhand study must indeed be ever a makeshift; for the literature of a people inheres in its language, and loses its seeming and often its characteristic when caparisoned in the trappings of another speech, — an utterance totally dissimilar, the outcome of diverse conditions of physical environment, history, social and intellectual tradition. But in dealing with the purely imaginative products of antiquity, the inefficacy of translation may be somewhat offset if those products be reproduced, so far as possible, not in the prosaic but in the poetic atmosphere and in the imaginative garb of art. For though the phenomena of plastic art are not the same in one continent as in another, or from one century to the next, and though the fashion of poetry itself varies from age to age and from clime to clime, the genesis of imagination is universal, its products are akin, and its process is continuous. For this reason the study of the imaginative thought of the ancients through the artistic creations of the moderns is commended to students and readers as feasible and profitable.

The study of the classic myths stimulates to creative production, prepares for the appreciation of poetry and other kinds of art, and furnishes a clew to the spiritual development of the race.

1. Classic mythology has been for succeeding poetry, sculpture, and painting, a treasure house replete with golden tales and glimmering thoughts, passions in the rough and smooth, and fancies rich bejeweled. Like Virgil's Shadows that flit by the Lethean stream until at beck of Fate they revisit upper day and the ever-tranquil stars, these ghosts of "far-off things and battles long ago," peopling the murmurous glades of myth, await the artist who shall bestow on each his new and predetermined form and restore them, purified and breathing of Elysian air, to the world of life and ever-young mankind.

2. For the reader the study of mythology does, in this respect, as much as for poet, sculptor, or painter. It assists him to thrid the labyrinth of art, not merely with the clew of tradition, but with a thread of surer knowledge whose surest strand is sympathy.

The knowledge of mythic lore has led men in the past broadly to appreciate the motives and conditions of ancient art and literature, and the uniform and ordered evolution of the æsthetic sense. And, beside enriching us with heirlooms of fiction and pointing us to the sources of imaginative joy from which early poets of Hellenic verse, or Norse, or English, drank, the classic myths quicken the imaginative and emotional faculties to-day, just as of old. How many a man held by the sorrows of the Labdacidæ or the love of Alcestis, by some curious wonder in Pausanias, or some woe in Hyginus, has waked to the consciousness of artistic fancy and creative force within himself! How many, indifferent to the well-known round, the trivial task, the nearest care of home, have read the Farewell to Andromache and lived a new sympathy, an unselfish thrill, a purified delight! And not only as an impulse toward artistic output, or patriotic devotion, or domestic altruism, but as a restraining influence, a chastener of æsthetic excess, a moderator of the "unchartered freedom" that knows no mean between idolatry and loathing, of the foolish frenzy that affects new things, abnormal and sensational, in literature, music, and the plastic arts, — as such a tutor and governor is the study of beautiful myths invaluable. Long familiarity with the sweet simplicity, the orderly restraint, the severe regard, the filial awe that pervade the myths of Greece and Rome, — or with the newness of life and fullness and wonder of it, the naïveté and the romance, of Eddic lore, — cannot but graciously temper our modern estimate of artistic worth.

The study, when illustrated by masterpieces of literature and art, should lead to the appreciation of concrete artistic productions of both these kinds.

It goes without saying that a rational series of somewhat consecutive stories is more serviceable to the reader than a congeries of data acquired by spasmodic consultation of the classical dictionary, —a mass of information bolted, as it were, but by no means digested. If, moreover, these stories are narrated in genealogical and realistic sequence and are illustrated by lyric, narrative, and descriptive passages of modern literature, there is furnished not only that material of allusion and reference for which the student nowadays trusts to meager and disjointed textbook notes, but a potentiality that should render the general reading of *belles-lettres* more profitable. For a previous acquaintance with the material of literary tradition heightens the appreciation of each allusive passage as it is encountered; it enables the reader to sympathize with the mood and to enter into the purpose of the poet, the essayist, the novelist, the orator; it expands the intellectual lungs for the atmosphere breathed by the artist, at any rate for a literary and social atmosphere less asthmatic than that to which so many of us are unconsciously habituated. Of course all this advantage would far better result from the first-hand nutriment and discipline of the Greek and Latin classics; of course direct familiarity with the writers of Greece and Rome is the *sine qua non* of level-headed criticism and broad evaluation of modern literature; and, of course, a sympathy with the imaginings of old is the best incentive to an æsthetic estimate not only of art but of nature to-day; but if our American pupils and many of their teachers cannot quaff Massic and Falernian, they do well to scent the bouquet. In time a sense of flavor may perchance be stimulated, and ultimately a desire for nearer acquaintance with the literatures that we inherit.

The study of these ancient tales serves, then, much more than the purpose of special information. It refines the æsthetic judgment in general, and heightens the enjoyment of such works of literature as, not treating of mythical or classical subjects, still possess the characteristics of the classic: the unconscious simplicity, the inevitable charm, and the noble ideality. The Lycidas, the Adonais, the Thyrsis, the In Memoriam, the Ode to Duty, the Bothie of Tober-na-Vuolich, the Hymn of Man, Love is Enough, Prospice, Festus, the Ode of Life, the Dream of Gerontius, Lying in the Grass, and Simmenthal must mean little to one devoid of the spirit of classicism.

In respect of art a similar inspiration, aid, instruction, are afforded by the study. This volume is liberally supplied with cuts of famous paintings and sculptures of mythical subjects. Familiarity with specimens of ancient art, even through the medium of photography and engraving, must not only cultivate the historic sense but stimulate the æsthetic. The cruder efforts of the ancients, no less than the more refined, are windows through which we view the ancient mind. The frequent contemplation of their nobler efforts and of the modern masterpieces here reproduced may avail to lift some from the level of apathy or provinciality in matters of imagination ; some it may spur to a study of the originals, some to artistic creation. A public which, from year to year, displays a deeper interest in the art of foreign lands will despise no auxiliary to a more intelligent appreciation of that art. A country whose future in artistic achievement cannot be prophesied in a paragraph will more and more truly recognize the value of a study that is an introduction to much that is best in art as it exists.

3. Furthermore, it must be borne in mind that the myths of the ancients, as the earliest literary crystallization of social order and religious fear, record the incipient history of religious ideals and of moral conduct. For though ethnologists may insist that to search for truth *in* mythology is vain, the best of them will grant that to search for truth *through* mythology is wise and profitable. If we accept the statement (often stretched beyond its proper limit) that mythology is primitive philosophy, and the other statement that an ancient philosophy never dies, but by process of internal growth, of modification, and of accretion acquires a purer spirit and a new and higher form, — then, since truth was never yet conceived of error (*ex nihilo nihil fit*), the truth now recognized, while it did not exist in that fraction of myth which happens to be irrational, existed as an archetypal impulse, — set the myth in motion, and, as a process refining the mind of man, tended steadily to eliminate from primitive philosophy (that is, from the myths that embodied primitive philosophy) the savage, ephemeral, and irrational element. For all myths spring from the universal and inalienable desire to know, to enjoy, to teach. These impulses of knowledge, of imaginative relaxation, of conduct, are the throbbing of the heart of reason ; the first or the second is the primal pulse of every myth, and to the life of every myth each impulse may be, at some period, contributory. This study has led men to trace soberly the progress of their kind from the twilight of gray conjecture to the dawn of spiritual conviction and rational individuality ; to discern a continuity of thought, an outward reach of imagination, an upward

lift of moral and religious ideas; to confess the brotherhood of humanity and an inspiring purpose which holds good for every race and through all time.

SUGGESTIONS TO TEACHERS

1. *Of the Classic Myths in their Relation to Literature.* It is essential that the teacher of mythology, no matter what textbook or system he uses or what classic epic he proposes to present, should first make himself acquainted with the meaning of myth, its origin and elements; the difference between myth and fable, between myths explanatory and myths æsthetic, myths reasonable and myths unreasonable, the theories of myth-making as a process of deterioration or as a process of development. He should also inform himself concerning the ways in which the leading myths have been disseminated, and how the survivors have been preserved. Materials for this preparation he will find in Chapters XXX–XXXII of this book as readily, perhaps, as elsewhere; but no matter where he obtains this information he should in a simple and interesting talk pass on the cream of it to the pupils about to begin the study of the stories themselves. He will in that way bring them to a reasonable appreciation of the value of myths and their relation to our civilization, and awaken in them anticipatory interest in the proposed reading. It is a great mistake to plunge students of high-school age, without preliminary orientation and a justification of the study, into a world which may otherwise appear to them unreasonable in conception and unrelated in experience. Pupils may, if time permits, read these concluding chapters, and so obtain a systematic outlook upon the subject, during a brief review in the senior year, but not earlier.

This book should be studied for its materials and the inspiration that it affords, — not word by word for its style, or as a dictionary or scientific authority; nor paragraph by paragraph with a painful committing to memory of each myth and each episode in the myth. Discrimination must be made. Some of these myths, and especially the episodes from the epics (Chapters XXII–XXIX), are to be read rapidly and in large assignments, sometimes at home with reports in class, sometimes in class and at sight, but always for the enjoyment. Others are to be studied in detail, but solely when they are of special and vital significance, historically, morally, or æsthetically. Emphasis should be laid only occasionally and sparingly upon interpretations of mythical materials. What both teacher and student should aim at is the picture—manners, morals, ideals, heroic figures, epic events, broad and vivid against the canvas of antiquity: that, and the reality of classic order, grandeur, and restraint.

The myths are here presented in a logical and genealogical arrangement; and they should be studied in this order, so that the pupil may carry away, not a jumble of sporadic recollections, but some conception of the systems of creative imagination which obtained in earlier civilizations. The knowledge of the myths and the proper perspective of their relation, one to another, may further be fixed by the study of the family ties that motivate many of the incidents of mythical adventure, and that must have been commonplaces of information to the inventors and narrators of these stories.

The myths may well be reproduced as exercises in narration, comparison, description; and they may be regarded as stimulus for imaginative invention concerning local wonders and beauties of nature. Pupils may also be encouraged to consider, and to comment upon, the moral qualities of the heroes and heroines of mythology. Thus they may be led to recognize the difference between ancient and modern standards of right and wrong. To this end, and for the supply of further nutriment, it is important that teachers collect from their reading of the classic originals, or from translations of the Iliad, the Odyssey, the Greek dramatists, the Æneid, the Metamorphoses, etc., material supplementary to the text, and give it freely to their classes. To facilitate this practice the sources of the myths have been indicated in the footnotes of this volume, and a few of the best translations have been mentioned in the Commentary. Instructors should also read to the classes illustrative English poems, or portions of them based upon the myths under consideration; and they should encourage the pupils to collect from their English reading additional examples of the literary survival or adaptation of ancient story. For this purpose special sections of the Commentary have been prepared, indicating some of the best known literary applications of each myth.

The Commentary is numbered in sections corresponding to those of the text. The Textual Notes should be studied in connection with each lesson, the Interpretative more sparingly, as I have said. They should not be suffered to spoil the interest in the stories as such. They are of interest in themselves only to maturer minds. Allusions and interpretations which the younger pupil does not appreciate will, if the book is used for purposes of reference in his further English, Latin, or Greek studies, be clear before the end of his course.

From the outset care should be taken that pupils give to the classical names their proper accent, and that they anglicize both vowels and consonants according to the recognized rules laid down in the Latin grammars, the English dictionaries, and the pages preceding the Index of this book.

Mythological and classical geography should not be neglected. The maps accompanying this volume will be serviceable ; but there should be in the classroom one of Kiepert's maps of the World as Known to the Ancients (Orbis Veteribus Notus), or maps of Ancient Italy, Greece, and Asia Minor. The teacher will find the International Atlas (G. P. Putnam's Sons, New York), A. Keith Johnston's School and College Atlas of Ancient Geography, or the new edition of the same by James Cranstoun, issued as Ginn and Company's Classical Atlas, indispensable in the prosecution of general reading.

When it is the intention to study, in connection with the book, an Homeric epic or a portion of it, the teacher should first make sure that the class has an adequate preliminary training in general mythology (such, for instance, as may be provided by the first twenty-one chapters); he should then outline rapidly and entertainingly the epic as a whole, emphasizing its position in the literature of the world and its relation to the world of its own times, before proceeding to read it in detail with the class. Excellent suggestions as to this method of study are offered in the Introduction to Maxwell & Chubb's Pope's Homer's Iliad, Books I, VI,

XXII, and XXIV (Longmans), and in the Introduction to the Riverside Edition of the Odyssey : Ulysses among the Phæacians (Houghton Mifflin Company).

The more important myths and the best illustrative poems should provide not only nutriment for thought, but material for memory. Our youth in the push for hasty achievement bolt their meals ; they masticate little, swallow everything, digest nothing, — and having agonized, forget. If fewer things were dispatched, especially in the study of literature, and if more were intrusted to the memory, there would be something to assimilate and time to assimilate it ; there would be less dyspepsia and more muscle. Teachers and parents are overconsiderate, nowadays, of the memory in children : they approach it gingerly ; they have feared so much to wring its withers that in most children the memory has grown too soft for saddling. In our apprehension lest pupils may turn out parrots, we have too often turned them out loons. It is better that a few of the facts in their heads be wrong than that no facts be there at all. With all our study of children and our gabble about methods of teaching them, while we insist, properly enough, that youth is the seedtime of observation, we seem to have forgotten that it is also the harvest-time of memory. It is easy for children to remember what they learn, it is a delight for them to commit to memory ; we act criminally when we send them forth with hardly a fact or a date or a glorious verse in the memory of one out of ten of them. Such, unfortunately, is the case in many of our schools ; and such was not the case in the day of our fathers. Pupils should be encouraged to recite *memoriter* the best poems and verses that accompany the myths here given ; and they should not be allowed to pass allusions already explained without recalling verses that contain them.

But above all things should be cultivated, by means of this study, the spiritual capabilities of our youth. *Pabulum* for thought, accurate habits of memory, critical judgment, simplicity and directness of oral and written expression, may all be furnished or developed by other educative agencies ; but what stimulus to fancy, to poetic sensitiveness and reflection, to a near kinship with the spirit of nature humanized, can be found more cogent than the contemplation of the poetic traditions that abide in verse? Mythology, fraught with the fire of imagination, kindles the present from the past.

In this new world of ours, shall slopes and mountains, gorges, cañons, flowery fields and forests, rivers, bays, Titanic lakes, and shoreless reach of ocean be seen of eyes that lack insight, be known of men for whom nature does not live? Surely the age of myth is not wholly past; surely the beauties and the wonders of nature are a fable of things never fully revealed; surely this new republic of ours, no less than her prototypes by Tyrrhenian and Ægean seas, utters, in her queenly form and flowing robes, a spirit, a truth, a potential poetry, and a beauty of art, the grace of which we Americans, with deeper imaginative training and sympathy and awe, may yet more highly value and more clearly comprehend.

2. *Of the Classic Myths in their Relation to Art*.[1] The illustration of a book on ancient mythology offers great difficulties, because the modern reader expects one thing and the ancient artist, on whose works one must rely, intentionally offers a very different thing. We have grown to be a reading people, forming our ideas largely on the written word, while in antiquity the spoken word opened the door to understanding. A story which has been committed to writing is fixed for all time, having lost its power of growth; whereas a tale that passes from mouth to mouth, with no record by which to check its accuracy in particulars, is free to expand. It changes with the moods of those who tell it, and the intellectual and moral standards of those who listen. People to-day are unimaginative and literal. They also expect that the pictures which illustrate their books shall follow the individual conceptions of the author closely. When the story is dramatized a certain latitude is granted to the actor; the artist, however, who illustrates the book has no such freedom. He is expected to take precisely the author's view of a fictitious character, and, consequently, his individuality may show itself only in the technique. In antiquity there were no standard books of fiction or of myths. When writing came into use with the sixth century before Christ, the individual versions of this or that great epic poem or drama were preserved; but the great mass of the people knew them, not because they had read the manuscripts,

[1] See Preface.

but because they had heard them acted or recited. Book illustrations, therefore, were unknown. Yet so powerful was the impression which the myths made on the people that most of the artists drew their inspiration from them. Artists and poets alike wished to make real the powerful characters of Greek tradition. To make a literally true illustration of any one version of a great myth was not the aim of a classic artist.

Another difficulty is found in the fact that few ancient myths continued to be equally interesting to the people all the time. It is therefore necessary for us, in choosing illustrations, to draw on all periods of ancient art, the crude beginning and the decline as well as the brief span of fine art. The comparatively meager store of genuinely classic works of art acts as one of the greatest obstacles to the compilation of a continuous record of classic myths in classic art. To give such a record, however, rather than to *illustrate* his book, must be the aim of the author who publishes to-day a version of ancient mythology together with such pictures or reliefs or statues as are preserved. The modern reader of such a book should therefore appreciate this fact : he must make allowance for the gradual development of ancient art. The picture is not there for the sake of strengthening the written work, but for its own sake. It often offers an independent version of the myth which he reads, and at all times may give him an insight into the mental make-up of the classic people.

Sculpture was the finest art of the Greeks, if one may judge by the remains. In this province the artists worked according to the best principles of art, making their appeal directly to the nobler side of man. Before an ancient statue one feels the power of an idea immediately, and not by the circuitous route of remembering a sequence of words which may have aimed to suggest a similar idea. The Greeks were the least literal in their sculpture. Their marbles, therefore, cannot yield *illustrations* which the modern editor can use, except when they embody, like the Demeter of Knidos (Fig. 29) or the Athena of Velletri (Fig. 10), a well-defined character-conception. The modern reader, on the other hand, cannot fail to notice that this conception never does justice to the character of the goddess as it appears in all the myths, and very rarely even to that characteristic which may dominate the particular version of any one myth. If such pictures, however, were entirely omitted from the book, the best means of appreciating the essential nobility of the Greek mind would be lost.

None of the Greek masterpieces of painting are extant. Their attenuated influence, however, may be traced in the Italian wall paintings from Pompeii and elsewhere. Painting permits greater literalness than sculpture. The picture from Herculaneum, for instance, — Io, Argus, and Mercury (Fig. 47), — tells a definite story and one which is also told by the poets. But the painter has considered the making of a pleasing picture first, and given only a secondary thought to accuracy of tradition. This must be so; for while we may without displeasure listen to the description of a monster, we cannot see his actual representation without discomfort. When we hear how the companions of Ulysses were turned into swine, the tragic note is never lost. To paint this scene, however, and not to border on the ridiculous or the burlesque is given only to the greatest artist — if it is at all possible.

Fortunately for our purposes of illustration, there was a class of secondary artists in Greece which did not always shrink from selecting subjects ill adapted for art, and from rendering them with slight variations so that they are neither bad to look at nor altogether untrue. These were the painters of vases. Some of them were masters of their craft (cf. Fig. 116), others were of only mediocre skill. All, however, like their nobler brethren, were primarily concerned with the decorative and technical side of their art and but secondarily with their subject. If the story, for instance, called for four persons and their space for five, they unhesitatingly added the fifth person, and, vice versa, removed one without compunction if they had place for fewer figures than the story demanded. Being, moreover, commercial people, they painted according to fashion. Whatever version of a myth happened to be popular, that they selected, so that it has been possible to trace by their vases the changes which several myths underwent from the sixth century onward.

A careful student notices the similarity of types in many of these pictures and realizes that the ancient painter of vases started out with a certain stock-in-trade which he altered as little as possible, adding something new only where it was absolutely necessary.

From these observations it is clear that the works of men who were least gifted artistically are the best adapted for the purposes of book illustrations; for a painter is literal in the inverse ratio of his worth as artist. Nothing, therefore, could be less fair than to judge Greek vase painting by the collection of pictures here offered. Only paintings like Figures 85 and 101, for instance, can give a hint of the best that these men produced.

Going gradually down the scale of artists one finally comes to the level of the makers of Roman sarcophagi, in whose honor it can only be said that to descend lower is impossible. Several myths, however, — the story of the fall of Phaëthon (Fig. 59), for instance, — are not illustrated in art before the decadent period of imperial Roman sculpture. It is therefore necessary to draw also upon this source.

Of course unity of art or school or excellence cannot be preserved in a set of pictures which groups the Demeter of Knidos (Fig. 29), the blinding of Polyphemus (Fig. 171), and the fall of Phaëthon (Fig. 59). But individually the pictures help to fix in memory the particular stories that they are chosen to illustrate; and collectively they show how strongly the myths here retold influenced the noblest fancy of the great artists as well as the receptive minds of mediocre artisans. The suggestive power of classic myths, moreover, was not confined to antiquity. When learning and culture returned to the world in the Renaissance, this power also returned. Raphael (see Fig. 12) and Michelangelo (see Fig. 183) were under its sway, and so are many modern artists (see Figs. 72 and 154). They did not all understand the classic spirit equally, therefore some of their pictures are modern in everything save the title, while others have caught the truth with singular accuracy and are modern only in technique. Adding these Italian and more recent pictures to the collection further destroys mere unity, but it insures, on the other hand, a full appreciation of the abiding and ennobling power of ancient mythology.

THE CLASSIC MYTHS

PART I

MYTHS OF DIVINITIES AND HEROES

CHAPTER I

GREEK MYTHS OF THE CREATION

1. Purpose of the Study. Interwoven with the fabric of our English literature, of our epics, dramas, lyrics, and novels, of our essays and orations, like a golden warp where the woof is only too often of silver, are the myths of certain ancient nations. It is the purpose of this work to relate some of these myths, and to illus trate the uses to which they have been put in English literature, and, incidentally, in art.

2. The Fable and the Myth. Careful discrimination must be made between the fable and the myth. A fable is a story, like that of King Log, or the Fox and the Grapes, in which characters and plot, neither pretending to reality nor demanding credence, are fabricated confessedly as the vehicle of moral or didactic instruction. Dr. Johnson narrows still further the scope of the fable: "It seems to be, in its genuine state, a narrative in which *beings irrational, and sometimes inanimate*, are, for the purpose of moral instruction, feigned to act and speak with human interests and passions." Myths, on the other hand, are stories of anonymous origin, prevalent among primitive peoples and by them accepted as true, concerning supernatural beings and events, or natural beings and events influenced by supernatural agencies. Fables are made by individuals; they may be told in any stage of a nation's history, — by a Jotham when the Israelites were still under the Judges, 1200 years before Christ, or by Christ himself in the days of the most critical Jewish scholarship; by a Menenius when Rome was still involved in petty squabbles of plebeians and patricians, or by Phædrus and Horace in the Augustan age of Roman imperialism and Roman letters; by an Æsop, well-nigh fabulous, to fabled fellow-slaves and Athenian tyrants, or by La Fontaine to the Grand Monarch and the most highly civilized race of seventeenth-century Europe.

Fables are vessels made to order into which a lesson may be poured. Myths are born, not made. They are born in the infancy of a people. They owe their features not to any one historic individual, but to the imaginative efforts of generations of story-tellers. The myth of Pandora, the first woman, endowed by the immortals with heavenly graces, and of Prometheus, who stole fire from heaven for the use of man; the myth of the earthborn giants that in the beginning contested with the gods the sovereignty of the universe; of the moon-goddess who, with her buskined nymphs, pursues the chase across the azure of the heavens, or descending to earth cherishes the youth Endymion, — these myths, germinating in some quaint and childish interpretation of natural events or in some fireside fancy, have put forth unconsciously, under the nurture of the simple folk that conceived and tended them, luxuriant branches and leaves of narrative, and blossoms of poetic comeliness and form.

The myths that we shall relate present wonderful accounts of the creation, histories of numerous divine beings, adventures of heroes in which magical and ghostly agencies play a part, and where animals and inanimate nature don the attributes of men and gods. Many of these myths treat of divinities once worshiped by the Greeks and the Romans, and by our Norse and German forefathers in the dark ages. Myths, more or less like these, may be found in the literatures of nearly all nations; many are in the memories and mouths of savage races at this time existent. But the stories here narrated are no longer believed by any one. The so-called divinities of Olympus and of Asgard have not a single worshiper among men. They dwell only in the realm of memory and imagination; they are enthroned in the palace of art.

The stories of Greek, Roman, Norse, and German mythology that have most influenced our English literature will follow in the order named. The Romans, being by nature a practical, not a poetic, people, incorporated in their literature the mythology of the Greeks. We shall, however, append to our description of the Greek gods a brief account of the native Latin divinities that retained an individuality in Roman literature.

3. Origin of the World.[1] There were among the Greeks several accounts of the beginning of things. Homer tells us that River Ocean, a deep and mighty flood, encircling land and sea like a serpent with its tail in its mouth, was the source of all. According to other myths Night and Darkness were the prime elements

FIG. 1. JUPITER SURVEYING THE WORLD

of Nature, and from them sprang Light. Still a third theory, attributed to Orpheus, asserts that Time was in the beginning, but had himself no beginning; that from him proceeded Chaos, a yawning abyss wherein brooded Night and Mist and fiery air, or Æther; that Time caused the mist to spin round the central fiery air till the mass, assuming the form of a huge world egg, flew, by reason of its rapid rotation, into halves. Of these, one was Heaven, the other Earth. From the center of the egg proceeded Eros (Love) and other wondrous beings.

---

[1] Supplementary information concerning many of the myths may be found in the corresponding sections of the Commentary. For the pronunciation of names see Index, and Rules preceding the Index.

But the most consistent account of the origin of the world and of the gods is given by the poet Hesiod, who tells us that Chaos, the yawning abyss, composed of Void, Mass, and Darkness in confusion, preceded all things else. Next came into being broad-bosomed Earth, and beautiful Love who should rule the hearts of gods and men. But from Chaos itself issued Erebus,[1] the mysterious darkness that is under Earth, — and Night, dwelling in the remote regions of sunset.

From Mother Earth proceeded first the starry vault of Heaven, durable as brass or iron, where the gods were to take up their abode. Earth brought forth next the mountains and fertile fields, the stony plains, the sea, and the plants and animals that possess them.

4. Origin of the Gods. So far we have a history of the throes and changes of the physical world; now begins the history of gods and of men. For in the heart of creation Love begins to stir, making of material things creatures male and female, and bringing them together by instinctive affinity. First Erebus and Night, the children of Chaos, are wedded, and from them spring Light and Day; then *Uranus*, the personified Heaven, takes *Gæa*, the Earth, to wife, and from their union issue Titans and hundred-handed monsters and Cyclopes.

The *Titans*[2] appear to be the personification of mighty convulsions of the physical world, of volcanic eruptions and earthquakes. They played a quarrelsome part in mythical history; they were instigators of hatred and strife. Homer mentions specially two of them, Iapetus and Cronus; but Hesiod enumerates thirteen. Of these, the more important are Oceanus and Tethys, Hyperion and Thea, Cronus and Rhea, Iapetus, Themis, and Mnemosyne. The three *Cyclopes* represented the terrors of rolling thunder, of the lightning-flash, and of the thunderbolt; and, probably, for this reason, one fiery eye was deemed enough for each. The hundred-handed monsters, or *Hecatonchires*, were also three in number. In them, probably, the Greeks imaged the sea with its multitudinous waves, its roar, and its breakers that seem to shake the earth. These lightning-eyed, these hundred-handed

---

[1] So far as possible, Latin designations, or Latinized forms of Greek names, are used.
[2] On the Titans, etc., Preller's Griech. Mythol. 1, 37.

monsters, their father Uranus feared, and attempted to destroy by thrusting them into Tartarus, the profound abysm of the earth. Whereupon Mother Earth, or Gæa, indignant, called for help upon her elder children, the Titans. None dared espouse her cause save Cronus, the crafty. With an iron sickle he lay in wait for his sire, fell upon him, and drove him, grievously wounded, from the encounter. From the blood of the mutilated Uranus leaped into being the Furies, whose heads writhe with serpents; the Giants, a novel race of monsters; and the Melic Nymphs, invidious maidens of the ashen spear.

5. The Rule of Cronus. Now follows the reign of Cronus, lord of Heaven and Earth. He is, from the beginning, of incalculable years. In works of art his head is veiled, to typify his cunning and his reserve; he bears the sickle not only as memento of the means by which he brought his father's tyranny to end, but as symbol of the new period of growth and golden harvests that he ushered in.

For unknown ages Cronus and Rhea, his sister-queen, governed Heaven and Earth. To them were born three daughters, Vesta, Ceres, and Juno, and three sons, Pluto, Neptune, and Jupiter. Cronus, however, having learned from his parents that he should be dethroned by one of his own children, conceived the well-intentioned but ill-considered device of swallowing each as it was born. His queen, naturally desirous of discouraging the practice, — when it came to the turn of her sixth child, palmed off on the insatiable Cronus a stone carefully enveloped in swaddling clothes. Jupiter (or Zeus), the rescued infant, was concealed in the island of Crete, where, nurtured by the nymphs Adrastea and Ida, and fed on the milk of the goat Amalthea, he in due season attained maturity. Then, assisted by his grandmother Gæa, he constrained Cronus to disgorge the burden of his cannibal repasts. First came to light the memorable stone, which was placed in safe keeping at Delphi; then the five brothers and sisters of Jupiter, ardent to avenge themselves upon the unnatural author of their existence and their captivity.

6. The War of the Titans. In the war which ensued Iapetus and all the Titans, except Oceanus, ranged themselves on the side of their brother Cronus against Jupiter and his recently recovered kinsfolk. Jupiter and his hosts held Mount Olympus. For ages victory wavered in the balance. Finally Jupiter, acting again under the advice of Gæa, released from Tartarus, where Uranus had confined them, the Cyclopes and the Hecatonchires. Instantly they hastened to the battle-field of Thessaly, the Cyclopes to support Jupiter with their thunders and lightnings, the hundred-handed monsters with the shock of the earthquake. Provided with such artillery, shaking earth and sea, Jupiter issued to the onslaught. With the gleam of the lightning the Titans were blinded, by the earthquake they were laid low, with the flames they were well-nigh consumed : overpowered and fettered by the hands of the Hecatonchires, they were consigned to the yawning cave of Tartarus. Atlas, the son of Iapetus, was doomed to bear the heavens on his shoulders. But a more famous son of the same Titan, Prometheus, who had espoused the cause of Jove, acquired dignity hereafter to be set forth.

7. The Division of Empire. In the council of the gods that succeeded, Jupiter was chosen Sovereign of the World. He delegated to his brother Neptune (or Poseidon) the kingdom of the sea and of all the waters ; to his brother Pluto (or Hades), the government of the underworld, dark, unseen, mysterious, where the spirits of the dead should dwell, and of Tartarus, wherein were held the fallen Titans. For himself Jupiter retained Earth and the Heaven, into whose broad and sunny regions towered Olympus, the favored mountain of the greater gods.[1]

8. The Reign of Jupiter. New conflicts, however, awaited this new dynasty of Heaven — conflicts, the subject of many a tale among the ancients. Gæa, though she had aided her grandson Jupiter in the war against Cronus, was soon seized with compunctions of conscience ; and contemplating the cruel fate of her sons the Titans, she conceived schemes of vengeance upon their conqueror. Another son was born to her — *Typhon*, a monster more awful than his predecessors —; whose destiny it was to dispute the sway of the almighty Zeus. From the neck of Typhon dispread themselves a hundred dragon-heads ; his eyes shot fire, and from his black-tongued chaps proceeded the hissing of snakes, the

[1] On signification of Uranus, Cronus, Zeus, see Preller, I. 37, 38, and Commentary, §§ 4, 24.

bellowing of bulls, the roaring of lions, the barking of dogs, pipings and screams, and, at times, the voice and utterance of the gods themselves. Against Heaven this horror lifted himself; but quailing before the thunderbolt of Jove, he too descended to Tartarus, his own place and the abode of his brethren. To this day, however, he grumbles and hisses, thrusts upward a fiery tongue through the crater of a volcano, or, breathing siroccos, scorches trees and men.

Later still, the *Giants*, offspring of the blood that fell from the wounded Uranus, renewed the revolt against the Olympian gods. They were creatures nearer akin to men than were the Titans, or the Cyclopes, or Typhon. They clothed themselves in the skins of beasts, and armed themselves with rocks and trunks of trees. Their bodies and lower limbs were of snakes. They were awful to encounter or to look

FIG. 2. ATHENA AND GIANT

upon. They were named, like men, the *earthborn;* and their characteristics would suggest some prehistoric brutish race, hotheaded, not amenable to reason.[1] Of the Giants, the more mighty were Alcyoneus of the winter storms and icebergs, Pallas, and Enceladus, and Porphyrion the fire-king, — leader of the crew. In the war against them, Juno and Minerva, divinities of the new dynasty of Heaven, took active part, — and Hercules, an earthly son of Jupiter, whose arrows aided in their defeat. It was from the overthrow of Pallas that Athena (or Minerva) derived, according to certain records, her proud designation of Pallas-Athena.[2] In

---

[1] Roscher, Ausf. Lex., Article *Giganten* [J. Ilberg].
[2] The name more probably signifies Brandisher [of the Lance].

due course, like the Titans and Typhon, the Giants were buried
in the abyss of eternal darkness. What other outcome can be
expected when mere physical or brute force joins issue with the
enlightened and embattled hosts of heaven?

FIG. 3. ZEUS AND GIANTS .

9. The Origin of Man was a question which the Greeks did not
settle so easily as the Hebrews. Greek traditions do not trace all
mankind to an original pair. On the contrary, the generally
received opinion was that men grew out of trees and stones, or
were produced by the rivers or the sea. Some said that men and
gods were both derived from Mother Earth, hence both *autochthonous ;* and some, indeed, claimed an antiquity for the human race
equal to that of the divinities. All narratives, however, agree in
one statement, — that the gods maintained intimate relations with
men until, because of the growing sinfulness and arrogance of
mankind, it became necessary for the immortals to withdraw their
favor.

10. Prometheus, a Creator. There is a story which attributes
the making of man to Prometheus, whose father Iapetus had,
with Cronus, opposed the sovereignty of Jupiter. In that conflict,
Prometheus, gifted with prophetic wisdom, had adopted the cause

of the Olympian deities. To him and his brother Epimetheus was now committed the office of making man and providing him and all other animals with the faculties necessary for their preservation. Prometheus was to overlook the work of Epimetheus. Epimetheus proceeded to bestow upon the different animals the various gifts of courage, strength, swiftness, sagacity; wings to one, claws to another, a shelly covering to a third. But Prometheus himself made a nobler animal than these. Taking some earth and kneading it with water, he made man in the image of the gods. He gave him an upright stature, so that while other animals turn their faces toward the earth, man gazes on the stars. Then since Epimetheus, always rash, and thoughtful when too late, had been so prodigal of his gifts to other animals that no blessing was left worth conferring upon the noblest of creatures, Prometheus ascended to heaven, lighted his torch at the chariot of the sun, and brought down fire. With fire in his possession man would be able to win her secrets and treasures from the earth, to develop commerce, science, and the arts.

FIG. 4. PROMETHEUS MAKING MAN

11. The Age of Gold. Whether in this or in other ways the world was furnished with inhabitants, the first age was an age of innocence and happiness. Truth and right prevailed, though not enforced by law, nor was there any in authority to threaten or to punish. The forest had not yet been robbed of its trees to yield timbers for vessels, nor had men built fortifications round their towns. There were no such things as swords, spears, or helmets. The earth brought forth all things necessary for man, without his labor in plowing or sowing. Perpetual spring reigned, flowers sprang up without seed, the rivers flowed with milk and wine, and yellow honey distilled from the oaks. This Golden Age had begun in the reign of Cronus.[1] And when these heroes fell asleep in death, they were translated in a pleasant dream to a spiritual existence, in which, unseen by mortal eyes, they still attended men as monitors and guardians.

12. The Silver Age came next, inferior to the golden. Jupiter shortened the spring, and divided the year into seasons. Then, first, men suffered the extremes of heat and cold, and houses became necessary. Caves were their dwellings, — and leafy coverts of the woods, and huts woven of twigs. Crops would no longer grow without planting. The farmer was constrained to sow the seed, and the ox to draw the plow. This was a race of manly men, but insolent and impious. And when they died, Jupiter made them ghosts of the underworld, but withheld the privilege of immortal life.

13. Prometheus, Champion of Man. During this age when, as Hesiod says, the altars of the blessed were neglected, and the gods were denied their due, Prometheus stood forth — the champion of man against the Olympians.[2] For the son of Cronus had grudged mortals the use of fire, and was, in fact, contemplating their annihilation and the creation of a new race. Therefore, once upon a time, when gods and men were in dispute at Sicyon concerning the prerogatives of each, Prometheus, by an ingenious trick, attempted to settle the question in favor of man. Dividing into two portions a sacrificial bull, he wrapped all the eatable parts

---

[1] Consequently the creation of these men could not be assigned to Prometheus, — unless they were made by him before the war of the Titans.

[2] There is uncertainty as to the mythical period of these events. The order here given seems to me well grounded. Hes. Works and Days, 180; Theog. 790–910.

in the skin, cunningly surmounted with uninviting entrails; but the bones he garnished with a plausible mass of fat. He then offered Jupiter his choice. The king of Heaven, although he perceived the intended fraud, took the heap of bones and fat, and, forthwith availing himself of this insult as an excuse for punishing mankind, deprived the race of fire. But Prometheus regained the treasure, stealing it from Heaven in a hollow tube.

14. Pandora. Doubly enraged, Jupiter, in his turn, had recourse to stratagem. He is declared to have planned for man a curse in the shape of woman. How the race had persisted hitherto without woman is a mystery; but that it had done so, with no slight degree of happiness, the experience of the Golden Age would seem to prove. However, the bewitching evil was fashioned, — in Heaven, properly enough, — and every god and goddess contributed something to her perfection. One gave her beauty, another persuasive charm, a third the faculty of music. And they named her Pandora, "the gift of all the gods." Thus equipped, she was conveyed to earth and presented to Epimetheus, who, without hesitation, accepted the gift, though cautioned by his brother to beware of Jupiter and all his ways. And the caution was not groundless. In the hand of Pandora had been placed by the immortals a casket or vase which she was forbidden to open. Overcome by an unaccountable curiosity to know what this vessel contained, she one day lifted the cover and looked in. Forthwith there escaped a multitude of plagues for hapless man — gout, rheumatism, and colic for his body; envy, spite, and revenge for his mind — and scattered themselves far and wide. Pandora hastened to replace the lid; but one thing only remained in the casket, and that was *hope*.

15. Prometheus Bound. Because of his unselfish devotion to the cause of humanity, Prometheus drew down on himself the anger of Olympian Jove, by whose order he was chained to a rock on Mount Caucasus, and subjected to the attack of an eagle (or a vulture) which, for ages, preyed upon his liver, yet succeeded not in consuming it. This state of torment might have been brought to an end at any time by Prometheus, if he had been willing to submit to his oppressor; for he possessed a secret which involved the stability of Jove's throne. This was that by a certain woman Jove would beget a son who should displace him and end the sway of the Olympians. The god naturally desired more accurate information of this decree of Fate. But to reveal the secret Prometheus disdained. In this steadfastness the Titan was supported by the knowledge that in the thirteenth generation there should arrive a hero, — sprung from Jove himself, — to release him.[1] And in fullness of time the hero did arrive: none other than the mighty Hercules desirous of rendering the highest service to mankind. No higher service, thinks this radiant and masterful personage, — who, as we shall see, had already cleared the world of many a monster, — remains to be performed than to free the champion of mankind, suffering through the ages because he had brought light into the world. "The soul of man," says Hercules to the Titan—

> The soul of man can never be enslaved
> Save by its own infirmities, nor freed
> Save by its very strength and own resolve
> And constant vision and supreme endeavor!
> You will be free? Then, courage, O my brother!
> O let the soul stand in the open door
> Of life and death and knowledge and desire
> And see the peaks of thought kindle with sunrise!
> Then shall the soul return to rest no more,
> Nor harvest dreams in the dark field of sleep —
> Rather the soul shall go with great resolve
> To dwell at last upon the shining mountains
> In liberal converse with the eternal stars.[2]

And he kills the vulture; and sets Jove's victim free.

By his demeanor Prometheus has become the ensample of magnanimous endurance, and of resistance to oppression.

> Titan! to whose immortal eyes
>   The sufferings of mortality,
>   Seen in their sad reality,
> Were not as things that gods despise,
> What was thy pity's recompense?
> A silent suffering, and intense;

[1] §§ 156, 161, 191 and Commentary, § 10.
[2] From Herakles, a drama by George Cabot Lodge.

The rock, the vulture, and the chain,
All that the proud can feel of pain,
The agony they do not show,
The suffocating sense of woe,
Which speaks but in its loneliness,
And then is jealous lest the sky
Should have a listener, nor will sigh
   Until its voice is echoless. . . .

Thy godlike crime was to be kind,
   To render with thy precepts less
   The sum of human wretchedness,
And strengthen man with his own mind.
But, baffled as thou wert from high,
Still, in thy patient energy,
In the endurance and repulse
   Of thine impenetrable spirit,
Which earth and heaven could not convulse,
   A mighty lesson we inherit.[1] . . .

16. Longfellow's Prometheus. A happy application of the story of Prometheus is made by Longfellow in the following verses:[2]

Of Prometheus, how undaunted
   On Olympus' shining bastions
His audacious foot he planted,
Myths are told, and songs are chanted,
   Full of promptings and suggestions.

Beautiful is the tradition
   Of that flight through heavenly portals,
The old classic superstition
Of the theft and the transmission
   Of the fire of the Immortals!

First the deed of noble daring,
   Born of heavenward aspiration,
Then the fire with mortals sharing,
Then the vulture, — the despairing
   Cry of pain on crags Caucasian.

---

[1] From Byron's Prometheus. See also his translation from the Prometheus Vinctus of Æschylus, and his Ode to Napoleon Buonaparte.

[2] Prometheus, or The Poet's Forethought. See Commentary.

All is but a symbol painted
  Of the Poet, Prophet, Seer;
Only those are crowned and sainted
Who with grief have been acquainted.
  Making nations nobler, freer.

In their feverish exultations,
  In their triumph and their yearning,
In their passionate pulsations,
In their words among the nations,
  The Promethean fire is burning.

Shall it, then, be unavailing,
  All this toil for human culture?
Through the cloud-rack, dark and trailing,
Must they see above them sailing
  O'er life's barren crags the vulture?

Such a fate as this was Dante's,
  By defeat and exile maddened;
Thus were Milton and Cervantes,
Nature's priests and Corybantes,
  By affliction touched and saddened.

But the glories so transcendent
  That around their memories cluster,
And, on all their steps attendant,
Make their darkened lives resplendent
  With such gleams of inward lustre!

All the melodies mysterious,
  Through the dreary darkness chanted;
Thoughts in attitudes imperious,
Voices soft, and deep, and serious,
  Words that whispered, songs that haunted!

All the soul in rapt suspension,
  All the quivering, palpitating
Chords of life in utmost tension,
With the fervor of invention,
  With the rapture of creating!

Ah, Prometheus! heaven-scaling!
  In such hours of exultation
Even the faintest heart, unquailing,
Might behold the vulture sailing
  Round the cloudy crags Caucasian!

Though to all there is not given
  Strength for such sublime endeavor,
Thus to scale the walls of heaven,
And to leaven with fiery leaven
  All the hearts of men forever;

Yet all bards, whose hearts unblighted
  Honor and believe the presage,
Hold aloft their torches lighted,
Gleaming through the realms benighted,
  As they onward bear the message!

17. The Brazen Age. Next to the Age of Silver came that of brass,[1] more savage of temper and readier for the strife of arms, yet not altogether wicked.

18. The Iron Age. Last came the hardest age and worst, — of iron. Crime burst in like a flood; modesty, truth, and honor fled. The gifts of the earth were put only to nefarious uses. Fraud, violence, war at home and abroad were rife. The world was wet with slaughter; and the gods, one by one, abandoned it, Astræa, following last, goddess of innocence and purity.

19. The Flood. Jupiter, observing the condition of things, burned with anger. He summoned the gods to council. Obeying the call, they traveled the Milky Way to the palace of Heaven. There, Jupiter set forth to the assembly the frightful condition of the earth, and announced his intention of destroying its inhabitants, and providing a new race, unlike the present, which should be worthier of life and more reverent toward the gods. Fearing lest a conflagration might set Heaven itself on fire, he proceeded to drown the world. Not satisfied with his own waters, he called his brother Neptune to his aid. Speedily the race of men, and their possessions, were swept away by the deluge.

---

[1] Compare Byron's political satire, The Age of Bronze.

20. Deucalion and Pyrrha. Parnassus alone, of the mountains, overtopped the waves; and there Deucalion, son of Prometheus, and his wife Pyrrha, daughter of Epimetheus, found refuge — he a just man and she a faithful worshiper of the gods. Jupiter, remembering the harmless lives and pious demeanor of this pair, caused the waters to recede, — the sea to return to its shores, and the rivers to their channels. Then Deucalion and Pyrrha, entering a temple defaced with slime, approached the unkindled altar and, falling prostrate, prayed for guidance and aid. The oracle[1] answered, " Depart from the temple with head veiled and garments unbound, and cast behind you the bones of your mother." They heard the words with astonishment. Pyrrha first broke silence: " We cannot obey; we dare not profane the remains of our parents." They sought the woods, and revolved the oracle in their minds. At last Deucalion spoke: "Either my wit fails me or the command is one we may obey without impiety. The earth is the great parent of all; the stones are her bones; these we may cast behind us; this, I think, the oracle means. At least, to try will harm us not." They veiled their faces, unbound their garments, and, picking up stones, cast them behind them. The stones began to grow soft and to assume shape. By degrees they put on a rude resemblance to the human form. Those thrown by Deucalion became men; those by Pyrrha, women. It was a hard race that sprang up, and well adapted to labor.

21. The Demigods and Heroes. As preceding the Age of Iron, Hesiod mentions an *Age of Demigods and Heroes*. Since, however, these demigods and heroes were, many of them, reputed to have been directly descended from Deucalion, their epoch must be regarded as subsequent to the deluge. The hero, Hellen, son of Deucalion and Pyrrha, became the ancestor of the Hellenes, or Greeks. The Æolians and Dorians were, according to legend, descended from his sons Æolus and Dorus; from his son Xuthus, the Achæans and Ionians derived their origin.

Another great division of the Greek people, the Pelasgic, resident in the Peloponnesus or southern portion of the peninsula, was said to have sprung from a different stock of heroes, that of

---

1 Oracles, see §§ 24, 30, and Commentary.

Pelasgus, son of Phoroneus of Argos and grandson of the river-god Inachus.

The demigods and heroes were of matchless worth and valor. Their adventures form the subject of many of the succeeding chapters. The Older Heroes, especially, were endowed with godlike qualities, which they devoted to the service of mankind in the destruction of monsters, the founding of cities, or the introduction of civilization. Such were Perseus, the hero of Argos and his descendant Hercules, who came to be worshiped as the national hero of the Greeks. Such, too, Cadmus, the founder of Thebes, and Cecrops of Athens, and one of his successors, Theseus, a " second Hercules." Each city of Greece had its patron hero, to whom it accorded the honors of divinity. The Younger Heroes were chieftains in the Theban and the Trojan wars and in numerous other military or predatory expeditions.

FIG. 5. POSEIDON, DIONYSUS, AND GODDESS

CHAPTER II

THE GODS OF HEAVEN [1]

22. Olympus. The heaven of the Greek gods was the summit of an ideal mountain called Olympus.[2] A gate of clouds, kept by goddesses, the Hours or Seasons, opened to permit the passage of the Celestials to earth, and to receive them on their return. The gods had their separate dwellings; but all, when summoned, repaired to the palace of Jupiter, — even the deities whose usual abode was the earth, the waters, or the underworld. In the great hall of the Olympian king the gods feasted each day on ambrosia and nectar. Here they conversed of the affairs of heaven and earth; and as they quaffed the nectar that Hebe poured, Apollo made melody with his lyre and the Muses sang in responsive strain. When the sun was set, the gods withdrew to their respective dwellings for the night.

FIG. 6. TWO HOURS

The following lines from the Odyssey express the conception of Olympus entertained by Homer:

> So saying, Minerva, goddess, azure-eyed,
> Rose to Olympus, the reputed seat
> Eternal of the gods, which never storms
> Disturb, rains drench, or snow invades, but calm
> The expanse and cloudless shines with purest day.
> There the inhabitants divine rejoice
> Forever.[3]

[1] Consult, in general, corresponding sections of the Commentary.
[2] Symbolized on earth by Mount Olympus in Thessaly.   [3] Cowper's translation.

23. The Great Gods. The gods of Heaven were the following : [1]

Jupiter (Zeus).[2]

His daughter, Minerva (Athena), who sprang from his brain, full-grown and full-armed.

His sister and wife, Juno (Hera).

His children by Juno,— Mars (Ares), Vulcan (Hephæstus), and Hebe.

His children by Latona, — Apollo, or Phœbus, and Diana (Artemis).

His daughter by Dione, — Venus (Aphrodite).[3]

His son by Maia, — Mercury (Hermes).

His sister, Vesta (Hestia), the oldest born of Cronus and Rhea.

Of these all were deities of the highest order save Hebe, who must be ranked with the lesser gods. With the remaining ten " Great Gods " are sometimes reckoned the other sister of Jupiter, Ceres (Demeter), properly a divinity of earth, and Neptune (Poseidon), ruler of the sea.

24. Jupiter [4] **(Zeus).** The Greek name signifies the radiant light of heaven. Jupiter was the supreme ruler of the universe, wisest of the divinities and most glorious. In the Iliad he informs the other gods that their united strength would not budge him: that, on the contrary, he could draw them and earth and the seas to himself, and suspend all from Olympus by a golden chain. Throned in the high, clear heavens, Jupiter was the gatherer of clouds and snows, the dispenser of gentle rains and winds, the moderator of light and heat and the seasons, the thunderer, the wielder of the thunderbolt. Bodily strength and valor were dear to him. He was worshiped with various rites in different lands, and to him were sacred everywhere the loftiest trees and the grandest mountain peaks. He required of his worshipers cleanliness of surroundings and person and heart. Justice was his; his to repay violation of duty in the family, in social relations, and in the state. Prophecy was his; and his will was made known at the oracle of Dodona, where answers were given to those who inquired concerning the future. This oracular shrine was the most ancient in Greece. According to one account two black doves had taken wing from

---

[1] See Commentary, § 23, for Gladstone's latest utterance on the number of the Olympians.

[2] The names included in parentheses represent the Greek, the others being Roman equivalents, Latin names, or names common to both Greek and Roman usage.

[3] See Commentary, § 34.   [4] On the Latin name, see Commentary, § 24.

Thebes in Egypt. One flew to Dodona in Epirus, and, alighting in a grove of oaks, proclaimed to the inhabitants of the district that they should establish there an oracle of Jupiter. The other dove flew to the temple of Jupiter Ammon in the Libyan oasis, and delivered a similar command. According to another account, these were not doves but priestesses who, carried off from Thebes by the Phœnicians, set up oracles at Oasis and Dodona. The

responses of the oracle were given by the rustling of the oak trees in the wind. The sounds were interpreted by priests.

That Jupiter himself, though wedded to the goddess Juno, should be charged with numerous other love affairs, not only in respect of goddesses but of mortals, is, in part, explained by the fact that to the supreme divinity of the Greeks have been ascribed attributes and adventures of numerous local and foreign divinities that were gradually identified with him. It is, therefore, not wise to assume that the love affairs of Jupiter and of other divinities always symbolize combinations of natural or physical forces that have repeated themselves in

FIG. 7. ZEUS

ever-varying guise. It is important to understand that the more ideal Olympian religion absorbed features of inferior religions, and that Jupiter, when represented as appropriating the characteristics of other gods, was sometimes, also, accredited with their wives.

Beside the children of Jupiter already enumerated, there should here be mentioned, as of peculiar consequence, Bacchus (Dionysus), the god of wine, a deity of earth, — Proserpine, the wife of Pluto and queen of the underworld, — and Hercules, the greatest of the heroes.

25. Conceptions of Jupiter. The Greeks usually conceived the Jupiter of war as riding in his thunder-car, hurling the thunderbolt or lashing his enemies with a scourge of lightning. He wore a breastplate or shield of storm-cloud like the skin of a gray goat (the *Ægis*), fearful to behold, and made by the god of fire. His special messenger was the eagle. It was, however, only with the passage of generations that the Greeks came to represent their greatest of the gods by the works of men's hands. The statue of Olympian Jove by Phidias was considered the highest achievement of Grecian sculpture. It was of colossal dimensions and, like other statues of the period, "chryselephantine," that is, composed of ivory and gold. For the parts representing flesh were of ivory laid on a framework of wood, while the drapery and ornaments were of gold. The height of the figure was forty feet, of the pedestal twelve. The god was represented as seated on his throne. His brows were crowned with a wreath of olive; he held in his right hand a scepter, and in his left a statue of Victory. The throne was of cedar, adorned with gold and precious stones.

FIG. 8. ZEUS AFTER PHIDIAS

The idea which the artist essayed to embody was that of the supreme deity of the Hellenic race, enthroned as a conqueror, in perfect majesty and repose, and ruling with a nod the subject world. Phidias informs us that the idea was suggested by Homer's lines in the first book of the Iliad:

> Jove said, and nodded with his shadowy brows;
> Waved on th' immortal head th' ambrosial locks, —
> And all Olympus trembled at his nod.[1]

Unfortunately, our knowledge of this famous statue is confined to literary descriptions, and to copies on coins. Other representations of Jove have been obtained from Greek bronze statuettes, or the wall-paintings of Herculaneum and Pompeii.

[1] Iliad, 1, 622–625, Earl of Derby's translation. See also the passage in Chapman's translation.

26. Juno [1] (**Hera**), sister and wife of Jupiter. According to some, the name *Hera* means Splendor of Heaven, according to others, the Lady. Some think it approves her goddess of earth; others, goddess of the air; still others, for reasons by no means final, say that it signifies Protectress, and applies to Juno in her original function of moon-goddess, the chosen guardian of women, their aid in seasons of distress. Juno's union with Jupiter was the prototype of earthly marriages. She is the type of matronly virtues and dignity.

She was the daughter of Cronus and Rhea, but was brought up by Oceanus and Tethys in their dwelling in the remote west beyond the sea. Without the knowledge of her parents, she was wedded to Jupiter in this garden of the gods where ambrosial rivers flowed, and where Earth sent up in honor of the rite a tree of life, heavy with apples golden like the sunset. Juno was the most worthy of the goddesses, the most queenly; ox-eyed, says Homer; says Hesiod, golden-sandaled and golden-throned. Glorious beyond compare was her presence, when she had harnessed her horses, and driven forth the golden-wheeled chariot that Hebe made ready, and that the Hours set aside. Fearful, too, could be her wrath. For she was of a jealous disposition, which was not happily affected by the vagaries of her spouse; and she was, moreover, prone to quarrels, self-willed, vengeful, proud, even on occasion deceitful. Once, indeed, she conspired with Minerva and Neptune to bind the cloud-compeller himself. More than once she provoked him to blows; and once to worse than blows, — for her lord and master swung her aloft in the clouds, securing her wrists in golden handcuffs and hanging anvils to her feet.

FIG. 9. HERA OF ARGOS

The cities that the ox-eyed goddess favored were Argos, Sparta, and Mycenæ. To her the peacock and the cow were dear, and many a grove and pasture rejoiced her sacred herds.

[1] On the name *Juno*, see Commentary.

HERA OF THE VATICAN

27. Minerva (Athene or Athena), the virgin goddess. She sprang from the brain of Jove, agleam with panoply of war, brandishing a spear and with her battle-cry awakening the echoes of heaven and earth. She is goddess of the lightning that leaps like a lance from the cloud-heavy sky, and hence, probably, the name *Athene*.[1] She is goddess of the storms and of the rushing thunderbolt, and is, therefore, styled Pallas. She is the goddess of the thundercloud, which is symbolized by her tasseled breastplate of goatskin, the *ægis*, whereon is fixed the head of Medusa, the Gorgon, that turns to stone all beholders. She is also the goddess of war, rejoicing in martial music and protecting the war horse and the warship. On the other hand, she is of a gentle, fair, and thoughtful aspect. Her Latin name *Minerva* is connected with the Sanskrit, Greek, and Latin words for *mind*. She is eternally a virgin, the goddess of wisdom, of skill, of contemplation, of spinning and weaving, of horticulture and agriculture. She is protectress of cities, and was specially worshiped in her own Athens, in Argos, in Sparta, and in Troy. To her were sacrificed oxen and cows. The olive tree, created by her, was sacred to her, and also the owl, the cock, the serpent, and the crow.

FIG. 10. ATHENA VELLETRI

28. Mars (Ares),[2] the war-god, son of Jupiter and Juno. The meaning of the name *Ares* is uncertain; the most probable significations are the *Slayer*, the *Avenger*, the *Curse*. The Roman god of war, Mars, is the *bright* and *burning* one. Homer, in the Iliad, represents Ares as the insatiable warrior of the heroic age, who, impelled by rage and lust of violence, exults in the noise of battle, revels in the horror of carnage. Strife and slaughter are the condition of his existence. Where the fight is thickest, there he rushes in without hesitation, without question as to which

---

[1] For the names *Athene* and *Minerva*, see Commentary.   [2] See Commentary.

side is right. In battle array he is resplendent, — on his head the gleaming helmet and floating plume, on his arm the leathern shield, in his hand the redoubtable spear of bronze. Well-favored, stately, swift, unwearied, puissant, gigantic, he is still the foe of wisdom, the scourge of mortals. Usually he fights on foot, sometimes from a chariot drawn by four horses, — the offspring of the

North Wind and a Fury. In the fray his sons attend him, — Terror, Trembling, Panic, and Fear, — also his sister Eris, or Discord (the mother of Strife), his daughter Enyo, ruiner of cities, and a retinue of bloodthirsty demons. As typifying the chances of war, Mars is, of course, not always successful. In the battles before Troy, Minerva and Juno bring him more than once to grief; and when he complains to Jupiter, he is snubbed as a renegade most hateful of all the gods.[1] His loved one and mistress is the goddess of beauty herself. In her arms the warrior finds repose. Their daughter Harmonia is the ancestress of the unquiet dynasty of Thebes. The favorite land of Mars was, according to Homer, the rough, northerly Thrace.

FIG. 11. ARES LUDOVISI   His emblems are the spear and the burning torch; his chosen animals are haunters of the battle field, — the vulture and the dog.

29. Vulcan (Hephæstus), son of Jupiter and Juno, was the god of fire, especially of terrestrial fire, — volcanic eruption, incendiary flame, the glow of the forge or the hearth. But as the fires of earth are derived from that of heaven, perhaps the name *Hephæstus* (burning, shining, flaming) referred originally to the marvelous brilliance of the lightning. Vulcan was the blacksmith of the gods, the finest artificer in metal among them. His forge in

---

[1] Iliad, 5, 590. See also 21, 395.

Olympus was furnished not only with anvils and all other implements
of the trade, but with automatic handmaidens of silver and gold,
fashioned by Vulcan himself. Poets later than Homer assign to
Vulcan workshops under various volcanic islands. From the crater

FIG. 12. ARES (MARS)

of Mount Ætna poured
forth the fumes and
flames of his smithy.
He built the dwellings
of the gods; he made
the scepter of Jove, the
shields and spears of
the Olympians, the ar-
rows of Apollo and
Diana, the breastplate
of Hercules, the shield
of Achilles.

He was lame of gait,
—a figurative sugges-
tion, perhaps, of the flickering, unsteady nature of fire. According
to his own story,[1] he was born halt; and his mother, chagrined by
his deformity, cast him from Heaven out of the sight of the gods.
Yet, again,[2] he says that, attempting once to save his mother

from Jupiter's wrath,
he was caught by the
foot and hurled by the
son of Cronus from
the heavenly thresh-
old: " All day I flew;
and at the set of sun
I fell in Lemnos, and
little life was left in
me." Had he not been

FIG. 13. THE FORGE OF VULCAN

lame before, he had good reason to limp after either of these
catastrophes. He took part in the making of the human race, and
in the special creation of Pandora. He assisted also at the birth of
Minerva, to facilitate which he split Jupiter's head open with an ax.

1 Iliad, 18, 395.   2 Iliad, 1, 390.

His wife, according to the Iliad and Hesiod's Theogony, is Aglaia, the youngest of the Graces; but in the Odyssey it is Venus. He is a glorious, good-natured god, loved and honored among men as the founder of wise customs and the patron of artificers; on occasion, as a god of healing and of prophecy. He seems to have been, when he chose, the cause of " inextinguishable laughter " to the gods, but he was by no means a fool. The famous god of the strong arms could be cunning, even vengeful, when the emergency demanded.

FIG. 14. APOLLO IN THE VATICAN

30. Apollo, or Phœbus Apollo, the son of Jupiter and Latona, was preëminently the god of the sun. His name *Phœbus* signifies the radiant nature of the sunlight; his name *Apollo*, perhaps, the cruel and destructive heat of noonday. Soon after his birth, Jupiter would have sent him to Delphi to inculcate righteousness and justice among the Greeks; but the golden god Apollo chose first to spend a year in the land of the Hyperboreans, where for six continuous months of the year there is sunshine and spring, soft climate, profusion of herbs and flowers, and the very ecstasy of life. During this delay the Delphians sang pæans, — hymns of praise, — and danced in chorus about the tripod (or three-legged stool), where the expectant priestess of Apollo had taken her seat. At last, when the year was warm, came the god in his chariot drawn by swans, — heralded by songs of springtide, of nightingales and swallows and crickets. Then the crystal fount of Castalia and the stream Cephissus overflowed their bounds, and mankind made grateful offerings to the god. But his advent was not altogether peaceful. An enormous serpent, Python, had crept forth from the slime with which, after the flood, the Earth was covered; and in the caves of Mount Parnassus this terror of the people lurked. Him Apollo encountered and after fearful combat slew, with arrows, weapons which the god of the silver bow had not before used against any but feeble animals, — hares, wild goats, and such game. In commemoration of this illustrious conquest, he instituted the Pythian games, in which the victor in feats of strength, swiftness of foot, or in the chariot race, should be crowned with a wreath of beech leaves. Apollo brought not only the warm spring and summer, but also the blessings of the harvest. He warded off the dangers and diseases of summer and autumn; and he healed the sick. He was patron of music and of poetry. Through his oracle at Delphi, on the slopes of Parnassus in Phocis, the Pythian god made known the future to those who consulted him. He was a founder of cities, a promoter of colonization, a giver of good laws, the ideal of fair and manly youth, — a pure and just god, requiring clean hands and pure hearts of those that worshiped him. But though a god of life and peace, the far-darter did not shun the weapons of war. When presumption was to be punished, or

FIG. 15. APOLLO BELVEDERE

wrong righted, he could bend his bow and slay with the arrows of his sunlight. As in the days of his youth he slew the Python, so, also, he slew the froward Tityus, and so the children of Niobe. While Phœbus Apollo is the Olympian divinity of the sun, fraught with light and healing, spiritual, creative, and prophetic, he must not be confounded with a god of the older dynasty, Helios (offspring of Hyperion, Titanic deity of light), who represented the sun in its daily and yearly course, in its physical rather than spiritual manifestation. The bow of Apollo was bound with laurel in memory of Daphne, whom he loved. To him were sacred, also, many creatures, — the wolf, the roe, the mouse, the he-goat, the ram, the dolphin, and the swan.[1]

31. Shelley's Hymn of Apollo.

The sleepless Hours who watch me as I lie,
  Curtained with star-inwoven tapestries,
From the broad moonlight of the sky,
  Fanning the busy dreams from my dim eyes, —
Waken me when their mother, the gray Dawn,
Tells them that dreams and that the moon is gone.

FIG. 16. APOLLO

Then I arise, and climbing Heaven's blue dome,
  I walk over the mountains and the waves,
Leaving my robe upon the ocean foam;
  My footsteps pave the clouds with fire; the caves
Are filled with my bright presence, and the air
Leaves the green earth to my embraces bare.

The sunbeams are my shafts, with which I kill
  Deceit, that loves the night and fears the day;
All men who do or even imagine ill
  Fly me, and from the glory of my ray
Good minds and open actions take new might,
Until diminished by the reign of night.

I feed the clouds, the rainbows, and the flowers
  With their ethereal colors; the moon's globe
And the pure stars in their eternal bowers
  Are cinctured with my power as with a robe;
Whatever lamps on Earth or Heaven may shine,
Are portions of one power, which is mine.

I stand at noon upon the peak of Heaven,
  Then with unwilling steps I wander down
Into the clouds of the Atlantic even;
  For grief that I depart they weep and frown:
What look is more delightful than the smile
With which I soothe them from the western isle?

---

[1] On the birth of Apollo, his adventures, names, festivals, oracles, and his place in literature and art, see Commentary. For other particulars, see sections on *Myths of Apollo*.

I am the eye with which the universe
  Beholds itself and knows itself divine;
All harmony of instrument or verse,
  All prophecy, all medicine, are mine,
All light of art or nature; — to my song,
  Victory and praise in their own right belong.

32. Diana (Artemis), twin sister of Apollo, was born on Mount Cynthus in the island of Delos. Latona, the future mother of

Diana and Apollo, flying from the wrath of Juno, had besought, one after another, the islands of the Ægean to afford her a place of rest; but they feared too much the potent queen of heaven. Delos alone consented to become the birthplace of the future deities. This isle was then floating and unstable; but on Latona's arrival, Jupiter fastened it with adamantine chains to the bottom of the sea, that it might be a secure resting-place for his beloved. The daughter of Latona is, as her name *Artemis* indicates, a virgin goddess, the ideal of modesty, grace, and maidenly vigor.

FIG. 17. DIANA. After Correggio

She is associated with her brother, the prince of archery, in nearly all his adventures, and in attributes she is his feminine counterpart. As he is identified with sunlight, so is she, his fair-tressed sister, with the chaste brilliance of the moon. Its slender arc is her bow; its beams are her arrows with which she sends upon womankind a speedy and painless death. In her prerogative of moon-goddess she is frequently identified with Selene, daughter of Hyperion, just as Apollo is with Helios.

Despising the weakness of love, Diana imposed upon her nymphs vows of perpetual maidenhood, any violation of which she was swift and severe to punish. Graceful in form and free of movement, equipped for the chase, and surrounded by a bevy of fair companions, the swift-rushing goddess was wont to scour hill, valley, forest, and plain. She was, however, not only huntress, but guardian, of wild beasts, — mistress withal of horses and kine

FIG. 18. DIANA (ARTEMIS) OF VERSAILLES

and other domestic brutes. She ruled marsh and mountain; her gleaming arrows smote sea as well as land. Springs and woodland brooks she favored, for in them she and her attendants were accustomed to bathe. She blessed with verdure the meadows and arable lands, and from them obtained a meed of thanks. When weary of the chase she turned to music and dancing; for the lyre and flute and song were dear to her. Muses, Graces, nymphs, and the fair goddesses themselves thronged the rites of the chorus-leading queen. But ordinarily a woodland chapel or a rustic altar sufficed for her worship. There the hunter laid his offering — antlers, skin, or edible portions of the deer that Artemis of the golden arrows had herself vouchsafed him. The holy maid, however, though naturally gracious, gentle, and a healer of ills, was, like her brother, quick to resent injury to her sacred herds or insult to herself. To this stern temper Agamemnon, Orion, and Niobe bore regretful testimony. They found that the "fair-crowned queen of the echoing chase," though blithe and gracious, was by no means a frivolous personage.

Diana was mistress of the brute creation, protectress of youth, patron of temperance in all things, guardian of civil right. The cypress tree was sacred to her; and her favorites were the bear, the boar, the dog, the goat, and specially the hind.

33. Jonson's Hymn to Cynthia (Diana).

> Queen and Huntress, chaste and fair,
>   Now the sun is laid to sleep,
> Seated in thy silver chair
>   State in wonted manner keep:
>   Hesperus entreats thy light,
>   Goddess excellently bright.

> Earth, let not thy envious shade
>   Dare itself to interpose;
> Cynthia's shining orb was made
>   Heaven to clear when day did close:
>   Bless us then with wishèd sight,
>   Goddess excellently bright.

> Lay thy bow of pearl apart,
> And thy crystal-shining quiver;
>   Give unto the flying hart
> Space to breathe, how short soever:
>   Thou that mak'st a day of night,
>   Goddess excellently bright.[1]

FIG. 19. ARTEMIS

34. Venus (Aphrodite), goddess of love and beauty, was, according to the more ancient Greek conception, a daughter of Jupiter and Dione;[2] but Hesiod says that she arose from the foam of the sea at the time of the wounding of Uranus, and therefore was called, by the Greeks, Aphrodite, *the foam-born*.[3] Wafted by the west wind, and borne upon the surge, she won first the island of Cythera; thence, like a dream, she passed to Cyprus, where the grace and blossom of her beauty conquered every heart. Everywhere, at the touch of her feet the herbage quivered into flower. The Hours and Graces surrounded her, twining odorous garlands and weaving robes for her that reflected the hues and breathed the perfume of crocus and hyacinth, violet, rose, lily, and narcissus. To her influence is ascribed the fruitfulness of the animal and of the vegetable creation. She is goddess of gardens and flowers, of the rose,

---

[1] From Cynthia's Revels.   [2] Iliad, 5, 370, etc.   [3] A popular etymology.

the myrtle, and the linden. The heaths and slumberous vales, pleasant with spring and vernal breezes, are hers. In her broidered girdle lurk "love and desire, and loving converse that steals the wits even of the wise." For she is the mistress of feminine charm and beauty, the golden, sweetly smiling Aphrodite, who rules the hearts of men. She lends to mortals seductive form and fascination. To a few, indeed, her favor is a blessing; but to many her gifts are treacherous, destructive of peace. Her various influence is exemplified in the stories of Pygmalion and Adonis, Paris and Æneas, Helen, Ariadne, Psyche, Procris, Pasiphaë, and Phædra. Her power extended over sea as well as land, and her temples rose from many a shore. On the waters swan and dolphin were beloved of her; in air, the sparrow and the dove. She was usually attended by her winged son Cupid, of whom much is to be told. Especially dear to her were Cyprus, Cnidos, Paphos, Cythera, Abydos, Mount Eryx, and the city of Corinth.

35. The "Venus of Milo." Of artistic conceptions of Aphrodite, the most famous are the statues called the Venus of Melos and the Venus of the Medici.[1] A comparison of the two conceptions is instituted in the following poem.[2] The worshiper apostrophizes the Venus of Melos, that "inner beauty of the world," whose tranquil smile he finds more fair than "The Medicean's sly and servile grace":

> From our low world no gods have taken wing;
> Even now upon our hills the twain are wandering:[3]
> The Medicean's sly and servile grace,
> And the immortal beauty of thy face.
> One is the spirit of all short-lived love
> And outward, earthly loveliness:
> The tremulous rosy morn is her mouth's smile,
> The sky, her laughing azure eyes above;
> And, waiting for caress,
> Lie bare the soft hill-slopes, the while

---

[1] For Venus in poetry and art, see Commentary.

[2] From the Venus of Milo, by E. R. Sill, formerly professor of English Literature in the University of California.

[3] The references are to the Berkeley Hills, the Bay of San Francisco, and the glimpses of the Pacific.

VENUS OF MELOS

Her thrilling voice is heard
In song of wind and wave, and every flitting bird.
Not plainly, never quite herself she shows:
Just a swift glance of her illumined smile
Along the landscape goes;
Just a soft hint of singing, to beguile
A man from all his toil;
Some vanished gleam of beckoning arm, to spoil
A morning's task with longing, wild and vain.
Then if across the parching plain
He seek her, she with passion burns
His heart to fever, and he hears
The west wind's mocking laughter when he turns,
Shivering in mist of ocean's sullen tears.
It is the Medicean: well I know
The arts her ancient subtlety will show, —
The stubble field she turns to ruddy gold;
The empty distance she will fold
In purple gauze; the warm glow she has kissed
Along the chilling mist:
Cheating and cheated love that grows to hate
And ever deeper loathing, soon or late.
Thou, too, O fairer spirit, walkest here
Upon the lifted hills:
Wherever that still thought within the breast
The inner beauty of the world hath moved;
In starlight that the dome of evening fills;
On endless waters rounding to the west:
For them who thro' that beauty's veil have loved
The soul of all things beautiful the best.
For lying broad awake, long ere the dawn,
Staring against the dark, the blank of space
Opens immeasurably, and thy face
Wavers and glimmers there and is withdrawn.
And many days, when all one's work is vain,
And life goes stretching on, a waste gray plain,
With even the short mirage of morning gone,
No cool breath anywhere, no shadow nigh
Where a weary man might lay him down and die,
Lo! thou art there before me suddenly,
With shade as if a summer cloud did pass,
And spray of fountains whispering to the grass.

Oh, save me from the haste and noise and heat
That spoil life's music sweet:
And from that lesser Aphrodite there —
Even now she stands
Close as I turn, and O my soul, how fair!

36. Mercury (Hermes), born in a cave of Mount Cyllene in Arcadia, was the son of Jupiter and Maia (the daughter of Atlas). According to conjecture, his name *Hermes* means the *Hastener*.

FIG. 20. HERMES PSYCHOPOMPOS

Mercury, swift as the wind, was the servant and herald of Jupiter and the other gods. On his ankles (in plastic art), and his low-crowned, broad-brimmed *petasus*, or hat, were wings. As messenger of Heaven, he bore a wand (*caduceus*) of wood or of gold, twined with snakes and surmounted by wings, and possessed of magical powers over sleeping, waking, and dreams. He was beautiful and ever in the prime of youthful vigor. To a voice sweet-toned and powerful, he added the persuasiveness of eloquence. But his skill was not confined to speech; he was also the first of inventors — to him are ascribed the lyre and the flute. He was the forerunner, too, of mathematicians and astronomers. His agility and strength made him easily prince in athletic pursuits. His cunning rendered him a dangerous foe; he could well play the trickster and the thief, as Apollo found out to his vexation, and Argus, and many another unfortunate. His methods, however, were not always questionable; although the patron of gamblers and the god of chance, he, at the same time, was the furtherer of lawful industry and of commerce by land and sea. The gravest function of the Messenger was to conduct the souls of the dead, "that gibber like bats as they fare, down the dank ways, past the streams of Oceanus, past the gates of the sun and the land of dreams, to the mead of asphodel in the dark realm of Hades, where dwell the souls, the phantoms of men outworn." [1]

37. Vesta (Hestia), goddess of the hearth, public and private, was the first-born child of Cronus and Rhea and, accordingly, the elder sister of Jupiter, Juno, Neptune, Pluto, and Ceres. Vesta was an old maid by choice. Averse to Venus and all her ways, she scorned the flattering advances of both Neptune and Apollo, and resolved to remain single. Whereupon Jupiter gave her to sit in the middle of his palace, to receive in Olympus the choicest morsels of the feast, and, in the temples of the gods on earth, reverence as the oldest and worthiest of Olympian divinities. As goddess of the burning hearth, Vesta is the divinity of the home : of settled, in opposition to nomadic, habits of life. She was worshiped first of the gods at every feast. Before her shrine in city and state the holy flame was religiously cherished. From her altars those of the other gods obtained their fires. No new colony, no new home, was duly consecrated till on its central hearth there glowed coals from her ancestral hearth. In her temple at Rome a sacred fire, tended by six virgin priestesses called Vestals, was kept religiously aflame. As the safety of the city was held to be connected with its conservation, any negligence, by which it might go out, was severely punished. Whenever the fire did die, it was rekindled from the rays of the sun.

38. Of the **Lesser Divinities of Heaven** the most worthy of mention are :

1. *Cupid* (*Eros*), small but mighty god of love, the son of Venus and her constant companion. He was often represented with eyes covered because of the blindness of his actions. With his bow and arrows, he shot the darts of desire into the bosoms of gods and men. Another deity named *Anteros*, reputed the brother of Eros, was sometimes represented as the avenger of slighted love, and sometimes as the symbol of reciprocal affection. Venus

---

[1] Lang, Odyssey, 24, 1 ; adapted.

was also attended at times by another brother of Eros, *Himeros*, or Longing, and by *Hymen*, a beautiful youth of divine descent, the personification of the wedding feast and leader of the nuptial chorus. Of Eros the poet Gosse writes :

> Within a forest, as I strayed
> Far down a somber autumn glade,
> I found the god of love ;
>   His bow and arrows cast aside,
>   His lovely arms extended wide,
> A depth of leaves above,
> Beneath o'erarching boughs he made
> A place for sleep in russet shade.
>
> His lips, more red than any rose,
> Were like a flower that overflows
> With honey pure and sweet ;
>   And clustering round that holy mouth,
>   The golden bees in eager drouth
> Plied busy wings and feet ;
> They knew, what every lover knows,
> There's no such honey-bloom that blows.[1]

FIG. 21. EROS

2. *Hebe*, daughter of Jupiter and Juno, goddess of youth and cupbearer to the gods. According to one story, she resigned that office on becoming the wife of Hercules. According to another, Hebe was dismissed from her position in consequence of a fall which she met with one day when in attendance on the gods. Her successor was *Ganymede*, a Trojan boy whom Jupiter, in the disguise of an eagle, seized and carried off from the midst of his playfellows on Mount Ida, bore up to Heaven, and installed in the vacant place.

3. *The Graces*, daughters of Jove by Eurynome, daughter of Oceanus. They were goddesses presiding over the banquet, the dance, all social pleasures, and polite accomplishments. They were three in number, — Euphrosyne, Aglaia, and Thalia. Spenser describes the office of the Graces thus :

[1] Eros, by Edmund Gosse. For verses on the blindness of Cupid, see Lyly's Cupid and Campaspe in Commentary.

These three on men all gracious gifts bestow
Which deck the body or adorn the mind,
To make them lovely or well-favored show;
As comely carriage, entertainment kind,
Sweet semblance, friendly offices that bind,
And all the complements of courtesy;
They teach us how to each degree and kind
We should ourselves demean, to low, to high,
To friends, to foes; which skill men call civility.

4. *The Muses*, daughters of Jupiter and Mnemosyne (Memory). They presided over song and prompted the memory. They are

FIG. 22. RAPE OF GANYMEDE   FIG. 23. POLYHYMNIA

ordinarily cited as nine in number; and to each of them was assigned patronage in some department of literature, art, or science. Calliope was the muse of epic poetry, Clio of history, Euterpe of lyric poetry, Melpomene of tragedy, Terpsichore of choral dance and song, Erato of love poetry, Polyhymnia of sacred poetry, Urania of astronomy, Thalia of comedy.

5. *Themis*, one of the Titans, a daughter of Uranus. She sat, as goddess of justice, beside Jupiter on his throne. She was beloved of the father of gods and men, and bore him the Hours, goddesses who regulated the seasons, and the Fates.

6. *The Fates*, three in number,—Clotho, Lachesis, and Atropos. Their office was to spin the thread of human destiny, and they were provided with shears with which they cut it off when they pleased.[1] According to Hesiod, they were daughters of Night.

FIG. 24. THE THREE FATES

From the painting by Michelangelo (?)

7. *Nemesis*, daughter of Night. She represented the righteous anger and vengeance of the gods, particularly toward the proud, the insolent, and breakers of the law.

8. *Æsculapius*, son of Apollo. By his skill in medicine he restored the dead to life. Being killed by the lightning of Jove, he was translated to the ranks of Heaven. His function was the art of healing.

9. *The Winds*, — Boreas, or Aquilo, the north wind; Zephyrus, or Favonius, the west; Notus, or Auster, the south; and Eurus, the east. The first two, chiefly, have been celebrated by the poets, the former as the type of rudeness, the latter of gentleness. It is said that Boreas loved the nymph Orithyia and tried to play the lover's part, but met with poor success; for it was hard for him to breathe gently, and sighing was out of the question.

---

[1] For description of their spinning, see translation of Catullus, LXIV, in § 191.

Weary at last of fruitless endeavors, he acted out his true character, seized the maiden and bore her off. Their children were Zetes and Calais, winged warriors, who accompanied the Argonautic expedition and did good service in an encounter with those monstrous birds,

FIG. 25. BOREAS

the Harpies. Zephyrus was the lover of Flora (Chloris).

Here, too, may be mentioned Æolus, the king of the winds, although he is not a lesser divinity of Heaven. His palace was on the precipitous isle of Æolia, where, with his six sons and six daughters, he kept eternal carouse. The winds, which he confined in a cavern, he let loose as he saw fit or as he was bidden by superior deities. He is sometimes called Hippotades.[1]

10. *Helios*, *Selene*, and *Eos*, children of the Titan Hyperion. Helios and Selene were the more ancient Greek divinities of Sun and Moon respectively. Helios, the charioteer of the sun, is, as has been already said, frequently identified with his successor, Apollo. The attributes and adventures of Selene were merged

FIG. 26. ZEPHYROS

in those of the more modern Diana. Eos, or, in Latin nomenclature, Aurora, the rosy-fingered goddess of the Morn, was mother of the stars and of the morning and evening breezes. Saffron-robed she rises from the streams of Ocean, to bring light to gods and men.

1 See Commentary.

11. *Phosphor*, the morning-star, the star of Venus, son of Aurora and the hunter Cephalus. *Hesper*, the evening-star, was sometimes identified with Phosphor. He was king of the Western Land, and, say some, father of the Hesperides, who guarded the golden apples of the sunset.

The Spirit in Milton's Comus tells of

FIG. 27. BOREAS CARRYING OFF ORITHYIA

> . . . the gardens fair
> Of Hesperus, and his daughters three
> That sing about the golden tree.
> Along the crispèd shades and bowers
> Revels the spruce and jocund Spring;
> The Graces and the rosy-bosomed Hours
> Thither all their bounties bring.
> There eternal Summer dwells,
> And west winds with musky wing
> About the cedarn alleys fling
> Nard and cassia's balmy smells.
> Iris there with humid bow
> Waters the odorous banks, that blow
> Flowers of more mingled hue
> Than her purfled scarf can shew.

And Tennyson taking the lines as a text has written the melodious and mystic song of the Hesperides, beginning —

> The golden apple, the golden apple, the hallowed fruit,
> Guard it well, guard it warily,
> Singing airily,
> Standing about the charmèd root.
> Round about all is mute,
> As the snowfield on the mountain-peaks,
> As the sandfield at the mountain-foot.
> Crocodiles in briny creeks

Sleep and stir not: all is mute.
If ye sing not, if ye make false measure,
We shall lose eternal pleasure,
Worth eternal want of rest.
Laugh not loudly: watch the treasure
Of the wisdom of the West.

Readers of this poem will notice that Tennyson follows the tradition by which a sleepless dragon is introduced among the guardians of the Hesperian fruit. Still other versions substitute for Hesperus, the Titan Atlas.

12. *Various Other Personifications.* The constellation Orion, whose story will be narrated; Victoria (Nike), the goddess of Victory; Discors (Eris), the goddess of Strife; and Iris, goddess of the rainbow, who is represented frequently as a messenger of the gods.

FIG. 28. IRIS CARRYING CHILD

CHAPTER III

THE GODS OF EARTH[1]

39. Conception of the World. The Greek poets believed the earth to be flat and circular. In their opinion their own country

occupied the middle of it, and the central point was either Mount Olympus, the abode of the gods, or Delphi, famous for its oracle. The circular disk of the earth was crossed from west to east and divided into two equal parts by the *Sea*, as they called the Mediterranean and its continuation the Euxine, the only seas with which they were acquainted. Around the earth flowed *River Ocean*, from south to north on the western side, in a contrary direction on the eastern. It flowed in a steady, equable current, unvexed by storm or tempest. The sea and all the rivers on earth received their waters from it.

FIG. 29. DEMETER OF KNIDOS

The northern portion of the earth was inhabited by the Hyperboreans, dwelling in bliss and everlasting spring beyond the

[1] For references to poetry and works of art, see corresponding sections in Commentary.

mountains whose caverns sent forth the piercing blasts of the north wind. Their country was inaccessible by land or sea. They lived exempt from disease or old age, from toils and warfare. "I come" sings one of them,[1] —

> I come from a land in the sun-bright deep,
> Where golden gardens glow,
> Where the winds of the north, becalmed in sleep,
> Their conch-shells never blow.

On the south side of the earth, close to the stream of Ocean, dwelt the Æthiopians, whom the gods held in such favor that they left at times the Olympian abodes to partake of the Æthiopian sacrifices and banquets. On the western margin of the earth, by the stream of Ocean, lay the Elysian Plain, where certain mortals enjoyed an immortality of bliss.

The Dawn, the Sun, and the Moon were supposed to rise out of Ocean on the eastern side and to drive through the air, giving light to gods and men. The stars, also, except those forming the Wain or Bear and others near them, rose out of and sank into the stream of Ocean. There the sun-god embarked in a winged boat, which conveyed him by the northern part of the earth back to his place of rising in the east.

FIG. 30. CERES

40. Ceres (Demeter), the goddess of sowing and reaping, of harvest festivals, and of agriculture in general, was sister of Jupiter and daughter of Cronus and Rhea. She is connected through her daughter Proserpine, queen of Hades, with the holy ceremonies and

[1] According to Thomas Moore's Song of a Hyperborean.

rites of death and of the lower world. Of the institutions founded or favored by her the most important were the mysteries celebrated at Eleusis, concerning which we know that, in the presence of indi-

viduals initiated in the secret ritual and perhaps with their coöperation, scenes were enacted which represented the alternation of death and life in nature and, apparently, forecast the resurrection and immortality of man. Sacred to Ceres and to Proserpine were golden sheaves of corn and soporific poppies; while, among animals, cows, sheep, and pigs were acceptable to them.

41. Gæa (Ge), the Mother Earth, wife of Uranus, belongs to the older order of gods; so also, another goddess of the earth, *Rhea*, the wife of Cronus and mother of Jupiter. In Phrygia, Rhea became identified with *Cybele*, whose worship, as mother of the gods, was at a later period introduced into Rome. The Greek mother, Rhea, was attended by the Curetes; the Phrygian mother by the Corybantes,

FIG. 31. DIONYSUS AND THE VINE

who celebrated her orgies with enthusiastic din of trumpets, drums, and cymbals. Cybele presided over mountain fastnesses and fortified places.

42. Bacchus (Dionysus), the god of wine, was the son of Jupiter and Semele, daughter of Cadmus of Thebes. He was especially the god of animal life and vegetation. He represented not only the intoxicating power of wine but its social and beneficent influences, and was looked upon as a promoter of civilization, a lawgiver, and a lover of peace. His forehead was crowned with vine leaves or ivy. He rode upon the tiger, the panther, or the lynx, or was drawn by them in a car. His worshipers were Bacchanals, or Bacchantes. He was attended by Satyrs and Sileni and by women called Mænads, who, as they danced and sang, waved in the air the *thyrsus,* a staff entwined with ivy and surmounted by a pine cone. Ordinarily, as in the following verses by Dryden, the convivial qualities of the god overshadow all the rest:

> The praise of Bacchus then the sweet musician sung,
>   Of Bacchus ever fair, and ever young.
>   The jolly god in triumph comes;
>   Sound the trumpets, beat the drums;
>   Flushed with a purple grace
>   He shows his honest face:
> Now give the hautboys breath; he comes, he comes.
>   Bacchus, ever fair and young,
>   Drinking joys did first ordain;
>   Bacchus' blessings are a treasure,
>   Drinking is the soldier's pleasure;
>   Rich the treasure,
>   Sweet the pleasure,
>   Sweet is pleasure after pain.[1]

43. The Lesser Divinities of Earth were:

1. *Pan,* son of Mercury and a wood-nymph or Dryad. He was the god of woods and fields, of flocks and shepherds. He dwelt in caves, wandered on the mountains and in valleys, amused himself with the chase, led the dances of the Dryads, and made love to them. But his suit was frequently of no avail, for though good-natured he was not prepossessing; his hoofs and horns did not enhance his comeliness. He was fond of music and was himself inventor of the syrinx, or shepherd's pipe, which he played in a masterly manner. Like other gods who dwelt in forests, he was dreaded by those whose occupations caused them to pass through the woods by night; for gloom and loneliness oppress and appall the mind. Hence sudden unreasonable fright was ascribed to Pan and called a Panic terror.

FIG. 32. PAN THE HUNTER

2. *The Nymphs.* Pan's partners in the dance, the Dryads, were but one of several classes of nymphs. There were, beside

---

[1] From Alexander's Feast.

them, the Oreads, nymphs of mountains and grottoes; and the Water-Nymphs, who are mentioned in later sections.

3. *The Satyrs*, deities of the woods and fields. In early art they appear as bearded creatures with snub noses, goats' ears, and horses' tails. Later they resemble youths, sometimes with sprouting horns. The goat-legged satyr is found in Roman poetry.

FIG. 33. A SATYR

CHAPTER IV

THE GODS OF THE UNDERWORLD[1]

44. The Underworld was the region of darkness inhabited by the spirits of the dead and governed by Pluto (Hades) and Proserpina, his queen. According to the Iliad, this realm lay "beneath the secret places of the earth."[2] And from the Odyssey we gather that it is not in the bowels of the earth, but on the under side at the limits of the known world, across the stream Oceanus, where is a waste shore, the land of the Cimmerians, shrouded in mist and cloud, never lighted by the sun "neither when he climbs up the starry heavens nor when again he turns earthward from the firmament."[3] From that land one goes beside the stream till he reaches the dank house of Hades. The realm of darkness is bounded by awful rivers : the Styx, sacred even among the gods, for by it they sealed their oaths, and the Acheron, river of woe, — with its tributaries, Phlegethon, river of fire, and Cocytus, river of wailing. Hither past the White Rock, which perhaps symbolizes the bleaching skeletons of the dead, and past the gates of the sun, it is the duty of Hermes (Mercury) to conduct the outworn ghosts of mortals. One of the Greek dramatists, Sophocles, tells us that this shore of death is "down in the darkling west."[4] In later poems we read that Charon, a grim boatman, received the dead at the River of Woe, and ferried them across, if the money requisite for their passage had been placed in their mouths and their bodies had been duly buried in the world above.[5] Otherwise he left them gibbering on the hither bank. The abode of Pluto is represented as wide-gated and thronged with guests. At the gate Cerberus, a three-headed,

---

[1] For interpretation and illustration, see corresponding sections of Commentary.
[2] Iliad, 22, 482; 9, 568; 20, 61.
[3] Odyssey, 10, 508; 11, 20; 24, 1.
[4] Sophocles, Œdipus Rex, 177.
[5] Æneid, 6, 295.

47

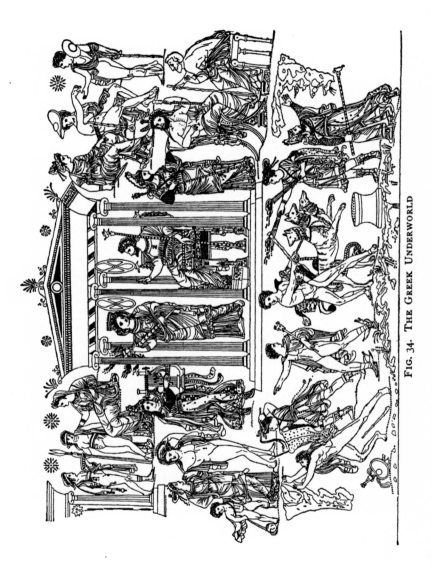

FIG. 34. THE GREEK UNDERWORLD

serpent-tailed dog, lay on guard, — friendly to the spirits entering, but inimical to those who would depart. The palace itself
is dark and gloomy,
set in the midst of un-
canny fields haunted
by strange apparitions.
The groves of somber
trees about the palace,
— the meads of As-
phodel, barren or, at
best, studded with
futile bushes and pale-
flowered weeds, where
wander the shades, —
and the woods along
the waste shore " of
tall poplars and willows

FIG. 35. HERMES CONDUCTING A SOUL
TO CHARON

that shed their fruit before the season" are, without any particular
discrimination, celebrated by the poets as the *Garden of Proserpine*.

> Here life has death for neighbor,
>   And far from eye or ear
> Wan waves and wet winds labor,
>   Weak ships and spirits steer;
> They drive adrift, and whither
> They wot not who make thither;
> But no such winds blow hither,
>   And no such things grow here.
>
> No growth of moor or coppice,
>   No heather-flower or vine,
> But bloomless buds of poppies,
>   Green grapes of Proserpine,
> Pale beds of blowing rushes,
> Where no leaf blooms or blushes
> Save this whereout she crushes
>   For dead men deadly wine.
>
> .   .   .   .
>
> Pale, beyond porch and portal,
>   Crowned with calm leaves, she stands

Who gathers all things mortal
  With cold immortal hands;
Her languid lips are sweeter
Than love's, who fears to greet her,
To men that mix and meet her
  From many times and lands.

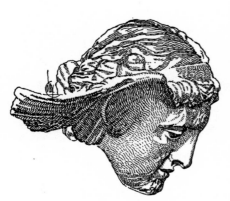

She waits for each and other,
  She waits for all men born;
Forgets the earth her mother,
  The life of fruits and corn;
And spring and seed and swallow
Take wing for her and follow
Where summer song rings hollow,
  And flowers are put to scorn.

.   .   .   .

We are not sure of sorrow,
  And joy was never sure;
To-day will die to-morrow;
  Time stoops to no man's lure;
And love, grown faint and fretful,
With lips but half regretful
Sighs, and with eyes forgetful
  Weeps that no loves endure.

FIG. 36. HYPNOS

From too much love of living,
  From hope and fear set free,
We thank with brief thanksgiving
  Whatever gods may be
That no life lives forever;
That dead men rise up never;
That even the weariest river
  Winds somewhere safe to sea.

Then star nor sun shall waken,
  Nor any change of light;
Nor sound of waters shaken,
  Nor any sound or sight;
Nor wintry leaves nor vernal,
Nor days nor things diurnal:
Only the sleep eternal
  In an eternal night.[1]

[1] From The Garden of Proserpine, by A. C. Swinburne.

45. Tartarus and the Elysian Fields. With the ghosts of Hades the living might but rarely communicate, and only through certain oracles of the dead, situate by cavernous spots and sheer abysms, deep and melancholy streams, and baleful marshes. These naturally seemed to afford access to the world below, which with the later poets, such as Virgil, comes to be regarded as under the ground. One of these descents to the Underworld was near Tænarum in Laconia; another, near Cumæ in Italy, was Lake Avernus, so foul in its exhalations that, as its name portends, no bird could fly across it.[1] Before the judges of the lower world, — Minos, Æacus, and Rhadamanthus, — the souls of the dead were brought to trial. The condemned were assigned to regions where all manner of torment awaited them at the hands of monsters dire, — the fifty-headed Hydra and the avenging Furies. Some evildoers, such as the Titans of old, were doomed to languish in the gulf of Tartarus immeasurably below. But the souls of the guiltless passed to the Elysian Fields, where each followed the chosen pursuit of

Fig. 37. A Fury

his former life in a land of spring, sunlight, happiness, and song. And by the Fields there flowed the river Lethe, from which the souls of those that were to return to the earth in other bodies drank oblivion of their former lives.

46. The Islands of the Blest. Homer mentions, elsewhere, an Elysium of the western seas, which is a happy land, " where life is easiest for men: no snow is there, nor yet great storm, nor any rain; but always ocean sendeth forth the breeze of the shrill West to blow cool on men." [2] Hither favored heroes pass without dying, and live under the happy rule of Rhadamanthus. The Elysium of Hesiod and Pindar is likewise in the Western Ocean,

[1] Æneid, 6.   [2] Odyssey, 4, 561.

on the Islands of the Blessed, the Fortunate Isles. From this dream of a western Elysium may have sprung the legend of the island Atlantis. That blissful region may have been wholly imaginary. It is, however, not impossible that the myth had its origin in the reports of storm-driven mariners who had caught a glimpse of occidental lands. In these Islands of the Blest, the Titans, released from Tartarus after many years, dwelt under the golden sway of the white-haired Cronus.[1]

> There was no heavy heat, no cold,
> The dwellers there wax never old,
>   Nor wither with the waning time,
> But each man keeps that age he had
>   When first he won the fairy clime.
> The night falls never from on high,
>   Nor ever burns the heat of noon;
> But such soft light eternally
>   Shines, as in silver dawns of June
> Before the sun hath climbed the sky!
>
> .   .   .   .
>
> All these their mirth and pleasure made
>   Within the plain Elysian,
>   The fairest meadow that may be,
> With all green fragrant trees for shade,
>   And every scented wind to fan,
>   And sweetest flowers to strew the lea;
> The soft winds are their servants fleet
>   To fetch them every fruit at will
>   And water from the river chill;
> And every bird that singeth sweet,
>   Throstle, and merle, and nightingale,
>   Brings blossoms from the dewy vale,—
> Lily, and rose, and asphodel, —
>   With these doth each guest twine his crown
>   And wreathe his cup, and lay him down
> Beside some friend he loveth well.[2]

47. Pluto (Hades) was brother of Jupiter. To him fell the sovereignty of the lower world and the shades of the dead. In his character of Hades, the viewless, he is hard and inexorable.

---

[1] Hes. Works and Days, 169.   [2] From The Fortunate Islands, by Andrew Lang.

By virtue of the helmet or cap given him by the Cyclopes, he moved hither and yon, dark, unseen, — hated of mortals. He was, however, lord not only of all that descends to the bowels of the earth, but of all that proceeds from the earth; and in the latter aspect he was revered as Pluto, or the giver of wealth. At his pleasure he visited the realms of day, — as when he carried off Proserpina; occasionally he journeyed to Olympus; but otherwise he ignored occurrences in the upper world, nor did he suffer his subjects, by returning, to find them out. Mortals, when they called on his name, beat the ground with their hands and, averting their faces, sacrificed black sheep to him and to his queen. Among the Romans he is known also as Dis, Orcus, and Tartarus. But Orcus is rather Death, or the Underworld, than ruler of the shades.

FIG. 38. HADES

48. Proserpina (Persephone) was the daughter of Ceres and Jupiter. She was queen of Hades, — a name applied both to the ruler of the shades and to his realm. When she is goddess of spring, dear to mankind, Proserpina bears a cornucopia overflowing with flowers, and revisits the earth in duly recurring season. But when she is goddess of death, sitting beside Pluto, she directs the Furies, and, like her husband, is cruel, unyielding, inimical to youth and life and hope. In the story of her descent to Hades will be found a further account of her attributes and fortunes.

49. The Lesser Divinities of the Underworld were:

1. *Æacus, Rhadamanthus*, and *Minos*, sons of Jupiter and judges of the shades in the lower world. Æacus had been during his earthly life a righteous king of the island of Ægina. Minos had been a famous lawgiver and king of Crete. The life of Rhadamanthus was not eventful.

2. *The Furies* (*Erinyes* or *Eumenides*), Alecto, Tisiphone, and Megæra, born of the blood of the wounded Uranus. They were attendants of Proserpina. They punished with the frenzies of remorse the crimes of those who had escaped from or defied public justice. The heads of the Furies were wreathed with serpents.

3. *Hecate*, a mysterious divinity sometimes identified with Diana and sometimes with Proserpina. As Diana represents the moonlight splendor of night, so Hecate represents its darkness and terrors. She haunted crossroads and graveyards, was the goddess of sorcery and witchcraft, and wandered by night, seen only by the dogs whose barking told of her approach.

Fig. 39. Death, Sleep, and Hermes laying a Body in the Tomb

4. *Sleep*, or *Somnus* (*Hypnos*), and *Death* (*Thanatos*), sons of Night.[1] They dwell in subterranean darkness. The former brings to mortals solace and fair dreams, and can lull the shining eyes of Jove himself; the latter closes forever the eyes of men. *Dreams*, too, are sons of Night.[2] They dwell beside their brother Death, along the Western Sea. Their abode has two gates, — one of ivory, whence issue false and flattering visions; the other of horn, through which true dreams and noble pass to men.[3]

[1] Iliad, 14, 231; 16, 672.
[2] Odyssey, 24, 12; 19, 560. Æneid, 6, 893. Ovid, Metam. 11, 592.
[3] For genealogical table, see Commentary.

CHAPTER V

THE GODS OF THE WATERS[1]

50. The Older Dynasty. There were two dynasties of the sea. The Older, which flourished during the rule of Cronus, was founded by the Titans, *Oceanus* and *Tethys*, from whom sprang three thousand rivers and ocean-nymphs unnumbered. The palace of Oceanus was beyond the limits of the bountiful earth,[2] surrounded by gardens and all things fair. From ages immemorial another dweller in the glimmering caves of Ocean was *Pontus* (the *deep sea* or the *waterway*), who became, by Mother Earth, father of Nereus. This *Nereus*, a genial old man of the sea, was distinguished for his prophetic gifts, his knowledge, his love of truth and justice. Taking to wife one of the daughters of Oceanus, the nymph Doris, he was blessed with a family of fifty fair daughters, the *Nereïds*.[3] Of these daughters the most famous are

FIG. 40. POSEIDON

Panope, Galatea, Thetis, and Amphitrite ; the last of whom gave her hand to Neptune (Poseidon), brother of Jove, and thus united the Older and the Younger dynasties of the sea.

51. Of the **Younger Dynasty** of the waters *Neptune* and *Amphitrite* were the founders. Neptune's palace was in the

---

[1] For references to poetry and works of art, see corresponding sections of Commentary.
[2] Iliad, 14, 303.   [3] Iliad, 18, 30-50.

FIG. 41. WEDDING OF POSEIDON AND AMPHITRITE

depths of the sea, near Ægæ in Eubœa; but he made his home on Olympus when he chose. The symbol of his power was the trident, or three-pronged spear, with which he could shatter rocks, call forth or subdue storms, and shake the shores of earth. He created the horse and was the patron of horse races. His own steeds were brazen-hoofed and golden-maned. They drew his chariot over the sea, which became smooth before him, while dolphins and other monsters of the deep gamboled about his path. In his honor black and white bulls, white boars, and rams were sacrificed.

52. The Lesser Divinities of the Waters[1] were :

1. *Triton*, the son of Neptune and Amphitrite, trumpeter of Ocean. By his blast on the sea-shell he stirred or allayed the waves.

2. *Proteus*, an attendant and, according to certain traditions, a son of Neptune. Like Nereus, he was a little old man of the sea. He possessed the prophetic gift and the power of changing his shape at will.

3. *The Harpies*, foul creatures, with heads of maidens, bodies, wings, and claws of birds, and

[1] For genealogical table, see Commentary.

faces pale with hunger. They are the offspring of Thaumas, a son of Pontus and Gæa.

4. The uncanny offspring of Phorcys and Ceto, — children of Pontus, — who rejoiced in the horrors of the sea:

a. The Grææ, three hoary witches, with one eye between them which they used in turn.

b. The Gorgons, whose glance was icy death.

c. The Sirens, muses of the sea and of death, who by their sweet singing enticed seafarers to destruction.

d. Scylla, also destructive to mariners, a six-headed monster whose lower limbs were serpents and ever-barking dogs.

FIG. 42. TRITON CARRYING OFF A NYMPH

5. *Atlas,* who stood in the far west, bearing on his shoulders the vault of heaven. He was once regarded as a divinity of the sea, but later as a mountain. He was the son of Iapetus and the father of three classes of nymphs, — the Pleiads, the Hyads, and, according to some stories, the Hesperids. The last-mentioned, assisted by their mother Hesperis and a dragon, guarded the golden apples of the tree that had sprung up to grace the wedding of Jove and Juno. **The daughters of Atlas were not themselves divinities of the sea.**

6. *The Water-Nymphs.* Beside the *Oceanids* and the *Nereïds*, who have already been mentioned, of most importance were the *Naiads*, daughters of Jupiter. They presided over brooks and fountains. Other lesser powers of the Ocean were Glaucus, Leucothea, and Melicertes, of whom more is said in another section.

In the following statement of the difference between ancient and modern conceptions of nature, the poet lends new charm to the fabled rulers of the sea.

> The world is too much with us; late and soon,
> Getting and spending, we lay waste our powers:
> Little we see in Nature that is ours;
> We have given our hearts away, a sordid boon!
> This sea that bares her bosom to the moon;
> The winds that will be howling at all hours,
> And are upgathered now like sleeping flowers;
> For this, for everything, we are out of tune;
> It moves us not. — Great God! I 'd rather be
> A Pagan suckled in a creed outworn;
> So might I, standing on this pleasant lea,
> Have glimpses that would make me less forlorn;
> Have sight of Proteus rising from the sea;
> Or hear old Triton blow his wreathèd horn.[1]

[1] Wordsworth, Miscellaneous Sonnets.

CHAPTER VI

THE ROMAN DIVINITIES

53. Gods Common to Greece and Italy. Of the deities already mentioned, the following, although they were later identified with certain Greek gods and goddesses [1] whose characteristics and adventures they assumed, had developed an independent worship in Italy : Jupiter (Zeus) ; Juno (Hera) ; Minerva (Athene) ; Diana (Artemis) ; Mars (Ares) ; Venus (Aphrodite) ; Vulcanus, or Mulciber (Hephæstus) ; Vesta (Hestia) ; Mercurius (Hermes) ; Neptunus (Poseidon) ; Ceres (Demeter) ; Liber (Bacchus) ; Libera (Persephone) ; Magna Mater, the great mother of the gods (Rhea, Cybele) ; Orcus (Pluto, Hades) ; Tellus, the Earth (Gæa).

54. Italian Gods. There were also divinities always peculiar to Roman mythology.[2] Of these the more important are :

1. *Saturn*, an ancient Italian deity (as his name indicates) of seeds and sowing, the introducer of agriculture. Fanciful attempts were made to identify him with the Grecian god Cronus ; and it was fabled that after his dethronement by Jupiter he fled to Italy, where he reigned during the Golden Age. In memory of his dominion, the feast of Saturnalia was held every year in the winter season. Then all public business·was suspended ; declarations of war and criminal executions were postponed ; friends made presents to one another ; and even slaves were indulged with great liberties. A feast was given them at which they sat at table while their masters served, to show the natural equality of men, and that all things belonged equally to all in the reign of Saturn. The wife of Saturn was *Ops*, goddess of sowing and harvest (later confounded with Rhea). Another Roman deity of earth was *Consus*, whose name means " the keeper of the stores." He is the

---

[1] Names of the corresponding Greek divinities are in parentheses.
[2] For illustrative material, see Commentary.

god of the stored-up harvest; and his altar is said to have been discovered underground by Romulus. It was in the Circus Maximus and was uncovered only on the days of his festivals, the harvest home of August and the granary feast of December. The underground altar is a reminiscence of the ancient custom of storing corn underground or at any rate of burying the sacrifices offered to deities of the earth. The harvest festival was celebrated with horse races, which, originating in a very simple way with the primitive farmers, became in time the distinctive feature of the Circus Maximus.

2. *Janus*, whose name is derived from the Latin root which means "going" and is connected with *janua*, a passage or door,

FIG. 43. BEARDED
JANUS

is the most distinctive and most important of the native Italic deities. He is not only the god of doors, or material openings, but more truly of beginnings, — especially of good beginnings which insure good endings. Hence undoubtedly he is represented as facing both ways; for the Romans very properly believed that beginning and ending were of the same piece, and that an undertaking ill begun could not achieve success. His temple, or covered passage, in the Forum had doors facing east and west for the beginning and ending of the day; and between stood his two-faced statue. In every home the morning prayer was addressed to him; in every domestic enterprise his assistance was implored. He was the god, also, of the opening year; hence his month, January, on the first day of which words only of good omen were uttered, and gifts were given (*strenae*, a name still preserved in the French word for New Year's presents, *étrennes*), and, for good luck, some stroke of work was bestowed on every undertaking planned for the year. He was publicly invoked not only on New Year's day, but on the first day of each month, by priests and people alike; and in these prayers his name was mentioned even before that of Jupiter. He is the god of civilization, and is sometimes called Consivius, or the Sower.[1] Of course he was invoked when wars were commenced. And during their progress the doors of his

---

[1] Gellius, 5, 12. Ovid, Fasti, 1, 179. Macrobius, Sat. 1, 9-15.

temple stood always open. In peace they were closed; but they were shut only once between the reign of Numa and that of Augustus. It was natural that his worship should gradually absorb that of Sol, the Sun, who opens the day and completes the year and blesses with his rays the seeds that are sown; and such was the case. But Janus and his wife Jana were not originally connected even in name with Dianus (Sol, Apollo) and Diana (the moon).

3. *Quirinus*, a war-god, said to be no other than Romulus, the founder of Rome, exalted after his death to a place among the immortals.

4. *Bellona*, a war-goddess.

5. *Lucina*, the goddess who brings to light, hence the goddess of childbirth : a title bestowed upon both Juno and Diana.

6. *Terminus*, the god of landmarks. His statue was a rude stone or post, set in the ground to mark the boundaries of fields.

7. *Faunus*, the grandson of Saturn. He was worshiped as a god of fields and shepherds and also of prophecy. His name in the plural, Fauni, expressed a class of gamesome deities, like the Satyrs of the Greeks. There was also a goddess called *Fauna*, or *Bona Dea* (good goddess). To Maia, wife of Vulcan, this designation, *Bona Dea*, was sometimes applied.

8. *Sylvanus*, presiding over forest-glades and plowed fields.

9. *Pales*, the goddess presiding over cattle and pastures. *Flora*, the goddess of flowers. *Pomona*, presiding over fruit trees. *Vertumnus*, the husband of Pomona, was guardian of fruit trees, gardens, and vegetables.

> Pomona loves the orchard,
>   And Liber loves the vine,
> And Pales loves the straw-built shed
>   Warm with the breath of kine;
> And Venus loves the whisper
>   Of plighted youth and maid
> In April's ivory moonlight,
>   Beneath the chestnut shade.[1]

10. *The Penates*, gods who were supposed to attend to the welfare and prosperity of the family. Their name is derived from

[1] From Macaulay's Prophecy of Capys.

Penus, the storehouse or inner chamber, which was sacred to them. Every master of a family was the priest to the Penates of his own house.

The *Lares*, or *Lars*, were also tutelary deities, but they differed from the Penates since they were regarded as the deified spirits of ancestors, who watched over and protected their descendants. The Lares were more particularly divinities presiding over the household or family ; but there were also public Lares, or guardian spirits of the city, Lares of the precincts, Lares of the fields, Lares of the highways, and Lares of the sea. To the Penates, to the domestic Lares (whose images were preserved in a private shrine),

FIG. 44. GENIUS LOCI

and to the *Manes* (shades that hovered over the place of burial), the family prayers of the Romans were addressed. Other spirits, the *Lemures* and *Larvæ*, more nearly correspond to our ghosts.

The Romans believed that every man had his *Genius* and every woman her *Juno ;* that is, a spirit who had given them being and was regarded as a protector through life. On birthdays men made offerings to their Genius, women to their Juno.

11. Other Italian deities were the gods of the rivers, such as *Father Tiber*, and the goddesses of the springs and brooks, such as *Juturna*, whose pool in the Forum was sacred. This nymph was also a goddess of healing and, according to later tradition, was beloved by Jupiter. Earlier stories, however, make her the wife of Janus and the mother of *Fontus*, the god of flowing waters, who had an altar on the Janiculan hill and was worshiped at an annual festival called the Fontinalia, when the wells were wreathed with garlands. Held in especial honor were the *Camenæ*, fountain-nymphs, goddesses of prophecy and healing (later identified with the Muses). The leader of them was *Carmenta*, who sang both the future and the past. With her is sometimes associated the nymph

Egeria, from whom the Roman king Numa is said to have received instruction concerning the forms of worship which he introduced.

12. The Romans worshiped, also, *Sol,* the Sun ; *Luna,* the Moon ; *Mater Matuta,* the Dawn ; *Juventus,* Youth ; *Fides,* Honesty ; *Feronia,* goddess of groves and freedmen ; and a great number of personified abstractions of conduct and experience, such as Fortune and Health.

Many of these Latin divinities were derived from the earlier cult and ritual of the Etruscan inhabitants of Italy.

CHAPTER VII

MYTHS OF THE GREAT DIVINITIES OF HEAVEN

55. Myths of Jupiter and Juno. Not a few of the adventures of Jupiter turn upon his love affairs. Among the immortals his queen had rivals in his affection; for instance, Latona, a goddess of darkness, daughter of the Titans Cœus and Phœbe. This goddess became, as we have already seen, the mother of Apollo and Diana. The ire of Juno against her was never appeased. In consequence of it, numerous trials were visited upon Latona, some of which find a place among the adventures of her children.

FIG. 45. GANYMEDE

56. Love Affairs of Jupiter. Not only with immortals but with mortals were Jupiter's relations sometimes of a dubious character. His devotion to the beautiful daughters of men involved him in frequent altercations with his justly jealous spouse. Of his fondness for Danaë, whom he approached in a shower of gold, particulars are given in the story of her son Perseus; of his love for Alcmene, the granddaughter of that Perseus, we are informed in the myths of her son Hercules; and of his attentions to Leda, whom he wooed in guise of a swan, we learn in the accounts of their children Pollux and Helen. Other love passages, upon which narratives depend, concern Io, Callisto, Europa, Semele, Ægina, and Antiope.

64

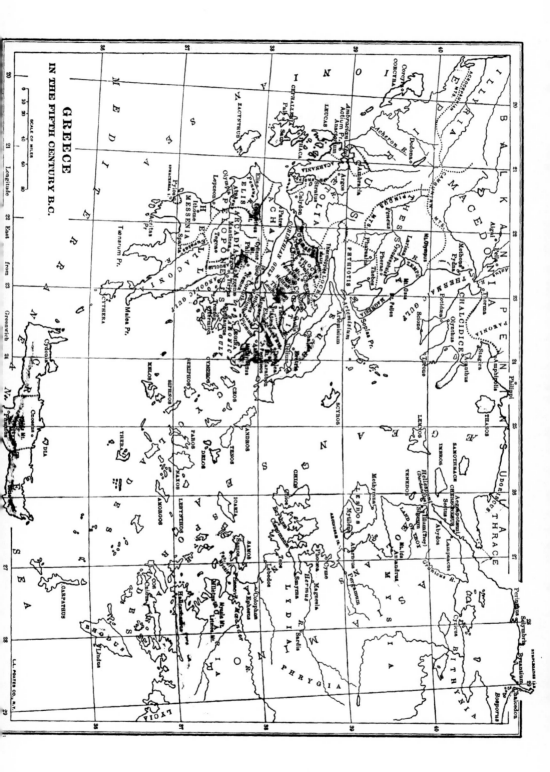

GREECE

IN THE FIFTH CENTURY B.C.

57. Io[1] was of divine ancestry. Her father was the river-god Inachus, son of Oceanus. It is said that Juno one day, perceiving the skies suddenly overcast, surmised that her husband had raised a cloud to hide some escapade. She brushed away the darkness and saw him on the banks of a glassy river with a beautiful heifer standing near. Juno suspected, with reason, that the heifer's form concealed some fair nymph of mortal mold. It was Io, whom Jupiter, when he became aware of the approach of his wife, had changed into that form.

The ox-eyed goddess joined her husband, noticed the heifer, praised its beauty, and asked whose it was and of what herd. Jupiter, to stop questions, replied that it was a fresh creation from the earth. Juno begged it as a gift. What could the king of gods and men do? He was loath to surrender his sweetheart to his wife; yet how refuse so trifling a present as a heifer? He could not, without exciting suspicion, and he therefore consented. The goddess delivered the heifer to Argus, to be strictly watched.

FIG. 46. HERMES KILLS ARGUS

Now Argus had a hundred eyes in his head, and never went to sleep with more than two at a time, so that he kept watch of Io constantly. He suffered her to graze through the day and at night tied a rope round her neck. She would have stretched out her arms to implore freedom of Argus, but that she had no arms to stretch out and her voice was a bellow. She yearned in vain to make herself known to her father. At length she bethought herself of writing, and inscribed her name — it was a short one — with her hoof on the sand. Inachus recognized it, and, discovering that his daughter whom he had long sought in vain was hidden under this disguise, mourned over her. While he thus lamented, Argus, observing, drove her away and took his seat on a bank from whence he could see in every direction.

[1] Ovid, Metam. 1, 700 *et seq.*

Jupiter, grieved by the sufferings of his mistress, sent Mercury to dispatch Argus. Mercury took his sleep-producing wand and presented himself on earth as a shepherd driving his flock. As he strolled, he blew upon his syrinx or Pandean pipes. Argus listened with delight. "Young man," said he, "come and take a seat by me on this stone. There is no better place for your flock to graze in than hereabouts, and here is a pleasant shade such as shepherds love." Mercury sat down, talked, told stories till it grew late, and played upon his pipes his most soothing strains, hoping to lull the watchful eyes to sleep, but in vain; for Argus still contrived to keep some of his eyes open, though he shut the rest.

FIG. 47. IO, ARGUS, AND MERCURY

But among other stories, Mercury told him how the instrument on which he played was invented. "There was a certain nymph," said he, "whose name was Syrinx,— much beloved by the satyrs and spirits of the wood. She would have none of them, but was a faithful worshiper of Diana and followed the chase. Pan, meeting her one day, wooed her with many compliments, likening her to Diana of the silver bow. Without stopping to hear him she ran away. But on the bank of the river he overtook her. She called for help on her friends, the water-nymphs. They heard and consented. Pan threw his arms around what he supposed to be the form of the nymph and found he embraced only a tuft of reeds. As he breathed a sigh, the air sounded through the reeds and produced a plaintive melody. Whereupon the god, charmed with the novelty and with the sweetness of the music, said, 'Thus, then, at least, you shall be mine.' Taking some of the reeds of unequal lengths and placing them together, side by side, he made an instrument and called it Syrinx, in honor of the nymph." Before Mercury had finished his story he saw the eyes of Argus all asleep. At once he slew him and set Io free. The eyes of Argus Juno took and scattered as ornaments on the tail of her peacock, where they remain to this day.

But the vengeance of Juno was not yet satiated. She sent a gadfly to torment Io, who, in her flight, swam through the sea, named after her, Ionian. Afterward, roaming over many lands, she reached at last the banks of the Nile. Then Jupiter interceded for her; and upon his engaging not to pay her any further attention, Juno consented to restore her to her form.

In a poem dedicated to Leigh Hunt, by Keats, the following allusion to the story of Pan and Syrinx occurs:

> So did he feel who pulled the boughs aside,
> That we might look into a forest wide, . . .
> Telling us how fair trembling Syrinx fled
> Arcadian Pan, with such a fearful dread.
> Poor nymph — poor Pan — how he did weep to find
> Nought but a lovely sighing of the wind
> Along the reedy stream; a half-heard strain,
> Full of sweet desolation, balmy pain.

58. Callisto of Arcadia was another maiden who excited the jealousy of Juno. Her the goddess changed into a bear. Often, frightened by the dogs, Callisto, though lately a huntress, fled in terror from the hunters. Often, too, she fled from the wild beasts, forgetting that she was now a wild beast herself; and, bear as she was, she feared the bears.

One day a youth espied her as he was hunting. She saw him and recognized him as her son Arcas, grown to manhood. She stopped and felt inclined to embrace him. He, alarmed, raised his hunting spear and was on the point of transfixing her, but Jupiter arrested the crime and, snatching away both of them, placed them in the heavens as the Great and Little Bear.

Juno, enraged at seeing her rival so set in honor, hastened to ancient Tethys and Oceanus and, complaining that she was supplanted in Heaven, cried, "So do my punishments result — such is the extent of my power! I forbade her to wear human form,

— she and her hateful son are placed among the stars. Better that she should have resumed her former shape, as I permitted Io to do. Perhaps my husband means to take her to wife, and put me away! But you, my foster parents, if you feel for me, and see with displeasure this unworthy treatment of me, show it, I beseech you, by forbidding this guilty couple from coming into your waters." The powers of the Ocean assented, and consequently the two constellations of the Great and Little Bear move round and round in the neighborhood of the pole, but never sink, as do the other stars, beneath the Ocean.[1]

59. Eurṓpa was the daughter of Agenor, king of Phœnicia, son of the god Neptune. The story of Jupiter's love for her is thus told by the idyllic poet, Moschus :

To Europa, princess of Asia, once on a time, a sweet dream was sent by Cypris. . . . Then she beheld two continents at strife for her sake, Asia and the further shore, both in the shape of women. Of these one had the guise of a stranger, the other of a lady of that land, and closer still she clung about her maiden, and kept saying how she was her mother, and herself had nursed Europa. But that other with mighty hands, and forcefully, kept haling the maiden, nothing loth; declaring that, by the will of ægis-bearing Jupiter, Europa was destined to be her prize.

But Europa leaped forth from her strown bed in terror, with beating heart, in such clear vision had she beheld the dream. . . . And she said, "Ah! who was the alien woman that I beheld in my sleep? How strange a longing for her seized my heart, yea, and how graciously she herself did welcome me, and regard me as it had been her own child! Ye blessed gods, I pray you, prosper the fulfillment of the dream!"

Therewith she arose, and began to seek the dear maidens of her company, girls of like age with herself, born in the same year, beloved of her heart, the daughters of noble sires, with whom she was always wont to sport, when she was arrayed for the dance, or when she would bathe her bright body at the mouths of the rivers, or would gather fragrant lilies on the leas. . . .

Now the girls, so soon as they were come to the flowering meadows, took great delight in various sorts of flowers, whereof one would pluck sweet-breathed narcissus, another the hyacinth, another the violet, a fourth the creeping thyme; and on the ground there fell many petals of the meadows rich with spring. Others, again, were emulously gathering the fragrant tresses of the yellow crocus; but in the midst of them all the princess culled with her hand

---

[1] Ovid, Metam. 2, 410 et seq.

the splendor of the crimson rose, and shone preëminent among them all like the foam-born goddess among the Graces. Verily, she was not for long to set her heart's delight upon the flowers. . . . For of a truth, the son of Cronus, so soon as he beheld her, was troubled, and his heart was subdued by the sudden shafts of Cypris, who alone can conquer even Jupiter. Therefore, both to avoid the wrath of jealous Juno, and being eager to beguile the maiden's tender heart, he concealed his godhead, and changed his shape, and became a bull. . . .

He came into the meadow, and his coming terrified not the maidens, nay, within them all wakened desire to draw nigh the lovely bull, and to touch him, and his heavenly fragrance was scattered afar, exceeding even the sweet perfume of the meadows. And he stood before the feet of fair Europa, and kept licking her neck, and cast his spell over the maiden. And she still caressed him, and gently with her hands she wiped away the deep foam from his lips, and kissed the bull. Then he lowed so gently, ye would think ye heard the Mygdonian flute uttering a dulcet sound.

FIG. 48. EUROPA ON THE BULL

He bowed himself before her feet, and bending back his neck, he gazed on Europa, and showed her his broad back. Then she spake among her deep-tressed maidens, saying,—

" Come, dear playmates, maidens of like age with me, let us mount the bull here and take our pastime, for, truly, he will bear us on his back, and carry all of us! And how mild he is, and dear, and gentle to behold, and no whit like other bulls! A mind as honest as a man's possesses him, and he lacks nothing but speech."

So she spake, and smiling, she sat down on the back of the bull, and the others were about to follow her. But the bull leaped up immediately, now he had gotten her that he desired, and swiftly he sped to the deep. The maiden turned, and called again and again to her dear playmates, stretching out her hands, but they could not reach her. The strand he gained, and forward he sped like a dolphin, faring with unwetted hooves over the wide waves. And the sea, as he came, grew smooth, and the sea monsters gamboled around, before the feet of Jupiter; and the dolphin rejoiced, and rising from the deeps, he tumbled on the swell of the sea. The Nereïds arose out of the salt water, and all of them came on in orderly array, riding on the backs of sea beasts. And himself, the thunderous shaker of the world, appeared above the sea, and made smooth the wave, and guided his brother on the salt sea path, and round him were gathered the Tritons, these hoarse trumpeters of the deep, blowing from their long conchs a bridal melody.

Meanwhile, Europa, riding on the back of the divine bull, with one hand clasped the beast's great horn, and with the other caught up the purple fold of her garment, lest it might trail and be wet in the hoar sea's infinite spray. And her deep robe was swelled out by the winds, like the sail of a ship, and lightly still did waft the maiden onward. But when she was now far off from

FIG. 49. NEREIDS ON SEA BEASTS

her own country, and neither sea-beat headland nor steep hill could now be seen, but above, the air, and beneath, the limitless deep, timidly she looked around, and uttered her voice, saying, —

" Whither bearest thou me, bull god? What art thou? How dost thou fare on thy feet through the path of the sea beasts, nor fearest the sea? The sea is a path meet for swift ships that traverse the brine, but bulls dread the salt sea ways. What drink is sweet to thee, what food shalt thou find from the deep? Nay, art thou then some god, for god-like are these deeds of thine." . . .

So spake she, and the horned bull made answer to her again: " Take courage, maiden, and dread not the swell of the deep. Behold, I am Jupiter, even I, though, closely beheld, I wear the form of a bull, for I can put on the semblance of what thing I will. But 't is love of thee that has compelled me to measure out so great a space of the salt sea, in a bull's shape. So Crete shall presently receive thee, Crete that was mine own foster-mother, where thy bridal chamber shall be.[1]

According to tradition, from this princess the continent of Europe acquired its name. Her three sons are famous in Greek

---

[1] Translated by Andrew Lang: Theocritus, Bion, and Moschus, London, 1880.

myth : Minos, who became king of Crete, and after his death a judge in the lower world ; Rhadamanthus, who also was regarded as king and judge in the world of ghosts ; and Sarpedon, who was ancestor of the Lycians.

The adventures of Europa's brother Cadmus, who by the command of his father went forth in quest of the lost maiden, fall under the myths of Mars.[1]

60. Semele was the daughter of Cadmus, founder of Thebes. She was descended, through both parents, from the gods ; for her mother Harmonia was daughter to Mars and the laughter-loving Venus. To Semele Jupiter had appeared, and had paid court in unostentatious manner and simple guise. But Juno, to gratify her resentment against this new rival for her lord's affections, contrived a plan for her destruction. Assuming the form of Beroë, the aged nurse of Semele, she insinuated doubts whether it was indeed Jove himself who came as a lover.

FIG. 50. BACCHUS EMBRACING SEMELE

Heaving a sigh, she said, " I hope it will turn out so, but I can't help being afraid. People are not always what they pretend to be. If he is indeed Jove, make him give some proof of it. Ask him to come arrayed in all his splendors, such as he wears in Heaven. That will put the matter beyond a doubt." Semele was persuaded to try the experiment. She asks a favor, without naming what it is. Jove gives his promise, and confirms it with the irrevocable oath, attesting the river Styx, terrible to the gods themselves. Then she made known her request. The god would have stopped her as she spake, but she was too quick for him. The words

[1] § 70.

escaped, and he could neither unsay his promise nor her request. In deep distress he left her and returned to the upper regions. There he clothed himself in his splendors, not putting on all his terrors, as when he overthrew the giants, but what is known among the gods as his lesser panoply. With thunders and lightnings he entered the chamber of Semele. Her mortal frame could not endure the splendors of the immortal radiance. She was consumed to ashes.[1] Her son was the god Bacchus.[2] Semele, in the blissful seats of Heaven, whither she was transported by the sorrowful Jove, has been represented as recounting thus the story of her doom :

> What were the garden-bowers of Thebes to me?
> What cared I for their dances and their feasts,
> Whose heart awaited an immortal doom?
> The Greek youths mocked me, since I shunned in scorn
> Them and their praises of my brows and hair.
> The light girls pointed after me, who turned
> Soul-sick from their unending fooleries. . . .
>
> There came a change : a glory fell to me.
> No more 't was Semele, the lonely girl,
> But Jupiter's Beloved, Semele.
> With human arms the god came clasping me :
> New life streamed from his presence; and a voice,
> That scarce could curb itself to the smooth Greek,
> Now and anon swept forth in those deep nights,
> Thrilling my flesh with awe; mysterious words —
> I knew not what; hints of unearthly things
> That I had felt on solemn summer noons,
> When sleeping Earth dreamed music, and the heart
> Went crooning a low song it could not learn,
> But wandered over it, as one who gropes
> For a forgotten chord upon a lyre.
>
> Yea, Jupiter! But why this mortal guise,
> Wooing as if he were a milk-faced boy?
> Did I lack lovers? Was my beauty dulled,
> The golden hair turned dross, the lithe limbs shrunk?
> The deathless longings tamed, that I should seethe
> My soul in love like any shepherd girl?

[1] Ovid, Metam. 3, 260 *et seq.*   [2] §§ 42, 110–113.

One night he sware to grant whate'er I asked:
And straight I cried, " To know thee as thou art!
To hold thee on my heart as Juno does!
Come in thy thunder — kill me with one fierce
Divine embrace! — Thine oath! — Now, Earth, at last!"

The Heavens shot one swift sheet of lurid flame;
The world crashed: from a body scathed and torn
The soul leapt through, and found his breast, and died.
   Died? — So the Theban maidens think, and laugh,
Saying, " She had her wish, that Semele!"
But sitting here upon Olympus' height,
I look down, through that oval ring of stars,
And see the far-off Earth, a twinkling speck —
Dust-mote whirled up from the Sun's chariot wheel —
And pity their small hearts that hold a man
As if he were a god; or know the god —
Or dare to know him — only as a man!
O human love! art thou forever blind? [1]

61. Ægina. The extent to which those who were concerned only indirectly in Jupiter's love affairs might yet be involved in the consequences of them is illustrated by the fortunes of Ægina. This maiden, the daughter of Asopus, a river-god, attracted the attention of Jupiter, who straightway ran off with her. Now, on the one hand, Sisyphus, king of Corinth, having witnessed the intrigue, was indiscreet enough to disclose it. Forthwith the vengeance of the king of gods and men fell upon him. He was condemned to Hades and, attempting to escape thence, had resort to a series of deceptions that resulted in his eternal punishment. [2] On the other hand, the inhabitants of the island that had the misfortune to bear Ægina's name incurred the displeasure of Juno, who devastated their land with a plague. The following account of this calamity is placed in the mouth of Æacus, king of the island: [3]

"At the beginning the sky seemed to settle down upon the earth and thick clouds shut in the heated air. For four months together a deadly south wind prevailed. The disorder affected the wells and springs. Thousands of snakes crept over the land and

---

[1] From E. R. Sill's Semele.   [2] Commentary, §§ 118, 255.
[3] Ovid, Metam. 7, 172 *et seq.*

shed their poison in the fountains. The force of the disease was first spent on the lower animals, — dogs, cattle, sheep, and birds. The oxen fell in the midst of their work. The wool dropped from the bleating sheep. The horse groaned at his stall and died an inglorious death. Everything languished; dead bodies lay in the roads, the fields, and the woods; the air was poisoned by them. Next the disease attacked the country people, and then the dwellers in the city. At first the cheek was flushed and the breath drawn with difficulty. The tongue grew rough and swelled, and the dry mouth stood open, with its veins enlarged, and gasped for the air. Men could not bear the heat of their clothes or their beds, but preferred to lie on the bare ground. Nor could the physicians help, for the disease attacked them also. At last men learned to look upon death as the only deliverer from disease. All restraint laid aside, they crowded round the wells and fountains, and drank, without quenching thirst, till they died. On all sides lay my people strewn like overripened apples beneath the tree, or acorns under the storm-shaken oak. You see yonder a temple on the height. It is sacred to Jupiter. Often, while the priest made ready for sacrifice, the victim fell, struck down by disease without waiting for the blow. At length all reverence for sacred things was lost. Bodies were thrown out unburied, wood was wanting for funeral piles, men fought with one another for the possession of them. Finally there were none left to mourn; sons and husbands, old men and youths, perished alike unlamented.

" Standing before the altar, I raised my eyes to Heaven. ' O Jupiter,' I said, ' if thou art indeed my father, give me back my people, or take me also away !' At these words a clap of thunder was heard. ' I accept the omen,' I cried. By chance there grew by the place where I stood an oak with wide-spreading branches, sacred to Jupiter. I observed on it a troop of ants busy with their labor. Observing their numbers with admiration, I said, ' Give me, O father, citizens as numerous as these, and replenish my empty city.' The tree shook, and the branches rustled, though no wind agitated them. Night came on. The tree stood before me in my dreams, with its numerous branches all covered with living, moving creatures, which, falling to the ground, appeared to

FARNESE BULL

gain in size, and by and by to stand erect, and finally to assume the human form. Then I awoke. My attention was caught by the sound of many voices without. While I began to think I was yet dreaming, Telamon, my son, throwing open the temple gates, exclaimed, ' Father, approach, and behold things surpassing even your hopes ! ' I went forth ; I saw a multitude of men, such as I had seen in my dream. While I gazed with wonder and delight, they approached and, kneeling, hailed me as their king. I paid my vows to Jove, and proceeded to allot the vacant city to the new-born race. I called them Myrmidons from the ant (*myrmex*), from which they sprang. They are a diligent and industrious race, eager to gain, and tenacious of their gains."

The Myrmidons were the soldiers of Achilles, the grandson of King Æacus, in the Trojan War.

62. Antiope was, according to the Odyssey, another daughter of Asopus, therefore a sister of Ægina. But later poets make this darling of Jove daughter of Nycteus, king of Thebes. While she was engaged in the Mænad dances, Jupiter as a satyr wooed and won her. She bore him two sons, Amphion and Zethus, who, being exposed at birth on Mount Cithæron, grew up among the shepherds, not knowing their parentage. After various adventures Antiope fell into the hands of her uncle Lycus, the usurping king of Thebes, who, egged on by his wife Dirce, treated her with extreme cruelty. Finally, when doomed by Dirce to be dragged to death behind a bull, Antiope found means to inform her children of her kinship to them. As it happened, they had been ordered to execute the cruel sentence upon their mother. But with a band of their fellow herdsmen, they attacked and slew Lycus instead, and, tying Dirce by the hair of her head to a bull, let her perish by her own device.[1]

While among the herdsmen, *Amphion* had been the special care of Mercury, who gave him a lyre and taught him to play upon it. His brother Zethus had occupied himself in hunting and tending the flocks. Amphion himself is one of the most famous of mythical musicians. Having become king of Thebes, it is said that when

---

[1] Roscher, Ausf. Lex. Lfg. 3, 379 [Schirmer]. Originals in Pausanias, Apollodorus, and Hyginus.

he played on his lyre, stones moved of their own accord and took
their places in the wall with which he was fortifying the city.

FIG. 51. AMPHION AND ZETHUS

. . . 'T is said he had a tuneful tongue,
   Such happy intonation,
Wherever he sat down and sung
   He left a small plantation;
Wherever in a lonely grove
   He set up his forlorn pipes,
The gouty oak began to move,
   And flounder into hornpipes.

The mountain stirred its bushy crown,
   And, as tradition teaches,
Young ashes pirouetted down
   Coquetting with young beeches;

And briony-vine and ivy-wreath
　　Ran forward to his rhyming,
And from the valleys underneath
　　Came little copses climbing.

The linden broke her ranks and rent
　　The woodbine wreaths that bind her,
And down the middle, buzz! she went
　　With all her bees behind her:
The poplars, in long order due,
　　With cypress promenaded,
The shock-head willows, two and two,
　　By rivers gallopaded.

Came wet-shot alder from the wave,
　　Came yews, a dismal coterie;
Each plucked his one foot from the grave,
　　Poussetting with a sloe-tree:
Old elms came breaking from the vine,
　　The vine streamed out to follow,
And, sweating rosin, plumped the pine
　　From many a cloudy hollow.

And was n't it a sight to see,
　　When, ere his song was ended,
Like some great landslip, tree by tree,
　　The country-side descended;
And shepherds from the mountain-eaves
　　Looked down, half-pleased, half-frightened,
As dashed about the drunken leaves
　　The random sunshine lightened.[1]

The musician's life was, however, not all harmony and happiness. Owing to the pride of his wife Niobe, daughter of King Tantalus, there befell him and his house a crushing calamity, which is narrated among the exploits of Apollo and Diana.

63. Jupiter, a Friend of Man. The kindly interest evinced by the Thunderer toward mortals is displayed in the story of Baucis and Philemon. Once on a time Jupiter, in human shape, visited the land of Phrygia, and with him Mercury, without his wings.

---

[1] From Tennyson's Amphion. See Horace, Ars Poet. 394.

They presented themselves as weary travelers at many a door, seeking rest and shelter, but found all closed; for it was late, and the inhospitable inhabitants would not rouse themselves to open for their reception. At last a small thatched cottage received them, where Baucis, a pious old dame, and her husband Philemon had grown old together. Not ashamed of their poverty, they made it endurable by moderate desires and kind dispositions. When the two guests crossed the humble threshold and bowed their heads to pass under the low door, the old man placed a seat, on which Baucis, bustling and attentive, spread a cloth, and begged them to sit down. Then she raked out the coals from the ashes, kindled a fire, and prepared some pot-herbs and bacon for them. A beechen bowl was filled with warm water, that their guests might wash. While all was doing, they beguiled the time with conversation.

The old woman with trembling hand set the table. One leg was shorter than the rest, but a piece of slate put under restored the level. When it was steady she rubbed the table down with sweet-smelling herbs. Upon it she set some of chaste Minerva's olives, some cornel berries preserved in vinegar, and added radishes and cheese, with eggs lightly cooked in the ashes. The meal was served in earthen dishes; and an earthenware pitcher, with wooden cups, stood beside them. When all was ready the stew, smoking hot, was set on the table. Some wine, not of the oldest, was added, and for dessert, apples and wild honey.

Now while the repast proceeded, the old folks were astonished to see that the wine, as fast as it was poured out, renewed itself in the pitcher of its own accord. Struck with terror, Baucis and Philemon recognized their heavenly guests, fell on their knees, and with clasped hands implored forgiveness for their poor entertainment. There was an old goose, which they kept as the guardian of their humble cottage, and they bethought them to make this a sacrifice in honor of their guests. But the goose, too nimble for the old folk, with the aid of feet and wings eluded their pursuit and at last took shelter between the gods themselves. They forbade it to be slain, and spoke in these words: "We are gods. This inhospitable village shall pay the penalty of its impiety; you alone shall go free from the chastisement. Quit your house and come with us to the top of yonder hill." They hastened to obey. The country behind them was speedily sunk in a lake, only their own house left standing. While they gazed with wonder at the sight, that old house of theirs was changed. Columns took the place of the corner posts, the thatch grew yellow and appeared a gilded roof, the floors became marble, the doors were enriched with carving and ornaments of gold. Then spoke Jupiter in benignant accents : " Excellent old man, and woman worthy of such a husband, speak, tell us your wishes. What favor have you to ask of us ? " Philemon took counsel with Baucis a few moments, then declared to the gods their common wish. " We ask to be priests and guardians of this thy temple, and that one and the same hour may take us both from life." Their prayer was granted. When they had attained a great age, as they stood one day before the steps of the sacred edifice and were telling the story of the place, Baucis saw Philemon begin to put forth leaves, and Philemon saw Baucis changing in like manner. While still they exchanged parting words, a leafy crown grew over their heads. " Farewell, dear spouse," they said together, and at the same moment the bark closed over their mouths. The Tyanean shepherd still shows the two trees, — an oak and a linden, standing side by side.[1]

The story of Baucis and Philemon has been imitated by Swift in a burlesque style, the actors in the change being two wandering saints, and the house being changed into a church, of which Philemon is made the parson :

> . . . They scarce had spoke, when, fair and soft,
> The roof began to mount aloft;
> Aloft rose every beam and rafter;
> The heavy wall climbed slowly after.
> The chimney widened and grew higher,
> Became a steeple with a spire.
> The kettle to the top was hoist,
> And there stood fastened to a joist,
> But with the upside down, to show
> Its inclination for below;
> In vain, for a superior force,
> Applied at bottom, stops its course;

1 Ovid, Metam. 8, 620–724.

Doomed ever in suspense to dwell,
'T is now no kettle, but a bell.
A wooden jack, which had almost
Lost by disuse the art to roast,
A sudden altèration feels,
Increased by new intestine wheels;
And, what exalts the wonder more,
The number made the motion slower;
The flier, though 't had leaden feet,
Turned round so quick you scarce could see 't;
But slackened by some secret power,
Now hardly moves an inch an hour.
The jack and chimney, near allied,
Had never left each other's side.
The chimney to a steeple grown,
The jack would not be left alone;
But up against the steeple reared,
Became a clock, and still adhered;
And still its love to household cares
By a shrill voice at noon declares,
Warning the cook-maid not to burn
That roast meat which it cannot turn.
The groaning chair began to crawl,
Like a huge snail, along the wall;
There stuck aloft in public view,
And with small change, a pulpit grew.
A bedstead of the antique mode,
Compact of timber many a load,
Such as our ancestors did use,
Was metamorphosed into pews,
Which still their ancient nature keep
By lodging folks disposed to sleep.

64. Juno's Best Gift. What the queen of heaven deemed the greatest blessing reserved for mortals is narrated in the beautiful myth of Biton and Cleobis. One Cydippe, an ancient priestess of the white-armed goddess, had desired to behold the famous new statue of Hera at Argos. Her sons testified their affection for their mother by yoking themselves, since no oxen were at hand, to her chariot, and so dragging her through heat and dust many a weary league till they reached the temple, where stood the gold and ivory masterwork of Polyclitus. With admiration the devoted priestess and her pious sons were received by the populace crowding round the statue. The priest officiating in the solemn rites thought meet that so reverend a worshiper should herself approach the goddess, — ay, should ask of Hera some blessing on her faithful sons:

> . . . Slowly old Cydippe rose and cried:
> " Hera, whose priestess I have been and am,
> Virgin and matron, at whose angry eyes
> Zeus trembles, and the windless plain of heaven
> With hyperborean echoes rings and roars,
> Remembering thy dread nuptials, a wise god,
> Golden and white in thy new-carven shape,
> Hear me! and grant for these my pious sons,
> Who saw my tears, and wound their tender arms
> Around me, and kissed me calm, and since no steer
> Stayed in the byre, dragged out the chariot old,
> And wore themselves the galling yoke, and brought
> Their mother to the feast of her desire,
> Grant them, O Hera, thy best gift of gifts! "

> Whereat the statue from its jeweled eyes
> Lightened, and thunder ran from cloud to cloud
> In heaven, and the vast company was hushed.
> But when they sought for Cleobis, behold,
> He lay there still, and by his brother's side
> Lay Biton, smiling through ambrosial curls,
> And when the people touched them they were dead.[1]

65. Myths of Minerva. Minerva, as we have seen,[2] presided over the useful and ornamental arts, both those of men — such as agriculture and navigation — and those of women — spinning, weaving, and needlework. She was also a warlike divinity, but favored only defensive warfare. With Mars' savage love of violence and bloodshed she, therefore, had no sympathy. Athens, her chosen seat, her own city, was awarded to her as the prize of a peaceful contest with Neptune, who also aspired to it. In the

---

[1] From The Sons of Cydippe, by Edmund Gosse in his On Viol and Flute.
[2] § 27, and Commentary.

reign of Cecrops, the first king of Athens, the two deities had contended for the possession of the city. The gods decreed that it should be awarded to the one who produced the gift most useful to mortals. Neptune gave the horse; Minerva produced the olive. The gods awarded the city to the goddess, and after her Greek appellation, Athena, it was named.

66. Arachne. In another contest, a mortal dared to come into competition with the gray-eyed daughter of Jove. This was Arachne, a maiden who had attained such skill in the arts of carding and spinning, of weaving and embroidery, that the Nymphs themselves would leave their groves and fountains to come and gaze upon her work. It was not only beautiful when it was done, but beautiful also in the doing. To watch her one would have said that Minerva herself had taught her. But this she denied, and could not bear to be thought a pupil even of a goddess. "Let Minerva try her skill with mine," said she. "If beaten, I will pay the penalty." Minerva heard this and was displeased. Assuming the form of an old woman, she appeared to Arachne and kindly advised her to challenge her fellow mortals if she would, but at once to ask forgiveness of the goddess. Arachne bade the old dame to keep her counsel for others. "I am not afraid of the goddess; let her try her skill, if she dare venture." "She comes," said Minerva, and dropping her disguise, stood confessed. The Nymphs bent low in homage and all the bystanders paid reverence. Arachne alone was unterrified. A sudden color dyed her cheek, and then she grew pale; but she stood to her resolve and rushed on her fate. They proceed to the contest. Each takes her station and attaches the web to the beam. Then the slender shuttle is passed in and out among the threads. The reed with its fine teeth strikes up the woof into its place and compacts the web. Wool of Tyrian dye is contrasted with that of other colors, shaded off into one another so adroitly that the joining deceives the eye. And the effect is like the bow whose long arch tinges the heavens, formed by sunbeams reflected from the shower,[1] in which, where the colors meet they seem as one, but at a little distance from the point of contact are wholly different.

[1] From Ovid.

Minerva wove the scene of her contest with Neptune (Poseidon). Twelve of the heavenly powers were represented, Jupiter, with august gravity, sitting in the midst. Neptune, the ruler of the sea, held his trident and appeared to have just smitten the earth, from

FIG. 52. CONTEST OF ATHENA AND POSEIDON

which a horse had leaped forth. The bright-eyed goddess depicted herself with helmed head, her ægis covering her breast, as when she had created the olive tree with its berries and its dark green leaves.

> Amongst these leaves she made a Butterfly,
>   With excellent device and wondrous slight,
> Fluttering among the olives wantonly,
>   That seemed to live, so like it was in sight;
> The velvet nap which on his wings doth lie,
>   The silken down with which his back is dight,
> His broad outstretchèd horns, his hairy thighs,
> His glorious colors, and his glistering eyes.
>
> Which when Arachne saw, as overlaid
>   And masterèd with workmanship so rare,
> She stood astonished long, ne aught gainsaid;
>   And with fast-fixèd eyes on her did stare.[1]

[1] From Spenser's Muiopotmos.

So wonderful was the central circle of Minerva's web; and in the four corners were represented incidents illustrating the displeasure of the gods at such presumptuous mortals as had dared to contend with them. These were meant as warnings from Minerva to her rival to give up the contest before it was too late.

But Arachne did not yield. She filled her web with subjects designedly chosen to exhibit the failings and errors of the gods. One scene represented Leda caressing the swan; and another, Danaë and the golden shower. Still another depicted Europa deceived by Jupiter under the disguise of a bull. Its appearance was that of a real bull, so naturally was it wrought and so natural the water in which it swam.

With such subjects Arachne filled her canvas, wonderfully well done but strongly marking her presumption and impiety. Minerva could not forbear to admire, yet was indignant at the insult. She struck the web with her shuttle and rent it in pieces; then, touching the forehead of Arachne, she made her realize her guilt. It was more than mortal could bear; and forthwith Arachne hanged herself. "Live, guilty woman," said Minerva, "but that thou mayest preserve the memory of this lesson continue to hang, both thou and thy descendants, to all future times." Then, sprinkling her with the juices of aconite, the goddess transformed her into a spider, forever spinning the thread by which she is suspended.[1]

67. Myths of Mars. The relations of Mars to other deities may be best illustrated by passages from the Iliad, which, generally speaking, presents him in no very favorable light.

68. Mars and Diomede. In the war of the Greeks and the Trojans,[2] the cause of the former was espoused by Minerva, of the latter by Mars. Among the chieftains of the Greeks in a certain battle, Diomede, son of Tydeus, was prominent. Now when Mars, scourge of mortals, beheld noble Diomede, he made straight at him.

. . . And when they were come nigh in onset on one another, first Mars thrust over the yoke and horses' reins with spear of bronze, eager to take away his life. But the bright-eyed goddess Minerva with her hand seized the spear and thrust it up over the car, to spend itself in vain. Next Diomede of the

[1] Ovid, Metam. 6, 1–145.   [2] § 200.

loud war cry attacked with spear of bronze; and Minerva drave it home against Mars' nethermost belly, where his taslets were girt about him. There smote he him and wounded him, rending through his fair skin, — and plucked forth the spear again. Then brazen Mars bellowed loud as nine thousand warriors or ten thousand cry in battle as they join in strife and fray. Thereat trembling gat hold of Achæans and Trojans for fear, so mightily bellowed Mars insatiate of battle.

Even as gloomy mist appeareth from the clouds when after heat a stormy wind ariseth, even so to Tydeus' son Diomede brazen Mars appeared amid clouds, faring to wide Heaven. Swiftly came he to the gods' dwelling, steep Olympus, and sat beside Jupiter, son of Cronus, with grief at heart, and showed the immortal blood flowing from the wound, and piteously spake to him winged words: " Father Jupiter, hast thou no indignation to behold these violent deeds? For ever cruelly suffer we gods by one another's devices, in showing men grace. With thee are we all at variance, because thou didst beget that reckless maiden and baleful, whose thought is ever of iniquitous deeds. For all the other gods that are in Olympus hearken to thee, and we are subject every one; only her thou chastenest not, neither in deed nor word, but settest her on, because this pestilent one is thine own offspring. Now hath she urged on Tydeus' son, even overweening Diomede, to rage furiously against the immortal gods. The Cyprian first

FIG. 53. ATHENA

he wounded in close fight, in the wrist of her hand, and then assailed he me, even me, with the might of a god. Howbeit my swift feet bare me away; else had I long endured anguish there amid the grisly heaps of dead, or else had lived strengthless from the smitings of the spear."

Then Jupiter the cloud-gatherer looked sternly at him, and said: " Nay, thou renegade, sit not by me and whine. Most hateful to me art thou of all gods that dwell in Olympus; thou ever lovest strife and wars and battles. Truly thy mother's spirit is intolerable, unyielding, even Juno's; her can I scarce rule with words. Therefore I deem that by her prompting thou art in this plight. Yet will I no longer endure to see thee in anguish; mine offspring art thou, and to me thy mother bare thee. But wert thou born of any other god unto this violence, long ere this hadst thou been lower than the sons of Heaven."

So spake he and bade Pæan heal him. And Pæan laid assuaging drugs upon the wound, and healed him, seeing he was in no wise of mortal mold. Even as fig juice maketh haste to thicken white milk, that is liquid but curdleth speedily as a man stirreth, even so swiftly healed he impetuous Mars. And Hebe bathed him and clothed him in gracious raiment, and he sate down by Jupiter, son of Cronus, glorying in his might.

Then fared the twain back to the mansion of great Jupiter, even Juno and Minerva, having stayed Mars, scourge of mortals, from his man-slaying.[1]

69. Mars and Minerva. It would seem that the insatiate son of Juno should have learned by this sad experience to avoid measuring arms with the ægis-bearing Minerva. But he renewed the contest at a later period in the fortunes of the Trojan War:

. . . Jupiter knew what was coming as he sat upon Olympus, and his heart within him laughed pleasantly when he beheld that strife of gods. Then no longer stood they asunder, for Mars, piercer of shields, began the battle and first made for Minerva with his bronze spear, and spake a taunting word: "Wherefore, O dogfly, dost thou match gods with gods in strife, with stormy daring, as thy great spirit moveth thee? Rememberest thou not how thou movedst Diomede, Tydeus' son, to wound me, and thyself didst take a visible spear and thrust it straight at me and pierce through my fair skin? Therefore deem I now that thou shalt pay me for all that thou hast done."

Thus saying, he smote on the dread tasseled ægis that not even the lightning of Jupiter can overcome — thereon smote blood-stained Mars with his long spear. But she, giving back, grasped with stout hand a stone that lay upon the plain, black, rugged, huge, which men of old time set to be the landmark of a field; this hurled she, and smote impetuous Mars on the neck, and unstrung his limbs. Seven roods he covered in his fall, and soiled his hair with dust, and his armor rang upon him. And Minerva laughed, and spake to him winged words exultingly: "Fool, not even yet hast thou learnt how far better than thou I claim to be, that thus thou matchest thy might with mine. Thus shalt thou satisfy thy mother's curses, who deviseth mischief against thee in her wrath, for that thou hast left the Achæans and givest the proud Trojans aid."

---

[1] Iliad, 5, 850 et seq. (Lang, Leaf, and Myers' translation). In accordance with the system of nomenclature adopted in this work, Latin equivalents are given, wherever possible, for Greek names.

Thus having said, she turned from him her shining eyes. Him did Venus, daughter of Jupiter, take by the hand and lead away, groaning continually, for scarce gathered he his spirit back to him.[1]

70. The Fortunes of Cadmus. Toward mortals Mars could show himself, on occasion, as vindictive as his fair foe, the unwearied daughter of Jove. This fact not only Cadmus, who slew a serpent sacred to Mars, but all the family of Cadmus found out to their cost.

When Europa was carried away by Jupiter in the guise of a bull, her father Agenor commanded his son Cadmus to go in search of

FIG. 54. CADMUS SLAYING THE DRAGON

her and not to return without her. Cadmus sought long and far; then, not daring to return unsuccessful, consulted the oracle of Apollo to know what country he should settle in. The oracle informed him that he would find a cow in the field, should follow her wherever she might wander, and where she stopped should build a city and call it Thebes. Cadmus had hardly left the Castalian cave, from which the oracle was delivered, when he saw a young cow slowly walking before him. He followed her close, offering at the same time his prayers to Phœbus. The cow went on till she passed

[1] Iliad, 21, 390 (Lang, Leaf, and Myers' translation).

the shallow channel of Cephissus and came out into the plain of
Panope. There she stood still. Cadmus gave thanks, and stooping
down kissed the foreign soil, then lifting his eyes, greeted the surrounding mountains. Wishing to offer a sacrifice to his protecting
deity, Minerva, he sent his servants to seek pure water for a libation. Near by there stood an ancient grove which had never been
profaned by the ax, in the midst of which was a cave thick covered with the growth of bushes, its roof forming a low arch from
beneath which burst forth a fountain of purest water. But in the
cave lurked a serpent with crested head, and scales glittering like
gold; his eyes shone like fire; his body was swollen with venom;
he vibrated a triple tongue and showed a triple row of teeth. No
sooner had the Tyrians dipped their pitchers in the fountain and
the ingushing waters had made a sound, than the monster, twisting
his scaly body in a huge coil, darted upon them and destroyed
some with his fangs, others in his folds, and others with his
poisonous breath.

Cadmus, having waited for the return of his men till midday,
went in search of them. When he entered the wood and saw their
lifeless bodies and the dragon with his bloody jaws, not knowing
that the serpent was sacred to Mars, scourge of mortals, he lifted
a huge stone and threw it with all his force at the monster. The
blow made no impression. Minerva, however, was present, unseen,
to aid her worshiper. Cadmus next threw his javelin, which penetrated the serpent's scales and pierced through to his entrails.
The monster attempted to draw out the weapon with his mouth,
but broke it off, leaving the iron point rankling in his flesh. His
neck swelled with rage, bloody foam covered his jaws, and the
breath of his nostrils poisoned the air around. As he moved onward, Cadmus retreated before him, holding his spear opposite to
the serpent's opened jaws. At last, watching his chance, the hero
thrust the spear at a moment when the animal's head thrown back
came against the trunk of a tree, and so succeeded in pinning him
to its side.

While Cadmus stood over his conquered foe, contemplating its
vast size, a voice was heard (from whence he knew not, but it was
Minerva's) commanding him to take the dragon's teeth and sow

them in the earth. Scarce had he done so when the clods began to move and the points of spears to appear above the surface. Next, helmets with their nodding plumes came up; next, the shoulders and breasts and limbs of men with weapons, and in time a harvest of armed warriors. Cadmus prepared to encounter a new enemy, but one of them said to him, "Meddle not with our civil war." With that he who had spoken smote one of his earthborn brothers with a sword, and he himself fell pierced with an arrow from another. The latter fell victim to a fourth, and in like manner the whole crowd dealt with each other till all but five fell slain. These five joined with Cadmus in building his city, to which they gave the name appointed.

As penance for the destruction of this sacred serpent, Cadmus served Mars for a period of eight years. After he had been absolved of his impiety, Minerva set him over the realm of Thebes, and Jove gave him to wife Harmonia, the daughter of Venus and Mars. The gods left Olympus to honor the occasion with their presence; and Vulcan presented the bride with a necklace of surpassing brilliancy, his own workmanship.

FIG. 55. HARMONIA IN COMPANY OF DEITIES

Of this marriage were born four daughters, Semele, Ino, Autonoë, and Agave, and one son, Polydorus. But in spite of the atonement made by Cadmus, a fatality hung over the family. The very necklace of Vulcan seemed to catch the spirit of ill luck and convey a baleful influence to such as wore it. Semele, Ino, Actæon the son of Autonoë, and Pentheus the son of Agave, all perished by violence. Cadmus and Harmonia quitted Thebes, grown odious to them, and emigrated to the country of the Enchelians, who received them with honor and made Cadmus their king. But the misfortunes of their children still weighing upon their minds, Cadmus one day exclaimed, "If a serpent's life is so dear to the gods, I would I were myself a serpent." No sooner had he uttered the words than he began to change his form. Harmonia, beholding it, prayed the gods to let her share his fate. Both became serpents. It is said that, mindful of their origin, they neither avoid the presence of man nor do they injure any one. But the curse appears not to have passed from their house until the sons of their great-great-grandson Œdipus had by fraternal strife ended themselves and the family.[1]

71. Myths of Vulcan. The stories of Vulcan are few, although incidents illustrating his character are sufficiently numerous. Accord-

FIG. 56. THE FORGE OF VULCAN

From the painting by Velasquez

ing to an account already given, Vulcan, because of his lameness, was cast out of Heaven by his mother Juno. The sea-goddesses Eurynome and Thetis took him mercifully to themselves, and for nine years cared for him, while he plied his trade and gained proficiency in it. In order to revenge himself upon the mother who had so despitefully used him, he fashioned in the depths of the sea a throne of cunning device, which he sent to his mother. She, gladly accepting the glorious gift, sat down upon it, to find out

[1] Ovid, Metam. 3, 1–137; 4, 563–614.

that straightway all manner of invisible chains and fetters wound and clasped themselves about her so that she could not rise. The assistance of the gods was of no avail to release her. Then Mars sought to bring Vulcan to Heaven by force that he might undo his trickery; but before the flames of the fire-god, the impetuous warrior speedily retreated. One god, however, the jovial Bacchus, was dear to the blacksmith. He drenched Vulcan with wine, conducted him to Olympus, and by persuasion caused him to set the queen of gods and men at liberty.

That Vulcan was not permanently hostile to Juno is shown by the services that on various occasions he rendered her. He forged the shield of her favorite Achilles ; and, at her instance, he undertook a contest against the river Xanthus. Homer[1] describes the burning of elms and willow trees and tamarisks, the parching of the plains, the bubbling of the waters, that signalized the fight, and how the eels and other fish were afflicted by Vulcan till Xanthus in anguish cried for quarter.

Fig. 57. A Sacrifice to Apollo

72. Myths of Apollo. The myths which cluster about the name of Phœbus Apollo illustrate, first, his birth and the wanderings of his mother, Latona ; secondly, his victory over darkness and winter ; thirdly, his gifts to man, — youth and vigor, the sunshine of spring, and the vegetation of early summer ; fourthly, his baleful influence, — the sunstroke and drought of midsummer, the miasma of autumn ; fifthly, his life on earth, as friend and counselor of mankind, — healer, soothsayer, and musician, prototype of manly beauty, and lover of beautiful women.

73. The Wanderings of Latona. Persecuted by the jealousy of the white-armed Juno, Latona fled from land to land. At last, bearing in her arms the infant progeny of Jove, she reached Lycia,

[1] Iliad, 2, 1335.

weary with her burden and parched with thirst. There the following adventure ensued. By chance the persecuted goddess espied
in the bottom of the valley a pond of clear water, where the country people were at work gathering willows and osiers. She approached and kneeling on the bank would have slaked her thirst
in the cool stream, but the rustics forbade her. "Why do you
refuse me water?" said she. "Water is free to all. Yet I ask it of
you as a favor. I have no intention of washing my limbs in it,
weary though they be, but only of quenching my thirst. A draft
of water would be nectar to me, and I would own myself indebted
to you for life itself. Let these infants move your pity, who stretch
out their little arms as if to plead for me."

But the clowns persisted in their rudeness; they added jeers,
and threatened violence if she did not leave the place. They waded
into the pond and stirred up the mud with their feet, so as to
make the water unfit to drink. Enraged, the goddess no longer
supplicated the clowns, but lifting her hands to Heaven exclaimed,
"May they never quit that pool but pass their lives there!" And
it came to pass accordingly. They still live in the water, sometimes
totally submerged, then raising their heads above the surface or
swimming upon it; sometimes coming out upon the bank, but soon
leaping back again into the water. Their voices are harsh, their
throats bloated, their mouths distended by constant railing; their
necks have shrunk up and disappeared, and their heads are joined
to their bodies. Their backs are green, their disproportioned bellies
white. They dwell as frogs in the slimy pool.[1]

74. Apollo, the Light Triumphant. Soon after his birth the
sun-god spent a year among the Hyperboreans, whose shining land
has been already described.[2] On his return, slaying with his golden
arrows the Python that had infested the slopes near Delphi, he
sang for the first time that song of victory which, as *the Pæan*,
is still among all nations synonymous with jubilation, praise, and
thanksgiving. In his conflict with another monster of darkness
and winter, the god of the silver bow had the assistance of his
sister Diana. By their unerring fiery darts they subdued the giant
Tityus, who not only had obstructed the peaceful ways to the

---

[1] Ovid. Metam. 6. 313–381.   [2] § 30.

oracle of Delphi, but had ventured to insult the mother of the twin deities. They overthrew also the Aloadæ, Otus and Ephialtes, sons of Iphimedia and Neptune. These monsters, the reputed sons of Aloeus, represent, perhaps, the unregulated forces of vegetation ; they were renowned for their strength, stature, and courage. They grew at the rate of three cubits in height and one in breadth every year ; and, when nine years of age, they attempted, by piling Mount Ossa upon Olympus, and Mount Pelion on top, to scale the skies and dethrone the immortals. It is reported that not Apollo and Diana, but Jupiter himself with his lightning slew them. They atoned for their presumption in Hades, where, bound by serpents to a pillar, they were tormented by the perpetual hooting of a screech owl.[1]

FIG. 58. APOLLO WITH HYACINTHUS

75. Hyacinthus. The fiery force of the Far-darter was not felt by the monsters of darkness alone. His friendship for the young and the vigorous was frequently as dangerous as it was dear to the objects of it. He was, for instance, passionately fond of a youth named Hyacinthus. The god of the silver bow accompanied the lad in his sports, carried the nets when he went fishing, led the dogs when he went to hunt, followed him in his excursions in the mountains, and neglected for him both lyre and arrows. One day they played a game of quoits ; Apollo, heaving aloft the discus with strength mingled with skill, sent it high and far. Hyacinthus, excited with the sport and eager to make his throw, ran forward to seize the missile ; but it bounded from the earth and struck him in the forehead. He fainted and fell. The god, as pale as himself, raised him and tried all his art to stanch the wound and retain the flitting life, but in vain. As when one has broken the stem of a lily in the garden it hangs its head and turns its flowers to the earth, so the head of the dying boy, as if too heavy for his neck, fell over on his shoulder. "Thou diest, Hyacinth," spake Phœbus,

---

[1] Roscher, Ausf. Lex. Lfg. 2, 254, Article *Aloadæ* [Schultz].

"robbed of thy youth by me. Would that I could die for thee! But since that may not be, my lyre shall celebrate thee, my song shall tell thy fate, and thou shalt become a flower inscribed with my regret." While the golden god spoke, the blood which had flowed on the ground and stained the herbage ceased to be blood; and a flower of hue more beautiful than the Tyrian sprang up, resembling the lily, save that this is purple and that silvery white. Phœbus then, to confer still greater honor, marked the petals with his sorrow, inscribing "Ai! ai!" upon them. The flower bears the name of Hyacinthus, and with returning spring revives the memory of his fate.[1]

It was said that Zephyrus (the west wind), who was also fond of Hyacinthus and jealous of his preference of Apollo, blew the quoit out of its course to make it strike Hyacinthus.

While this youth met his death by accident, another of Apollo's favorites, his own son, brought death upon himself by presumption. The story is as follows:

76. Phaëthon[2] was the son of Apollo and the nymph Clymene. One day Epaphus, the son of Jupiter and Io,[2] scoffed at the idea of Phaëthon's being the son of a god. Phaëthon complained of the insult to his mother Clymene. She sent him to Phœbus to ask for himself whether he had not been truly informed concerning his parentage. Gladly Phaëthon traveled toward the regions of sunrise and gained at last the palace of the Sun. He approached his father's presence, but stopped at a distance, for the light was more than he could bear. Phœbus Apollo, arrayed in purple, sat on a throne that glittered with diamonds. Beside him stood the Day, the Month, the Year, the Hours, and the Seasons. Surrounded by these attendants, the Sun beheld the youth dazzled with the novelty and splendor of the scene, and inquired the purpose of his errand. The youth replied, "Oh, light of the boundless world, Phœbus, my father — if thou dost yield me that name — give me some proof, I beseech thee, by which I may be known as thine!" He ceased. His father, laying aside the beams that shone around his head, bade him approach, embraced him, owned him for his son, and swore by the river Styx[3] that whatever proof

---

[1] Ovid, Metam. 10, 162–219.   [2] Ovid, Metam. 2, 1–400.   [3] § 44.

he might ask should be granted. Phaëthon immediately asked to be permitted for one day to drive the chariot of the sun. The father repented of his promise and tried to dissuade the boy by telling him the perils of the undertaking. "None but myself," he said, " may drive the flaming car of day. Not even Jupiter, whose terrible right arm hurls the thunderbolts. The first part of the way is steep and such as the horses when fresh in the morning can hardly climb; the middle is high up in the heavens, whence I myself can scarcely, without alarm, look down and behold the earth and sea stretched beneath me. The last part of the road descends rapidly and requires most careful driving. Tethys, who is waiting to receive me, often trembles for me lest I should fall headlong. Add to this that the heaven is all the time turning round and carrying the stars with it. Couldst thou keep thy course while the sphere revolved beneath thee? The road, also, is through the midst of frightful monsters. Thou must pass by the horns of the Bull, in front of the Archer, and near the Lion's jaws, and where the Scorpion stretches its arms in one direction and the Crab in another. Nor wilt thou find it easy to guide those horses, with their breasts full of fire that they breathe forth from their mouths and nostrils. Beware, my son, lest I be the donor of a fatal gift; recall the request while yet thou canst." He ended; but the youth rejected admonition and held to his demand. So, having resisted as long as he might, Phœbus at last led the way to where stood the lofty chariot.

It was of gold, the gift of Vulcan, — the axle of gold, the pole and wheels of gold, the spokes of silver. Along the seat were rows of chrysolites and diamonds, reflecting the brightness of the sun. While the daring youth gazed in admiration, the early Dawn threw open the purple doors of the east and showed the pathway strewn with roses. The stars withdrew, marshaled by the Daystar, which last of all retired also. The father, when he saw the earth beginning to glow and the Moon preparing to retire, ordered the Hours to harness up the horses. They led forth from the lofty stalls the steeds full fed with ambrosia, and attached the reins. Then the father, smearing the face of his son with a powerful unguent, made him capable of enduring the brightness of the flame. He set the

rays on the lad's head, and, with a foreboding sigh, told him to
spare the whip and hold tight the reins; not to take the straight
road between the five circles, but to turn off to the left; to keep
within the limit of the middle zone and avoid the northern and the
southern alike; finally, to keep in the well-worn ruts and to drive
neither too high nor too low, for the middle course was safest
and best.[1]

Forthwith the agile youth sprang into the chariot, stood erect,
and grasped the reins with delight, pouring out thanks to his
reluctant parent. But the steeds soon perceived that the load they
drew was lighter than usual; and as a ship without ballast is tossed
hither and thither on the sea, the chariot, without its accustomed
weight, was dashed about as if empty. The horses rushed headlong
and left the traveled road. Then, for the first time, the Great and
Little Bears were scorched with heat, and would fain, if it were
possible, have plunged into the water; and the Serpent which lies
coiled round the north pole, torpid and harmless, grew warm, and
with warmth felt its rage revive. Boötes, they say, fled away,
though encumbered with his plow and unused to rapid motion.

When hapless Phaëthon looked down upon the earth, now spreading in vast extent beneath him, he grew pale, and his knees shook
with terror. He lost his self-command and knew not whether to
draw tight the reins or throw them loose; he forgot the names of
the horses. But when he beheld the monstrous forms scattered
over the surface of heaven, — the Scorpion extending two great
arms, his tail, and his crooked claws over the space of two signs
of the zodiac, — when the boy beheld him, reeking with poison
and menacing with fangs, his courage failed, and the reins fell
from his hands. The horses, unrestrained, went off into unknown
regions of the sky in among the stars, hurling the chariot over
pathless places, now up in high heaven, now down almost to the
earth. The moon saw with astonishment her brother's chariot
running beneath her own. The clouds began to smoke. The
forest-clad mountains burned, — Athos and Taurus and Tmolus
and Œte; Ida, once celebrated for fountains; the Muses' mountain
Helicon, and Hæmus; Ætna, with fires within and without, and

[1] *Medio tutissimus ibis.* — OVID.

Parnassus, with his two peaks, and Rhodope, forced at last to part with his snowy crown. Her cold climate was no protection to Scythia; Caucasus burned, and Ossa and Pindus, and, greater than both, Olympus, — the Alps high in air, and the Apennines crowned with clouds.

Phaëthon beheld the world on fire and felt the heat intolerable. Then, too, it is said, the people of Æthiopia became black because the blood was called by the heat so suddenly to the surface; and the Libyan desert was dried up to the condition in which it remains to this day. The Nymphs of the fountains, with disheveled hair, mourned their waters, nor were the rivers safe beneath their banks;

FIG. 59. THE FALL OF PHAËTHON

Tanaïs smoked, and Caïcus, Xanthus, and Mæander; Babylonian Euphrates and Ganges, Tagus, with golden sands, and Caÿster, where the swans resort. Nile fled away and hid his head in the desert, and there it still remains concealed. Where he used to discharge his waters through seven mouths into the sea, seven dry channels alone remained. The earth cracked open, and through the chinks light broke into Tartarus and frightened the king of shadows and his queen. The sea shrank up. Even Nereus and his wife Doris with the Nereïds, their daughters, sought the deepest caves for refuge. Thrice Neptune essayed to raise his head above the surface and thrice was driven back by the heat. Earth, surrounded as she was by waters, yet with head and shoulders bare, screening her face with her hand, looked up to heaven, and with husky voice prayed Jupiter, if it were his will that she should perish by fire, to end her agony at once by his thunderbolts, or else to consider his own Heaven, how both the poles were smoking that sustained his palace, and that all must fall if they were destroyed.

Earth, overcome with heat and thirst, could say no more. Then Jupiter, calling the gods to witness that all was lost unless some speedy remedy were applied, thundered, brandished a lightning bolt in his right hand, launched it against the charioteer, and struck him at the same moment from his seat and from existence. Phaëthon, with his hair on fire, fell headlong, like a shooting star which marks the heavens with its brightness as it falls, and Eridanus, the great river, received him and cooled his burning frame. His sisters, the Heliades, as they lamented his fate, were turned into poplar trees on the banks of the river; and their tears, which continued to flow, became amber as they dropped into the stream. The Italian Naiads reared a tomb for him and inscribed these words upon the stone:

> Driver of Phœbus' chariot, Phaëthon,
> Struck by Jove's thunder, rests beneath this stone.
> He could not rule his father's car of fire,
> Yet was it much so nobly to aspire.[1]

77. The Plague sent upon the Greeks before Troy. It was not, however, only by accident, or by the ill-advised action of those whom he loved, that Apollo's gifts of light and heat were turned into misfortunes. Mortals who offended him were leveled by the cruel sunstroke, by arrows of malarial venom, of manifold sickness and death.

When the host of the Achæans was encamped before Troy, the king of men, Atrides, unjustly declined to restore his captive, Chryseïs of the fair cheeks, to her father Chryses, the priest of far-darting Apollo. Then the aged Chryses went apart and prayed aloud, " Hear me, god of the silver bow, . . . let the Danaans pay by thine arrows for my tears!"

---

[1] *Hic situs est Phaëthon, currus auriga paterni,*
Quem si non tenuit, magnis tamen excidit ausis. — OVID.

So spake he in prayer; and Phœbus Apollo heard him, and came down from the peaks of Olympus wroth at heart, bearing on his shoulders his bow and covered quiver. And the arrows clanged upon his shoulders in his wrath, as the god moved; and he descended like to night. Then he sate him aloof from the ships, and let an arrow fly; and there was heard a dread clanging of the silver bow. First did he assail the mules and fleet dogs, but afterward, aiming at the men his piercing dart, he smote; and the pyres of the dead burnt continually in multitude. Nor until Agamemnon had sent back his winsome captive to her father did Apollo remove from the Danaans the loathsome pestilence.[1]

78. The Punishment of Niobe is another illustration of the swift and awful vengeance of Apollo, and also of his sister Diana. This Niobe was the daughter of a certain Tantalus, king of Phrygia, who had been received at the table of the gods by his father Jupiter. But there was a strain of ingratitude and conceit in both father and daughter. The father not only betrayed the secrets of the gods, but, to ridicule their reputed omniscience, attempted at a banquet to deceive them into eating the roasted flesh of his own son Pelops. The gods were not deceived. Pelops was restored to life, — Tantalus consigned to Tartarus. The daughter Niobe, although she owed her happy marriage with Jupiter's son Amphion, and her seven stalwart sons and seven blooming daughters, to the favor of the gods and of Latona in particular, boasted of her birth, her marriage, and her offspring, bragged of her superiority to Latona, and, on one occasion, scoffed at the annual celebration in honor of the goddess and her two children. Surveying the people of Thebes with haughty glance, she said, "What folly to prefer beings whom you have never seen to those who stand before your eyes! Will you prefer to me this Latona, the Titan's daughter, with her two children? I have seven times as many. Were I to lose some of my children, I should hardly be left as poor as Latona with her two only. Put off the laurel from your brows, — have done with this worship!" The people left the sacred services uncompleted.

The goddess was indignant. On the Cynthian mountain top she thus addressed her son and daughter: "My children, I who have been so proud of you both and have been used to hold

[1] Iliad, 1, 43–52 (Lang, Leaf, and Myers' translation).

myself second to none of the goddesses except Juno alone, begin now to doubt whether I am indeed a goddess. I shall be deprived of my worship altogether unless you protect me." She was proceeding in this strain, but Apollo interrupted her. "Say no more," said he; "speech only delays punishment." So said Diana also. Darting through the air, veiled in clouds, they alighted on the

FIG. 60. A SON OF NIOBE

towers of the city. Spread out before the gates was a broad plain where the youth of the city pursued their warlike sports. The sons of Niobe were there with the rest, — some mounted on spirited horses richly caparisoned, some driving gay chariots. Ismenos, the first-born, as he guided his foaming steeds was struck by an arrow from above. "Ah me!" he cried, — dropped the reins and fell lifeless. Another, hearing the sound of the bow, gave the rein to his horses and attempted to escape. The inevitable arrow overtook him as he fled. Two others, younger, stood wrestling breast to breast : one arrow pierced them both. Alphenor, an elder brother, hastened to the spot to render assistance, but fell in the act of brotherly duty. One only was left, Ilioneus. "Spare me, ye gods!" he cried, addressing all of them, in his ignorance that all needed not his supplication ; and Apollo would have spared him, but the arrow had already left the string, and it was too late.

When Niobe was acquainted with what had taken place, she was indignant that the gods had dared, and amazed that they had been able to do it. Her husband Amphion, overwhelmed with the blow, destroyed himself. But the mother knelt over the lifeless bodies and kissed them. Raising her pallid arms to heaven, " Cruel Latona," said she, " satiate thy hard heart while I follow to the grave my seven sons. Yet where is thy triumph ? Bereaved as I am, I am still richer than thou, my conqueror." Scarce had she spoken, when the bow sounded and struck terror into all hearts except Niobe's alone. She was brave from excess of grief. Her daughters stood in garments of mourning over the biers of their dead brothers. One after another they fell, struck by arrows, beside the corpses that they were bewailing. Only one remained, whom the mother held clasped in her arms and covered, as it were, with her whole body. " Spare me one and that the youngest ! Oh, spare me one of so many ! " she cried ; and while she spoke, that one fell dead. Desolate she sat among sons, daughters, husband, all dead, and seemed torpid with grief. The breeze moved not her hair, no color was on her cheek, her eyes glared fixed and immovable, there was no sign of life about her. Her very tongue cleaved to the roof of her mouth and her veins ceased to convey the tide of life. Her neck bent not, her arms made no gesture, her foot no step. She was changed to stone, within and without. Yet tears continued to flow ; and borne on a

FIG. 61. THE CHILDREN OF NIOBE

whirlwind to her native mountain, she still remains, a mass of
rock from which a trickling stream flows, the tribute of her never-
ending grief.[1]

> Amid nine daughters slain by Artemis
> Stood Niòbe; she rais'd her head above
> Those beauteous forms which had brought down the scath
> Whence all nine fell, rais'd it, and stood erect,

FIG. 62. NIOBE AND HER YOUNGEST DAUGHTER

> And thus bespake the goddess enthroned on high:
> " Thou heardest, Artemis, my daily prayer
> That thou wouldst guide these children in the pass
> Of virtue, through the tangling wilds of youth,
> And thou didst ever guide them: was it just
> To smite them for a beauty such as thine?
> Deserv'd they death because thy grace appear'd
> In ever modest motion? 't was thy gift,

[1] Ovid, Metam. 6, 165–312.

The richest gift that youth from heaven receives.
True, I did boldly say they might compare
Even with thyself in virgin purity:
May not a mother in her pride repeat
What every mortal said?
                              One prayer remains
For me to offer yet.
Thy quiver holds
More than nine arrows: bend thy bow; aim here!
I see, I see it glimmering through a cloud.
Artemis, thou at length art merciful:
My children will not hear the fatal twang." [1]

79. The Lamentation for Linus. How the people of Argos fell under the displeasure of Apollo is told in the story of Linus, a beautiful son of Apollo and Psamathe. In fear of her father the king, Psamathe exposed the child on the mountains where, brought up by shepherds among the lambs, he was in tender youth torn to pieces by dogs. Meanwhile, Psamathe herself was driven from her father's home; wherefore Apollo sent against the land of the Argives a monster that for a season destroyed the children, but at last was slain by a noble youth named Corœbus. To appease the wrathful deity, a shrine was erected midway between Argos and Delphi; and every year Linus and his mother were bewailed in melancholy lays by the mothers and children of Argos, especially by such as had lost by death their own beloved. The fate of Linus, like that of Hyacinthus and others who succumb in the springtime of life under the excessive love of some shining deity,[2] typifies the sudden withering of herbs and flowers and of animal life, — the calves and lambs, young children too, under the fierce shafts of summer. The very name of Linus is taken from the refrain *ai-linon*, or "woe is me," of the lament anciently sung by the country people when thus afflicted by the unhealthy heats, because of which the crops fail and the dogs go mad and tear the little lambs to pieces. In the Iliad there is a beautiful picture which shows us that the song was not reserved completely for the dog days. It is of a vineyard teeming plenteously with clusters:

[1] From W. S. Landor's Niobe.   [2] See Commentary, §§ 64, 80.

And there was a pathway through it by which the vintagers might go. And maidens and striplings in childish glee bare the sweet fruit in plaited baskets. And in the midst of them a boy made pleasant music on a clear-toned viol, and sang thereto a sweet Linos-song with delicate voice; while the rest with feet falling together kept time with the music and song.[1]

80. Æsculapius. The Thessalian princess Coronis (or the Messenian, Arsinoë) bore to Apollo a child who was named

Æsculapius. On his mother's death the infant was intrusted to the charge of Chiron, most famous of the Centaurs, himself instructed by Apollo and Diana in hunting, medicine, music, and the art of prophecy. When the sage returned to his home bearing the infant, his daughter Ocyrrhoë came forth to meet him, and at sight of the child burst into a prophetic strain, foretelling the glory that he should achieve Æsculapius, when grown up, became a renowned physician; in one instance he even succeeded in restoring the dead to life. Pluto resented this, and, at his request, Jupiter struck the bold physician with lightning and killed him, but after his death received him into the number of the gods.[2]

FIG. 63. ÆSCULAPIUS

81. Apollo in Exile. Apollo, indignant at the destruction of this son, wreaked his vengeance on the innocent workmen who had made the thunderbolt. These were the Cyclopes, who had their workshop under Mount Ætna, from which the smoke and flames of their furnaces are constantly issuing. Apollo shot his arrows at the Cyclopes, a deed which so incensed Jupiter that he condemned him to serve a mortal for the space of one year. Accordingly, Apollo went into the service of Admetus, king of Thessaly, and pastured his flocks for him on the verdant banks of the river

[1] Iliad, 18. 564 (Lang, Leaf, and Myers' translation).   [2] Cicero, Natura Deorum, 3, 22.

Amphrysus. How the god lived among men, and what they thought of him, is well told in the following verses.

82. Lowell's Shepherd of King Admetus.

There came a youth upon the earth,
  Some thousand years ago,
Whose slender hands were nothing worth.
Whether to plow, or reap, or sow.

Upon an empty tortoise-shell
  He stretched some chords, and drew
Music that made men's bosoms swell
Fearless, or brimmed their eyes with dew.

Then King Admetus, one who had
  Pure taste by right divine,
Decreed his singing not too bad
To hear between the cups of wine:

And so, well pleased with being soothed
  Into a sweet half-sleep,
Three times his kingly beard he smoothed,
And made him viceroy o'er his sheep.

His words were simple words enough,
  And yet he used them so,
That what in other mouths was rough
In his seemed musical and low.

Men called him but a shiftless youth,
  In whom no good they saw;
And yet, unwittingly, in truth,
They made his careless words their law.

They knew not how he learned at all,
  For idly, hour by hour,
He sat and watched the dead leaves fall,
Or mused upon a common flower.

It seemed the loveliness of things
  Did teach him all their use,
For, in mere weeds, and stones, and springs
He found a healing power profuse.

Men granted that his speech was wise,
    But, when a glance they caught
Of his slim grace and woman's eyes,
    They laughed, and called him good-for-naught.

Yet after he was dead and gone
    And e'en his memory dim,
Earth seemed more sweet to live upon,
    More full of love, because of him.

And day by day more holy grew
    Each spot where he had trod,
Till after-poets only knew
    Their first-born brother as a god.

83. Admetus and Alcestis.[1] Admetus was a suitor, with others, for the hand of Alcestis, the daughter of Pelias, who promised her

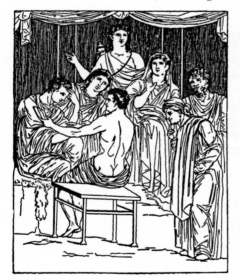

FIG. 64. ADMETUS MUST DIE

to him who should come for her in a chariot drawn by lions and boars. This task Admetus performed by the assistance of his divine herdsman, and was made happy in the possession of Alcestis. But Admetus falling ill and being near to death, Apollo prevailed on the Fates to spare him on condition that some one should consent to die in his stead. Admetus, in his joy at this reprieve, thought little of the ransom, and, perhaps remembering the declarations of attachment which he had often heard from his courtiers and dependents, fancied that it would be easy to find a substitute. But it was not so. Brave warriors, who would willingly have periled their lives for their

[1] See Commentary.

prince, shrunk from the thought of dying for him on the bed of sickness; and old servants who had experienced his bounty and that of his house from their childhood up were not willing to lay down the scanty remnant of their days to show their gratitude. Men asked, " Why does not one of his parents do it? They cannot in the course of nature live much longer, and who can feel like them the call to rescue the life they gave from an untimely end?" But the parents, distressed though they were at the thought of losing him, shrunk from the call. Then Alcestis, with a generous self-devotion, proffered herself as the substitute. Admetus, fond as he was of life, would not have submitted to receive it at such a cost; but there was no remedy. The condition imposed by the Fates had been met, and the decree was irrevocable. As Admetus revived, Alcestis sickened, rapidly sank, and died.

Just after the funeral procession had left the palace, Hercules, the son of Jupiter and Alcmena, arrived. He, to whom no labor was too arduous, resolved to attempt her rescue. Said he:

> "I will go lie in wait for Death, black-stoled
> King of the corpses!¹ I shall find him, sure,
> Drinking, beside the tomb, o' the sacrifice:
> And if I lie in ambuscade, and leap
> Out of my lair, and seize — encircle him
> Till one hand join the other round about —
> There lives not who shall pull him out from me,
> Rib-mauled, before he let the woman go!
> But even say I miss the booty, — say,
> Death comes not to the boltered blood, — why, then,
> Down go I, to the unsunned dwelling-place
> Of Koré² and the king there, — make demand,
> Confident I shall bring Alkestis back,
> So as to put her in the hands of him
> My host, that housed me, never drove me off:
> Though stricken with sore sorrow hid the stroke,
> Being a noble heart and honoring me!
> Who of Thessalians, more than this man, loves
> The stranger? Who that now inhabits Greece?
> Wherefore he shall not say the man was vile

¹ From Browning's Balaustion's Adventure. The Greek form of the proper names has been retained.　　　　² Proserpine.

FIG. 65. HERACLES

Whom he befriended, — native noble heart ! "
So, one look upward, as if Zeus might laugh
Approval of his human progeny, —
One summons of the whole magnific frame,
Each sinew to its service, — up he caught,
And over shoulder cast the lion-shag,
Let the club go, — for had he not those hands?
And so went striding off, on that straight way
Leads to Larissa and the suburb tomb.
Gladness be with thee, Helper of our world !
I think this is the authentic sign and seal
Of Godship that it ever waxes glad,
And more glad, until gladness blossoms, bursts
Into a rage to suffer for mankind,
And recommence at sorrow : drops like seed
After the blossom, ultimate of all.
Say, does the seed scorn earth and seek the sun?
Surely it has no other end and aim
Than to drop, once more die into the ground,
Taste cold and darkness and oblivion there :
And thence rise, tree-like grow through pain to joy,
More joy and most joy, — do man good again.
So to the struggle off strode Herakles.

Long time the Thessalians waited and mourned. As for Herakles, no doubt they supposed him dead. When — but can it be ?

. . . Ay, he it was advancing ! In he strode,
And took his stand before Admetos, — turned
Now by despair to such a quietude,
He neither raised his face nor spoke, this time,
The while his friend surveyed him steadily.
That friend looked rough with fighting : had he strained
Worst brute to breast was ever strangled yet?
Somehow, a victory — for there stood the strength,
Happy, as always ; something grave, perhaps ;
The great vein-cordage on the fret-worked front,
Black-swollen, beaded yet with battle-dew
The golden hair o' the hero ! — his big frame
A-quiver with each muscle sinking back
Into the sleepy smooth it leaped from late.
Under the great guard of one arm, there leant
A shrouded something, live and woman-like,

Propped by the heartbeats 'neath the lion-coat.
When he had finished his survey, it seemed,
The heavings of the heart began subside,
The helpful breath returned, and last the smile
Shone out, all Herakles was back again,
As the words followed the saluting hand.

"Admetus," said he, "take and keep this woman, my captive, till I come thy way again." But Admetus would admit no woman into the hall that Alcestis had left empty. Then cried Herakles, "Take hold of her. See now, my friend, if she look not somewhat like that wife thou hast lost."

Ah, but the tears come, find the words at fault!
There is no telling how the hero twitched
The veil off; and there stood, with such fixed eyes
And such slow smile, Alkestis' silent self!
It was the crowning grace of that great heart,
To keep back joy: procrastinate the truth
Until the wife, who had made proof and found
The husband wanting, might essay once more,
Hear, see, and feel him renovated now —
Able to do now all herself had done,
Risen to the height of her: so, hand in hand,
The two might go together, live and die.

Beside, when he found speech, you guess the speech.
He could not think he saw his wife again:
It was some mocking God that used the bliss
To make him mad! Till Herakles must help:
Assure him that no specter mocked at all;
He was embracing whom he buried once,
Still, — did he touch, might he address the true,
True eye, true body of the true live wife?
. . . And Herakles said little, but enough —
How he engaged in combat with that king
O' the dæmons: how the field of contest lay
By the tomb's self: how he sprang from ambuscade,
Captured Death, caught him in that pair of hands.

But all the time, Alkestis moved not once
Out of the set gaze and the silent smile;
And a cold fear ran through Admetos' frame:
"Why does she stand and front me, silent thus?"

Herakles solemnly replied, " Not yet
Is it allowable thou hear the things
She has to tell thee; let evanish quite
That consecration to the lower Gods,
And on our upper world the third day rise!
Lead her in, meanwhile; good and true thou art,
Good, true, remain thou! Practice piety
To stranger-guests the old way! So, farewell!
Since forth I fare, fulfill my urgent task
Set by the king, the son of Sthenelos." [1]

84. Apollo, the Musician. Not only in Arcadia, Laconia, and
Thessaly did Apollo care as a herdsman for the cattle of a mortal

FIG. 66. THE PALATINE
APOLLO

master; in Mount Ida, too, by the
order of Jupiter he herded for a year
the "shambling, crook-horned kine "of
King Laomedon, and, playing on the
lyre, aided Neptune to build the walls
of Troy, just as Amphion, in his turn,
had aided in the building of Thebes.
Apollo's life as herdsman was spent in
establishing wise laws and customs, in
musical contests on the flute and the
lyre, or in passages of love with nymphs
and maidens of mortal mold.

85. Apollo, Pan, and Midas. [2] It is
said that on a certain occasion Pan had
the temerity to compare his music with
that of Apollo and to challenge the god
of the lyre to a trial of skill. The challenge was accepted, and Tmolus, the
mountain-god, was chosen umpire. The
senior took his seat and cleared away
the trees from his ears to listen. At a
given signal Pan blew on his pipes, and with his rustic melody
gave great satisfaction to himself and his faithful follower Midas,
who happened to be present. Then Tmolus turned his head toward

---

[1] For the originals, see Iliad, 2, 715, and the Alcestis of Euripides.
[2] Ovid, Metam. 11, 146–193.

the sun-god, and all his trees turned with him. Apollo rose, his brow wreathed with Parnassian laurel, while his robe of Tyrian purple swept the ground. In his left hand he held the lyre and with his right hand struck the strings. Tmolus at once awarded the victory to the lyric god, and all but Midas acquiesced in the judgment. He dissented and questioned the justice of the award. Apollo promptly transformed his depraved pair of ears into those of an ass.

King Midas tried to hide his misfortune under an ample turban. But his hair-dresser found it too much for his discretion to keep such a secret; he dug a hole in the ground and, stooping down, whispered the story, and covered it up. But a thick bed of reeds springing up in the meadow began whispering the story, and has continued to do so from that day to this, every time a breeze passes over the place.

86. Shelley's Hymn of Pan. In the following verses Pan taunts Apollo as he might have done when Midas was sitting contentedly by :

> From the forests and highlands
>   We come, we come;
> From the river-girt islands,
>   Where loud waves are dumb,
>   Listening to my sweet pipings.
> The wind in the reeds and the rushes,
>   The bees on the bells of thyme,
> The birds on the myrtle bushes,
>   The cicale above in the lime,
> And the lizards below in the grass,
> Were as silent as ever old Tmolus was
>   Listening to my sweet pipings.
>
> Liquid Peneüs was flowing,
>   And all dark Tempe lay,
> In Pelion's shadow, outgrowing
>   The light of the dying day,
>   Speeded by my sweet pipings.
> The Sileni, and Sylvans, and Fauns,
>   And the Nymphs of the woods and waves,
> To the edge of the moist river-lawns,
>   And the brink of the dewy caves,
> And all that did then attend and follow
> Were silent with love, as you now, Apollo,
>   With envy of my sweet pipings.

> I sang of the dancing stars,
>   I sang of the dædal Earth,
> And of Heaven — and the giant wars,
>   And Love, and Death, and Birth, —
>   And then I changed my pipings, —
> Singing how down the vale of Menalus
>   I pursued a maiden, and clasp'd a reed:
> Gods and men, we are all deluded thus!
>   It breaks in our bosom and then we bleed:
> All wept, as I think both ye now would,
> If envy or age had not frozen your blood,
>   At the sorrow of my sweet pipings.

87. Marsyas also was unfortunate enough to underrate Apollo's musical ability. It seems that the flute, an invention of Minerva's, had been thrown away by that goddess because Cupid laughed at the grimaces which she made while playing it. Marsyas found the instrument, blew upon it, and elicited such ravishing sounds that he was tempted to challenge Apollo himself to a musical contest. The god, of course, triumphed, and he punished Marsyas by flaying him alive.

88. The Loves of Apollo. Beside Psamathe of Argos, Coronis of Thessaly, and the nymph Clymene, who have been already mentioned, Apollo loved the muse Calliope, who bore him Orpheus,[1] and the nymph Cyrene, whose son was Aristæus.[2] Of his relations with other maidens the following myths exist.

89. Daphne.[3] The lord of the silver bow was not always prosperous in his wooing. His first love, which, by the way, owed its origin to the malice of Cupid, was specially unfortunate. It appears that Apollo, seeing the boy playing with his bow and arrows, had tauntingly advised him to leave warlike weapons for hands worthy of them and content himself with the torch of love. Whereupon the son of Venus had rejoined, "Thine arrows may strike all things else, Apollo, but mine shall strike thee."

So saying, he took his stand on a rock of Parnassus, and drew from his quiver two arrows of different workmanship, — one to excite love, the other to repel it. The former was of gold and sharp pointed, the latter blunt and tipped with lead. With the

[1] § 118.   [2] § 145.   [3] Ovid, Metam. 1, 452–567.

APOLLO AND DAPHNE

leaden shaft he struck the nymph Daphne, the daughter of the river-god Peneüs, and with the golden one Apollo, through the heart. Forthwith the god was seized with love for the maiden, but she, more than ever, abhorred the thought of loving. Her delight was in woodland sports and in the spoils of the chase. Spurning all lovers, she prayed her father that she might remain always unmarried, like Diana. He consented, but, at the same time, warned her that her beauty would defeat her purpose. It was the face of this huntress maiden that Apollo saw. He saw the charming disorder of her hair, and would have arranged it; he saw her eyes bright as stars; he saw her lips, and was not satisfied with only seeing them. He longed for Daphne. He followed her; she fled swifter than the wind, nor delayed a moment at his entreaties. "Stay," said he, "daughter of Peneüs; I am not a foe. It is for love I pursue thee. I am no clown, no rude peasant. Jupiter is my father. I am lord of Delphi and Tenedos. I know all things, present and future. I am the god of song and the lyre. My arrows fly true to the mark; but alas! an arrow more fatal than mine has pierced my heart! I am the god of medicine and know the virtues of all healing plants. Alas! I suffer a malady that no balm can cure."

FIG. 67. DAPHNE

The nymph continues her flight and leaves his plea half-uttered. But even as she flies she charms him. The wind catches her garments, and her unbound hair streams loose behind her. The god, sped by Cupid, gains upon her in the race. His panting breath blows upon her hair. Her strength begins to fail, and, ready to sink, she calls upon her father, the river-god: "Help me, Peneüs! open the earth to inclose me, or change my form, which has brought me into this danger!" Scarcely had she spoken when a stiffness seized her limbs; and little by little she took on the appearance of a laurel tree. Apollo embraced the branches and lavished kisses on the wood. The branches shrank from his lips. "Since thou canst not be my wife," said he, "thou shalt assuredly be my tree. I will wear thee for my crown. I will decorate with thee my harp and my quiver. When the Roman conquerors conduct the triumphal pomp to the Capitol, thou shalt be woven into wreaths for their brows. And, as eternal youth is mine, thou also shalt be always green, and thy leaf know no decay." The laurel tree bowed its head in grateful acknowledgment.

The delicious humor of Lowell's extravaganza upon the story amply justifies the following citation:

Phœbus, sitting one day in a laurel tree's shade,
Was reminded of Daphne, of whom it was made,
For the god being one day too warm in his wooing,
She took to the tree to escape his pursuing;
Be the cause what it might, from his offers she shrunk,
And, Ginevra-like, shut herself up in a trunk;
And, though 't was a step into which he had driven her,
He somehow or other had never forgiven her;
Her memory he nursed as a kind of a tonic,
Something bitter to chew when he 'd play the Byronic,
And I can't count the obstinate nymphs that he brought over
By a strange kind of smile he put on when he thought of her.
"My case is like Dido's," he sometimes remarked;
"When I last saw my love, she was fairly embarked
In a laurel, as *she* thought — but (ah, how Fate mocks!)
She has found it by this time a very bad box;
Let hunters from me take this saw when they need it, —
You 're not always sure of your game when you 've treed it.
Just conceive such a change taking place in one's mistress!
What romance would be left? — who can flatter or kiss trees?
And, for mercy's sake, how could one keep up a dialogue
With a dull wooden thing that will live and will die a log, —
Not to say that the thought would forever intrude
That you 've less chance to win her the more she is wood?
Ah! it went to my heart, and the memory still grieves,
To see those loved graces all taking their leaves;
Those charms beyond speech, so enchanting but now,
As they left me forever, each making its bough!
If her tongue *had* a tang sometimes more than was right,
Her new bark is worse than ten times her old bite." [1]

1 From the Fable for Critics.

90. Marpessa. Another maiden who declined Apollo's love was Marpessa.[1] She is called by Homer "the fair-ankled daughter of Evenus."

> The god Apollo from the heaven of heavens
> Her mortal sweetness through the air allured; [2]

but Idas, "that was strongest of men that were then on earth," [1] carried her off, assisted by Poseidon who gave him a winged chariot. Her father Evenus vainly tried to catch up with the fleeing lovers; but Apollo found them in Messene, and wrested the maiden away. Then Jupiter, while the lovers were engaged in combat, separated them, saying, "Let her decide."

> They three together met; on the one side,
> Fresh from diffusing light on all the world
> Apollo; on the other without sleep
> Idas, and in the midst Marpessa stood.
> Just as a flower after drenching rain,
> So from the falling of felicity
> Her human beauty glowed, and it was new;
> The bee too near her bosom drowsed and dropped.[2]

According to the story as romantically told by the English poet Phillips, first spoke Apollo. The god told her that he dreaded that one so fair should ever taste of sorrow and death; how, if she lived with him, she should bide

> In mere felicity above the world
> In peace alive and moving, where to stir
> Is ecstasy, and thrilling is repose,[2]

immortal, scattering joy without intermission, lighting the world, bringing bliss to struggling men and sorrowing women, dispelling shadows and shadowy fear.

Then Idas, humbly, —

> "After such argument what can I plead?
> Or what pale promise make? Yet since it is
> In women to pity rather than to aspire,
> A little will I speak."

---

[1] Iliad, 9, 561; Apollodorus, 1, 7, § 8. [2] Stephen Phillips, Marpessa.

And he tells her simply that he *loves* her, — loves her not only for her beauty, but

> " Because Infinity upon thee broods;
> And thou art full of whispers and of shadows; — "

and because her voice is music, her face mystery beyond his power to comprehend ;

> " O beauty lone and like a candle clear
> In this dark country of the world! Thou art
> My woe, my early light, my music dying."

And Marpessa ? —

> As he was speaking, she with lips apart
> Breathed, and with dimmer eyes leaned through the air
> As one in dream, and now his human hand
> Took in her own; and to Apollo spoke, —

saying that she knew how sweet it might be forever with a god to aid suffering men and women and " gild the face that from its dead looks up"; but still she feared immortality, for, though dying not, she must grow old, and her god lover would tire of her when once her youth was faded. And as for that " existence without tears for evermore " which he promised, —

> " Yet I being human, human sorrow miss.
> The half of music, I have heard men say,
> Is to have grieved."

To sorrow she was born. It is out of sadness that men have made this world beautiful. If she chooses Idas, then they two will prosper together, grow old together, and last descend into the " natural ground," and " leave behind a wholesome memory on the earth."

> When she had spoken, Idas with one cry
> Held her, and there was silence; while the god
> In anger disappeared. Then slowly they,
> He looking downward, and she gazing up,
> Into the evening green wandered away.

91. Clytie.[1] In the story of Clytie the conditions are reversed. She was a water-nymph and in love with Apollo, who made her

---

[1] Ovid, Metam. 4, 256–270.

no return. So she pined away, sitting all day long upon the cold ground with her unbound tresses streaming over her shoulders. Nine days she sat, and tasted neither food nor drink, — her own tears and the chilly dew her only sustenance. She gazed on the sun when he rose; and as he passed through his daily course to his setting, she saw no other object, — her eyes fixed constantly on him. At last, they say, her limbs took root in the ground and her face became a flower, turning on its stem to follow the journeying sun.

In the following lines, Thomas Moore uses the flower as an emblem of constancy:

> The heart that has truly loved never forgets,
> But as truly loves on to the close;
> As the sunflower turns on her god when he sets
> The same look that she turned when he rose.

92. Myths of Diana. In company with her radiant brother, we find Diana subduing Tityus and the Python and assisting in the punishment of Niobe. The speedy transformation of Daphne has been attributed to this goddess, the champion of maidenhood. According to some, it was she, too, that changed Callisto into a bear, when for love of Jupiter that nymph deserted the huntress-band. Numerous are the myths that celebrate the severity of the goddess of the unerring bow toward those who offended her. How she served Agamemnon for slaying one of her hinds is told in the story of Troy;[1] how she punished Œneus for omitting a sacrifice to

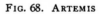

FIG. 68. ARTEMIS

her is narrated in the episode of the Calydonian hunt.[2] Similar attributes of the goddess are exemplified in the myths of Arethusa, Actæon, and Orion. It is only when she is identified with Selene, the peaceful moonlight, that we perceive a softer side of character, such as that displayed in her relations with Endymion.

93. The Flight of Arethusa.[3] A woodland nymph of Elis was this Arethusa; she delighted not in her comeliness, but in the

---

[1] § 196.   [2] § 168.   [3] Ovid, Metam. 5, 585-641.

joys of the chase. One day, returning from the wood heated with exercise, she descended to a stream silently flowing, so clear that you might count the pebbles on the bottom. She laid aside her garments ; but while she sported in the water, she heard an indistinct murmur rising as out of the depths of the stream. She made haste to reach the nearest bank. A voice followed her, "Why flyest thou, Arethusa ? Alpheüs am I, the god of this stream."

FIG. 69. ARETHUSA

The nymph ran, the god pursued. Arethusa, at last exhausted, cried for help to Diana, who, hearing, wrapped her votary in a thick cloud. Perplexed, the river-god still sought the trembling maiden. But a cold sweat came over her. In less time than it takes to tell, she had become a fountain. Alpheüs attempted then to mingle his stream with hers. But the Cynthian queen cleft the ground, and Arethusa, still endeavoring to escape, plunged into the abyss and, passing through the bowels of the earth, came out in Sicily, still followed by the passionate river-god.

94. Shelley's Arethusa. In the following version of the pursuit, Arethusa was already a river when Alpheüs espied her.

> Arethusa arose
> From her couch of snows
> In the Acroceraunian mountains, —
> From cloud and from crag,
> With many a jag,
> Shepherding her bright fountains,
> She leapt down the rocks,
> With her rainbow locks
> Streaming among the streams ; —
> Her steps paved with green
> The downward ravine
> Which slopes to the western gleams :
> And gliding and springing
> She went, ever singing,
> In murmurs as soft as sleep ;
> The Earth seemed to love her,
> And Heaven smiled above her,
> As she lingered towards the deep.

Then Alpheüs bold
On his glacier cold,
With his trident the mountain strook
And opened a chasm
In the rocks; — with the spasm
All Erymanthus shook.
And the black south wind
It concealed behind
The urns of the silent snow,
And earthquake and thunder
Did rend in sunder
The bars of the springs below;
The beard and the hair
Of the River-god were
Seen through the torrent's sweep,
As he followed the light
Of the fleet nymph's flight
To the brink of the Dorian deep.

" Oh, save me! Oh, guide me!
And bid the deep hide me,
For he grasps me now by the hair! "
The loud Ocean heard,
To its blue depth stirred,
And divided at her prayer;

FIG. 70. A YOUNG
RIVER-GOD

And under the water
The Earth's white daughter
Fled like a sunny beam;
Behind her descended
Her billows unblended
With the brackish Dorian stream: —
Like a gloomy stain
On the emerald main,
Alpheüs rushed behind, —
As an eagle pursuing
A dove to its ruin
Down the streams of the cloudy wind.

Under the bowers
Where the Ocean Powers
Sit on their pearlèd thrones,
Through the coral woods
Of the weltering floods,

Over heaps of unvalued stones;
    Through the dim beams
    Which amid the streams
Weave a network of colored light;
    And under the caves,
    Where the shadowy waves
Are as green as the forest's night:
    Outspeeding the shark,
    And the swordfish dark,
Under the ocean foam,
    And up through the rifts
    Of the mountain clifts
They past to their Dorian home.

    And now from their fountains
    In Enna's mountains,
Down one vale where the morning basks.
    Like friends once parted
    Grown single-hearted,
They ply their watery tasks.
    At sunrise they leap
    From their cradles steep
In the cave of the shelving hill;
    At noontide they flow
    Through the woods below
And the meadows of Asphodel:
    And at night they sleep
    In the rocking deep
Beneath the Ortygian shore; —
    Like spirits that lie
    In the azure sky
When they love but live no more.

95. The Fate of Actæon.[1] Diana's severity toward young Actæon, grandson of Cadmus whose kindred fell under the curse of
Mars, is thus narrated.

One day, having repaired to a valley inclosed by cypresses and
pines, where gushed a fountain of sparkling water, the chaste Diana
handed her javelin, her quiver, and her bow to one nymph, her
robe to another, while a third unbound the sandals from her feet.
Then Crocale, the most skillful of them, arranged her hair, and

1 Ovid, Metam. 3, 138–252.

Nephele, Hyale, and the rest drew water in capacious urns. While the huntress queen was thus employed in the labors of the toilet, Actæon, the son of Autonoë and Aristæus, having quitted his companions of the chase and rambling without any especial object, came to the place, led thither by his destiny. As he presented himself at the entrance of the cave, the nymphs, seeing a man, screamed and rushed towards the goddess to hide her with their bodies. But she was taller than the rest and overtopped them all by a head. Such a color as tinges the clouds at sunset or at dawn came over the

FIG. 71. ACTÆON

countenance of Diana, thus taken by surprise. Surrounded as she was by her nymphs, she yet turned half away and sought with a sudden impulse for her arrows. As they were not at hand, she dashed the water into the face of the intruder, saying, " Now go and tell, if you can, that you have seen Diana unappareled." Immediately a pair of branching stag's horns grew out of the huntsman's head, his neck gained in length, his ears grew sharp-pointed, his hands became feet, his arms, his long legs, and his body were covered with a hairy spotted hide. Fear took the place of his former boldness, and the hero fled. What should he do ? — go home to the palace or lie hid in the woods ? While he hesitated his dogs saw him. Over rocks and cliffs, through mountain gorges that seemed impracticable, he fled, and they followed. The air resounded with the bark of the dogs. Presently one fastened on his back, another seized his shoulder; the rest of the pack came up and buried their teeth in his flesh. His friends and fellow-huntsmen cheered on the dogs, and, looking everywhere for Actæon, called on him to join the sport. At the sound of his name, he turned his head and heard them regret that he should be away. He earnestly wished he was. But Diana had no pity for him, nor was her anger appeased till the dogs had torn his life out.

96. The Fortunes and Death of Orion. Orion, the son of Neptune, was a giant and a mighty hunter, whose prowess and manly favor gained for him the rare good will of Diana.

It is related that he loved Merope, the daughter of Œnopion, king of Chios, and sought her in marriage. He cleared the island of wild beasts and brought the spoils of the chase as presents to his beloved; but as Œnopion constantly deferred his consent, Orion attempted to gain possession of the maiden by violence. Her father, incensed at his conduct, made Orion drunk, deprived him of his sight, and cast him out on the seashore. The blinded hero, instructed by an oracle to seek the rays of morning, followed the sound of a Cyclops' hammer till he reached Lemnos, where Vulcan, taking pity on him, gave him Cedalion, one of his men, to be his guide to the abode of the sun. Placing Cedalion on his shoulders, Orion proceeded to the east, and there meeting the sun-god, was restored to sight by his beam.[1]

After this he dwelt as a hunter with the queen of the echoing chase; and it was even hinted that she loved him. Her brother, highly displeased, often chid her, but to no purpose. One day, therefore, observing Orion as he waded through the sea with his head just above the water, Apollo pointed out the black object to his sister, and maintained that she could not hit it. The archer goddess discharged a shaft with fatal aim: the waves rolled the dead body of Orion to the land. Then bewailing her fatal error with many tears, Diana placed him among the stars, where he appears as a giant, with a girdle, sword, lion's skin, and club.

[1] Apollodorus, 1, 4, § 3.

Sirius, his dog, follows him, and the Pleiads fly before him.[1] In the beginning of winter, all through the night, Orion follows the chase across the heavens; but with dawn he sinks toward the waters of his father Neptune. In the beginning of summer, he may be seen with daybreak in the eastern sky, where, beloved by Aurora, he remains gradually paling before the light of day till, finally, Diana, jealous of his happiness, draws her gentle darts and slays him.

97. The Pleiads,[2] who still fly before Orion in the heavens, were daughters of Atlas, and nymphs of Diana's train. One day

FIG. 72. THE PLEIADES
From the painting by Vedder

Orion saw them in Bœotia, became enamored of them, and gave pursuit. In their distress they prayed to the gods to change their form. Jupiter, accordingly, turned them into pigeons, and made them a constellation. Though their number was seven, only six stars are visible; for Electra, it is said, left her place that she might not behold the ruin of Troy, which had been founded by

[1] Ovid, Fasti, 5, 537; Iliad, 18, 486, and 22, 29; Odyssey, 5. 121, 274.
[2] The story is told by Hyginus in his Fables, and in his Poetical Astronomy.

her son Dardanus. The sight had such an effect on her sisters that they blanched, and have been pale ever since. But Electra became a comet; her hair floating wildly behind her, she still inconsolably ranges the expanse of heaven. According to some, the lost Pleiad is Merope, who was vested with mortality in consequence of her marriage with the mortal Sisyphus, king of Corinth.

FIG. 73. ENDYMION

Tennyson's reference to the Pleiads, in "Locksley Hall," is of course familiar to all readers.

98. Endymion. The frequent absence of Diana from her duties in heaven is said to have awakened suspicion among the deities of Olympus, who doubted whether she actually occupied these intervals with hunting. It is easy to imagine the satisfaction with which Venus, who so often had been reproached by Diana with her undue fondness of beautiful youths, would welcome news of a corresponding weakness on the part of the cold-hearted and apparently unyielding huntress queen. And such satisfaction Venus once enjoyed, if we may trust the later classical and the modern poets who have identified Diana with Selene, the more ancient goddess of the moon.

For, one calm, clear night Selene looked down upon the beautiful Endymion, who fed his flock on Mount Latmos, and saw him sleeping. The heart of the goddess was unquestionably warmed by his surpassing beauty. She came down to him; she kissed him; she watched over him while he slept. She visited him again and again. But her secret could not long be hidden from the company of Olympus. For more and more frequently she was absent from her station in the sky, and toward morning she was ever paler and more weary with her watching. When, finally, her love was discovered, Jupiter gave Endymion, who had been thus honored, a choice between death in any manner that was preferable, or perpetual youth united with perpetual sleep. Endymion chose the latter. He still sleeps in his Carian cave, and still the mistress of the moon slips from her nocturnal course to visit him. She takes care, too, that his fortunes shall not suffer by his inactive life : she yields his flock increase, and guards his sheep and lambs from beasts of prey.[1]

Keats, whose Endymion journeys on a mission under sea, thus describes a meeting of the goddess and her lover :

> On gold sand impearled
> With lily shells and pebbles milky white,
> Poor, Cynthia greeted him, and soothed her light
> Against his pallid face : he felt the charm
> To breathlessness, and suddenly a warm
> Of his heart's blood : 't was very sweet ; he stayed
> His wandering steps, and half-entrancèd laid
> His head upon a tuft of straggling weeds,
> To taste the gentle moon, and freshening beads,
> Lashed from the crystal roof by fishes' tails.
> And so he kept, until the rosy veils,
> Mantling the east, by Aurora's peering hand
> Were lifted from the water's breast, and fanned
> Into sweet air ; and sobered morning came
> Meekly through billows : — when like taper-flame
> Left sudden by a dallying breath of air,
> He rose in silence, and once more 'gan fare
> Along his fated way.[2]

99. Myths of Venus. Round the goddess of love cluster romances of her own tender passion, of the affairs of the winged Cupid, and of the loves of the worshipers at her shrine. Of the affection of Venus for Mars and of her relations with Anchises,[3]

---

[1] Authorities are Pausanias, 5, 1, §§ 2–4 ; Ovid, Ars. Am. 3, 83 ; Tristia, 2, 299 ; Apollonius, and Apollodorus.   [2] From the Endymion, Bk. 3.   [3] § 194.

the father of Æneas, mention is elsewhere made. The following
is the myth of Venus and Adonis.

100. Adonis.[1] The sweetly smiling goddess, playing one day
with her boy Cupid, wounded her bosom with one of his arrows.
Before the wound healed, she looked upon Adonis, the son of
Cinyras and Myrrha, and was captivated by him. She no longer
took any interest in her favorite resorts, — Paphos, and Cnidos,
and Amathus, rich in metals. She absented herself even from
Olympus, for Adonis was dearer to her than heaven. Him she
followed and bore him company. She who loved to recline in
the shade, with no care but to cultivate her charms, now rambled
through the woods and over the hills, girt like the huntress Diana.
She chased game that is safe to hunt, but kept clear of the wolves
and bears. She charged Adonis, too, to beware of dangerous
animals. " Be brave toward the timid," she would say, " courage
against the courageous is not safe." Having thus, on one occasion,
warned him, she mounted her chariot drawn by swans and drove
away through the air. But Adonis was too noble to heed such
counsels. The dogs had roused a wild boar from his lair, and the
youth threw his spear and wounded the animal with a sidelong
stroke. The beast drew out the weapon with his jaws, and, rushing
after Adonis, buried his tusks in the lad's side, and stretched him
dying upon the plain. The rest of the story is thus recounted :

THE LAMENT FOR ADONIS[2]

. . . Low on the hills is lying the lovely Adonis, and his thigh with the
boar's tusk, his white thigh with the boar's tusk, is wounded ; and sorrow on
Cypris he brings, as softly he breathes his life away.

His dark blood drips down his skin of snow ; beneath his brows his eyes
wax heavy and dim ; and the rose flees from his lip, and thereon the very kiss
is dying, the kiss that Cypris will never forego.

. . . She hath lost her lovely lord, with him she hath lost her sacred beauty.
Fair was the form of Cypris while Adonis was living, but her beauty has died
with Adonis ! *Woe, woe for Cypris*, the mountains all are saying. And the

---

[1] Ovid, Metam. 10, 503–559, 708–739.

[2] From an elegy intended to be sung at one of the spring celebrations in memory of
Adonis. Translated from Bion by Andrew Lang. *Cypris*, *Cytherea*, and the *Paphian* refer
to Venus. See Commentary. This elegy is also translated by Mrs. Browning and by Sir
Edwin Arnold.

PETWORTH APHRODITE

oak trees answer, *Woe for Adonis!*
And the rivers bewail the sorrows of
Aphrodite, and the wells are weeping
Adonis on the mountains. The flowers
flush red for anguish, and Cytherea
through all the mountain-knees, through
every dell, doth shrill the piteous dirge:
*Woe, woe for Cytherea, he hath
perished, the lovely Adonis!*

. . . When she saw, when she
marked the unstanched wound of
Adonis, when she saw the bright red
blood about his languid thigh, she cast
her arms abroad, and moaned, "Abide
with me, Adonis, hapless Adonis, abide!
. . . Awake, Adonis, for a little while,
and kiss me yet again, the latest kiss!
. . . This kiss will I treasure, even as
thyself, Adonis, since, ah, ill-fated, thou
art fleeing me, thou art fleeing far,
Adonis, and art faring to Acheron,
to that hateful king and cruel, while
wretched I yet live, being a goddess,
and may not follow thee! Persephone,
take thou my lover, my lord, for thyself art stronger than I, and all lovely
things drift down to thee. But I am
ill-fated, inconsolable is my anguish;
and I lament mine Adonis, dead to me,
and I have no rest for sorrow.

"Thou diest, oh, thrice-desired, and
my desire hath flown away as a dream!
Nay, widowed is Cytherea, and idle are
the Loves along the halls! With thee has
the girdle of my beauty perished. For
why, ah, overbold, didst thou follow the
chase, and being so fair, why wert thou
thus overhardy to fight with beasts?"

So Cypris bewailed her, the Loves
join in the lament:
*Woe, woe for Cytherea, he hath
perished, the lovely Adonis!*

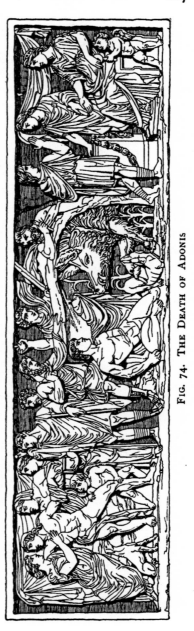

FIG. 74. THE DEATH OF ADONIS

A tear the Paphian sheds for each blood-drop of Adonis, and tears and blood on the earth are turned to flowers. The blood brings forth the rose; the tears, the wind-flower.

Woe, woe for Adonis, he hath perished, the lovely Adonis!

. . . Cease, Cytherea, from thy lamentations, to-day refrain from thy dirges. Thou must again bewail him, again must weep for him another year.

101. Cupid and Psyche.[1] A certain king and queen had three daughters. The charms of the two elder were more than common, but the beauty of the youngest was such that the poverty of language is unable to express its praise. In fact, Venus found her altars deserted, while men paid their vows to this virgin. When Psyche passed, the people sang her praises and strewed her way with chaplets and flowers.

This perversion of homage gave great offense to Venus, who complained that Paris might just as well not have yielded her the palm of beauty over Pallas and Juno, if a mortal were thus to usurp her honors. Wherefore she called Cupid and, pointing out Psyche to him, bade him infuse into the bosom of that haughty girl a passion for some low, unworthy being.

There were in Venus's garden two fountains, — one of sweet waters, the other of bitter. Cupid filled two amber vases, one from each fountain, and suspending them from the top of his quiver, hastened to the chamber of Psyche, whom he found asleep. He shed a few drops from the bitter fountain over her lips, though the sight of her almost moved him to pity; and then he touched her side with the point of his arrow. She awoke, and opening her eyes upon Cupid (himself invisible), so startled him that in his confusion he wounded himself with his arrow. Heedless of his wound, his thought now was to repair the mischief he had done. He poured, at once, the waters of joy over her silken ringlets.

But Psyche, henceforth frowned upon by Venus, derived no benefit from her charms. Her two elder sisters had long been married to princes; but Psyche's beauty failed to awaken love. Consequently her parents, afraid that they had unwittingly incurred the anger of the gods, consulted the oracle of Apollo.

[1] Apuleius, Metam. Golden Ass, 4, 28, etc.

They received answer, " The virgin is destined for the bride of no mortal lover. Her husband awaits her on the top of the mountain. He is a monster whom neither gods nor men can resist."

This dreadful decree of the oracle filled the people with dismay; but, at Psyche's request, preparations for her fate were made. The royal maid took her place in a procession, which more resembled a funeral than a nuptial pomp, and with her parents, amid the lamentations of their subjects, ascended the mountain, where she was left alone.

While Psyche stood there, panting with fear and with eyes full of tears, the gentle Zephyr lifted her and, with an easy motion, bore her to a flowery dale. By degrees her mind became composed, and she laid herself down on the grassy bank to sleep. When she awoke refreshed with sleep, she beheld near by a pleasant grove of tall and stately trees. Entering, she discovered in the midst.a fountain, and fast by a palace whose august front showed that it was not the work of mortal hands, but the happy retreat of some god. She approached the building and entered. Every object she met filled her with pleasure and amazement. Golden pillars supported the vaulted roof, and the walls were enriched with carvings and paintings that represented beasts of the chase and rural scenes. Other apartments were filled with still other beautiful and precious productions of nature and art.

While her eyes were thus occupied, the voice of an invisible being addressed her : " Sovereign lady, all that thou beholdest is thine. We whose voices thou dost hear are thy servants. Retire, we pray thee, to thy chamber, repose on thy bed of down, and when it may please thee repair to the bath. Food awaits in the adjoining alcove."

After repose and the refreshment of the bath, Psyche seated herself in the alcove, where, without any visible aid, a table immediately presented itself, covered with delicacies and nectareous wines. Her ears, too, were delighted with music from invisible performers.

For a long time she did not see her husband. He came in the hours of darkness and fled before the dawn of morning ; but his accents were full of love and inspired a like passion in her. Often she begged him to stay and let her behold him, but he would not consent. "Having looked upon me," he said, "mayhap thou wouldst fear, mayhap adore, me; but all I ask of thee is love. I would rather thou shouldst love me as an equal than adore me as a god." This reasoning somewhat quieted Psyche for a time. But the thought of her parents and of her sisters, left in ignorance

of her fate, preyed on her mind to such a degree that at last, telling her distress to her lord, she drew from him an unwilling consent that her sisters should be brought to see her.

Zephyr, promptly obedient, soon brought them across the mountain down to their sister's valley. They embraced her. She returned their caresses, and then committed them to the care of her attendant voices, who should refresh them in her bath and at her table, and show them her treasures. The view of these delights caused envy to enter their bosoms. They plied their fortunate sister with questions about her husband. Psyche replied that he was

Fig. 75. Psyche at the Couch of Cupid

From the painting by Thumann

a beautiful youth, who generally spent the daytime in hunting upon the mountains. The sisters, not satisfied with this reply, soon made her confess that she had never seen him. Then they proceeded to fill her bosom with dark suspicions. Probably her husband was a dreadful monster, such as the Pythian oracle had prophesied. Probably he was a direful serpent, who nourished her now to devour her by and by. They advised her to provide herself against the night with a lamp and a sharp knife, told her what to do if her husband turned out the monster that they surmised, and, so saying, departed.

These persuasions Psyche resisted as well as she could, but they did not fail to have their effect on her mind. She prepared a lamp and a sharp knife, and hid them out of sight of her husband. That night, when he had fallen into his first sleep, she silently rose and uncovering her lamp —

> Scarce kept back a cry
> At what she saw; for there before her lay
> The very Love brighter than dawn of day;
> And as he lay there smiling, her own name
> His gentle lips in sleep began to frame,
> And, as to touch her face, his hand did move;
> O then, indeed, her faint heart swelled for love,
> And she began to sob, and tears fell fast
> Upon the bed. — But as she turned at last
> To quench the lamp, there happed a little thing
> That quenched her new delight, for flickering
> The treacherous flame cast on his shoulder fair
> A burning drop; he woke, and seeing her there
> The meaning of that sad sight knew full well,
> Nor was there need the piteous tale to tell.[1]

Without a word, Cupid spread his white wings, and flew out of window. Psyche, in vain endeavoring to follow, fell to the earth. For but an instant Cupid, staying, reproached her with distrust of him. " No other punishment inflict I than to leave thee forever. Love cannot dwell with suspicion." And so he flew away.

When Psyche had recovered some degree of composure, she looked around her. The palace and gardens had vanished. She found herself not far from the city where her sisters dwelt. Thither she repaired, and told them the story of her misfortunes, whereat they inwardly rejoiced. " For now," thought they, " he will perhaps choose one of us." With this idea, they rose early the next morning and, ascending the mountain, each called upon Zephyr to receive her and bear her to his lord; then, leaping up,

---

[1] William Morris, The Story of Cupid and Psyche, in The Earthly Paradise.

failed of the support of Zephyr, fell down the precipice, and was dashed to pieces.

Psyche, meanwhile, wandered day and night, without food or repose, in search of her husband. But he was lying heartsick in the chamber of his mother; and that goddess was absent upon her own affairs. Then the white sea gull which floats over the waves dived into the middle deep,

> And rowing with his glistening wings arrived
> At Aphrodite's bower beneath the sea.

She, as yet unaware of her son's mischance, was joyously consorting with her handmaidens; but he, the sea gull,

> But he with garrulous and laughing tongue
> Broke up his news; how Eros fallen sick
> Lay tossing on his bed, to frenzy stung
> By such a burn as did but barely prick:
> A little bleb, no bigger than a pease,
> Upon his shoulder 't was, that killed his ease,
> Fevered his heart, and made his breathing thick.
>
> " For which disaster hath he not been seen
> This many a day at all in any place:
> And thou, dear mistress," said he, " hast not been
> Thyself among us now a dreary space:
> And pining mortals suffer from a dearth
> Of love; and for this sadness of the earth
> Thy family is darkened with disgrace. . . .
>
> " 'T is plain that, if thy pleasure longer pause,
> Thy mighty rule on earth hath seen its day:
> The race must come to perish, and no cause
> But that thou sittest with thy nymphs at play,
> While on the Cretan hills thy truant boy
> Has with his pretty mistress turned to toy,
> And, less for pain than love, now pines away." [1]

And Venus cried angrily, " My son, then, has a mistress! And it is Psyche, who witched away my beauty and was the rival of my godhead, whom he loves!"

[1] Robert Bridges, Eros and Psyche.

Therewith she issued from the sea, and, returning to her golden chamber, found there the lad sick, as she had heard, and cried from the doorway, "Well done, truly! to trample thy mother's precepts under foot, to spare my enemy that cross of an unworthy love; nay, unite her to thyself, child as thou art, that I might have a daughter-in-law who hates me! I will make thee repent of thy sport, and the savor of thy marriage bitter. There is one who shall chasten this body of thine, put out thy torch, and unstring thy bow. Not till she has plucked forth that hair, into which so oft these hands have smoothed the golden light, and sheared away thy wings, shall I feel the injury done me avenged." And with this she hastened in anger from the doors.

And Ceres and Juno met her, and sought to know the meaning of her troubled countenance. "Ye come in season," she cried; "I pray you, find for me Psyche. It must needs be that ye have heard the disgrace of my house." And they, ignorant of what was done, would have soothed her anger, saying, "What fault, Mistress, hath thy son committed, that thou wouldst destroy the girl he loves? Knowest thou not that he is now of age? Because he wears his years so lightly must he seem to thee ever to be a child? Wilt thou forever thus pry into the pastimes of thy son, always accusing his wantonness, and blaming in him those delicate wiles which are all thine own?" Thus, in secret fear of the boy's bow, did they seek to please him with their gracious patronage. But Venus, angry at their light taking of her wrongs, turned her back upon them, and with hasty steps made her way once more to the sea.[1]

And soon after, Psyche herself reached the temple of Ceres, where she won the favor of the goddess by arranging in due order the heaps of mingled grain and ears and the carelessly scattered harvest implements that lay there. The holy Ceres then counseled her to submit to Venus, to try humbly to win her forgiveness, and, mayhap, through her favor regain the lover that was lost.

Obeying the commands of Ceres, Psyche took her way to the temple of the golden-crowned Cypris. That goddess received her with angry countenance, called her an undutiful and faithless

[1] The last three paragraphs are from Pater's version in Marius the Epicurean.

servant, taunted her with the wound given to her husband, and insisted that for so ill-favored a girl there was no way of meriting a lover save by dint of industry. Thereupon she ordered Psyche to be led to the storehouse of the temple, where was laid up a great quantity of wheat, barley, millet, vetches, beans, and lentils prepared for food for her pigeons, and gave order, "Take and separate all these grains, putting all of the same kind in a parcel by themselves, — and see that thou get it done before evening." This said, Venus departed and left the girl to her task. But Psyche, in perfect consternation at the enormous task, sat stupid and silent; nor would the work have been accomplished had not Cupid stirred up the ants to take compassion on her. They separated the pile, sorting each kind to its parcel and vanishing out of sight in a moment.

At the approach of twilight, Cytherea returned from the banquet of the gods, breathing odors and crowned with roses. Seeing the task done, she promptly exclaimed, "This is no work of thine, wicked one, but his, whom to thine own and his misfortune thou hast enticed," — threw the girl a piece of black bread for her supper, and departed.

Next morning, however, the goddess, ordering Psyche to be summoned, commanded her to fetch a sample of wool gathered from each of the golden-shining sheep that fed beyond a neighboring river. Obediently the princess went to the riverside, prepared to do her best to execute the command. But the god of that stream inspired the reeds with harmonious murmurs that dissuaded her from venturing among the golden rams while they raged under the influence of the rising sun. Psyche, observing the directions of the compassionate river-god, crossed when the noontide sun had driven the cattle to the shade, gathered the woolly gold from the bushes where it was clinging, and returned to Venus with her arms full of the shining fleece. But, far from commending her, that implacable mistress said, "I know very well that by the aid of another thou hast done this; not yet am I assured that thou hast skill to be of use. Here, now, take this box to Proserpine and say, 'My mistress Venus entreats thee to send her a little of thy beauty, for in tending her sick son she hath lost some of her own.'"

Psyche, satisfied that her destruction was at hand, doomed as she was to travel afoot to Erebus, thought to shorten the journey by precipitating herself at once from the summit of a tower. But a voice from the tower, restraining her from this rash purpose, explained how by a certain cave she might reach the realm of Pluto ; how she might avoid the peril of the road, pass by Cerberus, and prevail on Charon to take her across the black river and bring her back again. The voice, also, especially cautioned her against prying into the box filled with the beauty of Proserpine.

So, taking heed to her ways, the unfortunate girl traveled safely to the kingdom of Pluto. She was admitted to the palace of Proserpine, where, contenting herself with plain fare instead of the delicious banquet that was offered her, she delivered her message from Venus. Presently the box, filled with the precious commodity, was restored to her ; and glad was she to come out once more into the light of day.

But having got so far successfully through her dangerous task, a desire seized her to examine the contents of the box, and to spread the least bit of the divine beauty on her cheeks that she might appear to more advantage in the eyes of her beloved husband.

> Therewith down by the wayside did she sit
> And turned the box round, long regarding it ;
> But at the last, with trembling hands, undid
> The clasp, and fearfully raised up the lid ;
> But what was there she saw not, for her head
> Fell back, and nothing she rememberèd
> Of all her life, yet nought of rest she had,
> The hope of which makes hapless mortals glad ;
> For while her limbs were sunk in deadly sleep
> Most like to death, over her heart 'gan creep
> Ill dreams ; so that for fear and great distress
> She would have cried, but in her helplessness
> Could open not her mouth, or frame a word.[1]

But Cupid, now recovered from his wound, slipped through a crack in the window of his chamber, flew to the spot where his beloved lay, gathered up the sleep from her body and inclosed it

---

[1] William Morris, The Earthly Paradise.

again in the box, then waked Psyche with the touch of an arrow
"Again," said he, "hast thou almost perished by thy curiosity.

FIG. 76. PSYCHE AND CUPID ON MOUNT
OLYMPUS

From the painting by Thumann

But now perform the task imposed upon thee by my mother, and I will care for the rest."

Then Cupid, swift as lightning penetrating the heights of heaven, presented himself before Jupiter with his supplication. Jupiter lent a favoring ear and pleaded the cause of the lovers with Venus. Gaining her consent, he ordered Mercury to convey Psyche to the heavenly abodes. On her advent, the king of the immortals, handing her a cup of ambrosia, said, "Drink this, Psyche, and be immortal. Thy Cupid shall never break from the knot in which he is tied; these nuptials shall indeed be perpetual."

Thus Psyche was at last united to Cupid; and in due season a daughter was born to them whose name was Pleasure.

The allegory of Cupid and Psyche is well presented in the following lines:

They wove bright fables in the days of old,
  When reason borrowed fancy's painted wings;
When truth's clear river flowed o'er sands of gold,
  And told in song its high and mystic things!
And such the sweet and solemn tale of her
  The pilgrim-heart, to whom a dream was given,
That led her through the world, — Love's worshiper, —
  To seek on earth for him whose home was heaven!

EROS WITH BOW

In the full city, — by the haunted fount, —
    Through the dim grotto's tracery of spars, —
'Mid the pine temples, on the moonlit mount,
    Where silence sits to listen to the stars;
In the deep glade where dwells the brooding dove,
    The painted valley, and the scented air,
She heard far echoes of the voice of Love,
    And found his footsteps' traces everywhere.

But never more they met! since doubts and fears,
    Those phantom-shapes that haunt and blight the earth,
Had come 'twixt her, a child of sin and tears,
    And that bright spirit of immortal birth;
Until her pining soul and weeping eyes
Had learned to seek him only in the skies;
Till wings unto the weary heart were given,
And she became Love's angel bride in heaven! [1]

The story of Cupid and Psyche first appears in the works of
Apuleius, a writer of the second century of our era. It is therefore of much more recent date than most of the classic myths.

102. Keats' Ode to Psyche. To this fact allusion is made in the
following poem :

O Goddess! hear these tuneless numbers, wrung
    By sweet enforcement and remembrance dear,
And pardon that thy secrets should be sung
    Even into thine own soft-conchèd ear:
Surely I dreamt to-day, or did I see
    The wingèd Psyche with awakened eyes?
I wandered in a forest thoughtlessly,
And, on the sudden, fainting with surprise,
      Saw two fair creatures, couchèd side by side
In deepest grass, beneath the whispering roof
Of leaves and tumbled blossoms, where there ran
      A brooklet, scarce espied!

'Mid hushed, cool-rooted flowers, fragrant-eyed,
    Blue, silver-white, and budded Tyrian,
They lay calm-breathing on the bedded grass;
    Their arms embracèd, and their pinions, too;
    Their lips touched not, but had not bade adieu,

[1] By T. K. Hervey.

As if disjoinèd by soft-handed slumber,
And ready still past kisses to outnumber
  At tender eye-dawn of Aurorean love:
    The wingèd boy I knew:
  But who wast thou, O happy, happy dove?
    His Psyche true!

O latest born and loveliest vision far
  Of all Olympus' faded hierarchy!
Fairer than Phœbe's sapphire-regioned star,
  Or Vesper, amorous glowworm of the sky;
Fairer than these, though temple thou hast none,
    Nor altar heaped with flowers;
Nor virgin-choir to make delicious moan
    Upon the midnight hours;
No voice, no lute, no pipe, no incense sweet
  From chain-swung censer teeming;
No shrine, no grove, no oracle, no heat
  Of pale-mouthed prophet dreaming.

O brightest! though too late for antique vows
  Too, too late for the fond believing lyre,
When holy were the haunted forest boughs,
  Holy the air, the water, and the fire;
Yet even in these days so far retired
  From happy pieties, thy lucent fans,
  Fluttering among the faint Olympians,
I see, and sing, by my own eyes inspired.
So let me be thy choir, and make a moan
    Upon the midnight hours;
Thy voice, thy lute, thy pipe, thy incense sweet
  From swingèd censer teeming,
Thy shrine, thy grove, thy oracle, thy heat
  Of pale-mouthed prophet dreaming.

Yes, I will be thy priest, and build a fane
  In some untrodden region of my mind,
Where branchèd thoughts, new grown with pleasant pain,
  Instead of pines shall murmur in the wind:
Far, far around shall those dark clustered trees
  Fledge the wild-ridgèd mountains steep by steep;
And there by zephyrs, streams, and birds and bees,
  The moss-lain Dryads shall be lulled to sleep;

And in the midst of this wide quietness
A rosy sanctuary will I dress
With the wreathèd trellis of a working brain,
　With buds, and bells, and stars without a name,
With all the gardener Fancy e'er could feign,
　Who breeding flowers, will never breed the same;
And there shall be for thee all soft delight
　That shadowy thought can win,
A bright torch, and a casement ope at night,
　To let the warm Love in!

The loves of the devotees of Venus are as the sands of the sea for number. Below are given the fortunes of a few : Hippomenes, Hero, Pygmalion, Pyramus, and Phaon. The favor of the goddess toward Paris, who awarded her the palm of beauty in preference to Juno and Minerva, will occupy our attention in connection with the story of the Trojan War.

103. Atalanta's Race.[1] Atalanta, the daughter of Schœneus of Bœotia, had been warned by an oracle that marriage would be fatal to her happiness. Consequently she fled the society of men and devoted herself to the sports of the chase. Fair, fearless, swift, and free, in beauty and in desire she was a Cynthia, — of mortal form and with a woman's heart. To all suitors (for she had many) she made answer : " I will be the prize of him only who shall conquer me in the race ; but death must be the penalty of all who try and fail." In spite of this hard condition some would try. Of one such race Hippomenes was to be judge. It was his thought, at first, that these suitors risked too much for a wife. But when he saw Atalanta lay aside her

FIG. 77. ARTEMIS
OF GABII

robe for the race with one of them, he changed his mind and began to swell with envy of whomsoever seemed likely to win.

The virgin darted forward. As she ran she looked more beautiful than ever. The breezes gave wings to her feet ; her hair flew

---

[1] Ovid, Metam. 10, 560–680.

over her shoulders, and the gay fringe of her garment fluttered behind her. A ruddy hue tinged the whiteness of her skin, such as a crimson curtain casts on a marble wall. Her competitor was distanced and was put to death without mercy. Hippomenes, not daunted by this result, fixed his eyes on the virgin and said, " Why boast of beating those laggards? I offer myself for the contest." Atalanta looked at him with pity in her face and hardly knew whether she would rather conquer so goodly a youth or not. While

FIG. 78. ATALANTA'S RACE

From the painting by Poynter

she hesitated, the spectators grew impatient for the contest and her father prompted her to prepare. Then Hippomenes addressed a prayer to Cypris: " Help me, Venus, for thou hast impelled me." Venus heard and was propitious.

She gathered three golden apples from the garden of her temple in her own island of Cyprus and, unseen by any, gave them to Hippomenes, telling him how to use them. Atalanta and her lover were ready. The signal was given.

> They both started; he, by one stride, first,
> For she half pitied him so beautiful,
> Running to meet his death, yet was resolved
> To conquer: soon she near'd him, and he felt
> The rapid and repeated gush of breath
> Behind his shoulder.
> From his hand now dropt
> A golden apple: she lookt down and saw
> A glitter on the grass, yet on she ran.

He dropt a second; now she seem'd to stoop:
He dropt a third; and now she stoopt indeed:
Yet, swifter than a wren picks up a grain
Of millet, rais'd her head: it was too late,
Only one step, only one breath, too late.
Hippomenes had toucht the maple goal
With but two fingers, leaning pronely forth.
She stood in mute despair; the prize was won.
    Now each walkt slowly forward, both so tired,
And both alike breathed hard, and stopt at times.
When he turn'd round to her, she lowered her face
Cover'd with blushes, and held out her hand,
The golden apple in it.
              " Leave me now,"
Said she, " I must walk homeward."
                      He did take
The apple and the hand.
                " Both I detain,"
Said he, "the other two I dedicate
To the two Powers that soften virgin hearts,
Eros and Aphrodite; and this one
To her who ratifies the nuptial vow."
    She would have wept to see her father weep;
But some God pitied her, and purple wings
(What God's were they?) hovered and interposed.[1]

But the oracle was yet to be fulfilled. The lovers, full of their own happiness, after all, forgot to pay due honor to Aphrodite, and the goddess was provoked at their ingratitude. She caused them to give offense to Cybele. That powerful goddess took from them their human form: the huntress heroine, triumphing in the blood of her lovers, she made a lioness; her lord and master a lion, — and yoked them to her car, where they are still to be seen in all representations in statuary or painting of the goddess Cybele.

104. Hero and Leander were star-crossed lovers of later classical fiction.[2] Although their story is not of supernatural beings, or of events necessarily influenced by supernatural agencies, and therefore not mythical in the strict sense of the word, it deserves to be

[1] From W. S. Landor's Hippomenes and Atalanta.

[2] The poetical passages are from Marlowe's Hero and Leander, First Sestiad. Marlowe's narrative was completed by Chapman. See Musæus of Alexandria, De Amore Herois et Leandri; Virg. Georg. 3, 258; Ovid, Her. 18, 19; Stat. Theb. 6, 770.

included here both because of its pathetic beauty and its long literary tradition. The poet Marlowe puts the story into English thus :

> On Hellespont, guilty of true love's blood,
> In view and opposite two cities stood,
> Sea-borderers, disjoin'd by Neptune's might
> The one Abydos, the other Sestos hight.
> At Sestos Hero dwelt; Hero the fair,
> Whom young Apollo courted for her hair,
> And offer'd as a dower his burning throne,
> Where she should sit, for men to gaze upon. . . .
> Some say, for her the fairest Cupid pin'd,
> And, looking in her face, was strooken blind.
> But this is true: so like was one the other,
> As he imagined Hero was his mother;
> And oftentimes into her bosom flew,
> About her naked neck his bare arms threw,
> And laid his childish head upon her breast,
> And, with still panting rockt, there took his rest.

In Abydos dwelt the manly Leander, who, as luck would have it, bethought himself one day of the festival of Venus in Sestos, and thither fared to do obeisance to the goddess.

> On this feast-day, — O cursèd day and hour ! —
> Went Hero thorough Sestos, from her tower
> To Venus' temple, where unhappily,
> As after chanc'd, they did each other spy.
> So fair a church as this had Venus none;
> The walls were of discolored jasper-stone, . . .
> And in the midst a silver altar stood:
> There Hero, sacrificing turtle's blood,
> Vail'd to the ground, veiling her eyelids close;
> And modestly they opened as she rose:
> Thence flew Love's arrow with the golden head;
> And thus Leander was enamourèd.
> Stone-still he stood, and evermore he gaz'd,
> Till with the fire, that from his countenance blaz'd,
> Relenting Hero's gentle heart was strook:
> Such power and virtue hath an amorous look.
>
> 　It lies not in our power to love or hate,
> For will in us is overrul'd by fate.
> When two are stript long e'er the course begin,
> We wish that one should lose, the other win:

And one especially do we affect
Of two gold ingots, like in each respect:
The reason no man knows; let it suffice,
What we behold is censur'd by our eyes.
Where both deliberate, the love is slight:
Who ever lov'd, that lov'd not at first sight?

He kneel'd; but unto *her* devoutly prayed:
Chaste Hero to herself thus softly said,
" Were I the saint he worships, I would hear him ";
And, as she spake those words, came somewhat near him.
He started up; she blush'd as one asham'd;
Wherewith Leander much more was inflam'd.
He touch'd her hand; in touching it she trembled:
Love deeply grounded, hardly is dissembled. . . .

So they conversed by touch of hands, till Leander, plucking up
courage, began to plead with words, with sighs and tears.

These arguments he us'd, and many more;
Wherewith she yielded, that was won before.
Hero's looks yielded, but her words made war:
Women are won when they begin to jar.
Thus having swallow'd Cupid's golden hook,
The more she striv'd, the deeper was she strook:
Yet, evilly feigning anger, strove she still,
And would be thought to grant against her will.
So having paus'd awhile, at last she said,
" Who taught thee rhetoric to deceive a maid?
Ay me! such words as these should I abhor,
And yet I like them for the orator."
With that Leander stoop'd to have embrac'd her,
But from his spreading arms away she cast her,
And thus bespake him: " Gentle youth, forbear
To touch the sacred garments which I wear." . . .

Then she told him of the turret by the murmuring sea where
all day long she tended Venus' swans and sparrows :

" Come thither." As she spake this, her tongue tripp'd,
For unawares, " Come thither," from her slipp'd;
And suddenly her former color chang'd,
And here and there her eyes through anger rang'd;
And, like a planet moving several ways
At one self instant, she, poor soul, assays,

Loving, not to love at all, and every part
Strove to resist the motions of her heart:
And hands so pure, so innocent, nay, such
As might have made Heaven stoop to have a touch,
Did she uphold to Venus, and again
Vow'd spotless chastity; but all in vain;
Cupid beats down her prayers with his wings. . . .

For a season all went well. Guided by a torch which his mistress reared upon the tower, he was wont of nights to swim the strait that he might enjoy her company. But one night a tempest

FIG. 79. HERO AND LEANDER
From the painting by Keller

arose and the sea was rough; his strength failed and he was drowned. The waves bore his body to the European shore, where Hero became aware of his death, and in her despair cast herself into the sea and perished.

A picture of the drowning Leander is thus described by Keats : [1]

> Come hither all sweet maidens soberly,
>   Down looking aye, and with a chasten'd light,
>   Hid in the fringe of your eyelids white,
> And meekly let your fair hands joinèd be,
> As if so gentle that ye could not see,
>   Untouch'd, a victim of your beauty bright,
>   Sinking away to his young spirit's night,
> Sinking bewilder'd 'mid the dreary sea :
> 'T is young Leander toiling to his death ;
>   Nigh swooning he doth purse his weary lips
> For Hero's cheek, and smiles against her smile.
>   O horrid dream ! see how his body dips
> Dead-heavy ; arms and shoulders gleam awhile ;
> He 's gone ; up bubbles all his amorous breath !

105. Pygmalion and the Statue. [2] Pygmalion saw so much to blame in women, that he came at last to abhor the sex and resolved to live unmarried. 'He was a sculptor, and had made with wonderful skill a statue of ivory, so beautiful that no living woman was to compare with it. It was indeed the perfect semblance of a maiden that seemed to be alive and that was prevented from moving only by modesty. His art was so perfect that it concealed itself, and its product looked like the workmanship of nature. Pygmalion at last fell in love with his counterfeit creation. Oftentimes he laid his hand upon it as if to assure himself whether it were living or not, and could not even then believe that it was only ivory.

The festival of Venus was at hand, — a festival celebrated with great pomp at Cyprus. Victims were offered, the altars smoked, and the odor of incense filled the air. When Pygmalion had performed his part in the solemnities, he stood before the altar and, according to one of our poets, timidly said :

> O Aphrodite, kind and fair,
>   That what thou wilt canst give,
> Oh, listen to a sculptor's prayer,
>   And bid mine image live !
> For me the ivory and gold
>   That clothe her cedar frame

---

[1] Sonnet, On a Picture of Leander.   [2] Ovid, Metam. 10, 243–297.

Are beautiful, indeed, but cold;
　Ah, touch them with thy flame!
Oh, bid her move those lips of rose,
　Bid float that golden hair,
And let her choose me, as I chose,
　This fairest of the fair!
And then an altar in thy court
　I 'll offer, decked with gold;
And there thy servants shall resort,
　Thy doves be bought and sold![1]

According to another version of the story, he said not, "bid mine image live," but "one like my ivory virgin." At any rate, with such a prayer he threw incense on the flame of the altar. Whereupon Venus, as an omen of her favor, caused the flame to shoot up thrice a fiery point into the air.

When Pygmalion reached his home, to his amazement he saw before him his statue garlanded with flowers.

Yet while he stood, and knew not what to do
With yearning, a strange thrill of hope there came,
A shaft of new desire now pierced him through,
And therewithal a soft voice called his name,
And when he turned, with eager eyes aflame,
He saw betwixt him and the setting sun
The lively image of his lovèd one.

He trembled at the sight, for though her eyes,
Her very lips, were such as he had made,
And though her tresses fell but in such guise
As he had wrought them, now was she arrayed
In that fair garment that the priests had laid
Upon the goddess on that very morn,
Dyed like the setting sun upon the corn.

Speechless he stood, but she now drew anear,
Simple and sweet as she was wont to be,
And once again her silver voice rang clear,
Filling his soul with great felicity,
And thus she spoke, "Wilt thou not come to me,
O dear companion of my new-found life,
For I am called thy lover and thy wife? ...

[1] Andrew Lang, The New Pygmalion.

" My sweet," she said, " as yet I am not wise,
Or stored with words aright the tale to tell,
But listen: when I opened first mine eyes
I stood within the niche thou knowest well,
And from my hand a heavy thing there fell
Carved like these flowers, nor could I see things clear,
But with a strange, confusèd noise could hear.

" At last mine eyes could see a woman fair,
But awful as this round white moon o'erhead,
So that I trembled when I saw her there,
For with my life was born some touch of dread,
And therewithal I heard her voice that said,
' Come down and learn to love and be alive,
For thee, a well-prized gift, to-day I give.' " [1]

A fuller account of Venus' address to the statue is the following:

O maiden, in mine image made!
    O grace that shouldst endure!
While temples fall, and empires fade,
    Immaculately pure:
Exchange this endless life of art
    For beauty that must die,
And blossom with a beating heart
    Into mortality!
Change, golden tresses of her hair,
    To gold that turns to gray;
Change, silent lips, forever fair,
    To lips that have their day!
Oh, perfect arms, grow soft with life,
    Wax warm, ere cold ye wane;
Wake, woman's heart, from peace to strife,
    To love, to joy, to pain! [2]

The maiden was called Galatea. Venus blessed the nuptials, and from the union Paphos was born, by whose name the city, sacred to Venus, is known.

106. Pyramus and Thisbe.[3] Pyramus was the handsomest youth and Thisbe the fairest maiden in Babylonia, where Semiramis

---

[1] From William Morris, Pygmalion and the Image, in The Earthly Paradise.
[2] Andrew Lang, The New Pygmalion, or The Statue's Choice. A witty and not unpoetic bit of burlesque.　　　　[3] Ovid, Metam. 4, 55-166.

reigned. Their parents occupied adjoining houses. Propinquity brought the young people together, and acquaintance ripened into love. They would gladly have married, but their parents forbade. One thing, however, parents could not forbid (for Venus and Cupid favored the match), — that love should glow with equal ardor in the bosoms of both. They conversed by signs and glances, and the fire

FIG. 80. THISBE

From the painting by Edward Burne-Jones

burned the more intensely that it was covered. In the wall between the two houses there was a crack, caused by some fault in the structure. It afforded a passage to the voice; and tender messages passed back and forth through the gap. When night came and they must say farewell, the lovers pressed their lips upon the wall, she on her side, he on his.

One morning, when Aurora had put out the stars and the sun had melted the frost from the grass, they met at the accustomed spot and arranged a meeting for that night at a well-known edifice, standing without the city's bounds, — the Tomb of Ninus. The one who first arrived should await the other at the foot of a white mulberry tree near a cool spring. Evening came. Thisbe, arriving first, sat alone by the monument in the dim light of the evening. Suddenly she descried a lioness, her jaws reeking with recent slaughter, approaching the fountain to slake her thirst. The maiden fled at the sight, dropping her veil as she ran. The lioness, after drinking at the spring, turned toward the woods, and, seeing the veil on the ground, tossed and rent it with her bloody mouth.

Now Pyramus approached the place of meeting. He saw in the sand the footsteps of the lion. He found the veil all rent and bloody. " O, hapless girl," cried he, " I have been the cause of thy death ; but I follow thee ! " So saying, he drew his sword and plunged it into his heart. The blood spurted from the wound and tinged the white mulberries of the tree all red, and, sinking into the earth, reached the roots, so that the sanguine hue mounted through the trunk to the fruit.

By this time Thisbe, still trembling with fear, yet wishing not to disappoint her lover, stepped cautiously forth, looking anxiously for the youth, eager to tell him the danger she had escaped. When she came to the spot and saw the changed color of the mulberries, she doubted whether it was the same place. While she hesitated, she saw the form of her lover struggling in the agonies of death. She screamed and beat her breast, she embraced the lifeless body, poured tears into its wounds, and imprinted kisses on the cold lips. " O, Pyramus," she cried, " what has done this ? It is thine own Thisbe that speaks." At the name of Thisbe Pyramus opened his eyes, then closed them again. She saw her veil stained with blood and the scabbard empty of its sword. " Thine own hand has slain thee, and for my sake," she said. " I, too, can be brave for once, and my love is as strong as thine. But ye, unhappy parents of us both, deny us not our united request. As love and death have joined us, let one tomb contain us. And thou, tree, retain the marks of slaughter. Let thy berries still serve for memorials of our blood." So saying, she plunged the sword into her breast. The two bodies were buried in one sepulcher, and the tree henceforth produced purple berries.

107. Phaon ferried a boat between Lesbos and Chios. One day the queen of Paphos and Amathus,[1] in the guise of an ugly crone, begged a passage, which was so good-naturedly granted that in recompense she bestowed on the ferryman a salve possessing magical properties of youth and beauty. As a consequence of the use made of it by Phaon, the women of Lesbos went wild for love of him. None, however, admired him more than the poetess Sappho, who addressed to him some of her warmest and rarest love-songs.

[1] § 100, and Commentary.

108. The Vengeance of Venus. Venus did not fail to follow with her vengeance those who dishonored her rites or defied her power. The youth Hippolytus who, eschewing love, preferred Diana to her, she brought miserably to his ruin. Polyphonte she transformed into an owl, Arsinoë into a stone, and Myrrha into a myrtle tree.[1] Her influence in the main was of mingled bane and blessing, as in the cases of Helen, Œnone, Pasiphaë, Ariadne, Procris, Eriphyle, Laodamia, and others whose stories are elsewhere told.[2]

109. Myths of Mercury. According to Homer,[3] Maia bore Mercury at the peep of day, — a schemer subtle beyond all belief. He began playing on the lyre at noon; for, wandering out of the lofty cavern of Cyllene, he found a tortoise, picked it up, bored the life out of the beast, fitted the shell with bridge and reeds, and accompanied himself therewith as he sang a strain of unpremeditated sweetness. At evening of the same day he stole the oxen of his half brother Apollo from the Pierian mountains, where they were grazing. He covered their hoofs with tamarisk twigs, and, still further to deceive the pursuer, drove them backward into a cave at Pylos. There rubbing laurel branches together, he made fire and sacrificed, as an example for men to follow, two heifers to the twelve gods (himself included). Then home he went and slept, innocent as a new-born child! To his mother's warning that Apollo would catch and punish him, this innocent replied, in effect, "I know a trick better than that!" And when the puzzled Apollo, having traced the knavery to this babe in swaddling clothes, accused him of it, the sweet boy swore a great oath by his father's head that he stole not the cows, nor knew even what cows might be, for he had only that moment heard the name of them. Apollo proceeded to trounce the baby, with scant success, however, for Mercury persisted in his assumption of ignorance. So the twain appeared before their sire, and Apollo entered his complaint: he had not seen nor ever dreamed of so precocious a cattle-stealer, liar, and full-fledged knave as this young rascal. To all of which Mercury responded that he was, on the contrary, a veracious

---

[1] Murray, Manual of Mythology, p. 87; Ovid, Metam. 10, 298–502.
[2] See Index for sections.   [3] Hymn to Mercury (Hermes).

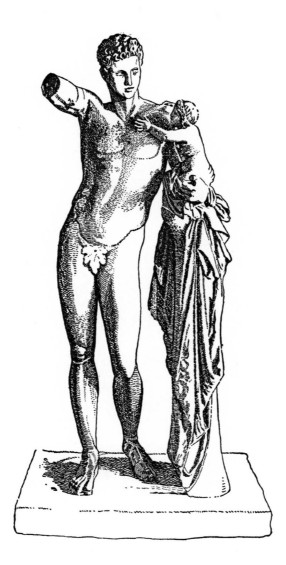

HERMES OF PRAXITELES

person, but that his brother Apollo was a coward to bully a helpless little new-born thing that slept, nor ever had thought of "lifting" cattle. The wink with which the lad of Cyllene accompanied this asseveration threw Jupiter into uncontrollable roars of laughter.

FIG. 81. HERMES AND DOG

Consequently, the quarrel was patched up: Mercury gave Apollo the new-made lyre; Apollo presented the prodigy with a glittering whiplash and installed him herdsman of his oxen. Nay even, when Mercury had sworn by sacred Styx no more to try his cunning in theft upon Apollo, that god in gratitude invested him with the magic wand of wealth, happiness, and dreams (the *caduceus*), it being understood, however, that Mercury should indicate the future only by signs, not by speech or song as did Apollo. It is said that the god of gain avenged himself for this enforced rectitude upon others: upon Venus, whose girdle he purloined; upon Neptune, whose trident he filched; upon Vulcan, whose tongs he borrowed; and upon Mars, whose sword he stole.

The most famous exploit of the Messenger, the slaughter of Argus, has already been narrated.

CHAPTER VIII

MYTHS OF THE GREAT DIVINITIES OF EARTH

110. Myths of Bacchus. Since the adventures of Ceres, although she was a goddess of earth, are intimately connected with the life of the underworld, they will be related in the sections pertaining to

FIG. 82. SILENUS TAK-
ING DIONYSUS TO
SCHOOL

Proserpine and Pluto. The god of vernal sap and vegetation, of the gladness that comes of youth or of wine, the golden-curled, sleepy-eyed Bacchus (Dionysus), — his wanderings, and the fortunes of mortals brought under his influence (Pentheus, Acetes, Ariadne, and Midas), here challenge our attention.

111. The Wanderings of Bacchus. After the death of Semele,[1] Jove took the infant Bacchus and gave him in charge to the Nysæan nymphs, who nourished his infancy and childhood and for their care were placed by Jupiter, as the Hyades, among the stars. Another guardian and tutor of young Bacchus was the pot-bellied, jovial Silenus, son of Pan and a nymph, and oldest of the Satyrs. Silenus was probably an indulgent precep-tor. He was generally tipsy and would have broken his neck early in his career, had not

the Satyrs held him on his ass's back as he reeled along in the train of his pupil. After Bacchus was of age, he discovered the culture of the vine and the mode of extracting its precious juice; but Juno struck him with madness and drove him forth a wan-derer through various parts of the earth. In Phrygia the goddess Rhea cured him and taught him her religious rites; and then

[1] § 60.

152

he set out on a progress through Asia, teaching the people the cultivation of the vine. The most famous part of his wanderings is his expedition to India, which is said to have lasted several years. Returning in triumph, he undertook to introduce his worship into Greece, but was opposed by certain princes who dreaded the disorders and madness it brought with it. Finally, he approached his native city Thebes, where his own cousin, Pentheus, son of Agave and grandson of Harmonia and Cadmus, was king. Pentheus, however, had no respect

FIG. 83. BEARDED DIONYSUS AND SATYR

for the new worship and forbade its rites to be performed.[1] But when it was known that Bacchus was advancing, men and women, young and old, poured forth to meet him and to join his triumphal march.

> Fauns with youthful Bacchus follow;
>   Ivy crowns that brow, supernal
> As the forehead of Apollo,
>   And possessing youth eternal.
>
> Round about him fair Bacchantes,
>   Bearing cymbals, flutes, and thyrses,
> Wild from Naxian groves or Zante's
>   Vineyards, sing delirious verses.[2]

It was in vain Pentheus remonstrated, commanded, and threatened. His nearest friends and wisest counselors begged him not to oppose the god. Their remonstrances only made him the more violent.

[1] Ovid, Metam. 3, 511–733.   [2] Longfellow, Drinking Song.

112. The Story of Acetes. Soon the attendants returned who had been dispatched to seize Bacchus. They had succeeded in taking one of the Bacchanals prisoner, whom, with his hands tied behind him, they brought before the king. Pentheus, threatening him with death, commanded him to tell who he was and what these new rites were that he presumed to celebrate.

The prisoner, unterrified, replied that he was Acetes of Mæonia; that his parents, being poor, had left him their fisherman's trade, which he had followed till he had acquired the pilot's art of steer-

FIG. 84. SATYR AND MÆNAD WITH CHILD
DIONYSUS

ing his course by the stars. It once happened that he had touched at the island of Dia and had sent his men ashore for fresh water. They returned, bringing with them a lad of delicate appearance whom they had found asleep. Judging him to be a noble youth, they thought to detain him in the hope of liberal ransom. But Acetes suspected that some god was concealed under the youth's exterior, and asked pardon for the violence done. Whereupon the sailors, enraged by their lust of gain, exclaimed, "Spare thy prayers for us!" and, in spite of the resistance offered by Acetes, thrust the captive youth on board and set sail.

Then Bacchus (for the youth was indeed he), as if shaking off his drowsiness, asked what the trouble was and whither they were carrying him. One of the mariners replied, "Fear nothing; tell us where thou wouldst go, and we will convey thee thither." "Naxos is my home," said Bacchus; "take me there, and ye shall be well rewarded." They promised so to do; but, preventing the pilot from steering toward Naxos, they bore away for Egypt, where they might sell the lad into slavery. Soon the god looked out over the sea and said in a voice of weeping, "Sailors, these are not the shores ye promised me; yonder island is not my home. It is small glory ye shall gain by cheating a poor boy." Acetes wept to hear him, but the crew laughed at both of them and sped the vessel fast over the sea. All at once it stopped in mid-sea, as fast as if it were fixed on the ground. The men, astonished, pulled at their oars and spread more sail, but all in vain. Ivy twined round the oars and clung to the sails, with heavy clusters of berries. A vine laden with grapes ran up the mast and along the sides of the vessel. The sound of flutes was heard, and the odor of fragrant wine spread all around. The god himself had a chaplet of vine leaves and bore in his hand a spear wreathed with ivy. Tigers crouched at his feet, and forms of lynxes and spotted panthers played around

FIG. 85. DIONYSUS AT SEA

him. The whole crew became dolphins and swam about the ship. Of twenty men Acetes alone was left. "Fear not," said the god; "steer towards Naxos." The pilot obeyed, and when they arrived there, kindled the altars and celebrated the sacred rites of Bacchus.

So far had Acetes advanced in his narrative, when Pentheus, interrupting, ordered him off to his death. But from this fate the pilot, rendered invisible by his patron deity, was straightway rescued.

Meanwhile, the mountain Cithæron seemed alive with worshipers, and the cries of the Bacchanals resounded on every side. Pentheus, angered by the noise, penetrated through the wood and reached an open space where the chief scene of the orgies met his eyes. At

the same moment the women saw him, among them his mother
Agave, and Autonoë and Ino, her sisters. Taking him for a wild
boar, they rushed upon him and tore him to pieces, — his mother
shouting, "Victory! Victory! the glory is ours!"

So the worship of Bacchus was established in Greece.

It was on the island of Naxos that Bacchus afterward found
Ariadne, the daughter of Minos, king of Crete, who had been deserted by her lover, Theseus. How Bacchus comforted her is related
in another section. How the god himself is worshiped is told by
Edmund Gosse in the poem from which the following extracts are
taken :

> Behold, behold! the granite gates unclose,
> And down the vales a lyric people flows ;
> Dancing to music, in their dance they fling
> Their frantic robes to every wind that blows,
> And deathless praises to the vine-god sing.

FIG. 86. BACCHIC PROCESSION

> Nearer they press, and nearer still in sight,
> Still dancing blithely in a seemly choir ;
> Tossing on high the symbol of their rite,
> The cone-tipped thyrsus of a god's desire ;
> Nearer they come, tall damsels flushed and fair,
> With ivy circling their abundant hair ;
> Onward, with even pace, in stately rows,
> With eye that flashes, and with cheek that glows,
> And all the while their tribute-songs they bring,
> And newer glories of the past disclose,
> And deathless praises to the vine-god sing.
> ... But oh! within the heart of this great flight,

Whose ivory arms hold up the golden lyre?
What form is this of more than mortal height?
What matchless beauty, what inspirèd ire!
The brindled panthers know the prize they bear,
And harmonize their steps with stately care;
Bent to the morning, like a living rose,
The immortal splendor of his face he shows,
And where he glances, leaf and flower and wing
Tremble with rapture, stirred in their repose,
And deathless praises to the vine-god sing. . . .[1]

113. The Choice of King Midas.[2] Once Silenus, having wandered from the company of Bacchus in an intoxicated condition, was found by some peasants, who carried him to their king, Midas.

FIG. 87. DIONYSUS VISITING A POET

Midas entertained him royally and on the eleventh day restored him in safety to his divine pupil. Whereupon Bacchus offered Midas his choice of a reward. The king asked that whatever he might touch should be changed into gold. Bacchus consented. Midas hastened to put his new-acquired power to the test. A twig of an oak, which he plucked from the branch, became gold in

---

[1] From The Praise of Dionysus. [2] Ovid, Metam. 11, 85–145.

his hand. He took up a stone; it changed to gold. He touched a sod with the same result. He took an apple from the tree; you would have thought he had robbed the garden of the Hesperides. He ordered his servants, then, to set an excellent meal on the table. But, to his dismay, when he touched bread, it hardened in his hand; when he put a morsel to his lips, it defied his teeth. He took a glass of wine, but it flowed down his throat like melted gold.

He strove to divest himself of his power; he hated the gift he had lately coveted. He raised his arms, all shining with gold, in prayer to Bacchus, begging to be delivered from this glittering destruction. The merciful deity heard and sent him to wash away his fault and its punishment in the fountainhead of the river Pactolus. Scarce had Midas touched the waters, before the gold-creating power passed into them, and the river sands became golden, as they remain to this day.

Thenceforth Midas, hating wealth and splendor, dwelt in the country and became a worshiper of Pan, the god of the fields. But that he had not gained common sense is shown by the decision that he delivered somewhat later in favor of Pan's superiority, as a musician, over Apollo.[1]

[1] See § 85.

FIG. 88. RAPE OF PROSERPINA

CHAPTER IX

FROM THE EARTH TO THE UNDERWORLD

114. Myths of Ceres, Pluto, and Proserpine. The search of Ceres for Proserpine, and of Orpheus for Eurydice, are stories pertaining both to Earth and Hades.

115. The Rape of Proserpine.[1] When the giants were imprisoned by Jupiter under Mount Ætna, Pluto (Hades) feared lest the shock of their fall might expose his kingdom to the light of day. Under this apprehension, he mounted his chariot drawn by black horses, and made a circuit of inspection to satisfy himself of the extent of the damage. While he was thus engaged, Venus, who was sitting on Mount Eryx playing with her boy Cupid, espied him and said, " My son, take thy darts which subdue all, even Jove himself, and send one into the breast of yonder dark monarch, who rules the realm of Tartarus. Dost thou not see that even in heaven some despise our power ? Minerva and Diana defy us ; and there is that daughter of Ceres, goddess of earth, who threatens to follow their example. Now, if thou regardest thine own interest or mine, join these two in one." The boy selected his sharpest and truest arrow, and sped it right to the heart of Pluto.

[1] Ovid, Metam. 5, 341–347.

159

In the vale of Enna is a lake embowered in woods, where Spring reigns perpetual. Here Proserpine (Persephone) was playing with her companions, gathering lilies and violets, and singing, one may imagine, such words as our poet Shelley puts into her mouth :

> Sacred Goddess, Mother Earth,
> Thou from whose immortal bosom,
> Gods, and men, and beasts, have birth,
> Leaf and blade, and bud and blossom,
> Breathe thine influence most divine
> On thine own child, Proserpine.
>
> If with mists of evening dew
> Thou dost nourish these young flowers
> Till they grow, in scent and hue,
> Fairest children of the hours,
> Breathe thine influence most divine
> On thine own child, Proserpine.[1]

Pluto saw her, loved her, and carried her off. She screamed for help to her mother and her companions ; but the ravisher urged on his steeds and outdistanced pursuit. When he reached the river Cyane, it opposed his passage, whereupon he struck the bank with his trident, and the earth opened and gave him a passage to Tartarus.

116. The Wanderings of Ceres.[2] Ceres (Demeter) sought her daughter all the world over. Bright-haired Aurora, when she came forth in the morning, and Hesperus, when he led out the stars in the evening, found her still busy in the search. At length, weary and sad, she sat down upon a stone, and remained nine days and nights in the open air, under the sunlight and moonlight and falling showers. It was where now stands the city of Eleusis, near the home of an old man named Celeus. His little girl, pitying the old woman, said to her, " Mother,"— and the name was sweet to the ears of Ceres, — " why sittest thou here alone upon the rocks ? " The old man begged her to come into his cottage. She declined. He urged her. " Go in peace," she replied, " and be happy in thy

---

1 Song of Proserpine, while gathering flowers on the plain of Enna.
2 Ovid, Metam. 5. 440, 642 ; Apollodorus, 1, 5, § 2 ; Hyginus, Fab. 147.

daughter; I have lost mine." But their compassion finally prevailed. Ceres rose from the stone and went with them. As they walked, Celeus said that his only son lay sick of a fever. The goddess stooped and gathered some poppies. Then, entering the cottage, where all was in distress, — for the boy Triptolemus seemed past recovery, — she restored the child to life and health with a kiss. In grateful happiness the family spread the table and put upon it curds and cream, apples, and honey in the comb. While they ate, Ceres mingled poppy juice in the milk of the boy. When night came, she arose and, taking the sleeping boy, molded his limbs with her hands, and uttered over him three times a solemn charm, then went and laid him in the ashes. His mother, who had been watching what her guest was doing, sprang forward with a cry and

FIG. 89. HADES AND PERSEPHONE

snatched the child from the fire. Then Ceres assumed her own form, and a divine splendor shone all around. While they were overcome with astonishment, she said, "Mother, thou hast been cruel in thy fondness; for I would have made thy son immortal. Nevertheless, he shall be great and useful. He shall teach men the use of the plow and the rewards which labor can win from the soil." So saying, she wrapped a cloud about her and mounting her chariot rode away.

Ceres continued her search for her daughter till at length she returned to Sicily, whence she first had set out, and stood by the

banks of the river Cyane. The river nymph would have told the
goddess all she had witnessed, but dared not, for fear of Pluto;
so she ventured merely to take up the girdle which Proserpine had
dropped in her flight, and float it to the feet of the mother. Ceres,
seeing this, laid her curse on the innocent earth in which her
daughter had disappeared. Then succeeded drought and famine,
flood and plague, until, at last, the fountain Arethusa made inter-

FIG. 90. SACRIFICE TO DEMETER AND PERSEPHONE

cession for the land. For she had seen that it opened only unwill-
ingly to the might of Pluto; and she had also, in her flight from
Alpheus through the lower regions of the earth, beheld the missing Proserpine. She said that the daughter of Ceres seemed sad,
but no longer showed alarm in her countenance. Her look was
such as became a queen, — the queen of Erebus; the powerful
bride of the monarch of the realms of the dead.

When Ceres heard this, she stood awhile like one stupefied;
then she implored Jupiter to interfere to procure the restitution

of her daughter. Jupiter consented on condition that Proserpine should not during her stay in the lower world have taken any food; otherwise, the Fates forbade her release. Accordingly, Mercury was sent, accompanied by Spring, to demand Proserpine of Pluto. The wily monarch consented; but alas! the maiden had taken a pomegranate which Pluto offered her, and had sucked the sweet pulp from a few of the seeds. A compromise, however, was effected by which she was to pass half the time with her mother, and the rest with the lord of Hades.

Of modern poems upon the story of the maiden seized in the vale of Enna, none conveys a lesson more serene of the beauty of that dark lover of all fair life, Death, than the Proserpine of Woodberry, from which we quote the three following stanzas. "I pick," says the poet wandering through the vale of Enna,

> I pick the flowers that Proserpine let fall,
>   Sung through the world by every honeyed muse:
> Wild morning-glories, daisies waving tall,
>   At every step is something new to choose;
>   And oft I stop and gaze
>   Upon the flowery maze;
> By yonder cypresses on that soft rise,
>   Scarce seen through poppies and the knee-deep wheat,
>   Juts the dark cleft where on her came the fleet
> Thunder-black horses and the cloud's surprise
>   And he who filled the place.
> Did marigolds bright as these, gilding the mist,
> Drop from her maiden zone? Wert thou last kissed,
>   Pale hyacinth, last seen, before his face?
>
>   .   .   .   .
>
> Oh, whence has silence stolen on all things here,
>   Where every sight makes music to the eye?
> Through all one unison is singing clear;
>   All sounds, all colors in one rapture die.
>   Breathe slow, O heart, breathe slow!
>   A presence from below
> Moves toward the breathing world from that dark deep,
>   Whereof men fabling tell what no man knows,
>   By little fires amid the winter snows,
> When earth lies stark in her titanic sleep

And doth with cold expire;
He brings thee all, O Maiden flower of earth,
Her child in whom all nature comes to birth,
Thee, the fruition of all dark desire.

.   .   .   .

O Proserpine, dream not that thou art gone
Far from our loves, half-human, half-divine;
Thou hast a holier adoration won
In many a heart that worships at no shrine.
Where light and warmth behold me,
And flower and wheat infold me,
I lift a dearer prayer than all prayers past:
He who so loved thee that the live earth clove
Before his pathway unto light and love,
And took thy flower-full bosom, — who at last
Shall every blossom cull, —
Lover the most of what is most our own,
The mightiest lover that the world has known,
Dark lover, Death, — was he not beautiful? [1]

117. Triptolemus and the Eleusinian Mysteries. Ceres, pacified with this arrangement, restored the earth to her favor. Now she

FIG. 91. TRIPTOLEMUS AND THE ELEUSINIAN DEITIES

remembered, also, Celeus and his family, and her promise to his infant son Triptolemus. She taught the boy the use of the plow and how to sow the seed. She took him in her chariot, drawn by

[1] From Proserpine, stanzas written by Lake Pergusa; by George E. Woodberry (*Century Magazine*, July, 1909).

winged dragons, through all the countries of the earth ; and under her guidance he imparted to mankind valuable grains and the knowledge of agriculture. After his return Triptolemus built a temple to Ceres in Eleusis and established the worship of the goddess under the name of the Eleusinian mysteries, which in the splendor and solemnity of their observance surpassed all other religious celebrations among the Greeks.

118. Orpheus and Eurydice.[1] Of mortals who have visited Hades and returned, none has a sweeter or sadder history than Orpheus, son of Apollo and the Muse Calliope. Presented by his father with a lyre and taught to play upon it, he became the most famous of musicians, and not only his fellow mortals but even the wild beasts were softened by his strains. The very trees and rocks were sensible to the

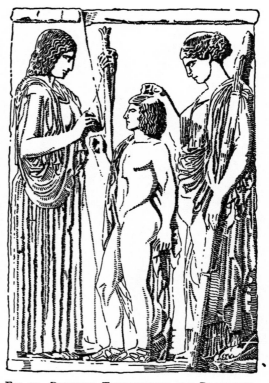

FIG. 92. DEMETER, TRIPTOLEMUS, AND PROSERPINA

charm. And so also was Eurydice, — whom he loved and won.

Hymen was called to bless with his presence the nuptials of Orpheus with Eurydice, but he conveyed no happy omens with him. His torch smoked and brought tears into the eyes. In keeping with such sad prognostics, Eurydice, shortly after her marriage, was seen by the shepherd Aristæus, who was struck with her beauty

[1] Ovid, Metam. 10, 1–77.

and made advances to her. As she fled she trod upon a snake in the grass, and was bitten in the foot. She died. Orpheus sang his grief to all who breathed the upper air, both gods and men, and finding his complaint of no avail, resolved to seek his wife in the regions of the dead. He descended by a cave situated on the side of the promontory of Tænarus, and arrived in the Stygian realm.

FIG. 93. ORPHEUS AND EURYDICE

From the painting by Lord Leighton

He passed through crowds of ghosts and presented himself before the throne of Pluto and Proserpine. Accompanying his words with the lyre, he sang his petition for his wife. Without her he would not return. In such tender strains he sang that the very ghosts shed tears. Tantalus, in spite of his thirst, stopped for a moment his efforts for water, Ixion's wheel stood still, the vulture ceased to tear the giant's liver, the daughters of Danaüs rested from their task of drawing water in a sieve, and Sisyphus sat on his rock to listen.[1] Then for the first time, it is said, the cheeks of the Furies were wet with tears. Proserpine could not resist and Pluto himself gave way. Eurydice was called. She came from among the new-arrived ghosts, limping with her wounded foot. Orpheus was permitted to take her away with him on condition that he should not turn round to look at her till they should have reached the upper air. Under this condition they proceeded on their way, he leading, she following. Mindful of his promise, without let or hindrance the bard passed through the horrors of hell. All Hades held its breath.

[1] See Commentary.

. . . On he stept,
And Cerberus held agape his triple jaws;
On stept the bard. Ixion's wheel stood still.
Now, past all peril, free was his return,
And now was hastening into upper air
Eurydice, when sudden madness seized
The incautious lover; pardonable fault,

FIG. 94. FAREWELL OF ORPHEUS AND EURYDICE

If they below could pardon: on the verge
Of light he stood, and on Eurydice
(Mindless of fate, alas! and soul-subdued)
Lookt back.

         There, Orpheus! Orpheus! there was all
Thy labor shed, there burst the Dynast's bond,
And thrice arose that rumor from the lake.
  "Ah, what!" she cried, " what madness hath undone
Me! and, ah, wretched! thee, my Orpheus, too!
For lo! the cruel Fates recall me now;
Chill slumbers press my swimming eyes. . . . Farewell!

Night rolls intense around me as I spread
My helpless arms . . . thine, thine no more . . . to thee."
She spake, and, like a vapor, into air
Flew, nor beheld him as he claspt the void
And sought to speak; in vain; the ferry-guard
Now would not row him o'er the lake again,
His wife twice lost, what could he? whither go?
What chant, what wailing, move the Powers of Hell?
Cold in the Stygian bark and lone was she.

Beneath a rock o'er Strymon's flood on high,
Seven months, seven long-continued months, 't is said,
He breath'd his sorrows in a desert cave,
And sooth'd the tiger, moved the oak, with song.[1]

The Thracian maidens tried their best to captivate him, but he
repulsed their advances. Finally, excited by the rites of Bacchus,
one of them exclaimed, " See yonder our despiser!" and threw
at him her javelin. The weapon, as soon as it came within the
sound of his lyre, fell harmless at his feet; so also the stones that
they threw at him. But the women, raising a scream, drowned
the voice of the music, and overwhelmed him with their missiles.
Like maniacs they tore him limb from limb; then cast his head
and lyre into the river Hebrus, down which they floated, murmuring
sad music to which the shores responded. The Muses buried
the fragments of his body at Libethra, where the nightingale is
said to sing over his grave more sweetly than in any other part of
Greece. His lyre was placed by Jupiter among the stars; but the
shade of the bard passed a second time to Tartarus and rejoined
Eurydice.

Other mortals who visited the Stygian realm and returned were
Hercules, Theseus, Ulysses, and Æneas.[2]

[1] From W. S. Landor's Orpheus and Eurydice in Dry Sticks.   [2] See Index.

CHAPTER X

MYTHS OF NEPTUNE, RULER OF THE WATERS

119. Lord of the Sea. Neptune (Poseidon) was lord both of salt waters and of fresh. The myths that turn on his life as lord of the sea illustrate his defiant invasions of lands belonging to other gods, or his character as earth shaker and earth protector. Of his contests with other gods, that with Minerva for Athens has been related. He contested Corinth with Helios, Argos with Juno, Ægina with Jove, Naxos with Bacchus, and Delphi with Apollo. That he did not always make encroachments in person upon the land that he desired to possess or to punish, but sent some monster instead, will be seen in the myth of Andromeda[1] and in the following story of Hesione,[2] the daughter of Laomedon of Troy.

FIG. 95. POSEIDON

Neptune and Apollo had fallen under the displeasure of Jupiter after the overthrow of the giants. They were compelled, it is said, to resign for a season their respective functions and to serve Laomedon, then about to build the city of Troy. They aided the king in erecting the walls of the city but were refused the wages agreed upon. Justly offended, Neptune ravaged the land by floods

---

[1] § 154.   [2] Iliad, 5, 649; Apollodorus, 3, 12, § 7.

and sent against it a sea monster, to satiate the appetite of which the desperate Laomedon was driven to offer his daughter Hesione. But Hercules appeared upon the scene, killed the monster, and rescued the maiden. Neptune, however, nursed his wrath; and it was still warm when the Greeks marched against Troy.

Of a like impetuous and ungovernable temper were the sons of Neptune by mortal mothers. From him were sprung the savage Læstrygonians, Orion, the Cyclops Polyphemus, the giant Antæus whom Hercules slew, Procrustes, and many another redoubtable being whose fortunes are elsewhere recounted.[1]

120. Lord of Streams and Fountains. As earth shaker, the ruler of the deep was known to effect convulsions of nature that made Pluto leap from his throne lest the firmament of the underworld might be falling about his ears. But as god of the streams and fountains, Neptune displayed milder characteristics. When Amymone, sent by her father Danaüs to draw water, was pursued by a satyr, Neptune gave ear to her cry for help, dispatched the satyr, made love to the maiden, and boring the earth with his trident called forth the spring that still bears the Danaïd's name. He loved the goddess Ceres also, through whose pastures his rivers strayed; and Arne the shepherdess, daughter of King Æolus, by whom he became the forefather of the Bœotians. His children, Pelias and Neleus, by the princess·Tyro, whom he wooed in the form of her lover Enipeus, became keepers of horses — animals especially dear to Neptune. Perhaps it was the similarity of horse-taming to wave-taming that attracted the god to these quadrupeds; perhaps it was because they increased in beauty and speed on the pastures watered by his streams. It is said, indeed, that the first and fleetest of horses, Arion, was the offspring of Neptune and Ceres, or of Neptune and a Fury.

121. Pelops and Hippodamia.[2] To Pelops, brother of Niobe, Neptune imparted skill in training and driving horses, — and with good effect. For it happened that Pelops fell in love with Hippodamia, daughter of Œnomaüs, king of Elis and son of Mars, — a girl of whom it was reported that none could win her save by worsting the father in a chariot race, and that none might fail in

---

[1] See Index.   [2] Hyginus, Fab. 84, 253; Pindar, Olymp. 1, 114.

that race and come off alive. Since an oracle, too, had warned
Œnomaüs to beware of the future husband of his daughter, he had
provided himself with horses whose speed was like the cyclone.
But Pelops, obtaining from Neptune winged steeds, entered the
race and won it, — whether by the speed of his horses or by the
aid of Hippodamia, who, it is said, bribed her father's charioteer,
Myrtilus, to take a bolt out of the chariot of Œnomaüs, is uncertain. At any rate, Pelops married Hippodamia. He was so injudi-
cious, however, as to throw Myrtilus into the sea ; and from that
treachery sprang the misfortunes of the house of Pelops. For
Myrtilus, dying, cursed the murderer and his race.

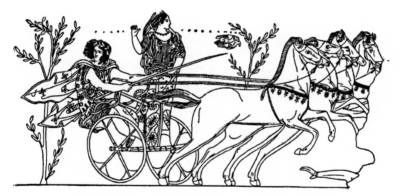

FIG. 96. PELOPS WINNING THE RACE, HIPPODAMIA LOOKING ON

CHAPTER XI

MYTHS OF THE LESSER DIVINITIES OF HEAVEN

122. Myths of Stars and Winds. The tales of Stars and Winds and the other lesser powers of the celestial regions are closely interwoven. That the winds which sweep heaven should kiss the stars is easy to understand. The stories of Aurora (Eos) and of Aura, of Phosphor and of Halcyone, form, therefore, a ready sequence.

FIG. 97. PHOSPHOR, EOS, AND HELIOS (THE SUN) RISING FROM THE SEA

123. Cephalus and Procris.[1] Aurora, the goddess of the dawn, fell in love with Cephalus, a young huntsman. She stole him away, lavished her love upon him, tried to content him, but in vain. He cared for his young wife Procris more than for the goddess. Finally, Aurora dismissed him in displeasure, saying, "Go, ungrateful mortal, keep thy wife; but thou shalt one day be sorry that thou didst ever see her again."

Cephalus returned and was as happy as before in his wife. She, being a favorite of Diana, had received from her for the chase a dog and a javelin, which she handed over to her husband. Of the dog it is told that when about to catch the swiftest fox in

[1] Ovid, Metam. 7, 394 *et seq.*

172

the country, he was changed with his victim into stone. For the heavenly powers, who had made both and rejoiced in the speed of both, were not willing that either should conquer. The javelin was destined to a sad office. It appears that Cephalus, when weary of the chase, was wont to stretch himself in a certain shady nook to enjoy the breeze. Sometimes he would say aloud, "Come, gentle Aura, sweet goddess of the breeze, come and allay the heat that burns me." Some one, foolishly believing that he addressed a maiden, told the secret to Procris. Hoping against hope, she stole out after him the next morning and concealed herself in the

FIG. 98. SUN, RISING, PRECEDED BY DAWN

From the painting by Guido Reni

place which the informer had indicated. Cephalus, when tired with sport, stretched himself on the green bank and summoned fair Aura as usual. Suddenly he heard, or thought he heard, a sound as of a sob in the bushes. Supposing it to proceed from some wild animal, he threw his javelin at the spot. A cry told him that the weapon had too surely met its mark. He rushed to the place and raised his wounded Procris from the earth. She, at last, opened her feeble eyes and forced herself to utter these words: "I implore thee, if thou hast ever loved me, if I have ever de-served kindness at thy hands, my husband, grant me this last request; marry not that odious Breeze!" So saying, she expired in her lover's arms.

FIG. 99. SUNRISE; EOS PURSUING CEPHALUS

124. Dobson's The Death of Procris.

A different version of the story is given in the following :

Procris, the nymph, had wedded
    Cephalus ; —
  He, till the spring had warmed to
    slow-winged days
Heavy with June, untired and amorous,
  Named her his love ; but . now, in
    unknown ways,
His heart was gone ; and evermore
  his gaze
  Turned from her own, and even
    farther ranged
His woodland war ; while she, in dull
  amaze,
  Beholding with the hours her hus-
    band changed,
  Sighed for his lost caress, by some
    hard god estranged.

So, on a day, she rose and found him not.
  Alone, with wet, sad eye, she watched
    the shade
Brighten below a soft-rayed sun that shot
  Arrows of light through all the deep-
    leaved glade ;
Then, with weak hands, she knotted
  up the braid
  Of her brown hair, and o'er her
    shoulders cast
Her crimson weed ; with faltering fin-
  gers made
  Her golden girdle's clasp to join,
    and past
  Down to the trackless wood, full pale
    and overcast.

And all day long her slight spear
  devious flew,
  And harmless swerved her arrows
    from their aim,

For ever, as the ivory bow she drew,
  Before her ran the still unwounded game.
Then, at the last, a hunter's cry there came,
  And, lo! a hart that panted with the chase.
Thereat her cheek was lightened as with flame,
  And swift she gat her to a leafy place,
  Thinking, " I yet may chance unseen to see his face."

Leaping he went, this hunter Cephalus,
  Bent in his hand his cornel bow he bare,
Supple he was, round-limbed and vigorous,
  Fleet as his dogs, a lean Laconian pair.
He, when he spied the brown of Procris' hair
  Move in the covert, deeming that apart
Some fawn lay hidden, loosed an arrow there;
  Nor cared to turn and seek the speeded dart,
  Bounding above the fern, fast following up the hart.

But Procris lay among the white wind-flowers,
  Shot in the throat. From out the little wound
The slow blood drained, as drops in autumn showers
  Drip from the leaves upon the sodden ground.
None saw her die but Lelaps, the swift hound,
  That watched her dumbly with a wistful fear,
Till, at the dawn, the hornèd wood-men found
  And bore her gently on a sylvan bier,
  To lie beside the sea, — with many an uncouth tear.

125. Ceyx and Halcyone. The son of Aurora and Cephalus was Phosphor, the Star of Morning. His son Ceyx, king of Trachis in Thessaly, had married Halcyone, daughter of Æolus.[1] Their reign was happy until the brother of Ceyx met his death. The direful prodigies that followed this event made Ceyx feel that the gods were hostile to him. He thought best therefore to make a voyage to Claros in Ionia to consult the oracle of Apollo. In spite of his wife's entreaties (for as daughter of the god of winds she knew how dreadful a thing a storm at sea was), Ceyx set sail. He was shipwrecked and drowned. His last prayer was that the waves might bear his body to the sight of Halcyone, and that it might receive burial at her hands.

[1] Ovid, Metam. 11, 583-748.

In the meanwhile, Halcyone counted the days till her husband's promised return. To all the gods she offered frequent incense, but more than all to Juno. The goddess, at last, could not bear to be further pleaded with for one already dead. Calling Iris, she enjoined her to approach the drowsy dwelling of Somnus and bid him send a vision to Halcyone in the form of Ceyx, to reveal the sad event.

FIG. 100. THE GOD OF SLEEP

Iris puts on her robe of many colors, and tinging the sky with her bow, seeks the cave near the Cimmerian country, which is the abode of the dull god, Somnus. Here Phœbus dare not come. Clouds and shadows are exhaled from the ground, and the light glimmers faintly. The cock never there calls aloud to Aurora, nor watchdog nor goose disturbs the silence. No wild beast, nor cattle, nor branch moved with the wind, nor sound of human conversation breaks the stillness. From the bottom of the rock the river Lethe flows, and by its murmur invites to sleep. Poppies grow before the door of the cave, from whose juices Night distills slumbers which she scatters over the darkened earth. There is no gate to creak on its hinges, nor any watchman. In the midst, on a couch of black ebony adorned with black plumes and black curtains the god reclines, his limbs relaxed in sleep. Around him lie dreams, resembling all various forms, as many as the harvest bears stalks, or the forest leaves, or the seashore sand grains.

Brushing away the dreams that hovered around her, Iris lit up the cave and delivered her message to the god, who, scarce opening his eyes, had great difficulty in shaking himself free from himself.

Then Iris hasted away from the drowsiness creeping over her, and returned by her bow as she had come. But Somnus called one of his sons, Morpheus, the most expert in counterfeiting forms of men, to perform the command of Iris; then laid his head on his pillow and yielded himself again to grateful repose.

Morpheus flew on silent wings to the Hæmonian city, where he assumed the form of Ceyx. Pale like a dead man, naked and dripping, he stood before the couch of the wretched wife and told her that the winds of the Ægean had sunk his ship, that he was dead.

Weeping and groaning, Halcyone sprang from sleep and, with the dawn, hastening to the seashore, descried an indistinct object washed to and fro by the waves. As it floated nearer she recognized the body of her husband. In despair, leaping from the mole, she was changed instantly to a bird, and poured forth a song of grief as she flew. By the mercy of the gods Ceyx was likewise transformed. For seven days before and seven days after the winter solstice, Jove forbids the winds to blow. Then Halcyon broods over her nest; then the way is safe to seafarers. Æolus confines the winds that his grandchildren may have peace.

126. Aurora and Tithonus.[1] Aurora seems frequently to have been inspired with the love of mortals. Her greatest favorite, and almost her latest, was Tithonus, son of Laomedon, king of Troy. She stole him away and prevailed on Jupiter to grant him immortality; but forgetting to have youth joined in the gift, after some time she began to discern, to her great mortification, that he was growing old. When his hair was white she left his society; but he still had the range of her palace, lived on ambrosial food, and was clad in celestial raiment. In time he lost the power of using his limbs; and then she shut him up in his chamber, whence his feeble voice might at times be heard. Finally, she turned him into a grasshopper.

127. Tennyson's Tithonus. The following is, according to a fine poetic conception, the lament of the old man when but a white-haired shadow:

> The woods decay, the woods decay and fall,
> The vapors weep their burthen to the ground,
> Man comes and tills the field and lies beneath,
> And after many a summer dies the swan.
> Me only cruel immortality

[1] Homeric Hymn to Venus; Horace, Odes, 1, 22; 2, 16; Apollodorus, 3, 12, § 4.

Consumes: I wither slowly in thine arms,
Here at the quiet limit of the world,
A white-haired shadow roaming like a dream
The ever silent spaces of the East,
Far-folded mists, and gleaming halls of morn.

Alas! for this gray shadow, once a man —
So glorious in his beauty and thy choice,
Who madest him thy chosen, that he seem'd
To his great heart none other than a God!
I ask'd thee, " Give me immortality."
Then didst thou grant mine asking with a smile,
Like wealthy men who care not how they give;
But thy strong Hours indignant work'd their wills,
And beat me down and marr'd and wasted me,
And tho' they could not end me, left me maim'd
To dwell in presence of immortal youth,
Immortal age beside immortal youth,
And all I was, in ashes. Can thy love,
Thy beauty, make amends, tho' even now,
Close over us, the silver star, thy guide,
Shines in those tremulous eyes that fill with tears
To hear me? Let me go: take back thy gift:
Why should a man desire in any way
To vary from the kindly race of men,
Or pass beyond the goal of ordinance
Where all should pause, as is most meet for all?

A soft air fans the cloud apart; there comes
A glimpse of that dark world where I was born.
Once more the old mysterious glimmer steals
From thy pure brows, and from thy shoulders pure
And bosom beating with a heart renew'd.
Thy cheek begins to redden thro' the gloom,
Thy sweet eyes brighten slowly close to mine,
Ere yet they blind the stars, and the wild team
Which love thee, yearning for thy yoke, arise,
And shake the darkness from their loosen'd manes,
And beat the twilight into flakes of fire.

Lo! ever thus thou growest beautiful
In silence, then before thine answer given
Departest, and thy tears are on my cheek.

Why wilt thou ever scare me with thy tears,
And make me tremble lest a saying learnt
In days far-off, on that dark earth, be true?
" The gods themselves cannot recall their gifts."

Ay me! ay me! with what another heart
In days far-off, and with what other eyes
I used to watch — if I be he that watched —
The lucid outline forming round thee; saw
The dim curls kindle into sunny rings;
Changed with thy mystic change, and felt my blood
Glow with the glow that slowly crimson'd all
Thy presence and thy portals, while I lay,
Mouth, forehead, eyelids, growing dewy-warm
With kisses balmier than half-opening buds
Of April, and could hear the lips that kiss'd
Whispering I knew not what of wild and sweet,
Like that strange song I heard Apollo sing,
While Ilion like a mist rose into towers.

Yet hold me not forever in thine East:
How can my nature longer mix with thine?
Coldly thy rosy shadows bathe me, cold
Are all thy lights, and cold my wrinkled feet
Upon thy glimmering thresholds, when the steam
Floats up from those dim fields about the homes
Of happy men that have the power to die,
And grassy barrows of the happier dead.
Release me, and restore me to the ground;
Thou seëst all things, thou wilt see my grave:
Thou wilt renew thy beauty morn by morn;
I earth in earth forget these empty courts,
And thee returning on thy silver wheels.

128. Memnon, the son of Aurora and Tithonus, was king of the Æthiopians. He went with warriors to assist his kindred in the Trojan War, and was received by King Priam with honor. He fought bravely, slew Antilochus, the brave son of Nestor, and held the Greeks at bay until Achilles appeared. Before that hero he fell.

Then Aurora, seeing her son's fate, directed his brothers, the Winds, to convey his body to the banks of the river Æsepus in Mysia. In the evening Aurora, accompanied by the Hours and

the Pleiads, bewept her son. Night spread the heaven with clouds;
all nature mourned for the offspring of the Dawn. The Æthiopians raised his tomb on the banks of the stream in the grove of

the Nymphs, and Jupiter
caused the sparks and
cinders of his funeral pile
to be turned into birds,
which, dividing into two
flocks, fought over the
pile till they fell into the
flame. Every year at
the anniversary of his
death they celebrated his
obsequies in like manner.
Aurora remained incon-
solable. The dewdrops
are her tears.[1]

The kinship of Mem-
non to the Dawn is certi-
fied even after his death.

FIG. 101. THE DEATH OF MEMNON

On the banks of the Nile are two colossal statues, one of which
is called Memnon's; and it was said that when the first rays of
morning fell upon this statue, a sound like the snapping of a harp-
string issued therefrom.[2]

> So to the sacred Sun in Memnon's fane
> Spontaneous concords choired the matin strain;
> Touched by his orient beam responsive rings
> The living lyre and vibrates all its strings;
> Accordant aisles the tender tones prolong,
> And holy echoes swell the adoring song.[3]

[1] Ovid, Metam. 13, 622, etc.   Odyssey, 4, 188; 11, 522.   Pindar, Pyth. 6, 30.
[2] Pausanias, 1, 42, § 2.   [3] Darwin, Botanic Garden.

CHAPTER XII

MYTHS OF THE LESSER DIVINITIES OF EARTH, ETC.

129. Pan, and the Personification of Nature. It was a pleasing trait in the old paganism that it loved to trace in every operation of nature the agency of deity. The imagination of the Greeks peopled the regions of earth and sea with divinities, to whose agency it attributed the phenomena that our philosophy ascribes to the operation of natural law. So Pan, the god of woods and fields,[1] whose name seemed to signify *all*, came to be considered a symbol of the universe and a personification of Nature. "Universal Pan," says Milton in his description of the creation:

> Universal Pan,
> Knit with the Graces and the Hours in dance,
> Led on the eternal Spring.

Later, Pan came to be regarded as a representative of all the Greek gods and of paganism itself. Indeed, according to an early Christian tradition, when the heavenly host announced to the shepherds the birth of Christ, a deep groan, heard through the isles of Greece, told that great Pan was dead, that the dynasty of Olympus was dethroned, and the several deities sent wandering in cold and darkness.

> The lonely mountains o'er,
> And the resounding shore,
>   A voice of weeping heard and loud lament;
> From haunted spring and dale,
> Edged with poplar pale,
>   The parting Genius is with sighing sent;
> With flower-inwoven tresses torn,
> The nymphs in twilight shade of tangled thickets mourn.[2]

[1] His name is not derived from the Greek *pān*, all, but from the root *pā*, to feed, to pasture (i.e. the flocks and herds).   [2] Milton, Hymn on the Nativity.

Many a poet has lamented the change. For even if the head did profit for a time by the revolt against the divine prerogative of nature, it is more than possible that the heart lost in due proportion.

His sorrow at this loss of imaginative sympathy among the moderns Wordsworth expresses in the sonnet, already cited, beginning "The world is too much with us." Schiller, also, by his poem, The Gods of Greece, has immortalized his sorrow for the decadence of the ancient mythology.

FIG. 102. PAN BLOWING
HIS PIPE, ECHO
ANSWERING

Ah, the beauteous world while yet ye ruled it, —
    Yet — by gladsome touches of the hand;
Ah, the joyous hearts that still ye governed,
    Gods of Beauty, ye, of Fable-land!
Then, ah, then, the mysteries resplendent
    Triumphed. — Other was it then, I ween,
When thy shrines were odorous with garlands,
    Thou, of Amathus the queen.

Then the gracious veil, of fancy woven,
    Fell in folds about the fact uncouth;
Through the universe life flowed in fullness,
    What we feel not now was felt in sooth:
Man ascribed nobility to Nature,
    Rendered love unto the earth he trod,
Everywhere his eye, illuminated,
    Saw the footprints of a God.

. . . .

Lovely world, where art thou? Turn, oh, turn thee,
    Fairest blossom-tide of Nature's spring!
Only in the poet's realm of wonder
    Liv'st thou, still, — a fable vanishing.
Reft of life the meadows lie deserted;
    Ne'er a godhead can my fancy see:
Ah, if only of those living colors
    Lingered yet the ghost with me![1]

. . . .

It was the poem from which these stanzas are taken that provoked the well-known reply of Elizabeth Barrett Browning,

[1] Translated by C. M. Gayley.

contained in The Dead Pan. Her argument may be gathered
from the following stanzas :

> By your beauty which confesses
> Some chief Beauty conquering you,
> By our grand heroic guesses
> Through your falsehood at the True,
> We will weep *not!* earth shall roll
> Heir to each god's aureole,
> > And Pan is dead.

> Earth outgrows the mythic fancies
> Sung beside her in her youth ;
> And those debonair romances
> Sound but dull beside the truth.
> Phœbus' chariot course is run !
> Look up, poets, to the sun !
> > Pan, Pan is dead.

130. Stedman's Pan in Wall Street.[1] That Pan, however, is not
yet dead but alive even in the practical atmosphere of our western
world, the poem here appended, written by one of our recently
deceased American poets, would indicate.

> Just where the Treasury's marble front
> > Looks over Wall Street's mingled nations ;
> Where Jews and Gentiles most are wont
> > To throng for trade and last quotations ;
> Where, hour by hour, the rates of gold
> > Outrival, in the ears of people,
> The quarter chimes, serenely tolled
> > From Trinity's undaunted steeple, —

> Even there I heard a strange, wild strain
> > Sound high above the modern clamor,
> Above the cries of greed and gain,
> > The curbstone war, the auction's hammer ;
> And swift, on Music's misty ways,
> > It led, from all this strife for millions,
> To ancient, sweet-do-nothing days
> > Among the kirtle-robed Sicilians.

[1] By Edmund Clarence Stedman.

FIG. 103. THE MUSIC LESSON

And as it still'd the multitude,
　And yet more joyous rose, and shriller,
I saw the minstrel where he stood
　At ease against a Doric pillar:
One hand a droning organ play'd,
　The other held a Pan's pipe (fashioned
Like those of old) to lips that made
　The reeds give out that strain impassioned.

'T was Pan himself had wandered here,
　A-strolling through the sordid city,
And piping to the civic ear
　The prelude of some pastoral ditty!
The demigod had cross'd the seas, —
　From haunts of shepherd, nymph, and satyr,
And Syracusan times, — to these
　Far shores and twenty centuries later.

A ragged cap was on his head:
　But — hidden thus — there was no doubting
That, all with crispy locks o'erspread,
　His gnarlèd horns were somewhere sprouting;
His club-feet, cased in rusty shoes,
Were cross'd, as on some frieze you see them.
And trousers, patched of divers hues,
　Conceal'd his crooked shanks beneath them.

FIG. 104. BACCHIC DANCE

He filled the quivering reeds with sound,
　And o'er his mouth their changes shifted,
And with his goat's-eyes looked around
　Where'er the passing current drifted;
And soon, as on Trinacrian hills
　The nymphs and herdsmen ran to hear him,
Even now the tradesmen from their tills,
　With clerks and porters, crowded near him.

The bulls and bears together drew
    From Jauncey Court and New Street Alley
As erst, if pastorals be true,
    Came beasts from every wooded valley;
The random passers stay'd to list, —
    A boxer Ægon, rough and merry, —
A Broadway Daphnis, on his tryst
    With Naïs at the Brooklyn Ferry.

A one-eyed Cyclops halted long
    In tatter'd cloak of army pattern,
And Galatea joined the throng, —
    A blowsy, apple-vending slattern;
While old Silenus stagger'd out
    From some new-fangled lunch-house handy
And bade the piper, with a shout,
    To strike up " Yankee Doodle Dandy! "

A newsboy and a peanut girl
    Like little Fauns began to caper:
His hair was all in tangled curl,
    Her tawny legs were bare and taper.
And still the gathering larger grew,
    And gave its pence and crowded nigher,
While aye the shepherd-minstrel blew
    His pipe, and struck the gamut higher.

O heart of Nature! beating still
    With throbs her vernal passion taught her, —
Even here, as on the vine-clad hill,
    Or by the Arethusan water!
New forms may fold the speech, new lands
    Arise within these ocean-portals,
But Music waves eternal wands, —
    Enchantress of the souls of mortals!

FIG. 105. SILENUS

So thought I, — but among us trod
    A man in blue with legal baton;
And scoff'd the vagrant demigod,
    And push'd him from the step I sat on.
Doubting I mused upon the cry —
    " Great Pan is dead! " — and all the people
Went on their ways: — and clear and high
    The quarter sounded from the steeple.

131. Other Lesser Gods of Earth. Of the company of the lesser gods of earth, besides Pan, were the Sileni, the Sylvans, the Fauns, and the Satyrs, all male; the Oreads and the Dryads or Hamadryads, female. To these may be added the Naiads, for, although they dwelt in the streams, their association with the deities of earth was intimate. Of the nymphs, the Oreads and the Naiads were immortal. The love of Pan for Syrinx has already been mentioned, and his musical contest with Apollo. Of Silenus we have seen something in the adventures of Bacchus. What kind of existence the Satyr enjoyed is conveyed in the following soliloquy:

FIG. 106. SATYR

> The trunk of this tree,
> Dusky-leaved, shaggy-rooted,
> Is a pillow well suited
> To a hybrid like me,
> Goat-bearded, goat-footed;
> For the boughs of the glade
> Meet above me, and throw

FIG. 107. SATYR SWINGING MAIDEN

A cool, pleasant shade
  On the greenness below;
    Dusky and brown'd
    Close the leaves all around;
And yet, all the while,
  Thro' the boughs I can see
A star, with a smile,
  Looking at me. . . .

Why, all day long,
  I run about
With a madcap throng,
  And laugh and shout.
Silenus grips
  My ears, and strides
On my shaggy hips,
    And up and down
    In an ivy crown
  Tipsily rides;
    And when in doze
    His eyelids close,
Off he tumbles, and I
Can his wine-skin steal,
  I drink — and feel
The grass roll — sea high;
    Then with shouts and yells,
    Down mossy dells,
I stagger after

FIG. 108. SATYR DRINKING

The wood-nymphs fleet,
Who with mocking laughter
  And smiles retreat;
And just as I clasp
    A yielding waist,
    With a cry embraced,
— Gush! it melts from my grasp
    Into water cool,
    And — bubble! trouble!
    Seeing double!
I stumble and gasp
    In some icy pool! [1]

1 From The Satyr, by Robert Buchanan.

132. Echo and Narcissus.[1] Echo was a beautiful Oread, fond of the woods and hills, a favorite of Diana, whom she attended in the chase. But by her chatter she came under the displeasure of Juno, who condemned her to the loss of voice save for purposes of reply.

FIG. 109. NARCISSUS

Subsequently having fallen in love with Narcissus, the beautiful son of the river-god Cephissus, Echo found it impossible to express her regard for him in any way but by mimicking what he said; and what he said, unfortunately, did not always convey her sentiments. When, however, he once called across the hills to her,

1 Ovid, Metam. 3, 339–510.

" Let us join one another," the maid, answering with all her heart, hastened to the spot, ready to throw her arms about his neck. He started back, exclaiming, "Hands off! I would rather die than thou shouldst have me!" "Have me," said she; but in vain. From that time forth she lived in caves and among mountain cliffs, and faded away till there was nothing left of her but her voice. But through his future fortunes she was constant to her cruel lover.

This Narcissus was the embodiment of self-conceit. He shunned the rest of the nymphs as he had shunned Echo. One maiden, however, uttered a prayer that he might some time or other feel what it was to love and meet no return of affection. The avenging goddess heard. Narcissus, stooping over a river brink, fell in love with his own image in the water. He talked to it, tried to embrace it, languished for it, and pined until he died. Indeed, even after death, it is said that when his shade passed the Stygian river it leaned over the boat to catch a look of itself in the waters. The nymphs mourned for Narcissus, especially the water-nymphs; and when they smote their breasts, Echo smote hers also. They prepared a funeral pile and would have burned the body, but it was nowhere to be found. In its place had sprung up a flower, purple within and surrounded with white leaves, which bears the name and preserves the memory of the son of Cephissus.

133. Echo, Pan, Lyde, and the Satyr. Another interesting episode in the life of Echo is given by Moschus :[1]

> Pan loved his neighbor Echo; Echo loved
> A gamesome Satyr; he, by her unmoved,
> Loved only Lyde; thus through Echo, Pan,
> Lyde, and Satyr, Love his circle ran.
> Thus all, while their true lovers' hearts they grieved,
> Were scorned in turn, and what they gave received.
> O all Love's scorners, learn this lesson true:
> Be kind to love, that he be kind to you.

134. The Naiads. These nymphs guarded streams and fountains of fresh water and, like the Naiad who speaks in the following verses, kept them sacred for Diana or some other divinity.

[1] Idyl VI (Lang's translation). For Moschus, see Commentary, § 298.

Dian white-arm'd has given me this cool shrine
Deep in the bosom of a wood of pine:
    The silver-sparkling showers
    That hive me in, the flowers
That prink my fountain's brim, are hers and mine;
  And when the days are mild and fair,
    And grass is springing, buds are blowing,
    Sweet it is, 'mid waters flowing,
  Here to sit and know no care,
    'Mid the waters flowing, flowing, flowing,
Combing my yellow, yellow hair.

The ounce and panther down the mountain side
Creep thro' dark greenness in the eventide;
    And at the fountain's brink
    Casting great shades, they drink,
Gazing upon me, tame and sapphire-eyed;
  For, awed by my pale face, whose light
    Gleameth thro' sedge and lilies yellow
    They, lapping at my fountain mellow,
  Harm not the lamb that in affright
    Throws in the pool so mellow, mellow, mellow,
Its shadow small and dusky-white.

Oft do the fauns and satyrs, flusht with play,
Come to my coolness in the hot noonday.
    Nay, once indeed, I vow
    By Dian's truthful brow,
The great god Pan himself did pass this way,
  And, all in festal oak-leaves clad,
    His limbs among these lilies throwing,
    Watch'd the silver waters flowing,
  Listen'd to their music glad,
    Saw and heard them flowing, flowing, flowing,
And ah! his face was worn and sad!

Mild joys like silvery waters fall;
But it is sweetest, sweetest far of all,
    In the calm summer night,
    When the tree-tops look white,
To be exhaled in dew at Dian's call,

Among my sister-clouds to move
  Over the darkness, earth bedimming,
  Milky-robed thro' heaven swimming,
Floating round the stars above,
  Swimming proudly, swimming proudly, swimming,
And waiting on the Moon I love.

So tenderly I keep this cool, green shrine,
Deep in the bosom of a wood of pine;
  Faithful thro' shade and sun,
  That service due and done
May haply earn for me a place divine
  Among the white-robed deities
  That thread thro' starry paths, attending
  My sweet Lady, calmly wending
Thro' the silence of the skies,
  Changing in hues of beauty never ending,
  Drinking the light of Dian's eyes.[1]

135. The Dryads, or Hamadryads, assumed at times the forms of peasant girls, shepherdesses, or followers of the hunt. But they were believed to perish with certain trees which had been their abode and with which they had come into existence. Wantonly to destroy a tree was therefore an impious act, sometimes severely punished, as in the cases of Erysichthon and Dryope.

136. Erysichthon,[2] a despiser of the gods, presumed to violate with the ax a grove sacred to Ceres. A venerable oak, whereon votive tablets had often been hung inscribed with the gratitude of mortals to the nymph of the tree, — an oak round which the Dryads hand in hand had often danced, — he ordered his servants to fell. When he saw them hesitate, he snatched an ax from one, and boasting that he cared not whether it were a tree beloved of the goddess or not, addressed himself to the task. The oak seemed to shudder and utter a groan. When the first blow fell upon the trunk, blood flowed from the wound. Warned by a bystander to desist, Erysichthon slew him; warned by a voice from the nymph of the tree, he redoubled his blows and brought down the oak. The Dryads invoked punishment upon Erysichthon.

---

[1] From The Naiad, by Robert Buchanan.　　　[2] Ovid, Metam. 8, 738–884.

The goddess Ceres, whom they had supplicated, nodded her assent. She dispatched an Oread to ice-clad Scythia, where Cold abides, and Fear and Shuddering and Famine. At Mount Caucasus, the Oread stayed the dragons of Ceres that drew her chariot; for afar off she beheld Famine, forespent with hunger, pulling up with teeth and claws the scanty herbage from a stony field. To her the nymph delivered the commands of Ceres, then returned in haste to Thessaly, for she herself began to be an hungered.

The orders of Ceres were executed by Famine, who, speeding through the air, entered the dwelling of Erysichthon and, as he slept, enfolded him with her wings and breathed herself into him. In his dreams the caitiff craved food; and when he awoke, his hunger raged. The more he ate, the more he craved, till, in default of money, he sold his daughter into slavery for edibles. Neptune, however, rescued the girl by changing her into a fisherman; and in that form she assured the slave-owner that she had seen no woman or other person, except herself, thereabouts. Then, resuming her own appearance, she was again and again sold by her father; while by Neptune's favor she became on each occasion a different animal, and so regained her home. Finally, increasing demands of hunger compelled the father to devour his own limbs; and in due time he finished himself off.

137. Dryope, the wife of Andræmon, purposing with her sister Iole to gather flowers for the altars of the nymphs, plucked the purple blossoms of a lotus plant that grew near the water, and offered them to her child. Iole, about to do the same thing, perceived that the stem of the plant was bleeding. Indeed, the plant was none other than a nymph, Lotis, who, escaping from a base pursuer, had been thus transformed.

Dryope would have hastened from the spot, but the displeasure of the nymph had fallen upon her. While protesting her innocence, she began to put forth branches and leaves. Praying her husband to see that no violence was done to her, to remind their child that every flower or bush might be a goddess in disguise, to bring him often to be nursed under her branches, and to teach him to say " My mother lies hid under this bark," — the luckless woman assumed the shape of a lotus.

138. Rhœcus.[1] The Hamadryads could appreciate services as well as punish injuries.

> Hear now this fairy legend of old Greece,
> As full of freedom, youth, and beauty still,
> As the immortal freshness of that grace
> Carved for all ages on some Attic frieze.[2]

Rhœcus, happening to see an oak just ready to fall, propped it up. The nymph, who had been on the point of perishing with the tree, expressed her gratitude to him and bade him ask what reward he would. Rhœcus boldly asked her love, and the nymph yielded to his desire. At the same time charging him to be mindful and constant, she promised to expect him an hour before sunset and, meanwhile, to communicate with him by means of her messenger, — a bee :

> Now, in those days of simpleness and faith,
> Men did not think that happy things were dreams
> Because they overstepped the narrow bourn
> Of likelihood, but reverently deemed
> Nothing too wondrous or too beautiful
> To be the guerdon of a daring heart.
> So Rhœcus made no doubt that he was blest,
> And all along unto the city's gate
> Earth seemed to spring beneath him as he walked,
> The clear, broad sky looked bluer than its wont,
> And he could scarce believe he had not wings,
> Such sunshine seemed to glitter through his veins
> Instead of blood, so light he felt and strange.

But the day was past its noon. Joining some comrades over the dice, Rhœcus forgot all else. A bee buzzed about his ear. Impatiently he brushed it aside :

> Then through the window flew the wounded bee,
> And Rhœcus, tracking him with angry eyes,
> Saw a sharp mountain peak of Thessaly
> Against the red disk of the setting sun, —
> And instantly the blood sank from his heart. . . .

[1] See note (Scholium) on the Argonautics of Apollonius, B 477. Keil's edition, p. 415, l. 32.
[2] J. R. Lowell, Rhœcus. The student should read the whole poem.

. . . Quite spent and out of breath he reached the tree,
And, listening fearfully, he heard once more
The low voice murmur, " Rhœcus! " close at hand:
Whereat he looked around him, but could see
Naught but the deepening glooms beneath the oak.
Then sighed the voice, " O Rhœcus! nevermore
Shalt thou behold me or by day or night,
Me, who would fain have blessed thee with a love
More ripe and bounteous than ever yet
Filled up with nectar any mortal heart:
But thou didst scorn my humble messenger
And sent'st him back to me with bruisèd wings.
We spirits only show to gentle eyes,
We ever ask an undivided love,
And he who scorns the least of Nature's works
Is thenceforth exiled and shut out from all.
Farewell! for thou canst never see me more."

Then Rhœcus beat his breast, and groaned aloud,
And cried, " Be pitiful! forgive me yet
This once, and I shall never need it more! "
"Alas! " the voice returned, " 't is thou art blind,
Not I unmerciful; I can forgive,
But have no skill to heal thy spirit's eyes;
Only the soul hath power o'er itself."
With that again there murmured, " Nevermore! "
And Rhœcus after heard no other sound,
Except the rattling of the oak's crisp leaves,
Like the long surf upon a distant shore,
Raking the sea-worn pebbles up and down.
The night had gathered round him: o'er the plain
The city sparkled with its thousand lights,
And sounds of revel fell upon his ear
Harshly and like a curse; above, the sky,
With all its bright sublimity of stars,
Deepened, and on his forehead smote the breeze:
Beauty was all around him and delight,
But from that eve he was alone on earth.

According to the older tradition, the nymph deprived Rhœcus of his physical sight; but the superior insight of Lowell's interpretation is evident.

139. Pomona and Vertumnus.[1] Pomona was a Hamadryad of Roman mythology, guardian especially of the apple orchards, but presiding also over other fruits. "Bear me, Pomona," sings one of our poets, —

> Bear me, Pomona, to thy citron groves,
> To where the lemon and the piercing lime,
> With the deep orange, glowing through the green,
> Their lighter glories blend. Lay me reclined
> Beneath the spreading tamarind that shakes,
> Fanned by the breeze, its fever-cooling fruit.[2]

This nymph had scorned the offers of love made her by Pan, Sylvanus, and innumerable Fauns and Satyrs. Vertumnus, too, she had time and again refused. But he, the deity of gardens and of the changing seasons, unwearied, wooed her in as many guises as his seasons themselves could assume. Now as a reaper, now as haymaker, now as plowman, now as vinedresser, now as apple-picker, now as fisherman, now as soldier, — all to no avail. Finally, as an old woman, he came to her, admired her fruit, admired especially the luxuriance of her grapes, descanted on the dependence of the luxuriant vine, close by, upon the elm to which it was clinging; advised Pomona, likewise, to choose some youth — say, for instance, the young Vertumnus — about whom to twine *her* arms. Then he told how the worthy Iphis, spurned by Anaxarete, had hanged himself to her gatepost; and how the gods had turned the hard-hearted virgin to stone even as she gazed on her lover's funeral. "Consider these things, dearest child," said the seeming old woman, "lay aside thy scorn and thy delays, and accept a lover. So may neither the vernal frosts blight thy young fruits, nor furious winds scatter thy blossoms!"

FIG. 110. A RUSTIC

When Vertumnus had thus spoken, he dropped his disguise and stood before Pomona in his proper person, — a comely youth. Such wooing, of course, could not but win its just reward.

---

[1] Ovid, Metam. 14, 623–771.   [2] Thomson, Seasons.

140. The Cranes of Ibycus.[1] The Furies, called also Diræ (the terrible ones), Erinyes (the persecutors, or the angered ones), and finally, by way of euphemism, Eumenides (the well-meaning), though they were spirits of the underworld, visited earth to punish filial disobedience, irreverence to old age, perjury, murder, treachery to guests, even unkindness toward beggars. They avenged the ghosts of such as, dying violent deaths, possessed on earth no representatives either by law or by kindred to avenge them. Therefore, as we shall see, they persecuted Orestes, who had slain his

FIG. 111. A RUSTIC

mother. Therefore, like the accusing voice of conscience, they marshaled to punishment the murderers of Ibycus.

This poet, beloved of Apollo, was, while journeying to the musical contest of the Isthmus at Corinth, attacked by two robbers in the Corinthian grove of Neptune. Overcome by them, he commended his cause as he fell to a flock of cranes that happened to be screaming hoarsely overhead. But when his body was found, all Greece, then gathered at the festival, demanded vengeance on the murderer.

Soon afterward, the vast assemblage in the amphitheater sat listening to a play in which the Chorus personated the Furies. The Choristers, clad in black, bore in their fleshless hands torches blazing with a pitchy flame. Advancing with measured step, they formed ranks in the orchestra. Their cheeks were bloodless, and in place of hair writhing serpents curled around their brows. Forming a circle, these awful beings sang their hymn. High it swelled, overpowering the sound of the instruments:

"Happy the man whose heart is pure from guilt and crime! Him we avengers touch not; he treads the path of life secure from us. But woe! woe! to him who has done the deed of secret murder. We, the fearful brood of Night, fasten ourselves upon him, soul and flesh. Thinks he by flight to escape us? Fly we

[1] Cf. Cicero, Tusculan Disputations, 4. 33, 71 ; and Statius, Silvæ, 5. 3, 152.

still faster in pursuit, twine our snakes around his feet, and bring him to the ground. Unwearied we pursue; no pity checks our course; still on, still on to the end of life, we give no peace, no rest."

Stillness like the stillness of death sat over the assembly. Suddenly a cry burst from one of the uppermost benches,—"Lo, comrade, the avengers of Ibycus!" A flock of cranes crossed the sky. "The murderer has informed against himself," shouted the assemblage. The inference was correct. The criminals, straightway seized, confessed the crime and suffered the penalty.

CHAPTER XIII

MYTHS OF LESSER DIVINITIES OF THE WATERS

141. Galatea and Polyphemus. The water-gods may be roughly classed as dwellers in the sea and dwellers in the streams. Of the former, daughters of Nereus and Doris, none was fairer than Galatea, sister of Amphitrite and Thetis. She loved Acis, the son of Faunus by a Naiad, and was loved in return; but her happiness was disturbed and finally ruined by the persistent and jealous attentions of the Cyclops Polyphemus.

For the first time in his life the Cyclops began to care for his appearance; he harrowed his coarse locks with a currycomb, mowed his beard with a sickle, and, looking into the sea when it was calm, soliloquized, " Beautiful seems my beard, beautiful my one eye, — as I count beauty, — and the sea reflects the gleam of my teeth whiter than the Parian stone." [1]

. . . He loved, not with apples, not roses, nor locks of hair, but with fatal frenzy; and all things else he held but trifles by the way. Many a time from the green pastures would his ewes stray back, self-shepherded, to the fold. But he was singing of Galatea; and pining in his place, he sat by the seaweed of the beach from the dawn of day with the direst hurt beneath his breast of mighty Cypris' sending, — the wound of her arrow in his heart!

Yet this remedy he found, and sitting on the crest of the tall cliff and looking to the deep, 'twas thus he would sing:

" Oh, milk-white Galatea, why cast off him that loves thee? More white than is pressed milk to look upon, more delicate than the lamb art thou, than the young calf wantoner, more sleek than the unripened grape! Here dost thou resort, even so, when sweet sleep possesses me, and home straightway dost thou depart when sweet sleep lets me go, fleeing me like an ewe that has seen the gray wolf. I fell in love with thee, maiden, I, on the day when first thou camest, with my mother, and didst wish to pluck the hyacinths from the hill, and I was thy guide on the way. But to leave loving thee when

---

[1] Theocritus, Idyl VI. See Andrew Lang's translation.

once I had seen thee, neither afterward, nor now at all, have I the strength, even from that hour. But to thee all this is as nothing, by Zeus, nay, nothing at all!

"I know, thou gracious maiden, why it is that thou dost shun me. It is all for the shaggy brow that spans my forehead, from this to the other ear, one long, unbroken eyebrow. And but one eye is on my forehead, and broad is the nose that overhangs my lip. Yet I (even such as thou seest me) feed a thousand cattle, and from these I draw and drink the best milk in the world. And cheese I never lack, in summer time or autumn, nay, nor in the dead of winter, but my baskets are always overladen.

"Also I am skilled in piping, as none other of the Cyclopes here, and of thee, my love, my sweet apple, and of myself, too, I sing, many a time, deep in the night. And for thee I tend eleven fawns, all crescent browed, and four young whelps of the bear. Nay, come thou to me and thou shalt lack nothing that now thou hast. . . .

"But if thou dost refuse because my body seems shaggy and rough, well, I have faggots of oak-wood, and beneath the ashes is fire unwearied, and I would endure to let thee burn my very soul, and this my one eye, the dearest thing that is mine.

"Ah me, that my mother bore me not a finny thing, so would I have gone down to thee, and kissed thy hand, if thy lips thou would not suffer me to kiss! And I would have brought thee either white

Fig. 112. Galatea and Polyphemus

lilies or the soft poppy with its scarlet petals. Nay, these are summer's flowers, and those are flowers of winter, so I could not have brought thee them all at one time.

"Now, verily, maiden, now and here will I learn to swim, if perchance some stranger come hither, sailing with his ship, that I may see why it is so dear to thee to have thy dwelling in the deep. Come forth, Galatea, and forget as thou comest, even as I that sit here have forgotten, the homeward way! . . .

"Oh, Cyclops, Cyclops, whither are thy wits wandering? Ah, that thou wouldst go and weave thy wickerwork and gather broken boughs to carry to thy lambs: in faith, if thou didst this, far wiser wouldst thou be!

" Milk the ewe that thou hast ; why pursue the thing that shuns thee? Thou wilt find, perchance, another, and a fairer, Galatea. Many be the girls that bid me stay with them, and softly they all laugh, if perchance I answer them. On land it is plain that I, too, seem to be somebody ! " [1]

Having, one day, in such wise sung, Polyphemus wandered, beside himself for passion, into the woods. On a sudden he came in sight of Galatea and Acis in the hollow of a rock, where they had hearkened to the strains of the Cyclops. The monster, infuriate, crying that this should be the last of their love-meetings, overwhelmed his rival with a tremendous rock. Purple blood spirted from under the stone, by degrees grew paler, and finally became the stream that still bears the name of the unfortunate youth. But Galatea remained inconsolable.[2]

FIG. 113. A SEA-GOD

142. Glaucus and Scylla.[3] Another deity of the sea was Glaucus, the son of that Sisyphus who was punished in Hades for his treachery to the gods. Glaucus had been a comely young fisherman ; but having noticed that a certain herb revived fishes after they were brought to land, he ate of it and suffered metamorphosis into something new and strange, half man, half fish, and after the fashion of a sea-god. Of his experience during this " sea change " the following is an account :

I plunged for life or death. To interknit
One's senses with so dense a breathing stuff
Might seem a work of pain ; so not enough
Can I admire how crystal-smooth it felt,
And buoyant round my limbs. At first I dwelt
Whole days and days in sheer astonishment ;
Forgetful utterly of self-intent,
Moving but with the mighty ebb and flow.
Then like a new-fledged bird that first doth show

---

[1] Theocritus, Idyl XI (Lang's translation).   [2] Ovid, Metam. 13, 750–867.
[3] Ovid, Metam. 13, 898 ; 14, 74 ; Tibullus, 3, 4–89.

His spreaded feathers to the morrow chill,
I tried in fear the pinions of my will.
'T was freedom! and at once I visited
The ceaseless wonders of this ocean bed.[1]

He became guardian of fishes and divers and of those who go down to the sea in ships. Later, being infatuated of the fair virgin Scylla (daughter of the sea-god Phorcys and granddaughter of Pontus), he paid his court to her, but the maiden rejected him. Whereupon, in desperation, Glaucus sought the aid of Circe, an enchantress. She, because she coveted for herself the handsome sea-green god, transformed her rival into a monster hideously fashioned of serpents and barking dogs.[2] In this shape Scylla thereafter infested the shore of Sicily and worked evil to mariners,[3] till finally she was petrified as a reef, none the less perilous to all seafarers.

A modern version of the fate of Glaucus and Scylla is given by Keats in the Endymion. Glaucus consents to Circe's blandishments for a season, but becoming disgusted with her treachery and cruelty, he endeavors to escape from her. The attempt proving unsuccessful, he is brought back and sentenced to pass a thousand years in decrepitude and pain. Consequently, returning to the sea, he there discovers the body of Scylla, whom the goddess has not transformed, but drowned, and learns that if he passes his thousand years in collecting the bodies of drowned lovers, a youth beloved of the gods will, in time, appear and help him. This prophecy is fulfilled by Endymion, who aids in restoring Glaucus to youth, and Scylla and the drowned lovers to life.

143. Nisus and Scylla.[4] The daughter of Phorcys is frequently confounded with another Scylla, daughter of King Nisus of Megara. Scylla of Megara betrayed her father to his enemy, Minos II of Crete, with whom, although the kings were at war, she had fallen violently in love. It seems that Nisus had on his head a purple lock of hair, upon which depended his fortune and his life. This lock his daughter clipped and conveyed to Minos. But recoiling from the treacherous gift, that king, after he had

---

[1] From Keats' Endymion.   [2] §§ 50, 52, and Commentary.
[3] See §§ 239, 250, Adventures of Ulysses and Æneas.   [4] Apollodorus, 3, 15, § 8.

conquered Megara, bound Scylla to the rudder of his ship and so dragged her through the waves toward Crete. The girl was ultimately transformed into the monster of the barking dogs, or, according to another authority, into a bird continually the prey of the sea eagle, whose form her father Nisus had assumed.

144. Leucothea.[1] Another sea change was that of Ino, the daughter of Cadmus and wife of Athamas, who, flying from her frantic husband, sprang, with her child Melicertes in her arms, from a cliff into the sea. The gods, out of compassion, made her a goddess of the sea under the name of Leucothea, and her son a god under that of Palæmon. Both were held powerful to save from shipwreck and were invoked by sailors. Palæmon was usually represented as riding on a dolphin. In his honor the Isthmian games were celebrated. By the Romans he was called Portumnus, and had jurisdiction of ports and shores.

145. Proteus and Aristæus.[2] Though Aristæus, the lover of Eurydice, was son of Apollo and guardian himself of herds and flocks, protector of vine and olive, and keeper of bees, still he was son of Cyrene, a water-nymph, and his most interesting adventure brought him into contact with another deity of the sea.

His bees having perished, Aristæus resorted for aid to his mother. She, surrounded by her maidens in the crystalline abode under her river, overheard his complaints and ordered that he should be brought into her presence. The stream at her command opened itself and let him enter, while it stood heaped like a mountain on either side. Cyrene and her nymphs, having poured out libations to Neptune, gave the youth to eat and listened to his complaint, then informed him that an aged prophet named Proteus, who dwelt in the sea and pastured the sea calves of Neptune, could explain the cause of the mortality among the bees and how to remedy it; but that the wizard would have to be chained and compelled to answer, and that even when chained, he would try to escape by assuming a series of dreadful forms. " Still, thou hast but to keep him fast bound," concluded Cyrene, "and at last, when he finds his arts of no avail, he will obey thy behest." The

---

[1] Ovid, Metam. 4, 432–542.
[2] Cf. Odyssey, 4, 410; Ovid, Fasti, 1, 369; Virgil, Georgics, 4, 317.

nymph then sprinkled her son with nectar, whereupon an unusual vigor filled his frame and courage his heart.

Cyrene led her son to the prophet's cave, which was in the island of Pharos, or of Carpathos,[1] and concealed him. At noon issued Proteus from the water, followed by his herd of sea calves, which spread themselves along the shore. He, too, stretched himself on the floor of the cave and went to sleep. Aristæus immediately clapped fetters on him and shouted at the top of his voice. Proteus, finding himself captured, resorted to his craft, becoming first a fire, then a flood, then a horrible wild beast, in rapid succession; nor did he succumb till all schemes had failed to set him free. Then he resumed his old form and, in response to the questioning of Aristæus, said: "Thou receivest the merited reward of thy deed, by which Eurydice met her death. To avenge her, the nymphs have sent this destruction on thy bees. Their anger thou must appease. Four bulls shalt thou select, of perfect form and size, and four cows of equal beauty; and four altars shalt thou build to the nymphs, and shalt sacrifice the animals, leaving their carcasses in the leafy grove. To Orpheus and Eurydice thou shalt pay such funeral honors as may allay their resentment. Returning after nine days, examine the bodies of the cattle slain and see what has befallen." Aristæus faithfully obeyed these directions. Returning to the grove on the ninth day he found that a swarm of bees had taken possession of one of the carcasses and were pursuing their labors there as in a hive.[2]

146. Acheloüs and Hercules.[3] A similar contest took place between Hercules and the river-god Acheloüs. The cause of the strife was Dejanira of Calydon, whom both heroes loved. Hercules boasted his divine descent. Acheloüs, not content with advancing his claim as lord of the mightiest and most ancient river of Greece, insinuated suspicions with regard to the value of Hercules' pretensions. Then began a mighty struggle. Finding he was no match for Hercules in the wrestler's art, Acheloüs glided away in the form of a serpent. Hercules, remarking that it was the labor of his infancy to strangle snakes,[4] clasped the neck of

---

[1] Cf. § 147, Milton's Carpathian Wizard.
[2] See Commentary.
[3] Ovid, Metam. 9, 1–100.
[4] § 156.

FIG. 114. NEREIDS AND SEA MONSTERS

Acheloüs and choked him. Then Acheloüs assumed the seeming of a bull. Whereupon Hercules, seizing him by the horns, dragged his head to the ground, overthrew him, and rent one horn away. This trophy the Naiads consecrated and filled with flowers for the goddess of Plenty, who, adopting it as her symbol, named it Cornucopia.

147. Milton's Sabrina Fair. No writer in modern times has made more graceful poetic use of the divinities of the streams than has Milton. The following song, chanted by a Spirit in invocation of "the gentle nymph" (of the poet's invention) "that with moist curb sways the smooth Severn stream," is but one refrain of many caught by the poet from the far-echoing chorus of classical verse :

Sabrina fair,
  Listen where thou art sitting
Under the glassy, cool, translucent wave,
  In twisted braids of lilies knitting
The loose train of thy amber-dropping hair ;
  Listen for dear honor's sake,
  Goddess of the silver lake,
        Listen and save.

Listen and appear to us
In name of great Oceanus.
By th' earth-shaking Neptune's mace,
And Tethys' grave, majestic pace,
By hoary Nereus' wrinkled look,
And the Carpathian wizard's hook,
By scaly Triton's winding shell,
And old soothsaying Glaucus' spell,

By Leucothea's lovely hands,
And her son that rules the strands,
By Thetis' tinsel-slippered feet,
And the songs of Sirens sweet,
By dead Parthenope's[1] dear tomb
And fair Ligea's[1] golden comb,
Wherewith she sits on diamond rocks,
Sleeking her soft, alluring locks,
By all the nymphs that nightly dance
Upon thy streams with wily glance;
Rise, rise, and heave thy rosy head
From thy coral-paven bed,
And bridle in thy headlong wave,
Till thou our summons answered have.
Listen and save.[2]

[1] See Commentary.   [2] Milton, Comus, 859–889.

CHAPTER XIV

MYTHS OF THE OLDER HEROES : THE HOUSE OF DANAÜS, AND ITS CONNECTIONS

148. The Older and the Younger Heroes. We have already narrated the adventures of certain demigods and heroes, such as Prometheus, Deucalion, Cadmus, Amphion, Orpheus. Others of importance were Perseus, Hercules, Minos, Œdipus, Theseus, Jason, Meleager, Peleus, Pelops, Castor and Pollux. These and their contemporaries may be called the *Older Heroes.* They are renowned either for individual exploits or for the part played by them in one or more of three great expeditions, — the War against Laomedon of Troy, the Voyage for the Golden Fleece, and the Hunt of the Calydonian Boar.

The *Younger Heroes* were of a later generation, which was concerned in four important enterprises, — the War of the Seven against Thebes, the Trojan War, the Wanderings of Ulysses, and the Adventures of Æneas.

The exploits of the Older Heroes may be arranged in respect of their probable sequence in time, and of their grouping according to families of heroes. If we observe the principle of genealogy, one race, that of Inachus of Argos, attracts our notice in the heroes descended from Pelasgus,[1] Belus, and Agenor. The family of Belus gives us the famous House of Danaüs, the family of Agenor the Houses of Minos and Labdacus. Another race, that of Deucalion, gives us the heroes of the Hellenic branch, most notably those descended from Æolus. With these families most of the Older Heroes are, by blood or by adventure, to some extent connected. Bearing this fact in mind and at the same time observing the chronological sequence of adventures, we obtain an arrangement of myths as illustrating the races, families, or houses — (1) of Danaüs of Argos, (2) of Æolus of Thessaly, (3) of Ætolus, (4) of Minos

---

[1] § 21, and Commentary, § 57.

of Crete, (5) of Cecrops and of Erichthonius of Attica, (6) of Labdacus of Thebes.[1]

149. The Genealogy of Danaüs. As the Hellenes, in the north, traced their descent from Deucalion and Pyrrha of Thessaly, so the Pelasgic races of the south from the river-god Inachus, son of Oceanus. The son of Inachus, Phoroneus, lived in the Peloponnesus and founded the town of Argos. This Phoroneus conferred upon the Argives the benefits attributed by other Greeks to Prometheus. He was succeeded by his son Pelasgus, from whom a division of the Greek people derive their name. With the love of Jupiter for the sister of Phoroneus, the fair Io, we are already acquainted. Her son was Epaphus, king of Egypt, from whom were descended (1) Agenor of Phœnicia, father of Europa and Cadmus, and (2) Belus of Egypt, father of Ægyptus and Danaüs. To the family of Agenor we shall return in the history of Minos, son of Europa, and of Œdipus, descendant of Cadmus.

FIG. 115. THE DANAÏDS

150. The Danaïds.[2] Ægyptus and his fifty sons drove Danaüs and his fifty daughters back to Argos, the ancestral home of the race. Finally, a reconciliation was arranged by means of a fiftyfold marriage between the sons of Ægyptus and the Danaïds. But in accordance with a treacherous command of Danaüs, all his daughters save Hypermnestra slew their husbands on the wedding night. For this crime the forty-nine Danaïds were condemned to spend eternity in Tartarus, trying to fill with water a vessel full of holes. From Hypermnestra and her husband, Lynceus, was sprung the royal house of Argos. Their son was Abas, their grandson, Acrisius, — of whom the following narrative is told.

---

[1] For references to genealogical tables, see Commentary, § 148.
[2] Apollodorus, 2, 1, § 5, etc.; Pausanias; Ovid, Heroides, 14; Horace, Odes, 3; 11; 23.

151. The Doom of King Acrisius.[1] The daughter of Acrisius was Danaë, of surpassing loveliness. In consequence of an oracle which had prophesied that the son of Danaë would be the means of his grandfather's death, the hapless girl was shut in an underground chamber, that no man might love or wed her. But Jupiter, distilling himself into a shower of gold, flooded the girl's prison, wooed, and won her. Their son was Perseus. King Acrisius, in dismay, ordered mother and child to be boxed up in a chest and set adrift on the sea. The two unfortunates were, however, rescued at Seriphus by a fisherman, who conveyed the mother and infant

FIG. 116. DANAË AND PERSEUS AND THE CHEST

to Polydectes, king of the country, by whom they were treated at first with kindness, but afterwards with cruelty.

152. Perseus and Medusa.[2] When Perseus was grown up, Polydectes sent him to attempt the conquest of the Gorgon Medusa,[3] a terrible monster who had laid waste the country. She had once been a maiden whose hair was her chief glory, but as she dared to vie in beauty with Minerva, the goddess deprived her of her charms and changed her ringlets into hissing serpents. She became a monster of so frightful an aspect that no living thing could behold her without being turned into stone. All around the cavern where she dwelt might be seen the stony figures of men and animals that had

---

[1] Simonides of Ceos, also Apollodorus, Pausanias, and Hyginus (Fables).

[2] Ovid, Metam. 4, 608–739; 5, 1–249. [3] For Gorgons and Grææ, see § 52.

chanced to catch a glimpse of her and had been petrified at the sight. Perseus, favored by Minerva and Mercury, set out against the Gorgon, and approached first the cave of the three Grææ:

> There sat the crones that had the single eye,
> Clad in blue sweeping cloak and snow-white gown;
> While o'er their backs their straight white hair hung down
> In long thin locks; dreadful their
>   faces were,
> Carved all about with wrinkles
>   of despair;
> And as they sat they crooned a
>   dreary song,
> Complaining that their lives
>   should last so long,
> In that sad place that no one
>   came anear,
> In that wan place desert of hope
>   and fear;
> And singing, still they rocked
>   their bodies bent,
> And ever each to each the eye
>   they sent.[1]

FIG. 117. MEDUSA

Snatching the eye, Perseus compelled the Grææ, as the price of its restoration, to tell him how he might obtain the helmet of Hades that renders its wearer invisible, and the winged shoes and pouch that were necessary. With this outfit, to which Minerva added her shield and Mercury his knife, Perseus sped to the hall of the Gorgons. In silence sat two of the sisters, —

FIG. 118. MEDUSA

> But a third woman paced about the hall,
> And ever turned her head from wall to wall
> And moaned aloud, and shrieked in her despair;
> Because the golden tresses of her hair
> Were moved by writhing snakes from side to side,
> That in their writhing oftentimes would glide

[1] William Morris, The Doom of King Acrisius, in The Earthly Paradise.

On to her breast, or shuddering shoulders white;
Or, falling down, the hideous things would light
Upon her feet, and crawling thence would twine
Their slimy folds about her ankles fine.[1]

This was Medusa. Her, while she was praying the gods to end her misery, or, as some say, while she was sleeping, Perseus approached, and, guided by her image reflected in the bright shield which he bore, cut off her head, and so ended her miserable existence. Thus are described the horror and the grace of her features in death:

FIG. 119. PERSEUS

From the sculpture by Cellini

It lieth, gazing on the midnight sky,
    Upon the cloudy mountain peak
        supine;
Below, far lands are seen tremblingly;
    Its horror and its beauty are divine.
Upon its lips and eyelids seems to lie
    Loveliness like a shadow, from which
        shine,
Fiery and lurid, struggling underneath,
The agonies of anguish and of death.

Yet it is less the horror than the grace
    Which turns the gazer's spirit into
        stone;
Whereon the lineaments of that dead
        face
    Are graven, till the characters be
        grown
Into itself, and thought no more can
        trace;
'T is the melodious hue of beauty
        thrown
Athwart the darkness and the glare of pain,
Which humanize and harmonize the strain.[2] . . .

[1] William Morris, The Doom of King Acrisius, in The Earthly Paradise.
[2] From Shelley's lines On the Medusa of Leonardo Da Vinci in the Florentine Gallery.

153. Perseus and Atlas. From the body of Medusa sprang the winged horse Pegasus, of whose rider, Bellerophon, we shall presently be informed.

After the slaughter of Medusa, Perseus, bearing with him the head of the Gorgon, flew far and wide, over land and sea. As night came on, he reached the western limit of the earth, and would gladly have rested till morning. Here was the realm of Atlas, whose bulk surpassed that of all other men. He was rich in flocks and herds, but his chief pride was his garden of the Hesperides, whose fruit was of gold, hanging from golden branches, half hid with golden leaves. Perseus said to him, " I come as a guest. If thou holdest in honor illustrious descent, I claim Jupiter for my father ; if mighty deeds, I plead the conquest of the Gorgon. I seek rest and food." But Atlas, remembering an ancient prophecy that had warned him against a son of Jove who should one day rob him of his golden apples, attempted to thrust the youth out. Whereupon Perseus, finding the giant too strong for him, held up the Gorgon's head. Atlas, with all his bulk, was changed into stone. His beard and hair became forests, his arms and shoulders cliffs, his head a summit, and

FIG. 120. PERSEUS WITH HEAD OF MEDUSA

his bones rocks. Each part increased in mass till the giant became the mountain upon whose shoulders rests heaven with all its stars.

154. Perseus and Andromeda. On his way back to Seriphus, the Gorgon-slayer arrived at the country of the Æthiopians, over whom Cepheus was king. His wife was Cassiopea —

> That starred Æthiope queen that strove
> To set her beauty's praise above
> The sea-nymphs, and their powers offended.[1]

These nymphs had consequently sent a sea monster to ravage the coast. To appease the deities, Cepheus was directed by the

---

[1] Milton, Il Penseroso, l. 19.

oracle to devote his daughter Andromeda to the ravening maw of the prodigy. As Perseus looked down from his aërial height, he beheld the virgin chained to a rock. Drawing nearer he pitied, then comforted her, and sought the reason of her disgrace. At first from modesty she was silent; but when he repeated his questions, for fear she might be thought guilty of some offense which she dared not tell, she disclosed her name and that of her country, and her mother's pride of beauty. Before she had done speaking, a sound was heard upon the water, and the monster appeared. The virgin shrieked; the father and mother, who had now arrived, poured

FIG. 121. PERSEUS FINDS ANDROMEDA

forth lamentations and threw their arms about the victim. But the hero himself undertook to slay the monster, on condition that, if the maiden were rescued by his valor, she should be his reward. The parents consented. Perseus embraced his promised bride; then —

> Loosing his arms from her waist he flew upward, awaiting the sea beast.
> Onward it came from the southward, as bulky and black as a galley,
> Lazily coasting along, as the fish fled leaping before it;
> Lazily breasting the ripple, and watching by sand bar and headland,
> Listening for laughter of maidens at bleaching, or song of the fisher,
> Children at play on the pebbles, or cattle that passed on the sand hills.
> Rolling and dripping it came, where bedded in glistening purple
> Cold on the cold seaweeds lay the long white sides of the maiden,
> Trembling, her face in her hands, and her tresses afloat on the water.[1]

[1] From Charles Kingsley's Andromeda.

PERSEUS FREEING ANDROMEDA

The youth darted down upon the back of the monster and plunged his sword into its shoulder, then eluded its furious attack by means of his wings. Wherever he could find a passage for his sword, he plunged it between the scales of flank and side. The wings of the hero were finally drenched and unmanageable with the blood and water that the brute spouted. Then alighting on a rock and holding by a projection, he gave the monster his deathblow.

The joyful parents, with Perseus and Andromeda, repaired to the palace, where a banquet was opened for them. But in the midst of the festivities a noise was heard of warlike clamor, and Phineus, who had formerly been betrothed to the bride, burst in, demanding her for his own. In vain, Cepheus remonstrated that all such engagements had been dissolved by the sentence of death passed upon Andromeda, and that if Phineus had actually loved the girl, he would have tried to rescue her. Phineus and his adherents, persisting in their intent, attacked the wedding party and would have broken it up with most admired disorder, but

> Mid the fabled Libyan bridal stood
> Perseus in stern tranquillity of wrath,
> Half stood, half floated on his ankle plumes
> Out-swelling, while the bright face on his shield
> Looked into stone the raging fray.[1]

Leaving Phineus and his fellows in merited petrifaction, and conveying Andromeda to Seriphus, the hero there turned into stone Polydectes and his court, because the tyrant had rendered Danaë's life intolerable with his attentions. Perseus then restored to their owners the charmed helmet, the winged shoes, and the pouch in which he had conveyed the Gorgon's head. The head itself he bestowed upon Minerva, who bore it afterward upon her ægis or shield. Of that Gorgon shield no simpler moral interpretation can be framed than the following:

> What was that snaky-headed Gorgon shield
> That wise Minerva wore, unconquered virgin,
> Wherewith she freezed her foes to congealed stone,
> But rigid looks of chaste austerity,
> And noble grace that dashed brute violence
> With sudden adoration and blank awe![2]

---

[1] Milman, Samor.   [2] Milton, Comus.

With his mother and his wife Perseus returned to Argos to seek his grandfather. But Acrisius, still fearing his doom, had retired to Larissa in Thessaly. Thither Perseus followed him, and found him presiding over certain funeral games. As luck would have it, the hero took part in the quoit throwing, and hurled a quoit far beyond the mark. The disk, falling upon his grandfather's foot, brought about the old man's death, and in that way the prophecy was fulfilled. Of Perseus and Andromeda three sons were born, through one of whom, Electryon, they became grandparents of the famous Alcmene, sweetheart of Jove and mother of Hercules.

155. Bellerophon and the Chimæra.[1] The horse Pegasus, which sprang from the Gorgon's blood, found a master in Bellerophon of Corinth. This youth was of the Hellenic branch of the Greek nation, being descended from Sisyphus and through him from Æolus, the son of Hellen.[2] His adventures should therefore be recited with those of Jason and other descendants of Æolus in the next chapter, but that they follow so closely on those of Perseus. His father, Glaucus, king of Corinth, is frequently identified with Glaucus the fisherman. This Glaucus of Corinth was noted for his love of horse racing, his fashion of feeding his mares on human flesh, and his destruction by the fury of his horses; for having upset his chariot, they tore their master to pieces. As to his son, Bellerophon, the following is related:

In Lycia a monster, breathing fire, made great havoc. The fore part of his body was a compound of the lion and the goat; the hind part was a dragon's. The king, Iobates, sought a hero to destroy this Chimæra, as it was called. At that time Bellerophon arrived at his court. The gallant youth brought letters from Prœtus, the son-in-law of Iobates, recommending Bellerophon in the warmest terms as an unconquerable hero, but adding a request to his father-in-law to put him to death. For Prœtus, suspecting that his wife Antea looked with too great favor on the young warrior, schemed thus to destory him.

Iobates accordingly determined to send Bellerophon against the Chimæra. Bellerophon accepted the proposal, but before

---

[1] Iliad, 6, 155–202; Apollodorus, 1, 9, § 3; Horace, Odes, 4; 11; 26.
[2] See Commentary, §§ 103, 155.

proceeding to the combat, consulted the soothsayer Polyidus, who counseled him to procure, if possible, the horse Pegasus for the conflict. Now this horse had been caught and tamed by Minerva and by her presented to the Muses. Polyidus, therefore, directed Bellerophon to pass the night in the temple of Minerva. While he slept, Minerva brought him a golden bridle. When he awoke, she showed him Pegasus drinking at the well of Pirene. At sight of the bridle, the winged steed came willingly and suffered himself to be taken. Bellerophon mounted him, sped through the air, found the Chimæra, and gained an easy victory.

FIG. 122. BELLEROPHON AND PEGASUS

After the conquest of this monster, Bellerophon was subjected to further trials and labors by his unfriendly host, but by the aid of Pegasus he triumphed over all. At length Iobates, seeing that the hero was beloved of the gods, gave him his daughter in marriage and made him his successor on the throne. It is said that Bellerophon, by his pride and presumption, drew upon himself the anger of the Olympians; that he even attempted to fly to heaven on his winged steed; but the king of gods and men sent a gadfly, which, stinging Pegasus, caused him to throw his rider, who wandered ever after lame, blind, and lonely through the Aleian field, and perished miserably.

156. Hercules (Heracles): His Youth.[1] Alcmene, daughter of Electryon and granddaughter of Perseus and Andromeda, was

---

[1] Authorities are Homer, — Iliad and Odyssey; Theocritus 24; 25, etc.; Apollodorus, 2, 4, § 7, etc.; Sophocles, Women of Trachis; Euripides, Hercules Furens; Ovid, Metam. 9, 102–272; Seneca, — Hercules Furens and Œtæus; Hyginus, etc.

beloved of Jupiter. Their son, the mighty Hercules, born in Thebes, became the national hero of Greece. Juno, always hostile to the offspring of her husband by mortal mothers, declared war against Hercules from his birth. She sent two serpents to destroy him as he lay in his cradle, but the precocious infant strangled them with his hands. In his youth he passed for the son of his step-father Amphitryon, king of Thebes, grandson of Perseus and Andromeda, and son of Alcæus. Hence his patronymic, Alcides. Rhadamanthus trained him in wisdom and virtue, Linus in music. Unfortunately the latter attempted one day to chastise Hercules; whereupon the pupil killed the master with a lute. After this melancholy breach of discipline, the youth was rusticated, — sent off to the mountains, where among the herdsmen and the cattle he grew to mighty stature, slew the Thespian lion, and performed various deeds of valor. To him, while still a youth, appeared, according to one story, two women at a meeting of the ways, — Pleasure and Duty. The gifts offered by Duty were the " Choice of Hercules." Soon afterward he contended with none other than Apollo for the tripod of Delphi; but reconciliation was effected between the combatants by the gods of Olympus, and from that day forth Apollo and Hercules remained true friends, each respecting the prowess of the other. Returning to Thebes, the hero aided his half brother Iphicles and his reputed father Amphitryon in throwing off the yoke of the city of Orchomenus, and was rewarded with the hand of the princess Megara. A few years later, while in the very pride of his manhood, he was driven insane by the implacable Juno. In his madness he slew his children, and would have slain Amphitryon, also, had not Minerva knocked him over with a stone and plunged him into a deep sleep, from which he awoke in his right mind. Next, for expiation of the bloodshed, he was rendered subject to his cousin Eurystheus and compelled to perform his commands. This humiliation, Juno, of course, had decreed.

157. His Labors. Eurystheus enjoined upon the hero a succession of desperate undertakings, which are called the twelve " Labors of Hercules." The first was the combat with the lion that infested the valley of Nemea, the skin of which Hercules was ordered to bring to Mycenæ. After using in vain his club and arrows against the lion, Hercules strangled the animal with his hands and returned, carrying its carcass on his shoulders; but Eurystheus, frightened at the sight and at this proof of the prodigious strength of the hero, ordered him to deliver the account of his exploits, in future, outside the town.

FIG. 123. HERACLES AND THE NEMEAN LION

His second labor was the slaughter of the Hydra, a water serpent that ravaged the country of Argos and dwelt in a swamp near the well of Amymone. It had nine heads, of which the middle one was immortal. Hercules struck off the heads with his club; but in the place of each dispatched, two new ones appeared. At last, with the assistance of his faithful nephew Iolaüs, he burned away the other heads of the Hydra and buried the ninth, which was immortal, under a rock.

His third labor was the capture of a boar that haunted Mount Erymanthus in Arcadia. The adventure was, in itself, successful. But on the same journey Hercules made the friendship of the centaur Pholus, who, receiving him hospitably, poured out for him without stint the choicest wine that the centaurs possessed. As a consequence, Hercules became involved in a

FIG. 124. HERACLES AND THE HYDRA

broil with the other centaurs of the mountain. Unfortunately his friend Pholus, drawing one of the arrows of Hercules from a brother centaur, wounded himself therewith and died of the poison.

The fourth labor of Hercules was the capture of a wonderful stag of golden antlers and brazen hoofs, that ranged the hills of Cerynea, between Arcadia and Achaia.

His fifth labor was the destruction of the Stymphalian birds, which with cruel beaks and sharp talons harassed the inhabitants of the valley of Stymphalus, devouring many of them.

His sixth labor was the cleaning of the Augean stables. Augeas, king of Elis, had a herd of three thousand oxen, whose stalls had not been cleansed for thirty years. Hercules, bringing the rivers Alpheüs and Peneüs through them, purified them thoroughly in one day.

FIG. 125. HERACLES BRINGING HOME THE BOAR

His seventh labor was the overthrow of the Cretan bull, — an awful but beautiful brute, at once a gift and a curse bestowed by Neptune upon Minos of Crete.[1] This monster Hercules brought to Mycenæ.

His eighth labor was the removal of the horses of Diomedes, king of Thrace. These horses subsisted on human flesh, were swift and fearful. Diomedes, attempting to retain them, was killed by Hercules and given to the horses to devour. They were then delivered to Eurystheus; but, escaping, they roamed the hills of Arcadia, till the wild beasts of Apollo tore them to pieces.

His ninth labor was of a more delicate character. Admeta, the daughter of Eurystheus, desired the girdle of the queen of the

[1] § 172.

Amazons, and Eurystheus ordered Hercules to get it. The Amazons were a nation dominated by warlike women, and in their hands were many cities. It was their custom to bring up only the female children, whom they hardened by martial discipline; the boys were either dispatched to the neighboring nations or put to death. Hippolyta, the queen, received Hercules kindly and consented to yield him the girdle; but Juno, taking the form of an Amazon, persuaded the people that the strangers were carrying off their queen. They instantly armed and beset the ship. Whereupon Hercules, thinking that Hippolyta had acted treacherously, slew her and, taking her girdle, made sail homeward.

FIG. 126. HERACLES WITH THE BULL

The tenth task enjoined upon him was to capture for Eurystheus the oxen of Geryon, a monster with three bodies, who dwelt in the island Erythea (the red), — so called because it lay in the west, under the rays of the setting sun. This description is thought to apply to Spain, of which Geryon was king. After traversing various countries, Hercules reached at length the frontiers of Libya and Europe, where he raised the two mountains of Abyla and Calpe as monuments of his progress, — the Pillars of Hercules; or, according to another account, rent one mountain into two and left half on each side, forming the Strait of Gibraltar. The oxen were guarded by the giant Eurytion and his two-headed dog, but Hercules killed the warders and conveyed the oxen in safety to Eurystheus.

One of the most difficult labors was the eleventh, — the robbery of the golden apples of the Hesperides. Hercules did not know where to find them; but after various adventures, arrived at Mount

Atlas in Africa. Since Atlas was the father of the Hesperides, Hercules thought he might through him obtain the apples. The hero, accordingly, taking the burden of the heavens on his own shoulders,[1] sent Atlas to seek the apples. The giant returned with them and proposed to take them himself to Eurystheus. "Even so," said Hercules; "but, pray, hold this load for me a moment, while I procure a pad to ease my shoulders." Unsuspectingly the giant resumed the burden of the heavens. Hercules took the apples.

His twelfth exploit was to fetch Cerberus from the lower world. To this end he descended into Hades, accompanied by Mercury and Minerva. There he obtained permission from Pluto to carry Cerberus to the upper air, provided he could do it without the use of weapons. In spite of the monster's struggling he seized him, held him fast, carried him to Eurystheus, and afterward restored him

FIG. 127 HERACLES AND CERBERUS

to the lower regions. While in Hades, Hercules also obtained the liberty of Theseus, his admirer and imitator, who had been detained there for an attempt at abducting Proserpine.[2]

After his return from Hades to his native Thebes, he renounced his wife Megara, for, having slain his children by her in his fit of madness, he looked upon the marriage as displeasing to the gods.

Two other exploits not recorded among the twelve labors are the victories over Antæus and Cacus. Antæus, the son of Poseidon and Gæa, was a giant and wrestler whose strength was invincible so long as he remained in contact with his mother Earth. He compelled all strangers who came to his country to wrestle with him, on condition that if conquered, they should suffer death.

[1] Atlas and the heavens, § 153.　　　[2] § 180.

Hercules encountered him and, finding that it was of no avail to throw him, — for he always rose with renewed strength from every fall, — lifted him up from the earth and strangled him in the air.

Later writers tell of an army of Pygmies which, finding Hercules asleep after his defeat of Antæus, made preparations to attack him, as if they were about to attack a city. But the hero, awakening, laughed at the little warriors, wrapped some of them up in his lion's skin, and carried them to Eurystheus.

Cacus was a giant who inhabited a cave on Mount Aventine and plundered the surrounding country. When Hercules was driving home the oxen of Geryon, Cacus stole part of the cattle while the hero slept. That their footprints might not indicate where they had been driven, he dragged them backward by their tails to his cave. Hercules was deceived by the stratagem and would have failed to find his oxen, had it not happened that while he was driving the remainder of the herd past the

FIG. 128. HERACLES AND ANTÆUS

cave where the stolen ones were concealed, those within, beginning to low, discovered themselves to him. Hercules promptly dispatched the thief.

Through most of these expeditions Hercules was attended by Iolaüs, his devoted friend, the son of his half brother Iphicles.

158. His Later Exploits. On the later exploits of the hero we can dwell but briefly. Having, in a fit of madness, killed his friend Iphitus, he was condemned for the offense to spend three years as the slave of Queen Omphale. He lived effeminately, wearing at times the dress of a woman and spinning wool with the hand-maidens of Omphale, while the queen wore his lion's skin. But during this period he contrived to engage in about as many adventures as would fill the life of an ordinary hero. He rescued

Daphnis from Lityerses and threw the bloodthirsty king[1] into the river Mæander; he discovered the body of Icarus[2] and buried it; he joined the company of Argonauts, who were on their way to Colchis to secure the golden fleece, and he captured the thievish gnomes, called Cercopes. Two of these grotesque rascals had made off with the weapons of Hercules while he was sleeping. When he had caught them he strapped them, knees upward, to a yoke and so bore them away. Their drollery, however, regained them their liberty. It is said that some of them having once deceived Jupiter were changed to apes.

159. The Loss of Hylas.[3] In the Argonautic adventure Hercules was attended by a lad, Hylas, whom he tenderly loved and on whose account he deserted the expedition in Mysia; for Hylas had been stolen by the Naiads.

. . . Never was Heracles apart from Hylas, not when midnoon was high in heaven, not when Dawn with her white horses speeds upwards to the dwelling of Zeus, not when the twittering nestlings look towards the perch, while their mother flaps her wings above the smoke-browned beam; and all this that the lad might be fashioned to his mind, and might drive a straight furrow, and come to the true measure of man. . . .

And Hylas of the yellow hair, with a vessel of bronze in his hand, went to draw water against supper-time for Heracles himself and the steadfast Telamon, for these comrades twain supped ever at one table. Soon was he ware of a spring in a hollow land, and the rushes grew thickly round it, and dark swallow-wort, and green maidenhair, and blooming parsley, and deer grass spreading through the marshy land. In the midst of the water the nymphs were arranging their dances, — the sleepless nymphs, dread goddesses of the country people, Eunice, and Malis, and Nycheia, with her April eyes. And now the boy was holding out the wide-mouthed pitcher to the water, intent on dipping it; but the nymphs all clung to his hand, for love of the Argive lad had fluttered the soft hearts of all of them. Then down he sank into the black water, headlong all, as when a star shoots flaming from the sky, plumb in the deep it falls; and a mate shouts out to the seamen, " Up with the gear, my lads, the wind is fair for sailing."

Then the nymphs held the weeping boy on their laps, and with gentle words were striving to comfort him. But the son of Amphitryon was troubled about the lad, and went forth, carrying his bended bow in Scythian fashion, and the club that is ever grasped in his right hand. Thrice he shouted, " Hylas! " as loud as

---

[1] § 160.   [2] § 173   [3] Theocritus, Idyl XIII (Lang's translation).

his deep throat could call, and thrice again the boy heard him, and thrice came his voice from the water, and, hard by though he was, he seemed very far away. And as when a bearded lion, a ravening lion on the hills, hears the bleating of a fawn afar off and rushes forth from his lair to seize it, his readiest meal, even so the mighty Heracles, in longing for the lad, sped through the trackless briars and ranged over much country.

Reckless are lovers: great toils did Heracles bear, in hills and thickets wandering; and Jason's quest was all postponed to this. . . .

Thus loveliest Hylas is numbered with the Blessed; but for a runaway they girded at Heracles — the heroes — because he roamed from Argo of the sixty oarsmen. But on foot he came to Colchis and inhospitable Phasis.

160. The Rescue of Daphnis.[1] Daphnis was the ideal Sicilian shepherd and to him was ascribed the invention of pastoral story and song. His father was Hermes (Mercury); his mother, a nymph who laid him when an infant in a charming valley in a laurel grove from which he received his name,[2] and on account of which Apollo loved him and endowed him with the gift of idyllic verse. He was brought up by nymphs and shepherds, and, avoiding the noisy haunts of men, he tended his flocks on Mount Ætna, winter and summer. He loved a maiden named Piplea, but she was borne away by robbers. He followed them to Phrygia, and there found his sweetheart in the power of the king of that realm, Lityerses. This Lityerses had a pleasant custom of making strangers try a contest with him in reaping corn. If he overcame them, he cut off their heads in the evening and concealed their bodies in the sheaves, singing a comfortable song meanwhile. In order to win back Piplea, Daphnis entered upon the reaping contest with the king and made himself comfortable, too, by singing a harvest song meanwhile. But Lityerses surpassed him at the work and was about to put him to death, singing no doubt a comfortable song of the reaper, Death, meanwhile, — when suddenly Hercules appeared upon the scene. He does n't seem to have spent much time singing: he assured Daphnis of his head by cutting off that of the pleasant king; and then he threw the body into the river Mæander. Daphnis regained his Piplea and one would suppose that they lived happy ever after. Another story, unfortunately,

---

[1] Theocritus, Idyl X, 41, and the Scholia; Virgil, Bucol. 5; 8; 10; and Comments.
[2] See the story of Daphne.

relates events in which Piplea's name does not occur. A Naiad
fell in love with the handsome shepherd and made him promise
eternal fidelity to her, threatening him with blindness if he violated
his vow. It was hard for poor Daphnis, for nearly every lass he
met made love to him. At last a princess intoxicated him and
he forgot his vow. Immediately the Naiad showed the quality of
her love by striking him blind. He consoled himself for a while
by singing his songs and playing the flute as he wandered from
place to place. Then weary, he called on his father for aid. Mercury accordingly transported him to heaven and caused a well to
gush forth on the spot from which he ascended. Here the Sicil-
ians offered yearly sacrifice in his honor.

Theocritus gives us a Lityerses song as he undoubtedly used to
hear it sung by the harvesters of the countryside in Sicily : [1]

Demeter, rich in fruit and rich in grain, may this corn be easy to win and
fruitful exceedingly !

Bind, ye binders, the sheaves, lest the wayfarer should cry, " Men of straw
were the workers here ; aye, and their hire was wasted ! "

See that the cut stubble faces the North wind, or the West ; — 't is thus that
the grain waxes richest.

They that thresh corn should shun the noonday sleep ; at noon the chaff
parts easiest from the straw.

As for the reapers, let them begin when the crested lark is waking, and cease
when he sleeps, but take holiday in the heat.

Lads, the frog has a jolly life : he is not cumbered about a butler to his
drink ; for he has liquor by him unstinted !

Boil the lentils better, thou miserly steward ; take heed lest thou chop thy
fingers, when thou 'rt splitting cummin seed.

When Matthew Arnold is writing of the death of his dear friend,
the poet, Arthur Hugh Clough, who died in Italy,[2] he says :

> And now in happier air,
> Wandering with the great Mother's train divine . . .
> Within a folding of the Apennine,
>
> Thou hearest the immortal chants of old !
> Putting his sickle to the perilous grain
> In the hot cornfield of the Phrygian king,

---

[1] Theocritus, Idyl X (Lang's translation).   [2] Thyrsis.

> For thee the Lityerses song again
>> Young Daphnis with his silver voice doth sing;
>>> Sings his Sicilian fold,
> His sheep, his hapless love, his blinded eyes: —
>> And how a call celestial round him rang,
>> And heavenward from the fountain-brink he sprang, —
> And all the marvel of the golden skies!

161. The Expedition against Laomedon. After his servitude under Omphale' was ended, Hercules sailed with eighteen ships against Troy. For Laomedon, king of that realm, had refused to give Hercules the horses of Neptune, which he had promised in gratitude for the rescue of his daughter Hesione from the sea-monster.[1] The hero, overcoming Troy, placed a son of Laomedon, Priam, upon the throne, and gave Hesione to Telamon, who, with Peleus, Oïcles, and other Greek heroes, had accompanied him. Also worthy of mention among the exploits of Hercules were his successful expeditions against Pylos and Sparta, his victory over the giants, his struggle with Death for the body and life of Alcestis,[2] and his delivery, according to prophecy, of Prometheus, who until that time had remained in chains upon the Caucasian Mountains.[3]

162. The Death of Hercules. Finally, the hero married Dejanira, daughter of Œneus of Calydon and sister of Meleager of the Calydonian hunt. With her he lived three prosperous years. But on one occasion, as they journeyed together, they came to a river across which the centaur Nessus carried travelers for a stated fee. Hercules proceeded to ford the river and gave Dejanira to Nessus to be carried across. Nessus, however, attempted to make off with her; whereupon Hercules, hearing her cries, shot an arrow into his heart. The centaur, as he died, bade Dejanira take a portion of his blood and keep it, saying that it might be used as a charm to preserve the love of her husband. Dejanira did so. Before long, jealous of Hercules' fondness for Iole of Œchalia, a captive maiden, she steeped a sacrificial robe of her husband's in the blood of Nessus. As soon as the garment became warm on the body of Hercules, the poison penetrated his limbs. In his frenzy he seized

[1] § 119.   [2] § 83.   [3] § 15.

Lichas, who had brought him the fatal robe, and hurled him into the sea; then tried to wrench off the garment, but it stuck to his flesh and tore away whole pieces of his body.

FIG. 129. HERCULES AND NESSUS

Alcides, from Œchalia crowned
With conquest, felt the envenomed robe, and tore,
Through pain, up by the roots Thessalian pines,
And Lichas from the top of Œta threw
Into the Euboic Sea.[1]

1 Milton.

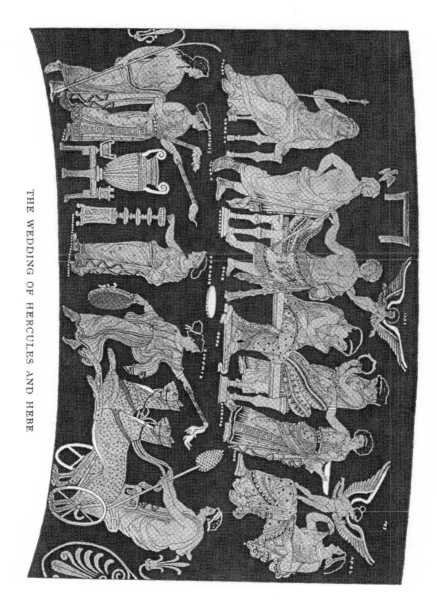

THE WEDDING OF HERCULES AND HEBE

In this state he embarked on board a ship and was conveyed home. Dejanira, on seeing what she had unwittingly done, hanged herself. Hercules, prepared to die, ascended Mount Œta, where he built a funeral pile of trees, gave his bow and arrows to Philoctetes,[1] and laid himself upon the pile, his head resting on his club and his lion's skin spread over him. With a countenance as serene as if he were taking his place at a festal board, he commanded Philoctetes to apply the torch. The flames spread apace, and soon invested the whole mass.[2]

The gods themselves grieved to see the champion of the earth so brought to his end. But Jupiter took care that only his mother's part in him should perish by the flames. The immortal element, derived from Jupiter himself, was translated to heaven; and by the consent of the gods — even of reluctant Juno — Hercules was admitted as a deity to the ranks of the immortals. The white-armed queen of heaven was finally reconciled to the offspring of Alcmene. She adopted him for her son and gave him in marriage her daughter Hebe.

> Deep degraded to a coward's slave,
> Endless contests bore Alcides brave,
> Through the thorny path of suffering led;
> Slew the Hydra, crushed the lion's might,
> Threw himself, to bring his friend to light,
> Living, in the skiff that bears the dead.
> All the torments, every toil of earth,
> Juno's hatred on him could impose,
> Well he bore them, from his fated birth
> To life's grandly mournful close.
>
> Till the god, the earthly part forsaken,
> From the man in flames asunder taken,
> Drank the heavenly ether's purer breath.
> Joyous in the new unwonted lightness,
> Soared he upwards to celestial brightness,
> Earth's dark heavy burden lost in death.
> High Olympus gives harmonious greeting

[1] See § 220. According to Sophocles, Philoctetes' father Pœas applied the torch.
[2] See the spirited poems, Deïaneira and Herakles, in the classical, but too little read, **Epic of Hades,** by Lewis Morris.

> To the hall where reigns his sire adored;
> Youth's bright goddess, with a blush at meeting,
> Gives the nectar to her lord.[1]

In the tragedy called The Maidens of Trachis, Sophocles describes this hero as "The noblest man of all the earth, of whom thou ne'er shalt see the like again." To some of us the manner of his earthly end may seem unworthy; but the Greek poets teach that, in the unabated vigor of one's powers, serenely to meet and accept one's doom is the happiest death. This view is well expressed by Matthew Arnold in the following fragment of a Greek chorus sung with reference to the death of Hercules:

> O frivolous mind of man,
> Light ignorance, and hurrying, unsure thoughts!
> Though man bewails you not,
>   How *I* bewail you! . . .
>
> For you will not put on
> New hearts with the inquirer's holy robe,
> And purged, considerate minds.
>
> And him on whom, at the end
> Of toil and dolor untold,
> The Gods have said that repose
> At last shall descend undisturb'd —
> Him you expect to behold
> In an easy old age, in a happy home;
> No end but this you praise.
>
> But him, on whom, in the prime
> Of life, with vigor undimm'd,
> With unspent mind, and a soul
> Unworn, undebased, undecay'd,
> Mournfully grating, the gates
> Of the city of death have forever closed —
> *Him*, I count *him*, well-starr'd.[2]

Here we take leave for a time of the descendants of Inachus. We shall revert to them in the stories of Minos of Crete and of the house of Labdacus.

[1] Schiller's Ideal and Life. Translated by S. G. Bulfinch, brother of Thomas Bulfinch.
[2] From Fragment of Chorus of a " Dejaneira."

FIG. 130. THE BUILDING OF THE ARGO

CHAPTER XV

THE FAMILY OF ÆOLUS

163. Descendants of Deucalion. Athamas, brother of Sisyphus, was descended from Æolus, whose father, Hellen, was the son of Deucalion of Thessaly. Athamas had by his wife Nephele two children, Phrixus and Helle. After a time, growing indifferent to his wife, Athamas put her away and took Ino, the daughter of Cadmus. The unfortunate sequel of this second marriage we have already seen.[1]

Nephele, apprehending danger to her children from the influence of their stepmother, took measures to put them out of her reach. Mercury gave her a ram with a golden fleece, on which she set the two children. Vaulting into the air, the animal took his course to the east; but when he was crossing the strait that divides Europe and Asia, the girl Helle fell from his back into the sea, which from her was afterward called the Hellespont — now the Dardanelles. The ram safely landed the boy Phrixus in Colchis,

[1] § 144.

where he was hospitably received by Æetes, the king of that country. Phrixus sacrificed the ram to Jupiter, but the fleece he gave to Æetes, who placed it in a consecrated grove under the care of a sleepless dragon.[1]

164. The Quest of the Golden Fleece.[2] Another realm in Thessaly, near to that of Athamas, was ruled over by his nephew Æson. Æson, although he had a son Jason, surrendered the crown to a half brother, Pelias,[3] on condition that he should hold it only during the minority of the lad. This young Jason was, by the way, a second cousin of Bellerophon and of the Atalanta who ran against Hippomenes, and a first cousin of Admetus, the husband of Alcestis.[4] When, however, Jason, being grown up, came to demand the crown, his uncle Pelias with wily intent suggested to him the glorious quest of the golden fleece. Jason, pleased with the thought, forthwith made preparations for the expedition. At that time the only species of navigation known to the Greeks consisted of small boats or canoes hollowed out from trunks of trees; when, accordingly, Jason employed Argus to build a vessel capable of containing fifty men, it was considered a gigantic undertaking. The vessel was named *Argo*, probably after its builder. Jason soon found himself at the head of a bold band of comrades, many of whom afterward were renowned among the heroes and demigods of Greece.

> From every region of Ægea's shore
> The brave assembled; those illustrious twins
> Castor and Pollux; Orpheus, tuneful bard;
> Zetes and Calaïs, as the wind in speed;
> Strong Hercules and many a chief renowned.
> On deep Iolcos' sandy shore they thronged,
> Gleaming in armor, ardent of exploits, —
> And soon, the laurel cord and the huge stone
> Uplifting to the deck, unmoored the bark;
> Whose keel of wondrous length the skillful hand
> Of Argus fashioned for the proud attempt;
> And in the extended keel a lofty mast
> Upraised, and sails full swelling; to the chiefs
> Unwonted objects. Now first, now they learned

[1] Apollodorus, 1, 9, § 1; Apollonius Rhodius, 1, 927.

[2] Ovid, Metam. 6, 667; 7, 143. The Argonautica of Apollonius of Rhodes.

[3] See § 120.   [4] See Table G, Commentary, § 103.

Their bolder steerage over ocean wave,
Led by the golden stars, as Chiron's art
Had marked the sphere celestial.[1]

Theseus, Meleager, Peleus, and Nestor were also among these Argonauts, or sailors of the *Argo*. The ship with her crew of heroes left the shores of Thessaly, and touching at the island of Lemnos, thence crossed to Mysia and thence to Thrace. Here they found the sage Phineus, who instructed the Argonauts how they might pass the Symplegades, or Clashing Islands, at the entrance of the Euxine Sea. When they reached these islands they, accordingly, let go a dove, which took her way between the

FIG. 131. JASON CONQUERS THE BULLS AND STEALS THE FLEECE

rocks and passed in safety, only losing some feathers of her tail. Jason and his men, seizing the favorable moment of the rebound, plied their oars with vigor and passed safe through, though the islands closed behind them and actually grazed the stern of the vessel. They then rowed along the shore till they arrived at the eastern end of the sea, and so landed in the kingdom of Colchis.

Jason made known his message to the Colchian king, Æetes, who consented to give up the golden fleece on certain conditions, namely, that Jason should yoke to the plow two fire-breathing bulls with brazen feet, and that he then should sow the teeth of the dragon that Cadmus had slain. Jason, although it was well known that a crop of armed men would spring up from the teeth, destined to turn their weapons against their producer, accepted the conditions, and a time was set for the undertaking. The hero,

[1] Dyer, The Fleece.

however, wisely spent the interval in wooing Medea, the daughter of Æetes; and with such success that they plighted troth before the altar of Hecate. The princess then furnished her hero with a charm which should aid him in the contest to come.

Accordingly, when the momentous day was arrived, Jason with calmness encountered the fire-breathing monsters and speedily yoked them to the plow. The Colchians stood in amazement; the Greeks shouted for joy. Next, the hero proceeded to sow the dragon's teeth and plow them in. Up sprang, according to prediction, the crop of armed men, brandished aloft their weapons, and rushed upon Jason. The Greeks trembled for their hero. Medea herself grew pale with fear. The hero himself for a time, with sword and shield, kept his assailants at bay; but he surely would have been overwhelmed by the numbers, had he not resorted to a charm which Medea had taught him : seizing a stone, he threw it in the midst of his foes. Immediately they turned their arms against one another, and soon there was not one of the dragon's brood alive.

It remained only to lull to sleep the dragon that guarded the fleece. This was done by scattering over him a few drops of a preparation which, again, Medea had supplied. Jason then seized the fleece, and, with his friends and his sweetheart accompanying, hastened to the vessel. It is said that, in order to delay the pursuit of her father Æetes, Medea tore to pieces her young brother Absyrtus and strewed fragments of him along the line of their flight. The ruse succeeded.

165. The Return of the Argonauts. On their way home the Argonauts beat a devious course, sailing after other dangers had been overcome, by the island that the Sirens infested. And here the heroes would have hung their halsers and remained, had not Orpheus vanquished the seductive strains of the sea-muses with his own more melodious and persuasive song.[1]

> Oh, happy seafarers are ye
>   And surely all your ills are past,
> And toil upon the land and sea,
>   Since ye are brought to us at last;

[1] William Morris, Life and Death of Jason.

chanted the Sirens, promising long rest and the kingdoms of sleep.

> But now, but now, when ye have lain
>   Asleep with us a little while
> Beneath the washing of the main,
>   How calm shall be your waking smile!

Then Orpheus replied, encouraging his men :

> A little more, a little more,
>   O carriers of the Golden Fleece!
> A little labor with the oar,
>   Before we reach the land of Greece.
>
> E'en now, perchance, faint rumors reach
>   Men's ears of this our victory,
> And draw them down upon the beach
>   To gaze across the empty sea.

Again the Sirens :

> Alas! and will ye stop your ears,
>   In vain desire to do aught,
> And wish to live 'mid cares and fears,
>   Until the last fear makes you nought?

But Orpheus, reminding the rowers of home and love and joy :

> Is not the May-time now on earth,
>   When close against the city wall
> The folks are singing in their mirth,
>   While on their heads the May flowers fall?

carried them past triumphant.

The Argonauts arrived safe in Thessaly. Jason delivered the fleece to Pelias, and dedicated the *Argo* to Neptune.

166. Medea and Æson.[1] Medea's career as a sorceress was, by no means, completed. At Jason's request she undertook next to restore his aged father Æson to the vigor of youth. To the full moon she addressed her incantations, to the stars, to Hecate, to Tellus, the goddess of the earth. In a chariot borne aloft by dragons she traversed the fields of air to regions where flourished potent plants, which only she knew how to select. Nine nights

[1] Ovid, Metam. 7, 143–293.

she employed in her search, and during that period shunned all intercourse with mortals.

Next she erected two altars, the one to Hecate, the other to Hebe, and sacrificed a black sheep, — pouring libations of milk and wine. She implored Pluto and his stolen bride to spare the old man's life. Then she directed that Æson be led forth; and

throwing him into a deep sleep, she laid him on a bed of herbs, like one dead. No eye profane looked upon her mysteries. With streaming hair thrice she moved round the altars, dipped flaming twigs in the blood, and laid them thereon to burn. Meanwhile, the caldron with its contents was preparing. In it she put magic herbs, with seeds and flowers of acrid juice, stones from the distant East, and sand from the shore of all-surrounding ocean, hoarfrost gathered by moonlight, a screech owl's head and wings, and the entrails of a wolf. She added fragments of the shells of tortoises and the liver of stags — animals tenacious of life — and the head and beak of a crow, which outlives nine generations of men. These, with many other things "without a name," she boiled together for her purposed work, stirring them with a dry olive branch. The branch, when taken out, instantly was green and erelong was covered with leaves and a plentiful growth of young olives; and as the liquor

FIG. 132. MEDEA

boiled and bubbled and sometimes bubbled over, the grass wherever the sprinklings fell leaped into verdure like that of spring.

Seeing that all was ready, Medea cut the throat of the old man, let out his blood, and poured into his mouth and his wound the juices of her caldron. As soon as he had completely imbibed them, his hair and beard lost their whiteness and assumed the color of youth; his paleness and emaciation were gone; his veins were full of blood, his limbs of vigor and robustness; and Æson, on awakening, found himself forty years younger.

167. Pelias.[1] In another instance, Medea made her arts the instrument of revenge. Pelias, the usurping uncle of Jason, still kept him out of his heritage. But the daughters of Pelias wished Medea to restore their father also to youth. Medea simulated consent, but prepared her caldron for him in a new and singular way. She put in only water and a few simple herbs. In the night she persuaded the daughters of Pelias to kill him. They at first hesitated to strike, but Medea chiding their irresolution, they turned away their faces and, giving random blows, smote him with their weapons. Starting from his sleep, the old man cried out, " My daughters, would you kill your father ? " Whereat their hearts failed them, and the weapons fell from their hands. Medea, however, struck the fatal blow.

FIG. 133. MEDEA AND DAUGHTERS OF PELIAS

They placed him in the caldron, but, as might be expected, with no success. Medea herself had taken care to escape before they discovered the treachery. She had, however, little profit of the fruits of her crime. Jason, for whom she had sacrificed so much, put her away, for he wished to marry Creüsa, princess of Corinth. Whereupon Medea, enraged at his ingratitude, called on the gods for vengeance ; then, sending a poisoned robe as a gift to the bride, killing her own children, and setting fire to the palace, she mounted her serpent-drawn chariot and fled to Athens. There she married King Ægeus, the father of Theseus ; and we shall meet her again when we come to the adventures of that hero.[2]

[1] Ovid, Metam. 7, 297–353.   [2] § 176

The incantation of Medea readily suggests that of the witches in Macbeth :

> Round about the caldron go;
> In the poison'd entrails throw. —
> Toad, that under cold stone
> Days and nights has thirty-one
> Swelter'd venom sleeping got,
> Boil thou first i' the charmèd pot. . . .
> Fillet of a fenny snake
> In the caldron boil and bake;
> Eye of newt and toe of frog,
> Wool of bat and tongue of dog,
> Adder's fork and blind-worm's sting,
> Lizard's leg and howlet's wing, —
> For a charm of powerful trouble
> Like a hell-broth boil and bubble. . . .
> Scale of dragon, tooth of wolf,
> Witches' mummy, maw and gulf
> Of the ravin'd salt-sea shark,
> Root of hemlock digged i' the dark. . .
> Make the gruel thick and slab.[1]

[1] Macbeth, IV, i. Consult.

CHAPTER XVI

THE FAMILY OF ÆTOLUS AND ITS CONNECTIONS

168. The Calydonian Hunt.[1] One of the heroes of the Argonautic expedition had been Meleager, a son of Œneus and Althæa,
rulers of Calydon in Ætolia. His parents were cousins, descended
from a son of Endymion named Ætolus, who had colonized that
realm. By ties of kinship and marriage they were allied with many
historic figures. Their daughter Dejanira had become, as we have
already noted, the wife of Hercules; while Leda, the sister of
Althæa, was mother of Castor and Pollux,[2] and of Clytemnestra
and Helen, intimately concerned in the Trojan War.

When her son Meleager was born, Althæa had beheld the three
Destinies, who, as they spun their fatal thread, foretold that the
life of the child should last no longer than a certain brand then
burning upon the hearth. Althæa seized and quenched the brand,
and carefully preserved it while Meleager grew to boyhood, youth,
and man's estate. It chanced, then, that Œneus, offering sacrifices
to the gods, omitted to pay due honors to Diana; wherefore she,
indignant at the neglect, sent a boar of enormous size to lay waste
the fields of Calydon. Meleager called on the heroes of Greece
to join in a hunt for the ravenous monster. Theseus and his friend
Pirithoüs,[3] Jason, Peleus the father of Achilles, Telamon the father
of Ajax, Nestor, then a youth, but who in his age bore arms with
Achilles and Ajax in the Trojan War,[4] — these and many more
joined in the enterprise. With them came, also, Atalanta, the
daughter of Iasius, of the race of Callisto, —

> Arcadian Atalanta, snowy-souled,
> Fair as the snow and footed as the wind.[5]

---

[1] Ovid, Metam. 8, 260–546.   [2] § 170.   [3] § 180.   [4] Chapter XXI.
[5] From Swinburne's Atalanta in Calydon.

A buckle of polished gold confined her vest, an ivory quiver hung on her left shoulder, and her left hand bore the bow. Her face blended feminine beauty with the graces of martial youth. Meleager saw and, with chivalric reverence, somewhat thus addressed her:

> For thy name's sake and awe toward thy chaste head,
> O holiest Atalanta! no man dares
> Praise thee, though fairer than whom all men praise,
> And godlike for thy grace of hallowed hair
> And holy habit of thine eyes, and feet
> That make the blown foam neither swift nor white,
> Though the wind winnow and whirl it; yet we praise
> Gods, found because of thee adorable
> And for thy sake praiseworthiest from all men:
> Thee therefore we praise also, thee as these,
> Pure, and a light lit at the hands of gods.[1]

FIG. 134. MELEAGER ON THE BOAR HUNT

But there was no time then for love; on to the hunt they pushed. To the hunt went also Plexippus and Toxeus, brothers of Queen Althæa, braggarts, envious of Meleager. Speedily the hunters drew near the monster's lair. They stretched strong nets from tree to tree; they uncoupled their dogs; they sought the footprints of their quarry in the grass. From the wood was a descent to marshy ground. Here the boar, as he lay among the reeds, heard the shouts of his pursuers and rushed forth against

[1] From Swinburne's Atalanta in Calydon.

them. One and another is thrown down and slain. Jason, Nestor,
Telamon open the attack, but in vain.

> . . . Then all abode save one,
> The Arcadian Atalanta: from her side
> Sprang her hounds, laboring at the leash, and slipped,
> And plashed ear-deep with plunging feet; but she
> Saying, " Speed it as I send it for thy sake,
> Goddess," drew bow and loosed; the sudden string
> Rang, and sprang inward, and the waterish air
> Hissed, and the moist plumes of the songless reeds
> Moved as a wave which the wind moves no more.
> But the boar heaved half out of ooze and slime,
> His tense flank trembling round the barbèd wound,
> Hateful; and fiery with invasive eyes,
> And bristling with intolerable hair,
> Plunged, and the hounds clung, and green flowers and white
> Reddened and broke all round them where they came.[1]

It was a slight wound, but Meleager saw and joyfully proclaimed
it. The attack was renewed. Peleus, Amphiaraüs, Theseus, Jason,
hurled their lances. Ancæus was laid low by a mortal wound.
But Meleager, —

> Rock-rooted, fair with fierce and fastened lips,
> Clear eyes and springing muscle and shortening limb —
> With chin aslant indrawn to a tightening throat,
> Grave, and with gathered sinews, like a god, —
> Aimed on the left side his well-handled spear,
> Grasped where the ash was knottiest hewn, and smote,
> And with no missile wound, the monstrous boar
> Right in the hairiest hollow of his hide,
> Under the last rib, sheer through bulk and bone,
> Deep in; and deeply smitten, and to death,
> The heavy horror with his hanging shafts
> Leapt, and fell furiously, and from raging lips
> Foamed out the latest wrath of all his life.[1]

Then rose a shout from those around; they glorified the conqueror, — crowded to touch his hand. But he, placing his foot
upon the head of the slain boar, turned to Atalanta, and bestowed

[1] From Swinburne's Atalanta in Calydon.

on her the head and the rough hide — trophies of his success.
Thereat she laughed —

> Lit with a low blush to the braided hair,
> And rose-colored and cold like very dawn,
> Golden and godlike, chastely with chaste lips,
> A faint grave laugh ; and all they held their peace,
> And she passed by them. Then one cried, " Lo now,
> Shall not the Arcadian shoot out lips at us,
> Saying all we were despoiled by this one girl ? "
> And all they rode against her violently
> And cast the fresh crown from her hair, and now
> They had rent her spoil away, dishonoring her,
> Save that Meleager, as a tame lion chafed,
> Bore on them, broke them, and as fire cleaves wood,
> So clove and drove them, smitten in twain ; but she
> Smote not nor heaved up hand ; and this man first,
> Plexippus, crying out, " This for love's sake, Sweet,"
> Drove at Meleager, who with spear straightening
> Pierced his cheek through ; then Toxeus made for him,
> Dumb, but his spear shake ; vain and violent words,
> Fruitless ; for him, too, stricken through both sides
> The earth felt falling. . . .
> . . . And these being slain,
> None moved, nor spake.[1]

Of this fearful sequel to the hunt, Althæa has heard nothing.
As she bears thank offering to the temples for the victory of her
son, the bodies of her murdered brothers meet her sight. She
shrieks, and beats her breast, and hastens to change the garments
of joy for those of mourning. But when the author of the deed
is known, grief gives way to the stern desire of vengeance on
her son. The fatal brand, which the Destinies have linked with
Meleager's life, she brings forth. She commands a fire to be prepared. Four times she essays to place the brand upon the pile ;
four times draws back, shuddering before the destruction of her
son. The feelings of the mother and the sister contend within
her. Now she is pale at the thought of the purposed deed, now
flushed again with anger at the violence of her offspring. Finally,

---

[1] From Swinburne's Atalanta in Calydon.

the sister prevails over the mother : — turning away her face, she throws the fatal wood upon the burning pile. Meleager, absent and unconscious of the cause, feels a sudden pang. He burns ; he calls upon those whom he loves, Atalanta and his mother. But speedily the brand is ashes, and the life of Meleager is breathed forth to the wandering winds.

When at last the deed was done, the mother laid violent hands upon herself.

169. Merope. A heroine connected by blood with Atalanta was Merope,[1] daughter of king Cypselus of Arcadia, and descended from Arcas, the son of Callisto and Jupiter. On account of her

FIG. 135. THE DEATH OF MELEAGER

relationship to Atalanta her story may be told here, though she is not a member of the family of Ætolus. Her husband, Cresphontes the Heraclid, king of Messenia, had been slain with two of his sons by rebellious nobles ; and one Polyphontes, leader of the revolt, reigned in his stead and took Merope to wife. But her third son by Cresphontes, Æpytus, had been concealed by her in Arcadia. Thence, in due season, he returned unknown to her, with the purpose of wreaking vengeance on the murderers of his sire. He pretended to have slain Æpytus, and so as a stranger won the favor of Polyphontes, but came near losing his life at his mother's hands. A recognition being happily effected, Æpytus, aided by his mother, put Polyphontes to death and took possession of the kingdom. This story has been frequently dramatized, first

[1] Hyginus, Fab.184 ; Apollodorus, 2, 8 ; Pausanias, 2, 18 ; 4, 3, etc.; Aristotle, Poetics, 14, 9.

by Euripides in a lost play called Cresphontes, and most recently by Matthew Arnold, whose Merope is a masterpiece of classical invention and of poetic execution.

170. Castor and Pollux. Leda, the sister of Althæa and aunt of Meleager, bore to Tyndareus, king of Sparta, Castor and Clytemnestra. To Jove she bore Pollux and Helen. Pollux and Castor — one, the son of a god and immortal, the other, of mortal breed and destiny — are famous for their fraternal affection. Endowed with various manly virtues, — Castor a horse-tamer, Pollux a boxer, — they made all expeditions in common. Together they joined the Calydonian hunt. Together they accompanied the Argonauts. During the voyage to Colchis it is said that, a storm arising, Orpheus prayed to the Samothracian gods and played on his harp, and that when the storm ceased, stars appeared on the heads of the brothers. Hence they came to be honored as patrons of voyagers.

They rendered, indeed, noteworthy service to the Argonauts returning from Colchis with Medea and the Golden Fleece. For when the voyagers attempted a landing at Crete they were confronted by the gigantic warder of the island. This was Talus, a form of living brass, fashioned by Hephæstus (Vulcan) and presented to King Minos, about whose Cretan domain he made his rounds three times a day. Ordinarily when Talus saw voyagers nearing the coast he fired himself red-hot and embraced them as they landed. For some reason he did not welcome the Argonauts in this warm fashion, but

> Whirling with resistless sway
> Rocks sheer uprent, repels them from the bay.[1]

Medea, objecting to the volley of stones, resorts to necromantic spells :

> Thrice she applies the power of magic prayer,
> Thrice, hellward bending, mutters charms in air ;
> Then, turning toward the foe, bids Mischief fly,
> And looks Destruction as she points her eye.[1]

Maddened, as might be surmised, by so insidious and unaccustomed a form of attack, the Man of Brass " tears up whole hills to

[1] Apollonius Rhodius, 4, 1629 (Broome's translation). See also Apollodorus, 1 ; 9, 26.

crush his foes "; then fleeing in sudden panic, he is overcome by the stupor of the enchantment and taken captive by Castor and Pollux. He had in his body only one vein, and that plugged on the crown of his head with a nail. Medea drew out the stopper.

At a later period when Theseus and his friend Pirithoüs had carried off Helen from Sparta, the youthful heroes, Castor and Pollux, with their followers hasted to the rescue. Theseus being absent from Attica, the brothers recovered their sister. Later still, we find Castor and Pollux engaged in a combat with Idas and Lynceus of Messene, some say over the daughters of Leucippus, others, over a herd of oxen. Castor was slain; but Pollux, inconsolable for the loss of his brother, besought Jupiter to be permitted to give his own life as a ransom for him. Jupiter so far consented as to allow the two brothers to enjoy the boon of life alternately, each spending one day under the earth and the next in the heavenly abodes. According to another version, Jupiter rewarded the attachment of the brothers by placing them among the stars as Gemini, the Twins. They received heroic honors as the *Tyndaridæ* (sons of Tyndareus); divine honors they received under the name of *Dioscuri* (sons of Jove).[1]

171. The Twin Brethren among the Romans. In Rome they were honored with a temple in the Forum and made the patrons of knighthood because of the assistance they rendered in the battle of Lake Regillus. In the moment of dire distress they had appeared, a princely pair :

> So like they were, no mortal
>   Might one from other know;
> White as snow their armor was,
>   Their steeds were white as snow.
> Never on earthly anvil
>   Did such rare armor gleam,
> And never did such gallant steeds
>   Drink of an earthly stream.
>
> And all who saw them trembled,
>   And pale grew every cheek;
> And Aulus the Dictator
>   Scarce gathered voice to speak:

[1] Hyginus, Fab. 80; Ovid, Fasti, 100. Theocritus, Idyl XXII, gives a different version.

" Say by what name men call you?
     What city is your home?
And wherefore ride ye in such guise
     Before the ranks of Rome? "

" By many names," they answered, —

" By many names men call us;
     In many lands we dwell:
Well Samothracia knows us;
     Cyrene knows us well;
Our house in gay Tarentum
     Is hung each morn with flowers;
High o'er the masts of Syracuse
     Our marble portal towers;
But by the brave Eurotas
     Is our dear native home;
And for the right we come to fight
     Before the ranks of Rome."

After the battle was won they were
the first to bear the tidings to the city.
With joy the people acclaimed them, —

But on rode these strange horsemen,
     With slow and lordly pace;
And none who saw their bearing
     Durst ask their name or race.
On rode they to the Forum,
     While laurel boughs and flowers,
From housetops and from windows,
     Fell on their crests in showers.

FIG. 136. CASTOR AND POLLUX
CAPTURING THE GIANT TALUS
(Left portion)

When they drew nigh to Vesta,
     They vaulted down amain,
And washed their horses in the well
     That springs by Vesta's fane.
And straight again they mounted,
     And rode to Vesta's door;
Then, like a blast, away they passed,
     And no man saw them more. . . .

And Sergius the High Pontiff
     Alone found voice to speak:

" The gods who live forever
  Have fought for Rome to-day!
These be the Great Twin Brethren
  To whom the Dorians pray.
Back comes the chief in triumph
  Who, in the hour of fight,
Hath seen the Great Twin Brethren
  In harness on his right.
Safe comes the ship to haven,
  Through billows and through gales

FIG. 137. CASTOR AND POLLUX CAPTURING THE GIANT TALUS

(Right portion)

If once the Great Twin Brethren
  Sit shining on the sails. . . .
Here, hard by Vesta's temple,
  Build we a stately dome
Unto the Great Twin Brethren
  Who fought so well for Rome!"[1]

For many a year the procession, in which the knights, olive-wreathed and purple-robed, marched in honor of the Twin Brethren, continued to be held; and still there stand three columns of their temple above the pool of Juturna and Vesta's ruined shrine.

[1] Macaulay, Lays of Ancient Rome, The Battle of Lake Regillus.

CHAPTER XVII

THE HOUSE OF MINOS

172. Minos of Crete was a descendant of Inachus in the sixth generation. A son of Jupiter and Europa, he was, after death, transferred, with his brother Rhadamanthus and with King Æacus, to Hades, where the three became judges of the Shades. This is the Minos mentioned by Homer and Hesiod, — the eminent lawgiver. Of his grandson, Minos II, it is related that when aiming at the crown of Crete, he boasted of his power to obtain by prayer whatever he desired, and as a test, he implored Neptune to send him a bull for sacrifice. The bull appeared, but Minos, astonished at its great beauty, declined to sacrifice the brute. Neptune, therefore incensed, drove the bull wild, — worse still, drove Pasiphaë, the wife of Minos, wild with love of it. The wonderful brute was finally caught and overcome by Hercules, who rode it through the waves to Greece. But its offspring, the Minotaur, a monster bull-headed and man-bodied, remained for many a day a terror to Crete, till finally a famous artificer, Dædalus, constructed for him a labyrinth, with passages and turnings winding in and about like the river Mæander, so that whoever was inclosed in it might by no means find his way out. The Minotaur, roaming therein, lived upon human victims. For it is said that, after Minos had subdued Megara,[1] a tribute of seven youths and seven maidens was sent every year from Athens to Crete to feed this monster; and it was not until the days of Theseus of Athens that an end was put to both tribute and Minotaur.[2]

173. Dædalus and Icarus.[3] Dædalus, who abetted the love of Pasiphaë for the Cretan bull, afterwards lost the favor of

---

[1] § 143.
[2] § 177. Apollodorus, 3, 1, § 3; 15, § 8; Pausanias, 1, 27, § 9, etc.; Ovid, Metam. 7, 456.
[3] Virgil, Æneid, 6, 14-36; Ovid, Metam. 8, 152-259; Hyginus, Fab. 40, 44.

Minos and was imprisoned by him. Seeing no other way of escape, the artificer made, out of feathers, wings for his son Icarus and himself, which he fastened on with wax. Then poising themselves in the air, they flew away. Icarus had been warned not to approach too near the sun, and all went well till they had passed Samos and Delos on the left and Lebynthos on the right. But then the boy, exulting in his career, soared upward. The blaze of the torrid sun softened the waxen fastening of his wings. Off they came, and down the lad dropped into the sea which after him is named Icarian, even to this day.

FIG. 138. DÆDALUS AND ICARUS

> . . . With melting wax and loosened strings
> Sunk hapless Icarus on unfaithful wings;
> Headlong he rushed through the affrighted air,
> With limbs distorted and disheveled hair;
> His scattered plumage danced upon the wave,
> And sorrowing Nereïds decked his watery grave;
> O'er his pale corse their pearly sea flowers shed,
> And strewed with crimson moss his marble bed;
> Struck in their coral towers the passing bell,
> And wide in ocean tolled his echoing knell.[1]

The story, save for its tragic conclusion, reads like a remarkable anticipation of the exploits of the Wright brothers, Blériot, and Latham with the aëroplane to-day, or of Count Zeppelin with his airships.

Dædalus, mourning his son, arrived finally in Sicily where, being kindly received by King Cocalus, he built a temple to Apollo and hung up his wings, an offering to the god. But Minos, having learned of the hiding place of the artificer, followed him to Sicily with a great fleet; and Dædalus would surely have perished, had not one of the daughters of Cocalus disposed of Minos by scalding him to death while he was bathing.

[1] Erasmus Darwin.

It is said that Dædalus could not bear the idea of a rival. His sister had placed her son Perdix under his charge to be taught the mechanical arts. He was an apt scholar and gave striking evidences of ingenuity. Walking on the seashore, he picked up the spine of a fish, and, imitating it in iron, invented the saw. He invented, also, a pair of compasses. But Dædalus, envious of his nephew, pushed him off a tower and killed him. Minerva, however, in pity of the boy, changed him into a bird, the partridge, which bears his name.

To the descendants of Inachus we shall again return in the account of the house of Labdacus.

CHAPTER XVIII

THE HOUSE OF CECROPS AND ERICHTHONIUS

174. From Cecrops[1] to Philomela. Cecrops, half-snake, half-man, came from Crete or Egypt into Attica, founded Athens, and chose Minerva rather than Neptune as its guardian. His successor was Erichthonius,[2] or Erechtheus, a snake-formed genius of the fertile soil of Attica. This Erichthonius[3] was a special ward of the goddess Minerva, who brought him up in her temple. His son Pandion had two daughters, Procne and Philomela, of whom he gave the former in marriage to Tereus, king of Thrace (or of Daulis in Phocis). This ruler, after his wife had borne him a son Itys (or Itylus), wearied of her, plucked

FIG. 139. THESEUS

out her tongue by the roots to insure her silence, and, pretending that she was dead, took in marriage the other sister, Philomela. Procne by means of a web, into which she wove her story, informed Philomela of the horrible truth. In revenge upon Tereus, the sisters killed Itylus and served up the child as food to the father; but the gods, in indignation, transformed Procne into a swallow, Philomela into a nightingale, forever bemoaning the murdered Itylus, and Tereus into a hawk, forever pursuing the sisters.[4]

---

[1] Ovid, Metam. 2, 555; Apollodorus, 3, 14, § 1; Pausanias; and Hyginus, Fab. 48.

[2] Ovid, Metam. 2, 554; 6, 676; Homer, Iliad, 2, 547; Odyssey, 7, 81; Hyginus, Poet. Astr. 2, 13.

[3] For Ruskin's interpretation, see Queen of the Air, § 38.

[4] Hyginus, Fab. 45; Apollodorus, 3, 14, § 8; Ovid, Metam. 6, 412–676. See Commentary.

175. Matthew Arnold's Philomela.

Hark! ah, the nightingale —
The tawny-throated!
Hark, from that moonlit cedar what a burst!
What triumph! hark! — what pain!
O wanderer from a Grecian shore,
Still, after many years in distant lands,
Still nourishing in thy bewilder'd brain
That wild, unquench'd, deep-sunken, old-world pain —
Say, will it never heal?
And can this fragrant lawn
With its cool trees, and night,
And the sweet, tranquil Thames,
And moonshine, and the dew,
To thy rack'd heart and brain
Afford no calm?

Dost thou to-night behold,
Here, through the moonlight on this English grass,
The unfriendly palace in the Thracian wild?
Dost thou again peruse,
With hot cheeks and sear'd eyes,
The too clear web, and thy dumb sister's shame?
Dost thou once more assay
Thy flight, and feel come over thee,
Poor fugitive, the feathery change
Once more, and once more seem to make resound
With love and hate, triumph and agony,
Lone Daulis, and the high Cephissian vale?
Listen, Eugenia —
How thick the bursts come crowding through the leaves!
Again — thou hearest?
Eternal passion!
Eternal pain!

According to another version of this story, it was Philomela who was robbed of her tongue and who wove the web by means of which the queen Procne learned the truth.

176. Theseus.[1] A descendant of Erechtheus, or of Cecrops, was Ægeus, king of Athens. By Æthra, granddaughter of Pelops, he

[1] Ovid, Metam. 7, 350–424; Plutarch, Theseus.

became the father of the Attic hero, Theseus. Ægeus, on parting from Æthra, before the birth of the child, had placed his sword and shoes under a large stone and had directed her to send the child to him if it should prove strong enough to roll away the stone and take what was under. The lad Theseus was brought up at Trœzen, of which Pittheus, Æthra's father, was king. When Æthra thought the time had come, she led Theseus to the stone. He removed it with ease and took the sword and shoes. Since at that time the roads were infested with robbers, his grandfather Pittheus pressed him earnestly to take the shorter and safer way to his father's country, by sea; but the youth, feeling in himself the spirit and soul of a hero and eager to signalize himself like Hercules, determined on the more perilous and adventurous journey by land.

FIG. 140. ÆTHRA AND THESEUS

His first day's journey brought him to Epidaurus, where dwelt Periphetes, a son of Vulcan. This ferocious savage always went armed with a club of iron, and all travelers stood in terror of his violence; but beneath the blows of the young hero he speedily fell.

Several similar contests with the petty tyrants and marauders of the country followed, in all of which Theseus was victorious. Most important was his slaughter of Procrustes, or the Stretcher. This giant had an iron bedstead on which he used to tie all travelers who fell into his hands. If they were shorter than the bed, he stretched them till they fitted it; if they were longer than the bed, he lopped off their limbs.

In the course of time Theseus reached Athens, but here new
dangers awaited him. For Medea, the sorceress, who had fled
from Corinth after her separation from Jason,[1] had become the
wife of Ægeus. Knowing by her arts who the stranger was, and
fearing the loss of her influence with her husband if Theseus
should be acknowledged as his son, she tried to poison the
youth ; but the sword which he wore discovered him to his father

and prevented the fatal
draft. Medea fled to
Asia, where the country
afterwards called Media
is said to have received
its name from her.
Theseus was acknowl-
edged by his sire and
declared successor to
the throne.

**177. Theseus and
Ariadne.**[2] Now the
Athenians were at that
time in deep affliction
on account of the trib-
ute of youths and maid-
ens which they were
forced to send to the
Minotaur, dwelling in
the labyrinth of Crete,
—a penalty said to have

FIG. 141. THESEUS AND THE MINOTAUR

been imposed by Minos upon the Athenians because Ægeus had
sent Androgeüs, the son of Minos, against the Marathonian bull
and so had brought about the young man's death.

From this calamity Theseus resolved to deliver his countrymen
or to die in the attempt. He, therefore, in spite of the entreaties
of his father, presented himself as champion of Athens and of her
fair sons and daughters, to do battle against the Minotaur, and
departed with the victims in a vessel bearing black sails, which he

---

[1] § 167.   [2] Odyssey, 11, 321 ; Plutarch, Theseus ; Catullus, LXIV.

promised his father to change for white in the event of his returning victorious. So, —

> Rather than cargo on cargo of corpses undead should be wafted [1]
> Over the ravening sea to the pitiless monster of Creta, —
> Leaving the curvèd strand Piræan, and wooing the breezes,
> Theseus furrowed the deep to the dome superb of the tyrant.
>   Then as the maid Ariadne beheld him with glances of longing, —
> Princess royal of Creta Minoan, tender, sequestered, —
> Locked in a mother's embrace, in seclusion virginal, fragrant,
> Like some myrtle set by streaming ways of Eurotas,
> Like to the varied tints that Spring invites with her breezes, —
> Then, as with eager gaze she looked her first upon Theseus,
> Never a whit she lowered her eyes nor ceased to consume him,
> Ere to the core profound her breast with love was enkindled.
> — God-born boy, thou pitiless heart, provoker of madness,
> Mischievous, mingling care with the fleeting pleasure of mortals, —
> Goddess of Golgi, thou, frequenter of coverts Idalian,
> In what wildering seas ye tossed the impassionate maiden
> Ever a-sighing, — aye for the fair-haired stranger a-sighing!
> Ah, what ponderous fears oppressed her languishing bosom,
> How, more pallid than gold her countenance flashed into whiteness,
> What time Theseus marched unto death or to glory undying,
> Manful, minded to quell the imbruted might of the monster!

Not unaided, however, did he undertake the task; for Ariadne, apprehensive lest he might lose his way in the dædalian labyrinth, furnished him with a thread, the gift of Vulcan, which, unrolled by Theseus as he entered the maze, should enable him on his return to retrace his former path. Meanwhile —

> Offering artless bribes, Ariadne invoked the Immortals,
> Kindled voiceless lip with unvoicèd tribute of incense,
> Suppliant, not in vain: for, like to an oak upon Taurus,
> Gnarlèd, swinging his arms, — like some cone-burthenèd pine tree
> Oozing the life from his bark, that, riven to heart by the whirlwind,
> Wholly uprooted from earth, falls prone with extravagant ruin,
> Perishes, dealing doom with precipitate rush of its branches, —
> So was the Cretan brute by Theseus done to destruction,
> E'en so, tossing in vain his horns to the vacuous breezes.

[1] Catullus, LXIV. From The Wedding of Peleus and Thetis. A Translation in Hexameters, by Charles Mills Gayley.

Then with abundant laud he turned, unscathed from the combat,
Theseus, — guiding his feet unsure by the filament slender,
Lest as he threaded paths circuitous, ways labyrinthine,
Some perverse, perplexing, erratic alley might foil him.

Why should I tarry to tell how, quitting her sire, Ariadne
Quitting the sister's arms, the infatuate gaze of the mother, —
She whose sole delight, whose life, was her desperate daughter, —
How Ariadne made less of the love of them
    all than of Theseus?
Why should I sing how sailing they came to
    the beaches of Dia, —
White with the foam, — how thence, false-
    hearted, the lover departing
Left her benighted with sleep, the Minoïd,
    princess of Creta?

FIG. 142. THE SLEEPING ARIADNE

Gazing amain from the marge of the flood-reverberant Dia,
Chafing with ire, indignant, exasperate, — lo, Ariadne,
Lorn Ariadne, beholds swift craft, swift lover retreating.
Nor can be sure she sees what things she sees of a surety,
When upspringing from sleep, she shakes off treacherous slumber,
Lone beholds herself on a shore forlorn of the ocean.
Carelessly hastens the youth, meantime, who, driving his oar-blades
Hard in the waves, consigns void vows to the blustering breezes.
But as, afar from the sedge, with sad eyes still the Minoïd
Mute as a Mænad in stone unmoving stonily gazes —
Heart o'erwhelmed with woe — ah, thus, while thus she is gazing, —

Down from her yellow hair slips, sudden, the weed of the fine-spun
Snood, and the vesture light of her mantle down from the shoulders
Slips, and the twisted scarf encircling her womanly bosom;
Stealthily gliding, slip they downward into the billow,
Fall, and are tossed by the buoyant flood at the feet of the fair one.
Nothing she recks of the coif, of the floating garment as little,
Cares not a moment then, whose care hangs only on Theseus, —
Wretched of heart, soul-wrecked, dependent only on Theseus, —
Desperate, woe-unselfed with a cureless sorrow incessant,
Frantic, bosoming torture of thorns Erycina had planted. . . .

Then, they say, that at last, infuriate out of all measure,
Once and again she poured shrill-voicèd shrieks from her bosom;
Helpless, clambered steeps, sheer beetling over the surges,
Whence to enrange with her eyes vast futile regions of ocean; —
Lifting the folds, soft folds of her garments, baring her ankles,
Dashed into edges of upward waves that trembled before her;
Uttered, anguished then, one wail, her maddest and saddest, —
Catching with tear-wet lips poor sobs that shivering choked her: —
" Thus is it far from my home, O traitor, and far from its altars —
Thus on a desert strand, — dost leave me, treacherous Theseus?
Thus is it thou dost flout our vow, dost flout the Immortals, —
Carelessly homeward bearest, with baleful ballast of curses?
Never, could never a plea forfend thy cruelly minded
Counsel? Never a pity entreat thy bosom for shelter? . . .
Hence, let never a maid confide in the oath of a lover,
Never presume man's vows hold aught trustworthy within them!
Verily, while in anguish of heart his spirit is longing,
Nothing he spares to assever, nor aught makes scruple to promise:
But, an his dearest desire, his nearest of heart be accorded —
Nothing he recks of affiance, and reckons perjury, — nothing.

" Oh ! what lioness whelped thee? Oh ! what desolate cavern?
What was the sea that spawned, that spat from its churning abysses,
Thee, — what wolfish Scylla, or Syrtis, or vasty Charybdis,
Thee, — thus thankful for life, dear gift of living, I gave thee? . . .
Had it not liked thee still to acknowledge vows that we plighted,
Mightest thou homeward, yet, have borne me a damsel beholden,
Fain to obey thy will, and to lave thy feet like a servant,
Fain to bedeck thy couch with purple coverlet for thee.

" But to the hollow winds why stand repeating my quarrel, —
I, for sorrow unselfed, — they, but breezes insensate, —

Potent neither voices to hear nor words to re-echo? . . .
Yea, but where shall I turn? Forlorn, what succor rely on?
' Haste to the Gnossian hills? ' Ah, see how distantly surging
Deeps forbid, distending their gulfs abhorrent before me!
' Comfort my heart, mayhap, with the loyal love of my husband? '
Lo, the reluctant oar, e'en now, he plies to forsake me! —
Nought but the homeless strand of an isle remote of the ocean!
No, no way of escape, where the circling sea without shore is, —
No, no counsel of flight, no hope, no sound of a mortal;
All things desolate, dumb, yea, all things summoning deathward!

FIG. 143. HEAD OF
DIONYSUS

Yet mine eyes shall not fade in death that sealeth
  the eyelids,
Nor from the frame outworn shall fare my linger-
  ing senses,
Ere, undone, from powers divine I claim retribu-
  tion —
Ere I call — in the hour supreme, on the faith of
  Immortals!

" Come, then, Righters of Wrong, O vengeful
  dealers of justice,
Braided with coil of the serpents, O Eumenides,
  ye of
Brows that blazon ire exhaling aye from the bosom,
Haste, oh, haste ye, hither and hear me, vehement
  plaining,
Destitute, fired with rage, stark-blind, demented
  for fury! —
As with careless heart yon Theseus sailed and
  forgot me,
So with folly of heart, may he slay himself and his household! "
. . . Then with a nod supreme Olympian Jupiter nodded:
Quaked thereat old Earth, — quaked, shuddered the terrified waters,
Ay, and the constellations in Heaven that glitter were jangled.
Straightway like some cloud on the inward vision of Theseus
Dropped oblivion down, enshrouding vows he had cherished,
Hiding away all trace of the solemn behest of his father.

For, as was said before, Ægeus, on the departure of his son for
Creta, had given him this command: " If Minerva, goddess of our
city, grant thee victory over the Minotaur, hoist on thy return,
when first the dear hills of Attica greet thy vision, white canvas

to herald thy joy and mine, that mine eyes may see the propitious sign and know the glad day that restores thee safe to me."

... Even as clouds compelled by
    urgent push of the breezes
Float from the brow uplift of a
    snow-envelopèd mountain,
So from Theseus passed all prayer
    and behest of his father.
Waited the sire meanwhile, looked
    out from his tower over ocean,
Wasted his anxious eyes in futile
    labor of weeping,
Waited expectant, — saw to the
    southward sails black-bellied —
Hurled him headlong down from
    the horrid steep to destruc-
    tion, —
Weening hateful Fate had severed
    the fortune of Theseus.
Theseus, then, as he paced that
    gloom of the home of his
    father,
Insolent Theseus knew himself
    what manner of evil
He with a careless heart had afore-
    time dealt Ariadne, —
Fixed Ariadne that still, still stared
    where the ship had receded, —
Wounded, revolving in heart her
    countless muster of sorrows.

178. Bacchus and Ariadne.

But for the deserted daughter of Minos a happier fate was yet reserved. This island, on which she had been abandoned, was Naxos, loved and

FIG. 144. THE REVELS OF BACCHUS AND ARIADNE

especially haunted by Bacchus, where with his train of reeling
devotees he was wont to hold high carnival.

> . . . Sweeping over the shore, lo, beautiful, blooming Iacchus, —
> Chorused of Satyrs in dance and of Nysian-born Sileni, —
> Seeking fair Ariadne, — afire with flame of a lover!
> Lightly around him leaped Bacchantès, strenuous, frenzied,
> Nodding their heads, " Euhoe! " to the cry, " Euhoe, O Bacchus! "
> Some — enwreathèd spears of Iacchus madly were waving;
> Some — ensanguined limbs of the bullock, quivering, brandished;
> Some — were twining themselves with sinuous snakes that twisted;
> Some — with vessels of signs mysterious, passed in procession —
> Symbols profound that in vain the profane may seek to decipher;
> Certain struck with the palms — with tapered fingers on timbrels,
> Others the tenuous clash of the rounded cymbals awakened; —
> Brayed with a raucous roar through the turmoil many a trumpet,
> Many a stridulous fife went, shrill, barbarian, shrieking.[1]

So the grieving, much-wronged Ariadne was consoled for the
loss of her mortal spouse by an immortal lover. The blooming god
of the vine wooed and won her. After her death, the golden crown
that he had given her was transferred by him to the heavens. As
it mounted the ethereal spaces, its gems, growing in brightness,
became stars; and still it remains fixed, as a constellation, between
the kneeling Hercules and the man that holds the serpent.

179. The Amazons. As king of Athens, it is said that Theseus
undertook an expedition against the Amazons. Assailing them
before they had recovered from the attack of Hercules, he carried
off their queen Antiope; but they in turn, invading the country
of Athens, penetrated into the city itself; and there was fought
the final battle in which Theseus overcame them.

180. Theseus and Pirithoüs. A famous friendship between
Theseus and Pirithoüs of Thessaly, son of Jupiter, originated in
the midst of arms. Pirithoüs had made an irruption into the plain
of Marathon and had carried off the herds of the king of Athens.
Theseus went to repel the plunderers. The moment the Thessalian
beheld him, he was seized with admiration, and stretching out his
hand as a token of peace, he cried, " Be judge thyself, — what

---

[1] Catullus, LXIV (Charles Mills Gayley's translation).

satisfaction dost thou require?" — "Thy friendship," replied the Athenian; and they swore inviolable fidelity. Their deeds corresponding to their professions, they continued true brothers in arms. When, accordingly, Pirithoüs was to marry Hippodamia, daughter of Atrax, Theseus took his friend's part in the battle that ensued between the Lapithæ (of whom Pirithoüs was king) and the Centaurs. For it happened that at the marriage feast, the Centaurs were among the guests; and one of them, Eurytion, becoming intoxicated, attempted to offer violence to the bride. Other Centaurs followed his example; combat was joined; Theseus leaped into the fray, and not a few of the guests bit the dust.

Later, each of these friends aspired to espouse a daughter of Jupiter. Theseus fixed his choice on Leda's daughter Helen, then a child, but afterwards famous as the cause of the Trojan War; and with the aid of his friend he carried her off, only, however, to restore her at very short notice. As for Pirithoüs, he aspired

FIG. 145. LAPITH AND CENTAUR

to the wife of the monarch of Erebus; and Theseus, though aware of the danger, accompanied the ambitious lover to the underworld. But Pluto seized and set them on an enchanted rock at his palace gate, where fixed they remained till Hercules, arriving, liberated Theseus but left Pirithoüs to his fate.

181. Phædra and Hippolytus. After the death of Antiope, Theseus married Phædra, sister of the deserted Ariadne, daughter of Minos. But Phædra, seeing in Hippolytus, the son of Theseus, a youth endowed with all the graces and virtues of his father and of an age corresponding to her own, loved him. When, however, he repulsed her advances, her love was changed to despair and hate. Hanging herself, she left for her husband a scroll containing false charges against Hippolytus. The infatuated husband, filled, therefore, with jealousy of his son, imprecated the vengeance of Neptune upon him. As Hippolytus one day drove his chariot along the shore, a sea monster raised himself above the waters and frightened the horses so that they ran away and dashed the chariot to pieces. Hippolytus was killed, but by Æsculapius was restored to life, and then, removed by Diana from the power of his deluded father, was placed in Italy under the protection of the nymph Egeria.

In his old age, Theseus, losing the favor of his people, retired to the court of Lycomedes, king of Scyros, who at first received him kindly, but afterwards treacherously put him to death.

CHAPTER XIX

THE HOUSE OF LABDACUS

182. The Misfortunes of Thebes. Returning to the descendants of Inachus, we find that the curse which fell upon Cadmus when he slew the dragon of Mars followed nearly every scion of his house. His daughters, Semele, Ino, Autonoë, Agave, — his grandsons, Melicertes, Actæon, Pentheus, — lived sorrowful lives or suffered violent deaths. The misfortunes of one branch of his family, sprung from his son Polydorus, remain to be told. The curse seems to have spared Polydorus himself. His son Labdacus, also, lived a quiet life as king of Thebes and left a son, Laïus, upon the throne. But erelong Laïus was warned by an oracle that there was danger to his throne and life if his son, new-born, should reach man's estate. He, therefore, committed the child to a herds-

FIG. 146. ŒDIPUS AND THE SPHINX

man with orders for its destruction; but the herdsman, moved with pity yet not daring entirely to disobey, pierced the child's feet, purposing to expose him to the elements on Mount Cithæron.

183. Œdipus and the Sphinx.[1] In this plight the infant was given to a tender-hearted fellow-shepherd, who carried him to King Polybus of Corinth and his queen, by whom he was adopted and called Œdipus, or Swollen-foot.

---

[1] Sophocles, Œdipus Rex, Œdipus Coloneus, Antigone; Euripides, Phœnissæ; Apollodorus, 3, 5, §§ 7, 8.

261

Many years afterward, Œdipus, learning from an oracle that he was destined to be the death of his father, left the realm of his reputed sire, Polybus. It happened, however, that Laïus was then driving to Delphi, accompanied only by one attendant. In a narrow road he met Œdipus, also in a chariot. On the refusal of the youthful stranger to leave the way at their command, the attendant killed one of his horses. Œdipus, consumed with rage, slew both Laïus and the attendant, and thus unknowingly fulfilled both oracles.

Shortly after this event, the city of Thebes, to which Œdipus had repaired, was afflicted with a monster that infested the highroad. She was called the Sphinx. She had the body of a lion and the upper part of a woman. She lay crouched on the top of a rock and, arresting all travelers who came that way, propounded to them a riddle, with the condition that those who could solve it should pass safe, but those who failed should be killed. Not one had yet succeeded in guessing it. Œdipus, not daunted by these alarming accounts, boldly advanced to the trial. The Sphinx asked him, " What animal is it that in the morning goes on four feet, at noon on two, and in the evening upon three ? " Œdipus replied, " Man, who in childhood creeps on hands and knees, in manhood walks erect, and in old age goes with the aid of a staff." The Sphinx, mortified at the collapse of her riddle, cast herself down from the rock and perished.

184. Œdipus, the King. In gratitude for their deliverance, the Thebans made Œdipus their king, giving him in marriage their queen, Jocasta. He, ignorant of his parentage, had already become the slayer of his father ; in marrying the queen he became the husband of his mother. These horrors remained undiscovered till, after many years, Thebes being afflicted with famine and pestilence, the oracle was consulted, and, by a series of coincidences, the double crime of Œdipus came to light. At once, Jocasta put an end to her life by hanging herself. As for Œdipus, horror-struck, —

> When her form
> He saw, poor wretch ! with one wild fearful cry,
> The twisted rope he loosens, and she fell,
> Ill-starred one, on the ground. Then came a sight
> Most fearful. Tearing from her robe the clasps,

All chased with gold, with which she decked herself,
He with them struck the pupils of his eyes,
With words like these: " Because they had not seen
What ills he suffered, and what ills he did,
They in the dark should look, in time to come,
On those whom they ought never to have seen,
Nor know the dear ones whom he fain had known."
With suchlike wails, not once or twice alone,
Raising his eyes he smote them, and the balls,
All bleeding, stained his cheek.[1]

185. Œdipus at Colonus. After these sad events Œdipus would have left Thebes, but the oracle forbade the people to let him go. Jocasta's brother, Creon, was made regent of the realm for the two sons of Œdipus. But after Œdipus had grown content to stay, these sons of his, with Creon, thrust him into exile. Accompanied by his daughter Antigone, he went begging through the land. His other daughter, Ismene, at first stayed at home. Cursing the sons who had abandoned him, but bowing his own will in submission to the ways of God, Œdipus approached the hour of his death in Colonus, a village near Athens. His friend Theseus, king of Athens, comforted and sustained him to the last. Both his daughters were also with him :

And then he called his girls, and bade them fetch
Clear water from the stream, and bring to him
For cleansing and libation. And they went,
Both of them, to yon hill we look upon,
Owned by Demeter of the fair green corn,
And quickly did his bidding, bathed his limbs,
And clothed them in the garment that is meet.
And when he had his will in all they did,
And not one wish continued unfulfilled,
Zeus from the dark depths thundered, and the girls
Heard it, and shuddering, at their father's knees,
Falling they wept; nor did they then forbear
Smiting their breasts, nor groanings lengthened out;
And when he heard their bitter cry, forthwith
Folding his arms around them, thus he spake:
" My children, on this day ye cease to have

---

[1] Sophocles, Œdipus, the King (E. H. Plumptre's translation).

A father. All my days are spent and gone;
And ye no more shall lead your wretched life,
Caring for me. Hard was it, that I know,
My children! Yet one word is strong to loose,
Although alone, the burden of these toils,
For *love* in larger store ye could not have
From any than from him who standeth here,
Of whom bereaved ye now shall live your life." [1]

There was sobbing, then silence. Then a voice called him, — and he followed. God took him from his troubles. Antigone returned to Thebes, — where, as we shall see, her sisterly fidelity showed itself as true as, aforetime, her filial affection.

Her brothers, Eteocles and Polynices, had meanwhile agreed to share the kingdom between them and to reign alternately year by year. The first year fell to the lot of Eteocles, who, when his time expired, refused to surrender the kingdom to his brother. Polynices, accordingly, fled to Adrastus, king of Argos, who gave him his daughter in marriage and aided him with an army to enforce his claim to the kingdom. These causes led to the celebrated expedition of the " Seven against Thebes," which furnished ample materials for the epic and tragic poets of Greece. And here the younger heroes of Greece make their appearance.

[1] Sophocles, Œdipus at Colonus, ll. 1600, etc. (E. H. Plumptre's translation).

CHAPTER XX

MYTHS OF THE YOUNGER HEROES: THE SEVEN AGAINST THEBES

186. Their Exploits. The exploits of the sons and grandsons of the chieftains engaged in the Calydonian Hunt and the Quest of the Golden Fleece are narrated in four stories, — the Seven against Thebes, the Siege of Troy, the Wanderings of Ulysses, and the Adventures of Æneas.

187. The Seven against Thebes.[1] The allies of Adrastus and Polynices in the enterprise against Thebes were Tydeus of Calydon, half brother of Meleager, Parthenopæus of Arcadia, son of Atalanta and Mars, Capaneus of Argos, Hippomedon of Argos, and Amphiaraüs, the brother-in-law of Adrastus. Amphiaraüs opposed the expedition for, being a soothsayer, he knew that none of the leaders except Adrastus would live to return from Thebes; but on his marriage to Eriphyle, the king's sister, he had agreed that whenever he and Adrastus should differ in opinion, the decision should be left to Eriphyle. Polynices, knowing this, gave Eriphyle the necklace of Harmonia and thereby gained her to his interest. This was the selfsame necklace that Vulcan had given to Harmonia on her marriage with Cadmus; Polynices had taken it with him on his flight from Thebes. It seems to have been still fraught with the curse of the house of Cadmus. But Eriphyle could not resist so tempting a bribe. By her decision the war was resolved on, and Amphiaraüs went to his fate. He bore his part bravely in the contest, but still could not avert his destiny. While, pursued by the enemy, he was fleeing along the river, a thunderbolt launched by Jupiter opened the ground, and he, his chariot, and his charioteer were swallowed up.

[1] Æschylus, Seven against Thebes; Euripides, Phœnissæ; Apollodorus, 3. 6 and 7; Hyginus, Fab. 69, 70; Pausanias, 8 and 9; Statius, Thebaid.

It is unnecessary here to detail all the acts of heroism or atrocity which marked this contest. The fidelity, however, of Evadne stands out as an offset to the weakness of Eriphyle. Her husband, Capaneus, having in the ardor of the fight declared that he would force his way into the city in spite of Jove himself, placed a ladder against the wall and mounted; but Jupiter, offended at his impious language, struck him with a thunderbolt. When his obsequies were celebrated, Evadne cast herself on his funeral pile and perished.

It seems that early in the contest Eteocles consulted the soothsayer Tiresias as to the issue. Now, this Tiresias in his youth had by chance seen Minerva bathing, and had been deprived by her of his sight, but afterwards had obtained of her the knowledge of future events. When consulted by Eteocles, he declared that victory should fall to Thebes if Menœceus, the son of Creon, gave himself a voluntary victim. The heroic youth, learning the response, threw away his life in the first encounter.

FIG. 147. ETEOCLES AND POLYNICES KILL EACH OTHER

The siege continued long, with varying success. At length both hosts agreed that the brothers should decide their quarrel by single combat. They fought, and fell each by the hand of the other. The armies then renewed the fight; and at last the invaders were forced to yield, and fled, leaving their dead unburied. Creon, the uncle of the fallen princes, now became king, caused Eteocles to be buried with distinguished honor, but suffered the body of Polynices to lie where it fell, forbidding any one, on pain of death, to give it burial.

188. Antigone,[1] the sister of Polynices, heard with indignation the revolting edict which, consigning her brother's body to

1 Sophocles, Antigone; Euripides, Suppliants.

the dogs and vultures, deprived it of the rites that were considered essential to the repose of the dead. Unmoved by the dissuading counsel of her affectionate but timid sister, and unable to procure assistance, she determined to brave the hazard and to bury the body with her own hands. She was detected in the act. When Creon asked the fearless woman whether she dared disobey the laws, she answered:

> Yes, for it was not Zeus who gave them forth,
> Nor justice, dwelling with the gods below,
> Who traced these laws for all the sons of men;
> Nor did I deem thy edicts strong enough,
> That thou, a mortal man, should'st overpass
> The unwritten laws of God that know no change.
> They are not of to-day nor yesterday,
> But live forever, nor can man assign
> When first they sprang to being. Not through fear
> Of any man's resolve was I prepared
> Before the gods to bear the penalty
> Of sinning against these. That I should die
> I knew (how should I not?), though thy decree
> Had never spoken. And before my time
> If I shall die, I reckon this a gain;
> For whoso lives, as I, in many woes,
> How can it be but he shall gain by death?
> And so for me to bear this doom of thine
> Has nothing fearful. But, if I had left
> My mother's son unburied on his death,
> In that I should have suffered; but in this
> I suffer not.[1]

Creon, unyielding and unable to conceive of a law higher than that he knew, gave orders that she should be buried alive, as having deliberately set at nought the solemn edict of the city. Her lover, Hæmon, the son of Creon, unable to avert her fate, would not survive her, and fell by his own hand. It is only after his son's death and as he gazes upon the corpses of the lovers, that the aged Creon recognizes the insolence of his narrow judgment. And those that stand beside him say:

[1] Sophocles, Antigone, ll. 450–470 (E. H. Plumptre's translation).

Man's highest blessedness
In wisdom chiefly stands;
And in the things that touch upon the gods,
'T is best in word or deed,
To shun unholy pride;
Great words of boasting bring great punishments,
And so to gray-haired age
Teach wisdom at the last.[1]

189. The Epigoni.[2] Such was the fall of the house of Labdacus. The bane of Cadmus expires with the family of Œdipus. But the wedding gear of Harmonia has not yet fulfilled its baleful mission. Amphiaraüs had, with his last breath, enjoined his son Alcmæon to avenge him on the faithless Eriphyle. Alcmæon engaged his word, but before accomplishing the fell purpose, he was ordered by an oracle of Delphi to conduct against Thebes a new expedition. Thereto his mother Eriphyle, influenced by Thersander, the son of Polynices, and bribed this time by the gift of Harmonia's wedding garment, impelled not only Alcmæon but her other son, Amphilochus. The descendants (*Epigoni*) of the former Seven thus renewed the war against Thebes. They leveled the city to the ground. Its inhabitants, counseled by Tiresias, took refuge in foreign lands. Tiresias himself perished during the flight. Alcmæon, returning to Argos, put his mother to death but, in consequence, repeated in his own experience the penalty of Orestes. The outfit of Harmonia preserved its malign influence until, at last, it was devoted to the temple at Delphi and removed from the sphere of mortal jealousies.

[1] Sophocles, Antigone, closing chorus.
[2] Pausanias, 9, 9, §§ 2, 3; Herodotus, 5, 61; Apollodorus.

CHAPTER XXI

HOUSES CONCERNED IN THE TROJAN WAR

190. Three Families. Before entering upon the causes of the war against Troy, we must notice the three Grecian families that were principally concerned, — those of Peleus, Atreus, and Tyndareus.

191. Peleus[1] was the son of Æacus and grandson of Jove. It was for his father Æacus, king of Phthia in Thessaly, that, as we have seen, an army of Myrmidons was created by Jupiter. Peleus joined the expedition of the Argonauts, and on that journey beheld and fell in love with the sea-nymph Thetis, daughter of Nereus and Doris. Such was the beauty of the nymph that Jupiter himself had sought her in marriage; but having learned from Prometheus, the Titan, that Thetis should bear a son who should be greater than his father, the Olympian desisted from his suit and decreed that Thetis should be the wife of a mortal. By the aid of Chiron, the Centaur, Peleus succeeded in winning the goddess for his bride. In this marriage, to be productive of momentous results for mortals, the immortals manifested a lively interest. They thronged with the Thessalians to the wedding in Pharsalia; they honored the wedding feast with their presence and, reclining on ivory couches, gave ear while the three Sisters of Fate, in responsive strain, chanted the fortunes of Achilles, — the future hero of the Trojan War, — the son that should spring from this union of a goddess with a mortal. The following is from a translation of the famous poem, The Wedding of Peleus and Thetis:[2]

> . . . Now, on the day foreset, Aurora forsaking the ocean
> Crimsons the orient sky: all Thessaly, seeking the palace,
> Fares to the royal seat, in populous muster exultant,
> Heavy of hand with gifts, but blithesome of cheer for the joyance.

[1] Ovid, Metam. 11, 221–265; Catullus, LXIV; Hyginus, Fab. 14; Apollonius Rhodius. Argon. 1, 558; Valerius Flaccus, Argon.; Statius, Achilleid.
[2] Catullus, LXIV (Charles Mills Gayley's translation).

Scyros behind they leave, they leave Phthiotican Tempe,
Crannon's glittering domes and the battlements Larissæan,
Cumber Pharsalia, throng the abodes and the streets of Pharsalus.
Fields, meanwhile are untilled, grow tender the necks of the oxen,
None with the curving teeth of the harrow cleareth the vineyard,
None upturneth the glebe with bull and the furrowing plowshare,
None with gardener's knife lets light through the branches umbrageous;
Squalid the rust creeps up o'er plows forgotten of plowmen.

Bright is the palace, ay, through far retreating recesses
Blazing for sheen benign of the opulent gold and the silver:
Ivory gleams on the thrones, great goblets glint on the tables,
Glitters the spacious home, made glad with imperial splendor, —
Ay, but most — in the hall midmost — is the couch of the goddess,
Glorious, made of the tusk of the Indian elephant — polished —
Spread with a wonder of quilt empurpled with dye of the sea-shell.

On this coverlet of purple were embroidered various scenes illustrating the lessons of heroism and justice that the poet would
inculcate: to the good falleth good; to the evil, evil speedily.
Therefore, the story of Theseus and Ariadne, which has already
been recounted, was here displayed in cunning handiwork. For
Theseus, the false lover, bold of hand but bad of heart, gained by
retributive justice undying ruth and misery; whereas Ariadne, the
injured and innocent, restored to happiness, won no less a reward
than Bacchus himself. Gorgeously woven with such antique and
heroic figures was the famous quilt upon the couch of Thetis. For
a season the wedding guests feasted their eyes upon it.

Then when Thessaly's youth, long gazing, had of the wonder
Their content, they gan give place to the lords of Olympus.
As when Zephyr awakes the recumbent billows of ocean,
Roughens the placid deep with eager breath of the morning,
Urges the waves, and impels, to the threshold of journeying Phœbus, —
They, at first, blown outward unroughly when Dawn is a-rising,
Limp slow-footed, and loiter with laughter lightsomely plashing,
But, with the freshening gale, creep quicker and thicker together,
Till on horizon they float refulgent of luminous purple, —
So from the portal withdrawing the pomp Thessalian departed
Faring on world-wide ways to the far-off homes of their fathers.

Now when they were aloof, drew nigh from Pelion's summit
Chiron bearing gifts from copses and glades of the woodland —
Gifts that the meadows yield: what flowers on Thessaly's mountains,
Or, by waves of the stream, the prolific breath of the West Wind,
Warming, woos to the day, all such in bunches assorted
Bore he. Flattered with odors the whole house brake into laughter.
Came there next Peneüs, abandoning verdurous Tempe —
Tempe embowered deep mid superimpendent forests.

And after the river-god, who bore with him nodding plane trees
and lofty beeches, straight slim laurels, the lithe poplar, and the
airy cypress to plant about the palace that thick foliage might give
it shade, followed Prometheus, the bold and cunning of heart,
wearing still the marks of his ancient punishment on the rocks of

FIG. 148. THE GODS BRING WEDDING GIFTS

Caucasus. Finally the father of the gods himself came, with his
holy spouse and his offspring, — all, save Phœbus and his one
sister, who naturally looked askance upon a union to be productive
of untold misfortune to their favored town of Troy.

   . . . When now the gods had reclined their limbs on the ivory couches,
Viands many and rare were heaped on the banqueting tables,
Whilst the decrepit Sisters of Fate, their tottering bodies
Solemnly swayed, and rehearsed their soothfast vaticination.
— Lo, each tremulous frame was wrapped in robe of a whiteness,
Down to the ankles that fell, with nethermost border of purple,
While on ambrosial brows there rested fillets like snowflakes.
They, at a task eternal their hands religiously plying,
Held in the left on high, with wool enfolded, a distaff,
Delicate fibers wherefrom, drawn down, were shaped by the right hand —
Shaped by fingers upturned, — but the down-turned thumb set a-whirling,

Poised with perfected whorl, the industrious shaft of the spindle.
Still, as they span, as they span, was the tooth kept nipping and smoothing,
And to the withered lip clung morsels of wool as they smoothed it —
Filaments erstwhile rough that stood from the twist of the surface.
Close at their feet, meantime, were woven baskets of wicker
Guarding the soft white balls of the wool resplendent within them.
Thus then, parting the strands, these Three with resonant voices
Uttered, in chant divine, predestined sooth of the future —
Prophecy neither in time, nor yet in eternity, shaken.

" Thou that exaltest renown of thy name with the name of thy valor,
Bulwark Emathian, blest above sires in the offspring of promise,
Hear with thine ears this day what oracles fall from the Sisters
Chanting the fates for thee ; — but you, ye destiny-drawing
Spindles, hasten the threads of the destinies set for the future !

" Rideth the orb upon high that heralds boon unto bridegrooms —
Hesperus, — cometh anon with star propitious the virgin,
Speedeth thy soul to subdue — submerge it with love at the flood tide.
Hasten, ye spindles, and run, yea, gallop, ye thread-running spindles !

" Erstwhile, never a home hath roofed like generous loving,
Never before hath Love conjoinèd lovers so dearly, —
Never with harmony such as endureth for Thetis and Peleus.
Hasten, ye spindles, and run, yea, gallop, ye thread-running spindles !

" Born unto you shall be the undaunted heart of Achilles,
Aye by his brave breast known, unknown by his back to the foeman, —
Victor in onslaught, victor in devious reach of the race-course,
Fleeter of foot than feet of the stag that lighten and vanish, —
Hasten, ye spindles, and run, yea, gallop, ye thread-running spindles ! "

192. Achilles, Son of Peleus. So the sisters prophesied the future of the hero, Achilles, — from his father called Pelides ; from his grandfather, Æacides. How by him the Trojans should fall, as fall the ears of corn when they are yellow before the scythe ; how because of him Scamander should run red, warm with blood, choked with blind bodies, into the whirling Hellespont ; how finally he himself, in his prime, should fall, and how on his tomb should be sacrificed the fair Polyxena, daughter of Priam, whom he had loved. " So," says Catullus, " sang the Fates. For those were the days before piety and righteous action were spurned by mankind, the days when Jupiter and his immortals deigned to consort with zealous man, to enjoy the sweet odor of his burnt-offering, to march beside him to battle, to swell his shout in victory and his lament in defeat, to smile on his peaceful harvests, to

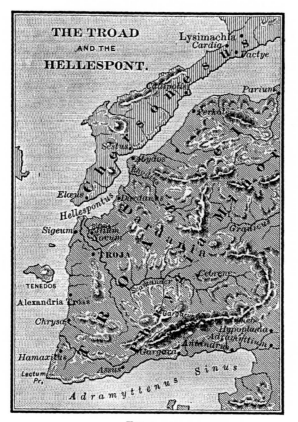

FIG. 149

recline at his banquets, and to bless the weddings of fair women and goodly heroes. But now, alas," concludes Catullus, " godliness and chastity, truth, wisdom, and honor have departed from among men " :

> Wherefore the gods no more vouchsafe their presence to mortals,
> Suffer themselves no more to be touched by the ray of the morning.
> But there were gods in the pure, — in the golden prime of the Ages.

The hero of the Trojan War, here prophesied, **Achilles,** fleet of foot, the dauntless, the noble, the beloved of Zeus, the breaker of the ranks of men, is the ideal hero of the Greeks, — the mightiest of the Achæans far. Of his youth many interesting stories are told : how his mother, endeavoring to make him invulnerable, plunged him in the river Styx, and succeeded save with regard to his ankles by which she held him ; and how he was educated in eloquence and the arts of war by his father's friend Phœnix, and by his father's other friend Chiron, the centaur, in riding and hunting and music and the art of healing. One of the most Greek-minded of our English poets, Matthew Arnold,[1] singing of a beauteous dell by Etna, tells how

> In such a glen, on such a day,
> On Pelion, on the grassy ground,
> Chiron, the aged Centaur, lay,
> The young Achilles standing by.
> The Centaur taught him to explore
> The mountains ; where the glens are dry
> And the tired Centaurs come to rest,
> And where the soaking springs abound
> And the straight ashes grow for spears,
> And where the hill goats come to feed
> And the sea eagles build their nest.
> He showed him Phthia far away.
> And said, " O boy, I taught this lore
> To Peleus, in long distant years ! "
> He told him of the gods, the stars,
> The tides ; — and then of mortal wars,
> And of the life which heroes lead
> Before they reach the Elysian place
> And rest in the immortal mead ;
> And all the wisdom of his race.

Upon the character of Achilles, outspoken, brave, impulsive ; to his friends passionately devoted, to his foes implacable ; lover of war and lover of home ; inordinately ambitious but submissive to divine decree ; — upon this handsome, gleaming, terrible, glooming, princely warrior of his race, the poet of the Iliad delights to dwell, and the world has delighted in the portraiture from that day to this.

[1] Empedocles on Etna.

193. Atreus was the son of Pelops and Hippodamia and grandson of Tantalus, therefore great-grandson of Jove. Both by blood and by marriage he was connected with Theseus. He took to wife Aërope, granddaughter of Minos II, king of Crete, and by her had two sons, Agamemnon, the general of the Grecian army in the Trojan War, and Menelaüs, at whose solicitation the war was undertaken. Of Atreus it may be said that with cannibal atrocity like that of his grandsire, Tantalus, he on one occasion wreaked his vengeance on a brother, Thyestes, by causing him to eat the flesh of two of his own children. A son of this Thyestes, Ægisthus by name, revived in due time against Agamemnon the treacherous feud that had existed between their fathers.

194. Tyndareus was king of Lacedæmon (Sparta). His wife was Leda, daughter of Thestius of Calydon, and sister of Althæa, the mother of Meleager and Dejanira. To Tyndareus Leda bore Castor and Clytemnestra; to Jove she bore Pollux and Helen. The two former were mortal; the two latter, immortal. Clytemnestra was married to Agamemnon of Mycenæ, to whom she bore Electra, Iphigenia, Chrysothemis, and Orestes. Helen, the fair immediate cause of the Trojan War, became the wife of Menelaüs, who with her obtained the kingdom of Sparta.

Of the families of Peleus, Atreus, and Tyndareus, the genealogies will be found in the Commentary corresponding with these sections of the story; also the genealogy of Ulysses, one of the leaders of the Greek army during the war and the hero of the Odyssey, which narrates his subsequent adventures; and that of the royal family of Troy against whom the war was undertaken. A slight study of these family trees will reveal interesting relationships between the principal participants in the war. For instance: that the passionate Achilles and the intolerant Ajax, second only to Achilles in military prowess, are first cousins; and that the family of Ajax is connected by marriage with that of the Trojan Hector, whom he meets in combat. That Ulysses is a distant cousin of his wife Penelope and of Clytemnestra, the wife of Agamemnon; and that he is a kinsman of Patroclus, the bosom friend of Achilles. In the family of Tyndareus we note most the tragic and romantic careers of the women, — Clytemnestra, who murdered her husband and married his cousin Ægisthus; Helen, whose beauty provoked war between her two husbands and their races; Penelope, whose fidelity to her absent lord is the marvel of the Odyssey. It will be noticed, too, that the daughter of Helen, Hermione, is strangely enough married first by the son of Achilles and, afterwards, by the son of Agamemnon, and so becomes sister-in-law to her noble cousins, Electra and Iphigenia.

The kinsmen and descendants of Peleus — Telamon, Ajax, Teucer, Achilles, Neoptolemus — are characterized by their personal valor, their intolerant and resentful temper. In the family of Atreus, the men are remarkable for their kingly attributes; the principal women for their unwavering devotion to religious duty. The members of the royal family of Troy are of richly varied and most unusual individuality: like Tithonus and Memnon, Paris, Hesione, Cassandra and Polyxena, poetic and pathetic; like Laomedon, Priam, Hector and Troilus, patriotic, persistent in the face of overwhelming odds.; but all fated to a dolorous end. Of those engaged in the Trojan War, Æneas and his aged father, Anchises, beloved of Venus, are practically the only survivors to a happier day.

FIG. 150. HELEN PERSUADED

CHAPTER XXII

THE TROJAN WAR

. . . At length I saw a lady within call,
 Stiller than chisel'd marble, standing there:
A daughter of the gods, divinely tall,
 And most divinely fair.

Her loveliness with shame and with surprise
 Froze my swift speech: she turning on my face
The starlike sorrows of immortal eyes,
 Spoke slowly in her place.

" I had great beauty; ask thou not my name:
 No one can be more wise than destiny.
Many drew swords and died. Where'er I came
 I brought calamity." [1]

195. Its Origin. At the nuptials of Peleus and Thetis all the
gods had been invited with the exception of Eris, or Discord.
Enraged at her exclusion, the goddess threw a golden apple among

[1] From Tennyson's Dream of Fair Women.

the guests, with the inscription, " For the fairest." Thereupon
Juno, Venus, and Minerva each claimed the apple. Not willing
to decide so delicate a matter, Jupiter sent the goddesses to Mount
Ida where Paris, son of Priam, king of Troy, was tending his
flocks. Till that moment the shepherd-prince had been happy.
He was young and beautiful and beloved, — " White-breasted like a
star," says Œnone, the nymph whom he had wedded :

> White-breasted like a star
> Fronting the dawn he moved; a leopard skin
> Dropp'd from his shoulder, but his sunny hair
> Cluster'd about his temples like a god's :
> And his cheek brighten'd as the foam-bow brightens
> When the wind blows the foam, and all my heart
> Went forth to embrace him coming ere he came.[1]

But to him was now committed the judgment between the goddesses. They appeared :

> And at their feet the crocus brake like fire,
> Violet, amaracus, and asphodel,
> Lotos and lilies : and a wind arose,
> And overhead the wandering ivy and vine,
> This way and that, in many a wild festoon
> Ran riot, garlanding the gnarlèd boughs
> With bunch and berry and flower thro' and thro'.[1]

Juno promised him power and riches, Minerva glory and renown
in war, Venus the fairest of women for his wife, — each attempting to bias the judge in her own favor. Paris, forgetting the fair
nymph to whom he owed fealty, decided in favor of Venus, thus
making the two other goddesses his enemies. Under the protection
of the goddess of love, he soon afterwards sailed to Greece. Here
he was hospitably received by Menelaüs, whose wife, Helen, as
fairest of her sex, was unfortunately the prize destined for Paris.
This fair queen had in time past been sought by numerous suitors ;
but before her decision was made known, they all, at the suggestion of Ulysses, son of Laërtes, king of Ithaca, had taken an oath

---

[1] From Tennyson's Œnone.

that they would sustain her choice and avenge her cause if necessary. She was living happily with Menelaüs when Paris, becoming their guest, made love to her, and then, aided by Venus, persuaded her to elope with him, and carried her to Troy. From this cause arose the famous Trojan War, — the theme of the greatest poems of antiquity, those of Homer and Virgil.

Menelaüs called upon the chieftains of Greece to aid him in recovering his wife. They came forward with a few exceptions. Ulysses, for instance, who had married a cousin of Helen's, Penelope, daughter of Icarius, was happy in his wife and child, and loth to embark in the troublesome affair. Palamedes was sent to urge him. But when Palamedes arrived at Ithaca, Ulysses pretended madness. He yoked an ass and an

FIG. 151. ACHILLES TAKEN FROM SCYROS

ox together to the plow and began to sow salt. The ambassador, to try him, placed the infant Telemachus before the plow, whereupon the father, turning the plow aside, showed that his insanity was a mere pretense. Being himself gained for the undertaking, Ulysses lent his aid to bring in other reluctant chiefs, especially Achilles, son of Peleus and Thetis. Thetis being herself one of the immortals, and knowing that her son was fated to perish before Troy if he went on the expedition, endeavored to prevent his going. She, accordingly, sent him to the court of King Lycomedes of the island of Scyros, and induced him to conceal himself in the garb of a maiden among the daughters of the king. Hearing that the young Achilles was there, Ulysses went disguised as a merchant to the palace and offered for sale female ornaments, among which had been placed some arms. Forgetting the part he had assumed, Achilles handled the weapons and thereby betrayed himself to Ulysses, who found no great difficulty in persuading him to disregard his mother's counsels and join his countrymen in the war.

It seems that from early youth Paris had been reared in obscurity, because there were forebodings that he would be the ruin of the state. These forebodings appeared, at last, likely to be realized; for the Grecian armament now in preparation was the greatest that had ever been fitted out. Agamemnon, king of Mycenæ and brother of Menelaüs, was chosen commander in chief. Preëminent among the warriors was the swift-footed Achilles. After him ranked his cousin Ajax, the son of Telamon, gigantic in size and of great courage, but dull of intellect; Diomede, the son of Tydeus, second only to Achilles in all the qualities of a hero; Ulysses, famous for sagacity; and Nestor, the oldest of the Grecian chiefs, to whom they all looked up for counsel.

But Troy was no feeble enemy. Priam the king, son of Laomedon and brother of Tithonus and Hesione, was now old; but he had been a wise prince and had strengthened his state by good government at home and powerful alliances with his neighbors. By his wife Hecuba he had a numerous family; but the principal stay and support of his throne was his son Hector, one of the noblest figures of antiquity. The latter had, from the first, a presentiment of the ruin of Troy, but still he persevered in heroic resistance, though he by no means justified the wrong which brought this danger upon his country. He was united in marriage with the noble Andromache, and as husband and father his character was not less admirable than as warrior. The principal leaders on the side of the Trojans, beside Hector, were his relative, Æneas, the son of Venus and Anchises, Deiphobus, Glaucus, and Sarpedon.

196. Iphigenia in Aulis. After two years of preparation, the Greek fleet and army assembled in the port of Aulis in Bœotia. Here Agamemnon, while hunting, killed a stag that was sacred to Diana. The goddess in retribution visited the army with pestilence and produced a calm which prevented the ships from leaving the port. Thereupon, Calchas the soothsayer announced that the wrath of the virgin goddess could only be appeased by the sacrifice of a virgin, and that none other but the daughter of the offender would be acceptable. Agamemnon, however reluctant, submitted to the inevitable and sent for his daughter Iphigenia, under the pretense that her marriage to Achilles was to be at once performed. But, in the moment of sacrifice, Diana, relenting, snatched the maiden away and left a hind in her

FIG. 152. THE SACRIFICE OF IPHIGENIA

place. Iphigenia, enveloped in a cloud, was conveyed to Tauris, where Diana made her priestess of her temple.[1]

Iphigenia is represented as thus describing her feelings at the moment of sacrifice :

" I was cut off from hope in that sad place,
   Which men call'd Aulis in those iron years :
My father held his hand upon his face ;
   I, blinded with my tears,

" Still strove to speak : my voice was thick with sighs
   As in a dream. Dimly I could descry
The stern black-bearded kings, with wolfish eyes
   Waiting to see me die.

" The high masts flicker'd as they lay afloat ;
   The crowds, the temples, waver'd, and the shore ;
The bright death quiver'd at the victim's throat ;
   Touch'd ; and I knew no more." [2]

[1] Euripides, Iphigenia at Aulis, Iphigenia among the Tauri.
[2] From Tennyson's Dream of Fair Women.

197. Protesilaüs and Laodamia. The wind now proving fair, the fleet made sail and brought the forces to the coast of Troy. The Trojans opposed their landing, and at the first onset one of the noblest of the Greeks, Protesilaüs, fell by the hand of Hector. This Protesilaüs had left at home his wife Laodamia (a niece of Alcestis), — who was most tenderly attached to him. The story runs that when the news of his death reached her, she implored the gods for leave to converse with him if but for three hours. The request was granted. Mercury led Protesilaüs back to the upper world; and when the hero died a second time Laodamia died with him. It is said that the nymphs planted elm trees round his grave, which flourished till they were high enough to command a view of Troy, then withered away, giving place to fresh branches that sprang from the roots.

Wordsworth has taken the story of Protesilaüs and Laodamia for a poem invested with the atmosphere of the classics. The oracle, according to the tradition, had declared that victory should be the lot of that party from which should fall the first victim in the war. The poet represents Protesilaüs, on his brief return to earth, relating to Laodamia the story of his fate:

" The wished-for wind was given: — I then revolved
  The oracle, upon the silent sea;
And, if no worthier led the way, resolved
  That, of a thousand vessels, mine should be
The foremost prow in pressing to the strand, —
Mine the first blood that tinged the Trojan sand.

" Yet bitter, ofttimes bitter, was the pang
  When of thy loss I thought, belovèd Wife!
On thee too fondly did my memory hang,
  And on the joys we shared in mortal life, —
The paths which we had trod — these fountains, flowers,
My new-planned cities, and unfinished towers.

" But should suspense permit the foe to cry,
  ' Behold they tremble! — haughty their array,
Yet of their number no one dares to die'?
  In soul I swept the indignity away:
Old frailties then recurred: — but lofty thought,
In act embodied, my deliverance wrought." . . .

> . . . Upon the side
> Of Hellespont (such faith was entertained)
> A knot of spiry trees for ages grew
> From out the tomb of him for whom she died;
> And ever, when such stature they had gained
> That Ilium's walls were subject to their view,
> The trees' tall summits withered at the sight;
> A constant interchange of growth and blight!

198. Homer's Iliad. The war continued without decisive result for nine years. Then an event occurred which seemed likely to prove fatal to the cause of the Greeks, — a quarrel between Achilles and Agamemnon. It is at this point that the great poem of Homer, the Iliad, begins.

Of this and the other epics from which the story is drawn an account will be found in Chapter XXXII below; and a list of the best English translations, in the corresponding sections of the Commentary. What delight one may derive from reading the Greek epics even in translation is nowhere better expressed than in the following sonnet of John Keats, "On First Looking into Chapman's Homer":

> Much have I travel'd in the realms of gold,
> And many goodly states and kingdoms seen;
> Round many western islands have I been
> Which bards in fealty to Apollo hold.
> Oft of one wide expanse had I been told
> That deep-brow'd Homer ruled as his demesne:
> Yet did I never breathe its pure serene
> Till I heard Chapman speak out loud and bold:
> — Then felt I like some watcher of the skies
> When a new planet swims into his ken;
> Or like stout Cortez when with eagle eyes
> He stared at the Pacific — and all his men
> Look'd at each other with a wild surmise —
> Silent, upon a peak in Darien.

199. The Wrath of Achilles. The Greeks, though unsuccessful against Troy, had taken the neighboring and allied cities; and in the division of the spoil a female captive, by name Chryseïs, daughter of Chryses, priest of Apollo, had fallen to the share of

Agamemnon. Chryses came bearing the sacred emblems of his office and begged the release of his daughter. Agamemnon refused. Thereupon Chryses implored Apollo to afflict the Greeks till they should be forced to yield their prey. Apollo granted the prayer of his priest and sent such pestilence upon the Grecian camp, that a council was called to deliberate how to allay the wrath of the gods and avert the plague. Achilles boldly charged the misfortunes upon Agamemnon as caused by his withholding Chryseïs. Agamemnon, in anger, consented, thereupon, to relinquish his captive, but demanded that Achilles should yield to him in her

FIG. 153. THE SURRENDER OF BRISEÏS

From the relief by Thorwaldsen

stead Briseïs, a maiden who had fallen to that hero's share in the division of the spoil. Achilles submitted, but declared that he would take no further part in the war, — withdrew his forces from the general camp and avowed his intention of returning to Greece.

200. The Enlistment of the Gods. The gods and goddesses interested themselves as much in this famous siege as did the parties themselves. It was well known in heaven that fate had decreed the fall of Troy, if her enemies only persevered. Yet there was room for chance sufficient to excite by turns the hopes and fears of the powers above who took part with either side. Juno and Minerva, in consequence of the slight put upon their charms by Paris, were hostile to the Trojans; Venus for the opposite cause favored them; she enlisted, also, her admirer Mars on the same side. Neptune favored the Greeks. Apollo was neutral, sometimes taking one side, sometimes the other. Jove himself, though he loved Priam, exercised a degree of impartiality, — not, however, without exceptions.

201. Thetis intercedes for Achilles. Resenting the injury done by Agamemnon to her son, Thetis, the silver-footed, repaired to Jove's palace, and besought him to grant success to the Trojan arms and so make the Greeks repent of their injustice to Achilles. The father of the gods, wavering at first, finally sighed and consented, saying, "Go thou now, but look to it that Juno see thee not, for oft she taunts me that I aid the Trojan cause." Vain precaution: the jealous queen had seen only too well, and quickly she confronted the Thunderer with her suspicions, —

> " Fateful favor to Achilles, hast thou granted now I trow!"

said she.

> Zeus that rolls the clouds of heaven, her addressing answered then:
> " Moonstruck! thou art ever *trowing;* never I escape thy ken.
> After all, it boots thee nothing; leaves thee of my heart the less, —
> So thou hast the worser bargain. What if I the fact confess?
> It was done because I willed it. Hold thy place — my word obey,
> Lest if I come near, and on thee these unconquered hands I lay,
> All the gods that hold Olympus naught avail thee here to-day."[1]

202. Agamemnon calls a Council. In the events which immediately follow we are introduced to the more important human personages on both sides. To begin with, Agamemnon, king of men, deceived by a dream sent by Jupiter, calls a council of the Greeks in which, desiring to arouse them to fresh onslaught upon the Trojans, he tests their patience first by depicting the joys of the return home to Greece, and nearly overreaches himself in his cunning; for had it not been for the wise Nestor, king of sandy Pylos, and Ulysses of many devices, peer of Jove in wisdom, the common soldiers, fired with hope of viewing their dear native land and wives and little children once more, would have launched the ships and sailed forthwith. Among the murmuring host of those who

---

[1] Gladstone's Translations from the Iliad.

clamor for retreat the leader is Thersites, uncontrolled of speech, full of disorderly words, striving idly against the chieftains, aiming ever to turn their authority into ridicule. He is the one ludicrous character of the Iliad, this boaster and scandalmonger, sneering and turbulent of tongue:

> His figure such as might his soul proclaim;
> One eye was blinking, and one leg was lame;
> His mountain shoulders half his breast o'erspread,
> Thin hairs bestrewed his long misshapen head.
> Spleen to mankind his envious heart possest,
> And much he hated all, but most the best.
> Ulysses or Achilles still his theme;
> But royal scandal his delight supreme.[1]

Him Ulysses hearing rebukes, raising his scepter to strike:

> " Peace, factious monster, born to vex the state,
> With wrangling talents formed for foul debate. . . .
> Have we not known thee, slave of all our host,
> The man who acts the least, upbraids the most? . . ."
> He said, and cowering as the dastard bends,
> The weighty scepter on his back descends:
> On the round bunch the bloody tumors rise;
> The tears spring starting from his haggard eyes:
> Trembling he sat, and, shrunk in abject fears,
> From his wild visage wiped the scalding tears.[1]

The revolt is thus stayed. A banquet of the Greek chieftains is then held, merely of the greatest — Nestor, Idomeneus of Crete, Ajax the son of Telamon and cousin of Achilles, and Ajax the less, son of Orleus, Ulysses, also, and Agamemnon himself. Menelaüs comes, unbid but not unwelcome. Sacrifices are offered, but in vain; Jove heeds them not. Finally, a muster of the Greek troops, by nations and by kings, is determined upon; and so the army is set in array.

203. Paris plays the Champion. Likewise the army of the Trojans; and battle is about to be joined when forth from the Trojan ranks steps Paris himself to challenge some champion of the opposing host to single combat, — the beauteous Paris,

---

[1] Iliad, 2 (Pope's translation).

> In form a god! The panther's speckled hide
> Flowed o'er his armor with an easy pride, —
> His bended bow across his shoulders flung,
> His sword beside him negligently hung,
> Two pointed spears he shook with gallant grace,
> And dared the bravest of the Grecian race.[1]

Him, Menelaüs whom he had betrayed, Menelaüs loved of Mars, raging like a lion, swift espies and, leaping from his chariot, hastens to encounter. But Paris, smitten with a sense of his own treachery, fearful, trembling, pale at sight of the avenger, betakes himself to his heels and hides in the thick of the forces behind. Upbraided, however, by the generous Hector, noblest of Priam's sons, the handsome Trojan recovers his self-possession and consents to meet Menelaüs in formal combat between the opposing hosts: Helen and the wealth she brought to be the prize; and, thus, the long war to reach its termination. The Greeks accept the proposal, and a truce is agreed upon that sacrifices may be made on either side for victory, and the duel proceed.

204. Helen surveys the Grecian Host. Meantime, Iris, the goddess of the rainbow, summons Helen to view the impending duel. At her loom in the Trojan palace the ill-starred daughter of Leda is sitting, weaving in a golden web her own sad story. At memory of her former husband's love, her home, her parents, the princess drops a tear; then, softly sighing, turns her footsteps to the Scæan gate. No word is said of her matchless beauty, but what it was Homer shows us by its effect. For as she approaches the tower where aged Priam and his gray-haired chieftains sit, these cry, —

> " No wonder such celestial charms
> For nine long years have set the world in arms;
> What winning graces! what majestic mien!
> She moves a goddess, and she looks a queen.
> Yet hence, oh Heaven! convey that fatal face,
> And from destruction save the Trojan race." [1]

—Words reëchoed by our English Marlowe, two thousand years later :

> Was this the face that launched a thousand ships,
> And burnt the topless towers of Ilium?

[1] Iliad, 3 (Pope's translation).

Sweet Helen, make me immortal with a kiss. —
Her lips suck forth my soul: see, where it flies!
Come, Helen, come, give me my soul again!
Here will I dwell, for heaven is in these lips,
And all is dross that is not Helena. . . .
Oh, thou art fairer than the evening air
Clad in the beauty of a thousand stars;
Brighter art thou than flaming Jupiter
When he appeared to hapless Semele; . . .
And none but thou shalt be my paramour![1]

Priam, receiving his daughter-in-law tenderly, inquires of her the names of one and another of the Greeks moving on the plain below. —

"Who, that
Around whose brow such martial graces shine,
So tall, so awful, and almost divine?"[2]

"The son of Atreus," answers she, shamefacedly. "Agamemnon, king of kings, my brother once, before my days of shame."

"What's he whose arms lie scattered on the plain?
Broad is his breast, his shoulders larger spread,
Though great Atrides overtops his head.
Nor yet appear his care and conduct small;
From rank to rank he moves and orders all."[2]

"That is Ulysses," replies Helen, "of the barren isle of Ithaca; but his fame for wisdom fills the earth."

Old Antenor, seated by Priam's side, thereupon recalls the modesty and the restrained but moving eloquence of the wondrous son of Laërtes.

The king then asked, as yet the camp he viewed,
"What chief is that, with giant strength endued;
Whose brawny shoulders, and whose swelling chest,
And lofty stature, far exceed the rest?"[2]

"That is Ajax the great," responds the beauteous queen, "himself a host, bulwark of the Achæans." And she points out Idomeneus, also, the godlike king of Crete; then scans the array for her

[1] Christopher Marlowe, Doctor Faustus.   [2] Iliad, 3 (Pope's translation).

own dear brothers Castor and Pollux; — in vain, for them the life-giving earth held fast there in Lacedæmon, their native land.

205. Menelaüs defeats Paris. Now from both sides sacrifices have been made to Jove, avenger of oaths, with prayer for victory and vow of fidelity to the contract made. But Jove vouchsafes not yet fulfillment. The lists are measured out by Hector and Ulysses. The duel is on. Paris throws his spear: it strikes, but fails to penetrate the shield of Menelaüs. Menelaüs then breaks his blade upon the helmet of the Trojan, seizes him by the horse-hair crest, and drags him toward the Grecian lines. But Aphrodite touches the chin strap of Paris' headpiece so that it breaks and leaves the futile helmet in the victor's hand. Then, wrapping her favorite in a mist, the goddess bears him from the pursuit of the furious Menelaüs, and, laying him safe in Helen's chamber, summons his mistress, who first upbraids, then soothes him with her love.

The Greeks claim the victory, and with justice. The Trojans, then and there, would have yielded Helen and her wealth, and the fate of Troy might have been averted, had it not been for the machinations of the goddesses, Juno and Minerva. These could not bear that the hated city should thus escape. Prompted by the insidious urging of Minerva, one of the Trojans, Pandarus, breaks the truce; he shoots his arrow full at the heart of the unsuspecting Menelaüs. Minerva, of course, deflects the fatal shaft. But the treachery has accomplished its purpose; the war is reopened with fresh bitterness.

206. The Two Days' Battle. The battle which then begins lasts for two whole days. In its progress we witness a series of single combats. Pandarus the archer wounds Diomede, the son of Tydeus. He in turn, raging over the plain, fells Pandarus with his spear and crushes Æneas, Priam's valiant kinsman, to his knees with a great stone. Venus shrouds her fallen son in her shining veil and will rescue him. But Diomedes, clear of vision, spies her out and drives his pointed spear against her hand, grazing the palm of it. Out leaps the ichor, life-stream of the blessed gods, and the goddess shrieking drops her burden and flees from the jeering Diomede; — nay, mounts even to Olympus where, sobbing in the arms of her mother, Dione, she finds solace of her pain, and straightway turns to hopes of vengeance. Æneas, meantime, is wrapped by Phœbus Apollo in a dusky cloud and borne aloof to that god's temple, where Diana and Latona heal him.

To Diomede still breathing slaughter, the god of war himself, Mars, now appears in form of a Thracian captain, opposing him and stirring Hector and the swiftly recovered Æneas and the god-like Sarpedon against the Greeks. And the Greeks give back, but the keen eye of Diomede pierces the disguise of the War-god, and he shouts a warning to his comrades. Then Minerva descends to where Diomede, the son of Tydeus, is resting beside his chariot, and she spurs him afresh to the fray. "Thou joy of my heart," says she, "fear thou neither Mars nor any other of the immortals, for I shall help thee mightily." So she takes the place of his charioteer, and together they drive upon the War-god. And that one cannot come at the son of Tydeus to strike him down, because of the ward that Minerva vouchsafes. But, for his part, Diomede strikes his spear against the nethermost belly of Mars and wounds him, rending his fair skin; and he plucks forth the spear again. Then brazen Mars bellows loud as nine or ten thousand soldiers all at once; and, like Venus before him, betakes himself to Olympus. There, complaining to Jove, he receives stern reprimand for his intolerant and hateful spirit, stirring men ever to strife, — "like thine own mother Juno, after whom, not after me, thou takest." Thus, the father of the gods; and he makes an end, and bids Pæan, the family physician, heal him.

Diomedes, still bearing down upon the Trojans, is about to fight with a young warrior when, struck by his appearance, he inquires his name. It is Glaucus, and the youth is grandson of the noble Bellerophon. Then Diomede of the loud war cry is glad and strikes his spear into the earth and declines to fight. "For lo," says he, "our grandfathers were guest-friends, and guest-friends are we. Why slay each other? There are multitudes of Trojans for me to slay, and for thee Achæans in multitude, if thou canst. Let us twain rather exchange arms as a testimony of our good faith." And this they do; and Diomede gets the best of the bargain, his armor being worth but nine oxen, and young Glaucus' five score.

207. Hector and Andromache. The Trojans being still pushed nearer to their own walls, Hector, bravest of Priam's sons, returns to the city to urge the women to prayer, and to carry the loitering Paris back with him to the defense. Here he meets his brave mother Hecuba, and then the fair Helen ; but most to our purpose and his, his wife, the white-armed Andromache, the noblest of the women of the Iliad, for whom he has searched in vain.

But when he had passed through the great city and was come to the Scæan gates, whereby he was minded to issue upon the plain, then came his dear-won wife, running to meet him, even Andromache, daughter of great-hearted

FIG. 154. HECTOR'S FAREWELL

From the relief by Thorwaldsen

Eëtion. . . . So she met him now ; and with her went the handmaid bearing in her bosom the tender boy, the little child, Hector's loved son, like unto a beautiful star. Him Hector called Scamandrius, but all the folk Astyanax, " defender of the city." So now he smiled and gazed at his boy silently, and Andromache stood by his side weeping, and clasped her hand in his, and spake and called upon his name. " Dear my lord, this thy hardihood will undo thee, neither hast thou any pity for thine infant boy, nor for hapless me that soon shall be thy widow ; for soon will the Achæans all set upon thee and slay thee. But it were better for me to go down to the grave if I lose thee ; for nevermore will any comfort be mine, when once thou, even thou, hast met thy fate, — but only sorrow. Moreover I have no father, now, nor lady mother. . . . And the seven brothers that were mine within our halls, all these on the selfsame day went within the house of Hades ; for fleet-footed, goodly Achilles slew them all amid their kine of trailing gait and white-faced sheep. . . .

Nay, Hector, thou art to me father and lady mother, yea and brother, even as thou art my goodly husband. Come now, have pity and abide here upon the tower, lest thou make thy child an orphan and thy wife a widow." . . .

Then great Hector of the glancing helm answered her: "Surely I take thought for all these things, my wife; but I have very sore shame of the Trojans and Trojan dames with trailing robes, if like a coward I shrink away from battle. Moreover mine own soul forbiddeth me, seeing I have learnt ever to be valiant and fight in the forefront of the Trojans, winning my father's great glory and mine own. Yea of a surety, I know this in heart and soul; the day shall come for holy Ilios to be laid low, and Priam and the folk of Priam of the good ashen spear. Yet doth the anguish of the Trojans hereafter not so much trouble me, neither Hecuba's own, neither king Priam's, neither my brethren's, the many and brave that shall fall in the dust before their foemen, as doth thine anguish in the day when some mail-clad Achæan shall lead thee weeping, and rob thee of the light of freedom. . . . But me in death may the heaped-up earth be covering, ere I hear thy crying and thy carrying into captivity." [1]

So spoke the great-hearted hero, and stretched his arms out to take his little boy. But

> The babe clung crying to his nurse's breast,
> Scared at the dazzling helm, and nodding crest.
> With secret pleasure each fond parent smiled,
> And Hector hasted to relieve his child, —
> The glittering terrors from his brows unbound
> And placed the beaming helmet on the ground.
> Then kissed the child, and, lifting high in air,
> Thus to the gods, preferred a father's prayer:
> "O thou! whose glory fills the ethereal throne,
> And all ye deathless powers! protect my son!
> Grant him, like me, to purchase just renown,
> To guard the Trojans, to defend the crown,
> Against his country's foes the war to wage,
> And rise the Hector of the future age!
> So when, triumphant from successive toils
> Of heroes slain, he bears the reeking spoils,
> Whole hosts may hail him with deserved acclaim
> And say, 'This chief transcends his father's fame':
> While, pleased, amidst the general shouts of Troy,
> His mother's conscious heart o'erflows with joy." [2]

[1] Iliad, 6, 390 *et seq.* (Lang, Leaf, and Myers' translation).
[2] Iliad, 6, 470–490 (Pope's translation).

So prayed he, the glorious Hector, foreboding of the future, but little thinking that, when he himself was slain and the city sacked, his starlike son should be cast headlong to death from Troy's high towers, and his dear wife led into captivity as he had dreaded, indeed, and by none other than Neoptolemus, the son of his mortal foe, Achilles. But now Hector laid the boy in the arms of his wife, and she, smiling tearfully, gathered him to her fragrant bosom; and her husband pitied her, and caressed her with his hand, and bade her farewell, saying:

> "Andromache! my soul's far better part,
> Why with untimely sorrows heaves thy heart?
> No hostile hand can antedate my doom,
> Till fate condemns me to the silent tomb.
> Fixed is the term to all the race of earth;
> And such the hard condition of our birth,
> No force can then resist, no flight can save;
> All sink alike, the fearful and the brave.
> No more — but hasten to thy tasks at home,
> There guide the spindle, and direct the loom;
> Me glory summons to the martial scene,
> The field of combat is the sphere for men.
> Where heroes war, the foremost place I claim,
> The first in danger, as the first in fame." [1]

He took up his horsehair crested helmet; and she departed to her home, oft looking back and letting fall big tears, thinking that he would no more come back from battle.

208. Neptune aids the Discouraged Greeks. But the end was not to be so soon. Hector, returning to the field, challenged the bravest of the Greeks to combat. Nine accepted the challenge; but the lot fell upon Ajax, the son of Telamon. The duel lasted till night, with deeds of valor on both sides; and the heroes parted, each testifying to his foeman's worth. The next day a truce was declared for the burning of the dead; but, soon after, the conflict was renewed, and before the might of Hector and his troops the Greeks were driven back to their trenches.

Then Agamemnon, king of men, called another council of his wisest and bravest chiefs and, grievously discouraged, proposed,

[1] Iliad, 6 (Pope's translation).

this time in earnest, that they reëmbark and sail home to Greece.[1] In the debate that ensued Nestor advised that an embassy should be sent to Achilles persuading him to return to the field ; and that Agamemnon should yield the maiden, the cause of dispute, with ample gifts to atone for the wrong he had done. Agamemnon assented ; and Ulysses, Ajax, and Phœnix were sent to carry to Achilles the penitent message. They performed that duty, but Achilles was deaf to their entreaties. He positively refused to

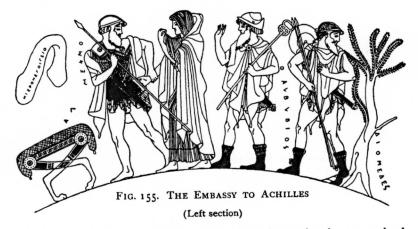

FIG. 155. THE EMBASSY TO ACHILLES

(Left section)

return to the attack and persisted in his determination to embark for Greece without delay.

Meanwhile the Greeks, having constructed a rampart around their ships, were now, instead of besieging Troy, in a manner themselves besieged, within their rampart. The next day after the unsuccessful embassy to Achilles, another battle was fought, in which Agamemnon raged mightily with his spear till, wounded, he was forced to retire to the hollow ships ; and Ulysses, too, bravely warring, had a narrow escape with life.[2] Then the Trojans, favored by Jove, succeeded in forcing a passage through the Grecian rampart and were about to set fire to the ships. But Neptune, seeing the Greeks hard pressed, came to their rescue.[3] Appearing in the form of Calchas the prophet, he raised the ardor of the warriors to such a pitch that they forced the Trojans to give way. Here

[1] Iliad, 9. [2] Iliad, 11. [3] Iliad, 13.

Ajax, son of Telamon, performed prodigies of valor. Bearing his massy shield and "shaking his far-shadowing spear," he encountered Hector.[1] The Greek shouted defiance, to which Hector replied, and hurled his lance at the huge warrior. It was well aimed and struck Ajax where the belts that bore his sword and shield crossed each other on the breast, but the double guard prevented its penetrating, and it fell harmless. Then Ajax, seizing a huge stone, one of those that served to prop the ships, hurled it

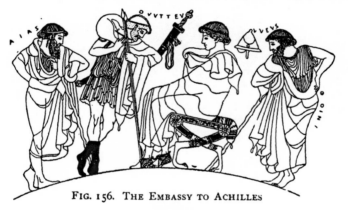

FIG. 156. THE EMBASSY TO ACHILLES

(Right section)

at Hector. It struck him near the neck and stretched him on the plain. His followers instantly seized him and bore him off stunned and wounded.

209. Jupiter inspirits the Trojans. While Neptune was thus aiding the Greeks and driving back the Trojans, Jupiter saw nothing of what was going on, for his attention had been drawn from the field by the wiles of Juno.[2] That goddess had arrayed herself in all her charms, and to crown all had borrowed of Venus her girdle, the Cestus, which enhanced the wearer's charms to such a degree that they were irresistible. So prepared, Juno had joined her husband, who sat on Olympus watching the battle. When he beheld her, the fondness of his early love revived and, forgetting the contending armies and all other affairs of state, he gave himself up to her and let the battle go as it would.

[1] Iliad, 14, 400–440.   [2] Iliad, 14, 150–350.

But this oblivion did not continue long. When, upon turning his eyes downward, the cloud-compeller beheld Hector stretched, almost lifeless, on the plain, he angrily dismissed Juno, commanding her to send Iris and Apollo to him.[1] The former bore a peremptory message to Neptune, ordering him to quit the contest.

FIG. 157. THE BATTLE BY THE SHIPS

Apollo was dispatched to heal Hector's bruises and to inspirit his heart. These orders were obeyed with such speed that while the battle was still raging, Hector returned to the field and Neptune betook himself to his own dominions.

210. Achilles and Patroclus. An arrow from the bow of Paris had wounded Machaon, son of Æsculapius, a brave warrior, who, having inherited his father's art, was of great value to the Greeks as their surgeon. Nestor, taking Machaon in his chariot, conveyed him from the field. As they passed the ships of Achilles, that hero, looking over the battle, saw the chariot of Nestor, and recognized the old chief, but could not discern who the wounded warrior was. Calling Patroclus, his companion and dearest friend, he sent him to Nestor's tent to inquire. Patroclus, performing the behest, saw Machaon wounded and, having told the cause of his coming, would have hastened away, but Nestor detained him to tell him the extent of the Grecian calamities. He reminded him also how, at the time of the departure for Troy, Achilles and himself had been charged by their respective sires: the one to aspire to the highest pitch of glory; the other, as the elder, to keep

[1] Iliad, 15.

watch over his friend and to guide his inexperience. "Now," said Nestor, "is the time for such guidance. If the gods so please, thou mayest win Achilles back to the common cause; but if not, let him at least send his soldiers to the field, and come thou, Patroclus, clad in his armor. Perhaps the very sight of it may drive back the Trojans."[1]

211. Patroclus in the Armor of Achilles. Patroclus, strongly moved by this address, hastened to his friend, revolving in his mind what he had seen and heard.[2] He told the prince the sad condition of affairs at the camp of their late associates; Diomede, Ulysses, Agamemnon, Machaon, all wounded, the rampart broken down, the enemy among the ships preparing to burn them and thus to cut off all means of return to Greece. While they spoke, the flames burst forth from one of the ships. Achilles, at the sight, relented so far as to intrust Patroclus with the Myrmidons for the onslaught and to lend him his armor that he might thereby strike the more terror into the minds of the Trojans. Without delay the soldiers were marshaled, Patroclus put on the radiant armor, mounted the chariot of Achilles, and led forth the men ardent for battle. But before his friend went, Achilles strictly charged him to be content with repelling the foe. "Seek not," said he, "to press the Trojans without me, lest thou add still more to the disgrace already mine." Then exhorting the troops to do their best, he dismissed them full of ardor to the fight.

Patroclus and his Myrmidons at once plunged into the contest where it raged hottest. At the sight of them the joyful Grecians shouted, and the ships reëchoed the acclaim; but the Trojans, beholding the well-known armor, struck with terror, looked everywhere for refuge. First those who had got possession of the ship and set it on fire allowed the Grecians to retake it and extinguish the flames. Then the rest fled in dismay. Ajax, Menelaüs, and the two sons of Nestor performed prodigies of valor. Hector was forced to turn his horses' heads and retire from the enclosure, leaving his men encumbered in the fosse to escape as they could. Patroclus drove all before him, slaying many; nor did one dare to make a stand against him.

[1] Iliad, 11. [2] Iliad, 16.

212. The Deaths of Sarpedon and Patroclus. At last the grandson of Bellerophon, Sarpedon, son of Jove and Laodamia, ventured to oppose the Greek warrior. The Olympian looked down upon his son and would have snatched him from the fate impending, but Juno hinted that if he did so, the other inhabitants of heaven might be induced to interpose in like manner whenever any of their offspring were endangered,—an argument to which Jove yielded. Sarpedon threw his spear, but missed Patroclus; the spear of the Greek, on the other hand, pierced Sarpedon's breast, and he fell, calling to his friends to save his body from the foe. Then a furious contest arose for the corpse. The Greeks succeeded in stripping Sarpedon of his armor, but Jove would not suffer the body to be dishonored. By his command Apollo snatched it from the midst of the combatants and committed it to the care of the twin brothers Death and Sleep. By them it was transported to Lycia, Sarpedon's native land, and there received due funeral rites.

FIG. 158. MENELAÜS WITH THE BODY OF PATROCLUS

Thus far Patroclus had succeeded to the utmost in repelling the foe and relieving his countrymen, but now came a change of fortune. Hector, borne in his chariot, confronted him. Patroclus threw a vast stone at the Trojan, which missed its aim, but smote Cebriones, the charioteer, and felled him from the car. Hector leaped from the chariot to rescue his friend, and Patroclus also descended to complete his victory. Thus the two heroes met face to face. At this decisive moment the poet, as if reluctant to give Hector the glory, records that Phœbus Apollo, taking part against

Patroclus, struck the helmet from his head and the lance from his hand. At the same moment an obscure Trojan wounded him in the back, and Hector pressing forward pierced him with his spear. He fell mortally wounded.

Then arose a tremendous conflict for the body of Patroclus; but his armor was at once taken possession of by Hector, who, retiring a short distance, divested himself of his own mail, put on that of Achilles, then returned to the fight.[1] Ajax and Menelaüs defended the body, and Hector and his bravest warriors struggled to capture it. The battle still raged with equal fortune, when Jove enveloped the whole face of heaven in a cloud. The lightning flashed, the thunder roared, and Ajax, looking round for some one whom he might dispatch to Achilles to tell him of the death of his friend and of the imminent danger of his remains falling into the hands of the enemy, could see no suitable messenger. In desperation he exclaimed:

> " Father of heaven and earth! deliver thou
> Achaia's host from darkness; clear the skies;
> Give day; and, since thy sovereign will is such,
> Destruction with it; but, oh, give us day! " [2]

Jupiter heard the prayer and dispersed the clouds. Ajax sent Antilochus to Achilles with the intelligence of Patroclus' death and of the conflict raging for his remains; and the Greeks at last succeeded in bearing off the body to the ships, closely pursued by Hector and Æneas and the rest of the Trojans.

213. The Remorse of Achilles. Achilles heard the fate of his friend with such distress that Antilochus feared for a while lest he might destroy himself.[3] His groans reached the ears of Thetis, far down in the deeps of ocean where she abode, and she hastened to inquire the cause. She found him overwhelmed with self-reproach that he had suffered his friend to fall a victim to his resentment. His only consolation was the hope of revenge. He would fly instantly in search of Hector. But his mother reminded him that he was now without armor and promised, if he would but wait till the morrow, to procure for him a suit of armor from

---

[1] Iliad, 17. [2] Cowper's translation. The lines are often quoted. [3] Iliad, 18.

Vulcan more than equal to that he had lost. He consented, and Thetis immediately repaired to Vulcan's palace. She found him busy at his forge, making tripods for his own use, so artfully constructed that they moved forward of their own accord when wanted, and retired again when dismissed. On hearing the request of Thetis, Vulcan immediately laid aside his work and hastened to comply with her wishes. He fabricated a splendid suit of armor for Achilles; first a shield adorned with elaborate devices, of which a noble description is given by Homer, then a helmet crested with gold, then a corselet and greaves of impenetrable temper, all perfectly adapted to the hero's form, and of consummate workmanship. The suit was made in one night, and Thetis, receiving it, descended to earth and laid it at Achilles' feet at the dawn of day.

214. The Reconciliation of Agamemnon and Achilles. The first glow of pleasure that Achilles had felt since the death of Patroclus was at the sight of this splendid armor.[1] And now arrayed in it, he went forth to the camp, calling the chiefs to council. When the leaders were assembled, Achilles addressed them. Renouncing his displeasure against Agamemnon and bitterly lamenting the miseries that had resulted from it, he called on them to proceed at once to the field. Agamemnon made a suitable reply, laying the blame on Ate, the goddess of infatuation; and thereupon complete reconcilement took place between the heroes.

Then Achilles went forth to battle, heartened by the inspiration of Minerva and filled with a rage and thirst for vengeance that made him irresistible. As he mounted his chariot, one of his immortal coursers was, strange to say, endowed suddenly with speech from on high and, breaking into prophecy, warned the hero of his approaching doom. But, nothing daunted, Achilles pressed upon the foe. The bravest warriors fled before him or fell by his lance.[2] Hector, cautioned by Apollo, kept aloof; but the god, assuming the form of one of Priam's sons, Lycaon, urged Æneas to encounter the terrible warrior. Æneas, though he felt himself unequal, did not decline the combat. He hurled his spear with all his force against the shield, the work of Vulcan. The spear pierced two plates of the shield, but was stopped in the third. Achilles

[1] Iliad, 19.   [2] Iliad, 20.

threw his spear with better success. It pierced through the shield of Æneas, but glanced near his shoulder and made no wound. Then Æneas, seizing a stone, such as two men of modern times could hardly lift, was about to throw it, — and Achilles, with sword drawn, was about to rush upon him, — when Neptune, looking out upon the contest, had pity upon Æneas, who was sure to have the worst of it. The god, consequently, spread a cloud between the combatants and, lifting the Trojan from the ground, bore him over the heads of warriors and steeds to the rear of the battle. Achilles, when the mist cleared away, looked round in vain for his adversary, and acknowledging the prodigy, turned his arms against other champions. But none dared stand before him ; and Priam from his city walls beheld the whole army in full flight toward the city. He gave command to open wide the gates to receive the fugitives, and to shut them as soon as the Trojans should have passed, lest the enemy should enter likewise. But Achilles was so close in pursuit that that would have been impossible if Apollo had not, in the form of Agenor, Priam's son, first encountered the swift-footed hero, then turned in flight, and taken the way apart from the city. Achilles pursued, and had chased his supposed victim far from the walls before the god disclosed himself.[1]

215. The Death of Hector. But when the rest had escaped into the town Hector stood without, determined to await the combat. His father called to him from the walls, begging him to retire nor tempt the encounter. His mother, Hecuba, also besought him, but all in vain. " How can I," said he to himself, " by whose command the people went to this day's contest where so many have fallen, seek refuge for myself from a single foe ? Or shall I offer to yield up Helen and all her treasures and ample of our own beside ? Ah no ! even that is too late. He would not hear me through, but slay me while I spoke." While he thus ruminated, Achilles approached, terrible as Mars, his armor flashing lightning as he moved. At that sight Hector's heart failed him and he fled. Achilles swiftly pursued. They ran, still keeping near the walls, till they had thrice encircled the city. As often as Hector approached the walls Achilles intercepted him and forced him to

[1] Iliad, 21.

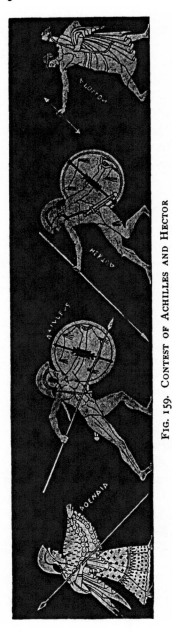

FIG. 159. CONTEST OF ACHILLES AND HECTOR

keep out in a wider circle. But Apollo sustained Hector's strength and would not let him sink in weariness. Then Pallas, assuming the form of Deiphobus, Hector's bravest brother, appeared suddenly at his side. Hector saw him with delight, and thus strengthened, stopped his flight, and, turning to meet Achilles, threw his spear. It struck the shield of Achilles and bounded back. He turned to receive another from the hand of Deiphobus, but Deiphobus was gone. Then Hector understood his doom and said, "Alas! it is plain this is my hour to die! I thought Deiphobus at hand, but Pallas deceived me, and he is still in Troy. But I will not fall inglorious." So saying he drew his falchion from his side and rushed at once to combat. Achilles, secure behind his shield, waited the approach of Hector. When he came within reach of his spear, Achilles, choosing with his eye a vulnerable part where the armor leaves the neck uncovered, aimed his spear at that part, and Hector fell, death-wounded. Feebly he said, " Spare my body! Let my parents ransom it, and let me receive funeral rites from the sons and daughters of Troy." To which Achilles replied, " Dog, name not ransom nor pity to me, on whom you have brought such dire distress. No! trust me, nought shall save thy carcass from the dogs.

Though twenty ransoms and thy weight in gold were offered, I should refuse it all."[1]

216. Achilles drags the Body of Hector. So saying, the son of Peleus stripped the body of its armor, and, fastening cords to the feet, tied them behind his chariot, leaving the body to trail along the ground. Then mounting the chariot he lashed the steeds and so dragged the body to and fro before the city. No words can tell the grief of Priam and Hecuba at this sight. His people could scarce restrain the aged king from rushing forth. He threw himself in the dust and besought them each by name to let him pass.

FIG. 160. ACHILLES OVER THE BODY OF HECTOR AT THE TOMB OF PATROCLUS

Hecuba's distress was not less violent. The citizens stood round them weeping. The sound of the mourning reached the ears of Andromache, the wife of Hector, as she sat among her maidens at work; and anticipating evil she went forth to the wall. When she saw the horror there presented, she would have thrown herself headlong from the wall, but fainted and fell into the arms of her maidens. Recovering, she bewailed her fate, picturing to herself her country ruined, herself a captive, and her son, the youthful Astyanax, dependent for his bread on the charity of strangers.

After Achilles and the Greeks had thus taken their revenge on the slayer of Patroclus, they busied themselves in paying due

[1] Iliad, 22, 350.

funeral rites to their friend.[1] A pile was erected, and the body
burned with due solemnity. Then ensued games of strength and
skill, chariot races, wrestling, boxing, and archery. Later, the
chiefs sat down to the funeral banquet, and finally retired to rest
But Achilles partook neither of the feast nor of sleep. The recollection of his lost friend kept him awake, — the memory of their
companionship in toil and dangers, in battle or on the perilous
deep. Before the earliest dawn he left his tent, and joining to his
chariot his swift steeds, he fastened Hector's body to be dragged
behind. Twice he dragged him round the tomb of Patroclus, leaving him at length stretched in the dust. But Apollo would not
permit the body to be torn or disfigured with all this abuse ; he
preserved it free from taint or defilement.[2]

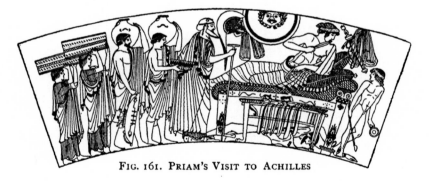

FIG. 161. PRIAM'S VISIT TO ACHILLES

While Achilles indulged his wrath in thus disgracing Hector,
Jupiter in pity summoned Thetis to his presence. Bidding her
prevail on Achilles to restore the body of Hector to the Trojans,
he sent Iris to encourage Priam to beg of Achilles the body of his
son. Iris delivered her message, and Priam prepared to obey.
He opened his treasuries and took out rich garments and cloths,
with ten talents in gold and two splendid tripods and a golden cup
of matchless workmanship. Then he called to his sons and bade
them draw forth his litter and place in it the various articles designed for a ransom to Achilles. When all was ready, the old
king with a single companion as aged as himself, the herald

---

[1] Iliad, 23.   [2] Iliad, 24, 15.

Idæus, drove forth from the gates, parting there with Hecuba his queen, and all his friends, who lamented him as going to certain death.

217. Priam in the Tent of Achilles.[1] But Jupiter, beholding with compassion the venerable king, sent Mercury to be his guide and protector. Assuming the form of a young warrior, Mercury presented himself to the aged couple; and, when at the sight of him they hesitated whether to fly or yield, approaching he grasped Priam's hand and offered to be their guide to Achilles' tent. Priam gladly accepted his service, and Mercury, mounting the carriage, assumed the reins and conveyed them to the camp. Then having cast the guards into a heavy sleep, he introduced Priam into the tent where Achilles sat, attended by two of his warriors. The aged king threw himself at the feet of Achilles and kissed those terrible hands which had destroyed so many of his sons. "Think, O Achilles," he said, "of thine own father, full of days like me, and trembling on the gloomy verge of life. Even now, mayhap, some neighbor chief oppresses him and there is none at hand to succor him in his distress. Yet, knowing that Achilles lives, he doubtless still rejoices, hoping that one day he shall see thy face again. But me no comfort cheers, whose bravest sons, so late the flower of Ilium, all have fallen. Yet one I had, one more than all the rest the strength of my age, whom fighting for his country thou hast slain. His body I come to redeem, bringing inestimable ransom with me. Achilles! reverence the gods! recollect thy father! for his sake show compassion to me!" These words moved Achilles, and he wept, remembering by turns his absent father and his lost friend. Moved with pity of Priam's silver locks and beard, he raised him from the earth and spake: "Priam, I know that thou hast reached this place conducted by some god, for without aid divine no mortal even in his prime of youth had dared the attempt. I grant thy request, for I am moved thereto by the manifest will of Jove." So saying he arose, went forth with his two friends, and unloaded of its charge the litter, leaving two mantles and a robe for the covering of the body. This they placed on the litter and spread the garments over it, that not unveiled it should be borne

[1] Iliad, 24, 330–804.

back to Troy. Then Achilles dismissed the old king, having first pledged himself to a truce of twelve days for the funeral solemnities.

As the litter approached the city and was descried from the walls, the people poured forth to gaze once more on the face of their hero. Foremost of all, the mother and the wife of Hector came, and at the sight of the lifeless body renewed their lamentations. The people wept with them, and to the going down of the sun there was no pause or abatement of their grief.

The next day, preparations were made for the funeral solemnities. For nine days the people brought wood and built the pile; and on the tenth they placed the body on the summit and applied the torch, while all Troy, thronging forth, encompassed the pyre. When it had completely burned, they quenched the cinders with wine, and, collecting the bones, placed them in a golden urn, which they buried in the earth. Over the spot they reared a pile of stones.

> Such honors Ilium to her hero paid,
> And peaceful slept the mighty Hector's shade.[1]

[1] Iliad, 24, 804 (Pope's translation).

AMAZON

CHAPTER XXIII

THE FALL OF TROY

218. The Fall of Troy. The story of the Iliad ends with the death of Hector, and it is from the Odyssey and later poems that we learn the fate of the other heroes. After the death of Hector, Troy did not immediately fall, but receiving aid from new allies, still continued its resistance. One of these allies was Memnon, the Ethiopian prince, whose story has been already told.[1] Another was Penthesilea, queen of the Amazons, who came with a band of female warriors. All the authorities attest the valor of these women and the fearful effect of their war cry. Penthesilea, having slain many of the bravest Greeks, was at last slain by Achilles. But when the hero bent over his fallen foe and contemplated her beauty, youth, and valor,

FIG. 162. ACHILLES AND PENTHESILEA

he bitterly regretted his victory. Thersites, the insolent brawler and demagogue, attempting to ridicule his grief, was in consequence slain by the hero.[2]

219. The Death of Achilles. But Achilles himself was not destined to a long life. Having by chance seen Polyxena, daughter of King Priam, — perhaps on occasion of the truce which was allowed the Trojans for the burial of Hector, — he was captivated with her charms; and to win her in marriage, it is said (but not by Homer) that he agreed to influence the Greeks to make peace with Troy. While the hero was in the temple of Apollo negotiating

[1] § 128.   [2] Pausanias, 5, 11, § 2; and Sophocles, Philoctetes, 445.

the marriage, Paris discharged at him a poisoned arrow,[1] which, guided by Apollo, fatally wounded him in the heel. This was his only vulnerable spot; for Thetis, having dipped him when an infant in the river Styx, had rendered every part of him invulnerable except that by which she held him.[2]

220. Contest for the Arms of Achilles. The body of Achilles so treacherously slain was rescued by Ajax and Ulysses. Thetis directed the Greeks to bestow her son's armor on that hero who of all survivors should be judged most deserving of it. Ajax and Ulysses were the only claimants. A select number of the other chiefs were appointed to award the prize. By the will of Minerva it was awarded to Ulysses, —wisdom being thus rated above valor. Ajax, enraged, set forth from his tent to wreak vengeance upon the Atridæ and Ulysses. But the goddess robbed him of reason and turned his hand against the flocks and herds of the Argives, which he slaughtered or led captive to his tent, counting them the rivals who had wronged him. Then the cruel goddess restored to him his wits. And he, fixing his sword in the ground, prepared to take his own life:

> " Come and look on me,
> O Death, O Death, — and yet in yonder world
> I shall dwell with thee, speak enough with thee;
> And thee I call, thou light of golden day,
> Thou Sun, who drivest on thy glorious car,
> Thee, for this last time, — never more again!
> O Light, O sacred land that was my home;
> O Salamis, where stands my father's hearth,
> Thou glorious Athens, with thy kindred race;
> Ye streams and rivers here, and Troïa's plains,
> To you that fed my life I bid farewell;
> This last, last word does Ajax speak to you;
> All else, I speak in Hades to the dead." [3]

Then, falling upon his sword, he died. So, in the words of his magnanimous foe, Ulysses, passed to the god that ruleth in gloom

> The best and bravest of the Argive host,
> Of all that came to Troïa, saving one,
> Achilles' self.[3]

---

[1] Virgil, Æneid, 6, 57.   [2] Statius, Achilleid, 1, 269.   [3] Sophocles, Ajax.

On the spot where his blood sank into the earth a hyacinth sprang up, bearing on its leaves the first two letters of his name, Ai, the Greek interjection of woe.[1]

It was now discovered that Troy could not be taken but by the aid of the arrows of Hercules. They were in possession of Philoctetes, the friend who had been with Hercules at the last and had lighted his funeral pyre. Philoctetes[2] had joined the Grecian expedition against Troy; but he accidentally wounded his foot with

FIG. 163. ŒNONE WARNING PARIS

one of the poisoned arrows, and the smell from the wound proved so offensive that his companions carried him to the isle of Lemnos and left him there. Diomede and Ulysses, or Ulysses and Neoptolemus (son of Achilles), were now sent to induce him to rejoin the army. They succeeded. Philoctetes was cured of his wound by Machaon, and Paris was the first victim of the fatal arrows.

[1] See Commentary.

[2] Servius Honoratus, Commentary on Æneid (3, 402). According to Sophocles (Philoctetes), the wound was occasioned by the bite of a serpent that guarded the shrine of the nymph Chryse, on an islet of the same name near Lemnos.

221. Paris and Œnone. In his distress Paris bethought him of one whom in his prosperity he had forgotten. This was the nymph Œnone, whom he had married when a youth and had abandoned for the fatal beauty of Helen. Œnone, remembering the wrongs she had suffered, refused to heal the wound; and Paris went back to Troy and died. Œnone quickly repented and hastened after him with remedies, but came too late, and in her grief hanged herself.

222. The Palladium. There was in Troy a celebrated statue of Minerva called the Palladium. It was said to have fallen from heaven, and the belief was that the city could not be taken so long as this statue remained within it. Ulysses and Diomede entered the city in disguise and succeeded in obtaining the Palladium, which they carried off to the Grecian camp.

Fig. 164. The Wooden Horse

223. The Wooden Horse. But Troy still held out. The Greeks began to despair of subduing it by force, and by advice of Ulysses they resorted to stratagem.[1] They pretended to be making preparations to abandon the siege; and a number of the ships were withdrawn and concealed behind a neighboring island. They then constructed an immense wooden horse, which they gave out was intended as a propitiatory offering to Minerva; but it was, in fact, filled with armed men. The rest of the Greeks then betook themselves to their ships and sailed away, as if for a final departure. The Trojans, seeing the encampment broken up and the fleet gone, concluded that the enemy had abandoned the siege. The gates of the city were thrown open, and the whole population issued forth, rejoicing at the long-prohibited liberty of passing freely over

[1] Virgil, Æneid. 2.

LAOCOÖN

the scene of the late encampment. The great horse was the chief object of curiosity. Some recommended that it be taken into the city as a trophy; others felt afraid of it. While they hesitated, Laocoön, the priest of Neptune, exclaimed, "What madness, citizens, is this! Have you not learned enough of Grecian fraud to be on your guard against it? For my part, I fear the Greeks even when they offer gifts."[1] So saying, he threw his lance at the horse's side. It struck, and a hollow sound reverberated like a groan. Then perhaps the people might have taken his advice and destroyed the fatal horse with its contents, but just at that moment a group of people appeared dragging forward one who seemed a prisoner and a Greek. Stupefied with terror, the captive was brought before the chiefs. He informed them that he was a Greek, Sinon by name; and that in consequence of the malice of Ulysses, he had been left behind by his countrymen at their departure. With regard to the wooden horse, he told them that it was a propitiatory offering to Minerva, and had been made so huge for the express purpose of preventing its being carried within the city; for Calchas the prophet had told them that if the Trojans took possession of it, they would assuredly triumph over the Greeks.

224. Laocoön and the Serpents. This language turned the tide of the people's feelings, and they began to think how they might best secure the monstrous horse and the favorable auguries connected with it, when suddenly a prodigy occurred which left no room for doubt. There appeared advancing over the sea two immense serpents. They came upon the land and the crowd fled in all directions. The serpents advanced directly to the spot where Laocoön stood with his two sons. They first attacked the children, winding round their bodies and breathing pestilential breath in their faces. The father, attempting to rescue them, was next seized and involved in the serpent's coils.

> . . . Vain
> The struggle; vain, against the coiling strain
> And gripe, and deepening of the dragon's grasp,
> The old man's clinch; the long envenomed chain
> Rivets the living links, — the enormous asp
> Enforces pang on pang, and stifles gasp on gasp.[2]

---

[1] *Timeo Danaos et dona ferentes.* — Æneid, 2, 49.   [2] Byron, Childe Harold.

He struggled to tear them away, but they overpowered all his efforts and strangled him and the children in their poisonous folds. The event was regarded as a clear indication of the displeasure of the gods at Laocoön's irreverent treatment of the wooden horse, which they no longer hesitated to regard as a sacred object and prepared to introduce with due solemnity into the city. They did so with songs and triumphal acclamations, and the day closed with festivity. In the night the armed men who were inclosed in the body of the horse, being let out by the traitor Sinon, opened the

FIG. 165. THE SACK OF TROY
(Left half)

gates of the city to their friends who had returned under cover of the night. The city was set on fire ; the people, overcome with feasting and sleep, were put to the sword, and Troy completely subdued.

225. The Death of Priam. Priam lived to see the downfall of his kingdom and was slain at last on the fatal night when the Greeks took the city. He had armed himself and was about to mingle with the combatants,[1] but was prevailed on by Hecuba to take refuge with his daughters and herself as a suppliant at the altar of Jupiter. While there, his youngest son, Polites, pursued by Pyrrhus, the son of Achilles, rushed in wounded and expired

---

[1] Hecuba's exclamation, "Not such aid nor such defenders does the time require," has become proverbial.   *Non tali auxilio nec defensoribus istis*
                                Tempus eget. — Æneid, 2, 521.

at the feet of his father; whereupon Priam, overcome with indignation, hurled his spear with feeble hand against Pyrrhus and was forthwith slain by him.

226. The Survivors.[1] Queen Hecuba and her daughter Cassandra were carried captives to Greece. Cassandra had been loved by Apollo, who gave her the gift of prophecy; but afterwards offended with her, he had rendered the gift unavailing by ordaining that her predictions should never be believed. Polyxena, another daughter, who had been loved by Achilles, was demanded by the

FIG. 166. THE SACK OF TROY
(Right half)

ghost of that warrior and was sacrificed by the Greeks upon his tomb. Of the fate of the white-armed Andromache we have already spoken. She was carried off as the wife of Neoptolemus, but he was faithful to her for only a short time. After he had cast her aside she married Helenus, a brother of Hector, and still later returned to Asia Minor.

227. Helen, Menelaüs, and Agamemnon. On the fall of Troy, Menelaüs recovered possession of his wife, who, it seems, had not ceased to love him, though she had yielded to the might of Venus and deserted him for another.[2] After the death of Paris, she aided

---

[1] Euripides,— Troades, Hecuba, Andromache.

[2] According to Euripides (Helen), and Stesichorus, it was a semblance of Helen that Paris won; the real Helen went to Egypt.

the Greeks secretly on several occasions : in particular when Ulysses and Diomede entered the city in disguise to carry off the Palladium. She then saw and recognized Ulysses, but kept the secret
and even assisted them in obtaining the image. Thus she became
reconciled to Menelaüs, and they were among the first to leave the
shores of Troy for their native land. But having incurred the displeasure of the gods, they were driven by storms from shore to
shore of the Mediterranean, visiting Cyprus, Phœnicia, and Egypt.
In Egypt they were kindly treated and presented with rich gifts, of
which Helen's share was a golden spindle and a basket on wheels.

> . . . Many yet adhere
> To the ancient distaff at the bosom fixed,
> Casting the whirling spindle as they walk.
> . . . This was of old, in no inglorious days,
> The mode of spinning, when the Egyptian prince
> A golden distaff gave that beauteous nymph,
> Too beauteous Helen ; no uncourtly gift.[1]

Milton also alludes to a famous recipe for an invigorating draft,
called Nepenthe, which the Egyptian queen gave to Helen :

> Not that Nepenthes which the wife of Thone
> In Egypt gave to Jove-born Helena,
> Is of such power to stir up joy as this,
> To life so friendly or so cool to thirst.[2]

At last, arriving in safety at Sparta, Menelaüs and Helen resumed their royal dignity, and lived and reigned in splendor ; and
when Telemachus, the son of Ulysses, in search of his father,
arrived at Sparta, he found them celebrating the marriage of their
daughter Hermione to Neoptolemus, son of Achilles.

Agamemnon [3] was not so fortunate in the issue. During his
absence his wife Clytemnestra had been false to him ; and when
his return was expected, she with her paramour, Ægisthus, son of
Thyestes, laid a plan for his destruction. Cassandra warned the
king, but as usual her prophecy was not regarded. While Agamemnon was bathing previous to the banquet given to celebrate
his return, the conspirators murdered him.

---

[1] Dyer, The Fleece.　　[2] Milton, Comus.　　[3] Æschylus, Agamemnon.

228. Electra and Orestes. It was the intention of the conspirators to slay his son Orestes also, a lad not yet old enough to be an object of apprehension, but from whom, if he should be suffered to grow up, there might be danger. Electra, the sister of Orestes, saved her brother's life by sending him secretly to his uncle Strophius, king of Phocis. In the palace of Strophius, Orestes grew up with the king's son Pylades, and formed with him a friendship which has become proverbial. Electra frequently reminded her brother by messengers of the duty of avenging his father's death; he, too, when he reached maturity, consulted the oracle of Delphi, which confirmed him in the design. He therefore repaired in disguise to Argos, pretending to be a messenger from Strophius, who would announce the death of Orestes. He brought with him what purported to be the ashes of the deceased in a funeral urn. After vis-

FIG. 167. ORESTES AND ELECTRA AT THE TOMB OF AGAMEMNON

iting his father's tomb and sacrificing upon it, according to the rites of the ancients, he met by the way his sister Electra. Mistaking her for one of the domestics, and desirous of keeping his arrival a secret till the hour of vengeance should arrive, he produced the urn. At once his sister, believing Orestes to be really dead, took the urn from him, and, embracing it, poured forth her grief in language full of tenderness and despair. Soon a recognition was effected, and the prince, with the aid of his sister, slew both Ægisthus and Clytemnestra.[1]

[1] Æschylus, Choëphori; Sophocles, Electra; Euripides, — Electra, Orestes.

229. Orestes pursued by the Furies.[1] This revolting act, the slaughter of a mother by her son, though extenuated by the guilt of the victim and the express command of the gods, did not fail

to awaken in the breasts of the ancients the same abhorrence that it does in ours. The Eumenides seized upon Orestes and drove him frantic from land to land. In these wanderings Pylades accompanied him and watched over him. At length in answer to a second appeal to the oracle, Orestes was directed to

FIG. 168. ORESTES PURSUED BY FURIES

go to the temple of the Tauri in Scythia and to bring thence a statue of Diana which was believed to have fallen from heaven. Accordingly the friends went to the Tauric Chersonese. Since there the

barbarous people were accustomed to sacrifice to the goddess all strangers who fell into their hands, the two friends were seized and carried bound to the temple to be made victims. But the priestess of Diana of the Tauri was no other than Iphigenia, the sister of Orestes, who had been snatched away by Diana at the moment when she was about to be sacrificed.

FIG. 169. ORESTES AND PYLADES BEFORE THE KING OF THE TAURI

Ascertaining from the prisoners who they were, Iphigenia disclosed herself to them; and the three made their escape with the statue of the goddess, and returned to Mycenæ.[2]

[1] Æschylus, Eumenides.   [2] Euripides, Iphigenia among the Tauri.

230. His Purification. But Orestes was not yet relieved from the vengeance of the Erinyes. Finally, he took refuge with Minerva at Athens. The goddess afforded him protection and appointed the court of Areopagus to decide his fate. The Erinyes brought their accusation, and Orestes pleaded the command of the Delphic oracle as his excuse. When the court voted and the voices were equally divided, Orestes was aquitted by the command of Minerva. He was then purified with plentiful blood of swine.

CHAPTER XXIV

THE WANDERINGS OF ULYSSES

As one that for a weary space has lain
  Lulled by the song of Circe and her wine
  In gardens near the pale of Proserpine,
Where that Ææan isle forgets the main,
And only the low lutes of love complain,
  And only shadows of wan lovers pine, —
  As such an one were glad to know the brine
Salt on his lips, and the large air again,
So, gladly, from the songs of modern
    speech
  Men turn and see the stars, and feel
    the free
    Shrill wind beyond the close of
      heavy flowers;
    And, through the music of the lan-
      guid hours,
They hear like ocean on a western beach
  The surge and thunder of the Odyssey.[1]

FIG. 170. ULYSSES

231. From Troy to Phæacia. The Odyssey of Homer narrates the wanderings of Ulysses (**Odysseus**) in his return from Troy to his own kingdom, Ithaca.[2]

From Troy the vessels first made land at Ismarus, city of the Ciconians, where, in a skirmish with the inhabitants, Ulysses lost six men from each ship.[3]

232. The Lotos-eaters. Sailing thence they were overtaken by a storm which drove them for nine days till they reached the

---

[1] Sonnet by Andrew Lang.

[2] For the authorship of the Odyssey, see § 298 (3); and for translations, see corresponding section of the Commentary.   [3] Odyssey, 9.

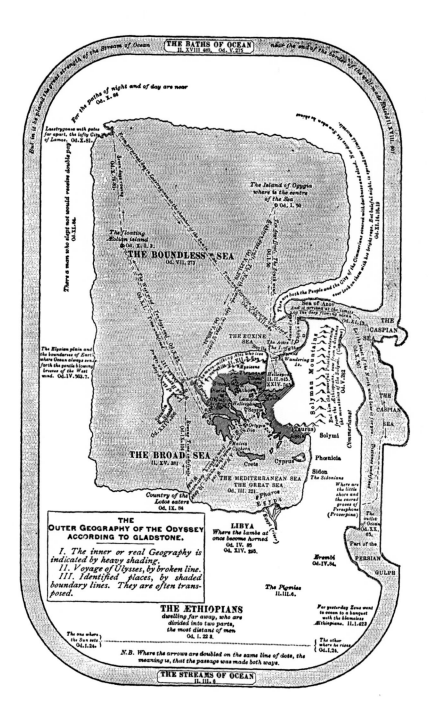

THE BATHS OF OCEAN
Il. XVIII. 489. Od. V. 275.

For the paths of night and of day are near
Od. X. 86.

Laestrygonia with gates
far apart, the lofty City
of Lamos. Od. X. 81.

The Island of Ogygia
where is the centre
of the Sea
Od. I. 50

The floating
Æolian island
Od. X. 1. 3.

THE BOUNDLESS SEA
Od. VII. 273

Sea of Azof
And it arrived at the limits
on the deep flowing ocean

THE
CASPIAN
SEA

THE EUXINE
SEA
Scylla The I. of the

THE
CASPIAN
SEA

The Elysian plain and
the boundaries of Earth
where Ocean always sends
forth the gentle blowing
breezes of the West
wind. Od. IV. 563. 7.

Mycenae

Wandering Is.

Hellespont
Il. II. 845.
XXIV.

Solymi

THE BROAD SEA
Il. XV. 381.

Cyprus

Crete

Taurus

Phœnicia

Sidon
The Sidonians

THE MEDITERRANEAN SEA
THE GREAT SEA
Od. III. 321.

Pharos

Where are
the little
shore and
the sacred
groves of
Persephone
(Proserpina)

Country of the
Lotos eaters
Od. IX. 84

THE
OUTER GEOGRAPHY OF THE ODYSSEY
ACCORDING TO GLADSTONE.

I. The inner or real Geography is
indicated by heavy shading.
II. Voyage of Ulysses, by broken line.
III. Identified places, by shaded
boundary lines. They are often trans-
posed.

LIBYA
Where the lambs at
once become horned
Od. IV. 85
Od. XIV. 293.

The outlet
of Ocean
Od. XX.
65.

Part of the

Erembi
Od. IV. 84.

PERSIAN

GULPH

The Pigmies
Il. III. 6.

THE ÆTHIOPIANS
dwelling far away, who are
divided into two parts,
the most distant of men
Od. I. 22 3.

For yesterday Zeus went
to ocean to a banquet
with the blameless
Æthiopians. Il. I. 423

The one where
the Sun sets
Od. I. 24.

The other
where he rises
Od. I. 24.

N.B. Where the arrows are doubled on the same line of dots, the
meaning is, that the passage was made both ways.

THE STREAMS OF OCEAN
Il. III. 6

country of the Lotos-eaters. Here, after watering, Ulysses sent three of his men to discover who the inhabitants were. These men on coming among the Lotos-eaters were kindly entertained by them and were given some of their own food, the lotos plant, to eat. The effect of this food was such that those who partook of it lost all thought of home and wished to remain in that country. It was by main force that Ulysses dragged these men away, and he was even obliged to tie them under the benches of his ship.

Tennyson in The Lotos-eaters has fittingly expressed the dreamy, languid feeling which the lotus-food is said to have produced.

> . . . How sweet it were, hearing the downward stream,
> With half-shut eyes ever to seem
> Falling asleep in a half-dream!
> To dream and dream, like yonder amber light
> Which will not leave the myrrh-bush on the height;
> To hear each other's whisper'd speech;
> Eating the Lotos, day by day,
> To watch the crisping ripples on the beach,
> And tender curving lines of creamy spray;
> To lend our hearts and spirits wholly
> To the influence of mild-minded melancholy;
> To muse and brood and live again in memory,
> With those old faces of our infancy
> Heap'd over with a mound of grass,
> Two handfuls of white dust, shut in an urn of brass!
>
> Dear is the memory of our wedded lives,
> And dear the last embraces of our wives
> And their warm tears: but all hath suffer'd change;
> For surely now our household hearths are cold:
> Our sons inherit us: our looks are strange:
> And we should come like ghosts to trouble joy.
>
> . . . But, propt on beds of amaranth and moly,
> How sweet (while warm airs lull us, blowing lowly)
> With half-dropt eyelid still,
> Beneath a heaven dark and holy,
> To watch the long bright river drawing slowly
> His waters from the purple hill —
> To hear the dewy echoes calling

From cave to cave thro' the thick-twined vine —
To watch the emerald-color'd water falling
Thro' many a wov'n acanthus-wreath divine!
Only to hear and see the far-off sparkling brine,
Only to hear were sweet, stretch'd out beneath the pine.

The Lotos blooms below the barren peak:
The Lotos blows by every winding creek:
All day the wind breathes low with mellower tone:
Thro' every hollow cave and alley lone
Round and round the spicy downs the yellow Lotos-dust is blown.
We have had enough of action, and of motion we,
Roll'd to starboard, roll'd to larboard, when the surge was seething free,
Where the wallowing monster spouted his foam-fountains in the sea.
Let us swear an oath, and keep it with an equal mind,
In the hollow Lotos-land to live and lie reclined
On the hills like Gods together, careless of mankind. . . .

233. The Cyclopes. They next arrived at the country of the
Cyclopes. The Cyclopes[1] inhabited an island of which they were
the only possessors. They dwelt in caves and fed on the wild productions of the island and on what their flocks yielded, for they
were shepherds. Ulysses left the main body of his ships at anchor,
and with one vessel went to the Cyclopes' island to explore for
supplies. He landed with his companions, carrying with them a
jar of wine for a present. Coming to a large cave they entered it,
and, finding no one within, examined its contents. They found it
stored with the riches of the flock, quantities of cheese, pails and
bowls of milk, lambs and kids in their pens, all in good order.
Presently arrived the master of the cave, Polyphemus, bearing an
immense bundle of firewood, which he threw down before the
cavern's mouth. He then drove into the cave the sheep and goats
to be milked, and, entering, rolled to the cave's mouth an enormous rock, that twenty oxen could not draw. Next he sat down
and milked his ewes, preparing a part for cheese and setting the
rest aside for his customary drink. Then turning round his one
huge eye he discerned the strangers, and growled out at them, demanding who they were and where from. Ulysses replied most
humbly, stating that they were Greeks from the great expedition

[1] § 141.

that had lately won so much glory in the conquest of Troy, that they were now on their way home, and finished by imploring his hospitality in the name of the gods. Polyphemus deigned no answer, but reaching out his hand seized two of the men, whom he hurled against the side of the cave and dashed out their brains. He proceeded to devour them with great relish, and having made a hearty meal, stretched himself on the floor to sleep. Ulysses was tempted to seize the opportunity and plunge his sword into him as he slept, but recollected that it would only expose them all to certain destruction, as the rock with which the giant had closed up the door was far beyond their power to remove, and they would therefore be in hopeless imprisonment.

Next morning the giant seized two more of the men and dispatched them in the same manner as their companions, feasting on their flesh till no fragment was left. He then moved away the rock from the door, drove out his flocks, and went out, carefully replacing the barrier after him. When he was gone Ulysses planned how he might take vengeance for his murdered friends and effect his escape with his surviving companions. He made his men prepare a massive bar of wood cut by the Cyclops for a staff, which they found in the cave. They sharpened the end of the staff and seasoned it in the fire, and hid it under the straw on the cavern floor. Then four of the boldest were selected, with whom Ulysses joined himself as a fifth. The Cyclops came home at evening, rolled away the stone, and drove in his flock as usual. After milking them and making his arrangements as before, he seized two more of Ulysses' companions, dashed their brains out, and made his evening meal upon them as he had on the others. After he had supped, Ulysses approaching him handed him a bowl of wine, saying, " Cyclops, this is wine ; taste and drink after thy meal of man's flesh." He took and drank it, and was hugely delighted with it, and called for more. Ulysses supplied him once and again, which pleased the giant so much that he promised him as a favor that he should be the last of the party devoured. He asked his name, to which Ulysses replied, " My name is Noman."

After his supper the giant sought his repose, and was soon sound asleep. Then Ulysses with his four select friends held the

end of the stake in the fire till it was one burning coal, then poising it exactly above the giant's only eye, they plunged it deep into
the socket, twirling it round as a carpenter does his auger. The
howling monster with his outcry filled the cavern, and Ulysses
with his aids nimbly got out of his way and concealed themselves
in the cave. He, bellowing, called aloud on all the Cyclopes
dwelling in the caves around him, far and near. They, on his cry,
flocked round the den, and inquired what grievous hurt had caused
him to sound such an alarm and break their slumbers. He replied,

FIG. 171. BORING OUT THE CYCLOPS' EYE

" O friends, I die, and Noman gives the blow." They answered,
" If no man hurts thee, it is the stroke of Jove, and thou must
bear it." So saying, they left him groaning.

Next morning the Cyclops rolled away the stone to let his flock
out to pasture, but planted himself in the door of the cave to feel
of all as they went out, that Ulysses and his men should not escape with them. But Ulysses had made his men harness the rams
of the flock three abreast, with osiers which they found on the
floor of the cave. To the middle ram of the three one of the
Greeks suspended himself, so protected by the exterior rams on
either side. As they passed, the giant felt of the animals' backs
and sides, but never thought of their bellies ; so the men all passed
safe, Ulysses himself being on the last one that passed. When
they had got a few paces from the cavern, Ulysses and his friends
released themselves from their rams and drove a good part of the

flock down to the shore to their boat. They put them aboard with all haste, then pushed off from the shore; and when at a safe distance Ulysses shouted out, " Cyclops, the gods have well requited thee for thy atrocious deeds. Know it is Ulysses to whom thou owest thy shameful loss of sight." The Cyclops, hearing this, seized a rock that projected from the side of the mountain, and rending it from its bed, he lifted it high in the air, then exerting all his force, hurled it in the direction of the voice. Down came the mass, just forward of the vessel. The ocean, at the plunge of the huge rock, heaved the

FIG. 172. ULYSSES AND TWO COMPANIONS UNDER RAMS

ship toward Polyphemus; but a second rock which he hurled, striking aft, propelled them fortunately in the direction that they desired to take. Ulysses was about to hail the giant again, but his friends besought him not to do so. He could not forbear, however, letting the giant know that they had escaped his missile, but waited till they had reached a safer distance than before. The giant answered them with curses, while Ulysses and his friends, plying their oars vigorously, regained their companions.

234. The Bag of Winds. Ulysses next arrived at the island of Æolus.[1] He treated Ulysses hospitably, and at his departure gave him, tied up in a leathern bag with a silver string, such winds as might be hurtful and dangerous, commanding fair winds to blow the barks toward their country. Nine days they sped before the wind, and all that time Ulysses had stood at the helm without sleep. At last quite exhausted he lay down to sleep. While he slept, the crew conferred together about the mysterious bag, and concluded it must contain treasures given by the hospitable King Æolus to their commander. Tempted to secure some portion for themselves, they loosed the string, when immediately the winds rushed forth. The ships were driven far from their

[1] Odyssey, 10.

course and back again to the island they had just left. Æolus, indignant at their folly, refused to assist them further, and they were obliged to labor over their course once more by means of their oars.

235. The Læstrygonians. Their next adventure was with the barbarous tribe of Læstrygonians. The vessels all pushed into the harbor, tempted by the secure appearance of the cove, completely landlocked; only Ulysses moored his vessel without. As soon as the Læstrygonians found the ships completely in their power, they attacked them, heaving huge stones which broke and overturned them, while with their spears they dispatched the seamen as they struggled in the water. All the vessels with their crews were destroyed, except Ulysses' own ship which had remained outside. He, finding no safety but in flight, exhorted his men to ply their oars vigorously; and they escaped.

236. The Isle of Æa. With grief for their slain companions mixed with joy at their own escape, they pursued their way till they arrived at the Ææan isle, where Circe dwelt, the daughter of the sun. Landing here, Ulysses climbed a hill and, gazing round, saw no signs of habitation except in one spot at the center of the island, where he perceived a palace embowered with trees. He sent forward one half of his crew, under the command of Eurylochus, to see what prospect of hospitality they might find. As they approached the palace, they found themselves surrounded by lions, tigers, and wolves, not fierce, but tamed by Circe's art, for she was a powerful magician. These animals had once been men, but had been changed by Circe's enchantments into the forms of beasts. The sounds of soft music were heard from within, and a sweet female voice singing. Eurylochus called aloud, and the goddess came forth and invited them in; they all gladly entered except Eurylochus, who suspected danger. The goddess conducted her guests to a seat, and had them served with wine and other delicacies. When they had feasted heartily, she touched them one by one with her wand, and they became immediately changed into swine, in "head, body, voice, and bristles," yet with their intellects as before. She shut them in her styes and supplied them with acorns and such other things as swine love.

Eurylochus hurried back to the ship and told the tale. Ulysses thereupon determined to go himself and try if by any means he might deliver his companions. As he strode onward alone, he met a youth who addressed him familiarly, appearing to be acquainted

ΕΤΛΙΡΟΙ ΤΕΟΗΡΙΩΜΕ ΚΙΡΚΗ ΟΔΙΣΣΕΥΣ ΟΔΙΣΣΕΥΣ ΚΙΡΚΗ ΟΔΙΣΣΕΙ ΤΟ ΜΩΛΤ ΕΡΜΗΣ

ΕΚΤΗΣ ΔΙΗΓΗΣΗΟΣ ΤΗΣ ΠΡΟΣ ΑΛΚΙΝΟΤΝ ΤΟΤ ΚΑΠΠΑ

FIG. 173. THE CASTLE OF CIRCE

with his adventures. He announced himself as Mercury, and informed Ulysses of the arts of Circe and of the danger of approaching her. As Ulysses was not to be dissuaded from his attempt, Mercury provided him with a sprig of the plant Moly, of wonderful power to resist sorceries, and instructed him how to act.

Meanwhile the companions of Ulysses made mournful plaint to their cruel mistress :

> Huddling they came, with shag sides caked of mire, —
> With hoofs fresh sullied from the troughs o'er-turned, —
> With wrinkling snouts, — yet eyes in which desire
> Of some strange thing unutterably burned,
> Unquenchable ; and still where'er She turned

They rose about her, striving each o'er each,
With restless, fierce importuning that yearned
Through those brute masks some piteous talé to teach,
Yet lacked the words thereto, denied the power of speech. . . .

. . . " If swine we be, — if we indeed be swine,
Daughter of Persé, make us swine indeed,
Well-pleased on litter-straw to lie supine, —
Well-pleased on mast and acorn-shales to feed,
Stirred by all instincts of the bestial breed ;
But O Unmerciful ! O Pitiless !
Leave us not thus with sick men's hearts to bleed ! —
To waste long days in yearning, dumb distress,
And memory of things gone, and utter hopelessness !

. . . " Make thou us men again, — if men but groping
That dark Hereafter which th' Olympians keep ;
Make thou us men again, — if men but hoping
Behind death's doors security of sleep ; —
For yet to laugh is somewhat, and to sleep ; —
To feel delight of living, and to plow
The salt-blown acres of the shoreless deep ; —
Better, — yea better far all these than bow
Foul faces to foul earth, and yearn — as we do now ! "

So they in speech unsyllabled. But She,
The fair-tressed Goddess, born to be their bane,
Uplifting straight her wand of ivory,
Compelled them groaning to the styes again ;
Where they in hopeless bitterness were fain
To rend the oaken woodwork as before,
And tear the troughs in impotence of pain, —
Not knowing, they, that even at the door
Divine Odysseus stood, — as Hermes told of yore.[1]

Ulysses, reaching the palace, was courteously received by Circe, who entertained him as she had done his companions, but after he had eaten and drunk, touched him with her wand, saying, " Hence, seek the stye and wallow with thy friends." But he, instead of obeying, drew his sword and rushed upon her with fury in his countenance. She fell on her knees and begged for mercy.

[1] From Austin Dobson's Prayer of the Swine to Circe.

He dictated a solemn oath that she would release his companions and practice no further harm against him or them; and she repeated it, at the same time promising to dismiss them all in safety after hospitably entertaining them. She was as good as her word. The men were restored to their shapes, the rest of the crew summoned from the shore, and all magnificently entertained day after day, till Ulysses seemed to have forgotten his native land and to have reconciled himself to an inglorious life of ease and pleasure.

237. Ulysses visits Hades. At length his companions recalled him to nobler sentiments, and he received their admonition gratefully. Circe, won over by his prayers, consented to send him on his homeward way. But she warned him that first he must perform another journey, must visit the Underworld and there learn from the shade of Tiresias, the blind prophet of Thebes, the way and measure of his path, and how to proceed to Ithaca over the teeming deep.

"But who will guide us?" queried Ulysses in amaze; "for no man ever yet sailed to hell in a black ship."

"Son of Laërtes," replied the Goddess, "Ulysses of many devices, nay, trouble not thyself for want of a guide, by thy ship abiding, but set up the mast and spread abroad the white sails and sit thee down; and the breeze of the North Wind will bear thy vessel on her way. But when thou hast now sailed in thy ship across the stream Oceanus where is a waste shore and the groves of Persephone, even tall poplar trees and willows that shed their fruit before the season, there beach thy ship by deep-eddying Oceanus, but go thyself to the dank house of Hades. Thereby into Acheron flows Pyriphlegethon, and Cocytus, a branch of the water of the Styx; and there is a rock, and the meeting of the two roaring waters. There dig a trench and pour a·drink offering to all the dead, mead and sweet wine and water, sprinkling white meal thereon. And when thou hast prayed to them, offer up a ram and a black ewe. Then will many spirits come to thee of the dead that be departed; but thou shalt draw thy sharp sword and suffer them not to approach the blood, ere thou hast word of Tiresias." [1]

[1] Odyssey, 10; adapted from Butcher and Lang's translation. So the following from Odyssey, 11.

So Ulysses and his companions did as they were bid. And the ship came to the limits of the world, to the deep-flowing Oceanus. There is the land and city of the Cimmerians, where no ray of sunshine ever falls, but deadly night is outspread over miserable mortals. And there Ulysses and those with him performed the drink offering and the prayer and the sacrifice; and Ulysses fended off the spirits of the dead from the blood until the soul of the Theban prophet arrived. And that one, having drunk of the dark blood, declared unto Ulysses the future of his way: how the Earth-shaker, god of the waters, should oppose him, but how he should win home without further disaster if, when passing the isle Thrinacia, he would but restrain the spirit of his men so that they should do no injury to the cattle of the Sun grazing thereon. If, however, these cattle were not respected but hurt, then there should follow ruin for both ship and men; and Ulysses himself on the ship of strangers should return late in time to his home, to find sorrows there, proud men wasting his patrimony and wooing his godlike wife to wed her. But that he should avenge their violence, and settle his affairs at home, and then betake himself again to wandering; and that from the sea should his own death come, — "the gentlest death that may be, which shall end thee fordone with smooth old age; and the folk shall dwell happily around thee."

In the land of Hades, Ulysses saw also the shade of his mother, and spoke with her of his father and of Penelope, his wife, and of his son Telemachus. And he saw also the shades of Antiope and Alcmene and Phædra and Procris; and of Agamemnon, and Achilles, and Ajax, the son of Telamon, and of many others, and spoke with them of their own fates and of the affairs of the upper world.

238. The Sirens. Returning from the abode of the shades, Ulysses revisited the Ææan isle and recounted to Circe his adventures and the wondrous visions and the laws of Hell. She in return speeded his homeward voyage, instructing him particularly how to pass safely by the coast of the Sirens.[1]

These nymphs had the power, as has been already said, of charming by their song all who heard them, so that mariners

[1] Odyssey, 12.

were impelled to cast themselves into the sea to destruction. Circe directed Ulysses to stop the ears of his seamen with wax, so that they should not hear the strain; to have himself bound to the mast, and to enjoin his people, whatever he might say or do, by no means to release him till they should have passed the Sirens' island. Ulysses obeyed these directions. As they approached the Sirens' island, the sea was calm, and over the waters came notes of music so ravishing and attractive that Ulysses struggled to get loose and, by cries and signs to his people, begged to be released; but they, obedient to his previous orders, sprang forward and bound him still faster. They held on their course, and the music grew fainter till it ceased to be heard, when with joy Ulysses gave his companions the signal to unseal their ears;

FIG. 174. ULYSSES AND THE SIRENS

and they relieved him from his bonds. It is said that one of the Sirens, Parthenope, in grief at the escape of Ulysses drowned herself. Her body was cast up on the Italian shore where now stands the city of Naples, in early times called by the Siren's name.

239. Scylla and Charybdis. Ulysses had been warned by Circe of the two monsters Scylla and Charybdis. We have already met with Scylla in the myth of Glaucus. She dwelt in a cave high up on the cliff, from whence she was accustomed to thrust forth her long necks (for she had six heads), and in each of her mouths to seize one of the crew of every vessel passing within reach. The other terror, Charybdis, was a gulf nearly on a level with the water. Thrice each day the water rushed into a frightful chasm, and thrice was disgorged. Any vessel coming near the whirlpool when the tide was rushing in must inevitably be engulfed; not Neptune himself could save it. On approaching the haunt of the dread monsters, Ulysses kept strict watch to discover them. The roar of the waters as Charybdis engulfed them gave warning at a distance, but Scylla could nowhere be discerned. While Ulysses

and his men watched with anxious eyes the dreadful whirlpool, they were not equally on their guard from the attack of Scylla,[1] and the monster, darting forth her snaky heads, caught six of his men and bore them away shrieking to her den. Ulysses was unable to afford any assistance.

240. The Cattle of the Sun. Both Tiresias and Circe had warned him of another danger.

FIG. 175. ULYSSES AND SCYLLA

After passing Scylla and Charybdis the next land he would make was Thrinacia, an island whereon were pastured the cattle of Helios, the Sun, tended by his daughters Lampetia and Phaëthusa. These flocks must not be violated, whatever the wants of the voyagers might be. If this injunction were transgressed, destruction was sure to fall on the offenders. Ulysses would willingly have passed the island of the Sun without stopping, but his companions so urgently pleaded for the rest and refreshment that would be derived from anchoring and passing the night on shore, that Ulysses yielded. He made them swear, however, not to touch the sacred flocks and herds, but to content themselves with what provision they yet had left of the supply which Circe had put on board. So long as this supply lasted the people kept their oath; but contrary winds detained them at the island for a month, and after consuming all their stock of provisions, they were forced to rely upon the birds and fishes they could catch. Famine pressed them, and at last, in the absence of Ulysses, they slew some of the cattle, vainly attempting to make amends for the deed by offering from them a portion to the offended powers. Ulysses, on his return to the shore, was horror-struck at perceiving what they had

[1] *Incidit in Scyllam, cupiens vitare Charybdim.*

FLYING MERCURY

done, and the more so on account of the portentous signs which followed. The skins crept on the ground, and the joints of meat lowed on the spits while roasting.

The wind becoming fair, they sailed from the island. They had not gone far when the weather changed, and a storm of thunder and lightning ensued. A stroke of lightning shattered their mast, which in its fall killed the pilot. At last the vessel itself went to pieces. The keel and mast floating side by side, Ulysses formed of them a raft to which he clung; and, the wind changing, the waves bore him to Calypso's island. All the rest of the crew perished.

241. Calypso's Island. Calypso, a sea-nymph, received Ulysses hospitably, entertained him magnificently, became enamored of him, and wished to retain him forever, offering him immortality. He remained with her seven long years. But he persisted in his resolution to return to his country and his wife and son.[1] Calypso at last received the command of Jove to dismiss him. Mercury brought the message to her and found her in her grotto.

> A garden vine, luxuriant on all sides,
> Mantled the spacious cavern, cluster-hung
> Profuse; four fountains of serenest lymph,
> Their sinuous course pursuing side by side,
> Strayed all around, and everywhere appeared
> Meadows of softest verdure, purpled o'er
> With violets; it was a scene to fill
> A god from heaven with wonder and delight.[2]

Calypso, with much reluctance, proceeded to obey the commands of Jupiter. She supplied Ulysses with the means of constructing a raft, provisioned it well for him, and gave him a favoring gale. He sped on his course prosperously for many days, till at last, when in sight of land, a storm arose that broke his mast and threatened to rend the raft asunder. In this crisis he was seen by a compassionate sea-nymph, Leucothea, who, in the form of a cormorant, alighted on the raft and presented him with a girdle, directing him to bind it beneath his breast, that, if he should be compelled to trust himself to the waves, it might buoy him up and enable him to reach the land.

[1] Odyssey, 1, 10.   [2] Odyssey, 5, 64 (Cowper's translation).

242. The Land of the Phæacians. Ulysses clung to the raft so long as its timbers held together, and when it no longer yielded him support, binding the girdle around him, he swam. Minerva smoothed the billows before him and sent him a wind that rolled the waves towards the shore. The surf beat high on the rocks and seemed to forbid approach; but at length finding calm water at the mouth of a gentle stream, he landed, spent with toil, breathless and speechless and almost dead. Reviving after some time, he kissed the soil, rejoicing, yet at a loss what course to take. At a short distance he perceived a wood, to which he turned his steps. There finding a covert sheltered by intermingling branches alike from the sun and the rain, he collected a pile of leaves and formed a bed, on which he stretched himself, and, heaping the leaves over him, fell asleep.

The land where he was thrown was Scheria, the country of the Phæacians.[1] These people dwelt originally near the Cyclopes; but, being oppressed by that savage race, they migrated to the isle of Scheria under the conduct of Nausithoüs, their king. They were, the poet tells us, a people akin to the gods, who appeared manifestly and feasted among them when they offered sacrifices, and did not conceal themselves from solitary wayfarers when they met them. They had abundance of wealth and lived in the enjoyment of it undisturbed by the alarms of war; for as they dwelt remote from gain-seeking man, no enemy ever approached their shores, and they did not even require to make use of bows and quivers. Their chief employment was navigation. Their ships, which went with the velocity of birds, were endued with intelligence; they knew every port and needed no pilot. Alcinoüs, the son of Nausithoüs, was now their king, a wise and just sovereign, beloved by his people.

Now it happened that the very night on which Ulysses was cast ashore on the Phæacian island, and while he lay sleeping on his bed of leaves, Nausicaä, the daughter of the king, had a dream sent by Minerva, reminding her that her wedding day might not be far distant, and that it would be but a prudent preparation for that event to have a general washing of the clothes of the family.

[1] Odyssey, 6.

This was no slight affair, for the fountains were at some distance and the garments must be carried thither. On awaking, the princess hastened to her parents to tell them what was on her mind, — not alluding to her wedding day, but finding other reasons equally good. Her father readily assented and ordered the grooms to furnish forth a wagon for the purpose. The clothes were put therein, and the queen, her mother, placed in the wagon likewise an abundant supply of food and wine. The princess took her seat and plied the lash, her attendant virgins following her on foot. Arrived at the riverside they turned out the mules to graze, and unlading the carriage, bore the garments down to the water, and, working with cheerfulness and alacrity, soon dispatched their labor. Then having spread the garments on the shore to dry, and having themselves bathed, they sat down to enjoy their meal ; after which they rose and amused themselves with a game of ball, the princess singing to them while they played. But when they had refolded the apparel and were about to resume their way to the town, Minerva caused the ball thrown by the princess to fall into the water, whereat they all screamed, and Ulysses awaked at the sound.

Utterly destitute of clothing, he discovered that only a few bushes were interposed between him and a group of young maidens, whom, by their deportment and attire, he discovered to be not mere peasant girls, but of a higher class. Breaking off a leafy branch from a tree, he held it before him and stepped out from the thicket. The virgins at sight of him fled in all directions, Nausicaä alone excepted, for her Minerva aided and endowed with courage and discernment. Ulysses, standing respectfully aloof, told his sad case, and besought the fair object (whether queen or goddess he professed he knew not) for food and clothing. The princess replied courteously, promising present relief and her father's hospitality when he should become acquainted with the facts. She called back her scattered maidens, chiding their alarm and reminding them that the Phæacians had no enemies to fear. This man, she told them, was an unhappy wanderer, whom it was a duty to cherish, for the poor and the stranger are from Jove. She bade them bring food, and the garments of some of her brothers that were among the contents of the wagon. When this was done, and Ulysses retiring to a sheltered place had washed his body free from the seafoam, and clothed himself, and eaten, Pallas dilated his form and diffused grace over his ample chest and manly brows.

The princess, seeing him, was filled with admiration and scrupled not to say to her damsels that she wished the gods would send her such a husband. To Ulysses she recommended that he repair to the city, following herself and her train so far as the way lay through the fields; but when they should approach the city, she desired that he no longer be seen in her company, for she feared the remarks which rude and vulgar people might make on seeing her return accompanied by such a gallant stranger. To avoid this she directed him to stop at a grove adjoining the city, in which were a farm and garden belonging to the king. After allowing time for the princess and her companions to reach the city, he was then to pursue his way thither, and should be easily guided by any he might meet to the royal abode.

Ulysses obeyed the directions and in due time proceeded to the city, on approaching which he met a young woman bearing forth a pitcher for water.[1] It was Minerva who had assumed that form. Ulysses accosted her and desired to be directed to the palace of Alcinoüs, the king. The maiden replied respectfully, offering to be his guide; for the palace, she informed him, stood near her father's dwelling. Under the guidance of the goddess and, by her power, enveloped in a cloud which shielded him from observation, Ulysses passed among the busy crowd and with wonder observed their harbor, their ships, their forum (the resort of heroes), and their battlements, till they came to the palace, where the goddess, having first given him some information of the country, king, and people he was about to meet, left him. Ulysses, before entering the courtyard of the palace, stood and surveyed the scene. Its splendor astonished him. Brazen walls stretched from the entrance to the interior house, of which the doors were gold, the doorposts silver, the lintels silver ornamented with gold. On either side were figures of mastiffs wrought in gold and silver, standing in rows as if to guard the approach. Along the walls

[1] Odyssey, 7.

were seats spread through all their length with mantles of finest texture, the work of Phæacian maidens. On these seats the princes sat and feasted, while golden statues of graceful youths held in their hands lighted torches which shed radiance over the scene. Full fifty female menials served in household offices, some employed to grind the corn, others to wind off the purple wool or ply the loom. For the Phæacian women as far exceeded all other women in household arts as the mariners of that country did the rest of mankind in the management of ships. Without the court a spacious garden lay, four acres in extent. In it grew many a lofty tree, pomegranate, pear, apple, fig, and olive. Neither winter's cold nor summer's drought arrested their growth.

> The languid sunset, mother of roses,[1]
>   Lingers, a light on the magic seas,
> The wide fire flames, as a flower uncloses,
>   Heavy with odor, and loose to the breeze.
>
> The red rose clouds, without law or leader,
>   Gather and float in the airy plain;
> The nightingale sings to the dewy cedar,
>   The cedar scatters his scent to the main.
>
> The strange flowers' perfume turns to singing,
>   Heard afar over moonlit seas:
> The Siren's song, grown faint in winging,
>   Falls in scent on the cedar-trees.
>
> As waifs blown out of the sunset, flying,
>   Purple, and rosy, and gray, the birds
> Brighten the air with their wings; their crying
>   Wakens a moment the weary herds.
>
> Butterflies flit from the fairy garden,
>   Living blossoms of flying flowers;
> Never the nights with winter harden,
>   Nor moons wax keen in this land of ours.
>
> Great fruits, fragrant, green and golden,
>   ·Gleam in the green, and droop and fall;
> Blossom, and bud, and flower unfolden,
>   Swing and cling to the garden wall.

[1] Andrew Lang, A Song of Phæacia.

Deep in the woods as twilight darkens,
   Glades are red with the scented fire;
Far in the dells the white maid hearkens
   Song and sigh of the heart's desire.

Ulysses stood gazing in admiration, unobserved himself, for the cloud which Minerva spread around him still shielded him. At length having sufficiently observed the scene, he advanced with rapid step into the hall where the chiefs and senators were assembled, pouring libation to Mercury, whose worship followed the evening meal. Just then Minerva dissolved the cloud and disclosed him to the assembled chiefs. Advancing to the place where the queen sat, he knelt at her feet and implored her favor and assistance to enable him to return to his native country. Then withdrawing, he seated himself in the manner of suppliants, at the hearth-side.

For a time none spoke. At last an aged statesman, addressing the king, said, "It is not fit that a stranger who asks our hospitality should be kept waiting in suppliant guise, none welcoming him. Let him, therefore, be led to a seat among us and supplied with food and wine." At these words the king, rising, gave his hand to Ulysses and led him to a seat, displacing thence his own son to make room for the stranger. Food and wine were set before him and he ate and refreshed himself.

The king then dismissed his guests, notifying them that the next day he would call them to council to consider what had best be done for the stranger.

When the guests had departed and Ulysses was left alone with the king and queen, the queen asked him who he was and whence he came, and (recognizing the clothes which he wore as those which her maidens and herself had made) from whom he received those garments. He told them of his residence in Calypso's isle and his departure thence; of the wreck of his raft, his escape by swimming, and of the relief afforded by the princess. The parents heard approvingly, and the king promised to furnish a ship in which his guest might return to his own land.

The next day the assembled chiefs confirmed the promise of the king.[1] A bark was prepared and a crew of stout rowers

[1] Odyssey, 8.

selected, and all betook themselves to the palace, where a bounteous repast was provided. After the feast the king proposed that the young men should show their guest their proficiency in manly sports, and all went forth to the arena for games of running, wrestling, and other exercises. After all had done their best, Ulysses being challenged to show what he could do, at first declined, but being taunted by one of the youths, seized a quoit of weight far heavier than any the Phæacians had thrown, and sent it farther than the utmost throw of theirs. All were astonished and viewed their guest with greatly increased respect.

After the games they returned to the hall, and the herald led in Demodocus, the blind bard, —

> Dear to the Muse,
> Who yet appointed him both good and ill,
> Took from him sight, but gave him strains divine.

He took for his theme the Wooden Horse, by means of which the Greeks found entrance into Troy. Apollo inspired him, and he sang so feelingly the terrors and the exploits of that eventful time that all were delighted, but Ulysses was moved to tears. Observing which, Alcinoüs, when the song was done, demanded of him why at the mention of Troy his sorrows awaked. Had he lost there a father, or brother, or any dear friend? Ulysses replied by announcing himself by his true name, and, at their request, recounted the adventures which had befallen him since his departure from Troy. This narrative raised the sympathy and admiration of the Phæacians for their guest to the highest pitch. The king proposed that all the chiefs should present him with a gift, himself setting the example. They obeyed, and vied with one another in loading the illustrious stranger with costly gifts.

The next day Ulysses set sail in the Phæacian vessel, and in a short time arrived safe at Ithaca, his own island.[1] When the vessel touched the strand he was asleep. The mariners, without waking him, carried him on shore, and landed with him the chest containing his presents, and then sailed away.

Neptune was so displeased at the conduct of the Phæacians in thus rescuing Ulysses from his hands, that, on the return of the

[1] Odyssey, 13.

vessel to port, he transformed it into a rock, right opposite the mouth of the harbor.

243. Fate of the Suitors. Ulysses had now been away from Ithaca for twenty years, and when he awoke he did not recognize his native land :

> " Some god hath cast me forth upon this land,
> And O ! what land? So thick is the sea mist,
> All is phantasmal. What king ruleth here?
> What folk inhabit? — cruel unto strangers,
> Or hospitable? The gods have lied to me
> When they foretold I should see Ithaca.
> This is some swimming and Cimmerian isle,
> With melancholy people of the mist.
> Ah! Ithaca, I shall not see thee more!"[1]

But Minerva, appearing in the form of a young shepherd, informed him where he was, and told him the state of things at his palace. More than a hundred nobles of Ithaca and of the neighboring islands had been for years suing for the hand of Penelope, his wife, imagining him dead, and lording it over his palace and people as if they were owners of both.

Penelope was one of those mythic heroines whose beauties were not those of person only, but of character and conduct as well. She was the niece of Tyndareus, — being the daughter of his brother Icarius, a Spartan prince. Ulysses, seeking her in marriage, had won her over all competitors. But, when the moment came for the bride to leave her father's house, Icarius, unable to bear the thoughts of parting with his daughter, tried to persuade her to remain with him and not accompany her husband to Ithaca. Ulysses gave Penelope her choice, to stay or go with him. Penelope made no reply, but dropped her veil over her face. Icarius urged her no further, but when she was gone erected a statue to Modesty on the spot where they had parted.

Ulysses and Penelope had not enjoyed their union more than a year when it was interrupted by the events which called Ulysses to the Trojan War. During his long absence, and when it was doubtful whether he still lived, and highly improbable that he

[1] Stephen Phillips, Ulysses.

would ever return, Penelope was importuned by numerous suitors, from whom there seemed no refuge but in choosing one of them for her husband. She, however, employed every art to gain time, still hoping for Ulysses' return. One of her arts of delay was by engaging in the preparation of a robe for the funeral canopy of Laërtes, her husband's father. She pledged herself to make her

FIG. 176. PENELOPE AND TELEMACHUS

choice among the suitors when the web was finished. During the day she worked at it, but in the night she undid the work of the day.

That Ulysses on returning might be able to take vengeance upon the suitors, it was important that he should not be recognized. Minerva accordingly metamorphosed him into an unsightly beggar, and as such he was kindly received by Eumæus, the swineherd, a faithful servant of his house.[1]

Telemachus, his son, had for some time been absent in quest of his father, visiting the courts of the other kings who had

[1] Odyssey, 14.

returned from the Trojan expedition. While on the search, he received counsel from Minerva to return home.[1] He arrived at this juncture, and sought Eumæus to learn something of the state of affairs at the palace before presenting himself among the suitors. Finding a stranger with Eumæus, he treated him courteously, though in the garb of a beggar, and promised him assistance. Eumæus was sent to the palace to inform Penelope privately of her son's arrival, for caution was necessary with regard to the suitors, who, as Telemachus had learned, were plotting to intercept and kill him. When the swineherd was gone, Minerva presented herself to Ulysses and directed him to make himself known to his son. At the same time she touched him, removed at once from him the appearance of age and penury, and gave him the aspect of vigorous manhood that belonged to him. Telemachus viewed him with astonishment, and at first thought he must be more than mortal. But Ulysses announced himself as his father, and accounted for the change of appearance by explaining that it was Minerva's doing.

> Then threw Telemachus
> His arms around his father's neck and wept.
> Desire intense of lamentation seized
> On both; soft murmurs uttering, each indulged
> His grief.[2]

The father and son took counsel together how they should get the better of the suitors and punish them for their outrages. It was arranged that Telemachus should proceed to the palace and mingle with the suitors as formerly; that Ulysses should also go as a beggar, a character which in the rude old times had different privileges from what we concede to it now. As traveler and story-teller, the beggar was admitted in the halls of chieftains and often treated like a guest; though sometimes, also, no doubt, with contumely. Ulysses charged his son not to betray, by any display of unusual interest in him, that he knew him to be other than he seemed, and even if he saw him insulted or beaten, not to interpose otherwise than he might do for any stranger. At the palace they found the usual scene of feasting and riot going on. The

[1] Odyssey, 15.   [2] Odyssey 16, 212 (Cowper's translation).

suitors pretended to receive Telemachus with joy at his return, though secretly mortified at the failure of their plots to take his life. The old beggar was permitted to enter and provided with a portion from the table. A touching incident occurred as Ulysses entered the courtyard of the palace. An old dog lay in the yard almost dead with age, and seeing a stranger enter, raised his head, with ears erect. It was Argus, Ulysses' own dog, that he had in other days often led to the chase.

> Soon as he perceived
> Long-lost Ulysses nigh, down fell his ears
> Clapped close, and with his tail glad sign he gave
> Of gratulation, impotent to rise,
> And to approach his master as of old.
> Ulysses, noting him, wiped off a tear
> Unmarked.
> . . . Then his destiny released
> Old Argus, soon as he had lived to see
> Ulysses in the twentieth year restored.[1]

As Ulysses sat eating his portion in the hall, the suitors soon began to exhibit their insolence to him. When he mildly remonstrated, one of them raised a stool and with it gave him a blow. Telemachus had hard work to restrain his indignation at seeing his father so treated in his own hall; but, remembering his father's injunctions, said no more than what became him as master of the house, though young, and protector of his guests.

FIG. 177. ULYSSES RECOGNIZED BY EURYCLEA

Once again was the wanderer all but betrayed; — when his agèd nurse Euryclea, bathing his feet, recognized the scar of

[1] Odyssey, 17, 290 (Cowper's translation).

a wound dealt him by a boar, long ago.[1] Grief and joy overwhelmed the crone, and she would have revealed him to Penelope
had not Ulysses enjoined silence upon her.

Penelope had protracted her decision in favor of any one of her
suitors so long that there seemed to be no further pretense for
delay. The continued absence of her husband seemed to prove
that his return was no longer to be expected. Meanwhile her
son had grown up and was able to manage his own affairs. She
therefore consented to submit the question of her choice to a trial
of skill among the suitors. The test selected was shooting with the

Fig. 178. Ulysses kills the Suitors

(Left half)

bow.[2] Twelve rings were arranged in a line, and he whose arrow
was sent through the whole twelve was to have the queen for his
prize. A bow that one of his brother heroes had given to Ulysses
in former times was brought from the armory and with its quiver
full of arrows was laid in the hall. Telemachus had taken care that
all other weapons should be removed, under pretense that in the
heat of competition there was danger, in some rash moment, of
putting them to an improper use.

All things being prepared for the trial, the first thing to be done
was to bend the bow in order to attach the string. Telemachus
endeavored to do it, but found all his efforts fruitless ; and mod-
estly confessing that he had attempted a task beyond his strength,

[1] Odyssey, 19.   [2] Odyssey, 21.

he yielded the bow to another. *He* tried it with no better success, and, amidst the laughter and jeers of his companions, gave it up. Another tried it, and another; they rubbed the bow with tallow, but all to no purpose; it would not bend. Then spoke Ulysses, humbly suggesting that he should be permitted to try; for, said he, "beggar as I am, I was once a soldier, and there is still some strength in these old limbs of mine." The suitors hooted with derision and commanded to turn him out of the hall for his insolence. But Telemachus spoke up for him, and, merely to gratify the old man, bade him try. Ulysses took the bow and handled it

FIG. 179. ULYSSES KILLS THE SUITORS

(Right half)

with the hand of a master. With ease he adjusted the cord to its notch, then fitting an arrow to the bow he drew the string and sped the arrow unerring through the rings.

Without allowing them time to express their astonishment, he said, "Now for another mark!" and aimed direct at Antinoüs, the most insolent of the suitors.[1] The arrow pierced through his throat and he fell dead. Telemachus, Eumæus, and another faithful follower, well armed, now sprang to the side of Ulysses. The suitors, in amazement, looked round for arms, but found none, neither was there any way of escape, for Eumæus had secured the door. Ulysses left them not long in uncertainty; he announced himself as the long-lost chief, whose house they had invaded, whose

[1] Odyssey, 22.

substance they had squandered, whose wife and son they had persecuted for ten long years; and told them he meant to have ample
vengeance. All but two were slain, and Ulysses was left master of
his palace and possessor of his kingdom and his wife.

244. Tennyson's Ulysses. Tennyson's poem of Ulysses represents the old hero, — his dangers past and nothing left but to
stay at home and be happy, — growing tired of inaction and re-
solving to set forth again in quest of new adventures.

> It little profits that an idle king,
> By this still hearth, among these barren crags,
> Match'd with an agèd wife, I mete and dole
> Unequal laws unto a savage race,
> That hoard, and sleep, and feed, and know not me.
> I cannot rest from travel: I will drink
> Life to the lees: all times I have enjoy'd
> Greatly, have suffer'd greatly, both with those
> That loved me, and alone; on shore, and when
> Thro' scudding drifts the rainy Hyades
> Vext the dim sea: I am become a name;
> For always roaming with a hungry heart
> Much have I seen and known: cities of men,
> And manners, climates, councils, governments,
> Myself not least, but honor'd of them all;
> And drunk delight of battle with my peers,
> Far on the ringing plains of windy Troy.
> I am a part of all that I have met;
> Yet all experience is an arch wherethro'
> Gleams that untravel'd world, whose margin fades
> Forever and forever when I move.
> How dull it is to pause, to make an end,
> To rust unburnish'd, not to shine in use!
> As tho' to breathe were life. Life piled on life
> Were all too little, and of one to me
> Little remains: but every hour is saved
> From that eternal silence, something more,
> A bringer of new things; and vile it were
> For some three suns to store and hoard myself,
> And this gray spirit yearning in desire
> To follow knowledge like a sinking star,
> Beyond the utmost bound of human thought.

This is my son, mine own Telemachus,
To whom I leave the scepter and the isle —
Well-loved of me, discerning to fulfil
This labor, by slow prudence to make mild
A rugged people, and thro' soft degrees
Subdue them to the useful and the good.
Most blameless is he, centered in the sphere
Of common duties, decent not to fail
In offices of tenderness, and pay
Meet adoration to my household gods,
When I am gone. He works his work, I mine.

There lies the port : the vessel puffs her sail :
There gloom the dark broad seas. My mariners,
Souls that have toil'd, and wrought, and thought
    with me —
That ever with a frolic welcome took
The thunder and the sunshine, and opposed
Free hearts, free foreheads — you and I are old ;
Old age has yet his honor and his toil ;
Death closes all : but something ere the end,
Some work of noble note, may yet be done,
Not unbecoming men that strove with Gods.
The lights begin to twinkle from the rocks :
The long day wanes : the slow moon climbs :
    the deep
Moans round with many voices. Come, my
    friends,
'T is not too late to seek a newer world.
Push off, and sitting well in order smite
The sounding furrows; for my purpose holds

FIG. 180. THE NIKE OF
SAMOTHRACE

To sail beyond the sunset, and the baths
Of all the western stars, until I die.
It may be that the gulfs will wash us down :
It may be we shall touch the Happy Isles,
And see the great Achilles, whom we knew.
Tho' much is taken, much abides ; and tho'
We are not now that strength which in old days
Moved earth and heaven, that which we are, we are ;
One equal temper of heroic hearts,
Made weak by time and fate, but strong in will
To strive, to seek, to find, and not to yield.

CHAPTER XXV

ADVENTURES OF ÆNEAS

Roman Virgil, thou that singest
    Ilion's lofty temples robed in fire,
Ilion falling, Rome arising,
    wars, and filial faith, and Dido's pyre;

Landscape lover, lord of language
    more than he that sang the Works and Days,
All the chosen coin of fancy
    flashing out from many a golden phrase; . . .

Light among the vanish'd ages;
    star that gildest yet this phantom shore;
Golden branch amid the shadows,
    kings and realms that pass to rise no more; . . .

Now the Rome of slaves hath perish'd,
    and the Rome of freemen holds her place,
I, from out the Northern Island
    sunder'd once from all the human race,

I salute thee, Mantovano,
    I that loved thee since my day began,
Wielder of the stateliest measure
    ever molded by the lips of man.[1]

245. From Troy to Italy. Homer tells the story of one of the Grecian heroes, Ulysses, in his wanderings on his return home from Troy. Virgil in his Æneid[2] narrates the mythical fortunes of the remnant of the *conquered* people under their chief Æneas, the son of Venus and the Trojan Anchises, in their search for a

---

[1] From Tennyson's To Virgil.

[2] For Virgil, see § 299; for translations of his Æneid, see corresponding section in Commentary.

ITALY

BEFORE THE GROWTH OF
THE ROMAN EMPIRE

Greeks		Gauls		Venetians	
Italians		Ligurians &c.		Phœnicians	
		Etruscans			

new home after the ruin of their native city. On that fatal night
when the wooden horse disgorged its contents of armed men, and
the capture and conflagration of the city were the result, Æneas
made his escape from the scene of
destruction, with his father and his
wife and young son. The father,
Anchises, was too old to walk with
the speed required, and Æneas took
him upon his shoulders. Thus bur-
dened, leading his son and followed
by his wife, he made the best of his
way out of the burning city; but in
the confusion his wife, Creüsa, was
swept away and lost.

FIG. 181. ÆNEAS, ANCHISES,
AND IULUS

246. The Departure from Troy.
On arriving at the place of rendez-
vous, numerous fugitives of both
sexes were found, who put themselves under the guidance of Æneas.
Some months were spent in prep-
aration, and at length they embarked. They first landed on the
neighboring shores of Thrace, and were preparing to build a city,
but Æneas was deterred by a prodigy. Preparing to offer sacrifice,
he tore some twigs from one of the bushes. To his dismay the
wounded part dropped blood. When he repeated the act, a voice
from the ground cried out to him, " Spare me, Æneas ; I am thy
kinsman, Polydore, here murdered with many arrows, from which
a bush has grown, nourished with my blood." These words recalled
to the recollection of Æneas that Polydore was a young prince of
Troy, whom his father had sent with ample treasures to the neighboring land of Thrace, to be there brought up, at a distance from
the horrors of war. The king to whom he was sent had murdered
him and seized his treasures. Æneas and his companions, considering the land accursed by the stain of such a crime, hastened away.

247. The Promised Empire. They next landed on the island of
Delos. Here Æneas consulted the oracle of Apollo, and received
an answer, ambiguous as usual, — " Seek thy ancient mother ;

there the race of Æneas shall dwell, and reduce all other nations to their sway." The Trojans heard with joy and immediately began to ask one another, "Where is the spot intended by the oracle?" Anchises remembered that there was a tradition that their forefathers came from Crete, and thither they resolved to steer. They arrived at Crete and began to build their city; but sickness broke out among them, and the fields that they had planted, failed to yield a crop. In this gloomy aspect of affairs, Æneas was warned in a dream to leave the country and seek a western land called Hesperia, whence Dardanus, the true founder of the Trojan race, was reported to have migrated. To Hesperia, now called Italy, they therefore directed their future course, and not till after many adventures, and the lapse of time sufficient to carry a modern navigator several times round the world, did they arrive there.

248. The Harpies. Their first landing was at the island of the Harpies. These were disgusting birds, with the heads of maidens, with long claws, and faces pale with hunger. They were sent by the gods to torment a certain Phineus, whom Jupiter had deprived of his sight in punishment of his cruelty; and whenever a meal was placed before him, the harpies darted down from the air and carried it off. They were driven away from Phineus by the heroes of the Argonautic expedition, and took refuge in the island where Æneas now found them. When the Trojans entered the port they saw herds of cattle roaming over the plain. They slew as many as they wished, and prepared for a feast. But no sooner had they seated themselves at the table than a horrible clamor was heard in the air, and a flock of these odious harpies came rushing down upon them, seizing in their talons the meat from the dishes and flying away with it. Æneas and his companions drew their swords and dealt vigorous blows among the monsters, but to no purpose, for they were so nimble it was almost impossible to hit them, and their feathers were, like armor, impenetrable to steel. One of them, perched on a neighboring cliff, screamed out, "Is it thus, Trojans, ye treat us innocent birds, first slaughter our cattle and then make war on ourselves?" She then predicted dire sufferings to them in their future course, and, having vented her wrath, flew away.

249. Epirus. The Trojans made haste to leave the country, and next found themselves coasting along the shore of Epirus. Here they landed and to their astonishment learned that certain Trojan exiles, who had been carried there as prisoners, had become rulers of the country. Andromache, the widow of Hector, had borne three sons to Neoptolemus in Epirus. But when he cast her off for Hermione, he left her to her fellow-captive, Helenus, Hector's brother. Now that Neoptolemus was dead she had become the wife of Helenus ; and they ruled the realm. Helenus and Andromache treated the exiles with the utmost hospitality, and dismissed them loaded with gifts.

250. The Cyclopes Again. From hence Æneas coasted along the shore of Sicily and passed the country of the Cyclopes. Here they were hailed from the shore by a miserable object, whom by his garments tattered, as they were, they perceived to be a Greek. He told them he was one of Ulysses' companions, left behind by that chief in his hurried departure. He related the story of Ulysses' adventure with Polyphemus, and besought them to take him off with them, as he had no means of sustaining his existence where he was, but wild berries and roots, and lived in constant fear of the Cyclopes. While he spoke Polyphemus

FIG. 182. SCYLLA

made his appearance, — terrible, shapeless, vast, and, of course, blind.[1] He walked with cautious steps, feeling his way with a staff, down to the seaside, to wash his eye-socket in the waves. When he reached the water he waded out towards them, and his immense height enabled him to advance far into the sea, so that the Trojans in terror took to their oars to get out of his way. Hearing the oars, Polyphemus shouted after them so that the shores resounded, and at the noise the other Cyclopes came forth

---

[1] *Monstrum horrendum, informe, ingens, cui lumen ademptum.* — Æneid, 3, 658.

from their caves and woods, and lined the shore, like a row of lofty pine trees. The Trojans plied their oars and soon left them out of sight.

Æneas had been cautioned by Helenus to avoid the strait guarded by the monsters Scylla and Charybdis. There Ulysses, the reader will remember, had lost six of his men, seized by Scylla while the navigators were wholly intent upon avoiding Charybdis. Æneas, following the advice of Helenus, shunned the dangerous pass and coasted along the island of Sicily.

251. The Resentment of Juno. Now Juno, seeing the Trojans speeding their way prosperously towards their destined shore, felt her old grudge against them revive, for she could not forget the slight that Paris had put upon her in awarding the prize of beauty to another. In heavenly minds can such resentment dwell![1] Accordingly she gave orders to Æolus, who sent forth his sons, Boreas, Typhon, and the other winds, to toss the ocean. A terrible storm ensued, and the Trojan ships were driven out of their course towards the coast of Africa. They were in imminent danger of being wrecked, and were separated, so that Æneas thought that all were lost except his own vessel.

At this crisis, Neptune, hearing the storm raging, and knowing that he had given no orders for one, raised his head above the waves and saw the fleet of Æneas driving before the gale. Understanding the hostility of Juno, he was at no loss to account for it, but his anger was not the less at this interference in his province. He called the winds and dismissed them with a severe reprimand. He then soothed the waves, and brushed away the clouds from before the face of the sun. Some of the ships which had got on the rocks he pried off with his own trident, while Triton and a sea-nymph, putting their shoulders under others, set them afloat again. The Trojans, when the sea became calm, sought the nearest shore, — the coast of Carthage, where Æneas was so happy as to find that one by one the ships all arrived safe, though badly shaken.

252. The Sojourn at Carthage. Dido. Carthage, where the exiles had now arrived, was a spot on the coast of Africa opposite

---

[1] *Tantaene animis coelestibus irae?* — Æneid, I, II.

Sicily, where at that time a Tyrian colony under Dido, their queen, were laying the foundations of a state destined in later ages to be the rival of Rome itself. Dido was the daughter of Belus, king of Tyre, and sister of Pygmalion, who succeeded his father on the throne. Her husband was Sichæus, a man of immense wealth, but Pygmalion, who coveted his treasures, caused him to be put to death. Dido, with a numerous body of friends and followers, both men and women, succeeded in effecting their escape from Tyre, in several vessels, carrying with them the treasures of Sichæus. On arriving at the spot which they selected as the seat of their future home, they asked of the natives only so much land as they could inclose with a bull's hide. When this was readily granted, the queen caused the hide to be cut into strips, and with them inclosed a spot on which she built a citadel, and called it Byrsa (a hide). Around this fort the city of Carthage rose, and soon became a powerful and flourishing place.

Such was the state of affairs when Æneas with his Trojans arrived there. Dido received the illustrious exiles with friendliness and hospitality. "Not unacquainted with distress," she said, " I have learned to succor the unfortunate." [1] The queen's hospitality displayed itself in festivities at which games of strength and skill were exhibited. The strangers contended for the palm with her own subjects on equal terms, the queen declaring that whether the victor were "Trojan or Tyrian should make no difference to her." [2] At the feast which followed the games, Æneas gave at her request a recital of the closing events of the Trojan history and his own adventures after the fall of the city. Dido was charmed with his discourse and filled with admiration of his exploits. She conceived an ardent passion for him, and he for his part seemed well content to accept the fortunate chance which appeared to offer him at once a happy termination of his wanderings, a home, a kingdom, and a bride. Months rolled away in the enjoyment of pleasant intercourse, and it seemed as if Italy and the empire destined to be founded on its shores were alike forgotten. Seeing which, Jupiter dispatched Mercury with a message to Æneas

---

[1] *Haud ignara mali, miseris succurrere disco.* — Æneid, 1, 630.
[2] *Tros Tyriusve mihi nullo discrimine agetur.* — Æneid, 1, 574.

recalling him to a sense of his high destiny, and commanding him
to resume his voyage.

Æneas parted from Dido, though she tried every allurement and
persuasion to detain him. The blow to her affection and her pride
was too much for her to endure, and when she found that he was
gone, she mounted a funeral pile which she had caused to be prepared, and having stabbed herself was consumed with the pile.
The flames rising over the city were seen by the departing Trojans, and, though the cause was unknown, gave to Æneas some
intimation of the fatal event.

253. Palinurus. Italy at Last. After touching at the island
of Sicily, where Acestes, a prince of Trojan lineage, bore sway,
and gave them a hospitable reception, the Trojans reëmbarked
and held on their course for Italy. Venus now interceded with
Neptune to allow her son at last to attain the wished-for goal and
find an end of his perils on the deep. Neptune consented, stipu-
lating only for one life as a ransom for the rest. The victim was
Palinurus, the pilot. As he sat watching the stars with his hand
on the helm, Somnus, sent by Neptune, approached in the guise of
Phorbas, and said, "Palinurus, the breeze is fair, the water smooth,
and the ship sails steadily on her course. Lie down awhile and
take needful rest. I will stand at the helm in thy place." Palinurus
replied, "Tell me not of smooth seas or favoring winds,— me who
have seen so much of their treachery. Shall I trust Æneas to
the chances of the weather and the winds?" And he continued
to grasp the helm and to keep his eyes fixed on the stars. But
Somnus waved over him a branch moistened with Lethæan dew,
and his eyes closed in spite of all his efforts. Then Somnus pushed
him overboard, and he fell; but as he kept his hold upon the helm,
it came away with him. Neptune was mindful of his promise, and
held the ship on her track without helm or pilot till Æneas discovered his loss and, sorrowing deeply for his faithful steersman,
took charge of the ship himself. Under his guidance the ships
at last reached the shores of Italy, and joyfully the adventurers
leaped to land.

254. The Sibyl of Cumæ. While his people were employed in
making their encampment, Æneas sought the abode of the Sibyl.

It was a cave connected with a temple and grove, sacred to Apollo and Diana. While Æneas contemplated the scene, the Sibyl accosted him. She seemed to know his errand, and, under the influence of the deity of the place, burst forth in a prophetic strain, giving dark intimations of labors and perils through which he was destined to make his way to final success. She closed with the encouraging words which have become proverbial: "Yield not to disasters, but press onward the more bravely." [1] Æneas replied that he had prepared himself for whatever might await him. He had but one request to make. Having been directed in a dream to seek the abode of the dead in order to confer with his father Anchises to receive from him a revelation of his future fortunes and those of his race, he asked her assistance to enable him to accomplish the task. The Sibyl re-

FIG. 183. THE CUMÆAN SIBYL

From the painting by Michelangelo

plied: "The descent to Avernus is easy; the gate of Pluto stands open night and day; but to retrace one's steps and return to the upper air, that is the toil, that the difficulty." [2] She instructed him to seek in the forest a tree on which grew a golden branch. This

[1] *Tu ne cede malis, sed contra audentior ito.* —Æneid, 6, 95.

[2]   *Facilis descensus Averno;*
Noctes atque dies patet atri janua Ditis;
Sed revocare gradum, superasque evadere ad auras,
Hoc opus, hic labor est. — Æneid, 6, 126–129.

branch was to be plucked off and borne as a gift to Proserpine,
and if fate was propitious, it would yield to the hand and quit its
parent trunk, but otherwise no force could rend it away. If torn
away, another would succeed.

Æneas followed the directions of the Sibyl. His mother, Venus,
sent two of her doves to fly before him and show him the way,
and by their assistance he found the tree, plucked the branch,
and hastened back with it to the Sibyl.

255. The Infernal Regions. The region where Virgil locates
the entrance to the infernal regions is, perhaps, the most strikingly
adapted to excite ideas of the terrific and preternatural of any on
the face of the earth. It is the volcanic region near Vesuvius,
where the whole country is cleft with chasms from which sulphur-
ous flames arise, while the ground is shaken with pent-up vapors,
and mysterious sounds issue from the bowels of the earth. The
lake Avernus is supposed to fill the crater of an extinct volcano.
It is circular, half a mile wide and very deep, surrounded by high
banks, which in Virgil's time were covered with a gloomy forest.
Mephitic vapors rise from its waters, so that no life is found on
its banks, and no birds fly over it. Here Æneas offered sacrifices
to the infernal deities, Proserpine, Hecate, and the Furies. Then
a roaring was heard in the earth, the woods on the hilltops were
shaken, and the howling of dogs announced the approach of the
deities. "Now," said the Sibyl, "summon thy courage, for thou
shalt need it." She descended into the cave of Avernus, and
Æneas followed. Before the threshold of hell they passed through
a group of beings who are enumerated as Griefs and avenging
Cares, pale Diseases, and melancholy Age, Fear and Hunger that
tempt to crime, Toil, Poverty, and Death, — forms horrible to view.
The Furies spread their couches there, and Discord, whose hair
was of vipers tied up with a bloody fillet. Here also were the
monsters, Briareus, with his hundred arms, Hydras hissing, and
Chimæras breathing fire. Æneas shuddered at the sight, drew his
sword and would have struck, but the Sibyl restrained him. They
then came to the black river Cocytus, where they found the ferryman Charon, old and squalid, but strong and vigorous, who was
receiving passengers of all kinds into his boat, stout-hearted heroes,

boys and unmarried girls, as numerous as the leaves that fall at autumn or the flocks that fly southward at the approach of winter. They stood pressing for a passage and longing to touch the opposite shore. But the stern ferryman took in only such as he chose, driving the rest back. Æneas, wondering at the sight, asked the Sibyl, "Why this discrimination?" She answered, "Those who are taken on board the bark are the souls of those who have received due burial rites; the host of others who have remained unburied are not permitted to pass the flood, but wander a hundred years, and flit to and fro about the shore, till at last they are taken over." Æneas grieved at recollecting some of his own companions who had perished in the storm. At that moment he beheld Palinurus, his pilot, who fell overboard and was drowned. He addressed him and asked him the cause of his misfortune. Palinurus replied that the rudder was carried away, and he, clinging to it, was swept away with it. He besought Æneas most urgently to extend to him his hand and take him in company to the opposite shore. The Sibyl rebuked him for the wish thus to transgress the laws of Pluto, but consoled him by informing him that the people of the shore where his body had been wafted by the waves should be stirred up by prodigies to give it due burial, and that the promontory should bear the name of Cape Palinurus, — and so it does to this day. Leaving Palinurus consoled by these words, they approached the boat. Charon, fixing his eyes sternly upon the advancing warrior, demanded by what right he, living and armed, approached that shore. To which the Sibyl replied that they would commit no violence, that Æneas' only object was to see his father, and finally exhibited the golden branch, at sight of which Charon's wrath relaxed, and he made haste to turn his bark to the shore and receive them on board. The boat, adapted only to the light freight of bodiless spirits, groaned under the weight of the hero. They were soon conveyed to the opposite shore. There they were encountered by the three-headed dog Cerberus, with his necks bristling with snakes. He barked with all three throats till the Sibyl threw him a medicated cake, which he eagerly devoured, and then stretched himself out in his den and fell asleep. Æneas and the Sibyl sprang to land. The first sound that struck their ears was the wailing of young children who had died on the threshold of life; and near to these were those who had perished under false charges. Minos presides over them as judge and examines the deeds of each. The next class was of those who had died by their own hand, hating life and seeking refuge in death. How willingly would they now endure poverty, labor, and any other infliction if they might but return to life! Next were situated the regions of sadness, divided off into retired paths, leading through groves of myrtle. Here roamed those who had fallen victims to unrequited love, not freed from pain even by death itself. Among these Æneas thought he descried the form of Dido, with a wound still recent. In the dim light he was for a moment uncertain, but approaching, perceived it was indeed she. Tears fell from his eyes, and he addressed her in the accents of love. "Unhappy Dido! was then the rumor true that thou hadst perished? And was I, alas! the cause? I call the gods to witness that my departure from thee was reluctant and in obedience to the commands of Jove; nor could I believe that my absence would have cost thee so dear. Stop, I beseech thee, and refuse me not a last farewell." She stood for a moment with averted countenance and eyes fixed on the ground, and then silently passed on, as insensible to his pleadings as a rock. Æneas followed for some distance, then with a heavy heart rejoined his companion and resumed his route.

They next entered the fields where roam the heroes who have fallen in battle. Here they saw many shades of Grecian and Trojan warriors. The Trojans thronged around him and could not be satisfied with the sight. They asked the cause of his coming and plied him with innumerable questions. But the Greeks, at the sight of his armor glittering through the murky atmosphere, recognized the hero, and, filled with terror, turned their backs and fled, as they used to do on the plains of Troy.

Æneas would have lingered long with his Trojan friends, but the Sibyl hurried him away. They next came to a place where the road divided, the one way leading to Elysium, the other to the regions of the condemned. Æneas beheld on one side the walls of a mighty city, around which Phlegethon rolled its fiery waters. Before him was the gate of adamant that neither gods nor men can break through. An iron tower stood by the gate, on which Tisiphone, the avenging Fury, kept guard. From the city were heard groans, and the sound of the scourge, the creaking of iron, and the clanking of chains. Æneas, horror-stricken, inquired of his guide what crimes were those whose punishments produced the sounds he heard. The Sibyl answered, "Here is the judgment hall of Rhadamanthus, who brings to light crimes done in life which the perpetrator vainly thought impenetrably hid. Tisiphone applies her whip of scorpions and delivers the offender over to her sister Furies." At this moment with horrid clang the brazen gates unfolded, and within, Æneas saw a Hydra with fifty heads guarding the entrance. The Sibyl told him that the gulf of Tartarus descended deep, so that its recesses were as far beneath their feet as heaven was high above their heads. In the bottom of this pit the Titan race, who warred against the gods, lie prostrate; Salmoneus also, who presumed to vie with Jupiter, and built a bridge of brass over which he drove his chariot that the sound might resemble thunder, launching flaming brands at his people in imitation of lightning, till Jupiter struck him with a real thunderbolt and taught him the difference between mortal weapons and divine. Here also is Tityus, the giant, whose form is so immense that, as he lies, he stretches over nine acres, while a vulture preys upon his liver, which as fast as it is devoured grows again, so that his punishment will have no end.

Æneas saw groups seated at tables loaded with dainties, while near by stood a Fury who snatched away the viands from their lips as fast as they prepared to taste them. Others beheld suspended over their heads huge rocks, threatening to fall, keeping them in a state of constant alarm. These were they who had hated their brothers, or struck their parents, or defrauded the friends who trusted them, or who, having grown rich, kept their money to themselves and gave no share to others, — the last being the most numerous class. Here also were those who had violated the marriage vow, or fought in a bad cause, or failed in fidelity to their employers. Here was one who had sold his country for gold, another who perverted the laws, making them say one thing to-day and another to-morrow.

Ixion was there, fastened to the circumference of a wheel cease-lessly revolving; and Sisyphus, whose task was to roll a huge stone up to a hilltop; but when the steep was well-nigh gained, the rock, repulsed by some sudden force, rushed again headlong down to the plain. Again he toiled at it, while the sweat bathed all his weary limbs, but all to no effect. There was Tantalus, who stood in a pool his chin level with the water, yet he was parched with

FIG. 184. IXION ON THE WHEEL

thirst and found nothing to assuage it; for when he bowed his hoary head, eager to quaff, the water fled away, leaving the ground at his feet all dry. Tall trees, laden with fruit, stooped their heads to him, — pears, pomegranates, apples, and luscious figs; but when, with a sudden grasp, he tried to seize them, winds whirled them high above his reach.

256. The Elysian Fields. The Sibyl now warned Æneas that it was time to turn from these melancholy regions and seek the city of the blessed. They passed through a middle tract of dark-ness and came upon the Elysian Fields, the groves where the happy reside. They breathed a freer air and saw all objects clothed in a purple light. The region had a sun and stars of its own. The inhabitants were enjoying themselves in various ways, some in sports on the grassy turf, in games of strength or skill, others dancing or singing. Orpheus struck the chords of his lyre and called forth ravishing sounds. Here Æneas saw the founders of the Trojan state, great-hearted heroes who lived in happier times. He gazed with admiration on the war chariots and glittering arms now reposing in disuse. Spears stood fixed in the ground, and the horses, unharnessed, roamed over the plain. The same pride in splendid armor and generous steeds which the old heroes felt in life accompanied them here. He saw another group feasting and listening to the strains of music. They were in a laurel grove, whence the great river Po has its origin and flows out among men. Here dwelt those who fell by wounds received in their country's cause, holy priests also, and poets who have uttered thoughts worthy of Apollo, and others who have contributed to cheer and adorn life by their discoveries in the useful arts, and have made their memory blessed by rendering service to mankind. They wore snow-white fillets about their brows. The Sibyl addressed a group of these and inquired where Anchises was to be found. They were directed where to seek him, and soon found him in a verdant valley, where he was contemplating the ranks of his posterity, their destinies and worthy deeds to be achieved in coming times. When he recognized Æneas approaching, he stretched out both hands to him, while tears flowed freely. "Dost thou come at last," said he, "long expected, and do I behold thee after such perils past? O my son, how have I trembled for thee, as I have watched thy course!" To which Æneas replied, "O father! thy image was always before me to guide and guard me." Then he endeavored to infold his father in his embrace, but his arms inclosed only an unsubstantial shade.

257. The Valley of Oblivion. Æneas perceived before him a spacious valley, with trees gently waving to the wind, a tranquil landscape, through which the river Lethe flowed. Along the banks of the stream wandered a countless multitude, numerous as insects in the summer air. Æneas, with surprise, inquired who were these.

Anchises answered: "They are souls to which bodies are to be given in due time. Meanwhile they dwell on Lethe's bank and drink oblivion of their former lives." "O father!" said Æneas, "is it possible that any can be so in love with life as to wish to leave these tranquil seats for the upper world?" Anchises replied by explaining the plan of creation. The Creator, he told him, originally made the material of which souls are composed, of the four elements, fire, air, earth, and water, all which when united took the form of the most excellent part, fire, and became *flame*. This material was scattered like seed among the heavenly bodies, the sun, moon, and stars. Of this seed the inferior gods created man and all other animals, mingling it with various proportions of earth, by which its purity was alloyed and reduced. Thus the more earth predominates in the composition, the less pure is the individual; and we see that men and women with their full-grown bodies have not the purity of childhood. So in proportion to the time which the union of body and soul has lasted, is the impurity contracted by the spiritual part. This impurity must be purged away after death, which is done by ventilating the souls in the current of winds, or merging them in water, or burning out their impurities by fire. Some few, of whom Anchises intimates that he is one, are admitted at once to Elysium, there to remain. But the rest, after the impurities of earth are purged away, are sent back to life endowed with new bodies, having had the remembrance of their former lives effectually washed away by the waters of Lethe. Some souls, however, there still are, so thoroughly corrupted that they are not fit to be intrusted with human bodies, and these pass by metempsychosis into the bodies of brute animals.

Anchises, having explained so much, proceeded to point out to Æneas individuals of his race who were hereafter to be born, and to relate to him the exploits they should perform in the world. After this he reverted to the present, and told his son of the events that remained to him to be accomplished before the complete establishment of himself and his followers in Italy. Wars were to be waged, battles fought, a bride to be won, and, in the result, a Trojan state founded, from which should rise the Roman power, to be in time the sovereign of the world.

As Æneas and the Sibyl pursued their way back to earth, he said to her: "Whether thou be a goddess or a mortal beloved by the gods, by me thou shalt always be held in reverence. When I reach the upper air, I will cause a temple to be built to thy honor, and will myself bring offerings." "I am no goddess," said the Sibyl; "I have no claims to sacrifice or offering. I am mortal, yet, could I but have accepted the love of Apollo, I might have been immortal. He promised me the fulfillment of my wish, if I would consent to be his. I took a handful of sand and, holding it forth, said, 'Grant me to see as many birthdays as there are sand-grains in my hand.' Unluckily I forgot to ask for enduring youth. This also he would have granted could I have accepted his love, but, offended at my refusal, he allowed me to grow old. My youth and youthful strength fled long ago. I have lived seven hundred years, and to equal the number of the sand-grains I have still to see three hundred springs and three hundred harvests. My body shrinks up as years increase, and in time I shall be lost to sight, but my voice will remain, and future ages will respect my sayings."

These concluding words of the Sibyl alluded to her prophetic power. In her cave she was accustomed to inscribe on leaves gathered from the trees the names and fates of individuals. The leaves thus inscribed were arranged in order within the cave, and might be consulted by her votaries. But if, perchance, at the opening of the door the wind rushed in and dispersed the leaves, the Sibyl gave no aid to restoring them again, and the oracle was irreparably lost.

CHAPTER XXVI

THE WAR BETWEEN TROJANS AND LATINS

258. The Fulfillment of Prophecy. Æneas, having parted from the Sibyl and rejoined his fleet, coasted along the shores of Italy and cast anchor in the mouth of the Tiber. The poet, having brought his hero to this spot, the destined termination of his wanderings, invokes his Muse to tell him the situation of things at that eventful moment. Latinus, third in descent from Saturn, ruled the country. He was now old and had no male descendant, but had one charming daughter, Lavinia, who was sought in marriage by many neighboring chiefs, one of whom, Turnus, king of the Rutulians, was favored by the wishes of her parents. But Latinus had been warned in a dream by his father, Faunus, that the destined husband of Lavinia should come from a foreign land. From that union should spring a race destined to subdue the world.

Our readers will remember that in the conflict with the harpies, one of those half-human birds had threatened the Trojans with dire sufferings. In particular, she predicted that before their wanderings ceased they should be pressed by hunger to devour their tables. This portent now came true; for as they took their scanty meal, seated on the grass, the men placed their hard biscuit on their laps and put thereon whatever their gleanings in the woods supplied. Having dispatched the latter, they finished by eating the crusts. Seeing which, the boy Iulus said playfully, "See! we are eating our tables." Æneas caught the words and accepted the omen. "All hail, promised land!" he exclaimed, "this is our home, this our country!" He then took measures to find out who were the present inhabitants of the land and who their rulers. A hundred chosen men were sent to the village of Latinus, bearing presents and a request for friendship and alliance. They went and were favorably received. Latinus immediately concluded that the

Trojan hero was no other than the promised son-in-law announced
by the oracle. He cheerfully granted his alliance, and sent back
the messengers mounted on steeds from his stables and loaded
with gifts and friendly messages.

Juno, seeing things go thus prosperously for the Trojans, felt
her old animosity revive, summoned Alecto from Erebus, and sent
her to stir up discord. The Fury first took possession of the queen,
Amata, and roused her to oppose in every way the new alliance.
Alecto then sped to the city of Turnus and, assuming the form of
an old priestess, informed him of the arrival of the foreigners and
of the attempts of their prince to rob him of his betrothed. Next she
turned her attention to the camp of the Trojans. There she saw
the boy Iulus and his companions amusing themselves with hunting. She sharpened the scent of the dogs and led them to rouse
up from the thicket a tame stag, the favorite of Silvia, the daughter of Tyrrheus, the king's herdsman. A javelin from the hand of
Iulus wounded the animal, which had only strength left to run homeward and die at its mistress's feet. Her cries and tears roused her
brothers and the herdsmen, and they, seizing whatever weapons
came to hand, furiously assaulted the hunting party. These were
protected by their friends, and the herdsmen were finally driven
back with the loss of two of their number.

These things were enough to rouse the storm of war, and the
queen, Turnus, and the peasants all urged the old king to drive
the strangers from the country. He resisted as long as he could,
but, finding his opposition unavailing, finally gave way and retreated to his retirement.

259. The Gates of Janus Opened. It was the custom of the
country, when war was to be undertaken, for the chief magistrate,
clad in his robes of office, with solemn pomp to open the gates of
the temple of Janus, which were kept shut as long as peace endured. His people now urged the old king to perform that solemn
office, but he refused to do so. While they contested, Juno herself,
descending from the skies, smote the doors with irresistible force
and burst them open. Immediately the whole country was in a
flame. The people rushed from every side, breathing nothing
but war.

Turnus was recognized by all as leader; others joined as allies, chief of whom was Mezentius, a brave and able soldier, but of detestable cruelty. He had been the chief of one of the neighboring cities, but his people drove him out. With him was joined his son Lausus, a generous youth worthy of a better sire.

260. Camilla. Camilla, the favorite of Diana, a huntress and warrior after the fashion of the Amazons, came with her band of mounted followers, including a select number of her own sex, and ranged herself on the side of Turnus. This maiden had never

accustomed her fingers to the distaff or the loom, but had learned to endure the toils of war and in speed to outstrip the wind. It seemed as if she might run over the standing corn without crushing it, or over the surface of the water without dipping her feet. Camilla's history had been singular from the beginning. Her father, Metabus, driven from his city by civil discord, carried with him in his flight his infant daughter. As he fled through the woods, his enemies in hot pursuit, he reached the bank of the river Amasenus, which, swelled by rains, seemed to debar a passage. He paused for a moment, then decided what to do. He tied the infant to his lance with wrappers of bark, and poising the weapon in his upraised hand, thus addressed

FIG. 185. AMAZON

Diana : " Goddess of the woods ! I consecrate this maid to thee "; then hurled the weapon with its burden to the opposite bank. The spear flew across the roaring water. His pursuers were already upon him, but he plunged into the river, and swam across, and found the spear with the infant safe on the other side. Thenceforth he lived among the shepherds and brought up his daughter in woodland arts. While a child she was taught to use the bow and throw the javelin. With her sling she could bring down the crane or the wild swan. Her dress was a tiger's skin. Many mothers sought her for a daughter-in-law, but she continued faithful to Diana and repelled the thought of marriage.

261. Alliance with Evander. Such were the formidable allies that ranged themselves against Æneas. It was night, and he lay stretched in sleep on the bank of the river under the open heavens. The god of the stream, Father Tiber, seemed to raise his head above the willows and to say: "O goddess-born, destined possessor of the Latin realms, this is the promised land; here is to be thy home, here shall terminate the hostility of the heavenly powers, if only thou faithfully persevere. There are friends not far distant. Prepare thy boats and row up my stream; I will lead thee to Evander, the Arcadian chief. He has long been at strife with Turnus and the Rutulians, and is prepared to become an ally of thine. Rise! offer thy vows to Juno and deprecate her anger. When thou hast achieved thy victory, then think of me." Æneas woke and paid immediate obedience to the friendly vision. He sacrificed to Juno, and invoked the god of the river and all his tributary fountains to lend their aid. Then for the first time a vessel filled with armed warriors floated on the stream of the Tiber. The river smoothed its waves and bade its current flow gently, while, impelled by the vigorous strokes of the rowers, the vessel shot rapidly up the stream.

About the middle of the day they came in sight of the scattered buildings of the infant town where in after times the proud city of Rome grew, whose glory reached the skies. By chance the old king, Evander, was that day celebrating annual solemnities in honor of Hercules and all the gods. Pallas, his son, and all the chiefs of the little commonwealth stood by. When they saw the tall ship gliding onward through the wood, they were alarmed at the sight and rose from the tables. But Pallas forbade the solemnities to be interrupted and, seizing a weapon, stepped forward to the river's bank. He called aloud, demanding who the strangers were and what their object. Æneas, holding forth an olive branch, replied: "We are Trojans, friends to you and enemies to the Rutulians. We seek Evander and offer to join our arms with yours." Pallas, in amaze at the sound of so great a name, invited them to land, and when Æneas touched the shore, he seized his hand and held it long in friendly grasp. Proceeding through the wood they joined the king and his party, and were most favorably received. Seats were provided for them at the tables, and the repast proceeded.

262. The Site of Future Rome. When the solemnities were ended, all moved towards the city. The king, bending with age, walked between his son and Æneas, taking the arm of one or the other of them, and with much variety of pleasing talk shortening the way. Æneas with delight looked and listened, observing all the beauties of the scene and learning much of heroes renowned in ancient times. Evander said: "These extensive groves were once inhabited by fauns and nymphs, and a rude race of men who sprang from the trees themselves and had neither laws nor social culture. They knew not how to yoke the cattle, nor raise a harvest, nor provide from present abundance for future want, but browsed like beasts upon the leafy boughs or fed voraciously on their hunted prey. Such were they when Saturn, expelled from Olympus by his sons, came among them and drew together the fierce savages, formed them into society, and gave them laws. Such peace and plenty ensued that men ever since have called his reign the Golden Age; but by degrees far other times succeeded, and the thirst of gold and the thirst of blood prevailed. The land was a prey to successive tyrants till fortune and resistless destiny brought me hither, an exile from my native land, Arcadia."

Having thus said, he showed him the Tarpeian rock, and the rude spot, then overgrown with bushes, where in after times the Capitol was to rise in all its magnificence. He next pointed to some dismantled walls and said, "Here stood Janiculum, built by Janus, and there Saturnia, the town of Saturn." Such discourse brought them to the cottage of Evander, whence they saw the lowing herds roaming over the plain where soon should stand the proud and stately Forum. They entered, and a couch, well stuffed with leaves and covered with the skin of a Libyan bear, was spread for Æneas.

Next morning, awakened by the dawn and the shrill song of birds beneath the eaves of his low mansion, old Evander rose. Clad in a tunic, and a panther's skin thrown over his shoulders, with sandals on his feet and his good sword girded to his side, he went forth to seek his guest. Two mastiffs followed him, — his whole retinue and bodyguard. He found the hero attended by his faithful Achates, and Pallas soon joining them, the old king spoke thus:

"Illustrious Trojan, it is but little we can do in so great a cause. Our state is feeble, hemmed in on one side by the river, on the other by the Rutulians. But I propose to ally thee with a people numerous and rich, to whom fate has brought thee at the propitious moment. The Etruscans hold the country beyond the river. Mezentius was their king, a monster of cruelty, who invented unheard-of torments to gratify his vengeance. He would fasten the dead to the living, hand to hand and face to face, and leave the wretched victims to die in that dreadful embrace. At length people cast him out, him and his house. They burned his palace, and slew his friends. He escaped and took refuge with Turnus, who protects him with arms. The Etruscans demand that he shall be given up to deserved punishment, and would ere now have attempted to enforce their demand; but their priests restrain them, telling them that it is the will of heaven that no native of the land shall guide them to victory and that their destined leader must come from across the sea. They have offered the crown to me, but I am too old to undertake such great affairs, and my son is native-born, which precludes him from the choice. Thou, equally by birth and time of life and fame in arms pointed out by the gods, hast but to appear to be hailed at once as their leader. With thee I will join Pallas, my son, my only hope and comfort. Under thee he shall learn the art of war and strive to emulate thy great exploits."

Then the king ordered horses to be furnished for the Trojan chiefs, and Æneas, with a chosen band of followers and Pallas accompanying, mounted and took the way to the Etruscan city,[1] having sent back the rest of his party in the ships. Æneas and his band safely arrived at the Etruscan camp and were received with open arms by Tarchon and his countrymen.

263. Turnus attacks the Trojan Camp. In the meanwhile Turnus had collected his bands and made all necessary preparations for the war. Juno sent Iris to him with a message inciting him to take advantage of the absence of Æneas and surprise the Trojan camp. Accordingly the attempt was made; but the Trojans were

---

[1] The poet here inserts a famous line which is thought to imitate in its sound the galloping of horses: *Quadrupedante putrem sonitu quatit ungula campum.* — Æneid, 8, 596.

found on their guard, and having received strict orders from Æneas not to fight in his absence, they lay still in their intrenchments and resisted all the efforts of the Rutulians to draw them into the field. Night coming on, the army of Turnus, in high spirits at their fancied superiority, feasted and enjoyed themselves, and finally stretched themselves on the field and slept secure.

264. Nisus and Euryalus. In the camp of the Trojans things were far otherwise. There all was watchfulness and anxiety, and impatience for Æneas' return. Nisus stood guard at the entrance of the camp, and Euryalus, a youth distinguished above all in the army for graces of person and fine qualities, was with him. These two were friends and brothers in arms. Nisus said to his friend: "Dost thou perceive what confidence and carelessness the enemy display? Their lights are few and dim, and the men seem all oppressed with wine or sleep. Thou knowest how anxiously our chiefs wish to send to Æneas and to get intelligence from him. Now I am strongly moved to make my way through the enemy's camp and to go in search of our chief. If I succeed, the glory of the deed will be reward enough for me, and if they judge the service deserves anything more, let them pay it thee."

Euryalus, all on fire with the love of adventure, replied: "Wouldst thou then, Nisus, refuse to share thy enterprise with me? And shall I let thee go into such danger alone? Not so my brave father brought me up, nor so have I planned for myself when I joined the standard of Æneas and resolved to hold my life cheap in comparison with honor." Nisus replied: "I doubt it not, my friend; but thou knowest the uncertain event of such an undertaking, and whatever may happen to me, I wish thee to be safe. Thou art younger than I and hast more of life in prospect. Nor can I be the cause of such grief to thy mother, who has chosen to be here in the camp with thee rather than stay and live in peace with the other matrons in Acestes' city." Euryalus replied, "Say no more. In vain dost thou seek arguments to dissuade me. I am fixed in the resolution to go with thee. Let us lose no time." They called the guard and, committing the watch to them, sought the general's tent. They found the chief officers in consultation, deliberating how they should send notice to Æneas of their situation. The offer of the two friends was gladly accepted, themselves loaded with praises and promised the most liberal rewards in case of success. Iulus especially addressed Euryalus, assuring him of his lasting friendship. Euryalus replied : "I have but one boon to ask. My aged mother is with me in the camp. For me she left the Trojan soil and would not stay behind with the other matrons at the city of Acestes. I go now without taking leave of her. I could not bear her tears nor set at naught her entreaties. But do thou, I beseech thee, comfort her in her distress. Promise me that and I shall go more boldly into whatever dangers may present themselves." Iulus and the other chiefs were moved to tears and promised to do all his request. "Thy mother shall be mine," said Iulus, "and all that I have promised thee shall be made good to her, if thou dost not return to receive it."

The two friends left the camp and plunged at once into the midst of the enemy. They found no watch, no sentinels posted, but, all about, the sleeping soldiers strewn on the grass and among the wagons. The laws of war at that early day did not forbid a brave man to slay a sleeping foe, and the two Trojans slew, as they passed, such of the enemy as they could without exciting alarm. In one tent Euryalus made prize of a helmet brilliant with gold and plumes. They had passed through the enemy's ranks without being discovered, but now suddenly appeared a troop directly in front of them, which, under Volscens, their leader, were approaching the camp. The glittering helmet of Euryalus caught their attention, and Volscens hailed the two and demanded who and whence they were. They made no answer, but plunged into the wood. The horsemen scattered in all directions to intercept their flight. Nisus had eluded pursuit and was out of danger, but, since Euryalus was missing, he turned back to seek him. He again entered the wood and soon came within sound of voices. Looking through the thicket he saw the whole band surrounding Euryalus with noisy questions. What should he do ; how extricate the youth ; or would it be better to die with him ?

Raising his eyes to the moon which now shone clear, he said, "Goddess, favor my effort !" and, aiming his javelin at one of the leaders of the troop, struck him in the back and stretched him

on the plain with a deathblow. In the midst of their amazement
another weapon flew, and another of the party fell dead. Volscens,
the leader, ignorant whence the darts came, rushed sword in hand
upon Euryalus. "Thou shalt pay the penalty of both," he said,
and would have plunged the sword into his bosom, when Nisus,
who from his concealment saw the peril of his friend, rushed forward exclaiming, "'Twas I! 'twas I! Turn your swords against
me, Rutulians. I did it; he only followed me as a friend." While
he spoke the sword fell and pierced the comely bosom of Euryalus.
His head fell over on his shoulder, like a flower cut down by the
plow. Nisus rushed upon Volscens and plunged his sword into
his body, and was himself slain on the instant by numberless blows.

265. The Death of Mezentius. Æneas, with his Etrurian allies,
arrived on the scene of action in time to rescue his beleaguered
camp; and now the two armies being nearly equal in strength,
the war began in good earnest. We cannot find space for all the
details, but must simply record the fate of the principal characters.
The tyrant Mezentius, finding himself engaged against his revolted
subjects, raged like a wild beast. He slew all who dared withstand
him, and put the multitude to flight wherever he appeared. At
last he encountered Æneas, and the armies stood still to see the
issue. Mezentius threw his spear, which, striking Æneas' shield,
glanced off and hit Antores, — a Grecian by birth who had left
Argos, his native city, and followed Evander into Italy. The poet
says of him, with simple pathos which has made the words proverbial, "He fell, unhappy, by a wound intended for another,
looked up to the skies, and, dying, remembered sweet Argos." [1]
Æneas now in turn hurled his lance. It pierced the shield of
Mezentius and wounded him in the thigh. Lausus, his son, could
not bear the sight, but rushed forward and interposed himself,
while the followers pressed round Mezentius and bore him away.
Æneas held his sword suspended over Lausus and delayed to
strike, but the furious youth pressed on, and he was compelled to
deal the fatal blow. Lausus fell, and Æneas bent over him in pity.
"Hapless youth," he said, "what can I do for thee worthy of thy

[1] *Sternitur infelix alieno volnere, caelumque*
Aspicit, et dulcis moriens reminiscitur Argos. — Æneid 10, 781.

praise? Keep those arms in which thou gloriest, and fear not but that thy body shall be restored to thy friends and have due funeral honors." So saying, he called the timid followers and delivered the body into their hands.

Mezentius meanwhile had been borne to the riverside, and had washed his wound. Soon the news reached him of Lausus' death, and rage and despair supplied the place of strength. He mounted his horse and dashed into the thickest of the fight, seeking Æneas. Having found him, he rode round him in a circle, throwing one javelin after another, while Æneas stood fenced with his shield, turning every way to meet them. At last after Mezentius had three times made the circuit, Æneas threw his lance directly at the horse's head. The animal fell with pierced temples, while a shout from both armies rent the skies. Mezentius asked no mercy, but only that his body might be spared the insults of his revolted subjects and be buried in the same grave with his son. He received the fatal stroke not unprepared, and poured out his life and his blood together.

266. The Deaths of Pallas and Camilla. While these things were doing in one part of the field, in another Turnus encountered the youthful Pallas. The contest between champions so unequally matched could not be doubtful. Pallas bore himself bravely, but fell by the lance of Turnus. The victor almost relented when he saw the brave youth lying dead at his feet, and spared to use the privilege of a conqueror in despoiling him of his arms. The belt only, adorned with studs and carvings of gold, he took and clasped round his own body. The rest he remitted to the friends of the slain.

After the battle there was a cessation of arms for some days to allow both armies to bury their dead. In this interval Æneas challenged Turnus to decide the contest by single combat, but Turnus evaded the challenge. Another battle ensued, in which Camilla, the virgin warrior, was chiefly conspicuous. Her deeds of valor surpassed those of the bravest warriors, and many Trojans and Etruscans fell pierced with her darts or struck down by her battle-ax. At last an Etruscan named Aruns, who had watched her long, seeking for some advantage, observed her pursuing an enemy whose splendid armor offered a tempting prize. Intent on the chase she observed not her danger, and the javelin of Aruns struck her and inflicted a fatal wound. She fell and breathed her last in the arms of her attendant maidens. But Diana, who beheld her fate, suffered not her slaughter to be unavenged. Aruns, as he stole away glad but frightened, was struck by a secret arrow, launched by one of the nymphs of Diana's train, and he died ignobly and unknown.

267. The Final Conflict. At length the final conflict took place between Æneas and Turnus. Turnus had avoided the contest as long as he could; but at last, impelled by the ill success of his arms and by the murmurs of his followers, he braced himself to the conflict. The outcome could not be doubtful. On the side of Æneas were the expressed decree of destiny, the aid of his goddess-mother in every emergency, and impenetrable armor fabricated by Vulcan, at her request, for her son. Turnus, on the other hand, was deserted by his celestial allies, Juno having been expressly forbidden by Jupiter to assist him any longer. Turnus threw his lance, but it recoiled harmless from the shield of Æneas. The Trojan hero then threw his, which, penetrating the shield of Turnus, pierced his thigh. Then Turnus' fortitude forsook him, and he begged for mercy; Æneas, indeed, would have spared his opponent's life, but at the instant his eye fell on the belt of Pallas, which Turnus had taken from the slaughtered youth. Instantly his rage revived, and exclaiming, " Pallas immolates thee with this blow," he thrust him through with his sword.

Here the poem of the Æneid closes, and we are left to infer that Æneas, having triumphed over his foes, obtained Lavinia for his bride. Tradition adds that he founded a city and called it Lavinium, after her name. His son Iulus founded Alba Longa, which became the birthplace of Romulus and Remus and the cradle of Rome.

NIKE OF BRESCIA

CHAPTER XXVII

MYTHS OF THE NORSE GODS[1]

268. The Creation. According to the Eddas there was once no heaven above nor earth beneath, but only a bottomless deep, Ginungagap, and a world of mist, Niflheim, in which sprang a fountain. Twelve rivers issued from this fountain, Vergelmir, and when they had flowed far from their source, they froze into ice, and one layer accumulating over another, the great deep was filled up.

Southward from the world of mist was the world of light, Muspelheim. From this proceeded a warm wind upon the ice and melted it. The vapors rose in the air and formed clouds, from which sprang Ymir, the rime-cold giant and his progeny, and the cow Audhumbla, whose milk afforded nourishment and food to the giant. The cow got nourishment by licking the hoar frost and salt from the ice. While she was one day licking the salt stones there appeared at first the hair of some being, on the second day his whole head, and on the third the entire form endowed with beauty, agility, and power. This new being was a god, Bori, from whom and his wife, a daughter of the giant race, sprang Bor, the father of Odin, Vili, and Ve. These three slew the giant Ymir, and out of his body formed the earth, of his blood the seas, of his bones the mountains, of his hair the trees, of his skull the heavens, and of his brain clouds, charged with hail and snow. Of Ymir's eyebrows the gods built a fence around the Midgard or mid-earth between Niflheim and Muspelheim, destined to become the abode of man.

Odin then regulated the periods of day and night and the seasons by placing in the heavens the sun and moon, and appointing to them their respective courses. As soon as the sun began to shed its rays upon the earth, it caused the vegetable world to

[1] For Records of Norse Mythology, see § 300, and Commentary, §§ 268, 282, and 300.

bud and sprout. Shortly after the gods (the Anse-race, Anses, Æsir, or Asa-folk) had created the world, they walked by the side of the sea, pleased with their new work, but found that it was still incomplete, for it was without human beings. They therefore took an ashen spar and made a man out of it; woman they made out of a piece of elm; and they called the man Ask and the woman Embla. Odin then gave them life and soul, Vili reason and motion, and Ve bestowed upon them the senses, expressive features, and speech. Midgard was given them as their residence, and they became the progenitors of the human race.

269. Yggdrasil. The mighty ash tree, Yggdrasil, was supposed to support the whole universe. It sprang from the body of Ymir, and had three immense roots, extending one into Midgard (the dwelling of mortals), another into Jötunheim (the abode of the giants), and the third below Niflheim, into the region of Death. By the side of each of these roots is a spring, from which it is watered. The root that extends into Midgard is carefully tended by the three Norns, — goddesses who are regarded as the dispensers of fate. They are Urd (the past), Verdandi (the present), Skuld (the future). The spring at the Jötunheim side is Mimir's well, in which wisdom and wit lie hidden, but that below Niflheim refreshes also the dark dragon of despair, Nidhogg (the back-biter), which perpetually gnaws at the root. Four harts run across the branches of the tree and nip the buds; they represent the four winds. Under the tree lies Ymir, and when he tries to shake off its weight the earth quakes. The boughs overshadow the earth, and the top rises into Asgard in the zenith.

270. Odin and his Valhalla. To Asgard, the abode of the gods, access is gained only by crossing the bridge, Bifrost (the rainbow). Asgard — Gladsheim for the gods, Vingolf for the goddesses — consists of golden and silver palaces; but the most beautiful of these is Valhalla, the great hall of Odin. When seated on his throne he overlooks heaven and earth. Beside him sits *Frigga* (or *Fricka*), his wife, who knows all things. Upon his shoulders are the ravens, Hugin and Munin, — Thought and Memory, — who fly every day over the whole world, and on their return report to him what they have seen and heard. At his feet lie his two wolves, Geri and

Freki, to whom Odin gives the meat that is set before him, for he himself stands in no need of food. Mead is for him both food and drink. He invented the Runic characters; the decrees of fate, inscribed therein, it is the business of the Norns to engrave upon a

FIG. 186. VALKYRIE BEARING A HERO TO VALHALLA

From the painting by Dielitz

metal shield. From Odin's name, spelt Woden, as it sometimes is, comes our English word, Wednesday.

Odin is frequently called Alfadur (All-father), but this name is sometimes used in a way that shows that the Scandinavians had an idea of a deity superior to Odin, uncreated and eternal. In Valhalla Odin feasts with his chosen heroes, all those who have fallen bravely in battle, for all who die a peaceful death are excluded. The flesh of the boar Serimnir is served up to them and is abundant for all. For although this boar is cooked every morning, he becomes whole again every night. For drink the heroes are supplied abundantly with mead from the she-goat Heidrun. When the heroes are not feasting, they amuse themselves with fighting. Every day they ride out into the court or field and fight until they cut each other in pieces. This is their pastime; but when mealtime comes, they recover from their wounds and return to feast in Valhalla.

271. The Valkyries. The Valkyries are warlike virgins, mounted upon horses and armed with helmets, shields, and spears. Odin is desirous of gathering many heroes in Valhalla that he may gloriously meet the giants in the day of the final contest; he therefore sends to every battle field for the bravest of those who shall be slain. The Valkyries, Choosers of the Slain, are his messengers. Later they are called his daughters. When they ride forth on their errand, their armor sheds a weird flickering light over the northern skies, making what men call the Aurora Borealis.[1]

272. Thor and the Other Gods. Of the following, *Thor*, *Vidar*, *Bragi*, *Balder*, and *Höder* are sons of Odin. *Thor*, the thunderer, Odin's eldest son, is the strongest of gods and men, and possesses three precious things. The first is a hammer, which both the Frost and the Mountain giants (Hrim-thursar and Berg-risar) know to their cost, when they see it hurled against them in the air, for it has split many a skull of their fathers and kindred. When thrown, it returns to his hand of its own accord. The second rare thing he possesses is the belt of strength. When he girds it about him his divine might is doubled. The third is his iron gloves, which he puts on whenever he would use his mallet efficiently. From Thor's name is derived our word Thursday.

Vidar comes next in strength to Thor.

Bragi is the god of poetry, and his song records the deeds of warriors. His wife, *Iduna*, keeps in a box the apples which the gods, when they feel old age approaching, have only to taste of to become young again.

Balder, dearest of the Anses, is the god of sunlight, spring, and gladness. *Höder*, his opposite, is the blind god of winter.

---

[1] Gray's ode, The Fatal Sisters, is founded on this superstition.

Of other gods, *Freyr* presides over rain and sunshine and all the fruits of the earth. His sister *Freya* (Freia) is the most propitious of the goddesses. She loves music, spring, and flowers, and the fairies of Elfheim. She is the goddess of love. Her day is Friday.

Tyr (*Ziu* or *Tiw*), from whose name is derived our Tuesday, is the wrestler among the gods; and preëminently the " god of battles."

Heimdall is the watchman of the gods, and is therefore placed on the borders of heaven to prevent the giants from forcing their way over the bridge Bifrost. He requires less sleep than a bird, and sees by night as well as by day a hundred miles around him. So acute is his ear that no sound escapes him, for he can even hear the grass grow,—and the wool on a sheep's back.

273. Loki and his Progeny. Loki (or Loge) is described as the calumniator of the gods and the contriver of all fraud and mischief. He is the son of Farbauti, the Charon of Norse mythology. He is handsome and well made, but of fickle mood and evil disposition. Although of the demon race, he forced himself into the company of the gods, and seemed to take pleasure in bringing them into difficulties, and in extricating them out of the danger by his cunning, wit, and skill. Loki has three children. The first is the wolf *Fenris*, the second the *Midgard Serpent*, the third *Hela* (Death). The gods were not ignorant that these monsters were maturing and that they would one day bring much evil upon gods and men. So Odin deemed it advisable to send one to bring them to him. When they came he threw the serpent in that deep ocean by which the earth is surrounded. But the monster has grown to such an enormous size that, holding his tail in his mouth, he encircles the whole earth. Hela he hurled below Niflheim and gave her power over nine worlds or regions, in which she distributes those who are sent to her, — that is, all who die of sickness or old age. Her hall is called Eliudnir, or Sleet-den. Hunger is her table, Starvation her knife, Delay her man, Slowness her maid, Pale Woe her door, Stumbling-stone her threshold, Care her bed; and Falling-peril forms the hangings of her apartments. She may easily be recognized, for her body is half flesh color and half blue, and she presents a stern and forbidding countenance.

The wolf Fenris gave the gods a great deal of trouble before they succeeded in chaining him. He broke the strongest fetters as if they were made of cobwebs. Finally the gods sent a messenger to the mountain spirits, who made for them the chain called Gleipnir. It is fashioned of six things, — the noise made by the footfall of a cat, the beards of women, the roots of stones, the breath of fishes, the nerves (sensibilities) of bears, and the spittle of birds. When finished it was as smooth and soft as a silken string. But when the gods asked the wolf to suffer himself to be bound with this apparently slight ribbon, he suspected their design, fearing that it was made by enchantment. He therefore consented to be bound with it only upon condition that one of the gods put his hand in his (Fenris') mouth as a pledge that the band was to be removed again. Tyr alone had courage enough to do this. But when the wolf found that he could not break his fetters and that the gods would not release him, he bit off Tyr's hand. Tyr, consequently, has ever since remained one-handed.

274. The Conflict with the Mountain Giants. When the gods were constructing their abodes and had already finished Midgard and Valhalla, a certain artificer came and offered to build them a residence so well fortified that they should be perfectly safe from the incursions of the Frost giants and the giants of the mountains. But he demanded for his reward the goddess Freya, together with the sun and moon. The gods yielded to the terms, provided that the artificer would finish the whole work without any one's assistance, and all within the space of one winter. But if anything remained unfinished on the first day of summer, he should forfeit the recompense agreed on. On being told these terms, the artificer stipulated that he be allowed the use of his horse Svadilfari, and this request, by the advice of Loki, was conceded. He accordingly set to work on the first day of winter, and during the night let his horse draw stone for the building. The enormous size of the stones struck the gods with astonishment, and they saw clearly that the horse did one half more of the toilsome work than his master. Their bargain, however, had been concluded and confirmed by solemn oaths, for without these precautions a giant would not have thought himself safe among the gods, — still less, indeed, if Thor should return from the expedition he had then undertaken against the evil demons.

As the winter drew to a close the building was far advanced, and the bulwarks were sufficiently high and massive to render the place impregnable. In short, when it wanted but three days to summer, the only part that remained to be finished was the gateway. Then sat the gods on their seats of justice and entered into consultation, inquiring of one another who among them could have advised the rest to surrender Freya, or to plunge the heavens in darkness by permitting the giant to carry away the sun and the moon.

They all agreed that no one but Loki, the author of so many evil deeds, could have given such counsel, and that he should be put to a cruel death unless he contrived some way to prevent the artificer from completing his task and obtaining the stipulated recompense. They proceeded to lay hands on Loki, who in his fright promised upon oath that, let it cost him what it might, he would so manage matters that the man should lose his reward. That night when the man went with Svadilfari for building-stone, a mare suddenly ran out of a forest and began to neigh. The horse thereat broke loose and ran after the mare into the forest, obliging the man also to run after his horse; thus, therefore, between one and another the whole night was lost, so that at dawn the work had not made the usual progress. The man, seeing that he must fail of completing his task, resumed his own gigantic stature, and the gods now clearly perceived that it was in reality a mountain giant who had come amongst them. Feeling no longer bound by their oaths, they called on Thor, who immediately ran to their assistance and, lifting up his mallet, paid the workman his wages, not with the sun and moon, and not even by sending him back to Jötunheim, for with the first blow he shattered the giant's skull to pieces and hurled him headlong into Niflheim.

275. The Recovery of Thor's Hammer. Soon afterward it happened that Thor's hammer fell into the possession of the giant Thrym, who buried it eight fathoms deep under the rocks of Jötunheim. Thor sent Loki to negotiate with Thrym, but he could only prevail so far as to get the giant's promise to restore the weapon if Freya would consent to be his bride. Loki returned and reported the result of his mission, but the goddess of love was horrified at the idea of bestowing her charms on the king of the Frost giants. In this emergency Loki persuaded Thor to dress himself in Freya's clothes and accompany him to Jötunheim. Thrym received his veiled bride with due courtesy, but was greatly surprised at seeing her eat for her supper eight salmon and a full-grown ox besides other delicacies, washing the whole down with three tuns of mead. Loki, however, assured him that she had not tasted anything for eight long nights, so great was her desire to see her lover, the renowned ruler of Jötunheim. Thrym had at last the curiosity to peep under his bride's veil, but started back in affright, and demanded why Freya's eyeballs glistened with fire. Loki repeated the same excuse, and the giant was satisfied. He ordered the hammer to be brought in and laid on the maiden's lap. Thereupon Thor threw off his disguise, grasped his redoubted weapon, and slaughtered Thrym and all his followers.

276. Thor's Visit to Jötunheim. One day Thor, with his servant Thialfi and accompanied by Loki, set out for the giants' country. Thialfi was of all men the swiftest of foot. He bore Thor's wallet containing their provisions. When night came on they found themselves in an immense, forest, and searched on all sides for a place where they might pass the night. At last they came to a large hall, with an entrance that took the whole breadth of one end of the building. Here they lay down to sleep, but towards midnight were alarmed by an earthquake which shook the whole edifice. Thor, rising up, called on his companions to seek with him a place of safety. On the right they found an adjoining chamber into which the others entered, but Thor remained at the doorway with his mallet in his hand, prepared to defend himself whatever might happen. A terrible groaning was heard during the night, and at dawn of day Thor went out and found lying near him a huge giant, still snoring in the way that had alarmed them. For once Thor was afraid to use his mallet, and as the giant soon waked up, Thor contented himself with simply asking his name.

"My name is Skrymir," said the giant, "but I need not ask thy name, for I know that thou art the god Thor. But what has become of my glove?" Thor then perceived that what they had taken overnight for a hall was the giant's glove, and the chamber where his two companions had sought refuge was the thumb. Skrymir then proposed that they should travel in company, and Thor consenting, they sat down to eat their breakfast. When they had done, Skrymir packed all the provisions into one wallet, threw it over his shoulder, and strode on before them, taking such tremendous strides that they were hard put to it to keep up with him. So they traveled the whole day, and at dusk Skrymir chose a place for them to pass the night in under a large oak tree. Skrymir then told them he would lie down to sleep. "But take ye the wallet," he added, "and prepare your supper."

Skrymir soon fell asleep and began to snore strongly, but when Thor tried to open the wallet, he found the giant had tied it up so tight he could not untie a single knot. At last Thor became wroth, and grasping his mallet with both hands, he struck a furious blow on the giant's head. Skrymir, awakening, merely asked whether a leaf had not fallen on his head, and whether they had supped and were ready to go to sleep. Thor answered that they were just going to sleep, and so saying went and laid himself down under another tree. But sleep came not that night to Thor, and when Skrymir snored again so loud that the forest reëchoed with the noise, he arose, and, grasping his mallet, launched it with such force at the giant's skull that it made a deep dint in it. Skrymir, awakening, cried out: "What's the matter? Are there any birds perched on this tree? I felt some moss from the branches fall on my head. How fares it with thee, Thor?" But Thor went away hastily, saying that he had just then awoke, and that as it was only midnight, there was still time for sleep. He, however, resolved that if he had an opportunity of striking a third blow, it should settle all matters between them. A little before daybreak he perceived that Skrymir was again fast asleep, and again grasping his mallet, he dashed it with such violence that it forced its way into the giant's skull up to the handle. But Skrymir sat up, and, stroking his cheek, said: "An acorn fell on my head. What! Art thou awake, Thor? Methinks it is time for us to get up and dress ourselves; but you have not now a long way before you to the city called

Utgard. I have heard you whispering to one another that I am not a man of small dimensions, but if you come to Utgard, you will see there many men much taller than I. Wherefore I advise you, when you come there, not to make too much of yourselves; for the followers of Utgard-Loki will not brook the boasting of such little fellows as you are. You must take the road that leads eastward; mine lies northward, so we must part here."

Hereupon he threw his wallet over his shoulders and turned away from them into the forest, and Thor had no wish to stop him or to ask for any more of his company.

Thor and his companions proceeded on their way, and towards noon descried a city standing in the middle of a plain. It was so lofty that they were obliged to bend their necks quite back on their shoulders in order to see to the top of it. On arriving they entered the city, and seeing a large palace before them with the door wide open, they went in and found a number of men of prodigious stature, sitting on benches in the hall. Going further, they came before the king Utgard-Loki, whom they saluted with great respect. The king, regarding them with a scornful smile, said, "If I do not mistake me, that stripling yonder must be the god Thor." Then addressing himself to Thor, he said: "Perhaps thou mayst be more than thou appearest to be. What are the feats that thou and thy fellows deem yourselves skilled in? — for no one is permitted to remain here who does not, in some feat or other, excel all other men."

"The feat that I know," said Loki, "is to eat quicker than any one else, and in this I am ready to give a proof against any one here who may choose to compete with me."

"That will indeed be a feat, if thou performest what thou promisest," said Utgard-Loki, "and it shall be tried forthwith."

He then ordered one of his men, who was sitting at the farther end of the bench and whose name was Logi, to come forward and try his skill with Loki. A trough filled with meat having been set on the hall floor, Loki placed himself at one end and Logi at the other, and each of them began to eat as fast as he could, until they met in the middle of the trough. But it was found that Loki had only eaten the flesh, while his adversary had devoured both flesh and bone, and the trough to boot. All the company therefore adjudged that Loki was vanquished.

Utgard-Loki then asked what feat the young man who accompanied Thor could perform. Thialfi answered that he would run a race with any one who might be matched against him. The king observed that skill in running was something to boast of, but if the youth would win the match, he must display great agility. He then arose and went, with all who were present, to a plain where there was good ground for running on, and calling a young man named Hugi, bade him run a match with Thialfi. In the first course Hugi so much outstripped his competitor that he turned back and met him not far from the starting-place. Then they ran a second and a third time, but Thialfi met with no better success.

Utgard-Loki then asked Thor in what feats he would choose to give proofs of that prowess for which he was so famous. Thor answered that he would try a drinking-match with any one. Utgard-Loki bade his cupbearer bring the large horn which his followers were obliged to empty when they had trespassed in any way against the law of the feast. The cupbearer having presented it to Thor, Utgard-Loki said, "Whoever is a good drinker will empty that horn at a single draft, though most men make two of it; but the most puny drinker can do it in three."

Thor looked at the horn, which seemed of no extraordinary size, though somewhat long; however, as he was very thirsty, he set it to his lips and, without drawing breath, pulled as long and as deeply as he could, that he might not be obliged to make a second draft of it; but when he set the horn down and looked in, he could scarcely perceive that the liquor was diminished.

After taking breath, Thor went to it again with all his might, but when he took the horn from his mouth, it seemed to him that he had drank rather less than before, although the horn could now be carried without spilling.

"How now, Thor," said Utgard-Loki, "thou must not spare thyself; if thou meanest to drain the horn at the third draft, thou must pull deeply; and I must needs say that thou wilt not be called so mighty a man here as thou art at home if thou showest no greater prowess in other feats than methinks will be shown in this."

Thor, full of wrath, again set the horn to his lips and did his best to empty it; but on looking in found the liquor was only a little lower, so he resolved to make no further attempt, but gave back the horn to the cupbearer.

"I now see plainly," said Utgard-Loki, "that thou art not quite so stout as we thought thee; but wilt thou try any other feat? — though methinks thou art not likely to bear any prize away with thee hence."

"What new trial hast thou to propose?" said Thor.

"We have a very trifling game here," answered Utgard-Loki, "in which we exercise none but children. It consists in merely lifting my cat from the ground; nor should I have dared to mention such a feat to the great Thor if I had not already observed that thou art by no means what we took thee for."

As he finished speaking a large gray cat sprang on the hall floor. Thor put his hand under the cat's belly and did his utmost to raise him from the floor, but the cat, bending his back, had, notwithstanding all Thor's efforts, only one of his feet lifted up, seeing which Thor made no further attempt.

"This trial has turned out," said Utgard-Loki, "just as I imagined it would. The cat is large, but Thor is little in comparison to our men."

"Little as ye call me," answered Thor, "let me see who among you will come hither now that I am in wrath and wrestle with me."

"I see no one here," said Utgard-Loki, looking at the men sitting on the benches, "who would not think it beneath him to wrestle with thee; let somebody, however, call hither that old crone, my nurse Elli, and let Thor wrestle with her if he will. She has thrown to the ground many a man not less strong than this Thor is."

A toothless old woman then entered the hall, and was told by Utgard-Loki to take hold of Thor. The tale is shortly told. The more Thor tightened his hold on the crone the firmer she stood. At length, after a very violent struggle, Thor began to lose his footing, and was finally brought down upon one knee. Utgard-Loki then told them to desist, adding that Thor had now no occasion to ask any one else in the hall to wrestle with him, and it was also getting late; so he showed Thor and his companions to their seats, and they passed the night there in good cheer.

The next morning, at break of day, Thor and his companions dressed themselves and prepared for their departure. Utgard-Loki ordered a table to be set for them, on which there was no lack of victuals or drink. After the repast Utgard-Loki led them to the gate of the city, and on parting asked Thor how he thought his journey had turned out and whether he had met with any men stronger than himself. Thor told him that he could not deny but that he had brought great shame on himself. "And what grieves me most," he added, "is that ye will call me a person of little worth."

"Nay," said Utgard-Loki, "it behooves me to tell thee the truth, now thou art out of the city, which so long as I live and have my way thou shalt never enter again. And, by my troth, had I known beforehand that thou hadst so much strength in thee, and wouldst have brought me so near to a great mishap I would not have suffered thee to enter this time. Know then that I have all along deceived thee by my illusions; first in the forest, where I tied up the wallet with iron wire so that thou couldst not untie it. After this thou gavest me three blows with thy mallet; the first, though the least, would have ended my days had it fallen on me, but I slipped aside and thy blows fell on the mountain, where thou wilt find three glens, one of them remarkably deep. These are the dints made by thy mallet. I have made use of similar illusions in the contests ye have had with my followers. In the first, Loki, like hunger itself, devoured all that was set before him, but Logi was in reality nothing else than Fire, and therefore consumed not only the meat but the trough which held it. Hugi, with whom Thialfi contended in running, was Thought, and it was impossible for Thialfi to keep pace with that. When thou, in thy turn, didst attempt to empty the horn, thou didst perform, by my troth, a deed so marvelous that had I not seen it myself I should never have believed it. For one end of that horn reached the sea, which thou wast not aware of, but when thou comest to the shore thou wilt perceive how much the sea has sunk by thy drafts. Thou didst perform a feat no less wonderful by lifting up the cat, and to tell thee the truth, when we saw that one of his paws was off the floor,

we were all of us terror-stricken, for what thou tookest for a cat
was in reality the Midgard serpent that encompasseth the earth,
and he was so stretched by thee that he was barely long enough to
inclose it between his head and tail. Thy wrestling with Elli was
also a most astonishing feat, for there was never yet a man, nor
ever will be, whom Old Age, for such in fact was Elli, will not
sooner or later lay low. But now, as we are going to part, let me
tell thee that it will be better for both of us if thou never come
near me again, for shouldst thou do so, I shall again defend myself
by other illusions, so that thou wilt only lose thy labor and get no
fame from the contest with me."

On hearing these words Thor, in a rage, laid hold of his mallet
and would have launched it at him, but Utgard-Loki had disappeared, and when Thor would have returned to the city to destroy
it, he found nothing around him but a verdant plain.

277. The Sword of Freyr. Freyr also possessed a wonderful
weapon, a sword which would of itself spread a field with carnage
whenever the owner desired it. Freyr parted with this sword, but
was less fortunate than Thor and never recovered it. It happened
in this way : Freyr once mounted Odin's throne, from whence one
can see over the whole universe, and looking round, saw far off in
the giant's kingdom a beautiful maid, at the sight of whom he was
struck with sudden sadness, insomuch that from that moment he
could neither sleep nor drink nor speak. At last Skirnir, his
messenger, drew his secret from him, and undertook to get him
the maiden for his bride, if he would give him his sword as a
reward. Freyr consented and gave him the sword, and Skirnir
set off on his journey and obtained the maiden's promise that
within nine nights she would come to a certain place and there
wed Freyr. Skirnir having reported the success of his errand,
Freyr exclaimed :

> " Long is one night,
> Long are two nights,
> But how shall I hold out three ?
> Shorter hath seemed
> A month to me oft
> Than of this longing time the half."

So Freyr obtained Gerda, the most beautiful of all women, for his wife, but he lost his sword.

278. The Death of Balder. Balder the Good, having been tormented with terrible dreams indicating that his life was in peril, told them to the assembled gods, who resolved to conjure all things to avert from him the threatened danger. Then Frigga, the wife of Odin, exacted an oath from fire and water, from iron and all other metals, from stones, trees, diseases, beasts, birds, poisons, and creeping things, that none of them would do any harm to Balder. Odin, not satisfied with all this, and feeling alarmed for the fate of his son, determined to consult the prophetess Angerbode, a giantess, mother of Fenris, Hela, and the Midgard serpent. She was dead, and Odin was forced to seek her in Hela's dominions.

But the other gods, feeling that what Frigga had done was quite sufficient, amused themselves with using Balder as a mark, some hurling darts at him, some stones, while others hewed at him with their swords and battle-axes, for do what they would, none of them could harm him. And this became a favorite pastime with them, and was regarded as an honor shown to Balder. But when Loki beheld the scene, he was sorely vexed that Balder was not hurt. Assuming, therefore, the shape of a woman, he went to Fensalir, the mansion of Frigga. That goddess, when she saw the pretended woman, inquired of her if she knew what the gods were doing at their meetings. She replied that they were throwing darts and stones at Balder, without being able to hurt him. "Ay," said Frigga, "neither stones, nor sticks, nor anything else can hurt Balder, for I have exacted an oath from all of them." "What," exclaimed the woman, "have all things sworn to spare Balder?" "All things," replied Frigga, "except one little shrub that grows on the eastern side of Valhalla and is called Mistletoe, which I thought too young and feeble to crave an oath from."

As soon as Loki heard this he went away and, resuming his natural shape, cut off the mistletoe and repaired to the place where the gods were assembled. There he found Höder standing apart, without partaking of the sports on account of his blindness, and going up to him said, "Why dost thou not also throw something at Balder?"

"Because I am blind," answered Höder, "and see not where Balder is, and have, moreover, nothing to throw."

"Come, then," said Loki, "do like the rest and show honor to Balder by throwing this twig at him, and I will direct thy arm toward the place where he stands."

Höder then took the mistletoe and, under the guidance óf Loki, darted it at Balder, who, pierced through and through, fell down lifeless. Never was there witnessed, either among gods or men, a more atrocious deed.

> So on the floor lay Balder dead; and round [1]
> Lay thickly strewn swords, axes, darts, and spears,
> Which all the gods in sport had idly thrown
> At Balder, whom no weapon pierced or clove;
> But in his breast stood fixt the fatal bough
> Of mistletoe, which Lok the accuser gave
> To Höder, and unwitting Höder threw —
> 'Gainst that alone had Balder's life no charm.
> And all the gods and all the heroes came,
> And stood round Balder on the bloody floor,
> Weeping and wailing; and Valhalla rang
> Up to its golden roof with sobs and cries;
> And on the tables stood the untasted meats,
> And in the horns and gold-rimmed skulls the wine.
> And now would night have fall'n and found them yet
> Wailing; but otherwise was Odin's will.

He bade them not to spend themselves in unavailing grief, for Balder, though the brightest god of heaven and best beloved, had but met the doom ordained at his birth by the Norns. Rather let the funeral pile be prepared, and let vengeance on Loki be left to Odin himself. So speaking, Odin mounted his horse Sleipnir and rode away to Lidskialf, and the gods in Valhalla returned to the feast:

> And before each the cooks, who served them, placed
> New messes of the boar Serimnir's flesh,
> And the Valkyries crowned their horns with mead.
> So they, with pent-up hearts and tearless eyes,
> Wailing no more, in silence ate and drank,
> While twilight fell, and sacred night came on.

[1] From Matthew Arnold's Balder Dead.

But the blind Höder, leaving the gods, went by the sea to Fensalir, the house of Frigga, mother of the gods, to ask her what way there might be of restoring Balder to life and heaven. Might Hela perchance surrender Balder if Höder himself should take his place among the shades? "Nay," replied Frigga, "no way is there but one, that the first god thou meetest on the return to Asgard take Sleipnir, Odin's horse, and ride o'er the bridge Bifrost where is Heimdall's watch, past Midgard fortress, down the dark, unknown road to Hel, and there entreat the goddess Hela that she yield Balder back to heaven." Höder, returning cityward, met Hermod, swiftest of the gods, —

> Nor yet could Hermod see his brother's face,
> For it grew dark; but Höder touched his arm.
> And as a spray of honeysuckle flowers
> Brushes across a tired traveler's face
> Who shuffles through the deep dew-moisten'd dust
> On a May evening, in the darken'd lanes,
> And starts him, that he thinks a ghost went by,
> So Höder brush'd by Hermod's side, and said:
> "Take Sleipnir, Hermod, and set forth with dawn
> To Hela's kingdom, to ask Balder back;
> And they shall be thy guides who have the power."
> He spake, and brush'd soft by and disappear'd.
> And Hermod gazed into the night, and said:
> "Who is it utters through the dark his hest
> So quickly, and will wait for no reply?
> The voice was like the unhappy Höder's voice.
> Howbeit ⸱ will see, and do his hest;
> For there rang note divine in that command."
> So speaking, the fleet-footed Hermod came
> Home, and lay down to sleep in his own house;
> And all the gods lay down in their own homes.
> And Höder, too, came home distraught with grief,
> Loathing to meet, at dawn, the other gods;
> And he went in, and shut the door, and fixt
> His sword upright, and fell on it, and died.
> But from the hill of Lidskialf Odin rose,
> The throne, from which his eye surveys the world;
> And mounted Sleipnir, and in darkness rode
> To Asgard. And the stars came out in heaven,

High over Asgard, to light home the king.
But fiercely Odin gallop'd, moved in heart:
And swift to Asgard, to the gate he came,
And terribly the hoofs of Sleipnir rang
Along the flinty floor of Asgard streets,
And the gods trembled on their golden beds
Hearing the wrathful father coming home —
For dread, for like a whirlwind Odin came.
And to Valhalla's gate he rode, and left
Sleipnir; and Sleipnir went to his own stall;
And in Valhalla Odin laid him down.

That night in a vision appeared Balder to Nanna his wife,
comforting her :

" Yes, and I fain would altogether ward
Death from thy head, and with the gods in heaven
Prolong thy life, though not by thee desired —
But right bars this, not only thy desire.
Yet dreary, Nanna, is the life they lead
In that dim world, in Hela's moldering realm;
And doleful are the ghosts, the troops of dead,
Whom Hela with austere control presides.
For of the race of gods is no one there
Save me alone, and Hela, solemn queen;
For all the nobler souls of mortal men
On battle field have met their death, and now
Feast in Valhalla, in my father's hall;
Only the inglorious sort are there below —
The old, the cowards, and the weak are there,
Men spent by sickness, or obscure decay.
But even there, O Nanna, we might find
Some solace in each other's look and speech,
Wandering together through that gloomy world,
And talking of the life we led in heaven,
While we yet lived, among the other gods."
He spake, and straight his lineaments began
To fade; and Nanna in her sleep stretch'd out
Her arms towards him with a cry, but he
Mournfully shook his head and disappear'd.
And as the woodman sees a little smoke
Hang in the air, afield, and disappear,
So Balder faded in the night away.

And Nanna on her bed sank back; but then
Frea, the mother of the gods, with stroke
Painless and swift, set free her airy soul,
Which took, on Balder's track, the way below;
And instantly the sacred morn appear'd.

With the morn Hermod, mounting Sleipnir, set out on his mission. For the space of nine days and as many nights he rode through deep glens so dark that he could not discern anything, until he arrived. at the river Gyoll, which he passed over on a bridge covered with glittering gold. The maiden who kept the bridge asked him his name and lineage, telling him that the day before five bands of dead persons had ridden over the bridge, and did not shake it as much as he alone. "But," she added, "thou hast not death's hue on thee; why then ridest thou here on the way to Hel?"

"I ride to Hel," answered Hermod, "to seek Balder. Hast thou perchance seen him pass this way?"

She replied, "Balder hath ridden over Gyoll's bridge, and yonder lieth the way he took to the abodes of death."

Hermod pursued his journey until he came to the barred gates of Hel. Here he alighted, girthed his saddle tighter, and remounting clapped both spurs to his horse, which cleared the gate by a tremendous leap without touching it. Hermod then rode on to the palace, where he found his brother Balder occupying the most distinguished seat in the hall, and passed the night in his company. The next morning he besought Hela to let Balder ride home with him, assuring her that nothing but lamentations were to be heard among the gods. Hela answered that it should now be tried whether Balder was so beloved as he was said to be. "If, therefore," she added, "all things in the world, both living and lifeless, weep for him, then shall he return to life; but if any one thing speak against him or refuse to weep, he shall be kept in Hel."

Hermod then rode back to Asgard and gave an account of all he had heard and witnessed.

The gods upon this dispatched messengers throughout the world to beg everything to weep in order that Balder might be delivered from Hel. All things very willingly complied with this request, both men and every other living being, as well as earths, and stones, and trees, and metals, just as we have all seen these things weep when they are brought from a cold place into a hot one.

Then the messengers returned, —

> . . . And they rode home together, through the wood
> Of Jarnvid, which to east of Midgard lies
> Bordering the giants, where the trees are iron;
> There in the wood before a cave they came,
> Where sate in the cave's mouth a skinny hag,
> Toothless and old; she gibes the passers-by.
> Thok is she called, but now Lok wore her shape;
> She greeted them the first, and laughed and said:
> " Ye gods, good lack, is it so dull in heaven
> That ye come pleasuring to Thok's iron wood?
> Lovers of change, ye are, fastidious sprites.
> Look, as in some boor's yard, a sweet-breath'd cow,
> Whose manger is stuffed full of good fresh hay,
> Snuffs at it daintily, and stoops her head
> To chew the straw, her litter at her feet —
> So ye grow squeamish, gods, and sniff at heaven!"
>   She spake, but Hermod answered her and said,
> " Thok, not for gibes we come; we come for tears.
> Balder is dead, and Hela holds her prey,
> But will restore, if all things give him tears.
> Begrudge not thine! to all was Balder dear."
>   Then, with a louder laugh, the hag replied:
> "Is Balder dead? and do ye come for tears?
> Thok with dry eyes will weep o'er Balder's pyre.
> Weep him all other things, if weep they will —
> I weep him not! let Hela keep her prey."
>   She spake, and to the cavern's depth she fled,
> Mocking; and Hermod knew their toil was vain.[1]

So was Balder prevented from returning to Asgard.

279. The Funeral of Balder. The gods took up the dead body and bore it to the seashore, where stood Balder's ship Hringham, which passed for the largest in the world. Balder's dead body was put on the funeral pile, on board the ship; and the body of Nanna was burned on the same pile with her husband's. There was a

---

[1] From Matthew Arnold's Balder Dead.

vast concourse of various kinds of people at Balder's obsequies.
First came Odin accompanied by Frigga, the Valkyries, and his
ravens; then Freyr in his car drawn by Gullinbursti, the boar;
Heimdall rode his horse Gulltopp, and Freya drove in her chariot
drawn by cats. There were also a great many Frost giants and
giants of the mountain present. Balder's horse was led to the pile
fully caparisoned, and
was consumed in the
same flames with his
master.

But Loki did not
escape his merited
punishment. When he
saw how wroth the gods
were, he fled to the
mountain and there
built himself a hut with
four doors, so that he
could see every ap-
proaching danger. He
invented a net to catch
the fishes, such as fish-
ermen have used since
his time. But Odin
found out his hiding
place and the gods as-
sembled to take him.
He, seeing this, changed
himself into a salmon

FIG. 187. LOKI AND SIGUNA

From the painting by Gebhardt

and lay hid among the stones of the brook. But the gods took
his net and dragged the brook, and Loki, finding he must be
caught, tried to leap over the net; but Thor caught him by the
tail, and compressed it so that salmon ever since have had that
part remarkably fine and thin. They bound him with chains and
suspended a serpent over his head, whose venom falls upon his
face drop by drop. His wife, Siguna, sits by his side and catches
the drops as they fall, in a cup; but when she carries it away to

empty it, the venom falls upon Loki, which makes him howl with horror and writhe so that the whole earth shakes.

280. The Elves. The Edda mentions another class of beings, inferior to the gods, but still possessed of great power; these were the Elves. The white spirits, or Elves of Light, were exceedingly fair, more brilliant than the sun, and clad in garments of a delicate and transparent texture. They loved the light, were kindly disposed to mankind, and generally appeared as fair and lovely children. Their country was called Elfheim, and was the domain of Freyr, in whose sunlight they always sported.

The black elves, ugly, long-nosed dwarfs, of a dirty brown color, appeared only at night. They avoided the sun as their most deadly enemy, because his beams changed them immediately into stones. Their language was the echo of solitudes, and their dwelling places subterranean caves and clefts. They were supposed to have come into existence as maggots produced by the decaying flesh of Ymir's body. They were afterwards endowed by the gods with a human form and great understanding. They were particularly distinguished for a knowledge of the mysterious powers of nature, and for the runes which they carved and explained. They were the most skillful artificers of all created beings, and worked in metals and in wood. Among their most noted works were Thor's hammer, and the ship *Skidbladnir*, which they gave to Freyr. This vessel was so large that it could contain all the deities with their war and household implements, but so skillfully was it wrought that when folded together it could be put into a side pocket.

281. Ragnarok. It was a firm belief of the Northern nations that a time would come when all the visible creation, the gods of Valhalla and Niflheim, the inhabitants of Jötunheim, Elfheim, and Midgard, together with their habitations, would be destroyed. The fearful day of destruction will not however be without warning. First will come a triple winter, during which snow will fall from the four corners of the heavens, the frost be severe, the wind piercing, the weather tempestuous, and the sun impart no gladness. Three such winters will pass without being tempered by a single summer. Three other like winters will follow, during which war and discord will spread over the universe. The earth itself will be afraid and begin to tremble, the sea leave its basin, the heavens tear asunder; men will perish in great numbers, and the eagles of the air feast upon their still quivering bodies. The wolf Fenris will now break his bands, the Midgard serpent rise out of his bed in the sea, and Loki, released from his bonds, will join the enemies of the gods. Amidst the general devastation the sons of Muspelheim will rush forth under their leader Surter, before and behind whom are flames and burning fire. Onward they ride over Bifrost, the rainbow bridge, which breaks under the horses' hoofs. But they, disregarding its fall, direct their course to the battle field called Vigrid. Thither also repair the wolf Fenris, the Midgard serpent, Loki, with all the followers of Hela, and the Frost giants.

Heimdall now stands up and sounds the Giallar horn to assemble the gods and heroes for the contest. The gods advance, led on by Odin, who, engaging the wolf Fenris, falls a victim to the monster. Fenris is, in turn, slain by Vidar, Odin's son. Thor wins great renown by killing the Midgard serpent, but, recoiling, falls dead, suffocated with the venom which the dying monster vomits over him. Loki and Heimdall meet and fight till they both are slain. The gods and their enemies having fallen in battle, Surter, who has killed Freyr, darts fire and flames over the world, and the universe is consumed. The sun grows dim, the earth sinks into the ocean, the stars fall from heaven, and time is no more.

After this Alfadur (not Odin but the Almighty) will cause a new heaven and a new earth to arise out of the sea. The new earth, filled with abundant supplies, will produce its fruits without labor or care. Wickedness and misery will no more be known, but the gods and men will live happily together.

This twilight of the gods is aptly described in a conversation held between Balder and Hermod, after Hermod has a second time ridden to Hel:

> And the fleet-footed Hermod made reply:[1] —
> " Thou hast then all the solace death allows,
> Esteem and function; and so far is well.
> Yet here thou liest, Balder, underground,
> Rusting for ever; and the years roll on,

[1] From Matthew Arnold's Balder Dead.

The generations pass, the ages grow,
And bring us nearer to the final day
When from the south shall march the fiery band
And cross the bridge of heaven, with Lok for guide,
And Fenris at his heel with broken chain ;
While from the east the giant Rymer steers
His ship, and the great serpent makes to land ;
And all are marshal'd in one flaming square
Against the gods, upon the plains of heaven.
I mourn thee, that thou canst not help us then."
    He spake ; but Balder answered him, and said : —
" Mourn not for me ! Mourn, Hermod, for the gods ;
Mourn for the men on earth, the gods in heaven,
Who live, and with their eyes shall see that day !
The day will come, when fall shall Asgard's towers,
And Odin, and his sons, the seed of Heaven ;
But what were I, to save them in that hour ?
If strength might save them, could not Odin save,
My father, and his pride, the warrior Thor,
Vidar the silent, the impetuous Tyr ?
I, what were I, when these can nought avail ?
Yet, doubtless, when the day of battle comes,
And the two hosts are marshal'd, and in heaven
The golden-crested cock shall sound alarm,
And his black brother-bird from hence reply,
And bucklers clash, and spears begin to pour —
Longing will stir within my breast, though vain.
But not to me so grievous as, I know,
To other gods it were, is my enforced
Absence from fields where I could nothing aid ;
For I am long since weary of your storm
Of carnage, and find, Hermod, in your life
Something too much of war and broils, which make
Life one perpetual fight, a bath of blood.
Mine eyes are dizzy with the arrowy hail ;
Mine ears are stunn'd with blows, and sick for calm.
Inactive, therefore, let me lie in gloom,
Unarm'd, inglorious ; I attend the course
Of ages, and my late return to light,
In times less alien to a spirit mild,
In new-recover'd seats, the happier day."
    He spake ; and the fleet Hermod thus replied : —

" Brother, what seats are these, what happier day?
Tell me, that I may ponder it when gone."
   And the ray-crownèd Balder answered him : —
" Far to the south, beyond the blue, there spreads
Another heaven, the boundless — no one yet
Hath reach'd it; there hereafter shall arise
The second Asgard, with another name.
Thither, when o'er this present earth and heavens
The tempest of the latter days hath swept,
And they from sight have disappear'd and sunk,
Shall a small remnant of the gods repair;
Höder and I shall join them from the grave.
There reassembling we shall see emerge
From the bright ocean at our feet an earth
More fresh, more verdant than the last, with fruits
Self-springing, and a seed of man preserved,
Who then shall live in peace, as now in war.
But we in heaven shall find again with joy
The ruin'd palaces of Odin, seats
Familiar, halls where we have supp'd of old,
Reënter them with wonder, never fill
Our eyes with gazing, and rebuild with tears.
And we shall tread once more the well-known plain
Of Ida, and among the grass shall find
The golden dice wherewith we played of yore;
And that shall bring to mind the former life
And pastime of the gods — the wise discourse
Of Odin, the delights of other days.
O Hermod, pray that thou may'st join us then!
Such for the future is my hope; meanwhile,
I rest the thrall of Hela, and endure
Death, and the gloom which round me even now
Thickens, and to inner gulf recalls.
Farewell, for longer speech is not allow'd."

CHAPTER XXVIII

MYTHS OF NORSE AND OLD GERMAN HEROES

282. The Saga of the Volsungs.[1] Sigi, son of Odin, was a mighty king of the Huns whom Odin loved and prospered exceedingly. Rerir, also, the son of Sigi, was a man of valor and one who got lordship and land unto himself; but neither Sigi nor Rerir were to compare with *Volsung*, who ruled over Hunland after his father Rerir went home to Odin.

To Volsung were born ten sons and one daughter, — Signy by name; and of the sons *Sigmund* was the eldest and the most valiant. And the Volsungs abode in peace till Siggeir, king of Gothland, came wooing Signy, who, though loath to accept him, was, by her father's desire, betrothed to him.

Now on the night of the wedding great fires were made in the hall of the Volsungs, and in the midst stood Branstock, a great oak tree, about which the hall had been built, and the limbs of the tree spread over the roof of the hall; and round about Branstock they sat and feasted, and sang of ancient heroes and heard the music of the harp that went from hand to hand.

> But e'en as men's hearts were hearkening some heard the thunder pass[2]
> O'er the cloudless noontide heaven; and some men turned about
> And deemed that in the doorway they heard a man laugh out.
> Then into the Volsung dwelling a mighty man there strode,
> One-eyed and seeming ancient, yet bright his visage glowed;
> Cloud-blue was the hood upon him, and his kirtle gleaming-gray
> As the latter morning sun-dog when the storm is on the way;
> A bill he bore on his shoulder, whose mighty ashen beam
> Burnt bright with the flame of the sea, and the blended silver's gleam.
> And such was the guise of his raiment as the Volsung elders had told
> Was borne by their fathers' fathers, and the first that warred in the wold.

[1] For the Sagas, see § 300; and for translations, etc., see § 282 of the Commentary.
[2] The extracts in verse are from William Morris' Sigurd the Volsung.

So strode he to the Branstock, nor greeted any lord,
But forth from his cloudy raiment he drew a gleaming sword,
And smote it deep in the tree-bole, and the wild hawks overhead
Laughed 'neath the naked heaven as at last he spake and said:
" Earls of the Goths, and Volsungs, abiders on the earth,
Lo there amid the Branstock a blade of plenteous worth!
The folk of the war-wand's forgers wrought never better steel
Since first the burg of heaven uprose for man-folk's weal.
Now let the man among you whose heart and hand may shift
To pluck it from the oak-wood e'en take it for my gift.
Then ne'er, but his own heart falter, its point and edge shall fail
Until the night's beginning and the ending of the tale.
Be merry, Earls of the Goth-folk, O Volsung Sons be wise,
And reap the battle-acre that ripening for you lies:
For they told me in the wild wood, I heard on the mountain-side
That the shining house of heaven is wrought exceeding wide,
And that there the Early-comers shall have abundant rest
While Earth grows scant of great ones, and fadeth from its best,
And fadeth from its midward, and groweth poor and vile: —
All hail to thee, King Volsung! farewell for a little while!"
So sweet his speaking sounded, so wise his words did seem
That moveless all men sat there, as in a happy dream
We stir not lest we waken; but there his speech had end
And slowly down the hall-floor, and outward did he wend;
And none would cast him a question or follow on his ways,
For they knew that the gift was Odin's, a sword for the world to praise.

Then all made trial, Siggeir and his earls, and Volsung and his
people, to draw forth the sword from Branstock, but with no success, till Sigmund, laying his hand carelessly on the precious hilt,
drew forth the naked blade as though it were loose in the oak.
Whereupon Siggeir offered money for the sword, but Sigmund
scorned the offer.

But in time Siggeir had his vengeance. Inviting King Volsung
and his sons to Gothland, he fell upon them, slew the king, and
suffered the sons, fastened under a log, to be devoured in succession by a she-wolf — all but Sigmund, who through the wile of
his sister Signy was rescued. He, driven to the life of an outlaw,
sought means to avenge his father, and Signy, on her part, strove
to aid him, — without avail, however, till Sinfiotli, the son of

herself and Sigmund, was grown to manhood. This youth bore
Sigmund company. For a season, as wolves, they scoured the
woods; finally resuming the form of men, they slew the children
of Siggeir and burned him in his hall. Signy, having helped to
avenge her father, died with her husband.

Sigmund, thereupon, became king, and took to himself a wife.
But she, suffering injury at the hands of Sinfiotli, poisoned him
with a horn of ale. Then Sigmund sorrowed nigh to death over
his son, and drove away that queen, and soon after she died. He
then married Hiordis the fair; but before long, doing battle against
Lyngi, the son of Hunding, — a chieftain who also had loved the
fair Hiordis, — he got his death wound:

> For lo, through the hedge of the war-shafts a mighty man there came,
> One-eyed and seeming ancient, but his visage shone like flame;
> Gleaming-gray was his kirtle, and his hood was cloudy-blue;
> And he bore a mighty twibil, as he waded the fight-sheaves through,
> And stood face to face with Sigmund, and upheaved the bill to smite.
> Once more round the head of the Volsung fierce glittered the Branstock's light,
> The sword that came from Odin; and Sigmund's cry once more
> Rang out to the very heavens above the din of war.
> Then clashed the meeting edges with Sigmund's latest stroke,
> And in shivering shards fell earthward that fear of worldly folk.
> But changed were the eyes of Sigmund, and the war-wrath left his face;
> For that gray-clad mighty helper was gone, and in his place
> Drave on the unbroken spear-wood 'gainst the Volsung's empty hands:
> And there they smote down Sigmund, the wonder of all lands,
> On the foemen, on the death-heap his deeds had piled that day.

To Hiordis, after Sigmund's death, was born *Sigurd*, like whom
was never man for comeliness and valor and great-heartedness and
might. He was the greatest of the Volsungs. His foster-father was
Regin, the son of Rodmar, a blacksmith, who taught him the lore
of runes and many tongues; and, by means of a story of ancient
wrongs, incited him to the destruction of the dragon Fafnir. For
Regin told that while the gods, Odin and Hœnir, were wandering
with Loki near Rodmar's house, Loki slew one of Rodmar's sons,
Otter. Whereupon Rodmar demanded that the gods should fill
the Otter-skin with gold and cover it with gold. Now Loki, being

sent to procure the gold, caught Andvari the dwarf, and from him procured by force a hoard of the precious metal and with it a magic ring, whose touch bred gold. But Andvari cursed the ring and the gold and all that might possess either. The gods forthwith filled Otter with the dwarf's gold, and surrendered both gold and ring to Rodmar. Immediately the curse began to work. Fafnir, brother of Regin and Otter, slew Rodmar and seized the treasure and, assuming a dragon's form, brooded upon the hoard. With this tale Regin egged on Sigurd to the undoing of Fafnir. He welded him, too, a resistless sword out of the shards of Sigmund's sword, Gram (the wrath). Then Sigurd swore that he would slay the dragon. But first, riding on his horse, Greyfell, of the blood of Odin's Sleipnir, he avenged upon the sons of Hunding the death of his father. This done, Sigurd rode to Glistenheath and slew Fafnir, the dragon, and eating of his heart, learned the language of the birds; and at their advice he slew Regin also, who plotted against him.

So, setting the ring of Andvari on his finger and bearing the gold before him on his horse, Greyfell, Sigurd comes to the Hill of Hindfell:

And sitteth awhile on Greyfell on the marvelous thing to gaze:
For lo, the side of Hindfell inwrapped by the fervent blaze,
And naught 'twixt earth and heaven save a world of flickering flame,
And a hurrying, shifting tangle, where the dark rents went and came . . .
Now Sigurd turns in his saddle, and the hilt of the Wrath he shifts,
And draws a girth the tighter; then the gathered reins he lifts,
And crieth aloud to Greyfell, and rides at the wildfire's heart;
But the white wall wavers before him and the flame-flood rusheth apart,
And high o'er his head it riseth, and wide and wild is its roar
As it beareth the mighty tidings to the very heavenly floor;
But he rideth through its roaring as the warrior rides the rye,
When it bows with the wind of the summer and the hid spears draw
        anigh;
The white flame licks his raiment and sweeps through Greyfell's mane,
And bathes both hands of Sigurd and the hilts of Fafnir's bane,
And winds about his war-helm and mingles with his hair,
But naught his raiment dusketh or dims his glittering gear; —
Then it falls and fades and darkens till all seems left behind,
And dawn and the blaze is swallowed in mid-mirk stark and blind. . . .

Then before him Sigurd sees a shield-hung castle, surmounted by a golden buckler, instead of a banner, which rings against the flagstaff. And he enters and finds the form of one asleep, in armor cap-a-pie.

> So he draweth the helm from the head, and, lo, the brow snow-white,
> And the smooth unfurrowed cheeks, and the wise lips breathing light;
> And the face of a woman it is, and the fairest that ever was born,
> Shown forth to the empty heavens and the desert world forlorn:
> But he looketh, and loveth her sore, and he longeth her spirit to move,
> And awaken her heart to the world, that she may behold him and love.
> And he toucheth her breast and her hands, and he loveth her passing sore;
> And he saith, "Awake! I am Sigurd," but she moveth never the more. . . .

Then with his bright blade Sigurd rends the ring-knit mail that incloses her, "till naught but the rippling linen is wrapping her about," —

> Then a flush cometh over her visage and a sigh upheaveth her breast,
> And her eyelids quiver and open, and she wakeneth into rest;
> Wide-eyed on the dawning she gazeth, too glad to change or smile,
> And but little moveth her body, nor speaketh she yet for a while;
> And yet kneels Sigurd, moveless, her wakening speech to heed,
> While soft the waves of the daylight o'er the starless heavens speed,
> And the gleaming vines of the Shield-burg yet bright and brighter grow,
> And the thin moon hangeth her horns dead-white in the golden glow.
> Then she turned and gazed on Sigurd, and her eyes met the Volsung's eyes.
> And mighty and measureless now did the tide of his love arise,
> For their longing had met and mingled, and he knew of her heart that she loved,
> As she spake unto nothing but him and her lips with the speech-flood moved.

Brynhild, it was, — the Valkyrie, — who long time had lain in that enchanted sleep that Odin, her father, had poured over her, dooming her to mortal awakening and to mortal love, for the evil she had wrought of old when she espoused the cause in battle of those whom the Norns had predestined to death. Her might none but the fearless awaken; and her had Sigurd awakened; and she loved him, for he was without fear and godlike. And she taught him many wise sayings; and they plighted troth, one to the other, both then and again; and Sigurd gave her the ring of Andvari.

But they were not destined to dwell together in wedlock, and Brynhild, foreseeing the future, knew even this.

Sigurd was to wed with another than Brynhild, and it fell in this wise. In the land of the Nibelungs (Niblungs, Nibelungen) dwelt Gudrun, daughter of Giuki, the Nibelung king. And Gudrun dreamed a dream in which a fair hawk feathered with feathers of gold alighted upon her wrist. She went to Brynhild for the interpretation of the dream. " The hawk," said Brynhild, " is Sigurd." And so it came to pass. Sigurd, visiting the court of the Nibelungs, was kindly entreated by King Giuki and his three sons, Gunnar, Hogni, and Guttorm; and he performed deeds of valor such that they honored him. But after many days, Grimhild, the mother of Gudrun, administered to Sigurd a magic potion that removed from him all memory of Brynhild. So Sigurd loved and wedded the fair Gudrun. Indeed he soon joined others in urging his wife's brother Gunnar, a doughty warrior, to sue for the hand of Brynhild herself. But Brynhild would have no one that could not ride through the flames drawn up around her hall. After Gunnar had made two unsuccessful attempts, Sigurd, assuming the form of King Gunnar, mounted Greyfell and rode for the second time through the flames of Hindfell. Then, still wearing the semblance of Gunnar, he gained the consent of Brynhild to the union, and exchanged rings with her, — she giving him none other than the ancient ring of Andvari back again. But even this did not recall to Sigurd's memory his former ride and his former love. Returning to the land of the Nibelungs, he announced the success of his undertaking and told all things to Gudrun, giving her the fatal ring that he had regained from Brynhild.

In ten days came Brynhild by agreement to the Hall of the Nibelungs, and though she knew well the deceit that had been practiced on her, she made no sign; nay, was wedded, according to her promise, to King Gunnar. But as they sat at the wedding-feast, the charm of Grimhild was outworn, — Sigurd looked upon Gunnar's bride and knew the Brynhild of old, the Valkyrie, whom he had loved; "and Brynhild's face drew near him with eyes grown stern and strange."

But, apparently, all went well till the young queens, one day bathing in the Water of the Nibelungs, fell into contention on a matter of privilege. Brynhild claimed precedence in entering the river on the ground that Gunnar was the liege lord of Sigurd. Gudrun, white with wrath, flashed out the true story of the ride through the flames, and thrust in Brynhild's face the Andvari ring. Consumed with jealousy, Brynhild plotted revenge. She loved Sigurd still, and he, since he had regained his memory, could not overcome his love for her. But the insult from Gudrun Brynhild would not brook. By her machinations, Guttorm, the brother of Gudrun, was incited to slay Sigurd. He, accordingly, stabbed the hero while asleep, but Sigurd, throwing Gram at the assassin, cut him in twain before he could escape.

Woe me! how the house of the Niblungs by another cry was rent,
The awakening wail of Gudrun, as she shrank in the river of blood
From the breast of the mighty Sigurd: he heard it and understood,
And rose up on the sword of Guttorm, and turned from the country of death,
And spake words of loving-kindness as he strove for life and breath;
" Wail not, O child of the Niblungs! I am smitten, but thou shalt live,
In remembrance of our glory, mid the gifts the gods shall give! . . .
It is Brynhild's deed," he murmured, "and the woman that loves me well;
Nought now is left to repent of, and the tale abides to tell.
I have done many deeds in my life-days, and all these, and my love, they lie
In the hollow hand of Odin till the day of the world go by.
I have done and I may not undo, I have given and I take not again;
Art thou other than I, Allfather, wilt thou gather my glory in vain?"

So ended the life of Sigurd. Brynhild, overcome with sorrow, dealt herself a mortal wound and was burned on the funeral pyre beside Sigurd the Volsung.

In time Gudrun became the queen of Atli, the Budlung. He, in order to obtain the hoard of Sigurd, which had passed into the hands of the Nibelungs, — Gudrun's brothers, — bade them visit him in Hunland. Fully warned by Gudrun, they still accepted the invitation and, arriving at the hall of Atli, were after a fearful conflict slain. But they did not surrender the hoard — that lay concealed at the bottom of the Rhine. Gudrun with the aid of Nibelung, her brother Hogni's son, in the end slew Atli, set fire to his hall, and brought ruin on the Budlung folk. Then leaping into the sea, she was borne with Swanhild, her daughter by Sigurd, to the realm of King Jonakr, who became her third husband. Swanhild, "fairest of all women, eager-eyed as her father, so that few durst look under the brows of her," met, by stress of love and treachery, a foul end in a foreign land, trampled under foot of horses.

Finally Gudrun sent her sons by Jonakr to avenge their half-sister's death; and so, bereft of all her kin and consumed with sorrow, she called upon her ancient lover, Sigurd, to come and look upon her, as he had promised, from his abiding-place among the dead. And thus had the words of her sorrow an end.

Her sons slew Jormunrek, the murderer of Swanhild, but were themselves done to death by the counsel and aid of a certain warrior, seeming ancient and one-eyed, — Odin the forefather of the Volsungs, — the same that had borne Sigi fellowship, and that struck the sword into Branstock of Volsung's hall, and that faced Sigmund and shattered Gram in the hour of Sigmund's need, and that brought to Sigurd the matchless horse Greyfell, and oft again had appeared to the kin of the Volsungs; — the same god now wrought the end of the Nibelungs. The hoard and the ring of Andvari had brought confusion on all into whose hands they fell.

283. The Lay of the Nibelungs.[1] In the German version of this story — called the Nibelungenlied — certain variations of name, incident, and character appear. Sigurd is Siegfried, dwelling in Xanten near the Rhine, the son of Siegmund and Siegelind, king and queen of the Netherlands. Gudrun is Kriemhild, sister of Gunther (Gunnar), king of the Burgundians, and niece of Hagen (Hogni), a warrior of dark and sullen mien, cunning, but withal loyal and brave, the foe of the glorious Siegfried. Siegfried weds Kriemhild, takes her to the Netherlands and lives happily with her, enjoying the moneys of the Nibelungen hoard, which he had taken not from a dwarf, as in the Norse version, but from two princes, the sons of King Nibelung. Meanwhile Gunther dwells in peace in the Burgundian land, husband of the proud Brunhild, whom Siegfried had won for him by stratagem not altogether unlike that

---

[1] For Records of German Mythology, see § 301, below; for literature and translations, see §§ 283 and 301 of the Commentary.

of the Norse story. For the Brunhild of the Yssel-land had declared that she would marry no man save him who should surpass
her in athletic contest. This condition Siegfried, wearing the Tarn-
kappe, a cloak that rendered him invisible, had fulfilled for Gunther. He had also succored poor Gunther after his marriage with
Brunhild. For that heroine, in contempt of Gunther's strength,
had bound him hand
and foot and suspended
him from a nail on their
bedroom wall. By
agreement Siegfried
had again assumed Gun-
ther's form and, after a
fearful tussle with the
queen, had reduced her
to submission, taking
from her the ring and
girdle which were the
secret sources of her
strength, and leaving
her to imagine that she
had been conquered by
her bridegroom, Gun-
ther. The ring and
girdle Siegfried had be-
stowed upon Kriemhild,
unwisely telling her at

FIG. 188. GUNTHER AND BRUNHILD

From the fresco by Julius Schnorr von Carolsfeld

the same time the story of Brunhild's defeat. Although the Nibelungenlied offers no explanation, it is evident that the injured queen
of Yssel-land had recognized Siegfried during this ungallant intrigue ; and we are led to infer that there had been some previous
acquaintance and passage of love between them.

At any rate, Siegfried and Kriemhild, retiring to the Netherlands, were ruling happily at Xanten by the Rhine ; and all might
have continued in peace had not Brunhild resented the lack of
homage paid by Siegfried, whom she had been led to regard as a
vassal, to Gunther, his reputed overlord.

In her heart this thought she fostered, deep in its inmost core ; [1]
That still they kept such distance, a secret grudge she bore.
How came it that their vassal to court declined to go,
Nor for his land did homage, she inly yearned to know.

She made request of Gunther, and begged it so might be,
That she the absent Kriemhild yet once again might see,
And told him, too, in secret, whereon her thoughts were bent, —
Then with the words she uttered her lord was scarce content.

But Gunther yielded, and Siegfried and Kriemhild were invited to Worms, nominally to attend a high festival.

. . . With what joy and gladness
    welcomed were they there!
It seemed when came dame
    Brunhild to Burgundy
    whilere,
Her welcome by dame Kriemhild
    less tender was and true ;
The heart of each beholder beat
    higher at the view. . . .

Received was bold Sir Siegfried,
    as fitted well his state,
With the highest honors; no
    man bore him hate.
Young Giselher and Gernot
    proffered all courtly care;
Never met friend or kinsman
    reception half so fair.

FIG. 189. SIEGFRIED AND KRIEMHILD

From the fresco by Julius Schnorr von Carolsfeld

One day at the hour of vespers certain knights proved themselves at tilting in the regal courtyard. Conspicuous among these was Siegfried. And the proud queens sitting together were thinking each on the good knight that she loved full well. Then outspoke fair Kriemhild, " My husband is of such might that surely he should rule these realms "; Brunhild answered, " So long as Gunther lives that can never be."

[1] The extracts in verse are, unless otherwise stated, from the translation by W. N. Lettsom, London, 1890. Werner Hahn's Uebersetzung has also been used.

> . . . Thereto rejoined fair Kriemhild, " See'st thou how proud he stands,
> How proud he stalks, conspicuous among those warrior bands,
> As doth the moon far-beaming the glimmering stars outshine?
> Sure have I cause to pride me when such a knight is mine."

> Thereto replied queen Brunhild, " How brave soe'er he be,
> How stout soe'er or stately, one greater is than he.
> Gunther, thy noble brother, a higher place may claim,
> Of knights and kings the foremost in merit and in fame."

So began the altercation. It attained its climax the same day, when each queen attempted to take precedence of the other in entering the cathedral for the celebration of the mass.

> Both met before the minster in all the people's sight;
> There at once the hostess let out her deadly spite.
> Bitterly and proud she bade fair Kriemhild stand;
> "No vassaless precedeth the lady of the land."

Then, full of wrath, Kriemhild, in terms anything but delicate, acquainted her haughty sister-in-law with the deception that had twice been practiced upon her by Siegfried and Gunther; nay, worse, corroborated her statement by displaying both ring and girdle that Brunhild had lost. The altercation came to the ears of the kings. Gunther made complaint to Siegfried. Then,

> . . . "Women must be instructed," said Siegfried, the good knight,
> "To leave off idle talking and rule their tongues aright.
> Keep thy fair wife in order, I 'll do by mine the same.
> Such overweening folly puts me indeed to shame."

But it was too late to mend the matter. With devilish intent Brunhild plotted vengeance. Siegfried, the author of her mortification, must die the death. The foes of Siegfried persuaded his wife, unaware of their design, to embroider in his vesture a silken cross over the one spot where the hero was vulnerable. Then the crafty Hagen, who had been suborned by Brunhild to the baleful deed, bided his time. One day, Gunther, Hagen, and Siegfried, heated in running, stayed by a brook to drink. Hagen saw his chance.

> . . . Then, as to drink, Sir Siegfried down kneeling there he found,
> He pierced him through the crosslet, that sudden from the wound
> Forth the life-blood spurted, e'en o'er his murderer's weed.
> Nevermore will warrior dare so foul a deed. . . .

. . . With blood were all bedabbled the flowerets of the field.
Some time with death he struggled as though he scorned to yield
E'en to the foe whose weapon strikes down the loftiest head.
At last prone in the meadow lay mighty Siegfried dead.

Brunhild glories in the fall of Siegfried and exults over the mourning widow. Kriemhild, sitting apart, nurses schemes of vengeance. Her brothers affect to patch up the breach in order that they may obtain the hoard of the Nibelungs. But this treasure, after it has been brought to Worms, is sunk, for precaution's sake, by Hagen, in the Rhine. Although in time Kriemhild becomes the wife of King Etzel (Atli, Attila) of Hunland, still she does not forget the injury done her by her kin. After thirteen years she inveigles her brothers and their retainers, called now Nibelungs because of their possession of the hoard, to Etzel's court, where, after a desperate and dastardly encounter, in which their hall is reduced to ashes, they are all destroyed save Gunther and Hagen. Immediately, thereafter, Gunther's head is cut off at her orders; and she herself, with Siegfried's sword Balmung, severs the head of the hated Hagen from his body. With these warriors the secret of the hidden hoard passes. Kriemhild, having wreaked her vengeance, falls by the hand of one of her husband's knights, Hildebrand, who, with Dietrich of Bern, had played a prominent part among the associates of King Etzel.

" I cannot say you now what hath befallen since;
The women all were weeping, and the Ritters and the prince,
Also the noble squires, their dear friends lying dead:
Here hath the story ending; this is the Nibelungen's Need." [1]

[1] From Carlyle's translation of fragments of the poem.

CHAPTER XXIX

THE RING OF THE NIBELUNG

284. Wagner's Tetralogy. In his famous Ring of the Nibelung the German composer, Richard Wagner, returns to the Norse version of the stories recounted in the chapter preceding this. He is responsible not only for the musical score of the four operas of which the Ring consists, but for the text and scenic arrangement as well. As musical dramas the four plays constitute the grandest series of the kind that the world possesses. But even if they were not wedded to such music, the *Rhine-gold*, the *Valkyrie*, the *Siegfried*, and the *Twilight* (or *Dusk*) *of the Gods* would be entitled, for creative invention, imaginative insight and power, and poetic diction, to rank with notable dramas, ancient or modern. The tetralogy (or series of four) presents the whole story of the accursed Nibelung gold, from that dawn when it was wrested from the daughters of the Rhine to that dusk when it was restored, having wrought meanwhile the doom of Nibelungs, Volsungs, and the gods themselves.

285. The Rhine-gold. We are at the bottom of the Rhine: a greenish twilight, and moving water, and everywhere sharp points of rocks jutting from the depths. Around the central rock three Rhine-daughters swim, guarding it carefully, but laughing and playing, and chasing one the other as they guard. To them from a chasm climbs Alberich, the Nibelung, he who in the old Norse lay was known as Andvari. He views the maidens with increasing pleasure. He addresses them, he clambers after them, he strives to catch them; they lure him on, they mock him and escape his grasp; he woos them each in turn, all unsuccessfully. He gazes upward — " Could I but catch one " ; then once more failing, remains in speechless rage. Rage soon transformed to wonder : for through the water from above there filters a brightening glow, a magical light, streaming from the summit of the central rock where in the splendor of the morning sun the Rhine-gold laughs a-kindle.

> " What is it, ye sleek ones,
> That there doth gleam and glow? " [1]

Has he never heard of the Rhine-gold? they ask. Of the wondrous star whose glory lightens the waves? He has not. He scorns it. " The golden charm," cries one of the maidens, —

> " The golden charm
> Wouldst thou not flout
> Knewest thou all of its wonders."

" The world's wealth," jeers another,

> " Could be won by a man
> If out of the Rhine-gold
> He fashioned the Ring
> That measureless might can bestow . . .
> He who the sway
> Of love forswears,
> He who delight
> Of love forbears,
> Only he can master the magic
> That forces the gold to a ring!"

" But we fear not thee—oh, no—for thou burnest in love for us." So, lightly sing the Rhine-daughters; but Alberich, with his eyes on the gold, has heeded well their chatter. " The world's wealth," he mutters; " might I win that by the spell of the gold? Nay, though love be the forfeit, my cunning shall win me delight." Then terribly loud he cries,

> " Mock ye, mock on!
> The Nibelung neareth your toy; — "

then, clambering with haste to the summit,

> " My hand, it quenches your light;
> I wrest from the rock your gold;
> I fashion the ring of revenge;
> Now, hear me, ye floods —
> Accursèd be love henceforth."

[1] For the translations of the Ring, especially the verse, I am indebted to the edition of Frederick Jameson (Schott & Co., London).

Tearing the gold from the rock, he plunges into the depths and disappears. After him dive the maidens. In vain. Far, far below, from Nibelheim rises the mocking laughter of Alberich, Lord of the Gold.

The scene changes. An open space on a mountain height becomes visible. The dawning day lights up a castle, glittering with pinnacles, on the top of a cliff. Below flows silent the Rhine. At one side, on a flowery bank, Wotan (Odin), king of the gods, lies sleeping, and Fricka (Frigga) his wife. They wake. Wotan turns toward his castle, new-built by the giants, and exults; but Fricka reminds him of the terrible price that is yet to be paid for its building, — none other, forsooth, than the person of Freia, the fair one, the goddess of spring and love, she who tends the garden of the gods, and whose apples, eaten from day to day, confer eternal youth, — she is the wage that the giants will claim.

"I mind me well of the bargain," returns Wotan, "but I give no thought to fulfill it. My castle stands; for the wage — fret not thyself."

"Oh, laughing, impious lightness," reproves him Fricka, "thy bargain is fast, and is still to rue."

Nay, on the moment rushes Freia to them, pleading, pursued by the giants. "Give her to us!" they cry, — Fasolt and Fafner, mighty twain that unslumbering had reared the walls of Wotan's castle, to win them a woman, winsome and sweet.

"Now pay us our wage!"

"Nay," coolly answers Wotan, "other guerdon ask. Freia may I not grant!"

But the giants insist. They accuse the god of faithlessness. He jests with them, temporizing, awaiting anxiously the arrival of Loge (Loki), spirit of cunning, at whose suggestion that bargain had been struck. For even then Loge had secretly assured Wotan that Freia should in the emergency be ransomed. The giants, indignant at the delay, press on Freia. She calls on her brothers, Froh (Freyr) and Donner (Thor). They rush to her rescue: Froh clasps the fair one; Donner plants himself before the importunates.

"Know ye the weight of my hammer's blow?" thunders he.

There is battle in the air.

Then enters Loge, demon of fire, mischief-maker, traitor, and thief, whom long ago Wotan had lifted from his evil brood and of him made a friend and counselor.

"Now hear, crabbèd one; keep thy word," says Wotan, sharply.

Loge appears to be nonplussed. He has restlessly searched to the ends of the world to find a ransom for Freia; "but naught is so rich that giant or man will take it as price for a woman's worth and delight." He has sought amid the forces of water and earth and air; "but naught is so mighty that giant or man will prefer it above a woman's worth and delight!" And yet; — slyly Loge lets fall the word, — there is the ruddy Gold:

"Yea, one I looked on, but *one*, who love's delights forswore, for ruddy gold renouncing the wealth of woman's grace."

And he recounts the marvels of the Rhine-gold. The giants offer to take it in lieu of Freia; nay, gods and goddesses as well are held by the charm of the glittering hoard; by the lure, and the dread too, of the Ring that, once fashioned, gives measureless might to its lord. Even now, doubtless, he who has forsworn love has muttered the magic rune and rounded the sovereign circlet of gold. If so, the gods themselves shall be his slaves, — slaves of the Nibelung Alberich.

"The ring I must win me," decides Wotan.

"But at the cost of love?" queries Froh.

Loge counsels the theft of the gold from Alberich and its restoration to the daughters of the Rhine. But the gods are not thus far-sighted, and the giants insist upon the hoard as their due. They seize Freia, and bear her away as pledge till that ransom be paid. . . .

"Alack, what aileth the gods?"

It is Loge who speaks. A pale mist falls upon the scene, gradually growing denser. The light of the heavenly abodes is quenched. Wotan and all his clan become increasingly wan and aged. Freia of the Garden is departed: the apples of youth are decaying; "old and gray, worn and withered, the scoff of the world, dies out the godly race!"

"Up, Loge," calls Wotan, dismayed, "descend with me. To Nibelheim go we together. To win back our youth, the golden ransom must I gain."

The scene changes to Nibelheim, the subterranean home of the Nibelungs. Wotan and Loge find Mime, Alberich's brother, bewailing the fate of the Nibelungs — for Alberich has fashioned the Ring and all below groan under his tyranny. Even now, reluctantly indeed, Mime is forging the *Tarnhelm* for his tyrant brother, — a wishingcap by whose magic the wearer may transfer himself through space and assume whatever form he please, or make himself invisible, at will. Alberich, in the flush of power, enters, driving before him with brandished whip a host of Nibelungs from the caverns. They are laden with gold and silver handiwork. At Alberich's command they heap it in a pile. He draws the Ring from his finger; the vanquished host trembles and, shrieking, cowers away.

"What seek ye here?" demands he, looking long and suspiciously at Wotan and Loge.

They have heard strange tidings, says Wotan, and they come to see the wonders that Alberich can work. Then Loge induces the Nibelung lord to exhibit the virtues of the Tarnhelm. Readily beguiled, he displays his necromantic power. First he transforms himself into a loathly dragon. The gods pretend dismay: — he can make himself great; can he make himself small, likewise? "Pah, nothing simpler! Look at me now!" He dons the Tarnhelm, and lo, a toad!

"There, grasp quickly," says Loge. Wotan places his foot on the toad, and Loge seizes the Tarnhelm. Alberich becomes visible in his own form, writhing under Wotan's foot. The gods bind him and drag him to the chasm by which they had descended.

The scene changes to the open space before Valhalla. Alberich, dragged in by Loge, is forced to deliver up the hoard and the Tarnhelm and the Ring. Wotan contemplates the Ring and puts it on. Alberich is set at liberty.

"Am I now free?" cries he, "free in sooth? Thus greets you then my freedom's foremost word: As by curse it came to me, accursed forever be this Ring! As its gold gave measureless might, let now its magic deal death to its lord. Its wealth shall yield pleasure to none. Care shall consume him who doth hold it. All shall lust after its delights; yet naught shall it boot him who wins the prize! To its lord no gain let it bring; and forever be murder drawn in its wake, till again once more in my hand, rewon, I hold it!"

So the baffled Nibelung curses, and departs. Then enter Fricka, Donner, and Froh, followed soon by the giants, who bring Freia back. They refuse, Fasolt and Fafner, to release the fair goddess until she is fully redeemed; and they claim not only Tarnhelm and gold, but Ring as well. With the Ring Wotan refuses to part. In that moment rises from a rocky cleft the goddess of the earth, Erda, the beloved of heaven's god, and mother by him of the Valkyries.

"Yield it, Wotan, yield it," she cries warningly. "Flee the Ring's dread curse."

"What woman warneth me thus?"

"All that e'er was, know I," pronounces Erda:

> "How all things are;
> How all things shall be.
> Hear me! hear me! hear me!
> All that e'er was, endeth:
> A darksome day
> Dawns for your godhood!
> Be counseled; give up the Ring."

She vanishes, the all-wise one; and Wotan surrenders the Ring. Freia is redeemed, and the gods glow again with youth. No sooner have the giants gained possession of the Ring than they proceed to quarrel over it. Fafner strikes out with his staff and stretches Fasolt on the ground. From the dying man he hastily wrests the Ring, puts it into his sack, and goes on quietly packing the gold. In a solemn silence the gods stand horrified. Care and fear fetter the soul of Wotan. That he may shake himself free of them he determines to descend to Erda; she yet can give him counsel. But first, — for Donner has cleared with his thunder and lightning the clouds that had overspread the scene, — he will enter "Valhalla," his castle, golden-gleaming in the evening sunlight.

"What meaneth the name, then?" asks Fricka, as they cross the rainbow bridge.

Wotan evades the question, for he still dreads the curse pronounced by the Nibelung upon all who have owned the Ring ; and that name, "Valhalla," indicates just the means by which he hopes to escape the curse. He has thought to avert the doom of the gods by gathering in this Valhalla, or Hall of the Slain, the spirits of heroes fallen in battle — especially of heroes of a race that shall spring from himself, the Volsungs (or Wälsungs) yet to be born. They shall do battle for the gods when sounds the crack of doom. But of all this Wotan says naught. He will say in the hour of his triumph.

As the gods enter Valhalla the plaints of the Rhine-maidens for the loss of their gold arise from the river below.

286. In **The Valkyrie** Wotan proceeds with his plan. During his wanderings on earth, under the name of Wälse, he has become the father of twin children, Siegmund and Sieglinde. These have, in early youth, been separated by the murderous turmoil of warring clans, but now they are to be reunited ; and Wotan, with a primitive disregard of the fact that they are brother and sister, intends to make them man and wife, in order that from them may issue the heroic race that, in the latter days, shall defend Valhalla from the onslaught of the powers of evil.

The play opens with the interior of a woodland lodge. In the center rises the stem of a mighty ash tree, about which has been built an apartment of roughly hewn logs. It is toward evening and a violent thunderstorm is just subsiding. This is the home of Hunding, chieftain of the Neiding clan. The door opens, and Siegmund, flying from his enemies, wounded and weaponless, enters. Seeing no one, he closes the door, strides toward the fire, and throws himself wearily down on a bearskin :

> "Whoe'er own this hearth,
> Here must I rest me."

He remains stretched out motionless. A woman enters from an inner chamber. It is Sieglinde. She takes compassion on the helpless fugitive, admires his noble bearing, gives him drink, and bids him tarry till her husband be home. They gaze upon each

other with ever-increasing interest and emotion. Suddenly Siegmund starts up as if to go.

"Who pursues thee?" she inquires.

"Ill fate pursues where'er I go. To thee, wife, may it never
come. Forth from thy house I fly."

She calls him back. "Then bide thou here. Thou canst not
bring ill fate where ill fate already makes its home."

He leans against the hearth. Again the eyes of the twain meet.

Hunding enters, regards the stranger with suspicion, notes the
resemblance between him and Sieglinde; but he consents to harbor
him for the night.

"Thy name and fortune?"

"Wehwalt," says Siegmund, "for woe still waits on my steps;
Wehwalt, the son of Wolfe." And thus concealing his race, he
tells a story in other respects true : how in his childhood a cruel
host had laid waste his home and killed his mother and carried
away the sister who was his twin, and how he and his father, the
Wolf, for years had battled in the woodlands against the Neidings.

The Neidings! They are Hunding's clan.

"My house holds thee, Wölfing, to-night. To-morrow defend
thee; with death thou shalt pay for this life!" And Hunding
withdraws, Sieglinde with him.

Siegmund is weaponless. The firelight sends a sudden glow
upon the ash tree, and a sword-hilt there sends back an answering
gleam. But Siegmund knows not what it means. Clad in white,
Sieglinde steals from the inner room. She has left Hunding
asleep, overcome by a slumberous draft.

"Thy coming is life," cries Siegmund.

"A weapon, now, let me show thee," she replies. And she tells
how, on the day of her unhappy wedding, a stranger, all in gray,
low-hatted and one-eyed, had entered the Hunding hall and struck
into the ash stem a sword that none but the bravest of heroes could
win, and how all in turn had tried in vain to draw forth the sword.
Now she knows for whom it was ordained, —

"It was for thee, my deliverer, my hero held in my arms!"

They embrace. He declares his lineage. He is son of him
whose eye proudly glistened from under the low-brimmed hat, —

son of Wälse, the wanderer. He is Siegmund, the Victorious. For him, the sword Nothung. — And he draws it easily forth.

"Art thou Siegmund?" she cries; "Sieglinde am I. Thine own twin sister thou winnest at once with the sword."

"Bride and sister be to thy brother; then flourish the Wälsungs for aye!"

So the twain make their compact.

In the second act we are transported to a wild and rocky place. Before Wotan, fully armed and carrying his spear, stands Brünnhilde, the warrior maid, likewise fully armed. She is one of the nine Valkyries, daughters of Wotan and Erda, fostered for battle that they might forfend the doom foretold by Erda herself, — the shameful defeat of the gods. Well have the Valkyrs, choosers of the slain, performed their task, stirring mortal hearts to battle and riding through the air above to designate the bravest for death, and with their spirits to fill the halls on Valhalla's height. Now, however, Wotan is ordering Brünnhilde to haste to the fray, — not on death's errand but on errand of life, — to shield Siegmund the Wälsung in the fight. The Valkyrie springs shouting from rock to rock, and disappears behind the mountain crags.

All seems to be arranged. But lo, Fricka, in her ram-drawn car! She descends and strides toward her scheming spouse. The goddess has heard the cry of Hunding, calling for vengeance on the twinborn pair who have rashly wrought him wrong; and as guardian of wedlock she demands the death of Siegmund in the coming conflict. Wotan tries to persuade her that Siegmund's success is needful to the gods, — the warrior band of mortal souls gathered by the Valkyries in the heights of Valhalla cannot alone suffice to avert the onslaught of the powers of darkness.

"Needed is one who, free from help of godhood, fights free of the godhead's control. Only such an one is meet for the deed which is denied to a god to achieve."

But Fricka is not to be deceived nor thwarted in her aim. She brushes aside the plea of Wotan and his subterfuge, — who has ever heard that heroes can accomplish what the gods cannot? And as for heroes unaided — none such is Siegmund.

"Who was it," she asks, "that brought him his conquering sword? and whose shield is ordained to cover him in the fight?"

"I cannot o'erthrow him," breaks out Wotan; "he has found my sword."

"Destroy its magic then," retorts the implacable queen. "Give word to thy shouting war-maid that Siegmund fall!"

Wotan is conquered. Sadly he revokes the order given to Brünnhilde.

"Then takest thou from Siegmund thy shield?" cries that one in amazement.

And the god: "Yea! though Alberich's host threaten our downfall; though again the Ring be won by the Nibelung, and Valhalla be lost forever. By bargains bound myself, I may not wrest the Ring from the foeman, from Fafner the giant. Therefore, to fulfill my purpose, I had thought to create a Free One who for me should fight. Now, with loathing, I find ever myself in all my hand has created. The Other for whom I have longed, that Other I never shall find. Himself must the Free One create him; my hand shapes nothing but slaves. For when this hand of mine touched Alberich's Ring, my heart grew greedy of gold. I fled from the curse, but the curse flies not from me. What I love best must I surrender; whom most I cherish, I must slay. One thing awaits me yet — the downfall! Yea, that portended Erda, — Erda, the all-wise.

"'When the dusky foe,' she said, —

'When the dusky foe of love
Grimly getteth a son,
The doom of the gods
Delays not long!'

And of late I have heard that the Nibelung has bought him a wife. Their son shall inherit, — their son, the child of spite, shall inherit the empty pomp of the gods!"

It was of Hagen, yet unborn, the baleful curse of the Volsungs, of Hagen, the traitor, that Erda had prophesied. And thus dimly is foreshadowed the Twilight of the Gods.

But Brünnhilde?

"Siegmund thou hast taught me to love," murmurs the Valkyrie. Then boldly, —

"For his sake thy wavering word I defy!"

The war-father turns in wrath upon this new rebellion, and on pain of eternal penalty enjoins upon his daughter her new duty:

"Fight truly for Fricka! Siegmund strike thou! Such be the Valkyrie's task!"

The war-maid seeks out Siegmund and announces to him his approaching death. But that hero's distress at the thought of parting from Sieglinde stirs her to the quick. And, in the moment of battle, Brünnhilde disobeys the All-father's injunction; — she shields the warrior whom she loves. Then suddenly appears Wotan, standing over Hunding and holding his spear across in front of Siegmund.

"Go back from the spear! In splinters the sword!" shouts the god.

In terror Brünnhilde sinks back. Siegmund's sword breaks on the outstretched spear, and Hunding pierces the Volsung's breast. Brünnhilde hastily gathers the bits of the broken sword, lifts Sieglinde to horse, and escapes through the gorges behind.

The scene changes to the Valkyries' rocky home. Through the drifting clouds come riding the eight sisters of Brünnhilde, in full armor each, and each bearing before her the body of some slain hero. They await Brünnhilde. She, fleeing from Wotan's pursuit, at last arrives. She implores them to shield Sieglinde from the wrath of the god, but unsuccessfully; and then she urges Sieglinde to fly. At first, benumbed by despair, the widowed woman refuses; but when Brünnhilde mentions the child that is to be born — the world's most glorious hero — she consents.

"Him thou shalt bear, thy son and Siegmund's. For him ward thou well these mighty splinters of his father's sword. He shall weld them anew and swing the victorious blade! His name from me let him take — 'Siegfried'; for Siegfried in *triumph* shall live!"

Comforted and hopeful, Sieglinde betakes herself to that forest far to the east, where the Nibelung's hoard had been borne by Fafner. There, in dragon's form, he guarded the gold and the Ring; and thither Wotan is not likely to pursue.

It thunders and lightens. Wotan, raging terribly, strides from crag to crag. The other Valkyries are driven from the scene. Brünnhilde hears her doom:

> " The heavenly host
> No more shall know thee;
> Outcast art thou
> From the clan of the gods:
> The bond by thee has been broken;
> Henceforth from sight of my face art thou banned!"

Immortal, she had followed the might of love; mortal, now she shall sleep, and that sleep shall endure till one comes to awaken her; and to him, whosoe'er it may be, she shall be subject thenceforth.

The Valkyrie drops to her knees:

"Ah, let no craven awake me!" she cries. "Surround me with horrors, with fires that shall fright: that none but the most fearless of heroes may find me here on the fell!"

Wotan accedes to her petition. He kisses her on both eyes and lays her unconscious, asleep, in the shade of a broad-branching fir tree. Then, —

> " Appear! Come, waving fire,
> And wind thee in flames round the fell!
> Loge, Loge, appear!"

A sea of flames encircles the spot, and Wotan proclaims:

> " He who my spear-point's
> Sharpness feareth
> Shall cross not this flaming fire!"

Alone, under her long steel shield, sleeps the Valkyrie.

287. Siegfried. The drama of Siegfried opens in the cavern of Mime, in the forest "far to the east" to which Sieglinde had fled. Mime, the dwarf, is he whom erstwhile his Nibelung brother, Alberich, then lord of the Ring, had held in thrall at the bottom of the Rhine. Some years before the events represented in this play, the dwarf had found Sieglinde dying in the woods, and had received from her Siegfried, her newborn son, and with him the pieces of Siegmund's broken sword, Nothung.

Young Siegfried, noble, proud, and strong, has been nurtured in ignorance of his lineage and destiny, as Mime's son. But of that lineage and destiny the cunning dwarf is well aware; and while he trains Siegfried to doughty deeds, he ceaselessly forges at the splinters of the sword, hoping to reweld them himself and through Siegfried's might to win victory over Fafner, the present lord of the Ring, and so achieve unmeasured wealth and the mastery of the world. But Siegfried despises his foster-father and seeks ever to discover the story of his own descent. The attempts of Mime to shape anew the pieces of Nothung fail; and he daily forges other swords, which Siegfried scorns and breaks at the first trial. In the course of time, however, there comes to Mime's cave a " Wanderer " — it is Wotan himself — and tells the dwarf that only one, a man who knows not fear, can remake the all-conquering sword. He tells him, too, of the mighty spear, fashioned of the world ash tree's hallowed branches, with which he, Wotan, rules the earth. But no word he says of the doom that is to befall that spear at the blow of the conquering sword, — the doom, forsooth, of the gods themselves.

Mime, after trying in vain to arouse in Siegfried the sense of fear, suggests to the youth that he try to reforge Nothung. Siegfried seizes the splinters, pounds them, and files them to powder; melts them over the charcoal of the ash tree's stem, and, singing at his work, refashions the sword. While this is doing, through the pauses of Siegfried's song can be heard the voice of Mime, muttering: "The sword will be forged . . . and Fafner vanquished. . . . When Siegfried has slain that dragon . . . he will be athirst. . . . I will brew him a drink. . . . One drop will lay him in sleep. . . . With the sword that he forges I'll kill him. . . . Mine, then, the Ring and the hoard!"

At last the sword is shaped and sharpened. Siegfried swings it before him:

" Nothung, Nothung, conquering sword; again to life have I woke thee! Strike at the traitor, cut down the knave! See, Mime, thou smith; so sunders Siegfried's sword!" and he strikes the anvil in twain from top to bottom. It falls asunder with a great noise, and the dwarf drops with terror to the ground.

The scene changes to the forest in front of Fafner's cave. Alberich is watching gloomily by, and the Wanderer rides in to taunt him with false hope of the Ring.

"A hero nears to set free the hoard," says the Wanderer. "Fafner will fall. Perchance if Alberich warn the dragon, he may win the Ring in token of gratitude."

Alberich makes the approaches. Fafner yawns: "I have and I hold; let me slumber!·"

With scornful laughter the Wanderer rides away. But "one day," snarls Alberich, — "one day shall I see you all fade, ye light-hearted eternals. The wise one keepeth his watch and surely worketh his spite!"

As the day breaks Siegfried and Mime enter, Siegfried wearing his sword hung in a girdle of rope, and blithely blowing a horn. Fafner, in the shape of a huge lizardlike dragon, comes out of his cave and forward to the stream for water. At sight of the nonchalant youth piping his wood-notes gay, the monster emits a snort that serves his need of a laugh, — "I came for drink; now, too, I find food."

The conflict is speedily joined. More than once Siegfried is well-nigh lost; but his chance comes. The dragon exposes his heart, and Siegfried sinks his sword into it up to the hilt. In the moment of death, Fafner warns the young hero to beware of him who stirred him to the fight. But Siegfried pays little heed. The blood of the dragon bespatters his hand; it burns. Siegfried involuntarily carries his hand to his lips. There is a wood bird singing. Siegfried regards him with astonishment. "Almost," he says, "it seems as wood birds were speaking to me," and he hearkens.

"Hei!" sings the wood bird; "now Siegfried owns all the Nibelung's hoard. Let him but search the cavern, and hoard, Tarnhelm, and Ring will make him the lord of the world!"

"Thanks, dearest birdling," Siegfried replies, and possesses himself of Tarnhelm and Ring. The hoard he leaves where it was.

"Hei!" sings the wood bird; "Ring and Tarnhelm Siegfried has won. Now let him not trust the treacherous tongue of the falsest of friends!"

No sooner is that warning given than Mime, who has meanwhile been wrangling with Alberich over the division of the spoils, creeps forward.

"See, thou art weary; drink of the broth I have brewed, and take rest," he says smilingly to Siegfried. But under his breath he is muttering, "Drink, and choke thee to death," as he pours the draft into the drink horn and offers it.

"Taste thou my sword, loathsome babbler!" cries the young hero, and strikes him dead at a blow; then pitches his body on top of the hoard and stops up the mouth of the cave with the grinning corpse of the dragon.

"Thanks, friendliest birdling! But happiness yet have I not. Brothers and sisters hast thou; but I — am so alone; nor brother nor sister, nor father nor mother. One comrade had I; he laid out to catch me, and now I have slain him, perforce. Ah, birdling, find me a comrade true!"

"Hei!" chatters the wood bird; "a glorious bride for Siegfried have I. On a rocky fastness she sleeps, and guarded by fire is her home. Who fighteth the flames wakens the maid; Brünnhilde, Brünnhilde, he wins for his own!"

"Where'er thou fliest, follows my foot," shouts Siegfried, bubbling with joy.

The scene changes. In a wild spot at the foot of a rocky mountain Wotan, the Wanderer, desiring the success of Siegfried and still knowing that that success involves the doom of the gods, seeks counsel from Erda. The all-wise one refuses to answer, — refers him to the Norns. "The Norns are waking, they wind the rope. The Norns will give thee answer!"

"Ah, no!" replies the Wanderer. "Their weaving is ever in thrall to fate. To thee I come that I may learn how to stay the wheel that is already rolling."

"Ask Brünnhilde!"

"In vain, All-wise One; the piercing sting of care was planted by thee. Ruin and downfall were foretold by thee. Say to me, now, how a god may conquer his care!"

"Thou art — *not* what thou hast said." No more will Erda vouchsafe.

Not what he has said! Then, surely, the gods are beyond redemption. But not even so shall the harvest be reaped by the Nibelungs. "Nay, to the Volsung shall be my heritage," decrees Wotan: "to him who has known me never, though chosen by me; to the lad of dauntless daring, though untaught by my counsel. Pure from greed, gladdened by love-dreams, he has won the Nibelung's Ring. Against him the curse of Alberich cannot avail."

While yet the Wanderer is speaking, Erda descends to endless sleep. Dawn illumines the scene. Siegfried's bird comes fluttering to the foreground, but, frighted by vision of the god, takes wing and disappears. Siegfried presses on.

"My birdling has flown from my eyes," he remarks. "I needs must find out the rock for myself."

"The way that the wood bird pointed," announces Wotan, encountering him, "shalt thou not pass!"

"Hoho! Wouldst thou stay me? Who art thou, then, that here withstandest?"

"Fear the fell's defender! By my might the slumbering maid is held enchained. He who should wake her, he who should win her, mightless would make me forever. Go back, then, foolhardy boy!"

As the Wanderer speaks, the splendor spreads from the flame-girdled rock above.

"Go back thyself, thou babbler! There where the fires are blazing, — to Brünnhilde now must I hie!" And Siegfried pushes forward.

The Wanderer bars the way to the mountain: "Once already that sword of thine, Nothung, has broken on the haft of this sacred spear!"

"'T is, then, my father's slayer!" thinks Siegfried; and nothing loath to face that foe, he raises the new-forged sword and strikes to pieces the All-father's spear!

"Fare on," says Wotan, quietly picking up the fragments, "I cannot withstand thee."

The god vanishes in darkness. The hero, light-hearted, blowing his horn, scales the cliffs, passes the fire, — wakes Brünnhilde. She, at first, with maidenly might struggles against his passion for her and her growing tenderness for him. She deplores the byrnie, shield and helm, symbols of her godhead, that he has torn from her. But, mortal now, she surrenders to a mortal's love:

" O Siegfried, Siegfried, child of delight,
Love thyself, — and turn thee from me;
Oh, bring not thine own to naught!"

And Siegfried:

" I — love thee: didst thou but love me!
Mine am I no more: oh, would that thou wert mine! . . .
Waken, O maid; live in laughter:
Sweetest delight, be mine, be mine!"

Then she, with a joyful cry:

" Oh, child of delight! Oh, glorious hero!
Thou foolish lord of loftiest deeds!
Laughing must I love thee,
Laughing welcome my blindness;
Laughing let us be lost,
With laughter go down to death. . . .
Farewell, Valhalla's light-giving world:
Thy stately towers let fall in dust!
Farewell, O glittering pomp of the gods!
Complete your bliss, eternal host!
Now rend, ye Norns, your rope of runes:
Dusk of Gods in darkness arise;
Night of downfall dawn in mist!"

And thus, turning their backs on Valhalla, and radiant with the light of human love, the twain, laughing, face toward death.

288. The Twilight of the Gods. The play opens with a prelude. By the Valkyrie's rock sit the three Norns and sing of past, present, and future, weaving through the night their rope of runes. As they foretell the burning of Valhalla and the end of the gods, the rope breaks, and the Norns disappear into the earth.

The sun rises, and in the first act of the play Siegfried and Brünnhilde enter from their cave. She sends him forth in quest of heroic adventures in the world, giving him her horse, Grane, and receiving from him the Ring as a pledge of his love.

The scene changes, and we behold the interior of the Gibichungs' hall on the Rhine. Gunther and Gutrune, his sister, are in converse with Hagen, their half brother, — dark and treacherous son of Grimhilde, their mother, and of Alberich the Nibelung, erstwhile owner of the Ring. Hagen alone knows, it would seem, that Siegfried has already ridden through the flames and won Brünnhilde. The others know merely that that hero has slain Fafner and is lord of the Tarnhelm, hoard, and Ring. Hagen, anxious to regain the heritage of the Nibelungs, urges marriage on Gunther, naming Brünnhilde as a fitting bride for him. As, however, Siegfried alone can pass through the fire to come at her, he proposes that Gutrune shall win Siegfried's love and induce him to serve Gunther. Siegfried's horn is heard, and he presently enters and is made welcome. Gutrune, at the instigation of Hagen, brings Siegfried a potion which causes him to love her, and drives clean out of his mind all memory of Brünnhilde. In the madness of his passion for Gutrune, Siegfried swears blood-brotherhood with Gunther, and promises by the aid of the Tarnhelm to make Brünnhilde Gunther's wife, if only in return Gutrune shall be his. The newly sworn "brothers" depart for Brünnhilde's rock.

In the next scene we are again before the home of Brünnhilde. Waltraute, a Valkyrie, comes to beg Brünnhilde to give back the Ring to the Rhine-maidens, and so avert the doom of the gods. "What, then, aileth the immortals?" cries Brünnhilde in alarm.

"Since Wotan doomed thee, no more hath he sent us to war," replies Waltraute. "No more hath he gathered the souls of the slain about him in Valhalla. Alone he has ridden unceasing through the world. But, one day, home he came bearing his spear all splintered in his hand. Wordless, with a sign he bade Valhalla's heroes hew the world ash tree in pieces and pile it like firewood around the Hall of the Blest. And from that hour silent he sits on his throne, about him the awe-struck gods and heroes, the war-maids cowering at his knees. None tastes the apples of youth. To-day Wotan remembered thee; his eye grew soft and, as dreaming, he spake:

> ' If once more the daughters of Rhine
> Should win from her finger the Ring,
> Of the load of the curse
> Were the world and immortals made free.'

Brünnhilde, yield up the Ring, and end all the grief of the world!"

" The Ring ? " wails Brünnhilde. " Knowest thou what 't is to me ? One flash of its fire outvalues all heaven's delight; for the gleam of that Ring is Siegfried's love !

" From love I never shall turn ;
Of his love they never shall rob me,
Though into ruins
Valhalla's splendor should fall ! "

Thus Brünnhilde refuses, and sends Waltraute away to take her defiance to Valhalla.

But retribution is swift, for on the moment Siegfried, changed to Gunther's shape by the Tarnhelm, comes and claims Brünnhilde as his bride. She resists and threatens him with the Ring. But now Siegfried, forgetful of the past, struggles for another with his own dear wife, overcomes her, and wrests the Ring from her. He then commands her to go into the cave, whither, after drawing his sword to lay between them as symbol of his loyalty to Gunther, he follows her.

The second act is outside the Gibichungs' hall. It is early morning of the next day. After a short scene in which the ever-plotting Alberich urges Hagen to get the Ring, Siegfried returns and tells Hagen and Gutrune of the winning of Brünnhilde and her approach with Gunther. Hagen calls together the vassals to welcome Gunther and his bride. The royal pair presently arrive and are received with loud acclaim. Straightway Brünnhilde recognizes Siegfried (who, however, does not know her) and, seeing the Ring on Siegfried's finger, she asks Gunther what he has done with the ring he took from her. His confusion reveals the truth to her, and she proclaims that she is wedded to Siegfried and not to Gunther. Siegfried swears on the point of Hagen's spear that her accusation is false. She repeats it, taking the same oath. Siegfried, Gutrune, and their vassals go out to prepare for the double wedding celebration ; Gunther, Hagen, and Brünnhilde remaining solemnly condemn Siegfried to death for what seems treachery to one and all. Hagen, left alone, glories in the prospect of regaining the Ring.

The third act discloses an open place on the banks of the Rhine. The three Rhine-maidens pray to the sun for the return of the

Rhine-gold. Siegfried, who has strayed from his companions on a hunting expedition, comes to the river bank. The maidens unsuccessfully attempt, by wiles and warnings of ill fate, to get the Ring from him, and finally swim away, foretelling his death that very day. Gunther, Hagen, and their vassals come to the place, and all sit down to rest. At Hagen's suggestion Siegfried relates the story of his life. But, lo! when he comes to the episode of his first passage through the fire, a draft given him by Hagen restores his memory, and innocently he tells of the waking and winning of Brünnhilde. All start up in amaze; Hagen stabs Siegfried in the back with his spear, and steals away. Siegfried falls, and after a few words sung to Brünnhilde, whom he sees as in a vision, he dies. His body is placed on a bier and borne away by the vassals with great pomp and state as the sun sets.

In the last scene we have the interior of the Gibichungs' hall as before. It is night. Gutrune comes from her chamber anxious for Siegfried. Presently Hagen's voice is heard calling for torches to light the returning hunters. He enters and, in reply to Gutrune's questions, tells her that Siegfried has been slain by a wild boar. Then come the vassals, bearing Siegfried's body. It is placed on a bier in the center of the hall. Hagen claims the Ring as his right for slaying Siegfried, but Gunther defies him to touch Gutrune's heritage. They fight and Gunther falls. As Hagen approaches the corpse to take the Ring, the dead Siegfried raises his arm threateningly. All start back in horror, and just then Brünnhilde enters and comes down to the bier. Here, after ordering a pyre to be built on the river bank, she sings a funeral song over Siegfried. The body, from which she has taken the Ring, is then placed on the pyre. Setting the Ring on her own finger, Brünnhilde calls on the Rhine-maidens to take it in turn from her ashes:

> " Let fire, burning this hand
> Cleanse, too, the Ring from its curse."

She applies the torch:

> " So cast I the brand
> On Valhall's glittering walls. —
> When ye see in the kindling fire,
> Siegfried and Brünnhild' consumed;

When ye see the river-daughters
Bear the Ring away to the deep:
To northward then
Look through the night!
When the heaven there gleams
With a holy glow,
Then know ye all
That Valhall's end ye behold!"

Her horse is brought. She mounts it and springs into the flames, which flare up and seize on the hall itself. The river overflows and rolls over the fire. The Rhine-maidens swim up and regain the Ring. Hagen rushes into the flood to get it from them, but is dragged down to the depths by their arms as they swim away. In the sky is seen a vision of Valhalla in flames.

The breed of the gods is gone like breath. The loveless Ring has worked its curse. Each in his turn its lords have bitten the dust. And Brünnhilde reads the moral:

"Not goods nor gold
Nor glory of gods
Can fashion a blessing for weal,
Can win a blessing from woe, —
But Love alone!"

PART II

THE HISTORY OF MYTH

CHAPTER XXX

THE ORIGIN AND ELEMENTS OF MYTH

289. Kinds of Myth. If we classify the preceding stories according to the reason of their existence, we observe that they are of two kinds, — explanatory and æsthetic.

(1) *Explanatory myths* are the outcome of naïve guesses at the truth, of mistaken and superstitious attempts to satisfy the curiosity of primitive and unenlightened peoples, to unveil the mysteries of existence, make clear the facts of the universe and the experiences of life, to account for religious rites and social customs of which the origin is forgotten, to teach the meaning and the history of things. There are certain questions that nearly every child and every savage asks : What is the world and what is man ? Who made them ? What else did the maker do ? and what the first men ? Whence came the commodities of life ? Why do we celebrate certain festivals, practice certain ceremonials, observe solemnities, and partake of sacraments, and bow to this or the other god ? What is death, and what becomes of us after death ? The answers to such questions crystallized themselves gradually into stories of the creation, of the gods, and of the heroes — forefathers of men, but magnified, because unfamiliar, mysterious, and remote.

Old literatures abound in explanatory myths of so highly imaginative a character that we moderns are tempted to read into them meanings which probably they never possessed. For the diverse and contradictory significations that have in recent years been proposed for one and the same myth could not all, at any one time, have been entertained by the myth-makers. On the other hand,

431

the current explanations of certain myths are sufficiently apparent to be probable. " To the ancients," says John Fiske,[1] " the moon was not a lifeless body of stones and clods; it was the horned huntress Artemis, coursing through the upper ether, or bathing herself in the clear lake; or it was Aphrodite, protectress of lovers, born of the sea foam in the East, near Cyprus. The clouds were not bodies of vaporized water; they were cows, with swelling udders, driven to the milking by Hermes, the summer wind; or great sheep with moist fleeces, slain by the unerring arrows of Bellerophon, the sun; or swan-maidens, flitting across the firmament; Valkyries hovering over the battle field to receive the souls of falling heroes; or, again, they were mighty mountains, piled one above another, in whose cavernous recesses the divining wand of the storm-god Thor revealed hidden treasures. The yellow-haired sun, Phœbus, drove westerly all day in his flaming chariot; or, perhaps, as Meleager, retired for awhile in disgust from the sight of men; wedded at eventide the violet light (Œnone, Iole) which he had forsaken in the morning; sank as Hercules upon a blazing funeral pyre, or, like Agamemnon, perished in a bloodstained bath; or, as the fish-god, Dagon, swam nightly through the subterranean waters to appear eastward again at daybreak. Sometimes Phaëthon, his rash, inexperienced son, would take the reins and drive the solar chariot too near the earth, causing the fruits to perish, and the grass to wither, and the wells to dry up. Sometimes, too, the great all-seeing divinity, in his wrath at the impiety of men, would shoot down his scorching arrows, causing pestilence to spread over the land."

(2) *Æsthetic myths* have their origin in the universal desire for amusement, in the revulsion of the mind from the humdrum of actuality. They furnish information that may not be practical, but is delightful; they elicit emotion — sympathy, tears, and laughter — for characters and events remote from our commonplace experience but close to the heart of things, and near and significant and enchanting to us in the atmosphere of imagination that embraces severed continents, inspires the dead with life, bestows color and breath upon the creatures of a dream, and wraps young and old

[1] Myths and Myth-Makers, p. 18. Proper nouns have been anglicized.

in the wonder of hearing a new thing. The æsthetic myth, first, removes us from the sordid world of immediate and selfish needs, and then unrolls a vision of a world where men and things exist simply for the purpose of delighting us. And the enduring measure of delight which the æsthetic myth affords is the test of 'what we call its *beauty*.

A myth, whether explanatory or æsthetic, is of unconscious growth, almost never concocted with a view to instruction.

According to their subjects, æsthetic myths are either historic or romantic. (*a*) If *historic*, they utilize events which have a skeleton of fact. They supply flesh and sinew of divine or heroic adventure and character, blood and breath of probability and imagination. In historic myths the dependence of gods, heroes, and events upon the stern necessity of an overruling power, of fate or providence, is especially to be observed. Of this class is the Iliad of Homer.

(*b*) If *romantic*, the myths are characterized by bolder selection or creation of fundamental events; indeed, events appear to be chosen with a view to displaying or developing the character of the hero. In such myths circumstances are not so important as what the hero does with circumstances. The hero is more independent than in the historic myth; his liberty, his choice, — in judgment, in conduct, and in feeling, — his responsibility, are the center of interest. In romantic myths like the Odyssey this sense of freedom does not impel the poet to capricious use of his material. But lesser bards than Homer have permitted their heroes to run riot in adventures that weary the imagination and offend the moral judgment.

290. Divisions of Inquiry. We are next led to ask how these myths came into existence, and how it is that the same myth meets us under various forms in literatures and among peoples widely separate in time and place. These are questions of the *Origin* and *Distribution* of myths; and in this chapter we shall discuss the former.

291. Elements of the Myth. The myths preserved in the literatures of many civilized nations, such as the Greek, present to the imaginative and the moral sense aspects fraught with contradiction. In certain myths the gods display themselves as beautiful,

wise, and beneficent beings; in others they indulge in cruel, foolish, and unbeautiful practices and adventures. These contradictory elements have been called the reasonable and the senseless.
A myth of Mother Earth (Demeter) mourning the loss of her
daughter, the Springtide, is reasonable; a myth of Demeter
devouring, in a fit of abstraction, the shoulder of the boy Pelops,
and replacing it with ivory, is capricious, apparently senseless.
"It is this silly, senseless, and savage element," as Max Müller
says, "that makes mythology the puzzle which men have so long
found it."

292. Reasonable Myths. If myths were always reasonable, it
would not be difficult to reach an agreement concerning some way
by which they may have come into existence.

Imagination. If we assume that the peoples who invented these
stories of supernatural beings and events had, with due allowance
for the discrepancy in mental development, imaginations like our
own, there is nothing in the history of reasonable myths to baffle
our understanding. For, at the present time, not only children
and simple-minded men, like sailors or mountaineers, but cultivated men of ordinary poetic sensibility, bestow attributes of life
upon inanimate things and abstract ideas. The sun is nowadays
thirsty, the ship is a woman, the clouds threaten, charity suffereth
long, the waves are angry, time will tell, and death swallows all
things. The sun still rises, and, as Mr. Jasper maintains, "do
move." By personification we, every day, bestow the attributes of
human beings upon inanimate nature, animals, and abstractions.
By our metaphors we perpetuate and diffuse the poetic illusion;
we talk not perhaps of the arrows of Apollo, but of a sunstroke;
our poetry abounds in symbols of the moon, of the swift-wingèd
wind, of the ravening sea. In our metonymies we use the sign
for the thing signified, the crown for the king, the flag for the
honor of the country; and the crown and the flag are to-day possessed of attributes and individuality just as efficient as those that
endowed the golden handmaids of Vulcan or the eagle of Jove.
Nor is hyperbole any less in use among us than it was among the
ancients; we glorify our political heroes with superlatives, they
dignified theirs with divinity.

Belief. But this resemblance in habits of imagination, while it may help us to appreciate the mental condition of primitive peoples, accentuates the distinction between our imagination and theirs. They, at some time or other, believed in these personifications. We do not believe. But their belief is easier to comprehend when we remember that the myths of savages are not a deliberate invention of any one individual, but are constructed by generations of people, and that many of them cluster about beings who were actually worshiped. Among primitive nations the sense of awe in the presence of magnificent objects of nature — mountains, the sky, the sun, the sea — is universal. It springs from the fact that savages do not deem themselves superior to nature. They are not conscious of souls whose flight is higher than that of nature. On the contrary, since sun, sea, and winds move, the savage invests them with free will and personality like man's. In proportion, however, as their size is grander or their movement more tremendous, these objects must be possessed of freedom, personality, and power exceeding those of man. Why, then, should not the savage believe, of beings worthy of worship and fear and gratitude, all and more than all that is accredited to man? Why not confer upon them human and superhuman passions and powers? If we were living, like the Greek of old, close to the heart of nature, such personification of natural powers would be more easy for us to appreciate.

" If for us also, as for the Greek," says Ruskin,[1] " the sunrise means daily restoration to the sense of passionate gladness and of perfect life — if it means the thrilling of new strength through every nerve, — the shedding over us of a better peace than the peace of night, in the power of the dawn, — and the purging of evil vision and fear by the baptism of its dew ; — if the sun itself is an influence, to us also, of spiritual good, — and becomes thus in reality, not in imagination, to us also, a spiritual power, — we may then soon overpass the narrow limit of conception which kept that power impersonal, and rise with the Greek to the thought of an angel who rejoiced as a strong man to run his course, whose voice, calling to life and to labor, rang round the earth, and whose going forth was to the ends of heaven."

[1] Ruskin, Queen of the Air.

Regarding thus the religious condition of the savage, we may comprehend the existence of myths and his acceptance of them.

293. Unreasonable Myths. But he would maintain this attitude of acceptance only in the matter of good and beneficent gods and of righteous or reasonable myths.

For how could a human being believe of the god whom he worshiped and revered, deeds and attributes more silly and more shameful than man can conceive of his fellow man ? When, therefore, we find senseless and shameless myths existing side by side with stories of the justice and righteousness of the same god, we must conclude that, since the worshiper could not believe both sets of attributes, he preserved his religious attitude before the good god only by virtue of rejecting the senseless myth.

A man's religious belief would assist him to entertain only the reasonable myths. How, then, did the senseless and cruel stories come into existence ? And were they ever believed ?

There are many answers to these questions. They may, however, be classified according to the theory of civilization that they assume.

According to the *Theory of Deterioration,* or Human Depravity, man, although he had in the beginning knowledge of common facts, pure moral and religious ideas, and true poetic conceptions, has forgotten, with the lapse of time, the significance of words, facts, men, and events, adopted corrupt moral and religious notions, and given license to the diseased imagining of untrue and unlovely conceptions.

According to the *Theory of Improvement,* or Progress, man, beginning with crude dreams and fancies about experience, life, the world, and God, has gradually developed truer and higher conceptions of his own nature, of his relation to the world about him, of duty, of art, and of religion.

294. Theory of Deterioration. Let us consider first the interpretations of mythology that assume a backward tendency in early civilization. They are :

(1) The *Historical,* or better called after its author, Euhemerus (B.C. 316), the *Euhemeristic.* This explanation assumes that myths of the gods are exaggerated adventures of historic individuals, chieftains, medicine men, heroes ; and that supernatural

events are distortions of natural but wonderful occurrences. In fact, it attributes to our forefathers a disease of the memory which prompted them to pervert facts. Jupiter, Odin, and Hercules were accordingly men who, after death, had been glorified, then deified, then invested with numerous characteristics and adventures appropriate to their exalted conditions of existence.

The custom of worshiping ancestors, still existent in China and other countries, is adduced in support of this method of investigating myths, and it is undoubtedly true that the method explains the origin and growth of some myths. But it accounts rather for the reasonable than the senseless element of mythical adventure, while it fails to show how savages come to exaggerate their heroes into beings entirely out of the realm of that actual experience which is the basis of the historical assumption.

(2) *The Philological Interpretation* [1] assumes also a disease of the memory by reason of which men misunderstand and confuse the meanings of words, and misapply the words themselves. Professor Max Müller calls this affection a disease of language. In ancient languages every such word as *day, night, earth, sun, spring, dawn,* had an ending expressive of gender, which naturally produced the corresponding idea of sex. These objects accordingly became in the process of generations not only persons, but male and female. As, also, the phrases expressing the existence or the activity of these natural objects lost their ancient signification under new colloquial coloring, primitive and simple statements of natural events acquired the garb and dignity of elaborate and often incongruous narratives, no longer about natural events, but about persons. Ancient language may, for instance, have said *sunrise* follows the *dawn.* The word for sun was masculine ; the word for dawn, feminine. In time the sentence came to mean, Apollo, the god of the sun, *chases* Daphne, the maiden of the glowing dawn. But the word, *Daphne,* meant also a laurel that burned easily, hence might readily be devoted to the god of the sun. So Daphne, the maiden, assuming the form of Daphne, the laurel, escaped the

[1] See Max Müller's Chips from a German Workshop, Science of Religion, etc.; Cox's Aryan Myths, and numerous articles by the learned authors of Roscher's Ausführliches Lexikon.

pursuit of her ardent lover, by becoming the tree sacred to his worship.[1] The merit of the philological method is, that, tracing the name of a mythical character through kindred languages, it frequently ascertains for us the family of the myth, brings to light kindred forms of the myth, discovers in what language the name was born, and sometimes, giving us the original meaning of the divine name, "throws light on the legend of the bearer of the name and on its origin and first home."[2]

But unfortunately there is very often no agreement among scholars about the original meaning of the names of mythical beings. The same name is frequently explained in half a dozen different ways. The same deity is reduced by different interpreters to half a dozen elements of nature. A certain goddess represents now the upper air, now light, now lightning, and yet again clouds. Naturally the attempts at construing her adventures must terminate in correspondingly dissimilar and unconvincing results. In fine, the philological explanation assumes as its starting point masculine and feminine names for objects of nature. It does not attempt to show how an object like the ocean came to be male and not female, or how it came to be a person at all. And this latter, in studying the origin of myths, is what should first be ascertained. We must not, however, fall into the error of supposing that the philologists look for the origin and growth of all myths in words and the diseases of words. Max Müller grants that mythology does not always create its own heroes, but sometimes lays hold of real history. He insists that mythologists should bear in mind that there may be in every mythological riddle elements which resist etymological analysis, for the simple reason that their origin was not etymological, but historical.

(3) *The Allegorical Interpretation* is akin to the philological in its results. It leads us to explain myths as embodiments in symbolic guise of hidden meaning: of physical, chemical, or astronomical facts; or of moral, religious, philosophical truth. The stories would at first exist as allegories, but in process of time would

[1] Max Müller, Essay on Comparative Mythology, Oxford Essays, 1856; Science of Religion, 2, 548 *n.*

[2] Andrew Lang, Myth, Ritual, and Religion, 1, 24-25, and Professor C. P. Tiele, as cited by Lang.

come to be understood literally. Thus Cronus, who devours his own children, is identified with the power that the Greeks called Chronos (Time), which may truly be said to destroy whatever it has brought into existence. The story of Io is interpreted in a similar manner. Io is the moon, and Argus the starry sky, which, as it were, keeps sleepless watch over her. The fabulous wanderings of Io represent the continual revolutions of the moon. This method of explanation rests upon the assumption that the men who made the allegories were proficient in physics, chemistry, astronomy, etc., and clever in allegory; but that, for some unknown reason, their descendants becoming stupid, knowledge as well as wit deserted the race. In some cases the myth was, without doubt, from the first an allegory; but where the myth was consciously fashioned as an allegory, in all probability it was preserved as such. It is not, however, likely that allegories of deep scientific or philosophical import were invented by savages. Where the myth has every mark of great antiquity, — is especially silly and senseless and savage, — it is safe to believe that any profound allegorical meaning, read into it, is the work of men of a later generation, who thus attempted to make reasonable the divine and heroic narratives which they could not otherwise justify and of whose existence they were ashamed. We find, moreover, in some cases a great variety of symbolic explanations of the same myth, one with as great claim to credence as another, since they spring from the same source, — the caprice or fancy of the expounder.

Among the ancients Theagenes of Rhegium, six hundred years before Christ, suggested the allegorical theory and method of interpretation. In modern times he has been supported by Lord Bacon, whose "Wisdom of the Ancients" treats myths as "elegant and instructive fables," and by many Germans, especially Professor Creuzer.

(4) *The Theological Interpretation.* This premises that mankind, either in general or through some chosen nationality, received from God an original revelation of pure religious ideas, and that, with the systematic and continued perversion of the moral sense, this knowledge of truth, morality, and spiritual religion fell into corruption. So in Greek mythology the attributes of the various

gods would be imperfect irradiations of the attributes of the one God. A more limited conception is, that all mythological legends are derived from the narratives of Scripture, though the real facts have been disguised and altered. Thus, Deucalion is only another name for Noah, Hercules for Samson, Arion for Jonah, etc. Sir Walter Raleigh, in his "History of the World," says, "Jubal, Tubal, and Tubal-Cain were Mercury, Vulcan, and Apollo, inventors of pasturage, smithing, and music. The dragon which kept the golden apples was the serpent that beguiled Eve. Nimrod's tower was the attempt of the giants against heaven." There are doubtless many curious coincidences like these, but the theory cannot, without extravagance, be pushed so far as to account for any great proportion of the stories. For many myths antedate the scriptural narratives of which they are said to be copies; many more, though resembling the scriptural stories, originated among peoples ignorant of the Hebrew Bible. The theory rests upon two unproved assumptions: one, that all nations have had a chance to be influenced by the same set of religious doctrines; the other, that God made his revelation in the beginning once for all, and has done nothing to help man toward righteousness since then. The theological theory has been advocated by Voss and other Germans in the seventeenth century, by Jacob Bryant in 1774, and in this century most ably by Gladstone.[1]

295. We are now ready for the explanation of myth-making based upon the **Theory of Progress**. This is best stated by Mr. Andrew Lang,[2] whose argument is, when possible, given in his own language. To the question how the senseless element got into myths, the advocates of this theory answer that it was in the minds and in the social condition of the savages who invented the myths. But since we cannot put ourselves back in history thousands of years to examine the habits of thought and life of early savages, we are constrained to examine whether anywhere nowadays there may exist "any stage of the human intellect in which these divine

---

[1] W. E. Gladstone, Homer and the Homeric Age; Juventus Mundi; The Olympian Religion, *North American Review*, Feb.–May, 1892.

[2] Andrew Lang, Myth, Ritual, and Religion, 2 vols., London, 1887; and Encyc. Brit., 9th ed., article, *Mythology*. Mannhardt, Antike Wald- und Feldkultus, Berlin, 1877. E. B. Tylor, Anthropology; Primitive Culture.

adventures and changes of men into animals, trees, stars, this belief in seeing and talking with the dead, are regarded as possible incidents of daily human life." As the result of such scientific investigation, numerous races of savages have been found who at this present day accept and believe just such silly and senseless elements of myth as puzzle us and have puzzled many of the cultivated ancients who found them in their inherited mythologies. The theory of development is, then, that " the savage and senseless element in mythology is, for the most part, a legacy from ancestors of civilized races who, at the time that they invented the senseless stories, were in an intellectual state not higher than that of our contemporary Australians, Bushmen, Red Indians, the lower races of South America, and other worse than barbaric people of the nineteenth century." But what are the characteristics of the mental state of our contemporary savages? First and foremost, *curiosity* that leads them to inquire into the causes of things; and second, *credulity* that impels them to invent or to accept childish stories that may satisfy their untutored experience. We find, moreover, that savages nowadays think of everything around them as having life and the parts and passions of persons like themselves. " The sky, sun, wind, sea, earth, mountains, trees, regarded as persons, are mixed up with men, beasts, stars, and stones on the same level of personality and life." The forces of nature, animals, and things have for these Polynesians and Bushmen the same powers and attributes that men have; and in their opinion men have the following attributes :

" 1. Relationship to animals and ability to be transformed, and to transform others, into animals and other objects.

" 2. Magical accomplishments, such as power to call up ghosts, or to visit ghosts and the region of the dead; power over the seasons, the sun, moon, stars, weather, and so forth." [1]

The stories of savages to-day abound in adventures based upon qualities and incidents like these. If these stories should survive in the literature of these nations after the nations have been civilized, they would appear senseless and silly and cruel to the descendants of our contemporary savages. In like manner, "as the ancient

[1] Encyc. Brit., *Mythology*.

Greeks, Egyptians, and Norsemen advanced in civilization, their religious thought and artistic taste were shocked by myths which were preserved by local priesthoods, or in ancient poems, or in popular religious ceremonials. . . . We may believe that ancient and early tribes framed gods like themselves in action and in experience, and that the allegorical element in myths is the addition of later peoples who had attained to purer ideas of divinity, yet dared not reject the religion of their ancestors." [1] The senseless element in the myths would, by this theory, be, for the most part, a " survival." Instead, then, of deteriorating, the races that invented senseless myths are, with ups and downs of civilization, intellectually and morally improved, to such extent that they desire to repudiate the senseless element in their mythical and religious traditions, or to explain it as reasonable by way of allegory. This method of research depends upon the science of mind — psychology, and the science of man — anthropology. It may be called the *Anthropological Method*. The theory is that of " survival."

According to this theory many of the puzzling elements of myth resolve themselves into survivals of primitive philosophy, science, or history. From the first proceed the cruder systems of physical and spiritual evolution, the generations of gods and the other-world of ghosts ; from the second, the cruder attempts at explaining the phenomena of the natural and animal world by endowing them with human and frequently magical powers ; from the third, the narratives invented to account for the sanctity of certain shrines and rituals, and for tribal customs and ceremonials, the origin of which had been forgotten. These last are known as *ætiological* myths ; they pretend to assign the *aitía*, or *reason*, why Delphi, for instance, should have the oracle of Apollo, or why the ritual of Demeter should be celebrated at Eleusis and in a certain dramatic manner.

It is of course probable that occasionally the questionable element of the myth originated in germs other than savage curiosity and credulity : for instance, in the adventures of some great hero, or in a disease of language by which statements about objects came to be understood as stories about persons, or perhaps in a conscious

[1] Chr. A. Lobeck, Aglaophamus: On the Causes of Greek Mythology. Cited by Lang,

allegory, or, even, in the perversion of some ancient purer form of moral or religious truth. But, in general, the root of myth-making is to be found in the mental and social condition of primitive man, the confused personality that he extended to his surroundings, and the belief in magical powers that he conferred upon those of his tribesmen who were shrewdest and most influential. This mental condition of the myth-maker should be premised in all scientific explanations of myth-making.

The transition is easy from the personification of the elements of nature and the acceptance of fictitious history to the notion of supernatural beings presiding over, and governing, the different objects of nature — air, fire, water, the sun, moon, and stars, the mountains, forests, and streams — or possessing marvelous qualities of action, passion, virtue, foresight, spirituality, and vice.

The Greeks, whose imagination was lively, peopled all nature with such invisible inhabitants and powers. In Greece, says Wordsworth,[1]

> In that fair clime the lonely herdsman, stretched
> On the soft grass through half a summer's day,
> With music lulled his indolent repose:
> And, in some fit of weariness, if he,
> When his own breath was silent, chanced to hear
> A distant strain, far sweeter than the sounds
> Which his poor skill could make, his fancy fetched,
> Even from the blazing chariot of the sun,
> A beardless Youth, who touched a golden lute,
> And filled the illumined groves with ravishment.
> The nightly hunter, lifting a bright eye
> Up towards the crescent moon, with grateful heart
> Called on the lovely wanderer who bestowed
> That timely light, to share his joyous sport:
> And hence, a beaming Goddess with her Nymphs,
> Across the lawn and through the darksome grove,
> Not unaccompanied with tuneful notes
> By echo multiplied from rock or cave,
> Swept in the storm of chase; as moon and stars
> Glance rapidly along the clouded heaven,
> When winds are blowing strong. The traveler slaked
> His thirst from rill or gushing fount, and thanked

[1] Excursion, Bk. 4.

The Naiad. Sunbeams, upon distant hills
Gliding apace, with shadows in their train,
Might, with small help from fancy, be transformed
Into fleet Oreads sporting visibly.
The Zephyrs, fanning, as they passed, their wings,
Lacked not, for love, fair objects whom they wooed
With gentle whisper. Withered boughs grotesque,
Stripped of their leaves and twigs by hoary age,
From depth of shaggy covert peeping forth
In the low vale, or on steep mountain side;
And, sometimes, intermixed with stirring horns
Of the live deer, or goat's depending beard, —
These were the lurking Satyrs, a wild brood
Of gamesome deities; or Pan himself,
The simple shepherd's awe-inspiring God.

The phases of significance and beauty through which the physical or natural myth may develop are expressed with poetic grace
by Ruskin, in his " Queen of the Air."[1] The reader must, however,
guard against the supposition that any myth has sprung into existence fully equipped with physical, religious, and moral import.
Ruskin himself says, " To the mean person the myth always meant
little; to the noble person, much." Accordingly, as we know, to
the savage the myth was savage; to the devotee it became religious; to the artist, beautiful; to the philosopher, recondite and
significant — in the course of centuries.

" If we seek," says Ruskin, " to ascertain the manner in which
the story first crystallized into its shape, we shall find ourselves
led back generally to one or other of two sources — either to actual
historical events, represented by the fancy under figures personify-
ing them, or else to natural phenomena similarly endowed with life
by the imaginative power, usually more or less under the influence
of terror. The historical myths we must leave the masters of
history to follow; they, and the events they record, being yet involved in great, though attractive and penetrable, mystery. But
the stars and hills and storms are with us now, as they were with
others of old; and it only needs that we look at them with the

---

[1] Concerning which may be accepted the verdict that Mr. Ruskin passes upon Payne
Knight's Symbolical Language of Ancient Art, " Not trustworthy, being little more than a
mass of conjectural memoranda; but the heap is suggestive, if well sifted."

earnestness of those childish eyes to understand the first words spoken of them by the children of men. And then, in all the most beautiful and enduring myths, we shall find not only a literal story of a real person — not only a parallel imagery of moral principle — but an underlying worship of natural phenomena, out of which both have sprung, and in which both forever remain rooted. Thus, from the real sun, rising and setting; from the real atmosphere, calm in its dominion of unfading blue and fierce in its descent of tempest — the Greek forms first the idea of two entirely personal and corporeal gods (Apollo and Athena), whose limbs are clothed in divine flesh, and whose brows are crowned with divine beauty; yet so real that the quiver rattles at their shoulder, and the chariot bends beneath their weight. And, on the other hand, collaterally with these corporeal images, and never for one instant separated from them, he conceives also two omnipresent spiritual influences, of which one illuminates, as the sun, with a constant fire, whatever in humanity is skillful and wise; and the other, like the living air, breathes the calm of heavenly fortitude and strength of righteous anger into every human breast that is pure and brave.

" Now, therefore, in nearly every [natural] myth of importance, . . . you have to discern these three structural parts — the root and the two branches. The root, in physical existence, sun, or sky, or cloud, or sea; then the personal incarnation of that, becoming a trusted and companionable deity, with whom you may walk hand in hand, as a child with its brother or its sister; and lastly, the moral significance of the image, which is in all the great myths eternally and beneficently true."

What Ruskin calls, above, the historical myth may be the euhemeristic transformation of real events and personages, as of a flood and those concerned in it; or it may be the ætiological invention of a story to account for rituals of which the origin has been forgotten, as of the Dionysiac revels, with their teaching of liberation from the sordid limits of mortality. In either case, especially the latter, the imaginative and moral significance of the historical myth has in general developed with the advance of civilization.

Myth, in fine, whether natural, historical, or spiritual, " is not to be regarded as mere error and folly, but as an interesting product of the human mind. It is sham history, the fictitious narrative of events that never happened." [1] But that is not the full statement of the case. Myth is also actual history of early and imperfect stages of thought and belief; it is the true narrative of unenlightened observation, of infantine gropings after truth. Whatever reservations scholars may make on other points, most of them will concur in these: that some myths came into existence by a "disease of language"; that some were invented to explain names of nations and of places, and some to explain the existence of fossils and bones that suggested prehistoric animals and men; that many were invented to gratify the ancestral pride of chieftains and clans and to justify the existence of religious and tribal ceremonials, and the common cult of departed souls, and that very many obtained consistency and form as explanations of the phenomena of nature, as expressions of the reverence felt for the powers of nature, and as personifications, in general, of the passions and the ideals of primitive mankind.[2]

[1] E. B. Tylor, Anthropology, p. 387. New York, 1881.

[2] See also L. Preller, Griechische Mythologie, 1, 19. Max Müller, Comparative Mythology, Oxford Essays, 1856, pp. 1–87; also Science of Religion, 1873, pp. 335–403; Philosophy of Mythology; and Science of Language, 7th ed., 2, 421–571. Hermann Paul, Grundriss der Germanischen Philologie, Bd. 1, Lfg. 5, 982–995, Mythologie (von E. Mogk). W. Y. Sellar, Augustan Poets. Louis Dyer, Studies of the Gods in Greece. Talfourd Ely, Olympus. A. H. Petiscus, The Gods of Olympus (translated by Katherine A. Raleigh). E. Rohde, Psyche. B. I. Wheeler, Dionysos and Immortality.

CHAPTER XXXI

THE DISTRIBUTION OF MYTHS

296. Theories of Resemblance. Several theories of the appearance of the same explanatory or æsthetic myth under various guises, in lands remote one from another, have been advanced; but none of them fully unveils the mystery. The difficulty lies not so much in accounting for the similarity of thought or material in different stories, as for the resemblance in isolated incidents and in the arrangement of incidents or plot. The principal theories of the distribution of myths are as follows:

(1) That the resemblances between the myths of different nations are purely *accidental*. This theory leaves us no wiser than we were.

(2) That the stories have been *borrowed* by one nation from another. This will account for exchange only between nations historically acquainted with each other. It will not account for the existence of the same arrangement of incidents in a Greek myth and in a Polynesian romance.

(3) That all myths, if traced chronologically backward and geographically from land to land, will be found *to have originated in India*.[1] This theory fails to account for numerous stories current among the modern nationalities of Europe, of Africa, and of India itself. It leaves also unexplained the existence of certain myths in Egypt many centuries before India had any known history: such as, in all probability, the Egyptian myth of Osiris. The theory, therefore, is open to the objection made to the theory of borrowing.

(4) That similar myths are based upon *historical traditions* similar in various countries or inherited from some mother country. But, although some historical myths may have descended from a mother race, it has already been demonstrated (§ 294, (1)) that

---

[1] Benfey and Cosquin. See Lang's Myth, Ritual, and Religion, 2, 299.

the historical (euhemeristic) hypothesis is inadequate. It is, moreover, not likely that many historical incidents, like those related in the Iliad and the Odyssey, happened in the same order and as actual history in Asia Minor, Ithaca, Persia, and Norway. But we find myths containing such incidents in all these countries.[1]

(5) That the Aryan tribes (from which the Indians, Persians, Phrygians, Greeks, Romans, Germans, Norsemen, Russians, and Celts are descended) "started from a common center" in the highlands of Northern India, "and that from their ancient home they must have carried away, if not the developed myth, yet the quickening germ from which might spring leaves and fruits, varying in form and hue according to the soil to which it should be committed and the climate under which the plant might reach maturity."[2] Against this theory it may be urged that stories having only the undeveloped germ or idea in common would not, with any probability, after they had been developed independently of each other, possess the remarkable resemblance in details that many widely separated myths display. Moreover, the assumption of this common stock considers only Aryan tribes : it ignores Africans, Mongolians, American Indians, and other peoples whose myths resemble the Aryan, but are not traceable to the same original germ. The *Aryan germ-theory* has, however, the merit of explaining resemblances between many myths of different Aryan nations.

(6) That the existence of similar incidents or situations is to be explained as resulting from the common facts of human thought, experience, and sentiment. This may be called the *psychological theory*. It was entertained by Grimm, and goes hand in hand with the anthropological, or "survivalist," explanation of the elements of myth. "In the long history of mankind," says Mr. Andrew Lang, "it is impossible to deny that stories may conceivably have spread from a single center, and been handed on from races like the Indo-European and Semitic to races as far removed from them in every way as the Zulus, the Australians,

---

[1] Lang, Myth, Ritual, and Religion, 2, 300 ; Cox, Mythology of the Aryan Nations, 1, 100.

[2] The Rev. Sir G. W. Cox, Mythology of Aryan Nations, 1, 99 ; also, same theory, Max Müller's Chips from a German Workshop ; Andrew Lang, Myth, Ritual, and Religion, 2, 297.

the Eskimos, the natives of the South Sea Islands. But while the possibility of the diffusion of myths by borrowing and transmission must be allowed for, the hypothesis of the origin of myths in the savage state of the intellect supplies a ready explanation of their wide diffusion." Many products of early art — clay bowls and stone weapons — are peculiar to no one national taste or skill, they are what might have been expected of *human* conditions and intelligence. " Many myths may be called ' human ' in this sense. They are the rough product of the early human mind, and are not yet characterized by the differentiations of race and culture. Such myths might spring up anywhere among untutored men, and anywhere might survive into civilized literature." [1]

The distribution of myth, like its origin, is inexplicable by any one theory. The discovery of racial families and of family traditions narrows the problem, but does not solve it. The existence of the same story in unrelated nationalities remains a perplexing fact, towards the explanation of which the theories of " borrowing " and of " similar historic tradition," while plausible, are but unsubstantiated contributions. And until we possess the earliest records of those unrelated nationalities that have similar myths, or until we discover monuments and log books of some commercial nation that in prehistoric times circumnavigated the globe and deposited on remote shores and islands the seeds of the parent mythic plant, we must accept as our only scientific explanation the psychological, or so-called *human*, theory : — Given similar mental condition with similar surroundings, similar imaginative products, called myths, will result.[2]

[1] Encyc. Brit., 9th ed. Article, *Mythology.* Cf. Tylor's Primitive Culture, 1, 369 ; Tylor's Anthropology, p. 397.
[2] See T. C. Johnston's Did the Phœnicians Discover America ? 1892.

CHAPTER XXXII

THE PRESERVATION OF MYTHS

297. Traditional History. Before the introduction of writing, myths were preserved in popular traditions, in the sacred ceremonials of colleges of priests, in the narratives chanted by families of minstrels or by professional bards wandering from village to village or from court to court, and in occasional hymns sung by privileged harpists, like Demodocus of Phæacia,[1] in honor of a chieftain, an ancestor, or a god. Many of these early bards are mere names to us. Most of them are probably as mythical as the songs with which they are accredited. The following is a brief account of mythical prophets, of mythical musicians and poets, and of the actual poets and historians who recorded the mythologies from which English literature draws its classical myths, — the Greek, the Roman, the Norse, and the German.

298. In Greece. (1) *Mythical Prophets.* To some of the oldest bards was attributed the gift of prophecy. Indeed, nearly every expedition of mythology was accompanied by one of these seers, priests, or " medicine men," as we might call them.

Melampus was the first Greek said to be endowed with prophetic powers. Before his house there stood an oak tree containing a serpent's nest. The old serpents were killed by the slaves, but Melampus saved the young ones. One day when he was asleep under the oak, the serpents licked his ears with their tongues, enabling him to understand the language of birds and creeping things.[2] At one time his enemies seized and imprisoned him. But Melampus, in the silence of the night, heard from the woodworms in the timbers that the supports of the house were nearly eaten through and the roof would soon fall in. He told his captors. They took his warning, escaped destruction, rewarded the prophet, and held him in high honor.

---

[1] Odyssey 8, 250.   [2] Cf. the experience of Sigurd.

Other famous soothsayers were Amphiaraüs, who took part in the War of the Seven against Thebes; Calchas, who accompanied the Greeks during the Trojan War; Helenus and Cassandra, of King Priam's family, who prophesied for the Trojan forces; Tiresias, the blind prophet of Thebes; and Mopsus, who attended the Argonauts. The stories of these expeditions are given in preceding chapters.

(2) *Mythical Musicians and Poets.* Since the poets of antiquity sang their stories oɪ hymns to an accompaniment of their own upon the harp or lyre, they were skilled in the art of music as well as in that of verse.

Orpheus, whose adventures have been narrated, passes in tradition for the oldest of Greek lyrists, and the special favorite, even the son, of the god Apollo, patron of musicians. This Thracian bard is said to have taught mysterious truths concerning the origin of things and the immortality of the soul. But the fragments of Orphic hymns which are attributed to him are probably the work of philosophers of a much later period in Greek literature.

Another Thracian bard, *Thamyris*, is said in his presumption to have challenged the Muses to a trial of skill. Conquered in the contest, he was deprived of his sight. To *Musæus*, the son of Orpheus, was attributed a hymn on the Eleusinian mysteries, and other sacred poems and oracles. Milton couples his name with that of Orpheus:

> But, O sad Virgin! that thy power
> Might raise Musæus from his bower,
> Or bid the soul of Orpheus sing
> Such notes as, warbled to the string,
> Drew iron tears down Pluto's cheek,
> And made Hell grant what love did seek.[1]

Other legendary bards or musicians were Linus, Marsyas, and Amphion.

(3) *The Poets of Mythology. Homer,* from whose poems of the Iliad and Odyssey we have taken the chief part of our chapters on the Trojan War and the return of the Grecians, is almost as mythical a personage as the heroes he celebrates. The traditionary story is that he was a wandering minstrel, blind and old, who traveled

---

[1] Il Penseroso, ll. 103-108.

from place to place singing his lays to the music of his harp, in the courts of princes or the cottages of peasants, — a dependent upon the voluntary offerings of his hearers. Byron calls him "the blind old man of Scio's rocky isle"; and a well-known epigram, alluding to the uncertainty of the fact of his birthplace, runs:

> Seven wealthy towns contend for Homer dead,
> Through which the living Homer begged his bread.

These seven places were Smyrna, Chios (now Scio), Colophon, Ithaca, Pylos, Argos, and Athens.

Modern scholars have doubted whether the Homeric poems are the work of any single mind. This uncertainty arises, in part, from the difficulty of believing that poems of such length could have been committed to writing in the age usually assigned to these, when materials capable of transmitting long productions were not yet in use. On the other hand, it is asked how poems of such length could have been handed down from age to age by means of the memory alone. This question is answered by the statement that there was a professional body of men whose business it was to commit to memory and rehearse for pay the national and patriotic legends.

Pisistratus of Athens ordered a commission of scholars (about 537 B.C.) to collect and revise the Homeric poems; and it is probable that at that time certain passages of the Iliad and Odyssey, as we now have them, were interpolated. Beside the Iliad and the Odyssey, many other epics passed in antiquity under Homer's name. The so-called Homeric Hymns to the gods, which were composed by various poets after the death of Homer, are a source of valuable information concerning the attributes of the divinities addressed.

The date assigned to Homer, on the authority of Herodotus, is 850 B.C. The preservation and further fashioning of myths fell, after Homer's time, into the hands of the Rhapsodists, who chanted epic songs, and of the Cyclic poets, who elaborated into various epic *circles*, or completed wholes, neglected traditions of the Trojan War. Among these cyclic poems were the Cyprian Lays, which related the beginnings of the Trojan War and the first nine years of the siege, thus leading up to the Iliad ; the Æthiopis, which continued the Iliad and told of the death of Achilles; the Little Iliad and the Iliupersis, which narrated the fall of Troy and magnified the exploits of Ajax and Philoctetes; and the Nostoi, or Home-Comings, which told the adventures of various Greek heroes during the period of ten years between the end of the Iliad and the beginning of the Odyssey. Most of these poems were once attributed to Homer. They are all lost, but the names of some of their authors survive. There was also a cycle which told of the two wars against Thebes.

Hesiod is, like Homer, one of the most important sources of our knowledge of Greek mythology. He is thought by some to have been a contemporary of Homer, but concerning the relative dates of the two poets there is no certainty. Hesiod was born in Ascra in Bœotia ; he spent his youth as a shepherd on Mount Helicon, his manhood in the neighborhood of Corinth, and wrote two great poems, the Works and Days, and the Theogony, or Genealogy of the Gods. From the former we obtain a connected account of Greek traditions concerning the primitive commodities of life, the arts of agriculture and navigation, the sacred calendar, and the various pre-historic ages. From the latter poem we learn the Greek mythology of the creation of the world, the family of the gods, their wars, and their attitude toward primeval man. While Hesiod may have composed his works at a somewhat later period than Homer, it is noteworthy that his stories of the gods have more of the savage or senseless element than those attributed to Homer. The artist, or artists, of the Iliad and the Odyssey seem to have refined the stories into poetic gold; Hesiod has gathered them in the ore, like so many specimens for a museum.

A company of *Lyric Poets*, of whom Stesichorus (620 B.C.), Alcæus (611 B.C.), Sappho (610 B.C.), Arion (600 B.C.), Simonides of Ceos (556 B.C.), Ibycus (540 B.C.), Anacreon (530 B.C.), and Pindar (522 B.C.) are the most prominent, have contributed much to our knowledge of mythology. They have left us hymns to the gods, references to mythical heroes, and accounts of more or less pathetic legendary adventures.

Of the works of *Sappho* few fragments remain, but they estab-lish her claim to eminent poetical genius. Her story is frequently alluded to. Being passionately in love with a beautiful youth named Phaon, and failing to obtain a return of affection, she is said to have thrown herself from the promontory of Leucadia into the sea, under a superstition that those who should take that " Lover's Leap " would, if not destroyed, be cured of their love.

Of *Arion* the greatest work was a dithyramb or choral hymn to the god of wine. It is said that his music and song were of such sweetness as to charm the monsters of the sea; and that when thrown overboard on one occasion by avaricious seamen, he was borne safely to land by an admiring dolphin. Spenser represents Arion, mounted on his dolphin, accompanying the train of Neptune and Amphitrite:

> Then was there heard a most celestial sound
> Of dainty music, which did next ensue
> Before the spouse: that was Arion crowned
> Who, playing on his harp, unto him drew
> The ears and hearts of all that goodly crew;
> That even yet the dolphin which him bore
> Through the Ægean seas from pirates' view,
> Stood still by him astonished at his lore,
> And all the raging seas for joy forgot to roar.[1]

Simonides was one of the most prolific of the early poets of Greece, but only a few fragments of his compositions have descended to us. He wrote hymns, triumphal odes, and elegies, and in the last species of composition he particularly excelled. His genius was inclined to the pathetic; none could touch with truer effect the chords of human sympathy. The Lamentation of Danaë, the most important of the fragments which remain of his poetry, is based upon the tradition that Danaë and her infant son were confined by order of her father Acrisius in a chest and set adrift on the sea. The myth of her son, Perseus, has already been narrated.

Myths received their freest and perhaps most ideal treatment at the hands of the greatest lyric poet of Greece, *Pindar* (522 B.C.). In his hymns and songs of praise to gods and in his odes composed

---

[1] *Faerie Queene*, 4, 11, 23.

for the victors in the national athletic contests, he was accustomed to use the mythical exploits of Greek heroes as a text from which to draw morals appropriate to the occasion.[1]

The three great *Tragic Poets* of Greece have handed down to us a wealth of mythological material. From the plays of *Æschylus* (525 B.C.) we gather, among other noble lessons, the fortunes of the family of Agamemnon, the narrative of the expedition against Thebes, the sufferings of Prometheus, benefactor of men. In the tragedies of *Sophocles* (495 B.C.) we have a further account of the family of Agamemnon, myths of Œdipus of Thebes and his children, stories connected with the Trojan War, and the last adventure and the death of Hercules. Of the dramas of *Euripides* (480 B.C.) there remain to us seventeen, in which are found stories of the daughters of Agamemnon, the rare and beautiful narrative of Alcestis, and the adventures of Medea. All of these stories have been recounted in their proper places.

The *Comedies of Aristophanes*, also, are replete with matters of mythological import.

Of the later poets of mythology, only two need be mentioned here, — *Apollonius* of Rhodes (194 B.C.), who wrote in frigid style the story of Jason's Voyage for the Golden Fleece; and *Theocritus* of Sicily (270 B.C.), whose rural idyls are at once charmingly natural and romantic.[2]

(4) *Historians of Mythology.* The earliest narrators in prose of the myths, legends and genealogies of Greece lived about 600 B.C. Herodotus, the "father of history" (484 B.C.), embalms various myths in his account of the conflicts between Asia and Greece. Apollodorus (140 B.C.) gathers the legends of Greece later incorporated in the Library of Greek Mythology. That delightful traveler, Pausanias, makes special mention, in his Tour of Greece, of the sacred customs and legends that had maintained themselves as late as his time (160 A.D). Lucian, in his Dialogues of the Gods and Dialogues of the Dead, awakens "inextinguishable laughter" by his satire on ancient faith and fable.

---

[1] See E. B. Clapp, Greek Morality and Religion as Set forth by Pindar (*Hibbert Journal*, 8, 283).

[2] For other authorities and for a few standard translations of the Greek Classics, see Commentary, § 298.

299. Roman Poets of Mythology. *Virgil*, called also by his surname, Maro, from whose poem of the Æneid we have taken the story of Æneas, was one of the great poets who made the age of the Roman emperor, Augustus, celebrated. Virgil was born in Mantua in the year 70 B.C. His great poem is ranked next to those of Homer, in that noble class of poetical composition, the epic. Virgil is inferior to Homer in originality and invention. The Æneid, written in an age of culture and science, lacks that charming atmosphere of belief which invests the naïve, or *popular*, epic. The myths concerning the founding of Rome, which Virgil has received from earlier writers, he has here fused into a *literary* epic. But what the Æneid lacks of epic simplicity, it makes up in patriotic spirit, in lofty moral and civic ideals, in correctness of taste, and in stylistic form.

Ovid, often alluded to in poetry by his other name, Naso, was born in the year 43 B.C. He was educated for public life and held some offices of considerable dignity; but poetry was his delight, and he early resolved to cultivate it. He accordingly sought the society of contemporary poets and was acquainted with Horace and saw Virgil, though the latter died when Ovid was yet too young and undistinguished to have formed his acquaintance. Ovid spent an easy life at Rome in the enjoyment of a competent income. He was intimate with the family of Augustus, the emperor; and it is supposed that some serious offense given to a member of that family was the cause of an event which reversed the poet's happy circumstances and clouded the latter portion of his life. At the age of fifty he was banished from Rome and ordered to betake himself to Tomi on the borders of the Black Sea. His only consolation in exile was to address his wife and absent friends. His letters were all in verse. They are called the "Tristia," or Sorrows, and Letters from Pontus. The two great works of Ovid are his "Metamorphoses" or Transformations, and his "Fasti," or Poetic Calendar. They are both mythological poems, and from the former we have taken many of our stories of Grecian and Roman mythology. These poems have thus been characterized :

"The rich mythology of Greece furnished Ovid, as it may still furnish the poet, the painter, and the sculptor, with materials for his art. With exquisite taste, simplicity, and pathos he has narrated the fabulous traditions of early ages, and given to them that appearance of reality which only a master hand could impart. His pictures of nature are striking and true; he selects with care that which is appropriate; he rejects the superfluous, and when he has completed his work, it is neither defective nor redundant. The 'Metamorphoses' are read with pleasure by the young and old of every civilized land."

In an incidental manner, *Horace*, the prince of Roman lyric poets, and the lyric and elegiac writers, *Catullus*, *Tibullus*, and *Propertius*, have liberally increased our knowledge of Greek and Roman myth.[1]

Seneca, the teacher of Nero, is best known for his philosophical treatises; but he wrote, also, tragedies, the materials of which are well-known Greek legends. *Apuleius*, born in Africa, 114 A.D., interests us as the compiler of a clever romance, The Golden Ass;[2] the most pleasing episode of which, the story of Cupid and Psyche, has been elsewhere related.[3]

300. Records of Norse Mythology.[4] A system of mythology of especial interest, — as belonging to the race from which we, through our English ancestors, derive our origin, — is that of the Norsemen, who inhabited the countries now known as Sweden, Denmark, Norway, and Iceland. Their mythological lore has been transmitted by means of Runes, Skaldic poems, the Eddas, and the Sagas.

The Runes. The earliest method of writing prevalent among the Norsemen was by runes. The word means *hidden lore*, or *mystery*. The earliest runes were merely fanciful signs supposed to possess mysterious power. As a synonym for *writing*, the term was first applied to the Northern alphabet, itself derived from ancient Greek and Roman coins. Of the old Scandinavian runes several specimens have been found — one an inscription on a golden horn of the third or fourth century A.D., which was dug

---

[1] With regard to translations of these and other Latin poets, see Commentary, § 299.
[2] Based upon Lucian's Lucius or the Ass, and other Greek stories.
[3] Translation in Walter Pater's Marius the Epicurean.
[4] For literature, see Commentary.

up in Schleswig a hundred and sixty years ago; another, on a stone at Tune in Norway. From such an alphabet the Anglo-Saxon runes were derived. Inscriptions in later Scandinavian runes have been discovered in Sweden, Denmark, and the Isle of Man. The characters are of the stiff and angular form necessitated by the materials on which they were inscribed,—tombstones, spoons, chairs, oars, and so forth.[1] It is doubtful whether mythological poems were ever written in this way; dedications to pagan deities, ditties of the eleventh century, and love-spells have, however, been found.

The Skaldic Poems. The bards and poets of the Norsemen were the Skalds. They were the depositaries of whatever historic lore there was; and it was their office to mingle something of intellectual gratification with the rude feasts of the warriors, by rehearsing, with such accompaniments of poetry and music as their skill could afford, the exploits of heroes living or dead. Such songs were called Drapas. The origin of Skaldic poetry is lost in mythic or prehistoric darkness, but the Skalds of Iceland continued to play a most important part in the literary development of the north as late as the end of the fourteenth century. Without their coöperation, the greater part of the songs and sagas of genuine antiquity could hardly have reached us. The Skaldic diction, which was polished to an artistic extreme, with its pagan metaphors and similes retained its supremacy over literary form even after the influence of Christianity had revolutionized national thought.[2]

The Eddas. The chief mythological records of the Norse are the Eddas and the Sagas. The word *Edda* has usually been connected with the Icelandic for *great-grandmother;*[3] it has also been regarded as a corruption of the High German *Erda*, Mother Earth, from whom, according to the lay in which the word first occurs, the earliest race of mankind sprang,[4]—or as the *point* or *head* of Norse poetry,[5] or as a tale concerned with *death*,[6] or as derived from Odde, the home of the reputed collector of the

---

[1] Cleasby and Vigfusson's Icelandic-English Dictionary.
[2] F. W. Horn's Geschichte d. Literatur d. Skandinavischen Nordens, 27–42.
[3] Cleasby and Vigfusson's Dictionary; Lüning's Die Edda, 1859.
[4] The Lay of Righ in Snorri's Edda; Vigfusson and Powell's Corpus Poeticum Boreale, 2, 514.   [5] Jacob Grimm.
[6] The Celtic *aideadh:* Professor Rhys, *Academy*, January 31, 1880.

Elder Edda. But, of recent years, scholars have looked with most favor upon a derivation from the Icelandic óðr, which means mind, or poetry.[1] There are two Icelandic collections called Eddas : Snorri's and Saemund's. Until the year 1643 the name was applied to a book, principally in prose, containing Mythical Tales, a Treatise on the Poetic Art and Diction, a Poem on Meters, and a Rhymed Glossary of Synonyms, with an appendix of minor treatises on grammar and rhetoric — the whole intended as a guide for poets. Although a note in the Upsala manuscript, of date about 1300 A.D., asserted that this work was "put together" by Snorri Sturlason, who lived 1178–1241, the world was not informed of the fact until 1609, when Arngrim Johnsson made the announcement in his Constitutional History of Iceland.[2] While the main treatises on the poetic art are, in general, Snorri's, the treatises on grammar and rhetoric have been, with more or less certitude, assigned to other writers of the twelfth and thirteenth centuries. It is probable, too, that in the Mythical Tales, or the Delusion of Gylfi, Snorri merely enlarged and edited with poetical illustrations the work of earlier hands. The poets of the fourteenth and fifteenth centuries do not speak of Snorri, but they refer continually to the "rules of Edda," and frequently to the obscurity and the conventionality of Eddic phraseology, figures, and art. Even at the present day in Iceland it is common to hear the term "void of Eddic art," or "a bungler in Eddic art." A rearrangement of Snorri's Edda, by Magnus Olafsson (1574–1636), is much better known than the original work.

In 1642, Bishop Bryniolf Sveinsson discovered a manuscript of the mythological poems of Iceland. Misled by theories of his own and by a fanciful suggestion of the famous antiquary Biorn of Scardsa, he attributed the composition of these poems to Saemund the Wise, a historian who lived 1056–1133. Henceforth, consequently, Snorri's work is called the Younger, or Prose Edda, in contradistinction to Bryniolf's find, which is known as the Elder, the Poetical Edda, or the Edda of Saemund. The oldest manuscript of the Poetical Edda is of the thirteenth century. Its

[1] Arne Magnusson, see Morley's English Writers, 2, 336, and Murray's New English Dictionary.   [2] Corpus Poeticum Boreale, 1 ; xxvii, etc.

contents were probably collected not later than 1150. The composition of the poems cannot well be placed earlier than the ninth or tenth centuries after Christ; and a consideration of the habits, laws, geography, and vocabulary illustrated by the poems leads eminent scholars to assign the authorship to emigrants of the south Norwegian tribes who, sailing westward, "won Waterford and Limerick, and kinged it in York and East England."[1] The poems are Icelandic, however, in their general character and history. They are principally of heroic and mythical import: such as the stories of Balder's Fate, of Skirnir's Journey, of Thor's Hammer, of Helgi the Hunding's Bane, and the twenty lays that in fragmentary fashion tell the eventful history of the Volsungs and the Nibelungs.[2]

The Sagas. The Eddas contain many myths and mythical features that contradict the national character of both Germans and Norsemen, but the sagas have their roots in Norse civilization and are national property.[3] Of these mythic-heroic prose compositions the most important to us is the Volsunga Saga, which was put together probably in the twelfth century and is based in part upon the poems of the Elder Edda, in part upon floating traditions, and in part upon popular songs that now are lost.[4]

301. Records of German Mythology.[2] The story of the Volsungs and the Nibelungs springs from mythological sources common to the whole Teutonic race. Two distinct versions of the saga survive, — the Low or North German, which we have already noticed in the lays of the Elder Edda and in the Norse Volsunga Saga, and the High or South German, which has been preserved in German folk songs and in the Nibelungenlied, or Lay of the Nibelungs, that has grown out of them. The Norse form of the story exhibits a later survival of the credulous, or myth-making, mental condition. The Lay of the Nibelungs absorbed, at an earlier date, historical elements, and began sooner to restrict the personality of its heroes within the compass of human limitations.[5]

---

[1] Corpus Poeticum Boreale, 1; lxxi; lxiii–lxiv.

[2] For literature, see Commentary.

[3] Paul's Grundriss d. Germanischen Philologie: Bd. 1, Lfg. 5, *Mythologie.*

[4] Morris and Magnusson's The Story of the Volsungs and Nibelungs. Horn's Geschichte d. Literatur d. Skandinavischen Nordens, 27–42, 58, etc.

[5] Werner Hahn, Das Nibelungenlied.

Although there are many manuscripts, or fragments of manuscripts, of the Nibelungenlied that attest its popularity between the thirteenth and sixteenth centuries, it was not until the Swiss critic, J. J. Bodmer, published, in 1757, portions of two ancient poems, " The Revenge of Kriemhild " and " The Lament over the Heroes of Etzel," that the attention of modern scholars was called to this famous German epic. Since that time many theories of the composition of the Nibelungenlied have been advanced. It has been held by some that the German epic is an adaptation of the Norse version;[1] by others, that the Scandinavians, not the Germans, borrowed the story; and by others still, that the epics, while proceeding from a common cradle, are of independent growth. The last theory is the most tenable.[2] Concerning the history of the Nibelungenlied, it has been maintained that since, during the twelfth century, when no poet would adopt any other poet's stanzaic form, the Austrian Von Kürenberg used the stanzaic form of the Nibelungenlied, the epic must be his.[3] It has also been urged that the poem, having been written down about 1140, was altered in metrical form by younger poets, until, in 1200 or thereabouts, it assumed the form preserved in the latest of the three great manuscripts.[4] But the theory advanced by Lachmann is still of great value : that the poem consists of a number of ancient ballads of various age and uneven worth ; and that, about 1210, a collector, mending some of the ballads to suit himself, strung them together on a thread of his own invention.

In fine, the materials of the poem would persuade us not only of its origin in very ancient popular lays, but of their fusion and improvement by the imaginative effort of at least one, and probably of several poets, who lived and wrote between 1120 and 1200 A.D. The metrical structure, also, would indicate derivation from the German folk song and modification due to multifarious handling on the part of popular minstrels and poets of written verse.[5]

[1] The Grimm Brothers; v. d. Hagen; Vilmar.
[2] Werner Hahn; Jas. Sime, Encyc. Brit. *Nibelungenlied.*
[3] Pfeiffer.
[4] Bartsch, see Encyc. Brit.
[5] Werner Hahn, 18, 58-60.

302. Records of Oriental Mythology: Egyptian.[1] Although the myths of Egypt, India, and Persia are of intense interest and importance, they have not materially affected English literature. The following is, however, a brief outline of the means by which some of them have been preserved.

The Egyptian records are (1) *The Hieroglyphs*, or sacred inscriptions in Tombs of the Kings, and other solemn places, — conveying ideas by symbols, by phonetic signs, or by both; (2) *The Sacred Papyri*, containing hymns to the gods; (3) *The Books of the Dead* and of the *Lower Hemisphere*, — devoted to necromantic incantations, prayers for the souls of the departed, and other rituals.

303. Indian Records. (1) *The Vedas*, or Holy Scriptures of the Hindus, which fall into four divisions. The most ancient, the Rig-Veda, consists of hymns of an elevated and spiritual character composed by families of Rishis, or psalmists, as far back, perhaps, as 3000 B.C., not later than 1400 B.C. They give us the religious conceptions of the Aryans when they crossed the Himalayas and began to push toward Southern Hindustan. The Sama-Veda is a book of solemn chants and tunes. The Yajur-Veda comprises prayers for sacrificial occasions, and interpretations of the same. The Atharva-Veda shows, as might be expected of the youngest of the series, the influence upon the purer Aryan creed of superstitions borrowed, perhaps, from the aboriginal tribes of India. It contains spells for exorcising demons and placating them.

(2) *The Indian Epics* of classical standing. They are the Mahábhárata and the Rámáyana. Scholars differ as to the chronological precedence. The Great Feud of the Bháratas has the air of superior antiquity because of the numerous hands and generations that have contributed to its composition. The Adventures of Ráma, on the other hand, recalls a more primitive stage of credulity and of savage invention. The Mahábhárata is a storehouse of mythical tradition. It contains several well-rounded epic poems, the most beautiful of which is the Episode of Nala, — a prince who, succumbing to a weakness common to

[1] For translations of Oriental Myths, see Commentary. For mythical personages, see Index and Dictionary.

his contemporaries, has gambled away his kingdom. The Great Feud of the Bhâratas is, indeed, assigned to an author — but his name, Vyâsa, means simply the Arranger. The Râmâyana purports to have been written by the poet Vâlmîki. It tells how Sita, the wife of Prince Râma, is carried off to Ceylon by Râvana, king of the demons, and how Râma, by the aid of an army of monkeys, bridges the straits between India and Ceylon and, slaying the demon, recovers his lovely and innocent wife. The resemblance between the plot and that of the Iliad has inclined some scholars to derive the Indian from the Greek epic. But, until the relative antiquity of the poems is established, the Iliad might as well be derived from the Râmâyana. The theory is unsubstantiated. These epics of India lack the artistic spirit and grace of the Iliad and the Odyssey, but they display a keener sympathy with nature and a more romantic appreciation of the loves and sorrows of mankind.

304. Persian Records. *The Avesta*, or Sacred Book of the ancient Persians, composed in the Zend language and later translated into medieval Persian, — or Pahlavi, — contains the Gáthás, or hymns of Zoroaster and his contemporaries, and scriptures of as recent a date as the fifth century B.C. Zoroaster, a holy man of God, was the founder or the reformer of the Persian religion. He lived as early as the fourteenth or fifteenth century B.C., and his system became the dominant religion of Western Asia from the time of Cyrus (550 B.C.) to the conquest of Persia by Alexander the Great. The teachings of Zoroaster are characterized by beautiful simplicity, and by an unwavering faith in the ultimate victory of righteousness (Ormuzd) over evil (Ahriman).

COMMENTARY[1]

3. Chaos: a gap. Compare the " Beginning Gap " of Norse mythology. **Eros:** a yearning. **Erebus:** black, from root meaning *to cover.*

4. Uranus (Greek *Ouranos*) corresponds with the name of the Indian divinity Varunas, root *var,* ' to cover.' Uranus is the starry vault that covers the earth; Varunas became the rain-giving sky. **Titan:** the honorable, powerful; the king; later, the signification was limited to the sun. **Oceanus** probably means *flood.* **Tethys:** the nourisher, nurse. **Hyperion:** the wanderer on high;[2] the sun. **Thea:** the beautiful, shining; the moon. She is called by Homer Euryphaëssa, the far-shining. **Iapetus:** the sender, hurler, wounder. **Themis:** that which is established, law. **Mnemosyne:** memory. Other Titans were Cœus and Phœbe, figurative of the radiant lights of heaven; Creüs and Eurybië, mighty powers, probably of the sea; Ophion, the great serpent, and Eurynome, the far-ruling, who, according to Apollonius of Rhodes, held sway over the Titans until Cronus cast them into the Ocean, or into Tartarus.

Cronus (Greek *Kronos*) is, as his name shows, the god of ripening, harvest, maturity. **Rhea** comes from Asia Minor, and was there worshiped as the Mother Earth, dwelling creative among the mountains. Cronus (*Kronos*) has been naturally, but wrongly, identified with Chronos, the personification of *Time,* which, as it brings all things to an end, devours its own offspring; and also with the Latin Saturn, who, as a god of agriculture and harvest, was represented with pruning-knife in hand, and regarded as the lord of an ancient golden age.

The three **Cyclopes** were Brontes, Steropes, and Arges. Cyclops means the round-eyed. The **Hecatonchires** were Briareus, the strong, called also Ægæon; Cottus, the striker; Gyes, or Gyges, the vaulter, or crippler. Gyges is called by Horace (Carm. 2, 17, 14) Centimanus, — the hundred-handed.

Illustrative. Milton, in Paradise Lost, 10, 581, refers to the tradition of Ophion and Eurynome, who " had first the rule of high Olympus, thence by Saturn driven." **Hyperion:** see Shakespeare's Hamlet, " Hyperion's curls, the front of Jove

---

[1] For assistance in collecting references to English poetry the author is indebted to Miss M. B. Clayes, a graduate of the University of California.

[2] Popular etymology. The suffix *ion* is patronymic.

himself." Also Henry V, IV, i; Troilus and Cressida, II, iii; Titus Andronicus, V, iii; Gray, Progress of Poesy, "Hyperion's march they spy, and glittering shafts of war"; Spenser, Prothalamion, "Hot Titans beames." On **Oceanus,** Ben Jonson, Neptune's Triumph. On **Saturn,** see Shakespeare, Much Ado About Nothing, I, iii; 2 Henry IV, II, iv; Cymbeline, II, v; Titus Andronicus, II, iii; IV, iii; Milton, Paradise Lost, I. 512, 519, 583, and Il Penseroso, 24. See Robert Buchanan, Cloudland, "One like a Titan cold," etc.; Keats, Hyperion; B. W. Procter, The Fall of Saturn.

In Art. Helios (Hyperion) rising from the sea: sculpture of eastern pediment of the frieze of the Parthenon (British Museum). Mnemosyne: D. G. Rossetti (crayons and oil).

5. Homer makes Zeus (Jupiter) the oldest of the sons of Cronus; Hesiod makes him the youngest, in accordance with a widespread savage custom which makes the youngest child heir in chief. — LANG, Myth, Ritual, etc., I, 297. According to other legends Zeus was born in Arcadia, or even in Epirus at Dodona, where was his sacred grove. He was in either case reared by the nymphs of the locality. According to Hesiod, Theog. 730, he was born in a cave of Mount Dicte, in Crete.

6. Atlas, according to other accounts, was not doomed to support the heavens until after his encounter with Perseus.

8. See Milton's Hymn on the Nativity, "Not **Typhon** huge ending in snaky twine." The monster is also called Typhöeus (Hesiod, Theog. 1137). The name means *to smoke, to burn.* The monster personifies fiery vapors proceeding from subterranean places. Other famous **Giants** were Mimas, Polybotes, Ephialtes, Rhœtus, Clytius. See Preller, I, 60. Briareus (really a Centimanus) is frequently ranked among the giants.

Illustrative. Shakespeare, Troilus and Cressida, I, ii; Milton, Paradise Lost, 1, 199, and Hymn on the Nativity, 226; M. Arnold, Empedocles, Act 2; Pope, Dunciad, 4, 66. For giants, in general, see Milton, Paradise Lost, 3, 464; 11. 642, 688; Samson Agonistes, 148.

10–15. Prometheus: forethought.[1] **Epimetheus:** afterthought. According to Æschylus (Prometheus Bound) the doom of Zeus (Jupiter) was only contingent. If he should refuse to set Prometheus free and should, therefore, ignorant of the secret, wed Thetis, of whom it was known to Prometheus that her son should be greater than his father, then Zeus would be dethroned. If, however, Zeus himself delivered Prometheus, that Titan would reveal his secret and Zeus would escape both the marriage and its fateful result. The Prometheus Unbound of Æschylus is lost; but its name indicates that in the sequel the Titan is freed from his chains. And from hints in the Prometheus Bound we gather that this liberation was to come about in the way mentioned above, Prometheus warning Zeus to marry Thetis to Peleus (whose son, Achilles, proved greater than his father, — see 191); or by the intervention of Hercules who was to be descended in the thirteenth generation from Zeus and Io (see 161 and C. 149); or by the voluntary sacrifice of the Centaur Chiron, who, when Zeus should hurl Prometheus and his rock into Hades, was destined to substitute himself

[1] Popular etymology. The root of the name indicates *Fire-god.*

for the Titan, and so by vicarious atonement to restore him to the life of the upper world. In Shelley's great drama of Prometheus Unbound, the Zeus of tyranny and ignorance and superstition is overthrown by Reason, the gift of Prometheus to mankind. **Sicyon** (or Mecone): a city of the Peloponnesus, near Corinth.

Illustrative. Milton, Paradise Lost, " More lovely than **Pandora** whom the gods endowed with all their gifts." Shakespeare, Titus Andronicus, II, i, 16.

Poems. D. G. Rossetti, Pandora; Longfellow, Masque of Pandora, Prometheus, and Epimetheus; Thos. Parnell, Hesiod, or the Rise of Woman. **Prometheus,** by Byron, Lowell, H. Coleridge, Robert Bridges; Prometheus Bound, by Mrs. Browning; translations of Æschylus, Prometheus Bound, Augusta Webster, E. H. Plumptre; Shelley, Prometheus Unbound; R. H. Horne, Prometheus, the Fire-bringer; E. Myers, The Judgment of Prometheus; George Cabot Lodge, Herakles, a drama. See Byron's Ode to Napoleon Buonaparte. **The Golden Age:** Chaucer, The Former Age (*Ætas Prima*); Milton, Hymn on the Nativity.

In Art. Ancient: Prometheus Unbound, vase picture (Monuments Inédits, Rome and Paris). Modern: Thorwaldsen's sculpture, Minerva and Prometheus. Pandora: Sichel (oil), Rossetti (crayons and oil), F. S. Church (water colors).

16. Dante (*Durante*) **degli Alighieri** was born in Florence, 1265. Banished by his political opponents, 1302, he remained in exile until his death, which took place in Ravenna, 1321. His Vita Nuova (New Life), recounting his ideal love for Beatrice Portinari, was written between 1290 and 1300; his great poem, the Divina Commedia (the Divine Comedy) consisting of three parts, — Inferno, Purgatorio, Paradiso, — during the years of his exile. Of the Divine Comedy, says Lowell, " It is the real history of a brother man, of a tempted, purified, and at last triumphant human soul." **John Milton** (b. 1608) was carried by the stress of the civil war, 1641–1649, away from poetry, music, and the art which he had sedulously cultivated, into the stormy sea of politics and war. Perhaps the severity of his later sonnets and the sublimity of his Paradise Lost, Paradise Regained, and Samson Agonistes are the fruit of the stern years of controversy through which he lived, not as a poet, but as a statesman and a pamphleteer. **Cervantes** (1547–1616), the author of the greatest of Spanish romances, Don Quixote. His life was full of adventure, privation, suffering, with but brief seasons of happiness and renown. He distinguished himself at the battle of Lepanto, 1571; but in 1575, being captured by Algerine cruisers, he remained five years in harsh captivity. After his return to Spain he was neglected by those in power. For full twenty years he struggled for his daily bread. Don Quixote was published in and after 1605. **Corybantes:** the priests of Cybele, whose festivals were violent, and whose worship consisted of dances and noise suggestive of battle.

18. Astræa was placed among the stars as the constellation Virgo, the virgin. Her mother was Themis (Justice). Astræa holds aloft a pair of scales, in which she weighs the conflicting claims of parties. The old poets prophesied a return of these goddesses and of the Golden Age. See also Pope's Messiah, —

> All crimes shall cease, and ancient fraud shall fail,
> Returning Justice lift aloft her scale;

and Milton's Hymn on the Nativity, 14, 15. In Paradise Lost, 4, 998 *et seq.*, is a different conception of the golden scales, " betwixt Astræa and the Scorpion sign." Emerson moralizes the myth in his Astræa.

19–20. *Illustrative.* B. W. Procter, The Flood of Thessaly. See Ovid's famous narrative of the Four Ages and the Flood, Metamorphoses, 1, 89–415. **Deucalion:** Bayard Taylor, Prince Deukalion; Milton, Paradise Lost, 11, 12.

Interpretative. This myth combines two stories of the origin of the Hellenes, or indigenous Greeks, — one, in accordance with which the Hellenes, as earthborn, claimed descent from Pyrrha (the red earth); the other and older, by which Deucalion was represented as the only survivor of the flood, but still the founder of the race (Greek *laós*), which he created by casting stones (Greek *láes*) behind him. The myth, therefore, proceeds from an unintended pun. Although, finally, Pyrrha was by myth-makers made the wife of Deucalion, the older myth of the origin of the race from stones was preserved. See Max Müller, Sci. Relig., London, 1873, p. 64.

21. For genealogy of the race of Inachus, Phoroneus, Pelasgus, and Io, see Table D. Pelasgus is frequently regarded as the grandson, not the son, of Phoroneus. For the descendants of Deucalion and Hellen, see Table I of this commentary.

22. In the following genealogical table (A), the names of the great gods of Olympus are printed in heavy-face type. Latin forms of names or Latin substitutes are used.

Illustrative. On the **Gods of Greece**, see E. A. Bowring's translation of Schiller's Die Götter Griechenlands, and Bayard Taylor's Masque of the Gods. On **Olympus,** see Lewis Morris, The Epic of Hades. Allusions abound; *e.g.* Shakespeare, Troilus and Cressida, III, iii; Julius Cæsar, III, i; IV, iii; Hamlet, V, i; Milton, Paradise Lost, 1, 516; 7, 7; 10, 583; Pope, Rape of the Lock, 5, 48, and Windsor Forest, 33, 234; E. C. Stedman, News from Olympia. See also E. W. Gosse, Greece and England (On Viol and Flute).

23. The Olympian Gods. There were, according to Mr. Gladstone (*No. Am. Rev.* April, 1892), about twenty Olympian deities:[1] (1) The five really great gods, Zeus, Hera, Poseidon, Apollo, and Athene; (2) Hephæstus, Ares, Hermes, Iris, Leto, Artemis, Themis, Aphrodite, Dione, Pæëon (or Pæon), and Hebe, — also usually present among the assembled immortals; (3) Demeter, Persephone, Dionysus, and Thetis, whose claims are more or less obscured. According to the same authority, the **Distinctive Qualities of the Homeric Gods** were as follows: (1) they were immortal; (2) they were incorporated in human form; (3) they enjoyed power far exceeding that possessed by mortals; (4) they were, however (with the possible exception of Athene, who is never ignorant, never deceived, never baffled), all liable to certain limitations of energy and knowledge; (5) they were subject also to corporeal wants and to human affections. The **Olympian Religion,** as a whole, was more careful of nations, states, public affairs, than of individuals and individual character; and in this respect, according to Mr. Gladstone,

---

[1] For Latin names, see Index or Chapters II–V.

it differs from Christianity. He holds, however, that despite the occasional immoralities of the gods, their general government not only "makes for righteousness," but is addressed to the end of rendering it triumphant. Says Zeus, for instance, in the Olympian assembly, "Men complain of us the gods, and say that we are the source from whence ills proceed; but they likewise themselves suffer woes outside the course of destiny, through their own perverse offending." But, beside this general effort for the triumph of right, there is little to be said in abatement of the general proposition that, whatever be their collective conduct, the common speech of the gods is below the human level in point of morality.[1]

24-25. Zeus. In Sanskrit *Dyaus*, in Latin *Jovis*, in German *Tiu*. The same name for the Almighty (the Light or Sky) used probably thousands of years before Homer, or the Sanskrit Bible (the Vedas). It is not merely the blue sky, nor the sky personified, — not merely worship of a natural phenomenon, but of the Father who is in Heaven. So in the Vedas we find *Dyaus pitar*, in the Greek *Zeu pater*, in Latin *Jupiter* all meaning *father of light*. — MAX MÜLLER, Sci. Relig. 171, 172. **Oracle:** the word signifies also the answers given at the shrine.

Illustrative. Allusions to Jove on every other page of Milton, Dryden, Pope, Prior, Gray, and any poet of the Elizabethan and Augustan periods. On the **Love Affairs of Jupiter** and the other gods, see Milton, Paradise Regained, 2, 182. **Dodona:** Tennyson's Talking Oak:

> That Thessalian growth,
> On which the swarthy ringdove sat,
> And mystic sentence spoke. . . .

Poem: Lewis Morris, Zeus, in The Epic of Hades.

In Art. Beside the representations of Jupiter noted in the text may be mentioned that on the eastern frieze of the Parthenon; the Jupiter Otricoli in the Vatican; also the Jupiter and Juno (painting) by Annibale Carracci; the Jupiter (sculpture) by Benvenuto Cellini.

[1] The Olympian Religion (*No. Am. Rev.* May, 1892). See his Juventus Mundi.

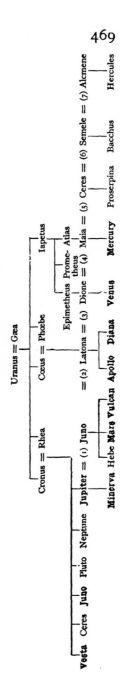

TABLE A. THE GREAT GODS OF OLYMPUS

26. Juno was called by the Romans Juno Lucina, the special goddess of child-birth. In her honor wives held the festival of the Matronalia on the first of March of each year. The Latin **Juno** is for *Diou-n-on*, from the stem *Diove*, and is the feminine parallel of Jovis, just as the Greek Dione (one of the loves of Zeus) is the feminine of Zeus. These names (and Diana, too) come from the root *div*, ' to shine,' ' to illumine.' There are many points of resemblance between the Italian Juno and the Greek Dione (identified with Hera, as Hera-Dione). Both are goddesses of the moon (?), of women, of marriage; to both the cow (with moon-crescent horns) is sacred. See Roscher, 21, 576–579. But Overbeck insists that the loves of Zeus are deities of the earth: " The rains of heaven (Zeus) do not fall upon the moon."

Illustrative. W. S. Landor, Hymn of Terpander to Juno; Lewis Morris, Heré, in The Epic of Hades.

In Art. Of the statues of Juno the most celebrated was that made by Polyclitus for her temple between Argos and Mycenæ. It was of gold and ivory. See Paus. 2, 17, 4. The goddess was seated on a throne of magnificent proportions; she wore a crown upon which were figured the Graces and the Hours; in one hand she held a pomegranate, in the other a scepter surmounted by a cuckoo. Of the extant representations of Juno the most famous are the Argive Hera (Fig. 9 in the text), the torso in Vienna from Ephesus, the Hera of the Vatican at Rome, the bronze statuette in the Cabinet of Coins and Antiquities in Vienna, the Farnese bust in the National Museum in Naples, the Ludovisi bust in the villa of that name in Rome, the Pompeian wall painting of the marriage of Zeus and Hera (given by Baumeister, Denkmäler 1, 649; see also Roscher, 13, 2127), and the Juno of Lanuvium.

27. Athenē (Athena) has some characteristics of the warlike kind in common with the Norse Valkyries, but she is altogether a more ideal conception. The best description of the goddess will be found in Homer's Iliad, 5, 730 *et seq.*

The derivation of **Athene** is uncertain (Preller). Related, say some, to *athēr*, αἰθήρ, the clear upper air; say others, to the word *anthos*, ἄνθος, 'a flower'—virgin bloom; or (see Roscher, p. 684) to *athēr*, ἀθήρ, 'spear point.' Max Müller derives **Athene** from the root *ah*, which yields the Sanskrit Ahana and the Greek Daphne, the Dawn (?). Hence Athene is the Dawn-goddess; but she is also the goddess of wisdom, because "the goddess who caused people to wake was involuntarily conceived as the goddess who caused people to know" (Science of Language, 1, 548–551). This is poor philology.

Epithets applied to Athene are the bright-eyed, the gray-eyed, the ægis-bearing, the unwearied daughter of Zeus.

The festival of the **Panathenæa** was celebrated at Athens yearly in commemo-ration of the union of the Attic tribes. See **C. 176–181**.

The name **Pallas** characterizes the goddess as the *brandisher* of lightnings. Her Palladium — or sacred image — holds always high in air the brandished lance.

Minerva, or **Menerva,** is connected with Latin *mens*, Greek *ménos*, Sanskrit *manas*, 'mind'; not with the Latin *mane*, 'morning.' The relation is not very plausible between the awakening of the day and the awakening of thought (Max Müller, Sci. Lang. 1, 552).

For the meaning of the Gorgon, see Commentary on the myth of Perseus.

Illustrative. Byron, Childe Harold, 4, 96, the eloquent passage beginning,

> Can tyrants but by tyrants conquer'd be,
> And Freedom find no champion and no child
> Such as Columbia saw arise when she
> Sprung forth a Pallas, arm'd and undefiled?

Shakespeare, Tempest, IV, i; As You Like It, I, iii; Winter's Tale, IV, iii; Pericles, II, iii; Milton, Paradise Lost, 4, 500; Comus, 701; Arcades, 23; Lewis Morris' Athene, in The Epic of Hades; Byron, Childe Harold, 2. 1-15, 87, 91; Ruskin's Lectures entitled "The Queen of the Air" (Athene); Thomas Woolner's Pallas Athene, in Tiresias.

In Art. The finest of the statues of this goddess was by Phidias, in the Parthenon, or temple of Athena, at Athens. The Athena of the Parthenon has disappeared; but there is good ground to believe that we have, in several extant statues and busts, the artist's conception. (See Frontispiece, the Lemnian Athena, and Fig. 53, the Hope Athena, ancient marble at Deepdene, Surrey.) The figure is characterized by grave and dignified beauty, and freedom from any transient expression; in other words, by repose. The most important copy extant is of the Roman period. The goddess was represented standing; in one hand a spear, in the other a statue of Victory. Her helmet, highly decorated, was surmounted by a Sphinx. The statue was forty feet in height, and, like the Jupiter, covered with ivory and gold. The eyes were of marble, and probably painted to represent the iris and pupil. The Parthenon, in which this statue stood, was also constructed under the direction and superintendence of Phidias. Its exterior was enriched with sculptures, many of them from the hand of the same artist. The Elgin Marbles now in the British Museum are a part of them. Also remarkable are the Minerva Bellica (Capitol, Rome); the Athena of the Acropolis Museum; the Athena of the Ægina Marbles (Glyptothek, Munich); the Minerva Medica (Vatican); the Athena of Velletri in the Louvre. (See Fig. 10.) In modern sculpture, especially excellent are Thorwaldsen's Minerva and Prometheus, and Cellini's Minerva (on the base of his Perseus). In modern painting, Tintoretto's Minerva defeating Mars.

28. While the Latin god **Mars** corresponds with Ares, he has also not a few points of similarity with the Greek Phœbus; for both names, Mars and Phœbus, indicate the quality *shining*. In Rome, the Campus Martius (field of Mars) was sacred to this deity. Here military maneuvers and athletic contests took place; here Mars was adored by sacrifice, and here stood his temple, where his priests, the Salii, watched over the sacred spear and the shield, *Ancile*, that fell from heaven in the reign of Numa Pompilius. Generals supplicated Mars for victory, and dedicated to him the spoils of war. See Roscher, pp. 478, 486, on the fundamental significance, philosophical and physical, of *Ares*. On the derivation of the Latin name *Mars*, see Roscher (end of article on Apollo).

Illustrative in Art. Of archaic figures, that upon the so-called François Vase in Florence represents **Ares** bearded and with the armor of a Homeric warrior. In the art of the second half of the fifth century B.C., he is represented as beardless, standing with spear and helmet and, generally, *chlamys* (short warrior's cloak); so the marble Ares statue (called the Borghese Achilles) in the Louvre. There is a later type (preferred in Rome) of the god in Corinthian helmet pushed back from the forehead, the right hand leaning on a spear, in the left a sword with point upturned, over the left arm a *chlamys*. The finest representation of the deity extant is the *Ares Ludovisi* in Rome, probably of the second half of the fourth century B.C., — a sitting figure, beautiful in form and feature, with an Eros playing at his feet. (See Fig. 11.) Modern sculpture: Thorwaldsen's relief, Mars and Cupid. Modern painting, Raphael's Mars (text, Fig. 12).

29. On the derivation of **Hephæstus,** see Roscher, p. 2037. From Greek *aphē*, ' to kindle,' or *pha*, ' to shine,' or *spha*, ' to burn.' The Latin **Vulcan,** while a god of fire, is not represented by the Romans as possessed of technical skill. It is said that Romulus built him a temple in Rome and instituted the Vulcanalia, — a festival in honor of the god. The name *Vulcanus*, or *Volcanus*, is popularly connected with the Latin *fulgere*, ' to flash ' or ' lighten,' *fulgur*, a ' flash of lightning,' etc. It is quite natural that, in many legends, fire should play an active part in the creation of man. The primitive belief of the Indo-Germanic race was that the fire-god, descending to earth, became the first man ; and that, therefore, the spirit of man was composed of fire. Vulcan is also called by the Romans Mulciber, from *mulceo*, ' to soften.'

Illustrative. Shakespeare, Twelfth Night, V, i; Much Ado About Nothing, I, i; Troilus and Cressida, I, iii; Hamlet, III, ii; Milton, Paradise Lost, 1, 740:

> From morn
> To noon he fell, from noon to dewy eve,
> A summer's day; and with the setting sun
> Dropt from the zenith, like a falling star,
> On Lemnos, the Ægean isle.

In Art. Various antique illustrations are extant of the god as a smith with hammer, or at the forge (text, Fig. 13); one of him working with the Cyclopes; a vase painting of him adorning Pandora; one of him assisting at the birth of Minerva; and one of his return to Olympus led by Bacchus and Comus. Of modern paintings the following are noteworthy: J. A. Wiertz, Forge of Vulcan; Velasquez, Forge of Vulcan (Museum, Madrid) (text, Fig. 56); the Forge of Vulcan by Tintoretto. Thorwaldsen's piece of statuary, Vulcan forging Arrows for Cupid, is justly famous.

30. Castalia: on the slopes of Parnassus, sacred to Apollo and the Muses. **Cephissus:** in Phocis and Bœotia. (Another Cephissus flows near Athens.)

Interpretative. The birth, wanderings, return of **Apollo,** and his struggle with the Python, etc., are explained by many scholars as symbolic of the annual course of the sun. Apollo is born of Leto, who is, according to hypothesis, the Night from which the morning sun issues. His conflict with the dragon reminds one of Siegfried's combat and that of St. George. The **dragon** is variously interpreted as symbolical of darkness, mephitic vapors, or the forces of winter, which are overcome by the rays of the springtide sun. The dragon is called Delphyne, or Python. The latter name may be derived simply from that part of Phocis (Pytho) where the town of Delphi was situate, or that again from the Greek root *pûth*, 'to rot,' because there the serpent was left by Apollo to decay; or from the Greek *pûth*, 'to inquire,' with reference to the consultation of the Delphian or Pythian oracle. "It is open to students to regard the **dolphin** as only one of the many animals whose earlier worship is concentrated in Apollo, or to take the creature for the symbol of spring when seafaring becomes easier to mortals, or to interpret the dolphin as the result of a *volks-etymologie* (popular derivation), in which the name *Delphi* (meaning originally a hollow in the hills) was connected with *delphis*, the dolphin." — LANG, Myth, Ritual, etc., 2, 197. Apollo is also called **Lycius**, which means, not the wolf-slayer, as it sometimes stated, for the wolf is sacred to Apollo, but either the wolf-god (as inheriting an earlier wolf-cult) or the golden god of Light. See Preller and Roscher. This derivation is more probable than that from *Lycia* in Asia Minor, where the god was said originally to have been worshiped. To explain certain rational myths of Apollo as referring to the annual and diurnal journeys of the sun is justifiable. To explain the savage and senseless survivals of the Apollo-myth in that way is impossible.

Festivals. The most important were as follows: (1) The **Delphinia,** in May, to celebrate the genial influence of the young sun upon the waters, in opening navigation, in restoring warmth and life to the creatures of the wave, especially to the dolphins, which were highly esteemed by the superstitious seafarers, fishermen, merchants, etc. (2) The **Thargelia,** in the Greek month of that name, our May, which heralded the approach of the hot season. The purpose of this festival was twofold: to propitiate the deity of the sun and forfend the sickness of summer; to celebrate the ripening of vegetation and return thanks for first-fruits. These festivals were held in Athens, Delos, and elsewhere. (3) The **Hyacinthian** fast and feast of Sparta, corresponding in both features to the Thargelian. It was held in July, in the oppressive days of the Dog Star, Sirius. (4) The **Carnean** of Sparta, celebrated in August. It added to the propitiatory features of the Hyacinthian, a thanksgiving for the vintage. (5) Another vintage-festival was the **Pyanepsian,** in Athens. (6) The **Daphnephoria:** "Familiar to many English people from Sir Frederick Leighton's picture. This feast is believed to have symbolized the year. . . . An olive branch supported a central ball of brass, beneath which was a smaller ball, and thence little globes were hung." "The greater ball means the sun, the smaller the moon, the tiny globes the stars, and the three hundred and sixty-five laurel garlands used in the feast are understood to symbolize the days." (*Proclus and Pausanias.*) — LANG, Myth, Ritual, etc., 2. 194, 195. Apollo is also called the **Sminthian,** or Mouse-god, because he was regarded either as the protector or as the destroyer of mice. In the Troad mice were fed in his temple; elsewhere he was honored as freeing the country from them. As Mr. Lang says (Myth, Ritual, etc., 2, 201), this is intelligible "if the vermin which had once been sacred became a pest in the eyes of later generations."

Oracle of Delphi. It had been observed at a very early period that the goats feeding on Parnassus were thrown into convulsions when they approached a certain long deep cleft in the side of the mountain. This was owing to a peculiar vapor arising out of the cavern, and a certain goatherd is said to have tried its effects upon himself. Inhaling the intoxicating air, he was affected in the same manner as the cattle had been; and the inhabitants of the surrounding country, unable to explain the circumstance, imputed the convulsive ravings to which he gave utterance while under the power of the exhalations to a divine inspiration. The fact was speedily spread abroad, and a temple was erected on the spot. The prophetic influence was at first variously attributed to the goddess Earth, to Neptune, Themis, and others, but it was at length assigned to Apollo, and to him alone. A priestess was appointed whose office it was to inhale the hallowed air, and she was named the Pythia. She was prepared for this duty by previous ablution at the fountain of Castalia, and being crowned with laurel was seated upon a tripod similarly adorned, which was placed over the chasm whence the divine afflatus proceeded. Her inspired words while thus situated were interpreted by the priests.

Other famous oracles were that of **Trophonius** in Bœotia and that of the Egyptian **Apis**. Since those who descended into the cave at Lebadea to consult the oracle of Trophonius were noticed to return dejected and melancholy, the proverb arose which was applied to a low-spirited person, " He has been consulting the oracle of Trophonius."

At Memphis the sacred bull Apis gave answer to those who consulted him, by the manner in which he received or rejected what was presented to him. If the bull refused food from the hand of the inquirer, it was considered an unfavorable sign, and the contrary when he received it.

It used to be questioned whether oracular responses ought to be ascribed to mere human contrivance or to the agency of evil spirits. The latter opinion would of course obtain during ages of superstition, when evil spirits were credited with an influence over human affairs. A third theory has been advanced since the phenomena of mesmerism have attracted attention: that something like the mesmeric trance was induced in the Pythoness, and the faculty of clairvoyance called into action.

Scholars have also sought to determine when the pagan oracles ceased to give responses. Ancient Christian writers assert that they became silent at the birth of Christ, and were heard no more after that date. Milton adopts this view in his Hymn on the Nativity, and in lines of solemn and elevated beauty pictures the consternation of the heathen idols at the advent of the Saviour:

> The Oracles are dumb;
> No voice or hideous hum
> Runs through the archèd roof in words deceiving.
> Apollo from his shrine
> Can no more divine,
> With hollow shriek the steep of Delphos leaving.
> No nightly trance, or breathèd spell
> Inspires the pale-eyed priest from the prophetic cell.

Illustrative. Spenser, Faerie Queene, 1, 2, 2; 1, 2, 29; 1, 11, 31; 1, 12, 2. Sir Philip Sidney, Astrophel and Stella; as, for instance, the pretty conceit beginning

> Phœbus was judge between Jove, Mars, and Love,
> Of those three gods, whose arms the fairest were.

Dekker, The Sun's Darling; Burns (as in the Winter Night) and other Scotch song-writers find it hard to keep Phœbus out of their verses; Spenser, Epithalamion; Shakespeare, Midsummer Night's Dream, II, i (Apollo and Daphne); Cymbeline (Cloten's Serenade); Love's Labour's Lost, IV, iii; Taming of the Shrew, Induction ii; Winter's Tale, II, i; III, i; III, ii; Titus Andronicus, IV, i; Drayton, Song 8; Tickell, To Apollo making Love; Swift, Apollo Outwitted; Pope, Essay on Criticism, 34; Dunciad, 4, 116; Prologue to Satires, 231; Miscellaneous, 7, 16; Armstrong, The Art of Preserving Health.

Poems. Drummond of Hawthornden, Song to Phœbus; Keats, Hymn to Apollo; A. Mary F. Robinson, A Search for Apollo, and In Apollo's Garden; Shelley, Homer's Hymn to Apollo; Aubrey De Vere, Lines under Delphi; Lewis Morris, Apollo, in The Epic of Hades; R. W. Dixon, Apollo Pythius.

The Python. Milton, Paradise Lost, 10, 531; Shelley, Adonais. **Oracles.** Milton, Paradise Lost, 1. 12, 515; 5, 382; 10, 182; Paradise Regained, 1. 395, 430, 456, 463; 3, 13; 4, 275; Hymn on the Nativity, 173. In Cowper's poem of Yardley Oak there are mythological allusions appropriate to this subject. On Dodona, Byron, Childe Harold, 2, 53; Tennyson, The Talking Oak. Byron alludes to the oracle of Delphi when speaking of Rousseau, whose writings he conceives did much to bring on the French Revolution: Childe Harold, 3, 81, —

> For then he was inspired, and from him came,
> As from the Pythian's mystic cave of yore,
> Those oracles which set the world in flame,
> Nor ceased to burn till kingdoms were no more.

In Art. One of the most esteemed of all the remains of ancient sculpture is the statue of Apollo, called the Belvedere from the name of the apartment of the Pope's palace at Rome in which it is placed (see Fig. 15). The artist is unknown. It is conceded to be a work of Roman art, of about the first century of our era (and follows a type fashioned by a Greek sculptor of the Hellenistic period, probably in bronze). A variation of the type has been discovered in a bronze statuette which represents Apollo holding in the left hand an ægis. Some scholars have therefore surmised that the Apollo of the original was similarly equipped. The Belvedere Apollo, however, is a standing figure, in marble, more than seven feet high, naked except for the cloak which is fastened around the neck and hangs over the extended left arm. It is restored to represent the god in the moment when he has shot the arrow to destroy the monster Python. The victorious divinity is in the act of stepping forward. The left arm which seems to have held the bow is outstretched, and the head is turned in the same direction. In attitude and proportion the graceful majesty of the figure is unsurpassed. The effect is completed by the countenance, where, on the perfection of youthful godlike beauty, there dwells the consciousness of triumphant power. To this statue Byron alludes in Childe Harold, 4, 161 :

> Or view the Lord of the unerring bow,
> The God of life, and poetry, and light, —
> The Sun, in human limbs arrayed, and brow
> All radiant from his triumph in the fight;
> The shaft hath just been shot — the arrow bright
> With an immortal's vengeance ; in his eye
> And nostril, beautiful disdain, and might
> And majesty flash their full lightnings by,
> Developing in that one glance the Deity.

The standing figure in our text reproduces this conception.[1] Also famous in sculpture are the "Adonis" Apollo of the Vatican (Fig. 14, text); the Greek bronze from Thessaly (Fig. 16, text); the Palatine Apollo in the Vatican (Fig. 66, text); the Apollo Citharœdus of the National Museum, Naples, and the Glyptothek, Munich ; the Lycian Apollo ; the Apollo Nomios ; Apollo of Thera ; the Apollo of Michelangelo (National Museum, Florence). A painting of romantic interest is Paolo Veronese's St. Christina refusing to adore Apollo. Of symbolic import is the Apollo (Sunday) by Raphael in the Vatican. Phœbus and Boreas by J. F. Millet.

32. Latona. A theory of the numerous **love-affairs** of Jupiter is given in **24** of the text. **Delos** is the central island of the Cyclades group in the Ægean. With its temple of Apollo it was exceedingly prosperous.

Interpretative. Latona (Leto), according to ancient interpreters, was night, — the shadow, therefore, of Juno (Hera), if Hera be the splendor of heaven. But the early myth-makers would hardly have reasoned so abstrusely. It is not at all certain that the name *Leto* means darkness (Preller 1, 190, note 4) ; and even if light is born of or after darkness, the sun (Apollo) and the moon (Artemis, or Diana) can hardly be considered to be twins of Darkness (Leto), for they do not illuminate the heavens at the same time. — LANG, Myth, Ritual, etc., 2, 199.

Illustrative. Byron's allusion to Delos in Don Juan, 3, 86:

> The isles of Greece ! the isles of Greece !
> Where burning Sappho loved and sung,
> Where grew the arts of war and peace,
> Where Delos rose, and Phœbus sprung !
> Eternal summer gilds them yet,
> But all, except their sun, is set.

See Milton's Sonnet, " I did but prompt the age to quit their clogs," for allusion to Latona.

In Art. In the shrine of Latona in Delos there was, in the days of Athenæus, a shapeless wooden idol.

Diana. The Latin **Diana** means either " goddess of the bright heaven," or " goddess of the bright day." She is frequently identified with Artemis, Hecate,

---

[1] Furtwängler (Meisterw. d. gr. Plastik) condemns the ægis.

Luna, and Selene. According to one tradition, Apollo and Diana were born at Ortygia, near Ephesus. **Diana of the Ephesians,** referred to (Acts xix, 28), was a goddess of not at all the maidenly characteristics that belonged to the Greek Artemis (Roscher, p. 591; A. Lang, 2, 217). Other titles of Artemis are Munychia, the moon-goddess; Calliste, the *fair,* or the *she-bear;* Orthia, the *severe,* worshiped among the Taurians with human sacrifices; Agrotera, the *huntress;* Pythia; Eileithyia, goddess of childbirth; Cynthia, born on Mount Cynthus.

Illustrative. Spenser, Faerie Queene, 1, 7, 5; 1, 12, 7; Shakespeare, Merchant of Venice, V, i, "Come, ho, and wake Diana with a hymn," etc.; Twelfth Night, I, iv; Midsummer Night's Dream, I, iv; All's Well that Ends Well, I, iii; IV, ii; IV, iv; Butler, Hudibras, 3, 2, 1448. *Poems:* B. W. Procter, The Worship of Dian; W. W. Story, Artemis; E. W. Gosse, The Praise of Artemis; E. Arnold, Hymn of the Priestess of Diana; Wordsworth, To Lycoris; Lewis Morris, Artemis, in The Epic of Hades; A. Lang, To Artemis. **Phœbe** (Diana): Spenser, Epithalamion; Keats, To Psyche. **Cynthia** (Diana): Spenser, Prothalamion, Epithalamion; Milton, Hymn on the Nativity; H. K. White, Ode to Contemplation.

In Art. In art the goddess is represented high-girt for the chase, either in the act of drawing an arrow from her quiver or watching her missile in its flight. She is often attended by the hind. Sometimes, as moon-goddess, she bears a torch. Occasionally she is clad in a *chiton*, or robe of many folds, flowing to her feet. The Diana of the Hind (*à la Biche*), in the Palace of the Louvre (see Fig. 18), may be considered the counterpart of the Apollo Belvedere. The attitude much resembles that of Apollo, the sizes correspond and also the styles of execution. The Diana of the Hind is a work of a high order, though by no means equal to the Apollo. The attitude is that of hurried and eager motion, the face that of a huntress in the excitement of the chase. The left hand of the goddess is extended over the forehead of the hind which runs by her side, the right arm reaches backward over the shoulder to draw an arrow from the quiver. Fig. 19 in the text is the Artemis Knagia (Diana Cnagia), named after Cnageus, a servant of Diana who assisted in transferring the statue from Crete to Sparta. In Dresden there is a statue of Artemis in the style of Praxiteles (Fig. 68, text); and in the Louvre an ancient marble called the Artemis of Gabii (Fig. 77, text).

In modern painting, noteworthy are the Diana and her Nymphs of Rubens; Correggio's Diana (Fig. 17); Jules Lefebvre's Diana and her Nymphs; Domenichino's Diana's Chase. Note also the allegorical Luna (Monday) of Raphael in the Vatican; and D. G. Rossetti's Diana, in crayons.

34. *Interpretative.* The worship of **Aphrodite** was probably of Semitic origin, but was early introduced into Greece. The Aphrodite of Hesiod and Homer displays both Oriental and Grecian characteristics. All Semitic nations, except the Hebrews, worshiped a supreme goddess who presided over the moon (or the Star of Love), and over all animal and vegetable life and growth. She was the Istar of the Assyrians, the Astarte of the Phœnicians, and is the analogue of the Greek Aphrodite and the Latin Venus. See Roscher, p. 390, etc. The native Greek deity of love would appear to have been, however, **Dione,** goddess of the moist and productive soil (**C. 26**), who passes in the Iliad (5. 370, 428) as the mother of Aphrodite, is worshiped at Dodona by the side of Zeus, and is regarded by Euripides as *Thyone*, mother of Dionysus (Preller 1, 259).

The epithets and names most frequently applied to Aphrodite are the Paphian, Cypris (the Cyprus-born), Cytherea, Erycina (from Mount Eryx), Pandemos (goddess of vulgar love), Pelagia (Aphrodite of the sea), Urania (Aphrodite of ideal love), Anadyomene (rising from the water); she is, also, the sweetly smiling, laughter-loving, bright, golden, fruitful, winsome, flower-faced, blushing, swift-eyed, golden-crowned.

She had temples and groves in Paphos, Abydos, Samos, Ephesus, Cyprus, Cythere, in some of which — for instance, Paphos — gorgeous annual festivals were held. See Childe Harold, 1, 66.

Venus was a deity of extreme antiquity among the Romans, but not of great importance until she had acquired certain attributes of the Eastern Aphrodite. She was worshiped as goddess of love, as presiding over marriage, as the goddess who turns the hearts of men, and, later, even as a goddess of victory. A festival in her honor, called the Veneralia, was held in Rome in April.

Illustrative. See Chaucer's Knight's Tale for frequent references to the goddess of love; also the Court of Love; Spenser's Prothalamion, and Epithalamion, "Handmaids of the Cyprian queen"; Shakespeare, Tempest, IV, i; Merchant of Venice, II, vi; Troilus and Cressida, IV, v; Cymbeline, V, v; Romeo and Juliet, II, i; Milton, L'Allegro; Paradise Regained, 2, 214; Comus, 124; Pope, Rape of the Lock 4, 135; Spring, 65; Summer, 61; Thomas Woolner, Pygmalion (Cytherea).

Poems. Certain parts of Shakespeare's Venus and Adonis and occasional stanzas in Swinburne's volume, Laus Veneris, may be adapted to illustrative purposes. Chaucer, The Complaint of Mars and Venus; Thomas Wyatt, The Lover prayeth Venus to conduct him to the Desired Haven. See the melodious chorus to Aphrodite in Swinburne's Atalanta in Calydon; Lewis Morris, Aphrodite, in The Epic of Hades; Thomas Gordon Hake, The Birth of Venus, in New Symbols; D. G. Rossetti, Sonnets; Venus Verticordia, Venus Victrix.

35. In Art. One of the most famous of ancient paintings was the Venus rising from the foam, of Apelles. The Venus found (1820) in the island of Melos, or of Milo (see text, opp. p. 32), now to be seen in the Louvre in Paris, is the work of some sculptor of about the fourth century B.C. Some say that the left hand uplifted held a mirrorlike shield; others, an apple; still others, a trident; and that the goddess was Amphitrite. A masterpiece of Praxiteles was the Venus of Cnidos, based upon which are the Venus of the Capitoline in Rome and the Venus de' Medici in Florence. Also the Venus of the Vatican, which is, in my opinion, superior to both. The Venus of the Medici was in the possession of the princes of that name in Rome when, about two hundred years ago, it first attracted attention. An inscription on the base assigns it to Cleomenes, an Athenian sculptor of 200 B.C., but the authenticity of the inscription is doubtful. There is a story that the artist was employed by public authority to make a statue exhibiting the perfection of female beauty, and that to aid him in his task the most perfect forms the city could supply were furnished him for models. Note Thomson's allusion in the Summer:

> So stands the statue that enchants the world;
> So bending tries to veil the matchless boast,
> The mingled beauties of exulting Greece.

And Byron's

> There too the goddess loves in stone, and fills
> The air around with beauty. — Childe Harold, 4, 49–53.

One of the most beautiful of the Greek Aphrodites is the Petworth (opp. p. 126, text).

Of modern paintings the most famous are: the Sleeping Venus and other representations of Venus by Titian; the Birth of Venus by Bouguereau; Tintoretto's Cupid, Venus, and Vulcan; Veronese's Venus with Satyr and Cupid. Modern sculpture: Thorwaldsen's Venus with the Apple; Venus and Cupid; Cellini's Venus; Canova's Venus Victrix, and the Venus in the Pitti Gallery; Rossetti's Venus Verticordia (crayons, water colors, oil).

36. Interpretative. Max Müller traces **Hermes**, child of the Dawn with its fresh breezes, herald of the gods, spy of the night, to the Vedic Saramâ, goddess of the Dawn. Others translate Saramâ, *storm*. Roscher derives from the same root as Sarameyas (son of Saramâ), with the meaning *Hastener*, the *swift wind*. The invention of the syrinx is attributed also to Pan.

Illustrative. To Mercury's construction of the lyre out of a tortoise shell, Gray refers (Progress of Poesy)," Parent of sweet and solemn-breathing airs, Enchanting shell!" etc. See Shakespeare, King John, IV, ii; Henry IV, IV, i; Richard III, II, i; IV, iii; Hamlet, III, iv; Milton, Paradise Lost, 3, " Though by their powerful art they bind Volatile Hermes"; 4, 717; 11, 133; Il Penseroso, 88; Comus, 637, 962. *Poems:* Sir T. Martin, Goethe's Phœbus and Hermes; Shelley's translation of Homer's Hymn to Mercury.

In Art. The Mercury in the Central Museum, Athens; Mercury Belvedere (Vatican); Mercury in Repose (National Museum, Naples). The Hermes by Praxiteles, in Olympia (text, opp. p. 150), and the Hermes Psychopompos leading to the underworld the spirit of a woman who has just died (text, Fig. 20; from a relief sculptured on the tomb of Myrrhina), are especially fine specimens of ancient sculpture.

In modern sculpture: Cellini's Mercury (base of Perseus, Loggia dei Lanzi, Florence); Giov. di Bologna's Flying Mercury (bronze, Bargello, Florence: text. opp. p. 330); Thorwaldsen's Mercury. In modern painting: Tintoretto's Mercury and the Graces; Francesco Albani's Mercury and Apollo; Claude Lorrain's Mercury and Battus; Turner's Mercury and Argus; Raphael's allegorical Mercury (Wednesday), Vatican, Rome; and his Mercury with Psyche (Farnese Frescoes).

37. Interpretative. The name **Hestia** (Latin *Vesta*) has been variously derived from roots meaning *to sit, to stand, to burn*. The two former are consistent with the domestic nature of the goddess; the latter with her relation to the hearth-fire. She is "first of the goddesses," the holy, the chaste, the sacred.

Illustrative. Milton, Il Penseroso (Melancholy), "*Thee* bright-haired Vesta long of yore To solitary Saturn bore," etc.

38. (1) **Cupid** (Eros). References and allusions to Cupid throng our poetry. Only a few are here given. Shakespeare, Romeo and Juliet, I, iv; Merchant of Venice, II, vi; Merry Wives, II, ii; Much Ado About Nothing, I, i; II, i; III, ii; Midsummer Night's Dream, I, i; II, ii; IV, i; Cymbeline, II, iv; Milton, Comus, 445, 1004; Herrick, The Cheat of Cupid; Pope, Rape of the Lock, 5, 102; Dunciad, 4, 308; Moral Essays, 4, 111; Windsor Forest, — on Lord Surrey, "In the same shades the Cupids tuned his lyre To the same notes of love and soft desire."

Poems. Chaucer, The Cuckow and Nightingale, or Boke of Cupid (?); Occleve, The Letter of Cupid; Beaumont and Fletcher, Cupid's Revenge, and the Masque, A Wife for a Month; J. G. Saxe, Death and Cupid, on their exchange of arrows, "And that explains the reason why Despite the gods above, The young are often doomed to die, The old to fall in love"; Thomas Ashe, The Lost Eros; Coventry Patmore, The Unknown Eros. Also John Lyly's Campaspe:

> Cupid and my Campaspe playd,
> At cardes for kisses, Cupid payd;
> He stakes his quiver, bow, and arrows,
> His mother's doves, and teeme of sparows;
> Looses them too; then, downe he throwes
> The corrall of his lippe, the rose
> Growing on 's cheek (but none knows how),
> With these, the cristall of his brow,
> And then the dimple of his chinne:
> All these did my Campaspe winne.
> At last hee set her both his eyes;
> Shee won, and Cupid blind did rise.
>   O love! has shee done this to thee?
>   What shall (alas!) become of mee?

See also Lang's translation of Moschus, Idyl I, and O. Wilde, The Garden of Eros.

In Art. Antique sculpture: the Eros in Naples, ancient marble from an original perhaps by Praxiteles (text, Fig. 21); Eros bending the Bow, in the Museum at Berlin; Cupid bending his Bow (Vatican); Eros with his Bow, in the Capitoline (text, opp. p. 136).

Modern sculpture: Thorwaldsen's Mars and Cupid. Modern paintings: Bouguereau's Cupid and a Butterfly; Raphael's Cupids (among drawings in the Museum at Venice); Burne-Jones' Cupid (in series with Pyramus and Thisbe); Raphael Mengs' Cupid sharpening his Arrow; Guido Reni's Cupid; Van Dyck's Sleeping Cupid. See also under *Psyche*, **C. 101.**

Hymen. See Sir Theodore Martin's translations of the *Collis O Heliconii*, and the *Vesper adest, juvenes,* of Catullus (LXI and LXII); Milton, Paradise Lost, 11, 591; L'Allegro, 125; Pope, Chorus of Youths and Virgins.

(2) **Hebe.** Thomas Lodge's Sonnet to Phyllis, "Fair art thou, Phyllis, ay, so fair, sweet maid"; Milton, Vacation Exercise, 38; Comus, 290; L'Allegro, 29;

Spenser, Epithalamion. *Poems:* T. Moore, The Fall of Hebe; J. R. Lowell, Hebe. *In Art:* Ary Scheffer's painting of Hebe; N. Schiavoni's painting.

Ganymede. Chaucer, Hous of Fame, 81; Tennyson, in the Palace of Art, "Or else flushed Ganymede, his rosy thigh Half-buried in the Eagle's down," etc.; Shelley in the Prometheus (Jove's order to Ganymede); Milton, Paradise Regained, 2, 353; Drayton, Song 4, "The birds of Ganymed." *Poems:* Lord Lytton, Ganymede; Bowring, Goethe's Ganymede; Roden Noël, Ganymede; Edith M. Thomas, Homesickness of Ganymede; S. Margaret Fuller, Ganymede to his Eagle; Drummond on Ganymede's lament, "When eagle's talons bare him through the air." *In Art:* The Rape of Ganymede, marble in the Vatican, probably from the original in bronze by Leochares (text, Fig. 22). Græco-Roman sculpture: Ganymede and the Eagle (National Museum, Naples). Modern sculpture: Thorwaldsen's Ganymede.

(3) **The Graces.** Rogers, Inscription for a Temple; Matthew Arnold, Euphrosyne. These goddesses are continually referred to in poetry. Note the painting by J. B. Regnault (Louvre), also the sculpture by Canova.

(4) **The Muses.** Spenser, The Tears of the Muses; Milton, Il Penseroso; Byron, Childe Harold, 1. 1, 62, 88; Thomson, Castle of Indolence, 2, 2; 2, 8; Akenside, Pleasures of Imagination, 3. 280, 327; Ode on Lyric Poetry; Crabbe, The Village, Bk. 1; Introductions to the Parish Register, Newspaper, Birth of Flattery; M. Arnold, Urania. **Delphi, Parnassus,** etc.: Gray, Progress of Poesy, 2, 3. **Vale of Tempe:** Keats, On a Grecian Urn; Young, Ocean, an ode. *In Art.* Sculpture: Polyhymnia, ancient marble in Berlin (text, Fig. 23); Clio and Calliope, in the Vatican in Rome; Euterpe, Melpomene, Polyhymnia, and Urania, in the Louvre, Paris; Terpsichore by Thorwaldsen. Painting: Apollo and the Muses, by Raphael Mengs and by Giulio Romano; Terpsichore (picture), by Schützenberger.

(5) **The Hours,** in art: Raphael's Six Hours of the Day and Night.

(6) **The Fates.** Refrain stanzas in Lowell's Villa Franca, "Spin, spin, Clotho, spin! Lachesis, twist! and Atropos, sever!" *In Art:* The Fates, painting attributed to Michelangelo, but now by some to Rosso Fiorentino from Michelangelo's design (text, Fig. 24, Pitti Gallery, Florence); painting by Paul Thumann.

(7) **Nemesis.** For genealogy see Table B, **C. 49.**

(8) **Æsculapius.** Spenser, Faerie Queene, 1, 5, 36–43; Milton, Paradise Lost, 9, 507.

(9) (10) **The Winds, Helios, Aurora, Hesper,** etc. **Æolus:** Chaucer, Hous of Fame, 480. See **C. 125** and genealogical tables H and I. **Hippotades** is Æolus (son of Hippotes). In Lycidas, 96, Milton calls the king of the winds Hippotades, because, following Homer (Odyssey, 10, 2) and Ovid (Metam. 14, 224), he identifies Æolus II with Æolus III. **Boreas and Orithyia:** Akenside, Pleasures of Imagination, 1, 722.

In Art. The fragment, Helios rising from the Sea, by Phidias, south end, east pediment of the Parthenon. Boreas and Zetos, Greek reliefs (text, Figs. 25 and 26); Boreas and Orithyia (text, Fig. 27), on a vase in Munich.

(11) **Hesperus.** Milton, Paradise Lost, 4, 605; 9, 49; Comus, 982; Akenside, Ode to Hesper; Campbell, Two Songs to the Evening Star. Tennyson, The Hesperides.

(12) "**Iris** there with humid bow waters the odorous banks," etc., Comus, 992. See also Milton's Paradise Lost, 4, 698; 11, 244. *In Art:* Fig. 28, text; and painting by Guy Head (Gallery, St. Luke's, Rome). She is the swift-footed, wind-footed, fleet, the Iris of the golden wings, etc.

39. Hyperborean. *Beyond the North.* Concerning the Elysian Plain, see **46.** *Illustrative:* Milton, Comus, "Now the gilded car of day," etc.

40. Ceres. *Illustrative.* Pope, Moral Essays, 4, 176, "Another age shall see the golden ear Imbrown the slope ... And laughing Ceres reassume the land"; Spring, 66; Summer, 66; Windsor Forest, 39; Gray, Progress of Poesy; Warton, First of April, "Fancy ... Sees Ceres grasp her crown of corn, And Plenty load her ample horn"; Spenser, Faerie Queene, 3, 1, 51; Milton, Paradise Lost, 4, 268; 9, 395.

Poems. Tennyson, Demeter and Persephone; Mrs. H. H. Jackson, Demeter. *Prose:* W. H. Pater, The Myth of Demeter (*Fortn. Rev.* Vol. 25, 1876); S. Colvin, A Greek Hymn (*Cornh. Mag.* Vol. 33, 1876); Swinburne, At Eleusis.

The name *Ceres* is from the stem *cer*, Sanskrit *kri*, 'to make.' By metonomy the word comes to signify *corn* in the Latin. Demeter (Γῆ μήτηρ, δᾶ μάτηρ) means *Mother Earth*. The goddess is represented in art crowned with a wheat-measure (or *modius*), and bearing a horn of plenty filled with ears of corn. Demeter (?) appears in the group of deities on the eastern frieze of the Parthenon. Also noteworthy are the Demeter from Knidos (text, Fig. 29, from the marble in the British Museum); two statues of Ceres in the Vatican at Rome, and one in the Glyptothek at Munich; and the Roman wall painting (text, Fig. 30).

41. Rhea was worshiped as **Cybele**, the Great Mother, in Phrygia and at Pessinus in Galatia. During the Second Punic War, 203 B.C., her image was brought from the latter place to Rome. In 191 B.C. the Megalensian Games were first celebrated in her honor, occupying six days, from the fourth of April on. Plays were acted during this festival. The Great Mother was also called Cybebe, Berecyntia, and Dindymene.

The Cybele of Art. In works of art, Cybele exhibits the matronly air which distinguishes Juno and Ceres. Sometimes she is veiled, and seated on a throne with lions at her side; at other times she rides in a chariot drawn by lions. She wears a mural crown, that is, a crown whose rim is carved in the form of towers and battlements. Rhea is mentioned by Homer (Iliad, 15, 187) as the consort of Cronus.

Illustrative. Byron's figure likening Venice to Cybele, Childe Harold, 4, 2, "She looks a sea-Cybele, fresh from ocean," etc. Also Milton's Arcades, 21.

42. *Interpretative.* It is interesting to note that Homer (Iliad and Odyssey) recognizes Dionysus neither as inventor, nor as exclusive god of wine. In Iliad, 6, 130 he refers, however, to the Dionysus cult in Thrace. Hesiod is the first to call wine the gift of Dionysus. **Dionysus** means the Zeus or *god* of Nysa, an imaginary vale of Thrace, Bœotia, or elsewhere, in which the deity spent his youth. The name **Bacchus** owes its origin to the *enthusiasm* with which the followers of the god lifted up their voices in his praise. Similar names are Iacchus, Bromius, Evius (from the cry *evoe*). The god was also called Lyæus, the *loosener* of care, Liber, the *liberator.* His followers are also known as Edonides (from

Mount Edon, in Thrace, where he was worshiped), Thyiades, the *sacrificers*, Lenæ and Bassarides. His festivals were the Lesser and Greater Dionysia (at Athens), the Lenæa, and the Anthesteria, in December, March, January, and February, respectively. At the first, three dramatic performances were presented.

Illustrative. A few references and allusions worth consulting : Spenser, Epithalamion; Fletcher, Valentinian, "God Lyæus, ever young"; Randolph, To Master Anthony Stafford (1632); Milton, L'Allegro, 16; Paradise Lost, 4, 279; 7, 33; Comus, 46, 522; Shakespeare, Midsummer Night's Dream, V, i; Love's Labour 's Lost, IV, iii; Antony and Cleopatra, II, vii, song; Shelley, Ode to Liberty, 7, Rome—"like a Cadmæan Mænad"; Keats, To a Nightingale, "Not charioted by Bacchus and his pards." On **Semele**, Milton, Paradise Regained, 2, 187; Spenser, Faerie Queene, 3, 11, 33.

Poems. Ben Jonson, Dedication of the King's New Cellar; Thomas Parnell, Bacchus, or the Drunken Metamorphosis; Landor, Sophron's Hymn to Bacchus; Swinburne, Prelude to Songs before Sunrise; Roden Noël, The Triumph of Bacchus; Robert Bridges, The Feast of Bacchus; others given in text. See Index.

In Art. Of ancient representations of the Bacchus, the best examples are the marble in the British Museum (text, Fig. 31); the Silenus holding the child Bacchus (in the Louvre); the head of Dionysus found in Smyrna (now in Leyden — see text, Fig. 143), from an original of the school of Scopas; the head (now in London) from the Baths of Caracalla, of the later Attic school; the Faun and Bacchus (Museum, Naples); a standing bronze figure in Vienna, and the statue of the Villa Tiburtina (Rome). The bearded or Indian Bacchus is represented as advanced in years, grave, dignified, crowned with a diadem and robed to the feet. See also Figs. 82–87, in text.

In modern sculpture note especially the Drunken Bacchus of Michelangelo. Among modern paintings worthy of notice are Bouguereau's Youth of Bacchus, and C. Gleyre's Dance of the Bacchantes. See also under *Ariadne*.

43. The invention of the syrinx is attributed also to Mercury. For poetical illustrations of Pan see **C. 129-138.** So also for Nymphs and Satyrs.

In Art. Pan the Hunter (text, Fig. 32); the antique, Pan and Daphnis (with the syrinx) in the Museum at Naples. See references above.

44-46. It was only in rare instances that mortals returned from Hades. See the stories of Hercules, Orpheus, Ulysses, Æneas. On the tortures of the condemned and the happiness of the blessed, see **254-257** in The Adventures of Æneas.

Illustrative. Lowell, addressing the Past, says :

> Whatever of true life there was in thee
>   Leaps in our age's veins ; . . .
> Here, 'mid the bleak waves of our strife and care
>   Float the green Fortunate Isles
> Where all thy hero-spirits dwell, and share
>   Our martyrdom and toils ;
> The present moves attended
>   With all of brave and excellent and fair
> That made the old time splendid.

Milton, Paradise Lost, 3, 568, "Like those Hesperian gardens," etc. See also the same, 2, 577 ff., — "Abhorrèd **Styx**, the flood of deadly hate," — where the rivers of Erebus are characterized according to the meaning of their Greek names; and L'Allegro, 3. **Charon**: Pope, Dunciad, 3, 19; R. C. Rogers, Charon. **Elysium**: Cowper, Progress of Error, Night, "The balm of care, Elysium of the mind"; Milton, Paradise Lost, 3, 472; Comus, 257; L'Allegro; Shakespeare, 3 Henry VI, I, ii; Cymbeline, V, iv; Twelfth Night, I, ii; Two Gentlemen of Verona, II, vii; Shelley, To Naples. **Lethe**: Shakespeare, Twelfth Night, IV, i; Julius Cæsar, III, i; Hamlet, I, v; 2 Henry IV, V, ii; Milton, Paradise Lost, 2, 583. **Tartarus**: Milton, Paradise Lost, 2, 858; 6, 54.

47. *Interpretative*. The name **Hades** means "the invisible," or "he who makes invisible." The meaning of Pluto (*Plouton*), according to Plato (Cratylus), is *wealth*, — the giver of treasure which lies underground. Pluto carries the cornucopia, symbol of inexhaustible riches; but careful discrimination must be observed between him and Plutus (*Ploutos*), who is merely an allegorical figure, — a personification of wealth and nothing more. **Hades** is called also the Illustrious, the Many-named, the Benignant, *Polydectes* or the Hospitable.

˙*Illustrative*. Milton, L'Allegro, and Il Penseroso; Paradise Lost, 4, 270; Thomas Kyd, Spanish Tragedy (Andrea's descent to Hades; — this poem deals extensively with the Infernal Regions); Shakespeare, 2 Henry IV, II, iv; Troilus and Cressida, IV, iv; V, ii; Coriolanus, I, iv; Titus Andronicus, IV, iii.

Poems. Buchanan, Ades, King of Hell; Lewis Morris, Epic of Hades.

48. Proserpina. Not from the Latin *pro-serpo*, 'to creep forth' (used of herbs in spring), but from the Greek form Persephone, *bringer of death*. The later name **Pherephatta** refers to the doves (*phatta*), which were sacred to her as well as to Aphrodite. She carries ears of corn as symbol of vegetation, poppies as symbol of the sleep of death, the pomegranate as the fruit of the underworld of which none might partake and return to the light of heaven. Among the Romans her worship was overshadowed by that of **Libitina**, a native deity of the underworld.

Illustrative. Keats, Melancholy, 1; Spenser, Faerie Queene, 1, 2, 2; Milton, Paradise Lost, 4, 269; 9, 396.

Poems. Aubrey De Vere, The Search after Proserpine; Jean Ingelow, Persephone; Swinburne, Hymns to Proserpine; L. Morris, Persephone (Epic of Hades); D. G. Rossetti, Proserpina. (Also in crayons, in water colors, and in oil.)

In Art. Sculpture: Eastern pediment of Parthenon frieze. Painting: Lorenzo Bernini's Pluto and Proserpine; P. Schobelt's Abduction of Proserpine.

49. *Textual*. (1) For Æacus, son of Ægina, see **61** and **C. 190**, Table O; for Minos and Rhadamanthus, see **59**. **Eumenides**: euphemistic term, meaning the *well-intentioned*. **Hecate** was descended through her father Perses from the Titans, Creüs and Eurybie; through her mother Asteria from the Titans, Cœus and Phœbe. She was therefore, on both sides, the granddaughter of Uranus and Gæa.

The following table is based upon Hesiod's account of **The Family of Night.** (Theogony.)

According to other theogonies, the Fates were daughters of Jove and Themis, and the Hesperides daughters of Atlas. The story of the true and false **Dreams** and the horn and ivory gates (Odyssey, 19, 560) rests on a double play upon words: (1) ἐλέφας (*elephas*), 'ivory,' and ἐλεφαίρομαι (*elephairomai*), 'to cheat with false hope'; (2) κέρας (*keras*), horn, and κραίνειν (*krainein*), 'to fulfill.' See Mortimer Collins, The Ivory Gate, a poem.

Illustrative. **Hades**: Milton, Paradise Lost, 2, 964; L. Morris, Epic of Hades. **Styx**: Shakespeare, Troilus and Cressida, V, iv; Titus Andronicus, I, ii; Milton, Paradise Lost, 2, 577; Pope, Dunciad, 2, 338. **Erebus**: Shakespeare, Merchant of Venice, V, i; 2 Henry IV, II, iv; Julius Cæsar, II, i. **Cerberus**: Spenser, Faerie Queene, 1, 11, 41; Shakespeare, Love's Labour's Lost, V, ii; 2 Henry IV, II, iv; Troilus and Cressida, II, i; Titus Andronicus, II, v; Maxwell, Tom May's Death; Milton, L'Allegro, 2. **Furies**: Milton, Lycidas; Paradise Lost, 2. 597, 671; 6, 859; 10, 620; Paradise Regained, 9, 422; Comus, 641; Dryden, Alexander's Feast, 6; Shakespeare, Midsummer Night's Dream, V, i; Richard III, I, iv; 2 Henry IV, V, iii. **Hecate**: Shakespeare, Macbeth, IV, i. **Sleep and Death**: Shelley, To Night; H. K. White, Thanatos.

In Art. Vase-painting of Canusium of the Underworld (text, Fig. 34); painting of a **Fury** by Michelangelo (Uffizi, Florence); also Figs. 35–39 in text.

50–52. See next page for Genealogical Table, Divinities of the Sea.

For stories of the Grææ, Gorgons, Scylla, Sirens, Pleiades, etc., consult Index.

Illustrative. **Oceanus**: Milton, Comus, 868. **Neptune**: Spenser, Faerie Queene, 1, 11, 54; Shakespeare, Tempest, I, ii; Midsummer Night's Dream, II, ii; Macbeth, II, ii; Cymbeline, III, i; Hamlet, I, i; Milton, Lycidas; Paradise Regained, 1, 190; Paradise Lost, 9, 18; Comus, 869; Prior, Ode on Taking of Namur; Waller's Panegyric to the Lord Protector. **Panope**: Milton, Lycidas, 99.

Harpies. Milton, Paradise Lost, 3, 403. **Sirens**: Wm. Morris, Life and Death of Jason — Song of the Sirens. **Scylla** and Charybdis (see Index): Milton, Paradise Lost, 2, 660; Arcades, 63; Comus, 257; Pope, Rape of the Lock, 3, 122. **Sirens**: Rossetti, A Sea-Spell; A. Lang, " They hear the Sirens for the second time."

Naiads. Landor, To Joseph Ablett; Shelley, To Liberty,

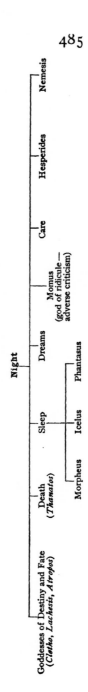

TABLE B. THE FAMILY OF NIGHT

Night

Nemesis

Hesperides

Care

Momus (god of ridicule — adverse criticism)

Dreams — Phantasus

Sleep — Icelus

Death (*Thanatos*) — Morpheus

Goddesses of Destiny and Fate (*Clotho, Lachesis, Atropos*)

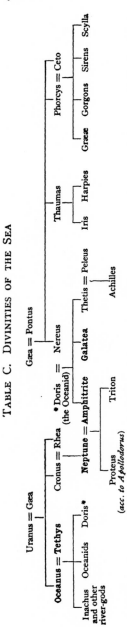

TABLE C. DIVINITIES OF THE SEA

Uranus = Gæa

Cronus = Rhea · Oceanus = Tethys · Gæa = Pontus

Oceanus = Tethys

Inachus and other river-gods · Oceanids · Doris*

Neptune = Amphitrite

Proteus (acc. to Apollodorus)

*Doris (the Oceanid) = Nereus

Triton · Galatea · Thetis = Peleus

Achilles

Thaumas · Phorcys = Ceto

Iris · Harpies · Grææ · Gorgons · Sirens · Scylla

8; Spenser, Prothalamion, 19; Milton, Lycidas; Paradise Regained, 2, 355; Comus, 254; Buchanan, Naiad (see **134**); Drummond of Hawthornden, "Nymphs, sister nymphs, which haunt this crystal brook, And happy in these floating bowers abide," etc.; Pope, Summer, 7; Armstrong, Art of Preserving Health, " Come, ye Naiads! to the fountains lead."

Proteus. Shakespeare, Two Gentlemen of Verona, I, i; II, ii; III, ii; IV, iv; Pope, Dunciad, 1, 37; 2, 109. The Water Deities are presented in a masque contained in Beaumont and Fletcher's Maid's Tragedy.

In Art. Poseidon: see text, Figs. 40 and 41 (originals in the British Museum and the Glyptothek, Munich); also the Isthmian Poseidon, Fig. 95. The Atlas (Græco-Roman sculpture) in National Museum, Naples; the Triton in Vatican (text, Fig. 42). Modern painting: J. Van Beers, The Siren; D. G. Rossetti, The Siren.

Textual. **Consus,** from *condere,* 'to stow away.' The sisters of **Carmenta,** the forward-looking Antevorta and the backward-looking Postvorta, were originally but different aspects of the function of the Muse.

54. *Illustrative.* **Saturn**: Milton, Il Penseroso; Keats, Hyperion; Peele, Arraignment of Paris. **Janus,** as god of civilization: Dryden, Epistle to Congreve, 7. **Fauns**: Milton, Lycidas; R. C. Rogers, The Dancing Faun. See Hawthorne's Marble Faun. **Bellona**: Shakespeare, Macbeth, " Bellona's bridegroom, lapp'd in proof"; Milton, Paradise Lost, 2, 922. **Pomona**: Randolph, To Master Anthony Stafford; Milton, Paradise Lost, 9, 393; 5, 378; Thomson, Seasons, Summer, 663. **Flora**: Milton, Paradise Lost, 5, 16; Spenser, Faerie Queene, 1, 4, 17; R. H. Stoddard, Arcadian Hymn to Flora; Pope, Windsor Forest, 38. **Janus**: Jonathan Swift, To Janus, on New Year's Day, 1726; **Egeria,** one of the Camenæ; Childe Harold, 4, 115–120; Tennyson, Palace of Art, " Holding one hand against his ear," etc. **Pan,** etc.: Milton, Paradise Lost, 4, 707; 4, 329.

In Sculpture. The Satyr, or so-called Faun, of Praxiteles in the Vatican (text, Fig. 106); Dancing Faun (Lateran, Rome); Dancing Faun, Drunken Faun, Sleeping Faun, and Faun and Bacchus (National Museum, Naples); The Barberini Faun, or Sleeping Satyr (Glyptothek, Munich).

Flora. Painting by Titian (Uffizi, Florence).

55. The first love of Zeus was **Metis,** daughter of Oceanus and Tethys. She is Prudence or Foreknowledge. She warned Zeus that if she bore him a child, it would be greater than he. Whereupon Zeus swallowed her; and, in time, from his head sprang Athene, "the virgin of the azure eyes, Equal in strength, and as her father wise" (Hesiod, Theog.). On **Latona,** see **32, 73,** and Commentary.

56. For Danaë see **151**; for Alcmene, **156**; for Leda, **194.**

57. In the following general table of the **Race of Inachus** (see p. 488), marriages are indicated in the usual manner (by the sign =, or by parentheses); the more important characters mentioned in this work are printed in heavy-faced type. While numerous less important branches, families, and mythical individuals have been intentionally omitted, it is hoped that this reduction of various relationships, elsewhere explained or tabulated, to a general scheme, may furnish the reader with a clearer conception of the family ties that motivate many of the incidents of mythical adventure, and that must have been commonplaces of information to those who invented and perpetuated these stories. It should be borne in mind that the traditions concerning relationships are by no means consistent, and that consequently the collation of mythical genealogies demands the continual exercise of discretion, and a balancing of probabilities. Notice that from the union of Jupiter and Io (Table D), Hercules is descended in the thirteenth generation.

Inachus is the principal river of Argolis in the Peloponnesus.

Interpretative. Io is explained as the horned moon, in its various changes and wanderings. **Argus** is the heaven with its myriad stars, some of them shut, some blinking, some always agleam. The wand of Hermes and his music may be the morning breeze, at the coming of which the eyes of heaven close (Cox, 2, 138; Preller 2, 40). The explanation would, however, be just as probable if Mercury (Hermes) were a cloud-driving wind. **Pan and the Syrinx:** naturally the wind playing through the reeds, if (with Müller and Cox) we take Pan to be the all-purifying, but yet gentle, wind. But see p. 181.

Illustrative. Shelley, To the Moon, "Art thou pale for weariness Of climbing heaven and gazing on the earth, Wandering companionless Among the stars that have a different birth?" Milton's "To behold the wandering moon, Riding near her highest noon, Like one that had been led astray, Through the heaven's wide pathless way" (Il Penseroso). See also for Io, Shelley's Prometheus Bound. **Argus:** Milton, Paradise Lost, 11, 131; Pope, Dunciad, 2, 374; 4, 637.

In Art. Fig. 47 in the text, from a wall-painting of Herculaneum (Museum, Naples). Correggio's painting, Jupiter and Io; not a pleasant conception.

58. *Interpretative.* The myth of **Callisto** and **Arcas** is of Arcadian origin. If the Arcadians, in very remote times, traced their descent from a she-bear, and if they also, like other races, recognized a bear in a certain constellation, they might naturally mix the fables and combine them later with the legend of the all-powerful Zeus (Lang, 2, 181). According to another account, Callisto was punished for her love of Jupiter by Diana (Artemis). Her name has been identified with the adjective *Calliste,* 'most fair,' which was certainly applied to Artemis herself. That Artemis was protectress of she-bears is known; also that, in Attica, she was

TABLE D. THE RACE OF INACHUS AND ITS BRANCHES

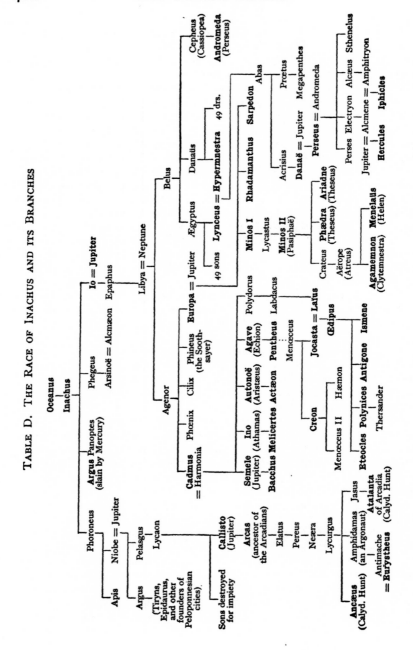

served by girls who imitated, while dancing, the gait of bears. It is quite possible, therefore, that Artemis inherited a more ancient worship of the bear that may have been the *totem*, or sacred animal, from which the Arcadians traced a mythological descent. Others hold that the word *arksha*, 'a star,' became confused with the Greek *arktos*, 'a bear.' So the myth of the son Arcas (the star and the bear) may have arisen (Max Müller). The last star in the tail of the Little Bear is the Polestar, or **Cynosure** (dog's tail).

Illustrative. Milton's " Let my lamp, at midnight hour, Be seen in some high lonely tower, Where I may oft *outwatch the Bear*" (Il Penseroso); and his " Where perhaps some beauty lies The cynosure of neighbouring eyes" (L'Allegro); also his " And thou shalt be our star of Arcady, Or Tyrian Cynosure " (Comus). Note Lowell's " The Bear, that prowled all night about the fold Of the North-star, hath shrunk into his den " (Prometheus). See also the song beginning, " Hear ye, ladies, that despise What the mighty Love had done," in Beaumont and Fletcher's drama, Valentinian, — for Callisto, Leda, and Danaë.

59. The Descendants of Agenor. For further details, see Table D.

TABLE E

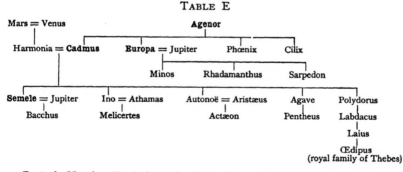

Textual. **Moschus** lived about the close of the third century B.C. in Syracuse. He was a grammarian and an idyllic poet. He calls himself a pupil of Bion, — whose Lament for Adonis is given in **100**. Both Bion and Moschus belong to the School of Theocritus — the Idyllic or Pastoral School of Poetry. **Cypris**: Venus, by whom the island of Cyprus was beloved. **Mygdonian flutes**: the ancients had three species or modes of music, depending, respectively, upon the succession of musical intervals which was adopted as the basis of the system. The Lydian measures were shrill and lively; the Dorian deep in tone, grave, and solemn; the Mygdonian, or Phrygian, were supposed by some to have been the same as the Lydian, but more probably they were a combination of Lydian and Dorian. **Shaker of the World**: Neptune. **Crete**: where Jupiter had been concealed from his father Cronus, and nourished by the goat Amalthea.

Interpretative. Herodotus says that **Europa** was a historical princess of Tyre, carried off by Hellenes to Crete. **Taurus** (the bull) was euhemeristically conceived to be a king of Crete who carried off the Tyrian princess as prize of war. Others said that probably the figurehead of the ship in which Europa was conveyed to Crete was a *bull*. It is not improbable that the story indicates a settlement of Phœnicians in Crete and the introduction by them of cattle. Modern critics, such as Preller and Welcker, make Europa a goddess of the moon = Diana or Astarte, and translate her name " the dark, or obscured one." But she has undoubtedly a connection with the earth, perhaps as wife of Jupiter (the Heaven). H. D. Müller connects both Io and Europa with the wandering Demeter (or Ceres), and considers Demeter to be a goddess both of the moon and of the earth (Helbig, in Roscher). Cox, after his usual method, finds here the Dawn borne across the heaven by the lord of the pure ether. Europa would then be the broad-spreading flush of dawn, seen first in the purple region of morning (Phœnicia). Her brother Cadmus, who pursues her, would be the sun searching for his lost sister or bride. Very fanciful, but inconclusive. **The bull** occurs not infrequently in myth as an incarnation of deity.

Illustrative. W. S. Landor, Europa and her Mother; Aubrey De Vere, The Rape of Europa; E. Dowden, Europa; W. W. Story, Europa (a sonnet). See also a graceful picture in Tennyson's Palace of Art.

In Art. Fig. 48, in text, from vase found at Cumæ; the marble group in the Vatican, Europa riding the Bull; painting by Paolo Veronese, The Rape of Europa; Europa, by Claude Lorrain.

60. See Tables D and E.

Interpretative. According to Preller, **Semele** is a personification of the fertile soil in spring, which brings forth the productive vine. In the irrational part of the myth, Jove takes the child Dionysus (Bacchus), after Semele's death, and sews him up in his thigh for safe-keeping. Preller finds here " the wedlock of heaven and earth, the first day that it thunders in March." Exactly why, might be easy to guess, but hard to demonstrate. The thigh of Jupiter would have to be the cool moist clouds brooding over the youthful vine. The whole explanation is altogether too conjectural. See A. Lang's Myth, Ritual, etc., 2, 221–225, for a more plausible but less poetic theory.

Illustrative. Milton, Paradise Regained, 2, 187; Bowring's translation of Schiller's Semele; E. R. Sill, Semele, of which a part is given in the text.

In Art. Fig. 50, in text.

61. *Textual.* The son of Ægina and Jove was Æacus (for genealogy, see Table O (1)). **Ægina**: an island in the Saronic Gulf, between Attica and Argolis. **Asopus**: the name of two rivers, one in Achaia, one in Bœotia, of which the latter is the more important. The Greek traveler, Pausanias, tells us that Asopus was the discoverer of the river which bears his name. **Sisyphus**, see **255**. This description of the plague is copied by Ovid from the account which Thucydides gives of the plague of Athens. That account, much fuller than is here given, was drawn from life and has been the source from which many subsequent poets and novelists have drawn details of similar scenes. The **Myrmidons** were, during the Trojan War, the soldiers of Achilles, grandson of this king Æacus.

Interpretative. The name Ægina may imply either the shore on which the waves break (Preller), or the sacred goat (*Ægeus*) which was the *totem* of the Ægeus family of Attica. The worship of Athene was introduced into Athens by this family. In sacrifices the goddess was clad in the skin of the sacred goat, but no goat might be sacrificed to her. Probably another example of the survival of a savage ritual (Lang, Myth, Ritual, etc., 1, 280).

Illustrative. **Myrmidons:**

> No, no, said Rhadamant, it were not well,
> With loving souls to place a martialist;
> He died in war, and must to martial fields,
> Where wounded Hector lives in lasting pain,
> And Achilles' Myrmidons do scour the plain.
>
> Kyd, Spanish Tragedy

On **Sisyphus,** read Lewis Morris' poem in The Epic of Hades.

62. *Textual.* **Mænad:** the Mænades, from μαίνομαι (*mainomai*), 'to rage,' were women who danced themselves into a frenzy in the orgies or festivals of Bacchus. **Cithæron:** a mountain range south of Thebes and between Bœotia and Attica.

Interpretative. **Antiope,** philologically interpreted, may indicate the moon with face turned full upon us. That Antiope is a personification of some such natural phenomena would also appear from the significance of the names associated with hers in the myth: **Nycteus,** the *night-man;* **Lycus,** the *man of light.* Amphion and Zethus are thought, in like fashion, to represent manifestations of light; see also Castor and Pollux. Perhaps the method employed by Zethus and Amphion in building Thebes may merely symbolize the advantage of combining mechanical force with well-ordered or harmonious thought.

In Art: The Farnese Bull group (text, opp. p. 74): marble, maybe by Tauriscus and Tralles, in Naples Museum. Fig. 51: a relief in the Palazzo Spada, Rome. Modern painting: Correggio's Antiope.

63. *Textual.* **Phrygia:** a province in Asia Minor. For **Minerva's** protection of the olive, see 65. **Tyana** is a town in Cappadocia, Asia Minor.

64. *Textual.* **Argos:** the capital of Argolis in the Peloponnesus. Of **Cydippe,** it is told, in Ovid's Heroides and elsewhere, that, when a girl sacrificing in the temple of Diana in Delos, she was seen and loved by a youth, Acontius. He threw before her an apple, on which these words were inscribed, " I swear by the sanctuary of Diana to marry Acontius." The maiden read aloud the words and threw the apple away. But the vow was registered by Diana, who, in spite of many delays, brought about the marriage of Cydippe and her unknown lover. **Polyclitus the Elder,** of Argos, lived about 431 B.C., and was a contemporary of two other great sculptors, Phidias and Myron. His greatest work was the chryselephantine statue of Hera for her temple between Argos and Mycenæ.

Illustrative. Beside Gosse's Sons of Cydippe, see verses by L. J. Richardson, in *The Inlander*, Ann Arbor, Vol. 2, p. 2. For the story of Acontius and Cydippe, see William Morris' Earthly Paradise; and Lytton's Cydippe, or The Apples, in The Lost Tales of Miletus.

In Art. The severe design in clay by Teignmouth, of which prints may be obtained, was made to illustrate Gosse's poem.

65-66. *Textual.* For **Cecrops**, see **174.** He named the city that he founded Cecropia, — a name which afterwards clung to Athens. For an excellent description of ancient weaving, see Catullus, LXIV, 304-323 (The Peleus and Thetis). For translation, see **191.** **Leda**, mother of Castor, Pollux, Helen, and Clytemnestra (see **194** and Commentary). **Danaë**, mother of Perseus (see **151**).

Interpretative. The waves were the coursers of Neptune, — the horses with which he scours the strand. **Arachne:** a princess of Lydia. It is probable that the myth symbolizes the competition in products of the loom between Attica and Asia Minor and the superior handicraft of the Athenian weavers.

Illustrative. Arachne: Shakespeare, Troilus and Cressida, V, ii; Pope, Dunciad, 4, 590. *Poem:* Garrick, Upon a Lady's Embroidery.

In Art. Fig. 52, in text: from a vase in Petrograd.

68. *Textual.* Diomede: for his genealogy, see Table K. **Taslets:** armor worn about the thighs. **Cyprian:** Venus. **Pæan** (Pæon, or Paiëon), classed by Homer among the Olympian gods, of whom he is, as his name implies, the "healer." Later, the name was applied to Æsculapius, then to any god who might repair or avert evil of any kind, as, for instance, to Apollo and to Thanatos (Death). See Armstrong's Art of Health, "So Pæan, so the powers of Health command," etc., and "the wise of ancient days Adored one power of physic, melody, and song." **Pæans** were chants in honor of Apollo, sung to deprecate misfortune in battle or to avert disease. **Lower than the sons of Heaven:** lower than the Titans, sons of Uranus (Heaven), who were plunged into Tartarus.

69. *Textual.* Lessing points out in his Laocoön the skill with which Homer, stating the size of the stone hurled by Minerva and the measure of the space covered by Mars, suggests the gigantic proportions of the warring divinities.

70. *Textual.* Family of **Cadmus:** see Tables D and E. **Castalian Cave** of Mount Parnassus, Phocis; here was the famous Delphic oracle of Apollo. **Cephissus:** a river running through Doris, Phocis, and Bœotia into the Eubœan Gulf; the valley of the Cephissus was noted for its fertility. **Panope:** a town on the Cephissus. **Tyrians:** Cadmus and his followers came from Tyre in Phœnicia. The **Necklace of Harmonia** was a fateful gift. It brought evil to whomsoever it belonged: to all the descendants of Cadmus; to Eriphyle, wife of Amphiaraüs of Argos, to whom Polynices gave it; and to the sons of Eriphyle. It was finally dedicated to Apollo in Delphi. Harmonia's robe possessed the same fatality, **187, 189.** **Enchelians:** a people of Illyria. For the myths of **Semele**, see **60**; of **Ino, 144**; of **Autonoë** and her son, **Actæon, 95**; of **Agave** and her son, **Pentheus, 112**; of **Polydorus**, the Labdacidæ, Œdipus, etc., **182.** **Eight years:** the usual period of penance. Apollo, after slaying the Python, had to clear himself of defilement by a period of purification.

Interpretative. **Cadmus and his Tyrians:** according to the usual explanation, this myth is based upon an immigration of Phœnicians, who settled Bœotia and gave laws, the rudiments of culture (alphabet, etc.), and industrial arts to the older races of Greece. Many Theban names, such as Melicertes, Cadmus, point to a possible Phœnician origin; cf. Semitic Melkarth, and Kedem, the *East*. But Preller holds that two mythical personages, a Greek Cadmus and a Phœnician Cadmus, have been confounded; that the Theban Cadmus is merely the representative of the oldest Theban state; that the selection of the spot on which a heifer had lain down was a frequent practice among settlers, superstitious about the site of their new town; that the dragon typifies the cruel and forbidding nature of the uncultivated surroundings; and that the story of the dragon's teeth was manufactured to flatter the warlike spirit of the Thebans, the teeth themselves being spear points.

Harmonia, daughter of the patron deities of Thebes, is the symbol of the peace and domesticity that attend the final establishment of order in the State.

According to the Sun-and-Cloud theory of Cox, Cadmus, the Sun, pursues his sister, Europa, the broad-flushing light of Dawn, who has been carried off on a spotless cloud (the Bull). The Sun, of course, must journey farther west than Crete. The heifer that he is to follow is, therefore, still another cloud (like the cattle of the Sun, — clouds). The dragon of Mars is still a third cloud; and this the Sun dissipates. A storm follows, after which new conflicts arise between the clouds that have sprung up from the moistened earth (the harvest of armed men!). This kind of explanation, indiscriminately indulged, delights the fancy of the inventor and titillates the risibles of the reader.

Illustrative. Milton, Paradise Lost, 9, 506. The serpent that tempted Eve compared with the serpents Cadmus and " Hermione." See Byron, Don Juan, 3, 86, " You have the letters Cadmus gave — Think you he meant them for a slave?"

In Art. Fig. 54, in text: from a vase in the Naples Museum. Fig. 55 is of a vase-painting from Eretria.

71. *Textual.* Eurynome is represented by some as one of the Titans, the wife of Ophion. Ophion and Eurynome, according to one legend, ruled over heaven before the age of Saturn (Cronus). So Milton, Paradise Lost, 10, 580, "And fabled how the Serpent, whom they called Ophion, with Eurynome (the wide-Encroaching Eve perhaps), had first the rule Of high Olympus, thence by Saturn driven." According to Vulcan's statement (Iliad, 18), Eurynome was daughter of Oceanus and Tethys. She was mother, by Jupiter, of the Graces. **Thetis:** see **50. Xanthus:** the principal river of Lycia in Asia Minor.

72-73. *Interpretative.* Latona (Leto): according to Homer, one of the deities of Olympus; a daughter of the Titans Cœus and Phœbe, whose names indicate phenomena of radiant light. She belonged, perhaps, to an ancient theogony of Asia Minor. At any rate she held at one time the rank of lawful wife to Zeus. Preller and, after him, Cox take Leto as *the dusk* or *darkness*. Cox traces the word to the root of Lethe (the forgetful), but Preller is doubtful. Possibly Leto and Leda, the mother of the bright Castor and Pollux, have something in common. The wanderings of Latona may be the weary journey of the night over the mountain tops, both before and after the Sun (Apollo) is born in Delos (the land of Dawn).

Illustrative. Milton, Arcades, 20, and Sonnet XII, " On the detraction which followed upon my writing certain treatises."

74. *Textual.* **Hyperboreans :** those who dwell in the land beyond the North. **Pæan,** see C. 68. **Tityus :** an earthborn giant; condemned to the underworld, he lay stretched over nine acres while two vultures devoured his liver.

Interpretative. **Python :** in many savage myths, a serpent, a frog, or a lizard that drinks up all the waters, and is destroyed by some national hero or god. As Mr. Lang says : " Whether the slaying of the Python was or was not originally an allegory of the defeat of winter by sunlight, it certainly, at a very early period, became mixed up with ancient legal ideas and local traditions. It is almost as necessary for a young god or hero to slay monsters as for a young lady to be presented at court; and we may hesitate to explain all these legends of a useful feat of courage as nature myths " (Myth, Ritual, etc., 2, 196). Compare the feats of Hercules, Jason, Bellerophon, Perseus, St. George and the Dragon, Sigurd, and Jack the Giant Killer. Commentators take Python to be the rigor of winter, or the darkness of night, or a " black storm-cloud which shuts up the waters " (Cox). It is not impossible that the Python was the sacred snake of an older animal worship superseded by that of Apollo. (See also **C. 38.**)

75. *Textual.* The Tyrian hue is purple, made from the juice of the *murex,* or purple shellfish. On the leaves of the hyacinth were inscribed characters like Ai, Ai, the Greek exclamation of woe. It is evidently not our modern hyacinth that is here described, but perhaps some species of iris, or of larkspur, or pansy. The meaning of the name is also uncertain, but the best authorities favor *youthful.* A festival called the **Hyacinthia** was celebrated, in commemoration of the myth, over a large part of the Peloponnesus. It lasted three days, probably in the first half of July. It consisted of chants of lamentation and fasting during the first and last days; during the second day, of processions, a horse race, joyous choral songs, dances, feasting, and sacrifice.

Interpretative. Most scholars consider Hyacinthus to be the personification of the blooming vegetation of spring, which withers under the heats of summer. The Hyacinthian festival seems to have celebrated — like the Linus festival and the Eleusinian — the transitory nature of life and the hope of immortality.

Illustrative. Keats, Endymion, " Pitying the sad death Of Hyacinthus, when the cool breath Of Zephyr slew him " (see context); Milton, Lycidas, " Like to that sanguine flower inscribed with woe "; On the Death of a Fair Infant, 4.

In Art. Fig. 58, in text, is of a marble group in the Hope Collection.

76. *Textual.* **Clymene :** a daughter of Oceanus and Tethys. **Chrysolite :** or *gold stone,* our topaz. **Daystar :** Phosphor, see **38** (11). **Ambrosia** (ἀμβρόσιος, ἄμβροτος, ἀ-βροτός), *immortal,* — here, " food for the immortals." **Turn off to the left :** indicating the course of the sun, west by south. The **Serpent,** or **Dragon :** a constellation between the Great and Little Bears. **Boötes :** the constellation called the Wagoner. The limits of the **Scorpion** were restricted by the insertion of the sign of the Scales. **Athos :** a mountain forming the eastern of three peninsulas south of Macedonia. **Mount Taurus :** in Armenia. **Mount Tmolus :** in

Lydia. **Mount Œte**: between Thessaly and Ætolia, where Hercules ascended his funeral pile. **Ida**: the name of two mountains, — one in Crete, where Jupiter was nurtured by Amalthea, the other in Phrygia, near Troy. **Mount Helicon**: in Bœotia, sacred also to Apollo. **Mount Hæmus**: in Thrace. **Ætna**: in Sicily. **Parnassus**: in Phocis; one peak was sacred to Apollo, the other to the Muses. The Castalian Spring, sacred to the Muses, is at the foot of the mountain; Delphi is near by. **Rhodope**: part of the Hæmus range of mountains. **Scythia**: a general designation of Europe and Asia north of the Back Sea. **Caucasus**: between the Black and Caspian seas. **Mount Ossa**: associated with **Mount Pelion** in the story of the giants, who piled one on top of the other in their attempt to scale Olympus. These mountains, with **Pindus**, are in Thessaly. **Libyan** desert: in Africa. Libya was fabled to have been the daughter of Epaphus, king of Egypt. **Tanaïs**: the Don, in Scythia. **Caïcus**: a river of Greater Mysia, flowing into the sea at Lesbos. **Xanthus** and **Mæander**: rivers of Phrygia, flowing near Troy. **Caÿster**: a river of Ionia, noted for its so-called "tuneful" swans. For Nereus, Doris, Nereids, etc., see **50** and **52**. **Eridanus**: the mythical name of the river Po in Italy (amber was found on its banks). **Naiads**, see **52** (6).

Interpretative. Apollo assumed many of the attributes of Helios, the older divinity of the sun, who is ordinarily reputed to be the father of Phaëthon (ordinarily anglicized Phaëton). The name *Phaëthon*, like the name *Phœbus*, means *the radiant one*. The sun is called both Helios Phaëthon and Helios Phœbus in Homer. It was an easy feat of the imagination to make Phaëthon the incautious son of Helios, or Apollo, and to suppose that extreme drought is caused by his careless driving of his father's chariot. The drought is succeeded by a thunderstorm; and the lightning puts an end to Phaëthon. The rain that succeeds the lightning is, according to Cox, the tears of the Heliades. It is hardly wise to press the analogy so far, unless one is prepared to explain the *amber* in the same way.

Illustrative. Milman in his Samor alludes to the story. See also Chaucer, Hous of Fame, 435; Spenser, Faerie Queene, 1, 4, 9; Shakespeare, Richard II, III, iii; Two Gentlemen of Verona, III, i; 3 Henry VI, I, iv; II, vi; Romeo and Juliet, III, ii. *Poems:* Prior, Female Phaëton; J. G. Saxe, Phaëton; and G. Meredith, Phaëton. For description of the palace and chariot of the Sun, see Landor, Gebir, Bk. 1.

In Art: Fig. 59, in text: a relief on a Roman sarcophagus in the Louvre.

77. *Textual.* For the siege of Troy, see Chap. XXII. **Atrides** (**Atreides**): the son of Atreus, Agamemnon. The ending *-ides* means *son of*, and is used in patronymics; for instance, Pelides (Peleides), Achilles; Tydides, Diomede, son of Tydeus. The ending *-is*, in patronymics, means *daughter of*; as Tyndaris, daughter of Tyndarus (Tyndareus), Helen; Chryseïs, daughter of Chryses.

Interpretative. Of this incident Gladstone, in his primer on Homer, says: "One of the greatest branches and props of morality for the heroic age lay in the care of the stranger and the poor. . . . Sacrifice could not be substituted for duty, nor could prayer. Such, upon the abduction of Chryseïs, was the reply of Calchas the Seer: nothing would avail but restitution."

78. The Dynasty of Tantalus and its Connections. (See also Table I.)

TABLE F

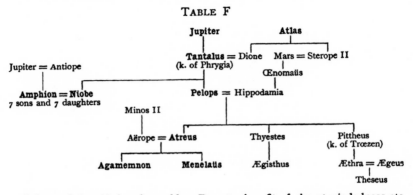

Pelops. It is said that the goddess Demeter in a fit of absent-mindedness ate the shoulder of Pelops. The part was replaced in ivory when Pelops was restored to life. **Mount Cynthus:** in Delos, where Apollo and Diana were born.

Interpretative. Max Müller derives **Niobe** from the root *snu*, or *snigh*, from which come the words for *snow* in the Indo-European languages. In Latin and Greek, the stem is *Niv*, hence Nib, Niobe. The myth, therefore, would signify the melting of snow and the destruction of its icy offspring under the rays of the spring sun (Sci. Relig. 372). According to Homer (Iliad, 24, 611), there were six sons and six daughters. After their death no one could bury them, since all who looked on them were turned to stone. The burial was, accordingly, performed on the tenth day after the massacre, by Jupiter and the other gods. This petrifaction of the onlookers may indicate the operation of the frost. Cox says that Niobe, the snow, compares her golden-tinted, wintry mists or clouds with the splendor of the sun and moon. Others look upon the myth as significant of the withering of spring vegetation under the heats of summer (Preller). The latter explanation is as satisfactory, for spring is the child of winter (Niobe).

Illustrative. Pope, Dunciad, 2, 311; Lewis Morris, Niobe on Sipylus (Songs Unsung); Byron's noble stanza on fallen Rome, "The Niobe of nations! there she stands, Childless and crownless, in her voiceless woe," etc. (Childe Harold, 4, 79); W. S. Landor, Niobe; Frederick Tennyson, Niobe. On **Tantalus,** see Lewis Morris, Tantalus, in The Epic of Hades. On Sir Richard Blackmore, a physician and poor poet, Thomas Moore writes the following stanza:

> 'T was in his carriage the sublime
> Sir Richard Blackmore used to rhyme,
>   And, if the wits don't do him wrong,
> 'Twixt death and epics passed his time,
>   Scribbling and killing all day long;
>   Like Phœbus in his car at ease,
>   Now warbling forth a lofty song,
>   Now murdering the young Niobes.

In Art. The restoration of the statue of Niobe, Mount Sipylus; of extreme antiquity. The Petrograd relief (see Fig. 61, in text) is probably the best group. Figs. 60 and 62 are from the ancient marbles in the Uffizi, Florence. The fragments of the latter group were discovered in 1583 near the Porta San Giovanni, Rome. The figure of the mother, clasping the little girl who has run to her in terror, is one of the most admired of the ancient statues. It ranks with the Laocoön and the Apollo Belvedere among the masterpieces of art. The following is a translation of a Greek epigram supposed to relate to this statue:

> To stone the gods have changed her, but in vain;
> The sculptor's art has made her breathe again.

There is also a fine figure of a daughter of Niobe in the Vatican, Rome; and there are figures in the Louvre. Reinach in his *Apollo* attributes the originals to Scopas.

79. Interpretative. The month in which the festival of **Linus** took place was called the **Lambs' Month**: the days were the **Lambs' Days,** on one of which was a massacre of dogs. According to some, Linus was a minstrel, son of Apollo and the Muse Urania, and the teacher of Orpheus and Hercules.

80. Centaurs. Monsters represented as men from the head to the loins, while the remainder of the body was that of a horse. Centaurs are the only monsters of antiquity to which any good traits were assigned. They were admitted to the companionship of men. **Chiron** was the wisest and justest of the Centaurs. At his death he was placed by Jupiter among the stars as the constellation Sagittarius (the Archer). **Messenia:** in the Peloponnesus. **Æsculapius:** there were numerous oracles of Æsculapius, but the most celebrated was at Epidaurus. Here the sick sought responses and the recovery of their health by sleeping in the temple. It has been inferred from the accounts that have come down to us that the treatment of the sick resembled what is now called animal magnetism or mesmerism.

Serpents were sacred to Æsculapius, probably because of a superstition that those animals have a faculty of renewing their youth by a change of skin. The worship of Æsculapius was introduced into Rome in a time of great sickness. An embassy, sent to the temple of Epidaurus to entreat the aid of the god, was propitiously received; and on the return of the ship Æsculapius accompanied it in the form of a serpent. Arriving in the river Tiber, the serpent glided from the vessel and took possession of an island, upon which a temple was soon erected to his honor.

Interpretative. The healing powers of nature may be here symbolized. But it is more likely that the family of Asclepiadæ (a medical clan) invented Asklepios as at once their ancestor and the son of the god of healing, Apollo.

Illustrative. Milton, Paradise Lost, 9, 506; Shakespeare, Pericles, III, ii; Merry Wives, II, iii.

In Art. Æsculapius (sculpture), Vatican; also the statue in the Uffizi, Florence (text, Fig. 63). Thorwaldsen's (sculpture) Hygea (Health) and Æsculapius, Copenhagen.

81. Interpretative. Perhaps the unceasing and unvarying round of the sun led to the conception of him as a servant. Max Müller cites the Peruvian Inca who

said that if the sun were free, like fire, he would visit new parts of the heavens.
" He is," said the Inca, " like a tied beast who goes ever round and round in the
same track" (Chips, etc., 2, 113). Nearly all Greek heroes had to undergo servitude,
— Hercules, Perseus, etc. No stories are more beautiful or more lofty than those
which express the hope, innate in the human heart, that somewhere and at some
time some god has lived as a man among men and for the good of men. Such
stories are not confined to the Greeks or the Hebrews.

Illustrative. R. Browning, Apollo and the Fates; Edith M. Thomas. Apollo the
Shepherd; Emma Lazarus, Admetus; W. M. W. Call, Admetus.

83. *Textual.* **Alcestis** was a daughter of the Pelias who was killed at the instigation of Medea (**167**). In that affair Alcestis took no part. For her family, see
Table G. She was held in the highest honor in Greek fable, and ranked with
Penelope and Laodamia, the latter of whom was her niece. To explain the myth
as a physical allegory would be easy, but is it not more likely that the idea of
substitution finds expression in the myth? — that idea of atonement by sacrifice,
which is suggested in the words of Œdipus at Colonus (**185**), " For one soul working in the strength of love Is mightier than ten thousand to atone." **Koré** (the
daughter of Ceres): Proserpina. **Larissa**: a city of Thessaly, on the river Peneüs.

Illustrative. Milton's sonnet, On his Deceased Wife:

> Methought I saw my late espousèd saint
> Brought to me like Alcestis from the grave,
> Whom Jove's great son to her glad husband gave,
> Rescued from death by force, though pale and faint.

Chaucer, Legende of Good Women, 208 *et seq.;* Court of Love (?), 100 *et seq.*

Poems. Robert Browning's noble poem, Balaustion's Adventure, purports to
be a paraphrase of the Alcestis of Euripides, but while it maintains the classical
spirit, it is in execution an original poem. The Love of Alcestis, by William
Morris; Mrs. Hemans, The Alcestis of Alfieri, and The Death Song of Alcestis;
W. S. Landor, Hercules, Pluto, Alcestis, and Admetus; Alcestis: F. T. Palgrave,
W. M. W. Call, John Todhunter (a drama).

In Art. Fig. 64, in text, Naples Museum; also the relief on a Roman sarcophagus in the Vatican.

84. *Textual.* This Laomedon was descended, through Dardanus (the forefather
of the Trojan race), from Jupiter and the Pleiad Electra. For further information
about him, see **119**, **161**, and Table I.

Interpretative. Apollo evidently fulfills, under Laomedon, his function as god
of colonization.

85–86. *Textual.* For Pan, see **43**; for Tmolus, **76**. **Peneüs**: a river in Thessaly,
which rises in Mount Pindus and flows through the wooded valley of Tempe.
Dædal: variously adorned, variegated. Midas was king of Phrygia (see **113**).

Illustrative. The story of King Midas has been told by others with some
variations. Dryden, in the Wife of Bath's Tale, makes Midas' queen the betrayer
of the secret:

> This Midas knew, and durst communicate
> To none but to his wife his ears of state.

87. Illustrative. M. Arnold, Empedocles (Song of Callicles); L. Morris, Marsyas, in The Epic of Hades; Edith M. Thomas, Marsyas; E. Lee-Hamilton, Apollo and Marsyas.

In Art. Raphael's drawing, Apollo and Marsyas (Museum, Venice); Bordone's Apollo, Marsyas, and Midas (Dresden); the Græco-Roman sculpture, Marsyas (Louvre); Marsyas (or Dancing Faun), in the Lateran, Rome.

89. Textual. Daphne was a sister of Cyrene, another sweetheart of Apollo's (**145**). **Delphi**, in Phocis, and **Tenedos**, an island off the coast of Asia Minor, near Troy, were celebrated for their temples of Apollo. The latter temple was sacred to **Apollo Smintheus**, the Mouse-Apollo, probably because he had rid that country of mice as St. Patrick rid Ireland of snakes and toads. **Dido**: queen of Carthage (**252**), whose lover, Æneas, sailed away from her.

Interpretative. Max Müller's explanation is poetic though not philologically probable. "Daphne, or Ahanâ, means the Dawn. There is first the appearance of the dawn in the eastern sky, then the rising of the sun as if hurrying after his bride, then the gradual fading away of the bright dawn at the touch of the fiery rays of the sun, and at last her death or disappearance in the lap of her mother, the earth." The word *Daphne* also means, in Greek, a *laurel;* hence the legend that Daphne was changed into a laurel tree (Sci. Relig., 378, 379). Others construe Daphne as the *lightning.* It is, however, very probable that the Greeks of the myth-making age, finding certain plants and flowers sacred to Apollo, would invent stories to explain why he preferred the laurel, the hyacinth, the sunflower, etc. "Such myths of metamorphoses" are, as Mr. Lang says, "an universal growth of savage fancy, and spring from a want of a sense of difference between men and things" (Myth, Ritual, etc., 2, 206).

Illustrative. Shakespeare, Midsummer Night's Dream, II, ii; Taming of the Shrew, Induction ii; Troilus and Cressida, I, i; Milton, Comus, 59, 662; Hymn on the Nativity, ll. 176–180, Vacation, 33–40; Paradise Lost, 4, 268–275; Paradise Regained, 2, 187; Lord de Tabley (Wm. Lancaster), Daphne, "All day long, In devious forest, Grove, and fountain side, The god had sought his Daphne," etc.; Lyly, King Mydas; Apollo's Song to Daphne; Frederick Tennyson, Daphne. Waller applies this story to the case of one whose amatory verses, though they did not soften the heart of his mistress, yet won for the poet widespread fame:

> Yet what he sung in his immortal strain,
> Though unsuccessful, was not sung in vain.
> All but the nymph that should redress his wrong,
> Attend his passion and approve his song.
> Like Phœbus thus, acquiring unsought praise,
> He caught at love and filled his arms with bays.

In Art. Fig. 67, in text; Bernini's Apollo and Daphne, in the Villa Borghese, Rome (see text, opp. p. 112). Painting: G. F. Watts' Daphne.

91. Illustrative. Hood, Flowers, "I will not have the mad Clytia, Whose head is turned by the sun," etc.; W. W. Story, Clytie; Mrs. A. Fields, Clytia. The so-called bust of Clytie (discovered not long ago) is possibly a representation of Isis.

93. *Textual.* **Elis:** northwestern part of the Peloponnesus. **Alpheüs:** a river of Elis flowing to the Mediterranean. The river Alpheüs does in fact disappear under ground, in part of its course, finding its way through subterranean channels, till it again appears on the surface. It was said that the Sicilian fountain Arethusa was the same stream, which, after passing under the sea, came up again in Sicily. Hence the story ran that a cup thrown into the Alpheüs appeared again in the Arethusa. It is, possibly, this fable of the underground course of Alpheüs that Coleridge has in mind in his dream of Kubla Khan:

> In Xanadu did Kubla Khan
> A stately pleasure-dome decree:
> Where Alph, the sacred river, ran
> Through caverns measureless to man,
> Down to a sunless sea.

In one of Moore's juvenile poems he alludes to the practice of throwing garlands or other light objects on the stream of Alpheüs, to be carried downward by it, and afterward reproduced at its emerging, " as an offering To lay at Arethusa's feet."

The Acroceraunian Mountains are in Epirus in the northern part of Greece. It is hardly necessary to point out that a river Arethusa arising there could not possibly be approached by an Alpheüs of the Peloponnesus. Such a criticism of Shelley's sparkling verses would however be pedantic rather than just. Probably Shelley uses the word *Acroceraunian* as synonymous with *steep, dangerous.* If so, he had the practice of Ovid behind him (Remedium Amoris, 739). **Mount Erymanthus:** between Arcadia and Achaia. The **Dorian** deep: the Peloponnesus was inhabited by descendants of the fabulous Dorus. **Enna:** a city in the center of Sicily. **Ortygia:** an island on which part of the city of Syracuse is built.

Illustrative. Milton, Arcades, 30; Lycidas, 132; Margaret J. Preston, The Flight of Arethusa; Keats, Endymion, Bk. 2, " On either side outgushed, with misty spray, A copious spring."

95. See genealogical table E for **Actæon.** In this myth Preller finds another allegory of the baleful influence of the dog days upon those exposed to the heat. Cox's theory that here we have large masses of cloud which, having dared to look upon the clear sky, are torn to pieces and scattered by the winds, is principally instructive as illustrating how far afield theorists have gone, and how easy it is to invent ingenious explanations.

Illustrative. Shakespeare, Merry Wives, II, i; III, ii; Titus Andronicus, II, iii; Shelley, Adonais, 31, " Midst others of less note, came one frail Form," etc., a touching allusion to himself; A. H. Clough, Actæon; L. Morris, Actæon (Epic of Hades).

96. Chios: an island in the Ægean. **Lemnos:** another island in the Ægean, where Vulcan had a forge.

Interpretative. The ancients were wont to glorify in fable constellations of remarkable brilliancy or form. The heavenly adventures of **Orion** are sufficiently explained by the text.

Illustrative. Spenser, Faerie Queene, 1, 3, 31; Milton, Paradise Lost, 1, 299, "Natheless he so endured," etc.; Longfellow, Occultation of Orion; R. H. Horne, Orion; Charles Tennyson Turner, Orion (a sonnet).

97. **Electra.** See genealogical table I. See same table for **Merope,** the mother of Glaucus and grandmother of Bellerophon (155).

Illustrative. **Pleiads:** Milton, Paradise Lost, 7, 374; Pope, Spring, 102; Mrs. Hemans has verses on the same subject; Byron, "Like the lost Pleiad seen no more below."

In modern sculpture, The Lost Pleiad of Randolph Rogers is famous; in painting, the Pleiades of Elihu Vedder (Fig. 72, in text).

98. **Mount Latmos:** in Caria. Diana is sometimes called **Phœbe,** the shining one. For the descendants of Endymion, the Ætolians, etc., see Table I.

Interpretative. According to the simplest explanation of the **Endymion** myth, the hero is the setting sun on whom the upward rising moon delights to gaze. His fifty children by Selene would then be the fifty months of the Olympiad, or Greek period of four years. Some, however, consider him to be a personification of sleep, the king whose influence comes over one in the cool caves of Latmos, "the Mount of Oblivion"; others, the growth of vegetation under the dewy moonlight; still others, euhemeristically, a young hunter, who under the moonlight followed the chase, but in the daytime slept.

Illustrative. The Endymion of Keats. Fletcher, in the Faithful Shepherdess, tells, "How the pale Phœbe, hunting in a grove, First saw the boy Endymion," etc. Young, Night Thoughts, "So Cynthia, poets feign, In shadows veiled, . . . Her shepherd cheered"; Spenser, Epithalamion, "The Latmian Shepherd," etc.; Marvel, Songs on Lord Fauconberg and the Lady Mary Cromwell (chorus, Endymion and Laura); O. W. Holmes, Metrical Essays, "And, Night's chaste empress, in her bridal play, Laughed through the foliage where Endymion lay."

Poems. Besides Keats' the most important are by Lowell, Longfellow, Clough (Epi Latmo, and Selene), T. B. Read, Buchanan, L. Morris (Epic of Hades). John Lyly's prose drama, Endymion, contains quaint and delicate songs.

In Art. Fig. 73, in text; Diana and the sleeping Endymion (Vatican).

Paintings. Carracci's fresco, Diana embracing Endymion (Farnese Palace, Rome); Guercino's Sleeping Endymion; G. F. Watts' Endymion.

100. *Textual.* **Paphos** and **Amathus:** towns in Cyprus, of which the former contained a temple to Venus. **Cnidos** (Cnidus or Gnidus): a town in Caria, where stood a famous statue of Venus, attributed to Praxiteles. **Cytherea:** Venus, an adjective derived from her island Cythera in the Ægean Sea. **Acheron,** and **Persephone** or **Proserpine:** see **44–48.** The windflower of the Greeks was of bloody hue, like that of the pomegranate. It is said the wind blows the blossoms open, and afterwards scatters the petals.

Interpretative. Among the Phœnicians Venus is known as Astarte, among the Assyrians as Istar. The **Adonis** of this story is the Phœnician *Adon,* or the Hebrew *Adonai,* 'Lord.' The myth derives its origin from the Babylonian worship of Thammuz or Adon, who represents the verdure of spring, and whom his mistress, the goddess of fertility, seeks, after his death, in the lower regions.

With their departure all birth and fruitage cease on the earth; but when he has been revived by sprinkling of water, and restored to his mistress and to earth, all nature again rejoices. The myth is akin to those of Linus, Hyacinthus, and Narcissus. Mannhardt (Wald- und Feld-kulte, 274), cited by Roscher, supplies the following characteristics common to such religious rites in various lands: (1) The spring is personified as a beautiful youth who is represented by an image surrounded by quickly fading flowers from the " garden of Adonis." (2) He comes in the early year and is beloved by a goddess of vegetation, goddess sometimes of the moon, sometimes of the star of Love. (3) In midsummer he dies, and during autumn and winter inhabits the underworld. (4) His burial is attended with lamentations, his resurrection with festivals. (5) These events take place in midsummer and in spring. (6) The image and the *Adonis* plants are thrown into water. (7) Sham marriages are celebrated between pairs of worshipers.

Illustrative. The realistic Idyl XV of Theocritus contains a typical Psalm of Adonis, sung at Alexandria, for his resurrection. Shakespeare's Venus and Adonis; Taming of the Shrew, Induction ii; 1 Henry VI, I, vi. In Milton, Comus, 998:

> Beds of hyacinth and roses,
> Where young Adonis oft reposes,
> Waxing well of his deep wound,
> In slumber soft, and on the ground
> Sadly sits th' Assyrian queen.

Drummond, The Statue of Adonis; Pope, Summer, 61; Winter, 24; Miscel. 7, 10; Moral Essays, 3, 73; Dunciad, 5, 202. See C. S. Calverley, Death of Adonis (Theocritus); L. Morris, Adonis (Epic of Hades).

In Art. Fig. 74, in text, from a Roman sarcophagus. The Dying Adonis, (sculpture), Michelangelo; the Adonis of Thorwaldsen in the Glyptothek, Munich.

101–102. *Textual.* Psyche does not eat anything in Hades, because, by accepting the hospitality of Proserpina, she would become an inmate of her household. The scene with the lamp and knife probably indicates the infringement of some ancient matrimonial custom. **Erebus**: the land of darkness, Hades. For **Zephyr**, **Acheron, Cerberus, Charon,** etc., see Index.

Interpretative. The fable of Cupid and Psyche is usually regarded as allegorical. The Greek name for *butterfly* is Psyche, and the same word means the *soul.* There is no illustration of the immortality of the soul so striking and beautiful as that of the butterfly, bursting on brilliant wings from the tomb in which it has lain, after a dull, groveling, caterpillar existence, to flutter in the blaze of day and feed on the most fragrant and delicate productions of the spring. Psyche, then, is the human soul, which is purified by sufferings and misfortunes, and is thus prepared for the enjoyment of true and pure happiness. It is probable that the story allegorizes a philosophical conception concerning *three* stages of the soul's life: first, a former existence of bliss; second, an earthly existence of trial; third, a heavenly future of fruition. Cox, by his usual method, finds here a myth of the search for the Sun (Eros) by the Dawn (Psyche). Many of the incidents of the story will be found in modern fairy tales and romances, such as Beauty and the Beast, Grimm's Twelve Brothers; the Gaelic stories: The Three Daughters of King O'Hara; Fair, Brown, and Trembling; The Daughter of the Skies; and the Norse tale — East of the Sun and West of the Moon. See Cox 1, 403–411.

Illustrative. Thomas Moore, Cupid and Psyche; Mrs. Browning, Psyche, Paraphrase on Apuleius; L. Morris, in The Epic of Hades; Frederick Tennyson, Psyche; Robert Bridges, Eros and Psyche. Most important is W. H. Pater's Marius the Epicurean, which contains the story as given by Apuleius.

In Art. Psyche is represented as a maiden with the wings of a butterfly, in the different situations described in the allegory. The Græco-Roman sculpture of Cupid and Psyche, in the Capitol at Rome, is of surpassing beauty; so also is Canova's Cupid and Psyche.

Paintings. Raphael's frescoes in the Farnesina Villa, twelve in number, illustrating the story; François Gérard's Cupid and Psyche; Paul Thumann's nine illustrations of the story (see Figs. 75, 76, in text); R. Beyschlag's Psyche with the Urn, Psyche Grieving, and Psyche and Pan; W. Kray's Psyche and Zephyr; Psyche: by A. de Curzon; by G. F. Watts, a series of three illustrations by H. Bates. The Charon and Psyche of E. Neide is a sentimental, simpering conception. A. Zick also has a Psyche.

103. According to another tradition, **Atalanta's** love was Milanion. The nuptial vow was ratified by Hera (Juno). This, the Bœotian, Atalanta is sometimes identified with the Arcadian Atalanta of the Calydonian Hunt. (See **168** and Table D). It is better to discriminate between them. The genealogy of this Atalanta will be seen in Tables G and I.

Illustrative. W. Morris, Atalanta's Race (Earthly Paradise); Moore, Rhymes on the Road, on Alpine Scenery, — an allusion to Hippomenes.

In Art. Painting by E. J. Poynter, Atalanta's Race (Fig. 78, in text); and Guido Reni's brilliant picture of the same subject.

104. *Textual* and *Illustrative.* The story of **Hero and Leander** is the subject of a romantic poem by Musæus, a grammarian of Alexandria, who lived in the fifth century A.D. This author, in distinction from the mythical poet of the same name, is styled the Pseudo-Musæus. The *epyllion* has been translated by Sir Robert Stapylton, Sir Edwin Arnold, and others. The feat of swimming the Hellespont was performed by Lord Byron. The distance in the narrowest part is not more than a mile, but there is a constant dangerous current setting out from the Sea of Marmora into the Archipelago. For an allusion to the story see Byron, Bride of Abydos, Canto II. For Byron's statement concerning the breadth of the water see footnote to " Stanzas written after swimming from Sestos to Abydos."

Poems. Hero and Leander: by Leigh Hunt, by Tom Hood, by Moore; sonnet by D. G. Rossetti, Hero's Lamp (House of Life); a poem not in later editions of Tennyson, Hero to Leander, 1830; Chapman's continuation of Marlowe's Hero and Leander.

Paintings. G. von Bodenhausen; F. Keller (Fig. 79, in text).

105. *Interpretative.* Another illustration of the vivifying influence of love. Preller deems Pygmalion's story nearly akin to the Adonis myth. He regards

TABLE G. THE CONNECTIONS OF ATALANTA THE BŒOTIAN

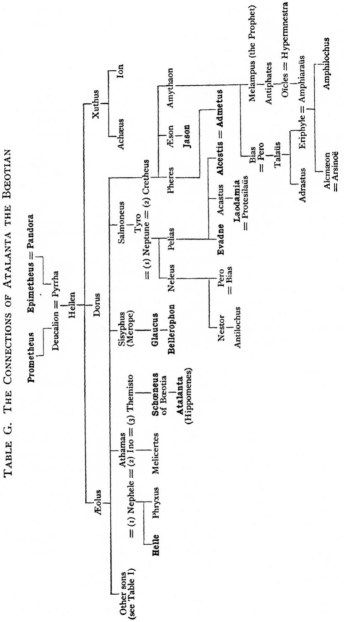

the festival of Venus, during which the statue of Galatea (or passive love) receives life, as the usual Adonis-festival.

Illustrative. Thomson, Castle of Indolence, 2, 12; R. Buchanan, Pygmalion the Sculptor; Morris, and Lang, as in text; Pygmalion: by T. L. Beddoes, by W. C. Bennett. The seventeenth-century satirist, Marston, wrote a Pygmalion, of no great worth. Frederick Tennyson, Pygmalion (in Daphne and other Poems); Arthur Henry Hallam, Lines spoken in the Character of Pygmalion; Thomas Woolner, Pygmalion.

In Art. The Pygmalion series of four scenes, by E. Burne-Jones.

106. *Textual.* Semiramis: wife of King Ninus and the queen of Assyria. Famous for her administrative and military ability. A mythical character with features of historic probability.

Illustrative. Chaucer, Thisbe, the Martyr of Babylon (Legende of Good Women). Allusions in Surrey, Of the Death of Sir Thomas Wyatt; Shakespeare, Midsummer Night's Dream, III, ii; V, i; Merchant of Venice, V, i. Moore, in the Sylph's Ball, draws a comparison between Thisbe's wall and the gauze of Davy's safety lamp. Mickle's translation of the Lusiad (Island of Love).

In Art. Burne-Jones' three paintings, Cupid, Pyramus, and Thisbe (Fig. 80, in text); E. J. Paupion's painting, Thisbe.

107. *Textual.* Lesbos and **Chios:** islands in the Ægean. For **Sappho** see **298** (3).

Illustrative. The second lyric of Sappho, beginning " Like to the gods he seems to me, The man that sits reclined by thee," has been translated by Phillips, by Fawkes, and by recent poets. The reference is probably to Phaon. Allusions in Pope, Moral Essays, 3, 121; 2, 24; Prologue to Satires, 309, 101; Byron's Isles of Greece, already referred to. Compare the translation in Catullus, LI.

Poems on Sappho or on Phaon: Charles Kingsley, Sappho; Buchanan, Sappho on the Leucadian Rock; Landor, — Sappho, Alcæus, Anacreon, and Phaon; Frederick Tennyson, Kleïs or the Return (in the Isles of Greece). See also Lyly's amusing prose drama, Sappho and Phao.

109. *Textual.* Mount Cyllene: between Arcadia and Achæa. **Pierian Mountains:** in Macedonia, directly north of Thessaly; the birthplace of the Muses. **Pylos:** an ancient city of Elis.

Interpretative. On the supposition that the herds of Apollo are the bright rays of the sun, a plausible physical explanation of the relations of **Mercury** (Hermes) to Apollo is the following from Max Müller: " Hermes is the god of the twilight, who betrays his equivocal nature by stealing, though only in fun, the herds of Apollo, but restoring them without the violent combat that (in the analogous Indian story) is waged for the herds between Indra, the bright god, and Vala, the robber. In India the dawn brings the light; in Greece the twilight itself is supposed to have stolen it, or to hold back the light, and Hermes, the twilight, surrenders the booty when challenged by the sun-god Apollo" (Lect. on Lang., 2 Ser., 521–522). Hermes is connected by Professor Müller with the Vedic god *Sarameya*, son of the twilight. Mercury, or Hermes, as morning or as evening twilight, loves the Dew, is herald of the gods, is spy of the night, is sender of sleep and dreams, is accompanied by the cock, herald of dawn, is the guide of the departed on their last journey. To the conception of twilight, Cox adds that of *motion*, and explains Hermes as the *air in motion* that springs up with the dawn, gains rapidly in force, sweeps before it the *clouds* (here the cattle of Apollo), makes soft music through the trees (lyre), etc. Other theorists make Hermes the Divine Activity, the god of the ether, of clouds, of storm, etc. Though the explanations of Professor Müller and the Rev. Sir G. W. Cox are more satisfactory here than usual, Roscher's *the swift wind* is scientifically preferable.

Illustrative. See Shelley, Homeric Hymn to Mercury, on which the text of this section is based, and passages in Prometheus Unbound; Keats, Ode to Maia.

In Art. The intent of the disguise in Fig. 81 (text) is to deceive Demeter with a sham sacrifice.

110-112. Textual. See Table E, for Bacchus, Pentheus, etc. **Nysa** " has been identified as a mountain in Thrace, in Bœotia, in Arabia, India, Libya; and Naxos, as a town in Caria or the Caucasus, and as an island in the Nile." **Thebes:** the capital of Bœotia. **Mæonia:** Lydia, in Asia Minor. **Dia:** Naxos, the largest of the Cyclades Islands in the Ægean. **Mount Cithæron:** in Bœotia. The **Thyrsus** was a wand, wreathed with ivy and surmounted by a pine cone, carried by Bacchus and his votaries. **Mænads** and **Bacchantes** were female followers of Bacchus. **Bacchanal** is a general term for his devotees.

Interpretative. "Bacchus (Dionysus) is regarded by many as the *spiritual form* of the new vernal life, the sap and pulse of vegetation and of the newborn year, especially as manifest in the vine and juice of the grape." — LANG, Myth, Ritual, etc., 2, 221 (from Preller 1, 554). The **Hyades** (rain-stars), that nurtured the deity, perhaps symbolize the rains that nourish sprouting vegetation. He became identified very soon with the *spirituous effects* of the vine. His sufferings may typify the "ruin of the summer year at the hands of storm and winter," or, perhaps, the agony of the bleeding grapes in the wine press. The orgies would, according to this theory, be a survival of the ungoverned actions of savages when celebrating a festival in honor of the deity of plenty, of harvest home, and of intoxication. But in cultivated Greece, Dionysus, in spite of the surviving orgiastic ceremonies, is a poetic incarnation of blithe, changeable, spirited youth. See Lang, Myth, Ritual, etc., 2, 221–241. That **Rhea** taught him would account for the Oriental nature of his rites; for Rhea is an Eastern deity by origin. The opposition of **Pentheus** would indicate the reluctance with which the Greeks adopted his doctrine and ceremonial. The Dionysiac worship came from Thrace, a barbarous clime; — but wandering, like the springtide, over the earth, Bacchus conquered each nation in turn. It is probable that the Dionysus-Iacchus cult was one of evangelical enthusiasm and individual cleansing from sin, of ideals in this life and of personal immortality in the next. By introducing it into Greece, Pisistratus reformed the exclusive ritual of the Eleusinian Mysteries.

Of the **Festivals of Dionysus**, the more important in Attica were the Lesser Dionysia, in December; the Lenæa, in January; the Anthesteria, or spring festival, in February; and the Great Dionysia, in March. These all, in greater or less degree, witnessed of the culture and the glories of the vine, and of the reawakening of the spirits of vegetation. They were celebrated, as the case might be, with a sacrifice of a victim in reminiscence of the blood by which the spirits of the departed were supposed to be nourished, with processions of women, profusion of flowers, orgiastic songs and dances, or dramatic representations.

Illustrative. **Bacchus:** Milton, Comus, 46. **Pentheus:** Landor, The Last Fruit of an Old Tree; H. H. Milman, The Bacchanals of Euripides; Calverley's and Lang's translations of Theocritus, Idyl XXVI; Thomas Love Peacock, Rhododaphne: The Vengeance of Bacchus; B. W. Procter, Bacchanalian Song. **Naxos:** Milton, Paradise Lost, 4, 275.

In Art. Figs. 31, 82–87, 143, in text.

113. *Textual.* Hesperides, see Index. **River Pactolus:** in Lydia. **Midas:** the son of one Gordius, who from a farmer had become king of Phrygia, because he happened to fulfill a prophecy by entering the public square of some city just as the people were casting about for a king. He tied his wagon in the temple of the prophetic deity with the celebrated **Gordian Knot,** which none but the future lord of Asia might undo. Alexander the Great undid the knot with his sword.

Interpretative. An ingenious, but not highly probable, theory explains the golden touch of Midas as the rising sun that gilds all things, and his bathing in Pactolus as the quenching of the sun's splendor in the western ocean. **Midas** is fabled to have been the son of the "great mother," Cybele, whose worship in Phrygia was closely related to that of Bacchus or Dionysus. The **Sileni** were there regarded as tutelary *genii* of the rivers and springs, promoting fertility of the soil. **Marsyas,** an inspired musician in the service of Cybele, was naturally associated in fable with Midas. The ass being the favorite animal of Silenus, the ass's ears of Midas merely symbolize his fondness for and devotion to such habits as were attributed to the Sileni. The ass, by the way, was reverenced in Phrygia; the acquisition of ass's ears may therefore have been originally a glory, not a disgrace.

Illustrative. John Lyly, Play of Mydas, especially the song, "Sing to Apollo, god of day"; Shakespeare, Merchant of Venice, III, ii (casket scene); Pope, Dunciad, 3, 342; Prologue to Satires, 82; Swift, The Fable of Midas; J. G. Saxe, The Choice of King Midas (a travesty). **Gordian Knot:** Henry V, I, i; Cymbeline, II, ii; Milton, Paradise Lost, 4, 348; Vacation, 90. **Pactolus:** Pope, Spring, 61; allusions also to the sisters of Phaëthon. **Silenus,** by W. S. Landor.

114–117. *Textual.* **Mount Eryx,** the vale of **Enna,** and **Cyane** are in Sicily. **Eleusis:** in Attica. For **Arethusa** see Index.

Interpretative. The Italian goddess Ceres assumed the attributes of the Greek Demeter in 496 B.C. Proserpine signifies the seed-corn which, when cast into the ground, lies there concealed, — is carried off by the god of the underworld; when the corn reappears, Proserpine is restored to her mother. Spring leads her back to the light of day. The following, from Aubrey De Vere's Introduction to his Search for Proserpine, is suggestive: "Of all the beautiful fictions of Greek Mythology, there are few more exquisite than the story of Proserpine, and none deeper in symbolical meaning. Considering the fable with reference to the physical world, Bacon says, in his Wisdom of the Ancients, that by the Rape of Proserpine is signified the disappearance of flowers at the end of the year, when the vital juices are, as it were, drawn down to the central darkness, and held there in bondage. Following up this view of the subject, the Search of her Mother, sad and unavailing as it was, would seem no unfit emblem of Autumn and the restless melancholy of the season; while the hope with which the Goddess was finally cheered may perhaps remind us of that unexpected return of fine weather which occurs so frequently, like an omen of Spring, just before Winter closes in. The fable has, however, its moral significance also, being connected with that great mystery of Joy and Grief, of Life and Death, which pressed so heavily on the mind of Pagan Greece, and imparts to the whole of her mythology a profound interest, spiritual as well as philosophical. It was the restoration of Man, not of flowers, the victory over Death, not over Winter, with which that high Intelligence felt itself to be really concerned." In Greece two kinds of **Festivals**, the **Eleusinia** and the **Thesmophoria**, were held in honor of Demeter and Persephone. The former was divided into the lesser, celebrated in February, and the greater (lasting nine days), in September. Distinction must be made between the Festivals and the Mysteries of Eleusis. In the Festivals all classes might participate. Those of the Spring represented the restoration of Persephone to her mother; those of the Autumn the rape of Persephone. An image of the youthful Iacchus (Bacchus) headed the procession in its march toward Eleusis. At that place and in the neighborhood were enacted in realistic fashion the wanderings and the sufferings of Demeter; the scenes in the house of Celeus, and finally the successful conclusion of the search for Persephone. The **Mysteries** of Eleusis were witnessed only by the initiated, and were invested with a veil of secrecy which has never been fully withdrawn. The initiates passed through certain symbolic ceremonies from one degree of mystic enlightenment to another till the highest was attained. The Lesser Mysteries were an introduction to the Greater; and it is known that the rites involved partook of the nature of purification from passion, crime, and the various degradations of human existence. By pious contemplation of the dramatic scenes presenting the sorrows of Demeter, and by participation in sacramental rites, it is probable that the initiated were instructed in the nature of life and death, and consoled with the hope of immortality (Preller). On the development of the Eleusinian Mysteries from the savage to the civilized ceremonial, see Lang, Myth, Ritual, etc., 2, 275, and Lobeck, Aglaophamus, 133.

The **Thesmophoria** were celebrated by married women in honor of Ceres (Demeter), and referred to institutions of married life.

That Proserpine should be under bonds to the underworld because she had partaken of food in Hades accords with a superstition not peculiar to the Greeks, but to be "found in New Zealand, Melanesia, Scotland, Finland, and among the Ojibbeways" (Lang, Myth, Ritual, etc., 2, 273).

Illustrative. Aubrey De Vere, as above; B. W. Procter, The Rape of Proserpine; R. H. Stoddard, The Search for Persephone; G. Meredith, The Appeasement of Demeter; Tennyson, Demeter and Persephone; Dora Greenwell, Demeter and Cora; T. L. Beddoes, Song of the Stygian Naiades; A. C. Swinburne, Song to Proserpine. See also notes under Persephone, **44**, Demeter and Pluto. **Eleusis**: Schiller, Festival of Eleusis, translated by N. L. Frothingham; At Eleusis, by Swinburne. See, for poetical reference, Milton, Paradise Lost, 4, 269, " Not that fair field Of Enna," etc.; Hood, Ode to Melancholy:

> Forgive if somewhile I forget,
>   In woe to come the present bliss;
> As frighted Proserpine let fall
>   Her flowers at the sight of Dis.

In Art. Bernini's Pluto and Proserpine (sculpture); P. Schobelt's Rape of Proserpine (picture). Eleusinian relief: Demeter, Cora, Triptolemus (Athens); and other figures, as in text.

118. *Textual.* **Tænarus**: in Laconia. For the crime of **Tantalus**, see **78**. In Hades he stood up to his neck in water which receded when he would drink; grapes hanging above his head withdrew when he would pluck them; while a great rock was forever just about to fall upon him. **Ixion,** for an insult to Juno, was lashed with serpents or brazen bands to an ever-revolving wheel. **Sisyphus,** for his treachery to the gods, vainly rolled a stone toward the top of a hill (see **255**). For the **Danaïds**, see **150**; **Cerberus, 44, 255. The Dynast's bond**: the contract with Pluto, who was Dynast or tyrant of Hades. **Ferry-guard**: Charon. **Strymon** and **Hebrus**: rivers of Thrace. **Libethra**: a city on the side of Mount Olympus, between Thessaly and Macedonia.

Interpretative. **The loss of Eurydice** may signify (like the death of Adonis and the rape of Proserpine) the departure of spring. Max Müller, however, identifies *Orpheus* with the Sanskrit *Arbhu*, used as a name for the Sun (Chips, etc., 2, 127). According to this explanation the Sun follows Eurydice, " the wide-spreading flush of the dawn who has been stung by the serpent of night," into the regions of darkness. There he recovers Eurydice, but while he looks back upon her she fades before his gaze, as the mists of morning vanish before the glory of the rising sun (Cox). It might be more consistent to construe *Eurydice* as the *twilight*, first, of evening which is slain by night, then, of morning which is dissipated by sunrise. Cox finds in the music of Orpheus the delicious strains of the breezes which accompany sunrise and sunset. The story should be compared with that of Apollo and Daphne, and of Mercury and Apollo. The Irish tale, The Three Daughters of King O'Hara, reverses the relation of Orpheus and Eurydice. See Curtin, Myths and Folk-Lore of Ireland, Boston, 1890.

Illustrative. **Orpheus**: Shakespeare, Two Gentlemen of Verona, III, ii; Merchant of Venice, V, i; Henry VIII, III, i (song); Milton, Lycidas, 58; L'Allegro, 145; Il Penseroso, 105; Pope, Ode on St. Cecilia's Day (Eurydice); Summer, 81; Southey, Thalaba (The Nightingale's Song over the Grave of Orpheus).

Poems. Wordsworth, The Power of Music; Shelley, Orpheus, a fragment; Browning, Eurydice and Orpheus; Wm. Morris, Orpheus and the Sirens (Life and Death of Jason); L. Morris, Orpheus, Eurydice (Epic of Hades); Lowell,

Eurydice; E. Dowden, Eurydice; W. B. Scott, Eurydice; E. W. Gosse, The Waking of Eurydice; R. Buchanan, Orpheus, the Musician; J. G. Saxe, Travesty of Orpheus and Eurydice. On **Tantalus** and **Sisyphus**, see Spenser, Faerie Queene, 1, 5, 31–35; L. Morris, Epic of Hades.

In Art. A Relief on a tombstone in the National Museum, Naples, of Mercury, Orpheus, and Eurydice. There is also a copy in Paris of the marble in the Villa Albani, Rome. (See Fig. 94, text.) Paintings: Fig. 93, in text, by Sir Frederick Leighton; by Robert Beyschlag; by G. F. Watts; The Story of Orpheus, a series of ten paintings, by E. Burne-Jones.

119–120. *Textual.* **Troy:** the capital of Troas in Asia Minor, situated between the rivers Scamander and Simois. Famous for the siege conducted by the Greeks under Agamemnon, Menelaüs, etc. (See Chap. XXII.) **Amymone:** a fountain of Argolis. **Enipeus:** a river of Macedonia.

Interpretative. The monsters that wreak the vengeance of Neptune are, of course, his destructive storms and lashing waves.

121. For genealogy of Pelops, etc., see Tables F and I. For the misfortunes of the Pelopidæ, see **193.**

Illustrative in Art. Pelops and Hippodamia; vase pictures (Monuments inédits, Rome, and Paris). East pediment, Temple of Zeus, Olympia.

123–124. *Textual.* **Cephalus,** the son of Mercury (Hermes) and Herse, is irretrievably confounded with Cephalus, the son of Deïon and grandson of Æolus I. The former should, strictly, be regarded as the lover of Aurora (Eos); the latter is the husband of Procris, and the great-grandfather of Ulysses. (See Tables H, I, and O (4).)

Interpretative. Procris is the dewdrop (from Greek *Prōx*, 'dew') which reflects the shining rays of the sun. The "head of the day," or the rising sun, Cephalus, is also wooed by Aurora, the Dawn, but flies from her. The Sun slays the dew with the same gleaming darts that the dew reflects, or gives back to him. According to Preller, Cephalus is the morning-star beloved alike by Procris, the moon, and by Aurora, the dawn. The concealment of Procris in the forest and her death would, then, signify the paling of the moon before the approaching day. Hardly so probable as the former explanation.

Illustrative. **Aurora:** Spenser, Faerie Queene, 1, 2, 7; 1, 4, 16; Shakespeare, Midsummer Night's Dream, III, ii; Romeo and Juliet, I, i; Milton, Paradise Lost, 5, 6, " Now Morn, her rosy steps in the eastern clime Advancing," etc.; L'Allegro, 19; Landor, Gebir, "Now to Aurora borne by dappled steeds, The sacred gates of orient pearl and gold . . . Expanded slow," etc. **Cephalus** and **Procris:** in Moore, Legendary Ballads; Shakespeare, Midsummer Night's Dream, " Shafalus and Procrus"; A. Dobson, The Death of Procris.

In Art. **Aurora:** Figs. 97 and 99, as in text; paintings, by Guido Reni, as Fig. 98 in text, and by J. L. Hamon, and Guercino. Procris and Cephalus, by Turner. L'Aurore et Céphale, painted by P. Guérin, 1810, engraved by F. Forster, 1821.

125. *Textual.* **Cimmerian** country: a fabulous land in the far west, near Hades; or, perhaps, in the north, for the people dwell by the ocean that is never visited by sunlight (Odyssey, 11, 14–19). Other sons of Somnus are **Icelus**, who personates birds, beasts, and serpents, and **Phantasus**, who assumes the forms of rocks, streams, and other inanimate things.

The accompanying table will indicate the connections and descendants of Aurora.

Interpretative. According to one account, **Ceyx** and **Halcyone**, by likening their wedded happiness to that of Jupiter and Juno, incurred the displeasure of the gods. The myth springs from observation of the habits of the Halcyon-bird, which nests on the strand and is frequently bereft of its young by the winter waves. The comparison with the glory of Jupiter and Juno is suggested by the splendid iris hues of the birds. Halcyon days have become proverbial as seasons of calm. Æolus I, the son of Hellen, is here identified with Æolus III, the king of the winds. According to Diodorus, the latter is a descendant, in the fifth generation, of the former. (See Genealogical Table I.)

Illustrative. Chaucer, The Dethe of Blaunche; E. W. Gosse, Alcyone (a sonnet in dialogue); F. Tennyson, Halcyone; Edith M. Thomas, The Kingfisher; Margaret J. Preston, Alcyone. **Morpheus**: see Milton, Il Penseroso; Pope, Ode on St. Cecilia's Day.

126–127. *Interpretative.* **Tithonus** may be the day in its ever-recurring circuit of morning freshness, noon heat, final withering and decay (Preller); or the gray glimmer of the heavens overspread by the first ruddy flush of morning (Welcker); or, as a solar myth, the sun in his setting and waning, — *Tithonus* meaning, by derivation, the illuminator (Max Müller). The sleep of Tithonus in his ocean-bed, and his transformation into a grasshopper, would then typify the presumable weariness and weakness of the sun at night.

Illustrative. Spenser, Epithalamion; Faerie Queene, I, 11, 51.

128. *Textual.* **Mysia**: province of Asia Minor, south of the Propontis, or Sea of Marmora. There is some doubt about the identification of the existing statue with that described by the ancients, and the mysterious sounds are still more doubtful. Yet there is not wanting modern testimony to their being still audible. It has been suggested that sounds produced by confined air making its escape from crevices or

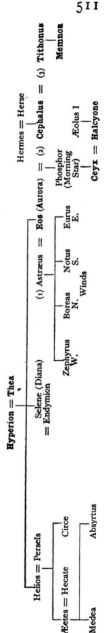

TABLE H. THE ANCIENT RACE OF LUMINARIES AND WINDS

caverns in the rocks may have given some ground for the story. Sir Gardner Wilkinson, a traveler of the highest authority, examined the statue itself, and discovered that it was hollow, and that " in the lap of the statue is a stone, which, on being struck, emits a metallic sound that might still be made use of to deceive a visitor who was predisposed to believe its powers."

Interpretative. **Memnon** is generally represented as of dark features, lighted with the animation of glorious youth. He is king of the mythical Æthiopians who lived in the land of gloaming, where east and west met, and whose name signifies " dark splendor." His birth in this borderland of light and darkness signifies either his existence as king of an eastern land or his identity with the young sun, and strengthens the theory according to which his father Tithonus is the gray glimmer of the morning heavens. The flocks of birds have been explained as the glowing clouds that meet in battle over the body of the dead sun.

Illustrative. Milton, Il Penseroso; Drummond, Summons to Love, " Rouse Memnon's mother from her Tithon's bed "; Akenside, Pleasures of the Imagination (analogy between Memnonian music and spiritual appreciation of truth); Landor, Miscellaneous Poems, 59, " Exposed and lonely genius stands, Like Memnon in the Egyptian sands," etc.

In Art. Fig. 101, from a vase in the Louvre.

129-130. *Textual.* **Doric pillar:** the three styles of pillars in Greek architecture were Dorian, Ionic, Corinthian (see English Dictionary). **Trinacria:** Sicily, from its *three promontories.* **Ægon** and **Daphnis:** idyllic names of Sicilian shepherds (see Idyls of Theocritus and Virgil's Eclogues). **Naïs:** a water-nymph. For Cyclops, Galatea, Silenus, Fauns, Arethusa, see Index. Compare, with the conception of Stedman's poem, Wordsworth's Power of Music.

Illustrative. Ben Jonson, Pan's anniversary; Milton, Paradise Lost, 4. 266, 707; Paradise Regained, 2, 190; Comus, 176, 268; Pope, Autumn, 81; Windsor Forest, 37, 183; Summer, 50; Dunciad, 3, 110; Akenside, Pleasures of Imagination, " Fair Tempe! haunt beloved of sylvan Powers," etc.; On Leaving Holland, 1, 2. *Poems:* Fletcher, Song of the Priest of Pan, and Song of Pan (in The Faithful Shepherdess); Landor, Pan and Pitys, " Pan led me to a wood the other day," etc.; Landor, Cupid and Pan; R. Buchanan, Pan; Browning, Pan and Luna; Swinburne, Pan and Thalassius; Hon. Roden Noël, Pan, in the Modern Faust. Of course Mrs. Browning's Dead Pan cannot be appreciated unless read as a whole; nor Schiller's Gods of Greece.

131. Fauns. Milton, Paradise Lost, 4, 708; 10. 573, 597; 11. 472, 788; Paradise Regained, 2, 257; Mrs. Browning, Flush or Faunus (sonnet). **Dryads:** Pope, Moral Essays, 4, 94; Winter, 12; Collins, The Passions; Keats, Nightingale, Psyche. **Satyrs:** Milton, Lycidas; Dryden, Mrs. Anne Killigrew, 6; Hawthorne, Marble Faun.

In Art. **Fauns** (sculpture): The Barberini Faun (Munich); the Drunken Faun, Sleeping Faun, Faun and Bacchus, and Dancing Faun (National Museum, Naples); the Dancing Faun (Lateran, Rome); the so-called Faun of Praxiteles or Marble Faun (Fig. 106 in text — a Satyr — best copy in the Capitoline, Rome). **Pan and**

Apollo. Græco-Roman sculpture (Museum, Naples). **Pan:** Fig. 102, in text; and Fig. 103, from an original perhaps of the School of Scopas or Praxiteles (Florence). Silenus and Bacchus (Glyptothek, Munich). **Nymphs** (pictures): Bouguereau, Nymphs and Satyr, and Nymphs; Burne-Jones, Nymphs; Giorgione, Nymphs pursued by a Satyr. **Satyrs:** Michelangelo (picture) (Uffizi, Florence), Mask of a Satyr; Rubens, Satyrs (Munich); Satyrs (sculpture), relief from theater of Dionysus; Satyr playing a flute (Vatican); and Figs. 103, 104, and 106–108 in the text.

132-133. *Textual.* **Cephissus:** four rivers in Phocis, Attica, and Argolis bear this name. The most famous runs near Athens.

Illustrative. **Echo:** Chaucer, Romaunt of the Rose, 1468 *et seq.;* Spenser, Prothalamion; Milton, Comus, 237; Collins, The Passions. *Poems:* L. Morris (Epic of Hades), Narcissus; Goldsmith, On a Beautiful Youth, etc.; Cowper, On an Ugly Fellow; Milton, Paradise Lost, 4, 449–470 (illus.); and Comus. **In Art:** Narcissus (sculpture), and Fig. 109, in text (Museum, Naples).

137. **Dryope** (poem), by W. S. Landor.

138. **Rhœcus.** Poems by Landor, The Hamadryad; Acon and Rhodope.

139. **Pomona.** Phillips, a poem on Cider. See Index. **In Art:** the painting by J. E. Millais.

Interpretative. The various guises and transformations of Vertumnus signify the succession of the seasons and the changing characteristics of each. The name itself implies *turning,* or *change.*

140. *Textual.* In order to understand the story of Ibycus, it is necessary to remember, first, that the theaters of the ancients were immense fabrics, capable of containing from ten to thirty thousand spectators, and as they were used only on festal occasions and admission was free to all, they were usually filled. They were without roofs and open to the sky, and performances were in the daytime. Secondly, that the appalling representation of the Furies is not exaggerated in the story. It is fabled that Æschylus, the tragic poet, having on one occasion represented the Furies in a chorus of fifty performers, the terror of the spectators was such that many fainted and were thrown into convulsions, and the magistrates forbade a like representation for the future (Pollux, 4, 110). Usually the chorus in a single tragedy consisted of only fifteen performers.

Illustrative. On the **Furies** see C. 49. On **Ibycus** see translation of Schiller's Cranes of Ibycus, by E. A. Bowring.

141. *Textual.* The adventures of the water-divinities turn largely on the idea of metamorphosis, which would readily be suggested to the imaginative mind by contemplation of the ever-changing aspect of fountain, stream, lake, or ocean. For genealogies of water-deities, see Table C.

Interpretative. The Cyclops, **Polyphemus,** does not possess much in common with Steropes, Brontes, and Arges, the offspring of Uranus and Gæa, save his one eye and his monstrous size. The sons of Gæa are personifications of thunder and lightning; Polyphemus is the heavy vapor that rolls its clouds along the hillside. The clouds are the sheep that he pastures; the sun glowering through the vapor is his single eye (Cox). More probably he is a mere giant of folklore.

Illustrative. John Gay, Song of Polypheme (in Acis and Galatea) ; A. Dobson, A Tale of Polypheme; R. Buchanan, Polypheme's Passion; Shelley, The Cyclops of Euripides; Translations of Theocritus by Mrs. Browning and by Calverley; J. S. Blackie, Galatea; B. W. Procter, The Death of Acis. See also on the **Cyclops,** Shakespeare, Titus Andronicus, IV, iii; Hamlet, II, ii.

In Art. Fig. 112, text; Carracci's frescoes in the Farnese Palace, Rome, of Polyphemus, Acis and Galatea; Claude Lorrain's painting, Evening, Acis and Galatea; Raphael's Triumph of Galatea.

142. *Textual.* For descent of Glaucus, see Tables G and I. For Scylla's descent, see Table C. See Keats, Endymion, Bk. 3.

Interpretative. Glaucus is explained by some as the calm gleaming sea; by others, as the angry sea that reflects the lowering heavens (see Roscher, p. 1690). Scylla is a personification of treacherous currents and shallows among jagged cliffs and hidden rocks.

144. For genealogy of Ino, see Table E. " Leucothea waked, and with fresh dews embalmed The Earth " (Milton, Paradise Lost, 11, 135).

145. Cyrene was sister to Daphne. Honey must first have been known as a wild product, the bees building their structures in hollow trees, or holes in the rocks, or any similar cavity that chance offered. Thus occasionally the carcass of a dead animal would be occupied by the bees for that purpose. It was no doubt from some such incident that the superstition arose that bees were engendered by the decaying flesh of the animal. Virgil assigns to Proteus the isle of Carpathus, between Crete and Rhodes; Homer, the isle of Pharus, near the river Nile.

Illustrative. See C. 50. Proteus, a poem by R. Buchanan. On **Aristæus,** Cowper's Task, comparison of the ice-palace of Empress Anne of Russia with Cyrene's palace. Milton probably thought of Cyrene in describing Sabrina (Comus). He calls Proteus "the Carpathian Wizard."

146-147. *Textual.* **Acheloüs** : the largest river in Greece, rose in Mount Lacmon, flowed between Acarnania and Ætolia, and emptied into the Ionian Sea. It was honored over all Greece. **Calydon** : a city of Ætolia, famed for the Calydonian Hunt. **Parthenope,** see **238.** **Ligea** (Ligeia) : the *shrill-sounding maiden :* here a Siren ; sometimes a Dryad.

Interpretative. Even among the ancients such stories as this were explained on a physical basis: the river Acheloüs flows through the realm of Dejanira, hence Acheloüs loves Dejanira. When the river winds it is a snake, when it roars it is a bull, when it overflows its banks it puts forth new horns. Hercules is supposed to have regulated the course of the stream by confining it within a new and suitable channel. At the same time the old channel, redeemed from the stream, subjected to cultivation, and blossoming with flowers, might well be called a *horn of plenty.* There is another account of the origin of the Cornucopia. Jupiter at his birth was committed by his mother Rhea to the care of the daughters of Melisseus, a Cretan king. They fed the infant deity with the milk of the goat Amalthea. Jupiter, breaking off one of the horns of the goat, gave it to his nurses,

148. (5)

TABLE I. THE RACE OF IAPETUS, DEUCALION, ATLAS, AND HELLEN

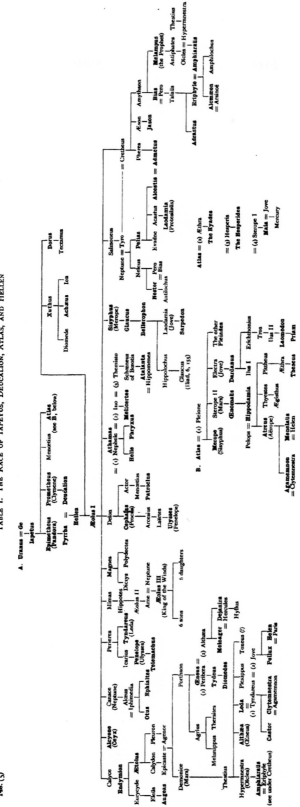

and endowed it with the power of becoming filled with whatever the possessor might wish.

Illustrative. The name *Amalthea* is given also to the mother of Bacchus. It is thus used by Milton, Paradise Lost, 4, 275:

> That Nyseian isle,
> Girt with the river Triton, where old Cham,
> Whom Gentiles Ammon call and Libyan Jove,
> Hid Amalthea, and her florid son,
> Young Bacchus, from his stepdame Rhea's eye.

See also Milton, Paradise Regained, 2, 356.

148. For the general genealogy of the race of Inachus, see Table D. For the general race of Iapetus, Deucalion, Hellen, Æolus, Ætolus, etc., see below, Table I (based in part on the table given in Roscher, article *Deukalion*). For the descendants of Agenor, see Table E. For the houses of Minos and of Labdacus, see Tables L and N. For the descendants of Belus (house of Danaüs), see Tables I and J ; of Cecrops and Erechtheus, Table M.

(1) The race of Inachus

The descendants of Pelasgus,	of Belus,	of Agenor
	House of Danaüs	Houses of Minos and Labdacus

(2) The race of Deucalion (Table G), and of his son, Hellen

The descendants of Æolus, of Dorus, of Xuthus,

(Achæans and Ionians)
The descendants of Endymion, Perieres, Deïon, Sisyphus, Cretheus, Athamas

(3) The descendants of Ætolus, son of Endymion (Table K)

Houses of Porthaon and Thestius

(4) The race of Cecrops

The descendants of Erichthonius

House of Pandion and Ægeus

149-154. *Textual.* **Seriphus:** an island of the Ægean.
The House of Danaüs is as follows:

TABLE J. THE HOUSE OF DANAÜS

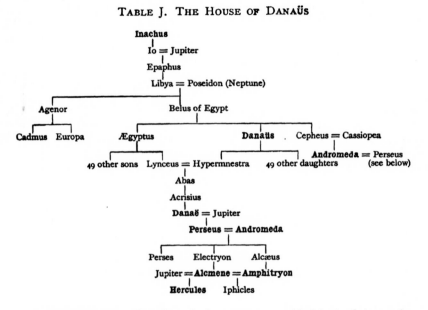

```
                        Inachus
                          |
                        Io = Jupiter
                          |
                        Epaphus
                          |
                        Libya = Poseidon (Neptune)
```

Interpretative. While **Danaüs** is, in fact, a native mythical hero of Argos, the story of his arrival from Egypt is probably an attempt to explain the influence of Egyptian civilization upon the Greeks. The name *Danaüs* means *drought*, and may refer to the frequently dry condition of the soil of Argos. The fifty daughters of Danaüs would then be the nymphs of the many *springs* which in season refresh the land of Argolis. Their suitors, the fifty sons of Ægyptus, would be the streams of Argolis that in the rainy months threaten to overflow their banks. But the springs by vanishing during the hot weather deprive the streams of water and consequently of life. That is to say, when the sources (Danaïds) choose to stop supplies, the heads of the streams (the fifty youths of Argolis) are cut off. The reference to Ægyptus and the sons of Ægyptus would indicate a reminiscence of the Nile and its tributaries, alternately overflowing and exhausted. The unsuccessful toil of the Danaïds in Tartarus may have been suggested by the sandy nature of the Argive soil, and the leaky nature of the springs, now high, now low. Or it may typify, simply, any incessant, fruitless labor. The name **Hypermnestra** signifies *constancy* and *love*. **Danaë,** the daughter of Acrisius, has been regarded as the dry earth, which under the rains of the golden springtime bursts into verdure and bloom; or as the dark depths of the earth; or as the dawn, from which, shot through with the golden rays of heaven, the youthful Sun is born.[1] Advocates of the last theory would understand the voyage of Danaë and Perseus as the tossing of the sunbeams on the waters of the eastern horizon. The young Sun would next overcome the **Gray-women,** forms of the gloaming, and then slay with his sword of light the black cloud of the heavenly vault, the **Gorgon,** whose aspect is night and death.

The **Grææ** and the Gorgons may, with greater probability, be taken as personifications of the hidden horrors of the unknown night-enveloped ocean and the misty horizon whence storms come. In that case the Grææ will be the gray clouds, and their one tooth (or one eye) the harmless gleam of the lightning; the Gorgons will be the heavy thunderclouds, and their petrifying gaze the swift and fatal lightning flash.

But there are still others who find in the Gorgon **Medusa** the wan visage of the moon, empress of the night, slain by the splendor of morning. The sandals of Hermes have, accordingly, been explained as the morning breeze, or even as the chariot of the sun. The invisible helmet may be the clouds under which the sun disappears. Compare the cloak of darkness in the Three Daughters of King O'Hara; and the Sword of Sharpness in the Weaver's Son and the Giant of White Hill (Curtin, Myths of Ireland).

Andromeda is variously deciphered: the tender dawn, which a storm-cloud would obscure and devour; the moon, which darkness, as a dragon, threatens to swallow; or some historic character that has passed into myth. Compare the contests of Perseus and the Dragon, Apollo and Pytho, Hercules and the Serpents, Cadmus and the Dragon of Mars, St. George and the Dragon, Siegfried and the Worm (Fafnir). For a Gaelic Andromeda and Perseus, see The Thirteenth Son of the King of Erin (Curtin, Myths of Ireland).

Perseus' flight to the **Gardens of the Hesperides** suggests, naturally, the circuit of the sun toward the flushing western horizon; and, of course, he would here behold the giant **Atlas,** who, stationed where heaven and earth meet, sustains upon his shoulders the celestial vault.

The **Doom of Acrisius** reminds one of that of Hyacinthus. The quoit suggests the rays of the sun, and the name *Acrisius* may be construed to mean the " confused or gloomy heavens " (Roscher, Preller, Müller, etc.).

Illustrative. " The starred Æthiop queen " : Cassiopea (Cassiepea, or Cassiope) became a constellation. The sea-nymphs, however, had her placed in a part of the heavens near the pole, where she is half the time held with her head downward to teach her humility.

Danaë. Tennyson, Princess, " Now lies the Earth all Danaë to the stars, And all thy heart lies open unto me." Translations of Simonides' Lament of Danaë, by W. C. Bryant and by J. H. Frere. **Danaïd** : Chaucer, Legende of Good Women, 2561 (Hypermnestra and Lynceus).

Gorgons and **Medusa.** Spenser, Epithalamion, " And stand astonished like to those which read Medusa's mazeful head "; Milton, Paradise Lost, 2. 611, 628; Comus (on Ægis and Gorgon); Drummond, The Statue of Medusa; Gray, Hymn

[1] This *dawn* theory is certainly far-fetched.

to Adversity; Armstrong, The Art of Preserving Health; D. G. Rossetti, Aspecta Medusa; L. Morris, in The Epic of Hades; Thomas Gordon Hake, The Infant Medusa (a sonnet); E. Lee-Hamilton, The New Medusa; Lady Charlotte Elliot, Medusa.

Andromeda. Milton, Paradise Lost, 3, 559 (the constellation); L. Morris in The Epic of Hades; W. Morris, Doom of King Acrisius; E. Dowden, Andromeda (The Heroines).

Atlas. Shakespeare, 3 Henry VI, 5, 1; Milton, Paradise Lost, 4, 987; 11, 402, comparison of Satan and Atlas.

In Art. Fig. 116, in text: vase in the Hermitage, Petrograd. Titian's painting, Danaë and the Shower of Gold; Correggio's Danaë. Ancient sculpture: a Danaïd in the Vatican; the Danaïds on an altar in the Vatican (Fig. 115, in text).

Perseus and Andromeda. Figs. 119–121, and opp. p. 212, in text; painting by Rubens (Berlin). Sculpture: Benvenuto Cellini's Perseus (Loggia de' Lanzi, Florence), and Perseus saving Andromeda; Canova's Perseus (Vatican).

Medusa. Græco-Roman sculpture: Head of Dying Medusa (Villa Ludovisi, Rome); the beautiful Medusa Rondanini in the Glyptothek, Munich (Figs. 117 and 118, text); numerous illustrations of abhorrent Gorgons in Roscher, p. 1707 *et seq.*, from vases, seals, marbles, etc.

Modern Painting. Leonardo da Vinci, Head of Medusa.

155. *Textual.* The descent of Bellerophon is as follows. (See also Table I.)

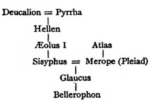

```
Deucalion = Pyrrha
        |
      Hellen
        |
     Æolus I      Atlas
        |           |
   Sisyphus = Merope (Pleiad)
            |
         Glaucus
            |
       Bellerophon
```

Lycia: in Asia Minor. The fountain **Hippocrene,** on the Muses' mountain, Helicon, was opened by a kick from the hoof of Pegasus. This horse belongs to the Muses, and has from time immemorial been ridden by the poets. From the story of Bellerophon being unconsciously the bearer of his own death-warrant, the expression "**Bellerophontic letters**" arose, to describe any species of communication which a person is made the bearer of, containing matter prejudicial to himself. **Aleian field:** a district in Cilicia (Asia Minor).

Interpretative. **Bellerophon** is either "he who appears in the clouds," or "he who slays the cloudy monster." In either sense we have another sun-myth and sun-hero. He is the son of Glaucus, who, whether he be descended from Sisyphus or from Neptune, is undoubtedly a sea-god. His horse, sprung from Medusa, the thundercloud, when she falls under the sword of the sun, is **Pegasus,** the rain-cloud. In his contest with the **Chimæra** we have a repetition of the combat of Perseus and the sea monster. Bellerophon is a heavenly knight errant who slays the powers of storm and darkness. The earth, struck by his horse's hoof, bubbles into springs

(Rapp in Roscher, and Max Müller). At the end of the day, falling from heaven, this knight of the sun walks in melancholy the pale fields of the twilight.

Illustrative. Wm. Morris, Bellerophon in Argos and in Lycia (Earthly Paradise); Longfellow, Pegasus in Pound; Bowring's translation of Schiller's Pegasus in Harness. Milton (**Bellerophon and Pegasus**), Paradise Lost, 7, 1; Spenser, "Then whoso will with virtuous wing assay To mount to heaven, on Pegasus must ride, And with sweet Poet's verse be glorified"; also Faërie Queene, 1, 9, 21; Shakespeare, Taming of the Shrew, IV, iv; 1 Henry IV, IV, i; Henry V, III, vii; Pope, Essay on Criticism, 150; Dunciad, 3, 162; Burns, To John Taylor; Young's Night Thoughts, Vol. 2 (on Bellerophontic letters). **Hippocrene**: Keats, To a Nightingale.

In Art. Bellerophon and Pegasus, vase picture (Monuments inédits, etc., Rome and Paris, 1839–1874); ancient relief, Fig. 122, in text.

156–162. For genealogy of Hercules, see Table J. **Rhadamanthus**: brother of Minos. (See Index.) **Thespiæ** and **Orchomenos**: towns of Bœotia. **Nemea**: in Argolis, near Mycenæ. **Stymphalian** lake: in Arcadia.

Pillars of Hercules. The chosen device of Charles V of Germany represented the Pillars of Hercules entwined by a scroll that bore his motto, "Plus Ultra" (still farther). This device, imprinted upon the German dollar, has been adopted as the sign of the American dollar ($). *Dollar*, by the way, means *coin of the valley,* — German *Thal.* The silver of the first dollars came from Joachimsthal in Bohemia, about 1518. **Hesperides**: the western sky at sunset. The apples may have been suggested by stories of the oranges of Spain. The **Cacus** myth is thoroughly latinized, but of Greek origin. The **Aventine**: one of the hills of Rome. **Colchis**: in Asia, east of the Euxine and south of Caucasus. **Mysia**: province of Asia Minor, north of Lydia. The river **Phasis** flows through Colchis into the Euxine. For genealogy of **Laomedon**, see Table O (5). **Pylos**: it is doubtful what city is intended. There were two such towns in Elis, and one in Messenia. The word means *gate* (see Iliad, 5, 397), and in the case of Hercules there may be some reference to his journey to the gate or *Pylos* of Hades. For **Alcestis, see 83**; for **Prometheus, 15**; for the family of Dejanira, Table K. **Alcides**: *i.e.* Hercules, descendant of Alcæus. **Œchalia**: in Thessaly or in Eubœa. **Mount Œta**: in Thessaly. The **Pygmies**: a nation of dwarfs, so called from a Greek word meaning the cubit, or measure of about thirteen inches, which was said to be the height of these people. They lived near the sources of the Nile, or, according to others, in India. Homer tells us that the cranes used to migrate every winter to the Pygmies' country, where, attacking the cornfields, they precipitated war. H. M. Stanley, in his last African expedition, discovered a race of diminutive men that correspond fairly in appearance with those mentioned by Homer. The **Cercopes**: the subject of a comic poem by Homer, and of numerous grotesque representations in Greek literature and sculpture.

Interpretative. All myths of the sun represent that luminary as struggling against and overcoming monsters, or performing other laborious tasks in obedience to the orders of some tryant of inferior spirit, but of legal authority. Since the life of Hercules is composed of such tasks, it is easy to class him with other sun-heroes. But to construe his whole history and all his feats as symbolic of the sun's progress through the heavens, beginning with the labors performed in his eastern home and ending with the capture of Cerberus in the underworld beyond the west, or to construe the subjects of the twelve labors as consciously recalling the twelve signs of the Zodiac is not only unwarranted, but absurd. To some extent Hercules is a sun-hero; to some extent his adventures are fabulous history; to a greater extent both he and his adventures are the product of generations of æsthetic, but primitive and fanciful, invention. The same statement holds true of nearly all the heroes and heroic deeds of mythology. As a matter of interest, it may be noted that the serpents that attacked Hercules in his cradle are explained as powers of darkness which the sun destroys, and the cattle that he tended, as the clouds of morning. His choice between pleasure and duty at the outset of his career enforces, of course, a lesson of conduct. His lion's skin may denote the tawny cloud which the sun trails behind him as he fights his way through the vapors that he overcomes (Cox). The slaughter of the Centaurs may be the dissipation of these vapors. His insanity may denote the raging heat of the sun at noonday. The Nemean lion may be a monster of cloud or darkness; the Hydra, a cloud that confines the kindly rains, or at times covers the heavens with numerous necks and heads of vapor. The Cerynean Stag may be a golden-tinted cloud that the sun chases; and the Cattle of the Augean stables, clouds that, refusing to burst in rain, consign the earth to drought and filth. The Erymanthian boar and the Cretan bull are probably varied forms of the powers of darkness; so also the Stamphalian (Stymphalian) birds and the giant Cacus. Finally, the scene of the hero's death is a " picture of a sunset in wild confusion, the multitude of clouds hurrying hither and thither, now hiding, now revealing the mangled body of the sun." In this way Cox, and other interpreters of myth, would explain the series. But while the explanations are entertaining and poetic, their very plausibility should suggest caution in accepting them. It is not safe to construe all the details of a mythical career in terms of any one theory. The more noble side of the character of Hercules presents itself to the moral understanding, as worthy of consideration and admiration. The dramatist Euripides has portrayed him as a great-hearted hero, high-spirited and jovial, rejoicing in the vigor of manhood, comforting the downcast, wrestling with Death and overcoming him, restoring happiness where sorrow had obtained. No grander conception of manliness has in modern times found expression in poetry than that of the Hercules in Browning's transcript of Euripides, Balaustion's Adventure.

Illustrative. Lang's translation of the Lityerses song (Theocritus, Idyl X). The song, like the Linus song, is of early origin among the laborers in the field. For **Hercules,** see Sir Philip Sidney, Astrophel and Stella; Spenser, Faerie Queene, I, II, 27; Shakespeare, Merchant of Venice, II, i; III, ii; Taming of the Shrew, I, ii; Coriolanus, IV, i; Hamlet, I, ii; Much Ado About Nothing, II, i; III, iii; King John, II, i; Titus Andronicus, IV, ii; Antony and Cleopatra, IV, x; I Henry VI, IV, vii; Pope, Satires, 5, 17; Milton, Paradise Lost, II, 410 (Geryon). **Amazons:** Shakespeare, King John, V, ii; Midsummer Night's Dream, II, ii;

1 Henry VI, I, iv; 3 Henry VI, I, iv; Pope, Rape of the Lock, 3, 67; **Hylas:** Pope, Autumn; Dunciad, 2, 336.

Poems. S. Rogers, on the Torso of Hercules; Browning, Balaustion's Adventure, and Aristophanes' Apology; L. Morris, Dejaneira (Epic of Hades); William Morris, The Golden Apples (Earthly Paradise); J. H. Frere's translation of Euripides' Hercules Furens, and Plumptre's, or R. Whitelaw's (1883), of Sophocles' Women of Trachis; George Cabot Lodge, Herakles. **Pygmies:** James Beattie, Battle of the Pygmies and the Cranes. **Dejanira:** Fragment of Chorus of a "Dejaneira," by M. Arnold. **Hylas:** Moore (song), "When Hylas was sent with his urn to the fount," etc.; Bayard Taylor, Hylas; R. C. Rogers, Hylas; translation of Theocritus, Idyl XIII, by C. S. Calverley, 1869. **Daphnis:** Theocritus, Idyl I. According to this, Daphnis so loves Naïs that he defies Aphrodite to make him love again. She does so, but he fights against the new passion, and dies a victim of the implacable goddess. This song is sung by Thyrsis. Also on Daphnis, read E. Gosse's poem, The Gifts of the Muses.

In Art. Fig. 65, of a statue reproducing the style of Scopas; figs. 123–129, and opp. p. 226, in text; Heracles in the eastern pediment of the Parthenon (?); the Torso Belvedere; Farnese Hercules (National Museum, Naples); Hercules in the metopes of the Temple of Silenus (Museum, Palermo); the Infant Hercules strangling a Serpent (antique sculpture), in the Uffizi at Florence; C. G. Gleyre's painting, Hercules at the Feet of Omphale (Louvre); Bandinelli (sculpture), Hercules and Cacus; Giovanni di Bologna (sculpture), Hercules and Centaur; Amazon (ancient sculpture), in the Vatican; and Figs. 162, 185 and opp. p. 306, in text; Centaur (sculpture), Capitol, Rome; the Mad Heracles, vase picture (Monuments inédits, Rome and Paris, 1839–1878).

163–167. For the descent of Jason from Deucalion, see Table G. **Iolcos:** a town in Thessaly. **Lemnos:** in the Ægean, near Tenedos. **Phineus:** a son of Agenor, or of Poseidon. For the family of Medea, see Table H.

Interpretative. **Argo** means *swift*, or *white*, or commemorates the ship-builder, or the city of Argos. The Argo-myth rests upon a mixture of traditions of the earliest seafaring and of the course of certain physical phenomena. So far as the tradition of primitive seafaring is concerned, it may refer to some half-piratical expedition, the rich spoils of which might readily be known as the **Golden Fleece.** So far as the physical tradition is concerned, it may refer to the course of the year (the **Ram** of the Golden Fleece being the fructifying clouds that come and go across the Ægean) or to the process of sunrise and sunset (?): **Helle** being the glimmering twilight that sinks into the sea; **Phrixus** (in Greek *Phrixos*), the radiant sunlight; the voyage of the Argo through the Symplegades, the nocturnal journey of the sun down the west; the oak with the Golden Fleece, a symbol of the sunset which the dragon of darkness guards; the fire-breathing bulls, the advent of morning; the offspring of the dragon's teeth, an image of the sunbeams leaping from eastern darkness. **Medea** is a typical wise-woman or witch; daughter of Hecate and granddaughter of Asteria, the starry heavens, she comes of a family skilled in magic. Her aunt Circe was even more powerful in necromancy than she.

The robe of Medea is the fleece in another form. The death of Creüsa, also called
Glauce, suggests that of Hercules (in the flaming sunset?). Jason is no more faithful
to his sweetheart than other solar heroes — Hercules, Perseus, Apollo — are to
theirs. The sun must leave the colors and glories, the twilights and the clouds of
to-day, for those of to-morrow. See Roscher, pp. 530–537. The physical explanation
is more than commonly plausible. But the numerous adventures of the Argonauts
are certainly survivals of various local legends that have been consolidated and
preserved in the artistic form of the myth. Jason, Diáson, is another Zeus, of the
Ionian race, beloved by Medea, whose name, "the counseling woman," suggests
a goddess. Perhaps Medea was a local Hera-Demeter, degraded to the rank of a
heroine. The Symplegades may be a reminiscence of rolling and clashing icebergs; the dove incident occurs in numerous ancient stories from that of Noah
down. If Medea be another personification of morning and evening twilight,
then her dragons are rays of sunlight that precede her. More likely they are
part of the usual equipage of a witch, symbolizing wisdom, foreknowledge, swiftness, violence, and Oriental mystery.

Illustrative. The Argo, see Theodore Martin's translation of Catullus, LXIV
(Peleus and Thetis), for the memorable launch; Pope, St. Cecilia's Day. Jason:
Shakespeare, Merchant of Venice, I, i; III, ii; Æson: Merchant of Venice, V,
i; Absyrtus: 2 Henry VI, V, ii. *Poems:* Chaucer, Legende of Good Women,
1366 (Ysiphile and Medee); W. Morris, Life and Death of Jason; Frederick
Tennyson, Æson and King Athamas (in Daphne and Other Poems). Thos.
Campbell's translation of the chorus in Euripides' Medea, beginning "Oh, hag-
gard queen! to Athens dost thou guide thy glowing chariot." Translations of
the Medea of Euripides have been made by Augusta Webster, 1868; by W. C.
Lawton (Three Dramas of Euripides) 1889; and by Wodhull.

In Art. The terra-cotta relief (Fig. 130, text) in the British Museum; the relief
from Naples, now in Vienna (Fig. 131). Figs. 132 and 133 as explained in text. Also
the splendid Vengeance of Medea in the Louvre; relief on a Roman sarcophagus.

168. *Textual.*

TABLE K. THE DESCENDANTS OF ÆTOLUS (SON OF ENDYMION)

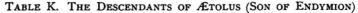

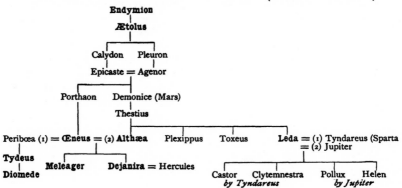

Also, in general, Table I.

For **Calydon,** see Index. The Arcadian **Atalanta** was descended from the Arcas who was son of Jupiter and Callisto. (See Table D.)

Interpretative. Atalanta is the "unwearied maiden." She is the human counterpart of the huntress Diana. The story has of course been allegorically explained, but it bears numerous marks of local and historic origin.

Illustrative. Swinburne, Atalanta in Calydon; Margaret J. Preston, The Quenched Branch; Shakespeare, 2 Henry IV, II, ii; 2 Henry VI, I, i.

In Art. The Meleager (sculpture), in the Vatican; the Roman reliefs as in text. The original of Fig. 135 is in the Louvre.

169. The **Merope** story has been dramatized by Maffei (1713), Voltaire (1743), Alfieri (1783), and by others.

170–171. C. S. Calverley's The Sons of Leda, from Theocritus. **Leda:** Spenser, Prothalamion; Landor, Loss of Memory. **Talus:** the iron attendant of Artegal, Spenser, Faerie Queene, 5, 1, 12.

172. The Descendants of Minos I. (See also Table D.)

TABLE L

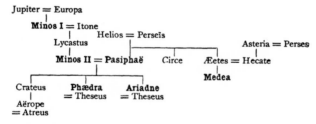

Interpretative. Discrimination between Minos I and Minos II is made in the text, but is rarely observed. **Minos,** according to Preller, is the solar king and hero of Crete; his wife, **Pasiphaë,** is the moon (who was worshiped in Crete under the form of a cow); and the **Minotaur** is the lord of the starry heavens which are his labyrinth. Others make Pasiphaë, whose name means *shiner upon all,* the bright heaven; and Minos (in accordance with his name, the Man, *par excellence*), the thinker and measurer. A lawgiver on earth, the Homeric Minos readily becomes a judge in Hades. Various fanciful interpretations, such as storm cloud, sun, etc., are given of the bull. Cox explains the Minotaur as night, devouring all things. The tribute from Athens may suggest some early suzerainty in politics and religion exercised by Crete over neighboring lands. For **Mæander,** see Pope, Rape of the Lock, 5, 65; Dunciad, 1, 64; 3, 55.

173. *Interpretative.* **Dædalus** is a representative of the earliest technical skill, especially in wood-cutting, carving, and the plastic arts used for industrial purposes. His flight from one land to another signifies the introduction of inventions into the countries concerned. The fall of Icarus was probably invented to explain the name of the **Icarian** Sea.

Illustrative. **Dædalus**: Chaucer, Hous of Fame, 409. **Icarus**: Shakespeare, 1 Henry VI, IV, vi; IV, vii; 3 Henry VI, V, vi; poem on Icarus by Bayard Taylor; travesty by J. G. Saxe.

In Art. Sculpture: Fig. 138, in text: Villa Albani, Rome; Canova's Dædalus and Icarus; painting by J. M. Vien; also by A. Pisano (Campanile, Florence).

174. The descendants of Erichthonius are as follows:

TABLE M

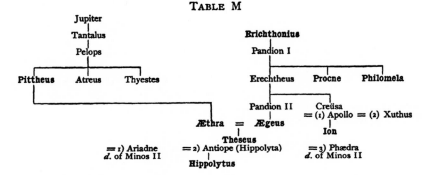

Cecrops (see **65**). According to one tradition, Cecrops was autochthonous and had one son, Erysichthon, who died without issue, and three daughters, Herse, Aglauros, and Pandrosos (personifications of Dew and its vivifying influences). According to another, he was of the line of Erichthonius, being either a son of Pandion I, or a son of Erechtheus and a grandson of Pandion I. Apollodorus makes him father of Pandion II. He was regarded as founder of the worship of Athene and of various civic institutions. He is probably a hero of the Pelasgian race.

Ion. According to one tradition, the race of Erechtheus became extinct, save for Ion, a son of Apollo and Creüsa, daughter of Erechtheus. This son, having been removed at birth, was brought up in Apollo's temple at Delphi, and, in accordance with the oracle of Apollo, afterwards adopted by Creüsa and her husband Xuthus (see the Ion of Euripides). Ion founded the new dynasty of Athens. But, according to Pausanias and Apollodorus, the dynasty of Erechtheus was continued by Ægeus, who was either a son, or an adopted son, of Pandion II. By Æthra he became father of Theseus, in whose veins flowed, therefore, the blood of Pelops and of Erichthonius.

Interpretative. The story of **Philomela** was probably invented to account for the sad song of the nightingale. With her the swallow is associated as another much loved bird of spring. Occasionally Procne is spoken of as the nightingale, and Philomela as the swallow, and Tereus as taking the form of a red-crested hoopoe.

Illustrative. Chaucer, Legende of Good Women (Philomene of Athens); Milton, Il Penseroso; Richard Barnfield, Song, "As it fell upon a day"; Thomson, Hymn on the Seasons; Swinburne, Itylus; Oscar Wilde, The Burden of Itys; Sir Thomas Noon Talfourd's drama, Ion.

176–181. Trœzen: in Argolis. According to some the Amazonian wife of Theseus was **Hippolyta,** but her Hercules had already killed. **Theseus** is said to have united the several tribes of Attica into one state, of which Athens was the capital. In commemoration of this important event, he instituted the festival of **Panathenæa,** in honor of Athene, the patron deity of Athens. This festival differed from the other Grecian games chiefly in two particulars. It was peculiar to the Athenians, and its chief feature was a solemn procession in which the Peplus, or sacred robe of Athene, was carried to the Parthenon, and left on or before the statue of the goddess. The Peplus was covered with embroidery, worked by select virgins of the noblest families in Athens. The procession consisted of persons of all ages and both sexes. The old men carried olive branches in their hands, and the young men bore arms. The young women carried baskets on their heads, containing the sacred utensils, cakes, and all things necessary for the sacrifices. The procession formed the subject of the bas-reliefs which embellished the frieze of the temple of the Parthenon. A considerable portion of these sculptures is now in the British Museum among those known as the "Elgin Marbles." We may mention here the other celebrated national games of the Greeks. The first and most distinguished were the **Olympic,** founded, it was said, by Zeus himself. They were celebrated at Olympia in Elis. Vast numbers of spectators flocked to them from every part of Greece, and from Asia, Africa, and Sicily. They were repeated every fifth year in midsummer, and continued five days. They gave rise to the custom of reckoning time and dating events by Olympiads. The first Olympiad is generally considered as beginning with the year 776 B.C. The **Pythian** games were celebrated in the vicinity of Delphi, the **Isthmian** on the Corinthian isthmus, the **Nemean** at Nemea, a city of Argolis. The exercises in these games were chariot-racing, running, leaping, wrestling, throwing the quoit, hurling the javelin, and boxing. Besides these exercises of bodily strength and agility, there were contests in music, poetry, and eloquence. Thus these games furnished poets, musicians, and authors the best opportunities to present their productions to the public, and the fame of the victors was diffused far and wide.

Interpretative. **Theseus** is the Attic counterpart of Hercules, not so significant in moral character, but eminent for numerous similar labors, and preëminent as the mythical statesman of Athens. His story may, with the usual perilous facility, be explained as a solar myth. **Periphetes** may be a storm cloud with its thunderbolts; the **Marathonian Bull** and the **Minotaur** may be forms of the power of darkness hidden in the starry labyrinth of heaven. Like Hercules, Theseus fights with the **Amazons** (clouds, we may suppose, in some form or other), and, like him, he descends to the underworld. **Ariadne** may be another twilight-sweetheart of the sun, and, like Medea and Dejanira, she must be deserted. She is either the "well-pleasing" or the "saintly." She was, presumably, a local nature-goddess of Naxos and Crete, who, in process of time, like Medea, sank to the condition of a heroine. Probably from her goddess-existence the marriage with Bacchus survived, to be incorporated later with the Attic myth of Theseus. As the female semblance of Bacchus, she appears to have been a promoter of vegetation; and, like Proserpina, she alternated between the joy of spring and the melancholy of winter. By some she is considered to be connected with star-worship as a moon-goddess.

Illustrative. Chaucer, The Knight's Tale (for Theseus and Ypolita); The Hous of Fame, 407, and the Legende of Good Women, 1884, for Ariadne; Shakespeare, Two Gentlemen of Verona, IV, i; Midsummer Night's Dream, II, ii (Hippolyta and Theseus); Shakespeare and Fletcher, Two Noble Kinsmen. In Beaumont and Fletcher's Maid's Tragedy, II, ii, a tapestry is ordered to be worked illustrating Theseus' desertion of Ariadne. Landor, To Joseph Ablett, "Bacchus is coming down to drink to Ariadne's love"; Landor, Theseus, and Hippolyta; Mrs. Browning, Paraphrase on Nonnus (Bacchus and Ariadne), Paraphrase on Hesiod; Sir Theodore Martin, Catullus, LXIV. Other poems: B. W. Procter, On the Statue of Theseus; Frederick Tennyson, Ariadne (Daphne and Other Poems); Mrs. Hemans, The Shade of Theseus; R. S. Ross, Ariadne in Naxos; J. S. Blackie, Ariadne; W. M. W. Call, Ariadne; Mrs. H. H. Jackson, Ariadne's Farewell. **Phædra and Hippolytus:** The Hippolytus of Euripides; Swinburne, Phædra; Browning, Artemis Prologizes; M. P. Fitzgerald, The Crowned Hippolytus; A. Mary F. Robinson, The Crowned Hippolytus; L. Morris, Phædra (Epic of Hades). On **Cecrops:** J. S. Blackie, The Naming of Athens; Erechtheus, by A. C. Swinburne.

In Art. Theseus: the original of Fig. 140, text is in the Hermitage, in Petrograd; of Fig. 141 in the Naples Museum. The Battle with the Amazons frequently recurs in ancient sculpture. The sleeping Ariadne, of the Vatican, Fig. 142, text. Also the Revels as in text, Fig. 144. Modern Sculpture: the Theseus of Canova (Volksgarten, Vienna); the Ariadne of Dannecker. Paintings: Tintoretto's Ariadne and Bacchus; Teschendorff's Ariadne; Titian's Bacchus and Ariadne.

182–189. The Royal Family of Thebes.

TABLE N

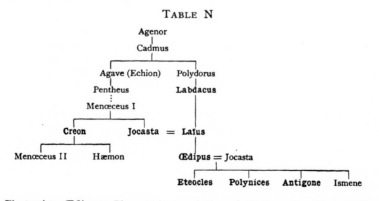

Illustrative. Œdipus: Plumptre's translation of Œdipus the King, Œdipus Coloneus, and Antigone; Shelley, Swellfoot the Tyrant; E. Fitzgerald, The

Downfall and Death of King Œdipus; Sir F. H. Doyle, Œdipus Tyrannus; Aubrey De Vere, Antigone; Emerson, The Sphinx; W. B. Scott, The Sphinx; M. Arnold, Fragment of an "Antigone." **Tiresias:** by Swinburne, Tennyson, and Thomas Woolner.

In Art. Ancient: Œdipus and the Sphinx (in Monuments Inédits, Rome and Paris, 1839–1878). Modern paintings: Teschendorff's Œdipus and Antigone, Antigone and Ismene, and Antigone; Œdipus and the Sphinx, by J. D. A. Ingres; The Sphinx, by D. G. Rossetti.

Of the stories told in these and the following sections no systematic, allegorical, or physical interpretations are here given, because (1) the general method followed by the unravelers of myth has already been sufficiently illustrated; (2) the attempt to force symbolic conceptions into the longer folk-stories, or into the artistic myths and epics of any country, is historically unwarranted and, in practice, is only too often capricious; (3) the effort to interpret such stories as the Iliad and the Odyssey must result in destroying those elements of unconscious simplicity and romantic vigor that characterize the early products of the creative imagination.

190–194. Houses concerned in the Trojan War.

TABLE O

(1) **Family of Peleus** and its connections:

(2) **Family of Atreus** and its connections:

(3) **Family of Tyndareus** and its connections:

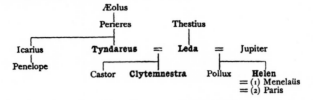

Castor and Pollux are called sometimes Dioscuri (sons of Jove), sometimes
Tyndaridæ (sons of Tyndareus). Helen is frequently called Tyndaris, daughter
of Tyndareus.

(4) **Descent of Ulysses and Penelope:**

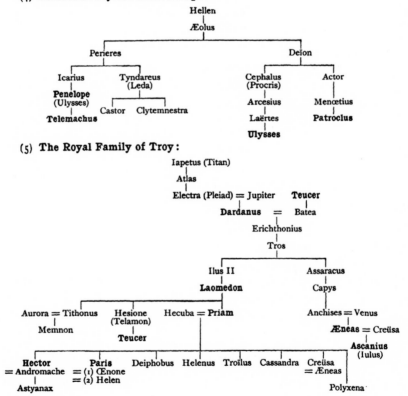

(5) **The Royal Family of Troy:**

195. On the **Iliad** and on **Troy:** Keats, Sonnet on Chapman's Homer; Milton,
Paradise Lost, 1, 578; 9, 16; Il Penseroso, 100; Hartley Coleridge, Sonnet on

Homer; T. B. Aldrich, Pillared Arch and Sculptured Tower; the Sonnets of Lang and Myers prefixed to Lang, Leaf, and Myers' translation of the Iliad. On the **Judgment of Paris:** George Peele, Arraignment of Paris; James Beattie, Judgment of Paris; Tennyson, Dream of Fair Women; J. S. Blackie, Judgment of Paris. See, for allusions, Shakespeare, All's Well that Ends Well, I, ii, iii; Henry V, II, iv; Troilus and Cressida, I, i; II, ii; III, i; Romeo and Juliet, I, ii; II, iv; IV, i; V, iii. On **Helen:** A. Lang, Helen of Troy, and his translation of Theocritus, Idyl XVIII; Landor, Menelaüs and Helen; John Todhunter, Helena in Troas; G. P. Lathrop, Helen at the Loom (*Atlantic Monthly*, Vol. 32, 1873). See Shakespeare, Midsummer Night's Dream, I, i; III, ii; IV, i; All's Well that Ends Well, I, i, iii; II, ii; Romeo and Juliet, II, iv; Troilus and Cressida, II, ii; Marlowe, Faustus (Helen appears before Faust).

In Art. **Homer:** the sketch by Raphael (in the Museum, Venice). **Paris and Helen.** Paintings: Helen of Troy, Sir Frederick Leighton; Paris and Helen, by David; The Judgment of Paris, by Rubens; by Watteau. Sculpture: Canova's Paris. Crayons: D. G. Rossetti's Helen; see also Fig. 150, as in text (ancient relief, Naples).

196. Iphigenia and Agamemnon. Sometimes, in accordance with Goethe's practice, the name *Tauris* is given to the land of the Tauri. To be correct one should say, "Iphigenia among the Tauri," or "Taurians." (See Index.) Iphigenia and Agamemnon by W. S. Landor; also his Shades of Agamemnon and Iphigenia; Dryden, Cymon and Iphigenia; Richard Garnett, Iphigenia in Delphi; Sir Edwin Arnold, Iphigenia; W. B. Scott, Iphigenia at Aulis. Any translations of Goethe's Iphigenia in Tauris, and of Euripides' Iphigenia in Aulis and Among the Tauri; also of Æschylus' Agamemnon, — such as those by Milman, Anna Swanwick, Plumptre, E. A. Morshead, J. S. Blackie, E. Fitzgerald, and Robert Browning. For Agamemnon, see Shakespeare, Troilus and Cressida, I, iii; II, i, iii; III, iii; IV, v; V, i; and James Thomson, Agamemnon (a drama). The **Troilus and Cressida** story is not found in Greek and Latin classics. Shakespeare follows Chaucer's Troilus and Criseyde, which is based upon the Filostrato and the Filocolo of Boccaccio. **Pandarus:** the character of this name, uncle of Cressida, to be found in Lydgate, Chaucer's Troilus and Criseyde, and Shakespeare's play of the same title, enjoys an unsavory reputation for which medieval romance is responsible. On **Menelaüs,** see notes to Helen and Agamemnon.

In Art. **Iphigenia.** Paintings: Fig. 152, text (Museum, Naples); E. Hübner; William Kaulbach; E. Teschendorff.

199. Achilles. Chaucer, Hous of Fame, 398; Dethe of Blaunche, 329; Landor, Peleus and Thetis; Robert Bridges, Achilles in Scyros; Sir Theodore Martin, translation of Catullus, LXIV; translation by C. M. Gayley as quoted in text. See also Shakespeare, Troilus and Cressida; 2 Henry VI, V, i; Love's Labour's Lost, V, ii; Milton, Paradise Lost, 9, 15.

In Art. In general, Figs. 151, 153, 155-156, 159-162, in text; Wiertz, Fight for the Body of Achilles (Wiertz Museum, Brussels); Burne-Jones, The Feast of Peleus (picture).

204. Ajax. Plumptre, Ajax of Sophocles; Shakespeare, Troilus and Cressida, Love's Labour 's Lost, IV, iii; V, ii; Taming of the Shrew, III, i; Antony and Cleopatra, IV, ii; King Lear, II, ii; Cymbeline, IV, ii; George Crabbe, The Village.

In Art. The ancient sculpture, Ajax (or Menelaüs) of the Vatican. Modern sculpture, The Ajax of Canova. Flaxman's outline drawings for the Iliad. .

207. Hector and Andromache. Mrs. Browning, Hector and Andromache, a paraphrase of Homer; C. T. Brooks, Schiller's Parting of Hector and Andromache. See also Shakespeare, Troilus and Cressida; Love's Labour 's Lost, V, ii; 2 Henry IV, II, iv; Antony and Cleopatra, IV, viii.

In Art. Flaxman's outline sketches of the Fight for the Body of Patroclus, Hector dragged by Achilles, Priam supplicating Achilles, Hector's Funeral, Andromache fainting on the Walls of Troy; Canova's Hector (sculpture); Thorwaldsen's Hector and Andromache (relief) (Fig. 154, text). Hector, Ajax, Paris, Æneas, Patroclus, Teucer, etc., among the Ægina Marbles (Glyptothek, Munich). The Pasquino group (Fig. 158, in text) is from a copy in the Pitti, Florence.

216. Priam and Hecuba. The translations of Euripides' Hecuba and Troades; Shakespeare, Troilus and Cressida; Coriolanus, I, iii; Cymbeline, IV, ii; Hamlet, II, ii; 2 Henry IV, I, i.

219-220. Polyxena. W. S. Landor, The Espousals of Polyxena. **Philoctetes:** translation of Sophocles by Plumptre; sonnet by Wordsworth; drama by Lord de Tabley.

221. Œnone. See A. Lang, Helen of Troy; W. Morris, Death of Paris (Earthly Paradise); Landor, Corythos (son of Œnone), the Death of Paris, and Œnone; Tennyson, Œnone, also the Death of Œnone, which is not so good.

The pathetic story of the death of Corythus, the son of Œnone and Paris, at the hands of his father, who was jealous of Helen's tenderness toward the youth, is a later myth.

223. Sinon. Shakespeare, 3 Henry VI, III, ii; Cymbeline, III, iv; Titus Andronicus, V, iii.

224. Laocoön. L. Morris, in The Epic of Hades. See Frothingham's translation of Lessing's Laocoön (a most important discussion of the Laocoön group and of principles of æsthetics). See also Swift's Description of a City Shower.

In Art. The original of the celebrated group (statuary) of Laocoön and his children in the embrace of the serpents is in the Vatican in Rome. (See text, opp. p. 310.)

226. Cassandra. Chaucer, Troilus and Criseyde; Dethe of Blaunche, 1246. Poems by W. M. Praed and D. G. Rossetti. See Troilus and Cressida, I, i; II, ii; V, iii; Lord Lytton's translation of Schiller's Cassandra.

In Art. The Cassandra of Dante Gabriel Rossetti (in ink).

228-230. Electra and Orestes. Translations of the Electra of Sophocles, the Libation-pourers and the Eumenides of Æschylus, by Plumptre; and of the Orestes and Electra of Euripides, by Wodhull. Lord de Tabley, Orestes (a drama); Byron, Childe Harold, 4; Milton, sonnet, "The repeated air Of sad Electra's poet," etc.

In Art. Græco-Roman sculpture: Fig. 169, in text, Orestes and Pylades find Iphigenia among the Taurians. Pompeian Fresco; Orestes and Electra (Villa Ludovisi, Rome); Orestes and Electra (National Museum, Naples). Vase-paintings: Figs. 167-168 in text; also Orestes slaying Ægisthus; Orestes at Delphi; Purification of Orestes. Modern paintings: Electra, by Teschendorff and by Seifert.

Clytemnestra, The Death of, by W. S. Landor; Clytemnestra, by L. Morris, in The Epic of Hades.

Troy: Byron, in his Bride of Abydos, thus describes the appearance of the deserted scene where once stood Troy:

> The winds are high, and Helle's tide
> Rolls darkly heaving to the main;
> And Night's descending shadows hide
> That field with blood bedew'd in vain,
> The desert of old Priam's pride;
> The tombs, sole relics of his reign,
> All — save immortal dreams that could beguile
> The blind old man of Scio's rocky isle !

On Troy the following references will be valuable: H. W. Acland, The Plains of Troy, 2 vols. (London, 1839); H. Schliemann, Troy and its Remains (London, 1875); Ilios (London, 1881); Troja, results of latest researches on the site of Homer's Troy (London, 1882); W. J. Armstrong, *Atlantic Monthly*, Vol. 33, p. 173 (1874), Over Ilium and Ida; R. C. Jebb, *Jour. Hellenic Studies*, Vol. 2, p. 7, Homeric and Hellenic Ilium; *Fortn. Review*, N. S. Vol. 35, p. 4331 (1884), Homeric Troy

231-244. The **Odyssey:** Lang, Sonnet, "As one that for a weary space has lain," prefixed to Butcher and Lang's Odyssey. Translations by W. Morris, G. H. Palmer, Chapman, Bryant, Pope. **Ulysses:** Tennyson; Landor, The Last of Ulysses. See also Shakespeare, Troilus and Cressida; 3 Henry VI, III, ii; Coriolanus, I, iii; Milton, Paradise Lost, 2, 1019; Comus, 637; R. Buchanan, Cloudland; Pope, Rape of the Lock, 4, 182; Stephen Phillips, Ulysses; Robert Bridges, The Return of Ulysses; R. C. Rogers, Odysseus at the Mast, Blind Polyphemus, Argus.

In Art. Statuettes, vase-paintings, and reliefs as in text, Figs. 170-180; also Ulysses summoning Tiresias (in Monuments Inédits, Rome and Paris, 1839-1878); Meeting with Nausicaa (Gerhard's vase pictures); outline drawings of Ulysses weeping at the song of Demodocus, boring out the eye of Polyphemus, Ulysses killing the suitors, Mercury conducting the souls of the suitors, Ulysses and his dog, etc., by Flaxman.

Penelope: Poems by R. Buchanan, E. C. Stedman, and W. S. Landor. In ancient sculpture, the Penelope in the Vatican. Modern painting by C. F. Marchal. In crayons by D. G. Rossetti.

Circe: M. Arnold, The Strayed Reveller; Hood, Lycus, the Centaur; D. G. Rossetti, The Wine of Circe; Saxe, The Spell of Circe. See Shakespeare, Comedy of Errors, V, i; 1 Henry VI, V, iii; Milton, Comus, 50, 153, 253, 522; Pope, Satire 8, 166; Cowper, Progress of Error; O. W. Holmes, Metrical Essay; Keats,

Endymion, "I sue not for my happy crown again," etc. Circe and the Companions of Ulysses, a painting by Briton Rivière. Circe, in crayons.

On **Sirens** and **Scylla** see C. 50-52 ; S. Daniel, Ulysses and the Siren; Lowell, The Sirens. Scylla and Charybdis have become proverbial to denote opposite dangers besetting one's course. Siren, in crayons; Sea-Spell, in oil, D. G. Rossetti.

Calypso: Pope, Moral Essays, 2, 45; poem by Edgar Fawcett (*Putnam's Mag.*, 14, 1869). Fénelon, in his romance of Telemachus, has given us the adventures of the son of Ulysses in search of his father. Among other places which he visited, following on his father's footsteps, was Calypso's isle; as in the former case, the goddess tried every art to keep the youth with her, and offered to share her immortality with him. But Minerva, who, in the shape of Mentor, accompanied him and governed all his movements, made him repel her allurements. Finally, when no other means of escape could be found, the two friends leaped from a cliff into the sea and swam to a vessel which lay becalmed offshore. Byron alludes to this leap of Telemachus and Mentor in the stanza of Childe Harold beginning "But not in silence pass Calypso's isles" (2, 29). Calypso's isle is said to be Goza.

Homer's description of the ships of the Phæacians has been thought to look like an anticipation of the wonders of modern steam navigation. See the address of Alcinoüs to Ulysses, promising "wondrous ships, self-moved, instinct with mind," etc. (Odyssey, 8).

Lord Carlisle, in his Diary in the Turkish and Greek Waters, thus speaks of Corfu, which he considers to be the ancient Phæacian island:

"The sites explain the Odyssey. The temple of the sea-god could not have been more fitly placed, upon a grassy platform of the most elastic turf, on the brow of a crag commanding harbor, and channel, and ocean. Just at the entrance of the inner harbor there is a picturesque rock with a small convent perched upon it, which by one legend is the transformed pinnace of Ulysses.

"Almost the only river in the island is just at the proper distance from the probable site of the city and palace of the king, to justify the princess Nausicaa having had resort to her chariot and to luncheon when she went with the maidens of the court to wash their garments."

245-254. Poems: Tennyson, To **Virgil**, of which a few stanzas are given in the text; R. C. Rogers, Virgil's Tomb. **Æneas** and **Anchises**: Chaucer, Hous of Fame, 165; 140-470 (pictures of Troy); Shakespeare, Troilus and Cressida; Tempest, II, i; 2 Henry VI, V, ii; Julius Cæsar, I, ii; Antony and Cleopatra, IV, ii; Hamlet, II, ii; Waller, Panegyric to the Lord Protector (The Stilling of Neptune's Storm).

Dido: Chaucer, Legende of Good Women, 923; Sir Thomas Wyatt, The Song of Iopas (unfinished); Marlowe, Tragedy of Dido, Queen of Carthage; Shakespeare, Antony and Cleopatra, IV, xii; Titus Andronicus, II, iii; Hamlet, II, ii. **Palinurus**: see Scott's Marmion, Introd. to Canto I (with reference to the death of William Pitt).

The **Sibyl**. The following legend of the Sibyl is fixed at a later date. In the reign of one of the Tarquins there appeared before the king a woman who offered him nine books for sale. The king refused to purchase them, whereupon the woman went away and burned three of the books, and returning offered the remaining books for the same price she had asked for the nine. The king again rejected them; but when the woman, after burning three books more, returned and asked for the three remaining the same price which she had before asked for the nine, his curiosity was excited, and he purchased the books. They were found to contain the destinies of the Roman state. They were kept in the temple of Jupiter Capitolinus, preserved in a stone chest, and allowed to be inspected only by especial officers appointed for that duty, who on great occasions consulted them and interpreted their oracles to the people.

There were various Sibyls; but the Cumæan Sibyl, of whom Ovid and Virgil write, is the most celebrated of them. Ovid's story of her life protracted to one thousand years may be intended to represent the various Sibyls as being only reappearances of one and the same individual.

Illustrative. Young, in the Night Thoughts, alludes to the Sibyl. See also Shakespeare, 1 Henry VI, II, ii; Othello, III, iv.

In Art. Figs. 181–183, in text. The Virgil of Raphael (drawing in the Museum, Venice); the Æneas of the Ægina Marbles (Glyptothek, Munich). P. Guérin's painting, Æneas at the Court of Dido; Raphael, Dido; Turner, Dido building Carthage. The Sibyls in Michelangelo's frescoes in the Sistine Chapel, Rome; the Cumæan Sibyl of Domenichino; Elihu Vedder's Cumæan Sibyl.

255–257. Rhadamanthus: E. W. Gosse, The Island of the Blest. **Tantalus:** Cowper, The Progress of Error; L. Morris, Epic of Hades; W. W. Story, Tantalus. **Ixion:** poem by Browning in Jocoseria. See Pope, St. Cecilia's Day, 67; Rape of the Lock, 2, 133. **Sisyphus:** Lord Lytton, Death and Sisyphus; L. Morris, in The Epic of Hades.

The teachings of Anchises to Æneas, respecting the nature of the human soul, were in conformity with the doctrines of the Pythagoreans. Pythagoras (born about 540 B.C.) was a native of the island of Samos, but passed the chief portion of his life at Crotona in Italy. He is therefore sometimes called " the Samian," and sometimes "the philosopher of Crotona." When young he traveled extensively and is said to have visited Egypt, where he was instructed by the priests, and afterwards to have journeyed to the East, where he visited the Persian and Chaldean Magi, and the Brahmins of India. He established himself at Crotona, and enjoined sobriety, temperance, simplicity, and silence upon his throngs of disciples. *Ipse dixit* (Pythagoras said so) was to be held by them as sufficient proof of anything. Only advanced pupils might question. Pythagoras considered *numbers* as the essence and principle of all things, and attributed to them a real and distinct existence; so that, in his view, they were the elements out of which the universe was constructed.

As the numbers proceed from the monad or unit, so he regarded the pure and simple essence of the Deity as the source of all the forms of nature. Gods, demons, and heroes are emanations of the Supreme, and there is a fourth emanation, the human soul. This is immortal, and when freed from the fetters of the body, passes to the habitation of the dead, where it remains till it returns to the world, to dwell in some other human or animal body; at last, when sufficiently purified, it returns to the source from which it proceeded. This doctrine of the transmigration of souls (metempsychosis), which was originally Egyptian and connected with the doctrine of reward and punishment of human actions, was the chief reason why the Pythagoreans killed no animals. Ovid represents Pythagoras saying that in the time of the Trojan War he was Euphorbus, the son of Panthus, and fell by the spear of Menelaüs. Lately, he said, he had recognized his shield hanging among the trophies in the Temple of Juno at Argos.

On **Metempsychosis**, see the essay in the Spectator (No. 343) on the Transmigration of Souls; Shakespeare, Merchant of Venice (Gratiano to Shylock).

Harmony of the Spheres. The relation of the notes of the musical scale to numbers, whereby harmony results from proportional vibrations of sound, and discord from the reverse, led Pythagoras to apply the word *harmony* to the visible creation, meaning by it the just adaptation of parts to each other. This is the idea which Dryden expresses in the beginning of his song for St. Cecilia's Day, " From harmony, from heavenly harmony, This everlasting frame began."

In the center of the universe (as Pythagoras taught) there was a central fire, the principle of life. The central fire was surrounded by the earth, the moon, the sun, and the five planets. The distances of the various heavenly bodies from one another were conceived to correspond to the proportions of the musical scale. See Merchant of Venice, Act V (Lorenzo and Jessica), for the Music of the Spheres; also Milton, Hymn on the Nativity. See Longfellow's Verses to a Child, and Occultation of Orion, for Pythagoras as inventor of the lyre.

260. Camilla. Pope, illustrating the rule that "the sound should be an echo to the sense," says:

> When Ajax strives some rock's vast weight to throw,
> The line, too, labors and the words move slow;
> Not so when swift Camilla scours the plain,
> Flies o'er th' unbending corn, or skims along the main.
> Essay on Criticism.

268-281. On Norse mythology, see R. B. Anderson, Norse Mythology, or the Religion of our Forefathers (Chicago, 1875); Anderson, Horn's Scandinavian Literature (Chicago, S. C. Griggs & Co., 1884); Dasent, Popular Tales from the Norse (transl. from P. C. Asbjörnsen, New York, 1859); Thorpe's translation of Sæmund's Edda, 2 vols. (London, 1866); Icelandic Poetry or Edda of Sæmund, transl. into English verse (Bristol, A. S. Cottle, 1797); Augusta Larned, Tales from the Norse Grandmother (New York, 1881); H. W. Mabie, Norse Stories (Boston, 1882). A critical edition of the Elder Edda is Sophus Bugge's (Christiania, 1867). The Younger Edda: Edda Snorra Sturlasonar, 2 vols. (Hafniae, 1848-1852); by Thorleif Jonsson (Copenhagen, 1875); Translation: Anderson's Younger Edda (Chicago, S. C. Griggs & Co., 1880) (see references at foot of pp. 458-461 and in C. 282). Illustrative poems: Gray, Ode on the Descent of Odin, Ode on the Fatal Sisters; Matthew Arnold, Balder Dead; Longfellow, Tegnér's Drapa, on Balder's Death; William Morris, The Funeral of Balder, in The Lovers of Gudrun (Earthly Paradise); Robert Buchanan, Balder the Beautiful;

W. M. W. Call, Balder; and Thor. Sydney Dobell's Balder does not rehearse the Norse myth. It is a poem dealing with the spiritual maladies of the time, excellent in parts, but confused and uneven. Longfellow's Saga of King Olaf (the Musician's Tale, Wayside Inn) is from the Heimskringla, or Book of Stories of the Kings, edited by Snorri Sturlason. Many of the cantos of the Saga throw light on Norse mythology. See also the Hon. Roden Noël's Ragnarok (in the Modern Faust), for an ethical modification of the ancient theme.

Anses (the Asa-folk, Æsir, etc.). The word probably means *ghost, ancestral spirit*, — of such kind as the Manes of the Romans. The derivation may be from the root *AN*, 'to breathe,' whence *animus* (Vigfusson and Powell, Corp. Poet. Bor. 1, 515). According to Jordanes, the Anses were demigods, ancestors of royal races. The main cult of the older religion was ancestor-worship, Thor and Woden being worshiped by a tribe, but each family having its own *anses*, or deified ancestors (Corp. Poet. Bor. 2, 413). **Elf** was another name used of spirits of the dead. Later it sinks to the significance of "fairy." Indeed, say Vigfusson and Powell, half our ideas about fairies are derived from the heathen beliefs as to the spirits of the dead, their purity, kindliness, homes in hillocks (cf. the Irish "folk of the hills," *Banshees*, etc.) (Corp. Poet. Bor. 2, 418).

The **Norse Religion** consists evidently of two distinct strata: the lower, of gods, that are personifications of natural forces, or deified heroes, with regular sacrifices, with belief in ghosts, etc.; the upper, of doctrines introduced by Christianity. To the latter belong the Last Battle to be fought by Warrior-Angels and the Elect against the Beast, the Dragon, and the Demons of Fire (Corp. Poet. Bor. 2, 459).

Odin or **Woden** was first the god of the heaven, or heaven itself, then husband of earth, god of war and of wisdom, lord of the ravens, lord of the gallows (which was called Woden's tree or Woden's steed). **Frigga** is Mother Earth. **Thor** is the lord of the hammer—the thunderbolt, the adversary of giants and all oppressors of man. He is dear to man, always connected with earth, — the husband of *Sif* (the Norse Ceres). His goat-drawn car makes the rumbling of the thunder. **Freyr** means *lord;* patron of the Swedes, harvest-god. **Balder** means also *lord* or *king*. On the one hand, his attributes recall those of Apollo; on the other hand, his story appeals to, and is colored by, the Christian imagination. He is another figure of that radiant type to which belong all bright and genial heroes, righters of wrong, blazing to consume evil, gentle and strong to uplift weakness: Apollo, Hercules, Perseus, Achilles, Sigurd, St. George, and many another. **Höder** is the "adversary."

Nanna, Balder's wife, is the ensample of constancy; her name is *maiden*.

282. The Völsunga Saga. The songs of the Elder Edda, from which Eirikr Magnússon and William Morris draw their Story of the Völsungs and the Nibelungs (London, 1870), are The Lay of Helgi the Hunding's-Bane, The Lay of Sigrdrifa, The Short Lay of Sigurd, The Hell-Ride of Brynhild, The Lay of Brynhild, The Ancient Lay of Gudrun, The Song of Atli, The Whetting of Gudrun, The Lay of Hamdir, The Lament of Oddrun. For translations of these fragments, see pp. 167–270 of the volume mentioned above. For the originals and literal translations of these and other Norse lays of importance, see Vigfusson and Powell's Corpus Poeticum Boreale; and Vigfusson's Sturlunga Saga, 2 vols. For the story of Sigurd, read William Morris' spirited epic, Sigurd the Volsung. Illustrative of the Norse spirit are Motherwell's Battle-Flag of Sigurd, the Wooing Song of Jarl Egill Skallagrim, and the Sword Chant of Thorstein Raudi; also Dora Greenwell's Battle-Flag of Sigurd; and Charles Kingsley's Longbeard's Saga, in Hypatia. Baldwin's Story of Siegfried (New York, 1888) is a good introduction for young people.

283. The Nibelungenlied. The little book entitled Echoes from Mist Land, by Auber Forestier (Chicago, Griggs & Co., 1877) will be of value to the beginner. Other translations are made by A. G. Foster-Barham (London, 1887) and by W. N. Lettsom, The Fall of the Nibelungers (London, 1874), both in verse. See also T. Carlyle, Nibelungenlied (Crit. Miscell.), Essays, 2, 220. Modern German editions by Simrock, Bartsch, Marbach, and Gerlach are procurable. The edition by Werner Hahn (Uebersetzung d. Handschrift A, Collection Spemann, Berlin u. Stuttgart) has been used in the preparation of this account. The original was published in part by Bodmer in 1757; later, in full by C. H. Myller, by K. K. Lachmann (Nibelunge Nôt mit der Klage, 1826); by K. F. Bartsch (Der Nibelunge Nôt, 2 vols. in 3, 1870–1880), and in Pfeiffer's Deutsch. Classik. des Mittelalt.,Vol. 3, (1872); and by others (see James Sime's *Nibelungenlied*, Encyc. Brit.). Of some effect in stimulating interest were Dr. W. Jordan's Studies and Recitations of the Nibelunge, which comprised the Siegfried Saga, and Hildebrandt's Return. Especially of value is Richard Wagner's series of operas, The Ring of the Nibelung, **284–288.** In painting, Schnorr von Carolsfeld's wall pictures illustrative of the Nibelungenlied, in the royal palace at Munich, are well known; also the illustrations of the four operas by J. Hoffmann, and by Th. Pixis.

282–283. Historically, **Siegfried** has been identified, variously, with (1) the great German warrior Arminius (or Hermann), the son of Sigimer, chief of the tribe of the Cherusci, who inhabited the southern part of what is now Hanover and Brunswick. Born 18 B.C. and trained in the Roman army, in the year 9 A.D. he overcame with fearful slaughter the Roman tyrants of Germany, defeating the Roman commander Varus and his legions in the Teutoburg Forest in the valley of the Lippe; (2) Sigibert, king of the Ripuarian Franks, who in 508 A.D. was treacherously slain while taking a midday nap in the forest; (3) Sigibert, king of the Austrasian Franks whose history recalls more than one event of the Sigurd and Siegfried stories; for he discovered a treasure, fought with and overcame foreign nations, — the Huns, the Saxons, the Danes, — and finally in consequence of a quarrel between his wife Brünhilde and his sister-in-law Fredegunde, was, in 576 A.D., assassinated by the retainers of the latter; (4) Julius, or Claudius Civilis, the leader of the Batavi in the revolt against Rome, 69–70 A.D. It is probable that in Sigurd and Siegfried we have recollections combined of two or more of these historic characters.

Mythologically, **Sigurd** (of the shining eyes that no man might face unabashed) has been regarded as a reflection of the god Balder.

Gunnar and **Gunther** are, historically, recognized in a slightly known king of the Burgundians, Gundicar, who with his people was overwhelmed by the Huns in 437 A.D.

Atli and **Etzel** are poetic idealizations of the renowned Hunnish chieftain, Attila, who united under his rule the German and Slavonic nations, ravaged the Eastern Roman Empire between 445 and 450 A.D., and, invading the Western Empire, was defeated by the Romans in the great battle of Châlons-sur-Marne, 451. He died 454 A.D.

Dietrich of Berne (Verona) bears some very slight resemblance to Theodoric, the Ostrogoth, who, between 493 and 526 A.D., ruled from Italy what had been the Western Empire. In these poems, however, his earlier illustrious career is overlooked; he is merely a refugee in the court of the Hunnish king, and, even so, is confounded with uncles of his who had been retainers of Attila; for the historic Theodoric was not born until two years after the historic Attila's death.

These historic figures were, of course, merely suggestions for, or contributions to, the great heroes of the epics, not prototypes; the same is true of any apparently confirmed historic forerunners of Brynhild, or Gudrun, or Kriemhild. The mythological connection of these epics with the Norse myths of the seasons, Sigurd being Balder of the spring, and Hogni Höder of winter and darkness, is ingenious; but, except as reminding us of the mythic material which the bards were likely to recall and utilize, it is not of substantial worth.

In the Norse version, the name **Nibelung** is interchangeable with the patronymic **Giuking,** — it is the name of the family that ruins Sigurd. But, in the German version, the name is of purely mythical import: the Nibelungs are not a human race; none but Siegfried may have intercourse with them. The land of the Nibelungs is equally vague in the German poem; it is at one time an island, again a mountain, and in one manuscript it is confounded with Norway. But mythically it is connected with Niflheim, the kingdom of Hela, the shadowy realm of death. The earth, that gathers to her bosom the dead, cherishes also in her bosom the hoard of gold. Naturally, therefore, the hoard is guarded by Alberich, the dwarf, for dwarfs have always preferred the underworld. So (according to Werner Hahn, and others) there is a deep mythical meaning in the Lay of the Nibelungs: beings that dwell far from the light of day; or that, possessing the riches of mortality, march toward the land of death.

284-288. Wagner finished this series of operas in 1876. For a translation the reader is referred to the four librettos, Englished by Frederick Jameson (Schott & Co., London); or to the series published by Thomas Y. Crowell & Co., New York.

298. Homer is also called Melesigenes, son of Meles — the stream on which Smyrna was built. The Homeridæ, who lived on Chios, claimed to be descended from Homer. They devoted themselves to the cultivation of epic poetry.

Arion. See George Eliot's poem beginning

> Arion, whose melodic soul
> Taught the dithyramb to roll.

Other Greek Poets of Mythology to be noted are **Callimachus** (260 B.C.), whose Lock of Berenice is reproduced in the elegiacs of Catullus, and from whose Origins (of sacred rites) Ovid drew much of his information. Also **Nicander** (150 B.C.), whose Transformations, and **Parthenius,** whose Metamorphoses furnished material to the Latin poet. With Theocritus should be read **Bion** and **Moschus,** all three masters of the idyl and elegy. See Andrew Lang's translation of Theocritus, Bion, and Moschus; and the verses by Dobson and Gosse with which Lang prefaces the translation. **Lycophron** (260 B.C.) wrote a poem called Alexandra, on the consequences of the voyage of Paris to Sparta. The Loves of Hero and Leander were probably written by a grammarian, **Musæus,** as late as 500 A.D.

Translations of Greek Poets. The best verse translations of Homer are those of Chapman, Pope, the Earl of Derby, Cowper, and Worsley.

An excellent prose translation of the Iliad is that of Lang, Leaf, and Myers (London, Macmillan & Co., 1889); of the Odyssey, that by Butcher and Lang (London, Macmillan & Co., 1883); or the translation into rhythmical prose by G. H. Palmer (Boston, Houghton Mifflin Co., 1892).

The Tragic Poets. Plumptre's translations of Æschylus and Sophocles, 2 vols. (New York, Routledge, 1882); A. S. Way's translation of Euripides, into verse (London, 1894); Wodhull, Potter, and Milman's translation of Euripides in Morley's Universal Library (London, Routledge, 1888); Potter's Æschylus, Francklin's Sophocles, Wodhull's Euripides, 5 vols. (London, 1809). Other translations of Æschylus are J. S. Blackie's (1850); T. A. Buckley's (London, Bohn, 1848); E. A. A. Morshead's (1881); and Verrall's; — of Sophocles: Thos. Dale's, into verse, 2 vols. (1824); R. Whitelaw's, into verse (1883); Lewis Campbell's Seven Plays, into verse (1883); — of Euripides: T. A. Buckley's, 2 vols. (London, Bohn, 1854–1858); and Verrall's.

Other Poets. Lang's prose translation of Theocritus, Bion, and Moschus; C. S. Calverley's verse translation of Theocritus (Boston, 1906). Pindar, — Odes, transl. by F. A. Paley (London, 1868); by Ernest Myers (London, 1874). Translations of Greek Lyric Poets, — Collections from the Greek Anthology, by Bland and Merivale (London, 1833); The Greek Anthology, by Lord Neaves, Ancient Classics for English Readers Series (London, 1874); Bohn's Greek Anthology, by Burges (London, 1852).

On Homer, Hesiod, Theocritus, the tragic poets, Pindar, etc., see also Collins' excellent series of Ancient Classics for English Readers, Philadelphia (Lippincott); and the series entitled " English Translations from Ancient and Modern Poems," by Various Authors, 3 vols. (London, 1810). Also W. C. Wilkinson's College Greek Course, and College Latin Course, in English (1884–1886). Of Æschylus read the Prometheus Bound, to illustrate **15**; the Agamemnon, Choëphori, and Eumenides, to illustrate **193, 228–230**; and the Seven against Thebes, for **187.** Of Sophocles read Œdipus Rex, Œdipus at Colonus, Antigone, with **182–185**, etc.; Electra, with **228**; Ajax and Philoctetes, with the Trojan War; Women of Trachis, with **162.** Of Euripides read Medea, Ion, Alcestis, Iphigenia in Aulis and in Tauris, Electra.

299. Roman Poets. Horace (65 B.C.) in his Odes, Epodes, and Satires makes frequent reference and allusion to the common stock of mythology, sometimes telling a whole story, as that of the daughters of Danaüs. **Catullus** (87 B.C.), the most original of Roman love-poets, gives us the Nuptials of Peleus and Thetis (for selections in English hexameters, see 177 and 191), the Lock of Berenice, and the Atys. **Manilius** of the age of Augustus wrote a poem on Astronomy, which contains a philosophic statement of star-myths. **Valerius Flaccus** (d. 88 A.D.) based his Argonautics upon the poem of that name by Apollonius of Rhodes. **Statius** (61 A.D.) revived in the brilliant verses of his Thebaïd and his Achilleïd the epic myths and epic machinery, but not the vigor and naturalness of the ancient style. To a prose writer, **Hyginus**, who lived on terms of close intimacy with Ovid, a fragmentary work called the Book of Fables, which is sometimes a useful source of information, and four books of Poetical Astronomy, have been attributed. The works, as we have them, could not have been written by a friend of the cultivated Ovid.

Translations and Studies. For a general treatment of the great poets of Rome, the student is referred to W. L. Collins' series of Ancient Classics for English Readers (Philadelphia, Lippincott). For the Cupid and Psyche of **Apuleius**, read Walter Pater's Marius the Epicurean (London, 1885). Of translations, the following are noteworthy: Ovid, — the Metamorphoses, by Dryden, Addison, and others; into English blank verse by Ed. King (Edinburgh, 1871); prose by Riley (London, 1851); verse by Geo. Sandys (London, 1626). Virgil: complete works into prose by J. Lonsdale and S. Lee (New York, Macmillan); Æneid, translations, — into verse by John Conington (London, 1873); into dactylic hexameter by Oliver Crane (New York, 1888); the Æneids into verse by Wm. Morris (London, 1876); and by Theodore C. Williams (Boston, Houghton Mifflin Co.); Bks. 1–4, by Stanyhurst (Arber's Reprint) (1582); Æneis, by Dryden. Catullus: transl. by Robinson Ellis (London, 1871); by Sir Theodore Martin (Edinburgh, 1875). Horace: transl. by Theodore Martin (Edinburgh, 1881); by Smart (London, 1853); Odes and Epodes in Calverley's translations (London, 1886); Odes, etc., by Conington (London, 1872); Odes and Epodes, by Lord Lytton (New York, 1870); complete, by E. C. Wickham (Oxford, Clarendon Press); Odes, by A. S. Way (London, 1876) and Epodes (1898). Statius: Thebaid, transl. by Pope.

300. For **Scandinavian literature**, see footnotes to **300,** and references in **C. 268–282.**

Runes were "the letters of the alphabets used by all the old Teutonic tribes. . . . The letters were even considered magical, and cast into the air written separately upon chips or spills of wood, to fall, as fate determined, on a cloth, and then be read by the interpreters. . . . The association of the runic letters with heathen mysteries and superstition caused the first Christian teachers to discourage, and, indeed, as far as possible, suppress their use. They were therefore superseded by the Latin alphabet, which in First English was supplemented by retention of two of the runes, named 'thorn' and 'wen,' to represent sounds of 'th' and 'w,' for which the Latin alphabet had no letters provided. Each rune was named after some object whose name began with the sound represented. The first letter was F, Feoh, money; the second U, Ur, a bull; the third Th, Thorn, a thorn; the fourth O, Os, the mouth; the fifth R, Rad, a saddle; the sixth C, Cen, a torch; and the six sounds being joined together make Futhorc, which is the name given to the runic A B C." — MORLEY, English Writers, 1, 267. See also Vigfusson and Powell's Corpus Poeticum Boreale, 2, 691, under Runes and Rune-Stones; Cleasby and Vigfusson's Icelandic-English Dictionary; and George Stephens' Old Northern Runic Monuments, 2 vols. (London, 1866–1868).

301. For Translations of the Nibelungenlied, see C. 283. For other German lays of myth, — the Gudrun, the Great Rose Garden, the Horned Siegfried, etc., — see Vilmar's Geschichte der deutschen National-Litteratur, 42–101 (Leipzig, 1886). See also, in general, Grimm's Deutsche Mythologie (Göttingen, 1855); Ludlow's Popular Epics of the Middle Ages, 2 vols. (London, 1865); George T. Dippold's Great Epics of Mediæval Germany (Boston, 1891).

302. Egyptian. See Birch's Guide to the First and Second Egyptian Rooms, British Museum; Miss A. B. Edwards' A Thousand Miles up the Nile (London, 1876).

For the principal divinities, see Index to this work.

303. Indian. Max Müller's translation of the Rig-Veda-Sanhita; Sacred Books of the East, 35 vols., edited by Max Müller, — the Upanishads, Bhagavadgita, Institutes of Vishnu, etc., translated by various scholars (Oxford, 1874–1890); Müller's History of Sanskrit Literature (London, 1859); Weber's History of Indian Literature (London, 1878); H. H. Wilson's Rig-Veda-Sanhita, 6 vols. (London, 1850–1870), and his Theatre of the Hindus, 2 vols. (London, 1871); Muir's Sanskrit Texts, and his Principal Deities of the Rig-Veda, 5 vols. (London, 1868–1873); J. Freeman Clarke's Ten Great Religions (Boston, 1880); the Mahâbhârata, translated by Protap Chundra Roy, Nos. 1–76 (Calcutta, 1883–1893). See Indian Idylls, by Edwin Arnold; The Episode of Nala, — Nalopákhyánam, — translated by Monier Williams (Oxford, 1879). Of the Râmâyana, a paraphase (in brief) is given by F. Richardson in the Iliad of the East (London, 1870). Sir William Jones' translation of the Sakuntala; E. A. Reed's Hindu Literature, with translations (Chicago, 1891); W. Ward's History, Literature, and Mythology of the Hindoos, 3 vols. (London, 1822). On Buddhism, read Arnold's Light of Asia.

For the chief divinities of the Hindus, see Index to this work.

304. Persian. J. Freeman Clarke's Ten Great Religions; Johnson's Oriental Religions; Haug's Essays on the Sacred Language, Literature, etc., of the Parsis, by E. W. West (Boston, 1879). In illustration should be read Moore's Fire-Worshipers in Lalla Rookh.

A FEW RULES FOR THE ENGLISH PRONUNCIA-
TION OF GREEK AND LATIN PROPER NAMES

[These rules will cover most cases, but they are not intended to exhaust the subject. The reader is referred to the Latin grammars and the English dictionaries.]

I. *Quantity.* The reader must first ascertain whether the second last syllable of the word is long. In general a syllable is long in quantity:

(1) If it contains a diphthong, or a long vowel: *Bau*-cis, Ac-*tae*-on, *Mē*-tis, O-*rī*-on, *Flō*-ra.

(2) If its vowel, whether long or short, is followed by *j*, *x*, or *z*, or by any two consonants except a mute and a liquid: *A'*-jax, Meg-a-*ba'*-zus, A-*dras'*-tus.

Note (a). Sometimes two vowels come together without forming a diphthong. In such cases the diæresis is, in this volume, used to indicate the division: *e.g.* Men-e-lā'-*üs*, Pe-nē'-*üs*.

Note (b). The *syllable* formed by a short vowel before a mute with *l* or *r* is sometimes long and sometimes short: *e.g.* Cle-o-*pā'*-tra, or Cle-op'-*ă*-tra; Pa-*trŏ'*-clus, or Pat'-*rŏ*-clus.

II. *Accent.*

(1) The accent may be principal, or subordinate: Hel²-les-pon'-tus.

(2) **The principal accent falls on the second last syllable (*penult*): Am-phi-tri'-te; or on the third last syllable (*antepenult*): Am-phit'-ry-on.**

Note (a) In words of two syllables, it falls on the *penult*: Cir'-ce.

Note (b) **In words of more than two syllables, it falls on the *penult* when that syllable is long; otherwise, on the *antepenult*: Æ-nē'-as, Her'-cŭ-les.**

(3) The subordinate accent:

Note (a) If only two syllables precede the principal accent, the subordinate accent falls on the first syllable of the word: *Hip²-po*-crē'ne.

Note (b) If more than two syllables precede the principal accent, the laws governing the principal accent apply to those preceding syllables: *Cas²-sĭ-o*-pē'-a.

Note. **In the Index of this work, when the *penult* of a word is long, it is marked with the accent; when the penult is short, the *antepenult* is marked.** The reader should however bear in mind that a *syllable* may be long even though it contain a short vowel, as by Rule I, (2), above.

III. *Vowels and Consonants.* These rules depend upon those of Syllabication:

(1) A vowel generally has its *long* English sound when it ends a syllable: *Hē'-ro*, *I'-o*, *Cā'-cus*, *I-thō'-me*, *E-do'-ni*, *My-cē'-næ*.

541

(2) A vowel generally has its *short* English sound in a syllable that ends in a consonant: *Hel'-en, Sis'-y-phus, Pol-y-phe'-mus.* But *e* in the termination *es* has its long sound: Her'*mes*, A-tri'-*des.*

(3) The vowel *a* has an *obscure* sound when it ends an unaccented syllable: A-chæ'-*a*; so, also, the vowel *i* or *y*, not final, after an accented syllable: Hesper'-*i*-des; and sometimes *i* or *y* in an unaccented first syllable: *Ci*-lic'-i-a.

(4) Consonants have their usual English sounds; but *c* and *g* are soft before *e*, *i*, *y*, *æ*, and *œ*: *Ce'*-to, *Ge'*-ry-on, *Gy'-ges;* *ch* has the sound of *k*: *Chi'*-os; and *c*, *s*, and *t*, immediately preceded by the accent and standing before *i* followed by another vowel, commonly have the sound of *sh*: *Sic'*-y-on (but see Latin grammars and English dictionaries for exceptions).

IV. *Syllabication.*

(1) The penultimate syllable ends with a vowel: *e.g.* Pe-*ne'*-us, I-*tho'*-me, *A'*-treus, Hel'-*e*-nus;

Except when its vowel is followed by *x* or by two consonants (not a mute with *l* or *r*), then the vowel is joined with the succeeding consonant: *Nax*-os, *Cir*-ce, Aga-*mem*-non.

(2) Other syllables (not ultimate or penultimate) end with a vowel: *e.g.* Pi-ræ-us;

Except when (*a*) the vowel is followed by *x* or any two consonants (not a mute with *l* or *r*): *e.g. Ix*-i'-on, Pel-o-*pon*-ne'-sus; *and when* (*b*) the syllable is accented and its vowel followed by one or more consonants: *e.g.* An²-ax-*ag'*-o-ras, Am-*phic'*ty-on, Œd-'i-pus.

Note (*a*). But an accented *a, e,* or *o* before a single consonant (or a mute with *l* or *r*), followed by *e, i,* or *y* before another vowel, is not joined with the succeeding consonant, and consequently has the long sound: Pau-*sā'*-ni-as; De-*mē'*-tri-us.

Note (*b*). An accented *u* before a single consonant (or mute with *l* or *r*) is not joined with the succeeding consonant, and consequently has the long sound: *Jū'*-pi-ter.

(3) **All words have as many syllables as they have vowels and diphthongs.**

INDEX OF MYTHOLOGICAL SUBJECTS
AND THEIR SOURCES

[Ordinary figures refer to pages of the Text. Figures in italics preceded by *C.* refer to sections of the Commentary and incidentally to the corresponding sections in the Text.

In the case of words of which the correct pronunciation has not seemed to be clearly indicated by their accentuation and syllabication, the sounds of the letters have been denoted thus: ā, like *a* in *grāy*; á, like *å*, only less prolonged; ă, like *a* in *hăve*; ä, like *a* in *fär*; à, like *a* in *sofà*; ą and au like *a* in *ąll*; æ, ē, and œ, like *ee* in *meet*; é, like *ē*, only less prolonged; ĕ, like *e* in *ĕnd*; ê, like *e* in *thêre*; ẽ, like *e* in *ẽrr*; ī, like *i* in *pīne*; ĭ, like *i* in *pĭn*; ō, like *ō* in *nōte*; ó, like *ō*, only less prolonged; ŏ, like *o* in *nŏt*; ô, like *o* in *ôrb*; o͞o, like *oo* in *fo͞ot*; ōō, like *oo* in *mōōn*; ou, as in *out*; ū, like *u* in *ūse*; ü, like the French *u*; c and ch, like *k*; th, as in *the*; ç, like *s*; ḡ, like *g* in *ḡet*; ġ, like *j*; ş, like *z*; ċh, as in German *ach*; G, small capital, as in German *Hamburg*.]

A'bas, 207
Ab-syr'tus, 232; *C. 163–167* (Illustr.)
À-by'dŏs, 32, 142; *C. 34*
Ab'y-la, 219
À-çes'tēş, 352, 368, 369
À-çe'tēş, 152; the vengence of Bacchus, 154, 155
À-chæ'àns, their origin, 16; 274, 288; *C. 148* (2)
À-cha'tēş, 366
Ăch-e-lo'us, myth of, 203, 204; *C. 146–147*
Ăch'e-rŏn, 47, 127, 327
À-chil'lēş, 75, 91, 179, 237; his descent, 269, 272, 275, 276; character of, 274; in the Trojan War, 279–308; in Scyros, 279, 280; wrath of, 283; and Patroclus, 296; remorse of, 299; reconciliation with Agamemnon, 300; slays Hector and drags his body, 301–303; and Priam, 304–306; death of, 307, 308, 313, 328, 345, 453; *C. 190–194* (1), *199, 207*
A'çis, 198, 200; *C. 141*

A'cŏn, *C. 138*
Acontius (à-con'shĭ-us), *C. 64*
À-cris'ĭ-us, 207; doom of, 208–214; *C. 149–154*
Ac-ro-çe-rau'nian Mountains, 118; *C. 93*
Ac-tæ'on, 89; myth of, 120–122, 261; *C. 59*, table E; *95*
Ad-me'ta, 218
Ad-me'tus, 104, 230; Lowell's Shepherd of King A., 105, 106; and Alcestis, 106–110
À-do'nis, myth of, 126–128; Lang's translation of Bion's Lament for A., 126–128; *C. 100*
Ad-ras-te'a, 5
À-dras'tus, 264, 265
Æ-açĭ-dēş, Achilles, 272
Æ'à-cus, 51, 53, 246, 269; king of Ægina, 73, 75; *C. 190–194* (1)
Æ-æ'a, isle of, 318, 324, 328
Æ-e'tēş, 230–232; genealogy, *C. 172*
Æ'ḡæ, palace of Neptune near, 56
Æ-ġæ'ŏn, *C. 4*
Æ-ġe'àn Sea, 177

543

Seb : the father of the Osirian gods. He is the god of earth and its vegetation; represented as a man with the head of a goose; he corresponds with the Greek Cronus; his consort was Nut.

Nut : wife of Seb, mother of the Osirian gods; the vault of heaven; she may be likened to the Greek Rhea.

Osi'ris, or *Hesiri :* the good principle. Identified with the vivifying power of the sun and of the waters of the Nile. In general, the most human and most beneficent of the Egyptian deities. He is the son of Seb (or, according to some, of Neph, Chnuphis). He may be likened to the Greek Apollo, as a representative of spiritual light; to Dionysus in his vivifying function. He wages war with his brother Seth (Set), the principle of Evil, but is vanquished by him, boxed in a chest, drowned, and finally cut into small pieces. His sister-wife, Isis, recovers all but one piece of the body of O., and buries them. He becomes protector of the shades, judge of the underworld, the sun of the night, the tutelary deity of the Egyptians. He is avenged by his son Horus, who, with the aid of Thoth (reason), temporarily overcomes Seth. The myth may refer to the daily struggle of the sun with darkness, and also to the unending strife of good with evil, the course of human life, and of the life after death. O. is represented as a mummy crowned with the Egyptian miter.

I'sis, or *Hes :* the wife and feminine counterpart of Osiris. Represented as a woman crowned with the sun's disk or cow's horns, bearing also upon her head her emblem, the throne.

Ho'rus, or *Har :* son of Osiris and Isis, who, as the strong young sun of the day, avenges his father, the sun of the underworld. He is Horus the child, Horus the elder (as taking the place

of his father on earth), or sometimes Horus Harpocrates, the god of silence. As the latter, he holds a finger to his lips. He may be. compared with the Greek Apollo.

Harpoc'ra-tes : see *Horus*

Ha'thor, or *Athor :* a goddess often identified with Isis. She had the head of a cow and wears the sun's disk, and plumes. Her name means "Home of Horus." She has characteristics of the Greek Aphrodite.

Seth, or *Set :* the principle of physical, and later of moral, darkness and evil. He is the opponent of his brother, or father, Osiris. Represented as a monster with ass's body, jackal's ears and snout, and the tail of a lion.

Nephthys : a goddess of the dead; the sister of Isis, and wife of Seth. She aided Isis to recover the drowned Osiris.

A'pis : the sacred bull, into which the life of Osiris was supposed to have passed. The name also indicates the Nile. The bull Apis must have certain distinguishing marks; he was treated like a god; and on his death (he was drowned at twenty-five years of age) the land went into mourning until his successor was found. He was worshiped with pomp in Memphis. See *Serapis*

Sera'pis (or *Ser'apis;* see *Milton, Paradise Lost, 1, 720*): as Apis represents the living Osiris, so S. the Osiris who had passed into the underworld.

Ra : originally the deity of the physical attributes of the sun; but ultimately the representative of supreme godhead. Worshiped through all Egypt, and associated with other gods who are then manifestations of his various attributes. He. is the victorious principle or light, life, and right, but rules over, rather than sympathizes with, mankind. He is of human form, sometimes hawk-headed, always crowned

INDEX OF MODERN AUTHORS
AND ARTISTS

[Ordinary figures refer to pages of the Text. Figures in italics preceded by *C.* refer to sections of the Commentary and incidentally to the corresponding sections in the Text. For explanation of the diacritical marks see p. 543.]